MARKS & MONOGRAMS ON POTTERY & PORCELAIN

MEISSEN GROUP. Modelled by
J. J. Kändler, circa 1770.

MARKS & MONOGRAMS

on European and Oriental Pottery and Porcelain

By

WILLIAM CHAFFERS

The British Section edited by
GEOFFREY A. GODDEN, F.R.S.A.

The European and Oriental Sections
edited by
FREDERICK LITCHFIELD & R. L. HOBSON

15TH REVISED EDITION

VOLUME ONE

LONDON
WILLIAM REEVES

Published by William Reeves Bookseller Ltd.,
1a Norbury Crescent, London, S.W.16

© William Reeves Bookseller Ltd., 1965

Made in England
Second Printing

Printed in Great Britain by
Lowe & Brydone (Printers) Ltd., London

NOTE TO THE FIFTEENTH EDITION

In publishing the fifteenth edition of " Chaffers," the publishers have been fortunate in securing the services of Mr. Geoffrey A. Godden, F.R.S.A., who has completely revised the British section of this book. As a result of the considerable amount of fresh information now available on Bow, Longton Hall and Lowestoft, the accounts of these factories have been completely rewritten. The histories of other factories have been brought up to date and the relevant modern reference books cited in the text. The European and Oriental sections, beyond some few corrections, remain substantially the same.

Remarks made by Frederick Litchfield in the ninth edition are quite as apt and to the point today: " I desire to thank my correspondents, who are too numerous to name. If, as a work of reference, Chaffers is to retain its high prestige, it must be in a great measure by the co-operation of collectors in communicating any inaccuracies or omissions that may be discovered."

CONTENTS

	PAGE
Ancient Pottery	I
Romano-British Pottery	10
Mediaeval Earthenware Vessels	28
Maiolica—Italy	48
Sgraffiati or Incised Ware—Citta di Castello, Pavia, La Fratta, etc., Spain and Portugal	149
Persian, Syrian and Turkish Fayence	165
Fayence—France	171
Fayence—Russia, Sweden and Denmark	252
Fayence—Holland, Belgium and Germany	261
China, Pottery and Porcelain	314
Japan	377
European Porcelain	426
Italy	429
Spain and Portugal	452
Meissen	466
Austria	483
Some Minor Factories of Bohemia	490
Prussia	498
Bavaria	506
Brunswick, Wurtemberg, Baden, etc.	515
Thuringia	520
Switzerland	531
Holland and Belgium	533
Russia and Poland	543
Sweden, Denmark and Norway	548
France	552

INTRODUCTION

PART I.

𝔄ncient ℙottery

T would be a vain attempt to endeavour to particularize any country, or race of people, from whence the art of making pottery took its rise. It is one of the oldest branches of human industry, and sprang from the requirements of man, desirous of finding a convenient mode of conveying the fruits of the earth to his mouth, that the appetite might be appeased and life sustained; one of the first laws of nature. Earth, the commonest of materials, was ready to his hand; he could not fail to observe that the rain falling upon the clay would soften and render it plastic, while the influences of the sun and air would dry and harden it. It is therefore reasonable to suppose, that the primeval races of man would naturally fashion the soft clay into rude cups or bowls, and dry them in the heat of the sun. Subsequently, as the human race became dispersed over the face of the globe, either by conquest, colonization, or other causes, peculiar methods of mixing the clays, conventional forms and ornamentation, would be manifested by each, and we should thus be enabled to trace most of the vessels to their source and appropriate the varied productions of keramic artists with some degree of certainty.

"Like the history of all other arts, the history of pottery has not escaped the blending with it of a large amount of apocryphal anecdote and romance. Perhaps pottery—the art of moulding and hardening clay —may claim to be the mother of all the arts. Necessity would soon prompt the attempted manufacture of a vessel to hold liquids; for neither of the methods of satisfying thirst adopted by Gideon's men would long suffice. Convenience and refinement would alike urge an improvement; and the first footmark in the clay, hardened by a Mesopotamian sun, would suggest the material and manner of its construction; and from Eve's first rude pipkin to the latest production of Wedgwood or Copeland, it would simply be a series of improvements. Thus to draw upon the apocrypha of pottery, a servant boils brawn in an earthen pipkin, and carelessly permitting it to boil over the fierce fire, the alkali combines with the earthenware, and the result is a vitreous surface—the first specimen of glass-glazing.[1]

"The first historic records of fictile clay are the bricks of Babel; the next the brickmaking of the Israelites, indicating an advanced and systematic art.

"The inventor of pottery, artistically so called, was Corœbus of Athens, in whose honour the æsthetic Greeks struck medals and erected statues. Phidias himself designed vases for the Athenian potters.

"Dibŭtades of Sicyon observed upon a wall the profile of his daughter's lover, traced by her from the outline of his shadow. He filled it with clay, which he hardened with fire, and this was the first specimen of modelling in relief. Talus of Athens is said to have invented the potter's wheel, and so to have provoked thereby the jealousy of Dædalus, that he threw him from the Acropolis and killed him." (*Allon.*)

The potter's wheel was an early invention, and a great improvement upon the methods previously adopted in fashioning the rude sun-dried vessels by the hand alone. It enabled the potter to make symmetrically a great variety of forms and every combination of circular, oval, spherical, and cylindrical shapes, in true proportions. Its origin is unknown, although it has been ascribed to several nations where excellence in the potter's art has been attained; thus Athens, Corinth, and Sicyon, the three great rivals in the keramic art, have all been mentioned as inventors of this simple machine, but we must look to a still more remote period for its origin.

M. Brongniart assigns it to the Chinese, and infers that after leaving China, where it had been long known, it passed into Egypt, thence into Scythia, and nearly at the same time into Greece and its colonies in Southern Italy, reaching Eturia at a *later* date, and that it then penetrated the whole of Southern Europe, Rome and its colonies, Spain, &c.; as these countries became civilized and acquainted with the arts of the East, stopping at the southern part of Germany, and only partially entering it, and that while penetrating into Gaul, it remained unknown among the ancient Scandinavian nations. All the early vases of Greece bear traces of the lies of the wheel, except in some later specimens where moulds alone were used. The representations of the potter's wheel in the tombs at Thebes, show that the general method of using it in ancient times was much the same as at the present day.

Modelling by the hand and moulding were both frequently employed for raised ornaments, and bronze or baked terra-cotta stamps for impressing devices and patterns have been discovered. These ornaments were moulded or stamped on round or square cakes of clay, and applied while moist to the terminations of the handles or lips of the vases. Borders

---

[1] Professor Church completely disposes of this fable in his *English Earthenware.*—ED.

and zones of small patterns in relief were impressed by cylindrical stamps revolving in a frame or handle, and passed round the vessel.

We will first briefly advert to the nature of clay as regards the change it undergoes in the process of manufacture. Suppose we take a lump of clay or earth, soaked in water sufficiently to render it plastic, and then form it into a brick or tile, and lay it in the sun to dry: as the moisture evaporates, the brick hardens and the particles adhere slightly together; but we have produced simply a brick of desiccated clay, which may, by adding the quantity of water taken from it, be again converted to its original state. But if we place this brick in a kiln, the nature of the clay is altogether changed; the high temperature melts all the parts and cements them together, effecting a great chemical change, the substance being so altered from its original state that water could never mix with it, so as again to form clay.

During this operation of baking the clay in the kiln, the object into which it is made decreases materially in bulk; this is termed the *shrinkage*, and arises, first, from the drying up of the moisture, amounting to even 15 per cent. or more; and secondly, by the fusion of the substances, the component particles draw closer together, causing a considerable diminution in size. To illustrate this, let us suppose the potter wishes to make a bust or statuette in earthenware. The original model is placed in his hand, which he proceeds to mould in plaster; into this hollow mould he presses the clay, which shortly contracts itself so as to become detached from the sides; he then dries it in the air, and again its size diminishes, and one hardly understands how it can be a strict reproduction of the original. Another ordeal follows; it is subjected to the high temperature of the kiln, and it is still more sensibly reduced.

A beautiful exposition of the *shrinkage* of clay is exemplified in the modern Dresden and other china figures, which are veiled with a fine keramic network in close imitation of lace. The process, however, is simple when the method of performing it is known. A piece of lace is steeped in diluted clay or slip, termed by the French *barbotine*; thus prepared, it is thrown over the statuette; when dried in the air the bulk of the keramic coating decreases. But it is in the kiln the magic effect is accomplished; the great heat entirely destroys the vegetable fibre which formed the network and flowers; the paste thus freed from its nucleus is contracted to such a degree that the outer covering becomes more delicate than the thread which it surrounded.

The proper selection of clays for making pottery is a most important matter, as some contain a greater proportion of moisture or more fusible materials than others; it is therefore evident, that if the clays are not all of the same composition, or not well kneaded and mixed together, the shrinkage of the vessel in baking will be irregular, and cause it to be distorted or cracked. While speaking of the nature of clay and its fitness to be moulded or fashioned into form and to receive impressions, I may mention one or two curious facts in connection therewith.

In London and various other parts of England, on the sites of ancient Roman buildings, there are frequently found Roman tiles with footprints of dogs, wolves, and other animals, the feet and claws of monstrous birds and various creatures which inhabited this island nearly two thousand years since, many of which are now extinct; these impressions were made when the tiles were in a plastic state and placed out in the fields to dry, by animals prowling about at night in search of their prey and trampling over them. In some instances also the perfect impression of a man's *caliga* or nailed shoe is discovered; these tiles being subsequently baked, the imprints were indelibly marked upon their surfaces.

A curious property in clay is that when a potter commences to work the clay into the desired form, it may happen that during the operation, by some accident, the surface of the vessel comes in contact with a seal, a figured button, or perchance a piece of money; the workman, to efface the defect, presses the impression inwards, and smooths it over with his hands. The heat of the kiln brings again to the surface the figure it had before received. Hence Roman vessels have been discovered bearing the impress of a medal or a coin, with which it had inadvertently come in contact.

In our endeavours to trace the earliest examples of the potter's art, we must necessarily consult ancient histories of Oriental countries, but these are so mixed up with traditions and fables, that it is extremely difficult to elicit the truth; and it is only by comparing such statements with actual discoveries on the sites of cities cœval with them that we can verify the assertions of ancient writers. For instance, it is related by Herodotus that the city of Ecbatana, the capital of Media, was surrounded by seven walls, painted in seven different colours: the first and largest, of a white colour, was nearly equal in extent to the city of Athens; the second was black; the third purple; the fourth blue; the fifth orange; and the two innermost in different colours, the battlements of the one being plated with silver, the other with gold. If there be any truth in this relation, the walls were probably of brick, the surfaces being enamelled in colours, a custom adopted in many towns of China and India.

A building of similar character is described by Sir Henry Rawlinson as still existing in Chaldæa, called Birs Nimrùd, which, from the custom of placing cylinders in the corners of the storeys, is ascertained to have been restored by Nebuchadnezzar the king (606 B.C.), who designates it, "The stages of the seven spheres of Borsippa." This structure consisted of six distinct platforms or terraces, each about 20 feet high and receding 42 feet towards the summit, so arranged as to form an oblique pyramid, and upon the top a vitrified mass which has caused much discussion. Each storey was dedicated to a particular planet, and vitrified or glazed with the colour attributed to it by astrologers in this order: the lowest stage, 1st, was *black* for Saturn; 2nd, *orange* for Jupiter; 3rd, *red* for Mars; 4th, *yellow* for the Sun; 5th, *green* for Venus; 6th, *blue* for Mercury; and the temple on the summit probably *white* for the Moon.

Recent investigations on the site of another celebrated city of old

Babylon, have brought to light bricks covered with enamel glazes of different colours, showing that the use of oxides of copper, antimony, and tin in producing their colours was known as early as the eighth or seventh century before our era, and proves that the opaque white stanniferous enamel was used at that early period, although generally supposed to be a comparatively recent invention, and ascribed to Lucca della Robbia in the fifteenth century. The glazed Babylonian bricks formed the innermost coatings of walls, and the patterns upon them are rosettes, palmette ornaments, circles, trellis-work, men, animals, trees, &c.

These remarkable coffins are slipper-shaped, like a covered bath, with a large oval aperture at its widest part, by which the body was admitted; a lid was placed upon it and cemented down; at the lower extremity a small semicircular hole was pierced, to allow the condensed gases to escape and prevent the bursting of the coffin; the upper surface was covered with elevated ridges forming square panels, each containing an embossed figure of a warrior, with an enormous head-dress of very curious appearance, bearing a striking resemblance to the heads on the coins of the Parthian and Sassanian periods. The whole visible surface of the coffin is covered with a thick glazing of rich green enamel on the exterior, and of blue within the oval aperture; it is made of yellow clay mixed with straw and half baked. Three of these are now in the British Museum. Mr. Loftus remarks, it would be too much to say positively that Chaldæa was the necropolis of Assyria, but it is by no means improbable. The two great rivers, the Tigris and Euphrates, would afford an admirable conveyance from a distance, even from the upper plains of Assyria.

Pottery was an important branch of the domestic arts in Egypt, in which the potters displayed great skill. Coptus was the chief seat of this manufacture; vessels were made to hold the waters of the Nile, and for numerous household purposes; also to hold mummies of sacred animals. Earthenware deities and emblems were made in immense quantities, their composition being a sort of silicious earth or frit covered with a greenish-blue glaze. These small objects were frequently made of steatite dipped in blue glaze, which substance withstood the heat required for its fusion. The forms of their vases are well known by the representations on the catacombs and monuments; the favourite ornamentation being derived from the sacred flower of the Nile, the lotus, its buds and flowers; the borders and details being derived from the petals, stems, and divisions of the calyx. The material of which the earliest specimens were made was a sort of stoneware or frit, resembling porcelain biscuit, and has therefore been called *Egyptian porcelain;* these were covered by a thin glaze. Some of the small deities must have been made at a very remote date. On good authority, as well as from the sacred writings, we learn that the most flourishing period of the Egyptian art goes back as far as two thousand years before our era. The period of the Ptolemies is known by a marked influence of Greek artists; the silicious frit gives place to a pottery, coarse and soft, sometimes painted on the plain surface, and sometimes glazed;

this was continued down to the second and third centuries of our era, when Egypt was under Roman domination. (*Keramic Gallery*, enlarged edition, figs. 4 and 5.)

The Greek fictile vases found in large quantities in the sepulchres of Eturia during the last century were erroneously called Etruscan, and continued to be so called even after they were discovered, still more abundantly, in the sepulchres of Magna Græcia, Sicily, in Attica, and in the islands of the Ægean. It is indisputable that the vases found in Eturia are the productions of Greek artists, and the style of painting, as well as the designs, completely Greek; and it has been observed that although the Etruscans have inscribed every work of art with their own peculiar characters, no *painted* vase has yet been found with any other than a Greek inscription. So also the Greek vases found in Campania and Sicily and the south of Italy: they invariably came from Greece, and are the works of Greek artists. They are the earliest monuments of Greek civilization, ranging from the eighth or tenth century to the second century before our era.

For the purpose of classifying these vases according to the styles of decoration, we may divide them into five periods, assigning approximate dates of their antiquity :—

> 1st. Archaic period, previous to the eighth century B.C.
> 2nd. Archaic period, from the eighth to the seventh century B.C.
> 3rd. Archaic period, from the seventh to the sixth century B.C.
> 4th. The finest period, from the sixth to the fourth century B.C.
> 5th. The Decadence, from the fourth to the second century B.C.

1st. Archaic Period, previous to the Eighth Century B.C.

The earliest specimens of Greek fictile art are those discovered at Athens, Corinth, Melos, and other parts of Greece, Camirus in Rhodes, and some from Eturia; most of these are exceedingly rude, painted in brown or black on ash-coloured ground, with chevrons, concentric circles, meanders, stars, chequers, &c., and primitive representations of men and animals. The shapes of the vases are peculiar, and differ materially from those of the later periods. A very interesting and probably unique specimen discovered at Camirus is a terra-cotta coffin of oblong quadrangular form, painted round the margin with lions and bulls and a helmeted head; now in the British Museum.

2nd. Archaic Period, from the Eighth to the Seventh Century B.C.

The vases abundantly supplied from Camirus in Rhodes show a great improvement in the drawing of the figures; they are usually of cream-coloured clay, painted with crimson and white, sometimes black and crimson, and red on black, the details being scratched with a point. The forms are still peculiar, but approaching to the best period: the amphora, œnochoe, and small vessels like the alabastron, bombylios, &c.; the style of ornamentation being composed of two or more rows of animals (real and imaginary), birds, harpies, &c. (*Keramic Gallery*, enlarged edition, fig. 8.)

On a *pinax* of this class, in the British Museum, is represented a combat between Menelaus and Hector over the wounded Euphorbos, with their names inscribed in Greek characters : this is the earliest vase from Camirus in which writing is introduced.

3rd. Archaic Period, from the Seventh to the Sixth Century B.C.

The next period is still of a very severe style of art, but more artistic than those which precede it; the figures are in *black on a red* ground heightened with a reddish-violet, and the flesh of the females painted white to distinguish them from the men; the outlines of these figures are usually graved with a point, and present *silhouette* sort of divinities, mythological and heroic subjects. (*Keramic Gallery*, enlarged edition, fig. 9.)

These are among the most valuable of the Greek vases, and the patterns on the necks, handles, and borders are very elegant and characteristic. The designs are not painted all over the vase, but are confined to a tablet between the handles, the rest of it being painted with a lustrous black varnish; more complicated subjects are found—quadrigæ and chariots and groups of figures; symbols are introduced in the field, such as a dolphin to indicate the presence of water, and a flower or tree to represent land. Inscriptions in Archaic Greek letters are traced in the same colour; the white was not used for inscriptions until about the middle of the fourth century B.C.

The Fourth Period, from the Sixth to the Fourth Century B.C.

We come now to the best period of Greek art. In critising these beautiful productions, we must bear in mind the fact that all these drawings were executed on the moist clay before the vessel was baked, so that great freedom of touch and unhesitating decision as regards the object to be represented was essential, or the mark of the pencil once made could not be obliterated or retouched, and a complete and perfect line was to be traced without taking the brush from the surface. The white and other colours used upon these vases are not enamels, but coloured clays painted upon them after the design was made. The outline was first sketched upon the clay, and the black background carefully filled in, leaving the figures in red; the details of costume, features, and anatomical delineations were effected by thick or thin strokes and touches as required. (*Keramic Gallery*, enlarged edition, fig. 10.)

Sometimes we find black subjects on red, and red on black, on the same vase, forming a sort of transition from the Archaic to the more artistic period.

The Panathenaic amphoræ are of great interest, being given as prizes to the victors in athletic sports. On these we usually find on one side Pallas Athêné holding a spear and shield, and on the other representations of wrestling, running, boxing, chariot-racing, and other games of the circus, inscribed occasionally with the name of the artist. A very fine vase in the British Museum is inscribed ΤΟΝ ΑΘΕΝΕΘΕΝ ΑΘΛΟΝ (The prize given at Athens.) The subjects on others are derived from mythology or from divine and heroic legends of the Greeks, and occasionally domestic scenes and actual life, as displayed in indoor amusements and occupations, &c. (*Keramic Gallery*, enlarged edition, fig. 11.)

In Greek art, gods, heroes, and mortals are constantly represented in the attire and costume of the period when the painting was executed; they all consequently more or less depict the manners and customs of the Greeks themselves. Most of the vases of this period come from Vulci, Canino, Cervetri, and other parts of Etruria. To about the same date we may refer the vases of Campania, of which so many have been discovered at Nola. These, which are distinguished by a brilliant black glaze, are also celebrated for the elegance of their forms and the beauty and finish of the subjects represented; they are in red on black ground; many being entirely covered with this black varnish, which has been conjectured to be due to volcanic ashes spread over the surface of the vessel, and then exposed to a heat sufficient to fuse it. They are frequently ribbed and impressed with elegant patterns (*Keramic Gallery*, enlarged edition, figs. 14, 15.)

The Fifth Period, from the Fourth to the Second Century B.C.

This may be called the *Decadence*, and dates from the accession of Alexander the Great, 336 B.C. to 186 B.C., when it is presumed the fabrication of painted vases altogether ceased; shortly after the edict of the Roman Senate against the celebration of the Bacchanalian festivals in that year. As we approach the second century B.C., we find less freedom of design and a certain mannerism in the drawing, as well as a greater profusion of ornament. (*Keramic Gallery*, enlarged edition, fig. 12.)

It now remains for us to notice another description of ancient pottery in which it may be said painting gives way to sculpture, excepting in the application of simple colours to heighten the effect of the relief. These vases are of a grand and imposing character, and are modelled in a masterly manner, evidently intended from their fragile nature to be seen from an elevated position and out of reach of the ordinary spectator. These religious vases have seldom any apertures, and could not contain liquids or be used for domestic purposes; they are modelled in terra-cotta, only slighty baked, and painted over with white, pink, blue, or other light colours. The usual form is a sort of hydria or askos; the spout rises perpendicularly from the front, and from the bottom of the neck the handle arches over the globular body and is fastened at the back; this handle on the larger specimens is surmounted by a lofty draped female figure, supported on each side by winged genii resting on the body of the vase; in front, on each side of the spout, are projecting sea-horses or tritons, and under the imbricated spout is placed in relief the head of Medusa surmounted by a small Victory. They vary in height from three to five feet, and are discovered in Magna Græcia, especially in Apulia; at Cumæ in Campania, and other places. From being found at these places, they are sometimes called *Cumæan* and sometimes *Apulian*; but although possibly the work of Greek artists, they are of the Roman era, that is, about 200 B.C., and succeeded the painted vases, a branch of art which was never cultivated by them.

Within the sepulchral chambers of Etruria are discovered, arranged in niches round the sides like the Roman columbaria, small oblong quadrangle urns, about two feet long, and about the same height, including the cover, used to contain the ashes of the dead. In places where stone was abundant, they were of stone or of tufa, which from its soft nature was easily carved, sometimes of alabaster, but most frequently of terra-cotta. In the front of these sarcophagi is generally carved in relief an allegorical subject, such as a mortal conflict with winged genii bearing torches, and on the cover a recumbent figure of the deceased, his or her head resting on the left hand; most of these earthenware urns bear traces of colour, especially blue, brown, and pink, and frequently have Etruscan inscriptions.

In many of the sepulchres of Etruria bronze specula or mirrors are found in juxtaposition with the Greek vases; they are doubtless the work of Etruscan artists, and not Greek. They are circular discs of bronze with long handles of the same metal, terminating usually in animals' heads; one side is polished, the other engraved with mythological or heroic scenes. These hand-mirrors formed a real part of the toilet of the ladies of Etruria, and according to ancient custom, having been constant and valued objects during life, were consigned as companions in death. Fibulæ, hairpins, gold wreaths, and other articles of female ornament are also frequently discovered.

PART II

THE VASA FICTILIA OF ENGLAND

Romano=British Pottery

F the hundreds of thousands who daily traverse the crowded streets of this great metropolis, how very few are aware that from twelve to fifteen feet beneath them lies concealed the *débris* of a Roman city, remains of buildings, tesselated pavements, domestic utensils, personal ornaments, household gods, and coins innumerable, actually remaining in that position in which accident had placed them upwards of 1500 years ago; and having been covered over in succeeding ages, their existence was forgotten and unknown. Every generation has left some token of former habitation, however insignificant, and traces of the early British, Roman, Saxon, Norman, and early English races may be discovered by the attentive observer.

The surface of the ground in densely populated cities is raised by traffic, pulling down and rebuilding houses, the consequent waste of old material, and a variety of other causes, about on an average a foot in every century. Thus, the area comprised within the old Roman wall of London has, beneath the present level, a series of strata of former occupiers of the soil.

A section of a cutting, exhibiting these strata in a very marked manner, was sketched by the author in Cannon Street in the year 1851, and is given on the opposite page, showing the relative position of the Roman and early English pottery discovered in London.

The earliest specimens of British pottery found in England are principally funereal, discovered in the burial-places of the ancient Britons, under mounds of earth called *barrows*, or heaps of stones called *cairns*; these are the most primitive kinds of sepulchral interment. The barrows are mostly seen on elevated situations, either on downs or uncultivated spots, and the investigation, although interesting, yields in general little to repay the antiquary for his trouble, as they seldom contain more than the rude sun-dried urn, filled with the ashes of the dead, mixed with the charcoal of the funeral pile, cremation being universal at that early period. These urns are sometimes ornamented with chevrons, semicircles, and longitudinal lines, cut or scratched on the vessel. We shall not enter into any lengthened description of these early British vessels, but proceed to give the reader an account of the more artistic productions of the Roman settlers in Britain, who brought with them improved methods of making and decorating pottery as well as other manufactures.

The author's attention was directed some years since, by accidental circumstances, to the antiquities discovered in the city of London, in consequence of the numerous excavations made in the metropolis for the construction of sewers, and in clearing the sites for the erection of

Fig. 1.

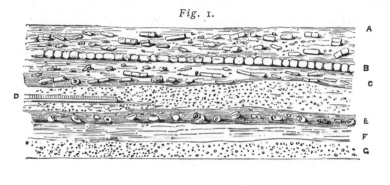

A is the present level of the street, with the remains of buildings, &c., which have accumulated since the great fire in 1666.
B is the paved roadway *in situ* before the fire of London.
C is the ground in which Norman and early English pottery is discovered.
D. In this stratum we have a sort of transition between the Roman and Saxon, and towards the bottom a piece of Roman tesselated pavement.
E. The Roman stratum is easily distinguished by the black soil, and it is more thickly embedded with remains than the others; here may be seen the lustrous red ware, drinking cups, tiles, and all sorts of domestic and personal implements.
F is the natural soil, a fine clay, resting upon G, the gravel.

some large buildings, especially the Royal Exchange, which afforded opportunities of saving from destruction many interesting relics of ancient art, and objects illustrative of the manners and customs of the Romans in Britain. His researches brought him in contact with others working in the same field, foremost among whom was Mr. C. Roach Smith, whose advice and assistance on all matters of antiquarian interest the writer is glad to have an opportunity of acknowledging.

The illustrations, therefore, in this brief and imperfect sketch of the *vasa fictilia* of England, will be supplied almost entirely from specimens discovered by the author in the metropolis.

Samian Pottery.

Evidence of Roman occupation is always manifested by the discovery of numerous fragments of vessels of a beautiful coralline red

ware, commonly known as *Samian*. These are discovered from twelve
to fifteen feet below the present level of London city, among undoubted
Roman remains.

From the quantity of this lustrous red ware which has been observed
on the sites of Roman cities and villas, it has been conjectured that it is
the identical *Samian* spoken of by Pliny and other authors as used by the
Romans at their meals and for other domestic purposes. It is indeed
expressly stated by Pliny that the ware made of Samian earth, and which
came from the island of Samos, was much esteemed by them to eat
their meals out of and display upon the board. That it was in common
use we have abundant authority; in fact, we find it proverbial, in the
same manner as we at the present day make use of the simile "as brittle
as glass." Plautus (*Menœch.* A. ii. sc. 2), "M. Placide pulta." "P. Metuis
credo, ne fores Samiæ fient." Again the same author says (*Bacch.* A.
ii. sc. 2)—

> "Vide quæso, ne quis tractet illam indiligens,
> Scis tu, ut confringi vas cito Samium solet."

Pliny says that the Samian ware was transported into foreign
countries, and that most nations under heaven used it at their tables. If
such be the case, we may reasonably ask: What has become of the
numerous vestiges which must necessarily have been deposited wherever
the Romans dwelt, if this red ware we are now considering be not identical
with it? No other red ware, at all corresponding with the descriptions
given by ancient authors, has been discovered. We are not disposed to
say that the ware found in England was actually made at Samos, but it
is a curious coincidence that the table ware used by the Romans in Italy,
and that used by the Roman settlers in Britain, should have been both of
a red colour. Martial says—

> "Cui portat gaudens ancilla *paropside rubra*
> Alecem."

And Persius—

> "*Rubrum* que amplexa *catinum*
> Cauda natat thynni, tumet alba fidelia vino."

The *paropsis rubra* and *rubrum catinum*, here mentioned, both refer
to dishes used by the Romans at their meals, such as Pliny speaks of
as Samian.[1] The former was a dish to hold vegetables (the *paropsis
leguminis* of Suetonius), and the other to hold larger viands, such as, in
this instance, a large fish. The *rubrum catinum* is also termed by Lucilius
Samium catinum—

> "Et non pauper uti, *Samio*, curtoque *catino*."

---

[1] The Editor is indebted to Mr. John Bellows of Gloucester for particulars of a fragment of a bowl,
found when digging the Metropolitan Railway Station of Aldgate, painted with a Chinese letter which
signifies "Rice," and which he contends goes to prove that during the Roman occupation this comestible
was imported from China.

The term *Samian* was probably applied to all vessels used at the table, much in the same way as in the present day *china* is a term used indiscriminately for all descriptions of ware, whether porcelain or fayence, European or Oriental. Two of these Samian bowls are engraved in *Montfauçon* (vol. v. pp. 124, 144), and are placed among the "Batterie de Cuisine." Speaking of the ware he says, "C'est fort creux, et peut avoir servie à mettre des sausses ou de la bouillie."

Tibullus alludes to these vessels—

"At tibi læta trahant Samiæ convivia testæ,
  Fictaque Cumana lubrica terra rota."

Fig. 2 is a large and elegantly formed vase of the lustrous red ware, ornamented in relief with scrolls; on the bottom of the interior is the potter's name, OF. VITAL., meaning Officinâ Vitalis: from the workshop of Vitalis. It was found in St. Martin's-le-Grand, August, 1845. (*Geol. Mus. Coll. Chaffers*, 295.)

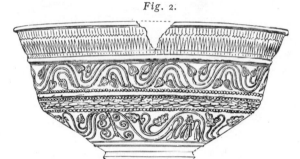

Fig. 2.

The most remarkable fact connected with this ware is its uniform colour wherever found, whether in France, Germany, or England, and this circumstance has caused considerable discussion as to the locality in which it was originally manufactured. M. Brongniart (*Traité des Arts Céramiques*), speaking of it, says: This resemblance in respect to the texture, the density, and above all the colour of this ware in every country, is a sort of enigma difficult to solve in a satisfactory manner; for when we consider the number of places at a great distance from each other where it is discovered, and the difference of soil in each, the difficulty arises how the Roman potters could everywhere make a paste so exactly similar, with materials necessarily so different; for it cannot be supposed they would carry with them their paste for making these vessels. It may, however, be presumed that, choosing a spot where they could procure a clay, colourless, and adapted to furnish a paste sufficiently dense, they gave it the nasturtium red colour by introducing a proportion of red ochre.

Fig. 3 is a perfect bowl of Roman red ware, found at Cologne: design, a soldier in armour, with sword and shield, engaged in combat with a retiarius, holding on his left arm a net with a sword, and in his right hand a three-pronged spear. There is also a draped figure presenting a palm branch to an emperor seated on a curule chair. The subject of the retiarius armed with a net and three-pronged fork, fighting with a secutor (*Geol. Mus. Coll. Chaffers, E.* 204), frequently occurs on the red pottery found in England. M. Brongniart mentions the discovery at Rheinzabern, a town in Alsace (Taberna Rheni), of several hundreds of

Fig. 3.

fragments, as well as some moulds of a lion's head, a wild boar, &c., and a vase with figures and animals, with a border of the usual pattern of festoons and tassels, and potter's name, COBNERTVS.

He also gives a plan of a kiln for the manufacture, as he supposes, of this red pottery at Heiligenberg, near Strasbourg, discovered by M. Schweighæuser, as well as sixteen moulds for making the vessels, but the patterns are not of the same character as the Samian, nor of so good a finish. The author had several of these terra-cotta moulds in his possession, discovered at Cologne, which are now in the British Museum.

The plan adopted by the Roman potters in Germany, where these moulds are discovered, is somewhat after this manner. Stamps, with handles either of bronze or baked clay, were modelled in relief with patterns, devices, and potters' names; these were employed to impress an incused pattern on the interior of a general mould of soft clay, capable of containing the vessel in one piece, the interior being first rounded smoothly into a perfect form by the lathe. The mould thus covered with the required pattern was fired, and became perfectly hard for future use. The moist paste, of which the vessel itself was to be made, was then pressed into the mould by hand, so as to obtain a perfect impression of all the minute details. The irregular surface of the interior was smoothed by being turned in the lathe (for the lathe-marks are always visible), while yet in a soft state, and before it was removed from the mould, thus preventing any injury which might otherwise happen to the ornamental vase by handling. Both the mould and vase inside it were then placed in the kiln and baked; the former, having been already fired, would not shrink, but act as a seggar to protect it from smoke and regulate the heat; the latter would necessarily shrink during the baking, and be easily removed when finished. The moulds would then be kept for future use. Dr. Fabroni, in his work on the Aretine Vases (*Storia degli Antichi Vasi Fittili Aretini*, Arezzo, 1840) gives a plate of some moulds for ornamenting the ware made at Arezzo, in one of which the bowl still remained, having been fired but not removed.

The plain red pateræ were simply turned in the lathe, and sometimes ornamented round the flat edge with ivy leaves laid on in *slip* of the same colour. In the annexed woodcut will be seen the potter's name, VRSVLVS, impressed across the centre, which is the usual position in the red ware;

occasionally the name is found outside the vase. The names of the potters have so close an affinity with each other, whether found in Italy, Germany, France, or England, that we may reasonably infer they had one common origin, but where that locality was has not yet been satisfactorily ascertained. In England no kilns for making it have been discovered, but in France and Germany kilns have been found, and moulds also, which it had been supposed were used for the manufacture of this particular ware, but the evidence is not clear enough to affirm positively that it actually was so. The moulds hitherto discovered appear to be for the manufacture of a coarser description of pottery, and the ornaments certainly not of so high a finish; in fact, they are just such imitations as we should expect to find in a distant colony.

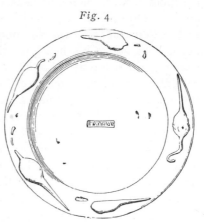

Fig. 4.

Mr. C. Roach Smith is of opinion that this elegant ware was made in Gaul and Germany, derived from the earlier and more artistic models of Italy, and finds among the names of the potters many which he considers of Gaulish origin, as Dagodubnus, Dagomarus, Divicatus, Cobnertus, Tasconus, &c., whilst others are derived from a mixture of races; but the greater part are obviously **Roman**, as Severus, Albanus, Cassius, Atilianus, Censorinus, Domitianus, Felix, Vitalis, &c. Mr. C. Roach Smith (*Collectanea Antiqua*, vol. v. p. 157) records the discovery of a monument erected to the memory of the daughter of a Romano-Gaulish potter, whose name occurs on a vessel of this red ware found in London. It represents in relief a young girl holding a mirror and a basket of fruit; above her head is this inscription: D.M. AXVLA CINTVGENI FIGVLI FILIA. Axula, the daughter of Cintugenus the potter.

A long list of several hundred potters' names, including those formerly in the author's collection, is given in Mr. C. Roach Smith's *Illustrations of Roman London*, a work to which the reader is referred for more detailed information on this most interesting subject. (*Geol. Mus. Coll. Chaffers*, 326.)

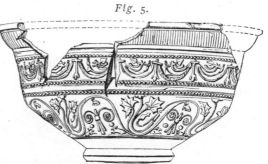

Fig. 5.

Fig. 5 is a large fragment of a Samian vase, $9\frac{1}{2}$ in. in diameter, enriched with elegant scrolls and festoons. Potter's mark, OF. RVFINI; found in London.

Some of the patterns with which this ware is decorated are exceedingly beautiful and interesting, illustrating the Roman mythology and the different games they were accustomed to celebrate; gladiatorial combats; conflicts between men and beasts in the arena; hunting subjects, and field-sports. On one fine fragment found in Lad Lane, London, is represented in the first compartment a seated figure drinking from the small end of a horn, held above his head; in the next are two male and female figures dancing, the one playing on the double pipe (tibiæ pares), the other holding a tambourine (tympanum over her head; another figure is beating time to the music with the castanets (crumata) in his hands, and an instrument called the scabellum under one foot; another division exhibits two pigmies, armed with spear, sword, and shield, attacking their inveterate enemies the cranes, who invaded their corn-fields; hounds and rabbits are introduced in another compartment. The patterns formed of the vine, its tendrils, leaves, and grapes, are tastefully grouped. On other vases are seen bas-reliefs of the heathen deities, Mars, Mercury, Apollo, Vulcan, Venus, &c.; some modelled from existing statues.

The vase (fig. 6) represents the Venus de Medicis, repeated, as a border; found at St. Mary-at-Hill, London, in 1845. (*Geol. Mus. Coll. Chaffers*, 328.)

Fig. 6.

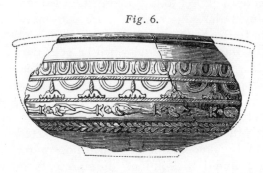

In general the ornaments are moulded as before explained, but in some few instances the figures in relief appear to have been cast in a mould and carefully finished previous to their being affixed to the surface of the vase. Mr. C. Roach Smith gives a sketch of a beautiful specimen of this variety formerly in his collection. (*Illustrations of Roman London*, p. 97.)

Some fragments of vessels of precisely the same material, colour, and glaze have been discovered, having incused patterns cut into the surface of the vase with great sharpness and skill, evidently by the lathe, as is our cut glass of the present day; but no perfect example has yet been met with.

The general forms of the Samian ware are bowls and dishes or pateræ, of various sizes and of considerable thickness, to bear the constant wear to which it was subjected in being repeatedly moved on and off the board at meals; unlike the Athenian vases, which were for ornament only, and the chief excellence of which consisted in their extreme lightness. Fig. 7 is a plain bowl of this red ware, nearly perfect, 9 inches in diameter; potter's mark, TITIVS, enclosed in a circle; found in Queen Street, City, 1850.

Fig. 7.

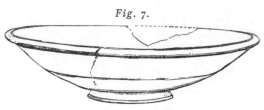

Drinking cups of the red lustrous ware are never found in England. The small open bowls may perhaps have been occasionally used to drink out of, but they would be inconvenient for the purpose. An elegant poculum with two handles, or small amphora, for passing round a table from one to another of the guests, is annexed, fig. 8; it is the red ware, ornamented in relief with a peacock amid ivy leaves laid on in *slip* of the same coloured paste, $7\frac{1}{2}$ in. high. Found at Cologne. (*Geol. Mus. Coll. Chaffers, E.* 204.)

Fig. 8.

The large ornamented bowls and plain pateræ were used to place the viands and substantial part of the repast in, while the small plain Samian cups of the same red ware were those described by ancient authors as the *salinum*, or salt-cellar, and the *acetabulum*, or vinegar-cup, which were put on the board to dip the lettuce and viands into, or to hold occasionally pickles, sauces, or other condiments.

The acetabulum was used as a measure, as we should say *a tea-cup full*. The cyathus or ladle held one-twelfth of a sextarius or pint, the acetabulum one-eighth of a pint. The Romans divided the sextarius into twelve equal parts, called cyathi; therefore the cups were called sextantes, quadrantes, trientes, &c., according to the number of cyathi they contained. Fig. 9 is an acetabulum of the Samian ware, with potter's mark; found in London, 1849.

Fig. 9.

A circumstance connected with these cups may not be unworthy of notice, as it shows the antiquity of the "thimble-rig" of the present day. The use of the acetabulum for this purpose is distinctly mentioned, they placed three of these cups on a three-legged table, and underneath each were put pebbles, which were removed from one to the other by sleight of hand or abstracted altogether, to the great astonishment and amusement of the spectators, who found the stones under different cups from those which they expected. These persons were called acetabularii because they played with the acetabulum.

Aretium, in Italy, is one of the towns mentioned by Pliny as celebrated for the finer description of earthenware. Dr. Fabroni has published a work descriptive of this ware (*Storia degli Antichi Vasi Fittili Aretini,* Arezzo, 1840), which is altogether distinct from the lustrous red ware called Samian, differing both in colour and execution; the ware of Arezzo being of a darker red, and the reliefs, although, as before noticed, produced in the same manner, are of higher finish. The potters' names, too, are generally impressed in a sort of footprint, or else outside the vase.

3

Figs. 10 and 11 represent a cup of Aretine manufacture, found in Lon-

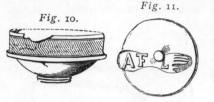

Fig. 10.

Fig. 11.

don in 1841, with the maker's name impressed at the bottom; it has a sort of engine-turned pattern round the top. Isidore of Seville speaks of a red ware as being the manufacture of Aretium; the passage runs thus:

" Aretina vasa, ex Aretio municipio Italiæ, dicuntur ubi fiunt, sunt enim rubra. De quibus Sedulius—

' Rubra quod appositum testa ministrat olus.'

Samia vasa quidam putant ad oppido Samo Græciæ habere nomen, alii, dicunt cretam esse Italiæ, quæ non longe a Roma nascitur quæ Samia appellat."—*Isidore*, 20. 4.

Here Isidore is doubtless speaking of two red wares, and even in his time (seventh century) there appears to have been a difference of opinion as to the locality of the Samian ware; the quotation from Sedulius would not solely apply to the Arezzo ware, but to any dish of red colour.

The pattern round the top of the Aretine vases is evidently the *ovolo*, or egg and arrow decoration, similar to that depicted on Greek vases (vide *Hamilton*), but unlike the border on the Samian, which is formed of festoons of drapery, with a cord and tassel pendent between each, appearing somewhat similar at the first glance, but the difference being easily detected upon close inspection.

Figs. 12 and 13 represent a cup of red pottery of Arezzo; it exhibits the higher style of art employed in ornamenting this kind of ware in

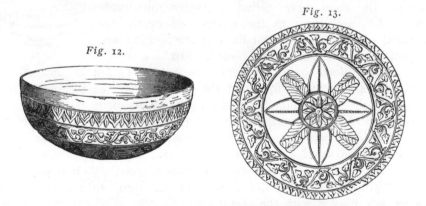

Fig. 12.

Fig. 13.

Roman Italy. The two views show the side and base of the cup; $2\frac{1}{2}$ inches high, 5 inches diameter.

The Samian vessels we have just described are so very superior to those which follow in texture, quality, glazing (*Geol. Mus. Coll. Chaffers*, 1028), and decoration, that we may liken them to fine porcelain as compared with coarse earthenware; they were of home manufacture, and although no kilns have been discovered in this country in which the red lustrous ware was manufactured, yet, on the other hand, several have been exhumed in which the more common description of vessels remained as placed by the Romano-British potter for baking, and the productions of each particular pottery may be recognised. Although these fictile vases are of common material, still a peculiar elegance of form may be observed in their outlines, and the ornamentation, though rude, has a good effect.

Upchurch Pottery.

Upon the banks of the Medway, near the village of Upchurch, there was, in the time of the occupation of Britain by the Romans, a very extensive pottery. Along the shore for many miles may be observed vast quantities of Roman ware in fragments; in fact, the mud or clay when the tide is out is found to be completely filled with Roman pottery. The pottery is of a fine and hard texture; its colour is usually a blue black, produced by baking it in the smoke of vegetable substances. The ornaments are simple but diversified; they appear to have been effected by means of a flat stick notched at the end, which was passed over the surface of the moist clay in parallel, zigzag, or crossed lines, leaving the pattern incuse. In some, the ornament consists of small dots or pellets encircling the vessel in squares, circles, and diamond patterns, which

Fig. 14.

Fig. 15.

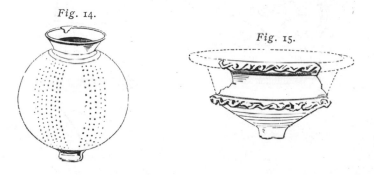

appear to have been stencilled on the surface, usually of a different colour to the body of the ware, but mostly white. Some of the vessels found here are of a red colour, bottle-shaped, having been subjected to a greater degree of heat in the burning.

Fig. 14 is a globular vase of reddish paste with black glaze; the pattern is formed of stencilled dots; it was found in Queen Street, Cheapside, June 1850, and is probably from the Upchurch manufactory.[1]

There is another description of ware, which is, no doubt, of native manufacture, but scarce and seldom found entire; it is of a light brown or ash-coloured clay, with crinkled ornament in relief round the edges, and unglazed. Fig. 15 shows the usual form of this singular kind of pottery; the pattern is made with a tool; it was found in St. Martin's-le Grand, October 1845.

[1 There are several specimens of Upchurch ware in the Jermyn Street Museum.]

Castor Pottery.

A more ornamental kind of drinking cup was made at Castor, in Northamptonshire. The discoveries of Mr. Artis in that neighbourhood revealed quantities of this ware in the kilns, as placed by the potters for baking. This gentleman traced the potteries to an extent of upwards of twenty miles on the banks of the Nen (see Artis' *Durobrivæ of Antoninus Identified and Illustrated*). These vessels are ornamented in relief with hunting subjects, representations of fishes, scrolls, foliage, and human figures; the mode of operation seems to have been by means of sharp and blunt skewer implements and a *slip* of suitable consistency. These implements were of two kinds, one thick enough to carry sufficient *slip* for the head, neck, and body of animals, and another small enough to delineate the details, as the tongue, eye, lower jaws, legs, and tail. There

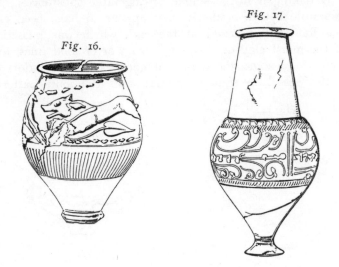

Fig. 16.

Fig. 17.

appears to have been no retouching after the *slip* trailed from the implement. These vessels were glazed after the figures were laid on, which are usually of a different colour from the body of the ware, as white on a light brown or chocolate ground. (*Geol. Mus. Coll. Chaffers*, 234 *and* 707.)

Fig. 16 is a poculum of the Castor ware of white paste, dark brown glaze with a metalloid lustre, representing hounds hunting a stag, laid on in slip after the vase was turned, and then glazed; a sort of engine-turned tool-work is seen at the bottom; height $4\frac{1}{2}$ inches; found in Cateaton Street, London, January, 1845.

Another elegant drinking cup of the Castor ware is annexed, fig. 17. It is 8 inches high: yellowish-brown paste. The glaze on the largest upper portion is black, with the scroll ornament in *slip* of a white pipe-clay; it has two bands of tool-work made before glazing; the stem of the vase has a red glaze; found at Winchester. Some others of a higher artistic order, with subjects from the heathen mythology, have been found; one at Bedford Purlieus, by Mr. Artis, had a representation of Hercules delivering Hesione from the monster; another at Colchester, with a hunting subject, two gladiators and two men leading a bear. These all have their names written over their heads, and are wonderfully well done, considering they are laid on in slip with a sort of skewer and not moulded. (*Geol. Mus. Coll. Chaffers, E.* 214 *and* 219.)

This kind of pottery has been occasionally discovered in Holland and Germany, where they were perhaps imported from England. Fig. 18 is introduced for comparison; it was found on the banks of the Rhine; it is $4\frac{1}{2}$ inches high, of a white paste covered with a metalloid glaze, representing dogs chasing a deer, worked in slip or *barbotine* in the way before mentioned. A drinking cup of another pattern, but of similar ware to that found at Castor, is here given, fig. 19. It is $5\frac{3}{4}$ inches high, of a white body covered with a red glaze; the mode of ornamentation is

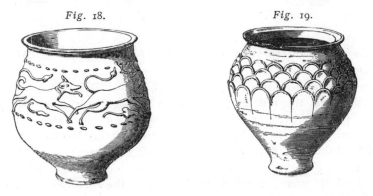

Fig. 18.   *Fig.* 19.

pleasing, and appears as if obtained by overlapping cut pieces of clay before glazing. The usual form of the wine cups will be seen from the foregoing specimens; they are almost invariably smaller at bottom than top, and many, formerly in the author's possession, which are now in the British Museum, have short convivial words laid on in relief, as IMPLE, REPLE, BIBE, VIVAS, AVE, DA VINUM, VITA, &c.; they contain about half a pint of liquid; others again are so pointed as not to be able to stand on a table, but must when once filled be emptied of their contents.

Fig. 20 is a vase or cup $4\frac{1}{2}$ inches high, of greyish-white body and black glaze. The pattern is formed of small bosses laid on in white slip, after turning, and before glazing and firing. (*Geol. Mus. Coll. Chaffers, E.* 221.)

New Forest Ware.[1]

There are many other places in England where kilns for making pottery have been discovered. Mr. J. Conyers, an antiquary, met with

[1] Professor Church places this pottery at Crockhill, and considers that it existed until the fifth century. There are some characteristic examples, E. 130-134, in the Jermyn Street Museum.]

✓

some in digging foundations north-west of St. Paul's in 1677; he states the depth to have been 26 feet, and gives sketches of the urns found in them (*Sloane MSS.*, 958, fol. 105); there were also lamps, bottles, and urns of the coarser sort.   Remains of extensive potteries have been

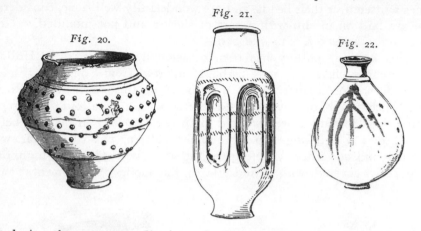

Fig. 21.

Fig. 20.

Fig. 22.

found in the western district of the New Forest, in Hampshire. (*Archæologia*, vol. xxxv.)

Fig. 21 is a drinking cup, 6 inches high, of red clay, covered with a blackish glaze, the red tint being seen through it; the sides are compressed into seven compartments, and a pattern in bands produced by tool-marks after turning on the lathe; found in Lothbury, 1847. (*Geol. Mus. Coll. Chaffers*,173, *and E.* 90.)

Fig. 23.

Fig. 22 is a small bottle, 6¾ inches high, of yellowish-white body, painted in black in the manner shown; from Castor, 1826.

Fig. 23 is a small vase of unglazed brownish-red pottery; found in London. (*Geol. Mus. Coll. Chaffers*, 119.)

Among the culinary utensils used by the Romans in this country was a broad shallow vessel termed a mortarium; it had on the bottom of the interior sharp angular pebbles embedded in the ware, for the purpose of triturating vegetable substances, or bruising them with liquids,

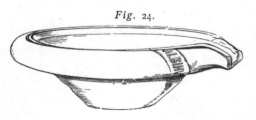

Fig. 24.

being provided with a spout to pour off the mixture when rubbed to the required consistency; it had a broad rim, which turned over outwards about half-way, apparently for the purpose of concentrating the heat round the vessel when placed upon the fire; on this rim is generally found the name of the potter.   These mortaria are exceedingly numerous, not only in London, but in other parts of England, wherever Roman buildings have been discovered; at Headington, near Oxford, Mr. Llewellyn Jewitt found fragments of at least two hundred of them. They vary in size from 7 inches to nearly 2 feet in diameter, and are about 5 inches deep; most of them, when found, give evidence of great wear, having generally a hole rubbed through the bottom.

Fig. 24 is a mortarium, $10\frac{3}{4}$ inches diameter, of light brown ware, unglazed; the potter's mark, ALBINVS, may be observed stamped upon the rim. It was found in Smithfield in April, 1844.

Mortaria are sometimes found of the red lustrous ware called Samian; these are provided with spouts of lions' heads or masks, through which the liquor was poured, and the grains of hard stone forced into the paste inside it as usual, for the purpose of trituration. (*Geol. Mus. Coll. Chaffers*, 380 *and* 631.)

Fig. 25 is of this red ware, and bears the potter's name, VLIGGI, M.,

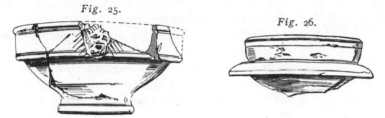

Fig. 25.

Fig. 26.

or Manû; made by the hand of the potter Uliggus; it was found in London. The next cut, fig. 26, is a fragment of a vessel of uncommon external form, of the red lustrous ware, for heating liquids, with a broad projecting

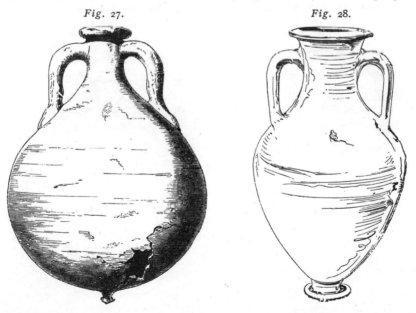

Fig. 27.

Fig. 28.

belt turned downwards to concentrate the heat round the bottom of the pan; found in London.

Large amphoræ have been discovered, capable of holding ten or twelve gallons, mostly in fragments; they were in general use for storing wine, oil, or other liquids. Two of them were found perfect in an excavation in Aldermanbury, one of which came into the author's possession, and is now in the Jermyn Street Museum. It is 2 feet 9 inches high, its largest diameter 2 feet; it is of a very thick light brown clay, and unglazed, the form as annexed (fig. 27). (*Geol. Mus. Coll. Chaffers*, 989.)

These large vessels were frequently used to contain funereal deposits, the upper part being cut off and fitted on again as a cover; glass cinerary urns, filled with charred bones collected from the funeral pyre, are found within them. In the Charles's Museum at Maidstone are two of these, discovered in a walled cemetery at Lockham Wood, and others were recently exhumed at Colchester, containing similar deposits, now in the Museum at Colchester Castle.

Fig. 29.

Smaller amphoræ are common amongst remains of Roman domestic vessels found in the metropolis, some of elegant forms. Fig. 28 was found in digging the foundation of London Bridge; it is 17 inches high, and unglazed. (*Geo. Mus. Coll. Chaffers*, 135 *and* 718.)

Fig. 29, another amphora-formed vessel of a light red ware, was found in Cannon Street, London; and fig. 30, also of a red body, painted with a zigzag band round the upper part, is from Old Broad Street. Fig. 31 is a small flattened amphora, used to carry at the side,

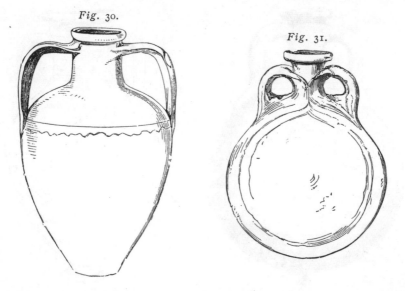

Fig. 30.

Fig. 31.

suspended by the handles round the neck; it is unglazed, with red markings round the sides; found in Moorgate Street in 1835. (*Geol. Mus. Coll. Chaffers*, 962 *and* 713.)

The lamps found in England are seldom of bronze, but almost invariably of terra-cotta, with small projections at the side instead of handles; they were usually placed upon flat earthenware trays, with upright ridges

Fig. 32.   Fig. 33.

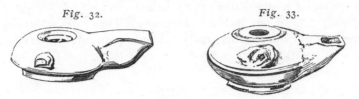

and handles, into which they fitted, and were thus carried about. These lamps are, with few exceptions, of a rude character, being mostly without ornaments or potters' names. Figs. 32 and 33 are specimens of the ordinary lamp, the former found in Queen Street, Cheapside, the latter in Lad Lane, in 1842. (*Geol. Mus. Coll. Chaffers, 237, 255, and 249.*) Fig. 34 has a hole through its centre for placing on a point; it is of black glaze ornamented with red bands; found in London.

Sometimes they are found with two or more burners; these larger lamps were suspended from the top of a high tripod or stand with a very long stem. (*Geol. Mus. Coll. Chaffers, E. 222.*)

Fig. 34.

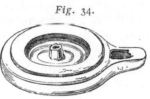

Fig. 35 has eight burners, and is provided with three small loops on the inner circle; it was suspended by small bronze chains; it is of a reddish clay, $7\frac{1}{2}$ inches diameter; discovered at Cologne.

Tiles were made of a red clay, very compact and well fired, and moreover extremely durable; for those made upwards of 1500 years since are as firm at the present day as when first made. Bonding tiles were used

Fig. 35.   Fig. 36.

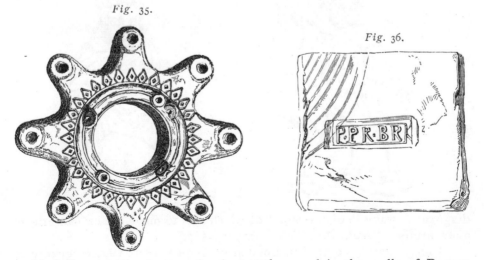

to bind the courses of stone firmly together, and in the walls of Roman buildings we usually find several courses of Kentish rag or other stone,

and then a double row of these bonding tiles. They were also used
to form the arches over doors and windows. One of these tiles in the
author's possession measures $15\frac{6}{10}$ inches in length, $10\frac{4}{10}$ inches in
breadth, and $1\frac{4}{10}$ of an inch in thickness. They are generally marked
with semicircles at one of their ends. The hypocaust tiles are square, and

Fig. 37.

Fig. 38.

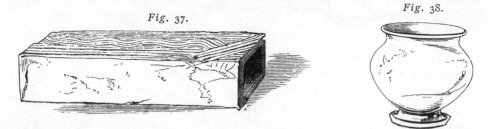

were used for constructing the pillars which supported the floor above the
hypocaust, and between which the flames of the furnace permeated. They
are frequently stamped with the name of the legion or cohort which was
at the time stationed at Londinium. Fig. 36 is a hypocaust tile, inscribed
P.PR.BR.: it was taken from a Roman building in Queen Street, Cheapside, in 1850: size $7\frac{3}{4}$ inches square. (*Geol. Mus. Coll. Chaffers*, 745.)

Flue-tiles are of various dimensions, but usually quadrilateral, long
and hollow, with lateral apertures for the heated air to pass through.
They were placed one upon another, end to end, along the inner sides of
the walls, to convey hot air from the hypocaust to distant rooms. They
are generally ornamented with incuse patterns of geometrical figures, and

Fig. 39.

Fig. 40.

diagonal or wavy lines, the object of which was to make the cement adhere
more firmly. (*Geol. Mus. Coll. Chaffers*, 117.)

Fig. 37 was discovered in London in August, 1846. Large quantities
of tubular draining-tiles have been discovered in and about London, fitting
into each other, and cemented, as at the present day. Roof-tiles were

made with longitudinal edges turned upwards; these, when placed side by side, were fastened together by semi-cylindrical tiles, larger at the lower end, which overlapped the narrow end of that placed next to it.

Cinerary urns are more frequently found without the city walls: the usual form is like that annexed. Fig. 38 contained bones, charcoal, and wood ashes. Another vase, found with this by the author in Wells Street, Jewin Street, a few yards from the circular bastion of the old Roman wall (which may still be seen in Cripplegate Churchyard), contained about seventy silver denarii, ranging from the Emperor Galba to the Empress Faustina Senior. They were all well preserved; those of the early Emperors were slightly worn from circulation, but the later coins of Antoninus Pius and Faustina seemed fresh from the die; from which circumstance we may infer that they were buried in the reign of Faustina, A.D. 140.— Vide British *Archæological Journal*, vol. ii. p. 272.

The next illustration (fig. 39) is a Roman terra-cotta figure of a boy on horseback; another, found by the author, was a rattle in form of a helmeted head. Clay statuettes are also discovered of heathen deities, but the penates are usually of bronze. Another terra-cotta figure of a child (No. 40) is of much better work than the preceding: the drapery hangs in graceful folds round the upper part of the figure. This was found also in the metropolis. (*Geol. Mus. Coll. Chaffers,* 715 *and* 250.)

PART III

Mediæval Earthenware Vessels

ROM the seventh to the fifteenth century, a period of nearly eight hundred years, but few examples of pottery that can with certainty be appropriated have been handed down to us; and when they do occasionally appear in the excavations in and about the metropolis, they possess so few distinctive characteristics, that it is almost vain our attempting to identify them with any particular century within this wide range. We will, however, endeavour to clear up a portion of the mystery which has hitherto enveloped these mediæval earthenware vessels. It must be remarked that we are to consider them merely in regard to their utility and domestic economy, and not to their elegance of form or fineness of material; for in those respects they present a lamentable decline from the Greek and Roman periods, when even vessels of the coarsest clay had a pleasing effect. We do not, therefore, speak of them as works of art, but as of homely manufacture and for domestic use, which, from their fragile nature and comparative insignificance as to value, have in few instances withstood the shock of time, or been thought worthy of preservation. These fictile vessels are extremely rare, and it is a matter of considerable difficulty to appropriate them to their particular era; it is only by comparison that we are likely to arrive at any satisfactory result.

As a reference to the Norman and early English manuscripts will materially assist us in our inquiries, a few of the more striking forms of Norman earthen cups are selected from various manuscripts,[1] which, by comparison with many of those hereafter engraved, will enable us to identify them as belonging to that period.

A point that requires investigation is the glazing on these vessels, and when it is probable this mode of application, either as a means of decoration or utility, was revived, if it were ever entirely lost. The green glaze appears to have been intended more for use than ornament, as it seldom covers the entire surface of the vessel, but only round the inside

[1] Strutt's "Horda Ang."

of the lip and upper portion of the exterior, where the liquids would come in immediate contact, or might be spilt over; this could not result

Fig. 41.

MEDIÆVAL EARTHEN VESSELS FOUND IN LONDON. (*Coll. Chaffers.*)

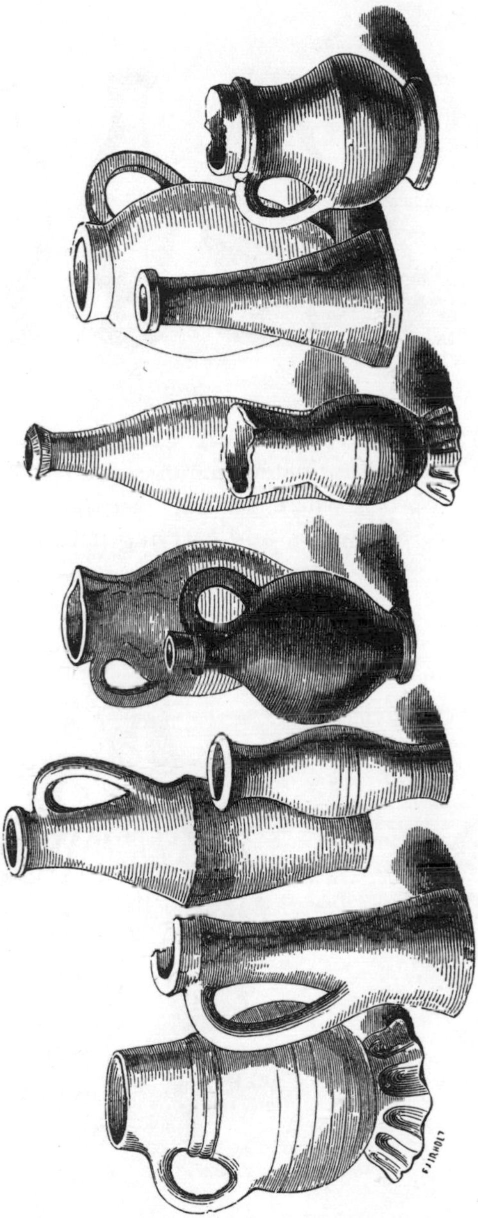

1. A wide-mouthed jug of brown earth, glazed all over, the foot ornamented with indentations —6 inches high.
2. Jug of reddish-brown earth, of rude manufacture, unglazed— 6 inches high.
3. Jug of yellow clay, glaze of the same colour on the upper part —8 inches high.
4. Pot of reddish earth, unglazed—5 inches high.
5. Jug of light-coloured clay, glazed on the upper part—6 ins. high.
6. Bottle of slate-coloured glaze—5½ inches high.
7. Pot of red earth, unglazed—7 ins. high.
8. Pot of yellowish earth—5 ins. high.
9. Jug of cream-coloured clay, yellow glaze mottled with green on the upper part—6 inches high.
10. Straight-sided vessel of yellow earth, slightly glazed—6 ins. high.
11. Jug of yellowish clay, with green glaze on the upper portion— 6 inches high.

from accident or decay. Imperfections or blemishes in the ware are generally covered over with a spot of glaze.

It is surprising the great depth at which these fictile vessels with a light green mottled glaze have been found in excavations; in some instances they have been discovered mixed with Roman remains. Fig. 43 is a water-pitcher, with mottled green glaze on the upper part; it is ten inches high, and was discovered at a depth of twelve or fourteen feet, in

Fig. 42.

Queen Street, Cheapside, in August, 1842. (*Coll. Chaffers.*) Vessels of similar form are represented in an illuminated manuscript of the eleventh century (*Cotton MSS., Nero, C.* iv), where servants are taking pitchers from the cupboard, filling them with water, and carrying it to the Saviour

Fig. 43.

Fig. 44.

to be changed into wine, at the marriage at Cana. Mr. Wellbeloved, in his Eburacum, says, that with undoubted remains of Roman earthenware he frequently found fragments and entire vessels of a coarse sort, generally of a yellowish-white clay, with a strong glaze of various shades of green, and adduces several instances; he states that at Carlisle, fifteen feet below the surface, and beneath several fragments of Samian ware, were discovered

Fig. 45.

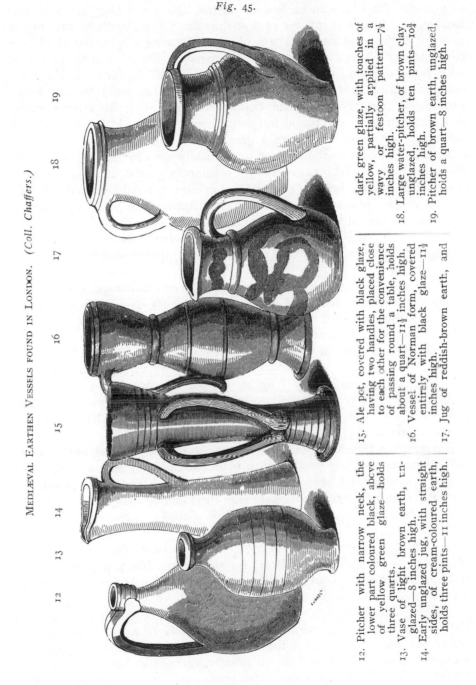

MEDIÆVAL EARTHEN VESSELS FOUND IN LONDON. (*Coll. Chaffers.*)

12. Pitcher with narrow neck, the lower part coloured black, above of yellow green glaze—holds three quarts.

13. Vase of light brown earth, unglazed—8 inches high.

14. Early unglazed jug, with straight sides, of cream-coloured earth, holds three pints—11 inches high.

15. Ale pot, covered with black glaze, having two handles, placed close to each other for the convenience of passing round a table, holds about a quart—11½ inches high.

16. Vessel of Norman form, covered entirely with black glaze—11½ inches high.

17. Jug of reddish-brown earth, and dark green glaze, with touches of yellow, partially applied in a wavy, or festoon pattern—7½ inches high.

18. Large water-pitcher, of brown clay, unglazed, holds ten pints—10¾ inches high.

19. Pitcher of brown earth, unglazed, holds a quart—8 inches high.

two ancient pitchers, which inclined him to regard them as the work of Roman potters. Without admitting these pitchers to be Roman, these circumstances tend to prove the great antiquity of the particular sort of glazing in question, and that it was used much earlier than has been supposed. An Etruscan or Roman lagena here given (fig. 44), with one handle, is evidence in favour of that opinion. The mouth of this jug is pinched at the sides into the shape of a leaf, forming a spout for the liquor to be poured off in a small stream; the front is ornamented by lines (cut with some sharp instrument), representing a fish, the fins of which are coloured with a green glaze, as also the lip and the wavy pattern which runs down from the top to the bottom; the ground is of a black glaze. A Roman cinerary urn, found in Queen Street, Cheapside, in 1842, had on the inner surface of the mouth a green glaze, and a spot or two on the exterior, as though some had been accidentally spilt; and a Roman lamp, the inner part of which is evenly and brilliantly glazed of a green colour, the outside having been so originally, but now partially rubbed off. To the latter two it may be urged, that this appearance was the result of vitrification, caused by intense heat; and such may perhaps have been the fact; but the jug is more conclusive, as it is very improbable (even supposing it to have been subjected to a great heat) that it should be coloured in a pattern.

Fig. 46 is a very early specimen of a pilgrim's bottle, partaking much of the form of the short and flat Roman amphora, No. 31, before given. It is of cream-coloured ware, unglazed, 10 inches high. The two sides of this bottle are separately turned and joined together in the line of the two handles. Found in Cannon Street, 1851. (*Geol. Mus. Coll. Chaffers, F.* 1.)

Fig. 47 is a tall early English jug of the Norman form; it is of light-coloured clay, partially covered with a yellow glaze, quite perfect, and of large capacity, being 16½ inches high; found in Cannon Street, 1853.

Fig. 48, a jug, 8 inches high; cream-colour body, upper part covered with transparent glaze spotted with black; found at London Wall, 1844. A jug of this form was discovered in Friday Street with pennies of Henry III. and Edward I.; its date may therefore be assigned to the latter part of the thirteenth century. (See *C. R. Smith's Catalogue of London Antiquities,* p. 114.)

Fig. 49, a costrel, 10 inches high, with two projections on each side, pierced for passing a cord or strap, for suspension, like a pilgrim's bottle; red body, glazed in a marble pattern with white and red; found in London, August, 1850. (*Geol. Mus. Coll. Chaffers, F.* 6, 10, 20.)

The gourd, pumpkin, coco-nut, and other fruits with a hard rind or shell, were undoubtedly the most primitive vessels, being naturally formed ready for use; and most of the forms of the fictile ware are derivable from this source. It would be an interesting task to pursue this subject further. We should probably find, that in those countries where a particular fruit was most abundant, the fictile vessels would partake of its figure and ornamentation. The gourd and coco-nut were in common use in England; there are frequent allusions to them.   "A standing gilt nut" is mentioned in the will of Sir Thomas Lyttleton, A.D. 1480, and in

Fig. 47.

Fig. 46.

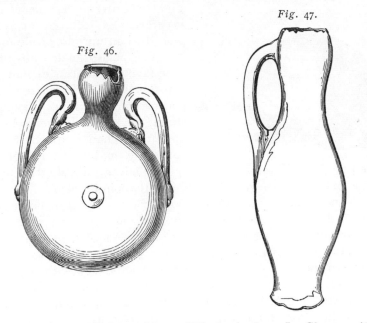

certain inventories of Wolsey, Queen Elizabeth, &c.   In Chaucer (*Canter-bury Tales*), the maniple says to the cook—

"I have here in my *gourd* a draught of win."

In the "Comptes Royaux de France," 1391, we read, "Pour ij seaux et j *courge* ferrez, pour porter l'eaue es chambres de Madame Ysabel et

Fig. 48.   Fig. 49.

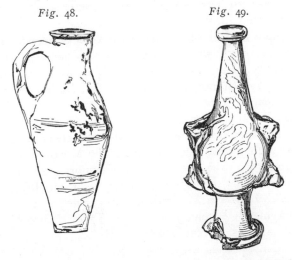

Madame Iohanne de France, x*s*.;" and in the inventory of Margaret of Austria, 1524, "Deux grosses pommes et ung concombre de terre cuyte, paincts."

4

The annexed cut represents a gourd-shaped bottle of brown earth, unglazed; perhaps a costrel used by travellers to carry liquids; it is slightly flattened on one of its sides to prevent it rolling, but cannot be placed in an upright position.

Fig. 50.

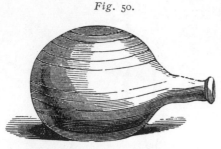

The pomegranate and pine-apple were favourite objects of imitation for cups; many of which, from their expensive workmanship, having withstood the general wreck consequent upon the change of fashion. The following is the description of one presented to Queen Elizabeth: "A cuppe of silver guilt, shutting and opening in the middest, pomegranade fashion, the handle being a wheat eare." In like manner, other natural productions, such as horns of beasts, eggs of ostriches, shells, &c., were formed into drinking cups, and were the types of earthenware vessels, which partook more or less of their form.

From the recent examination of Saxon graves much valuable information has been gained for the historian and antiquary with regard to the manners and customs of that people. The earthen vessels which have been discovered are generally of a very rude character, with some few exceptions; but this is not the case with the glass cups, which possess a degree of elegance in their form and design. The late Mr. Rolfe, of Sandwich, had one in his possession, discovered in a Saxon grave near Ramsgate,[1] and a similar specimen was found by Mr. Dennet in the Isle of Wight.[2] One peculiarity of these glasses is, that they cannot be placed upright upon the table, but must be held in the hand until emptied of their contents; they seem to partake of the character of the horn in their elongated and pointed form.

The descriptive notices of earthenware vessels by which they can be identified, or from which we can ascertain the name of any particular form, are very scanty. Earthen bowls and dishes were, no doubt, common; but we rarely meet with notices of them; for, by reason of their comparative insignificance, they were seldom enumerated or described in inventories. Bowls are frequently alluded to without mentioning the material of which they were made; earthen pitchers and pots were in very general use amongst all classes during the Middle Ages.

In the payments of the executors of Eleanor, wife of Edward I., in the thirteenth century, is the following entry: "Item, Julianæ *La Potere*, pro ccc. *picheriis* viijs. vid." And in the same document we have a record of the payment: "Item, Johanni *Le Squeler*[3] pro M^{le} et D. discus, tot platellis, tot salseriis, et cccc. *chiphis* xlijs."

---

[1] *Archæological Album*, by Thomas Wright, Esq., p. 207.

[2] *Transactions of the British Archæological Association at the Winchester Congress*, p. 152.

[3] The *squeler* was a seller of *esquelles*, from the French word *écuelle*, a porringer, dish, or basin Hence, the department in large establishments where these vessels were kept and cleaned was termed a *sqwellery* (scullery).

Some earthenware vessels have been discovered in England, which, although of a rude character, have certain peculiarities enabling us to appropriate them to their approximate date.

The glazed earthenware pitcher, fig. 51, was found in making an excavation at Lewes; it is in the form of a mounted knight, and is 10 inches high by 11½ inches long; its capacity is about a quart, and has evidently been used to contain liquids, which could be introduced at the crupper of the horse and discharged through the mouth, while the hole at the top of the rider's head served as a vent. The figure has a flowing beard, long-toed chausses, and prycke spur of the early part of the thirteenth century, for which abundant

Fig. 51.

authorities will be found from Henry III. to the earlier part of Edward I. The vessel was originally covered with a coarse green glaze, much of which has been worn away by use; the horse's legs were probably never longer than they are now. It is in the possession of Mr. W. Figg, of Lewes.[1]

The next illustration, fig. 52, represents a curious early English jug of the fourteenth century, found in an excavation in Cateaton Street in 1841, belonging to Mr. A. C. Kirkman.[2] It is also of earthenware, entirely covered with a coarse green glaze; its capacity is equivalent to about a quarter of a pint; under the lip is a face, the resemblance of which to the heads represented on the English coins of the first three Edwards is too obvious to escape attention; and when it was shown to Sir Samuel Meyrick, he at once pointed out the reverse curls of the beard as the fashion in the time of Edward II., and referred to the effigy of that King figured in Stothard's *Monumental Effigies* in corroboration of this opinion. In the Salisbury Museum is a vessel of greenish glaze, in the form of a mounted knight, with pear-shaped shield, cylindrical helmet, and prick spur, of the end of the twelfth century; and in the Scarborough Museum are several rude vessels of the same date, in forms of animals. Specimens of fictile vessels of the Mediæval period

Fig. 52.

are extremely rare; and although the fabrication of such as have hitherto been brought to light is rude and coarse, they possess a high degree of

[1] *Brit. Arch. Association Journal*, vol. ii. p. 343.   [2] *Ibid.* vol. iii. p. 63.

interest, from the circumstance of their representing, for the most part, something the artist was accustomed to see and imitate to the best of his ability : this is evidently the case with these two specimens.

In the fourteenth, fifteenth, and sixteenth centuries, jugs were very commonly ornamented with heads beneath the lips or spouts; we have given an illustration of one of the fourteenth century, and the Bellarmines of the sixteenth will presently be spoken of; an allusion to a similar vessel, from an inventory of the Duke of Burgundy in 1467, is here quoted, which was sufficiently valued to be mounted in silver and gilt : —

"Ung hault *goblet de terre*, ouvré et chiqueté à ung visaige d'un heremite, garny au dessus et au dessoubs d'argent doré, et le couvercle aussi d'argent doré."

A very interesting discovery was made at Lincoln of some terra-cotta moulds which had been used by a potter of the fourteenth century for impressing these ornamental heads on the glazed jugs of the time; they were found with numerous fragments of pottery near the remains of a kiln. From the head-dresses and disposition of the hair and beard they evidently belong to the reign of Edward III. The mode in which these heads were applied is shown by an impressed fragment of glazed ware found with them; they are in the collection of Mr. Arthur Trollope at Lincoln.

In the *Manners and Household Expenses* of Sir John Howard, 1466, there occurs the following entry : "Wateken bocher of Stoke delyverd of my mony to on of the *poteres* of Horkesley iv*s*. vi*d*. to pay hemselfe and is felawes for xi dosen potes."

The *Household Book* of the Earl of Northumberland, in 1512, gives us a pretty correct idea of the manner of living at the beginning of the sixteenth century, which, for such a noble family, astonishes us at the humble and unostentatious display made at the table; hence, it appears that *treen*, or wooden trenchers and pots of earth, were commonly used at the tables of the dependants. The former were not easily to be broken; but the case was different with the earthen pots, which, from their fragile nature, were, it seems, a continual source of expense; it was therefore ordered that—"Whereas *erthyn potts* be bought, that *ledder potts* be bought for them for serving of lyveries and meallys in my lord's hous."

Estienne Perlin, in his *Description des Royaulmes d'Angleterre et d'Ecosse*, published in Paris in 1558, says : "The English drink beer, not out of glasses, but from earthen pots, the covers and handles made of silver for the rich. The middle classes mount theirs in tin; the poorer sort use beer pots made of wood."

Harrison,[1] who wrote about the year 1579, gives us an account of the earthen pots which were in use in his time; he says : "As for drinke, it is usually filled in pots, goblets, jugs, bols of silver in noblemen's houses, also in fine Venice glasses of all forms, and for want of these elsewhere in *pots of earth* of sundrie colours and moulds, whereof many are garnished with silver, or at the leastwise in pewter."

---

[1] *Description of England*, Book II. cap.. 6.

In the books of the Drapers' Company[1] there is a description of an election feast in the year 1522, where, after describing the order in which they sat, and other matters, goes on to inform us that—"At the said high board were salvers of bread, pears, and filberds, placed upon the tables before they sat down; as also *green pots* of ale and wine, with ashen cups set before them at every mess; but they had gilt cups for red wine and ipocras." The green pots here mentioned were doubtless earthenware pitchers ornamented with a green glaze; for we read in the Loseley MSS. (*Kempe*, p. 300), that in the sixteenth century "the gentlemen of the Temple drank out of *green* earthen pots made from a *white clay* found at Farnham Park."

An English *costrel*, or flat round bottle, of the time of Henry VIII., with four loops, made of a fine description of pottery, and covered with a bright green glaze, was found in London, and formed part of Mr. Roach Smith's collection now in the British Museum; it is ornamented in relief on one side with the royal arms (England and France quarterly) within a double rose, surrounded with the garter and surmounted by a crown; the supporters are a dragon and a greyhound, and the inscription, "DNE SALVUM FAC REGEM REGINAM ET REGNUM." On the reverse side of the bottle are four medallions; one contains a heart and three daisies, with the motto "LEAL," another the monogram "I.H.S.," and the others radiated ornaments; from the mottoes and supporters it is clearly of the reign of Henry VIII.

There is in the British Museum a specimen of great interest, which bearing, as it does, the initials of Queen Elizabeth, the crown and Tudor rose, was probably made during that Queen's reign. It is a large, green-glazed stone tile, and in excellent preservation. Mr. R. L. Hobson, in his *Guide to the English Pottery and Porcelain* in the Museum, has illustrated this important specimen, and collectors who desire to study English pottery of the sixteenth and seventeenth centuries, many representations of which will be found in the Museum, will find much useful information in this excellent book. Many of these specimens were found in the ruined Cistercian abbeys and monasteries.

Pepys in his *Diary* (29th October, 1663)—being present at the Lord Mayor's dinner—says: "I sat at the merchant strangers' table, where ten good dishes to a mess, with plenty of wine of all sorts; but it was very unpleasing that we had no napkins nor change of trenchers, and drunk out of earthen pitchers and wooden dishes (cups)."

From these quotations it appears probable that pitchers and large pots were usually made of earth and leather; while the cups or dishes out of which the liquor was drunk were of ash; or sometimes among the more opulent, from cups or tankards of silver.

> " His cupboard's head six earthen pitchers graced,
>   Beneath them was his trusty tankard placed."—*Dryden's Juvenal.*

---

[1] *Herbert*, vol. i. p. 442.

In the orders and regulations for the royal household of Edward IV.,[1] "The orders for the picher house" are—"The butler *for the monthe* delyverythe nightly, at the buttery barre for the kynge for *all nyght*; with the ale in *new ashen cuppes* and two other for the watche, which of ryghte should be delyvered againe at the cupborde in the mornynge *with the pottes* to serve men of worshippe in the halle; when other men of worshippe bring to this office theyre old soyled *cuppes of ayshe*, to have new." And again, in the *Expenses* of Sir John Howard,[2] in the fifteenth century: "Item, paid to a nother *turnere* for ij*c* drynkng bolles, viij*s.*"

We have before observed, that although earthenware is frequently found, and was made, in England at a very early period in the form of pitchers, jugs, and occasionally drinking cups, yet it does not appear to have been applied to the fabrication of plates. The Romans had their pateræ as well as bowls for use at their tables, usually of the fine red ware called Samian, but we rarely find them amongst the *débris* of table ware of the Middle Ages. Thin plates, of such earthenware as the jugs were made of previous to the sixteenth century, would be liable to break with the least violence, and some more durable material would be selected, as metal or wood, and we accordingly find the latter in vogue for ordinary purposes. In the houses of the nobility these were of gold or silver, as now; but trenchers of wood were in general use among all classes. In the *Dictionary of John de Garlandia*, A.D. 1080, they are described "ROTUNDALIA, *gallice* taillieurs (trencheurs) et dicuntur a rotunditate." These plates were so called because they contained the *tranche* or slice of bread on which the meat was placed by the *ecuyer trenchant*, or carver, and passed to the guests. Instructions are given in the *Menagier de Paris*, 1393, and in the *Boke of Kervying*, as to the manner of cutting the bread; the latter says what the duty of the *butler* and *panter* is: "Ye must have three pantry knives, one to square trencher loaves, another to be a *chippere*, the third shall be sharp to smooth *trenchers*; then chyppe your sovereign's bread hot, and all other bread let it be a day old, household bread three days old, trencher bread four days old." In the same book much stress is laid upon the cutting of bread into *trenchers* or slices, in the placing of which the estimation of the guest was to be borne in mind; a person of high degree had five, another of lower station four, and so on.

The *cruskyn* or *cruske*—called also cruce, creuse, and croise—was a drinking cup of earth. Roquefort thus gives the signification of the old French word—"Creusequin: Coupe, gobelet, vaisseau servant à boire." The cruskyn of earth is frequently mentioned in inventories of the fourteenth century: thus in the *Kalendar of the Exchequer*, 1324: "Un *crusekyn* de terre garni d'argent, a covercle souz dorrez od iiij escuchions as costes de divers armes du pris, viij*s.*"[3] "Un cruskyn de terre blank hernoissez d'argent endorrez ove covercle embatell, enaymellez dedeins ove j babewyn pois ij lb."[4] In a manuscript in the possession of Sir Thomas

[1] *Liber Niger*, p. 78.   [2] *Manners and Expenses of England*, p. 527.
[3] *Kal. Exch.*, vol. iii. p. 128.   [4] *Ibid.* iii. 319.

Phillipps, we have also a little cruskyn of earth, with the foot and cover gilt and enamelled, and a pot of silver, "au guyse d'un *cruskyn*."

The same word is still used in Ireland to denote a small pot or cup, thus—"a *cruiskeen* of whisky." In O'Brien's *Irish Dictionary*, the word is rendered "a small pot or pitcher," *een* being the Irish diminutive; hence a small cruisk or cruske. The final syllable was omitted subsequently, and it was called a cruce.

> " They had sucked such a juice
> Out of the good ale *cruce,*
>   Wherein they found no dregges,
> That neyther of them his head
> Could carry home to his bed
>   For lack of better legges."—*The Unluckie Firmentie.*

The modern French word *cruche* comprises all earthenware pitchers and jugs. The *crock* was larger than the cruce; it is spelt crokke in *Piers Ploughman*;[1] and Chaucer thus uses the word :[2]

> " And when that dronken was all in the *crouke.*"

The *godet* was, according to Cotman, "an earthen bole, a stone cup or jug"; it seems to have been a small earthenware cup or tankard. The calix of a flower is called in the French language *godet*; the name occurs in several inventories of the fourteenth century. Among the stores for the king's ship, *The George*, in 1345, is an entry for nine godettes, called "flegghes," vs. iij*d.*; and a large godett for the king, xij*d.*[3]

It was in succeeding times called a goddard. Stowe, speaking of " Mount Goddard-street, in Ivie-lane," says: "It was so called of the tippling there; and the goddards mounting from the tappe to the table, from the table to the mouth, and sometimes over the head." Gayton[4] mentions—

> " A goddard or anniversary spice bowl
> Drank off by the gossips."

Florio (p. 80) has "a wooden godet or tankard;" and the following quotation (*temp*. Henry VI.) shows that it partook of the form of the wooden mazer : "Also ij litil *masers* called *godardes* covered, and another litil maser uncovered."[5]

The costrel was a portable vessel or flask of earth or of wood, having projections on either side, with holes, through which a cord or leathern strap passed, for the purpose of suspending it from the neck of the person

---

[1] " Vision," line 13,516.   [2] " Reeve's Tale," line 4166.
[3] Sir H. Nicholas' *History of the British Navy*, vol. ii. p. 173.
[4] *Festivous Notes on Don Quixote.*
[5] *Kal. Exch.*,vol. ii p. 251.

who carried it. It is spelt *costret* in *MS. Lansd.* 560, fol. 45; also,
in *Richard Cœur de Lion :*[1]

> "Now, steward, I warn thee,
>   Buy us vessel great plenté,
>   Dishes, cuppes, and saucers,
>   Bowls, trays, and platters,
>   Vats, tuns, and *costret.*"
>
> ["A youth that following with a costrel bore
>   The means of goodly welcome, flesh and wine."—TENNYSON.]

It is derived from the old French word *costeret*, from its being carried by
the side; and was probably a measure or allowance of beer carried by a
traveller, or given to a working-man for the day. Fig. 53 is a very early

Fig. 53.

Fig. 54.

specimen of such a vessel; it has been originally covered with a bright
red glaze, variegated with white streaks, and on each side are two projections, and holes for suspension by means of a leathern strap or cord;
it holds a pint, and is 11 inches high. (*Geol. Mus. Coll. Chaffers.*)

The other cut (fig. 54) represents a variety not quite so early; the
upper part is covered with a green glaze; it also contains a pint. These
were carried by pilgrims, travellers, and shepherds, pendent by their side
along with the scrip :

> "A bolle and a bagge
>   He bar by his syde,
>   And hundred of ampulles[2]
>   On his hat seten."—*Piers Ploughman*

---

[1] Ellis, *Met. Rom.*, 300.

[2] The ampulles were small oblong vessels of glass, carried by pilgrims in the Middle Ages, sewn to
the hat and other parts of their dress, in token of having visited some particular shrine.

Sometimes it was carried at the end of the bourdon or staff, which had a crook to receive it. The wooden barrel which the labourer carries with him when he goes to work is called at the present day in the Craven dialect a *costrel*.

The *jubbe* spoken of by Chaucer was a sort of jug, which held about a quart or more:

> "With bred and chese and good ale in a *jubbe*,
> Sufficing right ynow as for a day."[1]

Again:

> "A jubbe of Malvesie."[2]

The *juste*, according to Roquefort, was a vase, pot, or a sort of measure for wine:—these vessels were of earth, but more frequently of silver; sometimes of gold. In the *Kalendar of the Exchequer, temp.* Henry IV.: "Item, j autre *joust* d'argent enorrez ove les scochons des diverses armes ove botons de curall et cristall ove une covercle rouge sur le sumet."[3] And in an inventory of Charles V. of France, A.D. 1379, under the head of "Golden vessels," we have—"Six grandes justes à un email rond de France, cxxviij marc."

Oriental porcelain was known in Europe at a very early period: the first positive mention we have of it occurs in an inventory of effects of the Queen of Charles le Bel, King of France, who died 1370: "Item, un pot à eau de pierre de *porcelaine*, à un couvercle d'argent et bordé d'argent doré, pesant j marc, iiij ounces, xvij estellins, prisié xiiij fr. d'or."

Among the original letters edited by Sir Henry Ellis,[4] we read of a present of "iij potts of erthe payntid callyd *porceland*." It is also distinctly spoken of in 1587 as a present to Queen Elizabeth, mounted in silver and gold: "Item, one cup of grene *pursselyne*, the foote, shanke, and cover silver guilte, chased like droppes." "Item, one cup of *pursselyne*, th'one side paynted red, the foote and cover silver guilte." "Item, one porrynger of white *porselyn*, garnished with golde, the cover of golde with a lyon on the toppe thereof, 38 oz."

It was doubtless at this time much esteemed, on account of its scarcity; and this may be inferred from Shakespeare's allusion to it,[5]—"Your hononrs have seen such dishes; they are not *china dishes*, but very good dishes."

It did not at ·this time come direct from the East Indies, but from Venice. "China mettall" is described in Minsheu's *Spanish Dialogues* as "the fine dishes of earth, painted, such as are brought from Venice." China ware was not generally imported until 1631, when the East India ships made it an article of commerce, shortly after which a heavy duty was laid upon it by Cromwell, viz., twenty shillings on every dozen under a quart, and sixty shillings on those of a quart and upwards.

Ben Jonson[6] says: "Ay, sir! his wife was the rich Chinawoman, that

---

[1] Chaucer, line 3628.
[2] Chaucer, line 13,000.
[3] *Kal. Exch.*, ii. 86.
[4] Vol. ii. p. 242.
[5] *Measure for Measure*, act ii. sc. 2.
[6] *Silent Woman*, act i. sc. I.

the courtiers visited so often." In his time the China trade had not long been opened, and "China houses" were much resorted to for the purpose of purchasing the ware for presents; they are also frequently mentioned by writers of the time as places of assignation.

The following vessels, from an inventory of the jewels, &c., in the Castle of Edinburgh, 1578, were probably China ware; the Anglo-Saxon word *Lame* or *Laim*, signifying *loam*, *mud*, or *clay :* "Twa flaconis of *layme* anamalit with blew and quheit, and ane all blew." And in another account of the Queen of Scots' "moveables" under "vesshelis of glasse,"

Fig. 55.   Fig. 56.

1562 : "Item, a figure of ane doig maid in quhite *laym*." "i basing and lair with aips, wormes, and serpents." "One lawer with a cowp and a cover of copper enamellit."

The *Bellarmin*, or *long-beard*, here represented, was a description of jug of stoneware, which, being of peculiar ornament and form, has misled many, from its antique appearance. This vessel, which, from the reasons here-after stated, we have called the *Bellarmin*, was a stone pot or jug with a wide-spreading belly and a narrow neck, on the top of which was repre-sented a rudely-executed face with a long flowing beard, and a handle behind. The belly in front was orna-mented with a device, or a coat of arms of some town in Holland or Germany; sometimes only a crest; of a mottled brown colour, glazed all over, and being of stout substance and hard texture, it was exceedingly durable.

These vessels were in general use in the sixteenth and seventeenth centuries at public-houses and inns, to serve ale to the customers. The largest, or "galonier," twelve inches high, contains eight pints; the next, or "Pottlepot," about nine inches and a half high, holds four pints; another, eight inches and a half high, a quart; and the smallest, six inches in height, one pint. Fig. 55 (a pottlepot) bears a shield quartered, with the arms of Cleves, March, Ravensburgh, and Mœurs. One of these vessels bears the date 1589, struck upon it above a coat of arms; another, which was in the possession of the late Mr. Kempe, had a venerable bearded visage, and underneath a shield (which bore on a pale three mascles) was the date 1594. An interesting fact connected with this was its being found on the site of the Old Boar's Head Tavern, in East-cheap. Some have the arms of Amsterdam,—*gules*, on a pale *or*, a pale *sable*, charged with three saltires *argent*,—others of Prussia, Germany, &c. They are frequently alluded to in old plays; and the following description can leave no doubt as to its identity, and will justify us in christening it anew, as we have done. It occurs in the *Ordinary* act iii. scene 3 :—

> " Thou thing,
> Thy belly looks like to some strutting hill,
> O'ershadowed with thy rough beard like a wood ;
> Or like a larger jug, that some men call
> A *Bellarmine*, but we a *Conscience ;*
> Whereon the lewder hand of pagan workman
> Over the proud ambitious head hath carved
> An idol large, with beard episcopal,
> Making the vessel look like tyrant Eglon."

Another passage in the same play again alludes to this jug ; where a man, after having partaken rather too freely of its contents the night before, is advised thus in the following couplet :—

> "First to breakfast, then to dine,
> Is to conquer Bellarmine ; "

meaning, that the effects of the previous evening's potations and excesses are not dissipated until after a breakfast and a good dinner.

In *Epsom Wells* (act iv. sc. 1), Clodpate, after pushing about the cups of true English ale, says : "Uds bud, my head begins to turn round ; but let's into the house. 'Tis dark ; we'll have one *Bellarmine* there, and then Bonus Nocius."

This jug was so named after the celebrated Cardinal Robert Bellarmin, who about that time made himself so conspicuous by his zealous opposition to the reformed religion. He was born A.D. 1542, and died 1621. He was sent into the Low Countries to oppose the progress of the Reformers, and he consequently received his share of hatred and derision from the Protestants, and there were few men of talent who did not enter the lists against him. The controversy was maintained with great vigour, and its rancour was manifested by satirical allusions, like this of the bottle. His biographer, Fuligati, says, "He was very short of stature and hard-featured," and that "his soul was conspicuous in every feature of his face." If we can in any way rely upon the portraits of him thus handed down to posterity, he must indeed have been exceedingly hard-featured.[1]

Ben Jonson, in *Bartholomew Fair* (act iv. sc. 3), says of a man who was overcome with liquor : "He hash wrashled so long with the bottle here, that *the man with the beard* hash almost streek up hish heelsh ;" and to the same vessel he also compares a host in the *New Inn :*—

> " Who's at the best, some round grown thing *a jug,*
> *Fac'd with a beard*, that fills out to the guests."

---

[1] A similar instance may be cited in the well-known " Bourdaloue," or oval *vase de nuit*, made of fayence, painted with an eye at the bottom, or other device, usually surrounded with some free legend. L. Bourdaloue was a Jesuit preacher, born 1632, died 1704, who was sent into Languedoc to convert the unfortunate Protestants after the revocation of the Edict of Nantes ; and being the confidant of many, and mixed up with the secret intrigues of the time, this vessel, of an abject and secret use, was maliciously designated by the name of *Bourdaloue.*

In the *Gipsies Metamorphosed*, the same author gives the following humorous derivation of the form of these stone jugs. In the *Induction* one of the gipsies thus apostrophises the audience : " Gaze upon this brave spark struck out of Flintshire, upon Justice Jug's daughter, then sheriff of the county, who running away with a kinsman of our captain's, and her father pursuing her to the marches, he great with justice, she great with jugling, they were both for the time turned stone, upon the sight of each other here in Chester : till at last (see the wonder), a jug of the town ale reconciling them, the memorial of both their gravities,—*his in beard*, and *her's in belly*,—hath remained ever since preserved in picture upon the most stone jugs of the kingdom."

Cartwright also, in the *Lady Errant*, mentions them : —

> " The greater sort they say
> Are like *stone pots, with beards that do reach down*
> Even to their knees."

Bulwer, in the *Artificial Changeling*, 1653, speaks of a "formal doctor," that "the fashion of his beard was just for all the world like those upon your Flemish jugs, bearing in guise the forme of a broome, narrow above and broad beneath."

These passages, which have hitherto appeared obscure to the commentators, are henceforth easily explained.

We find in *Lansdowne MSS.* (108, fol. 60) a letter relating to them (which, as it seems a curious document, is here quoted at length), from a person of the name of Simpson, praying he may be allowed the sole importation af stone drinking pots; it is addressed to Queen Elizabeth : —

"The sewte of William Simpson, marchaunt :—Whereas one Garnet Tynes, a straunger livinge in Acon, in the parte beyond the seas, being none of her ma^ties subjecte, doth buy uppe all the pottes made at Culloin, called *Drinking stone pottes*, and he onelie transporteth them into this realm of England, and selleth them : It may please your ma^tie to graunte unto the sayd Simpson full power and onelie license to provyde, transport, and bring into this realm the same or such like drinking pottes ; and the sayd Simpson will put in good suretie that it shall not be prejudiciall to anie of your ma^ties subjects, but that he will serve them as plentifullie, and sell them at as reasonable price as the other hath sold them from tyme to tyme.

"Item. He will be bound to double her ma^ties custome by the year, whenever it hath been at the most.

"Item. He will as in him lieth, drawe the making of such like potte into some decayed town within this realm, wherebie manie a hundred poore men may be sette a work.

"Note. That no Englishman doth transport any potte into this realm, but only the sayd Garnet Tynes ; who also serveth all the Lowe Countries and other places with pottes."

From the quantities which have been found amongst the *débris* of the great fire of London, and throughout England, it is evident they were in very general use, which their durability and small cost would tend to ensure.

We are not informed whether Simpson was successful in his suit, but stoneware jugs in imitation of the German Bellarmines were actually made in this country in the reign of Elizabeth, which fact is proved by a mottled brown stoneware Bellarmine of the same form in the Schreiber Collection, now in the Victoria and Albert Museum. On the neck beneath the spout is a bearded head or mask, and on the body three medallions; that in the centre has the royal arms of England with supporters and E.R. (Elizabeth Regina) surrounded by the garter and motto "Honi soit," &c., that on the left has a Tudor rose crowned, and the other has a portcullis and date 1594—height 8½ inches.

About thirty years later, another application for the same purpose was made by Thomas Rous and Abraham Cullyn, to whom letters patent were granted on the 24th of October, 1626. The preamble to it is interesting, and runs thus :—

"Whereas we have been given to understand by our loving subjects, Thomas Rous (or Ruis) and Abraham Cullyn, of the City of London, Marchants, that heretofore and at this present, this our Kingdom of England, and other our dominions, are and have been served with stone pottes, stone jugges, and stone bottells out of foreign partes from beyond the seas, and they have likewise shewed unto us, that by their industry and charge, not onely the materials, but also the art and manufacture may be found out and performed, never formerly used within this our Kingdom of England by any, which profitable invention they have already attempted, and in some good measure proceeded in, and hope to perfect; by which many poore and unprofitable people may be sett on worke and put to labour and good employment. We therefore grant our Royal priviledge for the *sole* making of the stone pottes, stone juggs and stone bottells, for the terme of fourteene yeares for a reward for their invencion, and they have voluntarily offered unto us for the same a yearly rent of five pounds towards our revenue, soe long as they have benefitte by this our grant, neyther doe they desire by virtue of such grant to hinder the importacion of these commodities by others from foreign parts."

This was evidently the first exclusive permission to make stone pots and jugs in England. Judging from their names, they were both foreigners —Rous or Ruis and Cullyn; the latter probably was a native of Cologne, and took his name from the city.

These vessels differed from the Bellarmines above described, with their full-flowing bearded heads, but were of a sort of mottled grey or brown, with plain necks, and were called "cullings." J. Conyers, the antiquary, speaking of a discovery in St. Paul's Churchyard (before alluded to), says he picked up some pots like *cullings*. (*Wren's Parentalia*.)

The *tyg* was a cup of coarse earthenware coated with a dark chocolate-coloured glaze, sometimes decorated with buff-coloured ornaments. These cups were of various forms, with two or more handles, so that they could be passed round a table for three or four persons to drink out of; each person taking hold of a different handle, brought his mouth to another part of the rim to that previously used. Many of them are dated, varying from 1600 to 1680. They are still called by this name in Staffordshire. The word *tyg* is of Saxon derivation, signifying a utensil made of earth for conveying drink to the mouth. (Vide *Keramic Gall.*, enlarged edition, figs. 349, 350.)

The maker of drink-cups was named *tygel wyrthan*, a worker of tygs. The word *tile* is derived from *tygel*; and *tygel wyrthan*, tilewright or tellwright, has given the name to a numerous race in Staffordshire.

To give our readers some idea of the various ramifications of a single piece of earthenware before it arrives at completion, we may note that at the present day, to produce the commonest painted bowl used by the poorest peasant wife to contain the breakfast for her rustic husband, the clays of Dorset and Devonshire, the flints of Kent, the granite of Cornwall, the lead of Montgomery, the manganese of Warwickshire, and the soda of Cheshire must be conveyed from those respective districts, and by the ingenious processes, the results of unnumbered experiments, be made to combine with other substances, apparently as heterogeneous, obtained from other nations. (*Shaw.*)

The following is a description of the process adopted in the manufacture of earthenware in the last century in the Potteries:—

A piece of the prepared mixture of clay and ground flint, dried and tempered to a proper consistence, is taken to be formed into any required shape and fashion, by a man who sits over a machine called a wheel, on the going round of which he continues forming the ware. This branch is called *throwing*, and as water is required to prevent the clay sticking to the hand, it is necessary to place it for a short time in a warm situation. It then undergoes the operation of being *turned* and made much smoother than it was before by a person called a turner, when it is ready for the handle and spout to be added by the branch called *handling*.

Dishes, plates, tureens, and many other articles are made from moulds of ground plaster-of-Paris, and when finished, the whole are placed carefully (being then in a much more brittle state than when fired) in *seggars*, which in shape and form pretty much resemble a lady's bandbox without its cover, but much thicker, and are made from the marl or clay of the neighbourhood. The larger ovens or kilns are placed full of seggars so filled with ware, and heated by a fire which consumes from 12 to 15 tons of coal; when the oven has become cool again, the seggars are taken out and their contents removed, often exceeding in number 30,000 various pieces; but this depends upon the general sizes of the ware. In this state the ware is called *biscuit*, and the body of it has much the appearance of a new tobacco-pipe, not having the least gloss upon it. It is then immersed or dipped into a fluid generally consisting of white lead, ground flint, and a stone from Cornwall burnt and ground, all mixed together, and as much water put to it as reduces it to the thickness of cream, which it resembles. Each piece of ware being separately immersed or dipped into this fluid, so much of it adheres all over the piece, the water being absorbed by the biscuit, that when put into other seggars and exposed to another operation of fire, performed in the glossing kiln or oven, the ware becomes finished by acquiring its glossy covering, which is given it by the vitrification of the above ingredients. Enamelled ware undergoes a third fire after it has been painted, in order to bind the colour on.

A single piece of ware, such as a common enamelled teapot, mug, jug, &c., passes through at least fourteen different hands before it is finished, viz., the Slip-maker, who makes the clay; the Temperer or Beater of the clay; the Thrower, who forms the ware; the Ball-maker and Carrier; the Attendant upon the drying of it; the Turner, who removes its roughness; the Spout-maker; the Handler, who puts on the handle and spout; the First or Biscuit Fireman; the person who immerses or dips it into the lead fluid; the Second or Gloss Fireman; the Dresser or Sorter in the warehouse; the Enameller or Painter; the Muffle or enamel Fireman. Several more are required to the completion of each piece of ware, but are in inferior capacities, such as the turner of the wheel, turner of the lathe, &c.

The collector or reader who takes especial interest in the subject of these two preceding chapters, is recommended to consult Professor Church's *English Earthenware*, illustrated from specimens in the National collections, and also M. L. M. Solon's *The Art of the Old English Potter*, William Burton's *A History and Description of English Earthenware and Stoneware to the Nineteenth Century*, and Mr. R. L. Hobson's modest but valuable little *Guide to the Specimens in the British Museum*, where much additional information will be found which it would be impossible to incorporate into the limited space given in a work of this character to this special branch of Ceramics.

MARKS AND MONOGRAMS

N.B.—Many of the examples alluded to in the following descriptions are represented in " THE KERAMIC GALLERY," by W. CHAFFERS, the enlarged edition. The abbreviations " Ker. Gall.," &c., with the number of the object, refer to that work.

MAIOLICA

𝕴taly

THE essential feature of maiolica, and the cognate wares included under the names of fayence and delft, is the use of an opaque milky white tin-enamel which serves at once to conceal the buff body of the ware and to form an even white background for painted decoration. This use of tin-enamel was understood in Western Asia and Egypt certainly as early as the twelfth century, if not many years before, and it was known in Spain in the thirteenth century or earlier. In Italy it made a gradual and tentative appearance in the fourteenth century, slowly superseding the previous method of coating the earthenware with a wash of fine white clay or slip. The earliest painted Italian wares were decorated in manganese purple and transparent green on this white slip ground, chiefly with formal hatched patterns, coats of arms, and grotesque figures, human and animal. Such wares have been excavated at Orvieto, Faenza, Florence, and in many other parts of Italy. In the fifteenth century the tin-enamel was generally adopted for painted wares, and true maiolica may be said to have begun. There can be little doubt that the art was of Eastern origin, whether learnt directly from the near East or indirectly from the Moorish potters in Spain, and certainly the decoration of the fifteenth century maiolica shows very marked Oriental influences. The formalised flowers and foliage, birds, animals, and fish, among sprays of what seems to be oak foliage, heraldic animals, bands of lettering, portrait busts, &c., usually appear in a setting of slight arabesques or dotted patterns in Eastern style. In addition to the manganese and green we now find a blue colour, often very dark and thickly applied, and a pale yellow. It is not easy to place with certainty many of these early wares, and rival theorists dispute the claims of Faenza and Florence for that large and interesting group in which the oak-leaf design is conspicuous. Doubtless Siena and Orvieto had their share in the production of the fifteenth century wares, but there are no definite marks to decide the various claims. In fact the few marks which do occur are on the debated specimens, and they are in themselves not easily intelligible. The four following are on pieces in the British Museum.

Mark on a "waster" found at Faenza. Part of a dish painted in dark and light blue, orange, and yellow : a coat of arms and formal borders. Late fifteenth century. British Museum.

Two marks resembling the letter P, under the handle of a fifteenth century drug pot painted in blue, green, yellow, and manganese, with a shield of arms in a ground of leaf-trellis pattern in Hispano moresque taste. Probably Faenza. British Museum.

Under the handle of a fifteenth century albarello painted in thick blue and manganese and transparent green, with two figures in a foliage scroll. Perhaps Faenza. British Museum.

Indeterminate marks under the base of a double-gourd shaped drug pot painted in bright blue with a cartouche inscribed Sr. di dialtra, in a ground of ivy scrolls. Possibly Florentine. Sixteenth century. British Museum.

Towards the end of the fifteenth century important changes took place in the decoration of maiolica. Not only was the painter's palette enlarged by the addition of many new colour combinations, but figure drawing, which had hitherto been subordinated to the form of the vase, vessel, or dish, now became an essential part of the decorative scheme. Hence there gradually developed the pictorial or *istoriati* style of decoration, in which first the central parts and then the entire surface of the piece were covered with carefully drawn pictures copied or adapted from the works of the great painters of the day. This pictorial style reached its fullest development at Urbino in the middle of the sixteenth century.

Before proceeding to the Marks of the various manufactories, it may be found useful to know the Italian terms given to the forms of the vessels, and to the peculiar decorations upon them, as described by many writers, and their equivalents in the English language. Piccolpasso of Castel Durante, in his manuscript *Dell' Arte dell Vasaio*, now in the Library of the Victoria and Albert Museum, gives a description of most of them, accompanied by drawings of the patterns; these examples, which belong to the year 1548, must not be taken as types of all the early Italian maiolica, but rather of its decadence.

Scudella or *tazza*, a flat cup or bowl with high stem and foot.

Ongarescha or *piadene*, a cup mounted on a low foot.

Taglieri, a flat plate or trencher.

Canestrella, a fruit basket, made in a mould or pierced.

Bacile, a deep bowl plate.

Tondino, a plate with a wide rim and a deep cavity in the centre (*cavetto*).

Coppa amatoria, a bowl or cup, on the bottom of which is painted a female bust.

Albarello, a drug pot of cylindrical form, the sides slightly concave, to enable a person to hold it more conveniently.

Vasi di Spezieria, pharmacy vases.

A maiolica service much in fashion in the sixteenth century as a present to a lady in her confinement consisted of four pieces pitting one above the other; it was painted inside and out with the birth of some deity or an accouchement. The lowest piece was called the *scudella*, to receive broth, eggs, or other viands; this was covered by the *taglieri* or trencher to hold the bread; above this the *ongarescha* was inverted, and within its foot was placed the *saliera* or salt-cellar, and its cover, *coperchio*.

The patterns and decorations of maiolica were:—

Trofei, trophies, composed of weapons and musical instruments; these were made principally in the State of Urbino, at the price of an escu ducat the hundred.

Rabesche, arabesques, or Oriental designs copied from damascened metal-work, executed principally on white ground. Made more frequently at Genoa and Venice; at the latter the price was one florin the hundred; at Genoa, four livres, which was considered a high price.

Cerquate, oak leaves, employed in compliment to the Della Rovere family, then reigning at Urbino, such as branches of oak with leaves and acorns interlaced, with a central cartouche enclosing a bust, &c.; some at ten carlini the hundred, others an escu ducat the hundred.

Grotesche, grotesques or chimeræ, with bodies terminating in foliage, on coloured ground. The price in Urbino, two florins the hundred; at Venice, eight livres.

Foglie, leaves, groups of leaves, coloured on white ground, sometimes in *camaieu* on coloured ground. Made mostly at Venice and Genoa; price, three livres the hundred.

Fiori, flowers, roses, tulips, &c., intertwined, among which are birds perched or flying, painted in *camaieu* on blue ground. Made at Venice; price, five livres the hundred.

Frutti, fruit, of the same character and price.

Foglie da dozzena, a common sort of decoration of flowers and foliage covering the surface of the plate. Half-a-florin the hundred; at Venice, two livres.

Paesi, landscapes. Those made at Castel Durante, Genoa, and Venice cost six livres the hundred.

Porcellana, porcelain, executed in slight blue outline with scrolls and flowers in colour upon white ground. Cost two livres the hundred.

Tirata, interlaced ornaments or strap-work in colour on white ground, similar to the last. Cost two livres the hundred.

Sopra bianco, white upon white, palmette ornaments of opaque white enamel upon milky white ground. Cost a half-escu the hundred.

Sopra azurra, the same decoration on blue ground.

Quartiere, quartered, this common decoration consists of large rays dividing the plate into compartments of coloured designs, in the centre of which are sometimes busts, &c. Cost twenty bolognins or two to three livres the hundred.

Candelliere, candelabra, very similar to *grotesche*. In the example given by Piccolpasso, it appears painted on white ground, with an ornament composed of male or female figures or busts, with bodies and arms of branches and foliage symmetrically interlacing each other. These cost two florins the hundred; at Venice, eight livres.

Sgraffiato, incised ware with the outlines of the subject cut or scratched on the surface.

In some extracts from a *Book of Expenses* of Wilibald Imhoff of Nuremberg from 1564 to 1577, preserved among the archives of that city, we find in his account for the year 1565 that this wealthy and ostentatious patrician obtained his artistic maiolica direct from Venice.

Forty pieces of white maiolica painted with arms, and other maiolicas, cost eleven florins.

In 1567 an Urbino maiolica jug and cover, four florins.

A large cistern for water in the form of a ship, which cost nine florins. Two basins of white fayence with ewers, four florins the pair.

It will be seen by the comparative value of money that these objects of art were dearly paid for, even at that time; for twenty francs for a cistern or large basin then, represents in our time at least 300; and what some writers say about the low price of maiolica when it was originally made refers only to the common articles of commerce.

URBINO

In Urbino, or its immediate neighbourhood, at a place called Fermignano, existed at the latter part of the fifteenth century a manufactory of maiolica. Pungileone cites a certain potter of Urbino named Giovanni di Donino Garducci in the year 1477, and a member of the same family, Francesco Garducci, who in 1501 received the commands of the Cardinal of Carpaccio to make various vases. Ascanio del fu Guido is also mentioned as working in 1502; but the works of all these have disappeared, or are attributed to other fabriques, and it is not until 1530 that we can identify any of the artists named by Pungileone : Federigo di Giannantonio; Nicolo di Gabriele; Gian Maria Mariani, who worked in 1530; Simone di Antonio Mariani, in 1542, to whom M. V. Lazari attributes a plate in the Museum of Padua, signed S. A.; Luca del fu Bartholomeo in 1544; Césare Cari of Faenza, who painted in 1536 and 1551 in the botega of Guido Merlino.

The workshop of Guido Durantino was celebrated in the beginning of the sixteenth century, for the Connétable de Montmorency, an amateur of works of art, commanding in 1535 a service, of which several pieces bearing his arms are still extant : one is in the British Museum, and others from the same atelier are mentioned below. About the same time flourished the distinguished Francesco Xanto Avelli da Rovigo, whose works are so well known and so highly appreciated; he usually painted after the designs and engravings of Raphael, not always adhering strictly to the same grouping of the originals. Of the same school was Nicolo di Gabriele.

Another celebrated painter of maiolica of the middle of the sixteenth century was Orazio Fontana, originally of Castel Durante, whose family name appears to have been Pellipario, Fontana being a surname taken in consequence of the profession of several members of the family. The first whose name occurs is Nicola Pellipario, or Nicola da Urbino, who was alive in 1540, and had a son Guido, named in a notarial document as early as 1520; the latter had three sons, Orazio, Camillo, and Nicola. An early signed piece by this artist is in the British Museum, and a facsimile of the inscription on the plate, which represents a sacrifice to Diana, is given in Dr. Fortnum's Catalogue of Maiolica in the Victoria and Albert Museum, which should be referred to for notices of the chief maiolica artists, and of the many characteristics distinguishing their various works. An exhaustive work on *Maiolica* was published by Mr. Fortnum in 1896.

Guido, the father, survived Orazio, and his name is found on the plateau which was in the Fountaine Collection, which states that it was made in Urbino, in the shop of Maestro Guido Fontana, vase-maker. Orazio remained with his father up to the year 1565, when he separated and set up a botega on his own account in the Borgo San Polo; he died in 1571. Camillo, his brother, appears to have been invited to Ferrara by Duke Alfonso II. in 1567, to assist in resuscitating the maiolica manufacture of that city, founded by Alfonso I. many years before. Of Nicola, the third son, little is known, except that his name is incidentally mentioned in a document dated 1570. The period of the highest excellence of Urbino maiolica was from about 1520 to 1560, particularly in the dishes and shaped pieces painted in arabesques after the style of Raffaele. (Vide *Ker. Gall.*, enlarged edition, figs. 33, 34, 35, and 41.) There are in the Victoria and Albert Museum a great many excellent specimens belonging to the Salting and other collections.

EXAMPLES

A salt-cellar of triangular form, on dolphin's head and feet, painted with rich ornaments of cupids and negroes' heads, inscribed "FRA. XANTO," &c., dated 1532; was purchased at the Bernal sale for the *British Museum* for £61.

A superb dish in vivid colours, Pompey and Cleopatra, cupids, &c., and armorial bearings; at the back a description and "FRA. XANTO A DA ROVIGO IN URBINO, 1533," now in the *Victoria and Albert Museum;* sold at the Bernal sale for £50.

A fine dish; subject, Olympus with Apollo in the centre, above a choir of amorini; is in the *Victoria and Albert Museum;* £60.

A fine basin and ewer, painted with grotesques and cameos on white ground, elegant handles, of Urbino fabrique, best period, circa 1550 (*Soltykoff Coll.*); £136.

Two plates signed by Xanto: Hero and Leander and Metabus, with metallic lustre (*Soltykoff Coll.*); £116 each.

A fine Urbino vase, oviform with high handle, ornamented with a sphinx and masks, the body painted in bright colours with the brazen serpent, circa 1550; was purchased at the Bernal sale by the late Mr. A. Barker for £220. Another, similar, with subject of a metamorphosis, was bought by him at the same sale for £200.

A fine dish in the Bernal Coll.; subject, Pan playing upon the pipes and two kneeling figures bearing shields, with a beautiful arabesque border; was (although broken) bought for the *British Museum* for £62.

An Urbino plateau; subject, Moses striking the rock, with arabesque border on white (*Soulages*); is in the *Victoria and Albert Museum;* cost £100.

Two others of Leda and the swan, and Roman soldiers attacking a bridge (*Soulages*), in the same collection, cost £50 each; and two Urbino vases, painted with mythological subjects, cost £55 each.

We must not omit to mention (although no mark is to be found upon it) a unique and beautiful specimen of painting on maiolica, the well-known oviform vase, the handles and foot of it being restored in silver; round the body is a continuous frieze of nude figures fighting on a black background, after Giulio Romano, the shoulder and neck painted with arabesques, &c., *en grisaille* on blue ground, gadroon ornaments at bottom. This exquisite vase has been attributed to Orazio Fontana, but is unlike any of his known works. (There is another, similar, but of inferior merit, in the Brunswick Museum.) It was formerly the property of Mr. Gray, of Harringer House, at whose death it passed into the Stowe Collection for £35. At the Stowe sale it was purchased for fifty-one guineas only, by Mr. Mark Phillips, Warwickshire, and would at the present time probably realise ten times that amount. This vase is now in the British Museum, and is ascribed to the Lanfranchi *botega* at Pesaro.

In the Montferrand Collection, No. 55, there was a very interesting dish, representing the celebrated group of the Laocöon. The antiquity of this painting is evident from the fact that the right arm of the High-Priest is wanting; it is a copy of the group as it was actually discovered in 1506 in the vineyard of Felix de Fredis, near the gate of St. Jean de Lateran. It is believed that the arm now seen on this antique group was added by Michael Angelo.

·1531·
·f·X·A·R:
·T Urbino.

URBINO. The initials of Francesco Xanto Avelli da Rovigo in Urbino; inscribed on a plate; subject, Pyramus and Thisbe. In the Victoria and Albert Museum. *(Bernal Coll.)*

F.°X:
Roū:

URBINO. Francesco Xanto Rovigense. Inscribed on a plate in the Victoria and Albert Museum.

1539.
X·

URBINO. By Xanto. On a plate; subject, the Sword of Damocles. In the Collection of the late Mr. H. G. Bohn.

X

URBINO. By Xanto. On a tazza, with arabesques, dark blue and white *(sopra azurro).*

X· N

URBINO. The letter X. for Xanto is at the end of an inscription on a plateau dated 1540, painted in lustre colours with the Rape of Helen, marked in blue, but the letter N. is in red lustre, which proves that he sent his plates to be lustred either to Vincentio at Gubbio, or to Santa Natoia (?), whichever the letter may signify. Louvre Coll.

URBINO. Tazza with mythological subject, bearing the mark of Xanto.

URBINO. By Xanto. On a dish, with portrait of Laura, on blue ground.

fran·Auello R:y⸴:

URBINO. Francesco Avello Rovigense pinxit. On a plate, representing the Fall of Dædalus, finely lustred. In Lord Amherst of Hackney's Collection.

F. X. A. R. P. IN URBINO
1531.

URBINO. By Xanto. On a plate, dated 1531. Bernal Coll. An old man, Cupid, and female with a lute; in the centre a coat of arms, with Hercules; cost £7.

FRANCESCO XANTO.
AVELLI DA ROVIGO.
URBINO PINSE 1531.

URBINO. On a plate; subject, Æneas and Anchises. Bernal Coll., now in the British Museum; cost £14.

URBINO. The signature of Xanto on a deep lustred plate; subject, Hero and Leander. In the Louvre. The same occurs on a richly lustred plate, painted with Astolfo on Pegasus attacking the Harpies.

URBINO. This mark of Fra. Xanto Avelli da Rovigo in Urbino, 1533, is on the beautiful circular dish, painted with the marriage of Alexander and Roxana, now in the V. and A. Museum, purchased at the Bernal sale for £50. The letters X. H. A. are on a soldier's shield in front. A facsimile is given in Chaffers' *Ker. Gall.*, enlarged edition, fig. 32.

URBINO. A monogram of Xanto, on the border of a plate painted with Diana and the Transformation of Actæon into a stag; the subject inscribed on the back and dated 1544, which is the latest date of this artist's work we have met with. In the late Mr. H. A. Neck's Collection.

URBINO. Xanto occasionally painted in front of his plates, on some part of the subject, various large Greek characters in white enamel. The most complete example here given is from a plate signed by the artist, representing Joseph and Potiphar's wife. On the bed-curtains are the accompanying monograms, which in the opinion of Dr. Fortnum are not marks, but ornamental characters. In the late Mr. Evans Lombe's Collection.

URBINO. On a plate dated 1537; subject, the Rape of Helen; which formerly belonged to Mr. Addington.

URBINO. By Nicola da Urbino. This mark is on a hanap or ewer in the Museum of the University at Bologna, having the arms of Gian. Francesco Gonzaga impaling those of Isabella d'Este (married 1490; he died 1519; she died 1539).

URBINO. On a plate; belonging to M. Salomon de Rothschild.

URBINO. On a plate; subject, the Flight of Xerxes; signed by Xanto, ornamental figures. The plate is signed F. X. and R., dated 1537. In the Ashmolean Museum, Oxford (Fortnum Coll.).

In these inscriptions the Greek *alpha* and *omega* may be traced more or less perfect, and the *upsilon* traversed by a *sigma*.

URBINO. On a plate in the British Museum, representing a sacrifice to Diana, by Nicola da Urbino.

URBINO. This mark is reduced from the original, which is found on a large circular dish in the Bargello at Florence, representing the Martyrdom of Sta. Cecilia, painted by Nicola da Urbino. On the reverse is the monogram, varied from the others by connecting the upright lines of the letter N by a cross line to form an H (Nichola).

Dr. Fortnum says: "The inscription proves his connection with the Fontana fabrique, and also, we think, with that family;" and he is of opinion "that he was the Nicola Pellipario of Castel Durante, who came to Urbino with his son Guido and there established a botega, in his son's name;" he also inclines to the supposition that Guido Durantino and Guido Fontana of Castel Durante are one and the same.

URBINO. The monogram of Nicola da Urbino. On the back of a fragment of a plate, painted with Mount Parnassus, after Raffaelle, in the Sauvageot Coll., Louvre. M. Darcel erroneously attributes this mark to Nicola di Gabriele, of whom we have before spoken as working about 1530 at Urbino, but who did not sign the plate "A Sacrifice of Diana," "Nicola di V." In the British Museum. It is by Nicola da Urbino.

URBINO. Another mark of Nicola da Urbino, bearing date 1521. On a plate representing Charles V.; in the Basilewski Collection, now at St. Petersburg.

URBINO. This mark occurs on the back of a beautifully painted plate. The date is on a stone in front; subject, the Judgment of Paris, with Mercury and Cupid, and a Victory flying above.

In botega di M°
Guido durã
tino
1532

URBINO. On a dish; subject, David and Goliath, after Raphael, attributed to one of the Fontana family, or rather to the workshop of Fontana (Louvre). The same name is on a plate painted with the Parcæ or Fates, seated, spinning; in the Soane Museum.

Nella Botega
di M Guido
Duratino
Jn vrbino

URBINO. On a dish, with Jupiter and Semele. Bernal Collection, now in the British Museum.

NELLA-BOTEGA
DI GVIDO DVRANTINO
IN VRBINO 1535.

URBINO. This inscription occurs on a very fine plate in the possession of Baron Sellières, representing the Muses, from a painting by Perrino del Vaga, which is considered a veritable chef-d'œuvre of art, and may be considered as a prototype of the Fontana artists.

FATTO IN URBINO IN
BOTEGA DI M° GUIDO
DA CASTEL DURANTE

URBINO. On a cistern, painted with subjects after Giulio Romano. Formerly Narford Collection.

FRANCESCO DVRANTINO
VASARO 1553.

URBINO. This inscription and date are on a plateau, with the subject of Judith and Holofernes. (Campana Collection.) In the Louvre.

nẽ 1551
fato in Botega
de guido merling

URBINO. On a dish, with the signs of the zodiac round the rim; signed at the back. M. Demmin erroneously states that this was made at Bologna, arising from his mistaking the word *Botega* for *Bologna*. Dr. Fortnum attributes it to Venice.

FATE IN BOTEGA
DI GVIDO MERLIGNO
VASARO DA URBINO
IN SAN POLO
ADI. 30 DI MARZIO 1542.

URBINO. On a large dish; Mark Antony and a Naval Engagement. In the Brunswick Museum.

FATE IN BOTEGA
DI GUIDO DI NERLIGNO.

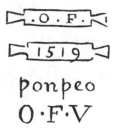

URBINO. *Made in Urbino in the work-shop (botega) of Maestro Guido Fontana, Vase-maker;* he is presumed to be the son of Nicola Pellipario and father of Orazio Fontana. This inscription was on a plateau in the late Mr. Andrew Fountaine's Collection at Narford Hall; subject, the Siege of the Castel of St. Angelo. (Illustrated in Delange's *Recueil de Faiences Italiennes*, plate 81.) In the sale of the Fountaine Collection, June, 1884, this plateau realised £315.

FATE IN BOTEGA DI
M° ORAZIO FONTANA
IN ORBINI.

URBINO. On the triangular plinth of an oviform vase, painted with the Triumph of Amphitrite. In the Collection of M. le Baron Sellières, formerly exhibited in the Sèvres Museum.

FATE IN BOTEGA
DI ORAZIO FONTANA.

URBINO. By the celebrated Orazio Fontana. This mark was on a vase formerly in the Strawberry Hill Collection, with serpent handles, and a subject painted after Giulio Romano. The pair then sold for £110. The late Mr. A. Barker had a similar vase by Orazio Fontana, and another is in the Sèvres Museum.

.O. F.

1519

ponpeo

O·F·V

URBINO. These labels, with O. F. and the date 1519, are on the front of an 8-inch maiolica plate, painted with the armed bust of Pompey and four labels on the border, two of which are here given; the three letters at the bottom are inscribed on the back in blue "*Ponpeo.* O. F. V." There is a decided assimilation to the succeeding mark given by Passeri, which he reads *Orazio Fontana Urbinate.* If this be the correct reading, it follows, either that Nicola Pellipario must have had two sons, Guido and Orazio, who both settled at Urbino before 1520, and adopted the surname, Fontana; or the more celebrated Orazio must have come with his uncle about the year 1519, a much earlier date than is generally assigned. The period in which he is considered to have flourished at Urbino by Passeri and others was between 1540 and 1560, and he died in 1571.

N.B.—Fortnum gives a similar mark, with initials O. F. V. and the name Pompio, with a date 1590. It looks as if there were some confusion in the dates; but in any case, the initials can scarcely be connected with Orazio Fontana.

URBINO. The initials of Orazio Fontana Urbino fecit. This mark is given by Passeri. M. A. Jacquemart thinks these initials have no reference to Orazio Fontana, and that this, as well as the preceding mark, must remain classed among the monograms of unknown artists. The same remark will also apply to many of those which follow, attributed to Orazio Fontana.

Another monogram of Orazio Fontana, but without the letter A. On a very interesting plate representing a view of the city of Urbino, towards which some horsemen are spurring. The monogram is in the brickwork of the rampart, while the letters D. V. (Duc d'Urbino), and also D. M. (perhaps Duke of Mantua), appear in two labels. The date of the plate is 1541. In the Salting Collection at the Victoria and Albert Museum.

URBINO. The monogram of Orazio Fontana. This mark occurs on a fine plate, representing the Rape of a Sabine Woman. Saracini Collection.

URBINO. The monogram of Orazio Fontana, accompanied by the date 1544; on the back of a plate, painted with the Chase of the Calydonian Boar. From the Bernal Coll., now in the British Museum; purchased at £8 5s.

URBINO. Orazio Fontana. This mark is attributed by Sir J. C. Robinson to this artist. It occurs on a magnificent plate in the Louvre; subject, the Massacre of the Innocents.

URBINO. Orazio Fontana; so attributed by Sir J. C. Robinson. This mark is on a plate, painted with St. Paul preaching at Athens, in the Narford Coll. At the sale, June, 1884, it was sold for £100.

URBINO. Orazio Fontana. This mark, similar to the preceding, is found on a tazza, painted with David and Goliath, formerly in the Narford Collection.

URBINO. This signature is on a plate, painted with statuary and a coat of arms, architectural subject in the background; it is finely painted by one of the Fontana family. Inscribed at back *Vitruvio de architectura principe*, &c. Formerly in Mr. H. A. Neck's Collection.

URBINO. This mark is on a fruit tazza in the Correr Museum at Venice, and is attributed by Sig. Lazari to Flaminio Fontana; subject, the Judgment of Paris.

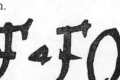

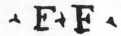

URBINO. On a plaque in Sir A. W. Franks' Coll., painted with a fine figure of St. Paul; on a stone in the foreground, the subject and date 1583. It has all the manner of the Fontana school, and has probably equal claim with the preceding.

URBINO, 1542. On a highly coloured plate, painted with St. Jerome plucking a thorn out of a lion's foot, inscribed on the back with description of the subject and "*Urbino*, 1542." Formerly in the Collection of the Marchese d'Azeglio.

Gjone

URBINO. On a plate, No. 345, Campana Collection; subject, Joshua commanding the sun to stand still, painted in the manner of Fontana. The abridged name of some artist unknown.

Urbino —
L

URBINO. On a plate; subject, David and Goliath, dated 1533; the description and signature on the back. Louvre Collection.

Nel anno de le
tribulatio ni
d'Italia adi
26 de luglio
J Urbino

URBINO. This curious inscription, which does not bear any allusion to the subject painted on the front, representing St. Mark, before whom a priest is kneeling, is on the back of a plate; similar inscriptions relating to contemporary events are occasionally met with: a piece in the Victoria and Albert Museum, representing a female, wounded, leaning against a buckler, before her two weeping figures, is inscribed on the reverse "DI TUA DISCORDIA ITALIA, IL PREMIO HOR HAI." This is dated 1536, and probably refers to the same event recorded above.

URBINO. On a square Urbino maiolica plaque, height 10 in. by $7\frac{1}{4}$ in. wide, painted in blue *camaieu* with the Temptation, Eve offering to Adam the forbidden fruit, copied from Marc Antonio's print after Raffaelle. In front is a tablet and date, 1523; on the reverse, a weaver's shuttle and distaff, probably a rebus of the painter. It is beautifully painted, and the finest specimen known to exist. In the Collection of the late Mr. R. Napier, of Shandon. Sir J. C. Robinson (Catalogue of the Shandon Coll., No. 3008) suggests that it may be by the Master of Forli, and describes the mark as a weaver's distaff and shuttle. Dr. Fortnum (Catalogue of the South Kensington Museum, p. 557) classes it as Forli, but he says it bears "as great a similitude to a brush and painter's palette" as to a shuttle and distaff.

URBINO. This mark is on a vase; subject, the Israelites gathering Manna in the Wilderness; of good design, but feeble in colouring. De Bruge Coll.

FATTO IN VRBINO
1587
T. R. F.

ITALY. Unknown master (Andrea di Bono ?), painted about 1500. The mark occurs on a plate; subject, Horatius Cocles defending the bridge. in the Victoria and Albert Museum; cost £6 15s.

A. D. B.

Bernal Coll., now

URBINO. A crescent and the initials E. F. B., dated 1594, is on the stem of an ewer, beautifully painted with yellow scrolls on blue ground, and a pelican encircled with the following inscription, "YMASQVE DE BVONA CANA;" in the possession of M. de Rothschild of Paris.

E.F.B.
1594

URBINO. The mark of an unknown master of the sixteenth century.

G+B+F+

URBINO. The initials of an unknown master; on the back of a large maiolica dish, raised centre, with Charity and a border of arabesques and cupids, 18 in.

↲1630↲
↲G↮B↯F↯

URBINO. This inscription and date are on the back of a very fine plateau, painted with the Storming of Goleta, engraved in Marryat. It has the mark of Fra. Xanto Avelli.

Jn Vrbino nella
bolteg di Francesco
de Siluano
✕
M·D·XXXXI

URBINO. The mark of Alfonzo Patanazzi. On the border of a large dish, painted with the subject of Romulus receiving the Sabine Women. In the Victoria and Albert Museum.

·ALF·P·F·
VRBINI
1606

ALFONSO PATANAZZI ↲

FECIT ↲

VRBINI 1606 ↲

The signature in full is on the reverse of the same dish. (*Ker. Gall.*, enlarged edition, fig. 36).

ALFONSO PATANAZZI
VRBINI FE.

ALFONSO PATANAZZI FE
VRBINI IN BOTEGA DI
IOS BATISTA BOCCIONE.
1607.

A.P.

Vrbini Patana
fecit anno 1584

F.P.
1617.

URBINO. Presumed to be the mark of Alfonzo Patanazzi, but no description is given of the subject or the name of the collection where it is to be found. In Dr. Fortnum's Catalogue of the Maiolica in the Victoria and Albert Museum (p. 369).

URBINO. The same artist; so signed at length on a plate mentioned by Passeri.

URBINO. "Alfonzo Patanazzi made this at Urbino, in the manufactory or workshop of Johannes Batista Boccione."

URBINO. The initials of Alfonzo Patanazzi, on a maiolica plate.

URBINO. This mark is on an inkstand with the four greatest poets at the corners, the body decorated with grotesques; from the collection of M. d'Azeglio, afterwards in the possession of Mons. H. Delange.

URBINO. The mark of Francesco Patanazzi. On a plate in the Delsette Collection.

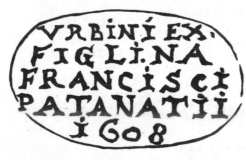

VINCENZIO PATANAZZI
DA VRBINO DI ETA
D'ANNI TREDECI DEL
1620.

VINCENTIO PATANAZZI
DE ANNI DODECI.

URBINO. Another mark of Francesco Patanazzi, 1608. On a large triangular cistern; subject, Adam and Eve driven out of Eden, and border of grotesques. Fountaine Collection. In the sale at Christie's in 1884 it was sold for £110.

URBINO. On a plate mentioned by Passeri, painted by Vincenzio Patanazzi, at the age of 13.

URBINO. Vincenzio Patanazzi, aged 12. Mentioned by Passeri.

URBINO. On a plate in the possession of Monsignore Cajani at Rome; subject, the Expulsion from Paradise. "Vincentio Patanatii de Anni 12."

uRcentico patanatun
ce anni j2

URBINO. Marked on the back of a plate; subject, Diana and Actæon. Formerly in the possession of the Marchese d'Azeglio.

1534.
Urbinj

URBINO. On a large vase painted with an historical subject. Soulages Collection.

FATTO IN URBINO.

URBINO. On a plate, painted / with arabesques, mentioned by M. Riocreux. Another mark of the same painter and date is on a bowl in the Victoria and Albert Museum; on the border are six oval sunk pools in the manner of Palissy, painted *en grisaille* with amorini; cost £40.

Gironimo
urbin fecie
1583

URBINO or FAENZA. This mark is on a plate of old white maiolica (Falcke's sale, No. 2880), marked in blue. Dr. Fortnum ascribes this to Faenza.

Φ
1526

URBINO. The arms of the Duke of Urbino. The initials of the inscription may be read, GUIDO, UBALDO, URBINO, DUX. Presented to Frater Andrea of Volterra.

G.V.V.D.
MVNVS. F. ANDREA
E VOLATERRANO.

Passeri quotes *two* plates of this service: subjects, Coriolanus and the Deluge; *two* more, one representing the Sacrifice of Jacob, the other the Burning of Troy, were in the Delsette Collection, whence they passed into that of the late Mr. A. Barker; *two* in the Geological Museum: subjects, the Triumph of Trajan, and Mutius Scævola; *three* in the Marquis of Bristol's Collection at Ickworth: subjects, Aaron the High-Priest, Camillo, and Men and Women at a stream; *one*, a fluted tazza, is in the British Museum; *one* is in the Rothschild Collection at Paris; and *one* in the Museum of the University of Bologna.

URBINO. This mark is on a plate; subject, Diana and Actæon, mentioned by Delange, attributed by some to Luca Cambiasi, a painter of Genoa, by others to Girolamo Lanfranco of Pesaro.

URBINO. A mark on a maiolica plate; subject, Diana and Actæon. In the Campana Collection.

URBINO. On the back of a plate, painted with St. Luke seated on a bull in the clouds, and holding an open volume. In the Ashmolean Museum, Oxford (Fortnum Collection).

URBINO. This mark occurs on the front of a large Urbino dish, painted with the martyrdom of St. Lawrence; the description and date, 1531, is on the back. It was sold at Lord Northwick's sale for 295 guineas.

URBINO. This mark, which is probably the number of the piece in the service, is on a large dish in the Narford Collection, admirably painted with the Conversion of St. Paul, attributed to Orazio Fontana.

URBINO. Tazza (elliptic), strap-work in relief on each side and end, which terminate in blue masks, surrounding two medallions: one represents Moses striking the Rock, the other the Return of the Spies from the Promised Land; on reverse, strap and scroll-work and four lions' masks in relief; beneath the foot F.G.C., circa 1580. Victoria and Albert Museum.

URBINO. On a very fine plateau, 16 in. diameter; subject, the Last Judgment, and long inscriptions signed both on the front and back. In the Collection of the Marquis of Bristol, Ickworth.

These two marks are given by Jacquemart as belonging to Urbino (*Merveilles de la Céramique*, p. 349). They are, however, not fabrique marks, but the initials of the pharmacy of the monastery.

URBINO. This curious inscription is on the back of a large dish of the middle of the sixteenth century,

TESAVRVS
CARBONES ERANT.

and a representation of a mine, with several lumps of coal and a hatchet. It relates either to a scarcity of coal at that time, or more probably it records the successful use of that mineral as a substitute for wood in heating the kiln. On the front of the dish is painted a Roman sacrifice.

URBINO. The mark of a painter, on a highly-coloured dish; subject, a Lion Hunt, after Marc Antonio. It has been suggested that the initials stand for Francesco Lanfranco, Rovigo. Berney

·*f*·*L*·*R*·

Collection. The same letters, in conjunction with the signature of Maestro Giorgio, dated 1529, are on a plate; subject, Jupiter and Semele. Formerly in the Addington Collection.

URBINO. On a plate; subject, Hector and Achilles in the River Xanthus, well coloured. Berney Collection.

Urbino-B

URBINO ? Denistoun (*Memoirs of the Dukes of Urbino*, iii. 391) observes that he saw "at

F. M. DOIZ. F.

Urbino, in 1845, a feeble plate in colour and design, signed F. M. DOIZ FIAMENGO FECIT, a proof that it was no despised production of the time." The mark in the margin was on the front, at the base of a specimen in the Gowen sale, No. 112, but the name sounds very much like one of the Delft artists.

URBINO. This may probably be the monogram of Césare Cari, of Faenza, who painted in the botega of Guido Merlino, from 1536 to 1551 (see p. 57).

1549

URBINO. Fayence with stanniferous enamel. This inscription is on the bottom of a sliding pillar lamp with four burners, painted in the style of Moustiers, from which place, or from Marseilles, M. Rolet

Fabrica di Maiolica
fina di Monsieur Rolet
in Urbino. a 28 Aprile 1713

probably came and established himself at Urbino; it is in the Victoria and Albert Museum; cost £12.

6

F · D ·
1 5 4 3

URBINO. On a plate formerly in the Narford Collection; subject, the Arrest of a Cavalier, painted with great care by Francesco Durantino.

fracesco durantino
1 5 4 4

URBINO. On a tazza in the British Museum; subject, Coriolanus met by his Mother.

GUBBIO,

in the Duchy of Urbino, is known to us principally by the works of Maestro Giorgio Andreoli, who seems to have monopolised the ruby metallic lustre with which he enriched not only his own productions, but put in the finishing-touches in metallic colours on plates of other artists from Urbino and Castel Durante.

Giorgio was son of Pietro Andreoli, a gentleman of Pavia, and was established at Gubbio when young, according to Passeri, with his brothers Salimbene and Giovanni.

In 1498 he obtained the rights of citizenship and filled some municipal offices. He was a statuary as well as a painter of fayence, several of his sculptures in marble being extant. His early pieces, mentioned below, are without the lustre which subsequently rendered him so famous. The first piece on which his metallic lustre is revealed to us by his signature is dated 1518; his last is dated 1541; quoted by Sir J. C. Robinson from a piece in the Pasolini Collection, signed by M°. Giorgio, which he says cannot implicitly be relied on. The figure of St. Sebastian, modelled in relief on a tile dated 1501 in the Victoria and Albert Museum, is attributed to Giorgio. The earliest specimen signed and dated is a plate with a border of trophies, painted in 1517 and lustred in 1518, and was formerly in the Napier (Shandon) Collection. It is now in the Victoria and Albert Museum. Another plate of the same service, but with a different mark, is in the British Museum.

In 1537 his son Vincentio or Cencio, the only one who followed his father's profession, was associated with him in his works. Vincentio is supposed to be denoted by the N seen on some of the Gubbio plates.

Perestino was another successor of M°. Giorgio, whose mark is found noticed below, but we have no certain information respecting him.

One of the finest specimens of Giorgio is the plate painted with the Three Graces, signed on the back with one of the many varieties of his signature, and dated 1525; sold in Mons. Roussel's sale for 400 guineas to the late Mr. A. Fountaine of Narford. At the Fountaine sale, 1884, it brought £766 10s., and was purchased by Mr. Beckett Denison. At his death it was bought by the Victoria and Albert Museum for £870, 19s. 6d., and is certainly one of the gems of our National Collection. (Vide *Ker. Gall.*, enlarged edition, fig. 42.)

GUBBIO. This mark is supposed to be that of Andreoli; it is on the back of a lustre plate formerly in the possession of Mr. I. Falcke.

GUBBIO. Attributed to Giorgio Andreoli. On the back of a lustre plate; subject, King Solomon. Campana Collection.

GUBBIO. Giorgio Andreoli, before he was enobled as Maestro. The mark, in gold lustre, is here reduced; it is on the reverse side of a plaque, representing St. Jerome seated. Soulages Collection.

GUBBIO. The initials of Maestro Giorgio. On a tazza, painted with a male and female figure seated, and a cupid. Soulages Collection.

GUBBIO. The initials of Maestro Giorgio, with a merchant's mark between; on a plate; subject, Balaam.

GUBBIO. Another mark of Maestro Giorgio; given by Passeri (now in the Victoria and Albert Museum).

GUBBIO. On a small plate of early period; in the centre the half-figure of a bishop (St. Petronio), after Perugino; border of leaf ornament, drawn in blue outline and lustred with ruby and gold; formerly in the possession of Monsignore Cajani at Rome. (Fortnum.)

GUBBIO. This monogram occurs in lustre colours on the back of a plateau, with female profile bust on a raised centre, of the well-known early type, richly lustred, which has been ascribed to Pesaro and Diruta. It is the only known instance of a mark on similar pieces. In the British Museum. (Fortnum.)

GUBBIO. On the back of a tazza, said by Brancaleoni to be in the "Casa tondi" at Gubbio, and referred to by Passeri; foliage and arabesques in blue, yellow, and ruby lustre. The form of the G is very similar to that on the small plate just described with the figure of St. Petronio.

GUBBIO. Maestro Giorgio. On a lustrous dish, with arabesques in blue; was in M. de Monville's Collection, Paris.

GUBBIO. Maestro Giorgio. His works date from about 1518 to 1541. Marked on a plate; subject, St. Francis: in the Victoria and Albert Museum; cost £30.

GUBBIO. Maestro Giorgio, 1520, with a merchant's mark. On a lustrous plate, painted with Aurora in a biga, and two winged attendants on the water. In the late Mr. A. Barker's Collection.

GUBBIO. Maestro Giorgio, 1520. On a flat plate, richly lustred gold ground, painted in the centre with a shield of arms of three fleurs-de-lis in chief and three crowns, supported by three cupids, candelabra, trophies, &c.

M°. Giorgio. 1520. Adi. 2 di Otobre B.D.S.R. In Ugubio.

GUBBIO. This curious inscription is written in blue on a piece of maiolica in the possession of M. Dutuit, of Rouen, differing materially from those we are accustomed to refer to Gubbio. The design is the Judgment of Paris, finished with great care in sober colours; the metallic lustre is subordinate to the rest; quoted by M. Jacquemart. The letters preceding the name of the place refer probably to the appellation of his manufactory, "Botega di S. R.," but we must leave the last two to be hereafter deciphered.

GUBBIO. On a plate, with a half-figure of St. John in the centre, ruby lustre, belonging to M. Leroy Ladurie, Paris.

GUBBIO. Another mark of Maestro Giorgio, with the date 1537. In the late Mr. A. Barker's Collection.

GUBBIO. Maestro Giorgio, 1525. On a plate, painted with "The Stream of Life," from an early print by Robetta. It was purchased at the Bernal sale for £142, and was formerly in Passeri's possession. (*Ker. Gall.*, enlarged edition, fig. 43.) In the recent sale of the Fountaine Collection, 1884, it brought £820. Now in the Salting Collection.

GUBBIO. Maestro Giorgio, 1526. On a plate; subject, an amorino swinging on the branch of a tree, painted *en grisaille*, richly lustred with ruby and gold colours. Soulages Collection.

GUBBIO. Maestro Giorgio. On a lustred plate, representing the Death of Dido, from an engraving by Marc Antonio.

GUBBIO. This mark of a signature and date, here reduced to half its size, is painted in gold lustre, the flowers in the cornucopiæ being in ruby; occurs on the back of one of the finest works of Maestro Giorgio known to us, a dish of the largest size, having in the centre a group of nymphs bathing, with a border of the richest *grotesche*. This noble piece is figured

on Delange's *Recueil*, pl 65, and at that time it belonged to the Baronne de Parpart, having been formerly in the Collection of Prince Bandini Giustiniani of Rome. This masterpiece of Giorgio is now, we are happy to say, in England; it was sold for Madame Parpart at £880, and was later acquired by Sir Richard Wallace at a price nearly doubling that amount. Hertford House Collection.

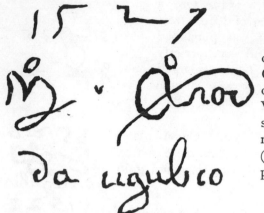

GUBBIO. A curious variety of the signature of Maestro Giorgio da Ugubio, dated 1527, on the back of a plateau in the Victoria and Albert Museum. A similar mark is given by Fortnum in his *Catalogue of Maiolica* (p. 200) which occurs on another piece by the same artist.

GUBBIO. The mark of M⁰. Giorgio of Ugubio, as it was formerly spelt; it is dated 1531. From the Collection of Signor Marnelli; painted by an Italian maiolica artist, and sent to Mⁿ. Giorgio to be touched with his far-famed lustre colours of gold and ruby. The latter pigment remained a secret with him, and has never been surpassed, or even equalled. This added considerably to the value of such pieces, as was evidenced at the sale of the Fountaine Coll. in 1884, where fine pieces realised from £500 to £800 each.

GUBBIO. This interesting mark (reduced) is on a magnificent circular dish in the Museum of the University of Bologna. The whole surface is covered with the subject, the Presentation of the Virgin, admirably drawn and richly lustred in gold and ruby. The inscription on reverse beneath the signature is remarkable, and the only instance recorded.

GUBBIO. This interesting mark, with the date 1543, may probably be referred to Guido Fontana. It occurs on a slightly lustred tazza of Urbino character, in the Ashmolean Museum, Oxford (Fortnum's Collection). The subject, somewhat coarsely painted, is Constantine crossing the bridge and seeing the Cross in the sky; the mark is on the reverse in gold lustre.

GUBBIO. This mark and date are on the back of a plate which came from Paris and was purchased by Mr. J. Webb. It is probably an imperfect signature of Maestro Giorgio.

GUBBIO. This mark occurs on a plate having on the border four medallions, two of which bear these initials; in the centre the Virgin between two angels. These letters have been considered to be the initials of Maria Gloriosa, but M. Darcel reads them Maestro Giorgio, and says the plate is identical with one in the Louvre, executed by the same hand, lustred and signed by that artist. In the Victoria and Albert Museum.

GUBBIO. This mark is on a plate; subject, Abraham visited by the angels, in metallic lustre; probably by Maestro Giorgio. Louvre Collection.

GUBBIO. This singular device is painted in colours, and beautifully lustred by Maestro Giorgio in the front of a *tondino* or deep plate. The initials are probably those of a merchant prince or. noble, the hand pointing to his trade-mark, and sent by him to be lustred at Gubbio. The design is here greatly reduced from the original. It is dated on the back 1518, and is a very choice specimen of Giorgio's art. In the British Museum.

GUBBIO. The name illegible, but in the style of Maestro Giorgio. From Passeri; the reading Maestro Gillio is highly improbable.

GUBBIO. This inscription, hastily and incorrectly drawn, has been attributed to Maestro Giorgio Andreoli, as well as to Cencio; subject, two hunters with dog and hare; border of trophies, in metallic lustre. Sauvageot Collection.

GUBBIO. The letter N. and 1539 on a plate; subject, Diana and Actæon, with metallic lustre. In the Campana Collection, Louvre.

GUBBIO. School of Maestro Giorgio. Sir J. C. Robinson attributed this to Vincentio or Maestro Cencio; some have given it to Santa Natoia, a branch of the Gubbio manufacture. It occurs on a plate, with the head of John the Baptist in a charger. (Soulages Coll.) The same letter is on a lustred plate, with an amorino holding a bow, in the Victoria and Albert Museum.

GUBBIO. The painter of the Giorgio school signing himself N., as in the preceding example.

NOCERA (Via Flaminia), a branch of the Gubbio manufactory. The pieces are usually marked N. The mark of G N, as in the margin, is in metallic lustre on the back of a plate, No. 83 in the Campana Collection.

GUBBIO. This signature of Perestino, considerably reduced here, is on a square bas-relief, representing the Virgin and Child, painted in metallic lustre; the name on the reverse is in red lustre. (Campana Coll., Louvre.) The semicircle above is not a C, as Mr. A. Darcel supposes, but the handle of the tablet. The idea that this letter is the initial of Cencio or Vincentio Andreoli, and the word underneath is a surname given him from his expertness and celerity in working, is too visionary; it is not "*prestino*," but without a doubt *Perestino*.

GUBBIO. Probably Maestro Perestino. On a vase in the Campana Collection; attributed in the catalogue to Maestro Giorgio.

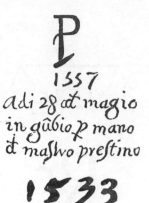

GUBBIO. Maestro Perestino or Prestino. Signed on a plate, painted in ruby and gold lustre, with Venus and Cupid; formerly in the possession of Mr. I. Falcke.

GUBBIO. The mark, probably, of Maestro Perestino. It is on a plateau, painted from a lost work of Raphael; the subject is the Redemption of Solomon and the establishment of the throne of David. King David is seated on a throne, like that of Solomon, spoken of in the tenth chapter of 1 Kings, ver. 18; on a lion tripod table before him is the flaming chafing-dish; a golden cup, holding the five shekels of silver; a priest holds the infant Solomon on the table, and inquires of Queen Bathsheba, who stands by his side, "Is this thy son?" &c. (Numb. xviii. 15). There are two attendants, one on the King, the other on the Queen. In the background is the type of the future temple; and in the distance is seen the tabernacle and the hill of the Lord, with two trees, on which are hanging the two sons of Rizpah, the daughter of Aiah, whom she bare unto Saul, and the five sons of Michal, the daughter of Saul; "and they hanged them in the hill before the Lord" (2 Sam. xxi. 9). Bracon Hall Collection.

GUBBIO. This mark occurs on a piece in the Campana Collection: a forked L and a sort of naked branch (see note on piece ascribed by M. Darcel to Rimini, p. 108).

GUBBIO. This monogram is on a fine plate, having the Torregiano arms, and foliage, trophies, &c.; sold at Mr. Galliardi's sale for £104.

GUBBIO. This monogram is on a lustred plate; subject, Abraham and the Angels. Campana Collection; perhaps an imperfect monogram of Maestro Giorgio, or one that has been badly traced or copied.

GUBBIO. This mark has been attributed to Maestro Cencio (Vincentio), son of Giorgio Andreoli, but the mark is in direct contradiction to the assertion. Passeri says that Giorgio was assisted in his manufacture of maiolica by his brothers; it is more likely to be the monogram of Salimbene, who we are told was one of them. One example was in the possession of M. Sauvageot of Paris; another in the Campana Collection.

GUBBIO. This mark occurs on a plate; subject, Hercules and Cerberus, in the Campana
Collection, Louvre. Another, without date, is in
the Victoria and Albert Museum; the latter being
rather indelicate in composition. Such is also
the case with a plate bearing the same mark,
having above the letters F R, dated 1535, given
by Greslou.

GUBBIO. On a bowl; subject, the Virgin
and Child, painted in lustre colours. Formerly
Narford Collection.

GUBBIO. Marked on the back of a plate, of
yellow ground, with trophies, shaded in blue; in
the centre is a shield of arms of two storks, dated
1540. Formerly in the Barker Collection.

GUBBIO. Marked in lustre colour on the back
of a plate; subject, Cupid with sword and shield,
blue border and scrolls.

GUBBIO. These letters are on a plate, dark
blue ground, with male and female heads in costume of the beginning of the sixteenth century,
within wreaths, trophies, &c. (Bernal Coll.), Victoria and Albert Museum; cost £26 10s. Dr.
Fortnum considered that this plate is erroneously
ascribed to Gubbio.

M.A.I.M.

GUBBIO. A plate of the sixteenth century, having in the centre the bust of a warrior, inscribed
as in the margin (most probably the name of
warrior or of the owner); on the border four coats
of arms of yellow ground, and beneath Y.A.E.
Formerly in the Collection of M. Meusnier, of Paris.

GABRIEL DA GUBBIO.

GUBBIO. This curious mark was on a lustred
plate by M°. Giorgio in Mr. Bernal's Collection,
but was not catalogued with the others at the
sale in 1855; subject, Abraham's sacrifice.

D

GUBBIO. This mark appears on a vase having, in relief,
the Virgin and Child, and also on a vase painted with ornaments in metallic lustre, and a large initial letter L; both in
the Campana Collection.

GUBBIO. On a portrait plate, with arabesques, as practised by Giorgio Andreoli, but of inferior merit. Campana
Collection. This piece is attributed by M. Darcel to Deruta.

GUBBIO. Perhaps the mark of Maestro Cencio. It occurs
on a plate in the De Monville Collection; also on a plate in
relief, No. 71, in the Campana Collection.

Modern Reproductions.

GUBBIO. Umbria. Manufacturers of maiolica, Messrs.
Carocci, Fabbri & Co., exhibiting specimens of lustred colours
in imitation of that of the fifteenth and sixteenth centuries,
in yellow, ruby, and other metallic lustres, at the International
Exhibition, 1862; marked in centre on the back. M. Pietro
Gay, the director, is the artist who personally attends to this
lustre, for which he obtained the medal.

Some good reproductions of Gubbio have also been made by the
Marquis of Ginori's Florence factory; they are generally marked with
the word GINORI, surmounted by a coronet. In the Italian Exhibition
of 1888 at Kensington some other Italian firms also exhibited lustred
maiolica.

PESARO.

We are indebted for much that we know of this fabrique to Giam-
battista Passeri, who has striven to do all honour to his native country;
and as its history was not written until nearly two centuries after its
establishment, we must make allowances for his *amour propre*. Many of
the pieces of ancient style with yellow metallic lustre, formerly attributed
to Pesaro, are now by common consent referred to Deruta.

Passeri quotes a certain *Joannis a Bocalibus* of Forli, who in 1396
established himself at Pesaro.

In 1462 mention is made of the loan of a large sum for the enlarge-
ment of a manufactory of vessels. The borrowers, Ventura di Mastro,
Simone da Siena of the Casa Piccolomini, and Matteo di Raniere of Cagli,
bought in the following year a considerable quantity of sand " du lac de
Perouse," which entered into the composition of fayence. To this date
Passeri places the introduction of the manufacture of maiolica.

In 1546, an edict was passed in favour of Pesaro by Jean Sforza,
forbidding the introduction from other fabriques of any but common
vessels for oil and water; to the same effect were two other edicts of
1508 and 1532, and another by Guido Ubaldo in 1552; in this last the
potters of Pesaro, M°. Bernardino Gagliardino, M°. Girolamo Lanfranchi,
and M°. Rinaldo, "vasari et boccalari," engage to supply the town and
country with vases, and pieces painted with historical subjects, under

certain conditions. The M°. Gironimo, vase-maker, who signs the plates in the margin (page 77), is probably the Girolamo Lanfranchi here mentioned; his son Giacomo succeeded him, who in 1562 invented the application of gold to maiolica, fixed by fire.

Another corroboration of Passeri's statement, and of the importance of the Lanfranchi establishment, occurs in an anonymous document published by the Marquis Giuseppe Campori (*Notizie della majolica e della porcellana di Ferrara*). It is preserved among the archives of Modena, and is dated Pesaro, 26th October, 1660. It relates how the Duke of Modena had been entertained at the house of the Signora Contessa Violante, "*con tutta quella domestichezza,*" which he desired; how he was presented with six *bacili* filled with delicacies made by the nuns, sent to him by the daughters of the Countess, and which were kept in the dishes. That some of his family wishing to buy *majoliche* painted by Raffaelle of Urbino, a great quantity of *bacili* and *tazzoni* was brought to them, not by Raffaelle, but painted by a certain ancient professor of that kind of painting denominated "*il Gabiccio*"—"*le furono portate gran quantità di bacili e di tazzoni o fruttere, non già de Raffaelle ma dipinti da un tale antico Professore di tali pitture denominato il Gabiccio,*" who, as the Marquis Campori suggests, was probably that Girolamo di Lanfranchi, the *maestro* of the establishment at the Gabice. It then goes on to relate that these dealers in antiquities, like some of their brethren of the present day, asked too much money, to wit, a hundred *doble* for a *rinfrescatore* or cistern; certainly well painted, but for which they offered twelve! and that they only succeeded in acquiring another *rinfrescatore*, and a large turtle that would serve as a basin or a dish, painted with grotesques and figures on the bowl and cover, for which they paid twenty-one *doble*. The Marquis Campori observes that the cover of this *tartaruga* was sold not long since in Modena to an amateur, and when last in Florence the writer learnt that such a piece was then in the hands of Signor Rusca of that city. He had himself seen at Rome the lower portion of a large turtle or tortoise shaped dish in the Palazzo Barberini, which may perchance belong to the cover in Florence, or be the other half of a similar piece. (Fortnum.)

We had an opportunity, a few years since, of inspecting a perfect *tartaruga*, which is still in the possession of a friend, answering exactly the description given above, ornamented on the interior with elegant arabesques of grotesque animals, modelled from life in form of a tortoise, of which a photograph was taken at the time.

Cicevone et julie Cesar cuado idete le lege 1522 in la botega et mastro givolame da legabice Jn pesavo

This inscription is on a *fruttiera* or tazza with the subject of Cicero expounding the law before Julius Cæsar, a composition of six figures: Cicero in the centre holds a folio before Cæsar, who is seated on a throne; the inscription is on the reverse. In the British Museum, the gift of Dr. Fortnum. It bears the signature of Girolamo of Gabice, 1542, mentioned by Passeri, whose name is so stated in an edict of 1552, probably the same as Girolamo Lanfranco. In 1562 a privilege was granted to his son Giacomo for the application of gold to fayence, fixed by the fire. About 1598 he was succeeded by his son Giacomo, who ceded the manufactory in 1599 to his sons Girolamo and Ludovico.

Dr. Fortnum (Catalogue S. K. Museum, p. 158) remarks, that in this inscription we have a very interesting example, corroborating the records given by Passeri of the Lanfranchi fabrique and of its locality. This is the Maestro Girolamo di Lanfranco of Gabice, a dependency of *Castello*, six miles west of Pesaro, and thus mentioned in a register :—

"1560 Mastro Girolamo di Lanfranco delle Gabice, vasaro, possiede una casa, &c." "1598 gli succede Giacomo suo figlio." "1599 gli succedono Girolamo e Ludovico figli di Giacomo."

In the Montferrand Collection, No. 162, there was a plate representing the Martyrdom of St. Maurice, the Tribune of a Roman Legion; on the border were the arms of Cardinal Giustiniani; it was heightened with gold, and the work of Giacomo Lanfranco, 1569.

This mark is on the reverse of a plate in the Museum of the University of Bologna, representing nymphs at the bath, by Jacomo, son of Maestro Girolamo, Fatto in Pesaro 1542 in bottega di Ma^ro Gironimo Vasaro, Jachomo pinsur. (In the second line of the inscription, the painter has transposed the letters *d* and *b*.)

*fatto in pefaro 1542
in dotte gabi^vo m^o givonimo
vafar o
iachomo pinfior*

There was in the Collection of M. Mathieu Meusnier, Paris (now dispersed), a fine Italian fayence-plate, with *réflét metallique*; in the centre a man on horseback in armour, praying, in the manner of Albert Dürer, and on the border a number of square tablets linked together like a chain, each tablet containing a letter, thus :—IOMARECHOMADOADIO, which reads IO-MA.RECHOMADO-A-DIO. Sixteenth century.

Passeri does honour to Guido Ubaldo II. della Rovere (who became Duke of Urbino in 1538) for his patronage of the fabrique of Pesaro. On the death of Guido Ubaldo in 1572, the pottery began to decline, and when Passeri returned to Pesaro in the year 1718, there was only one potter, who made ordinary vessels. Some years after, in 1757, he sent a painter from Urbania and recommenced the manufacture on an improved plan; some of these later pieces are noticed below.

PESARO. On the back of a dish, circa 1535; subject, Apollo and Argus. Bernal Collection; cost £6 10s. A similar inscription is on another dish, of Picus and Circe, also from the Bernal Collection; cost £11. Both in the British Museum.

FATO IN PESARO.

De Pisauro ed Chamillo.

The greater part of the early maiolica is not marked. One piece of a man on horseback, in gold and red metallic lustre, is quoted by M. Jacquemart.

PESARO. On a dish; subject, Horatius Cocles; mentioned by Passeri (sold, Spitzer Collection, Paris, 1893). Another large plateau —subject, the Triumphal March of the Emperor Aurelius—was in the Soltykoff Collection, with the same inscription, but dated 1552; sold for sixteen guineas.

FATTO IN PESARO.
1541.

PESARO. Made in the workshop of Master Gironimo, maker of vases, in Pesaro; quoted by Passeri.

NELLA BOTEGA DI
MAESTRO GIRONIMO
VASARO. I.P.

PESARO. This inscription is on a plate; subject, Mutius Scævola, of good design, but coarsely painted, blue, green, and yellow predominating. Formerly in the Marquis d'Azeglio's Collection.

˅1566˄
MVT˲ S Cʁ ˄
˂PÍ SAVRI ˄

O+A
1582

PESARO. This mark is given by Passeri as occurring on two pieces, which he assigns to this place.

QUESTO PIATTO FU FATTO
IN LA BOTEGA DI MASTRO
BALDASSAR VASARO
DA PESARO.
E FATTO PER MANO DI
TERENZIO FIOLO DI
MASTRO MATTEO
BOCCALARO
TERENCIO FECE 1550.

PESARO. Made in the workshop of Maestro Balthasar, vase-maker of Pesaro, by the hand of Terenzio, son of Maestro Matteo, bocalemaker, 1550. This inscription is found on a plate having a cupid in the centre, with a border of musical instruments and trophies on blue ground. An open music-book has the title of a song:

O bel fiore
Amore mio bello,
Amor mio caro
La Grisola, la grisola.

It is mentioned by Passeri. This artist was known as *Il Rondolino.*

PESARO
CALLEGARI E CASALI
OTTUBRE 1786.

PESARO. The manufacture of pottery was revived about the middle of the eighteenth century. M. A. Jacquemart says that two artists of Lodi, Filippo Antonio Callegari and Antonio Casali, were manufacturers here, but the precise date is unknown. There was another fabrique established by Giuseppe Bertolucci, of Urbania, in 1757, and it is known also that in 1763 Pietro Lei, a painter of Sassuolo, took the direction of one of these, probably the former. Their signatures at length, as in the margin, are found upon a soup-tureen in imitation of Sèvres, bleu de roi ground, with gold arabesques and medallions of flowers and landscapes.

PESARO, 1765. This mark, in violet, is beneath a fayence plate with stanniferous enamel, painted with a rose and forget-me-nots in the centre, and a border of birds and flowers in relief and coloured. The ware is very much like that of Marseilles, as is also the decoration. In the Ashmolean Museum, Oxford (Fortnum Collection). Vide *Ker. Gall.*, enlarged edition, fig. 59.

An *écuelle*, with green and gold leaves and scrolls, has the letters C C and Pesaro without a date.

The letters C C stand for Callegari and Casali, and those at the end for Pietro Lei, before named.

PESARO? On a late maiolica medicine vase; subject, Adam and Eve driven out of Paradise.

PESARO. On a jug, blue ground, painted with flowers on a white medallion; one of the latest of the maiolica productions in Italy. De Bruge Collection.

On a plate painted in colours with figure subject in Mr. F. A. White's Collection. Mark of Magrini & Co., about 1870.

fabbrica Magrin Pesaro.

CASTEL DURANTE.

M. Giuseppe Raffaeli (*Mémoires Historiques sur les Faïences de Castel Durante*) mentions the existence in 1361 of a certain Giovanni dai Bistuggi, or John of Biscuits, a name probably referring to "biscuit" ware, *i.e.*, ware which has been subjected to a preliminary firing but is not yet glazed. He also speaks of a certain Maestro Gentile, who furnished the Ducal palace with vessels in 1363. The most ancient dated piece is the beautiful bowl which belonged to Mr. H. T. Hope, dated 12th September, 1508.

At a later period, a potter named Guido di Savino worked at Castel Durante, who, according to Piccolpasso, transported to Antwerp the knowledge of the manufacture of Italian maiolica.

It was also from Castel Durante that Giovanni Tesio and Lucio Gatti, in 1530, introduced it into Corfu, and in 1545 that Mº. Francesco del Vasaro established himself in Venice.

About 1490 the following artists were working: Pier del Vasaro; the Sabatini; Picci; Superchina; Savini; Bernacchia; Marini; Morelli.

The manufacture was at its perfection in 1525-30, and continued to produce good wares even till 1580. In connection with *istoriati* pieces and mythological subjects, the following artists are recorded: Luca and Angiolo Picchi; Pier Francesco Calze; Ubaldo della Morcia; Simone da Colonello; the Fontana, &c.; also the Appoloni; Giorgio Picci; Lucio, Bernardino, and Ottaviano Dolci.

Piccolpasso, a potter of this place, in his interesting book describes all the various wares and patterns, illustrated by drawings in pen and ink, as well as its manufacture, processes, utensils, &c. About 1623 it was created a city, and took the name of Urbania after Pope Urban VIII.

In 1722 Urbania was the only fabrique which existed in the Duchy of Urbino, where articles of utility only were made; but Cardinal Stoppani brought painters from other places, and endeavoured to put fresh life into the trade of Urbania.

The best artists at Urbania were the Lazzarini, the Frattini, and the Biagini, who painted from prints by Sadeler, Martin de Vos, the Caracci, Bassano, Tempesta, &c. The arabesques with grotesque heads, frequently on blue ground, are boldly drawn; cornucopiæ, &c., designed and shaded with light blue, touched with yellow and orange, brown and green, mostly on a large scale of pattern. For the names of the designs and forms of the vases, see page 50.

A plate of Castel Durante maiolica, painted with Mars, Vulcan, and Venus, circa 1530 (Bernal Collection) is in the Victoria and Albert Museum; cost £44.

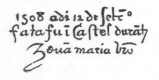

CASTEL DURANTE. This inscription is on the bottom of a large and very fine bowl, surrounded externally by blue scrolls on white; inside are painted the arms of Pope Julius II., supported by cupids with arabesques, &c., on deep blue ground. This important piece was made on the 12th of September, 1508, and painted by Giovanni Maria, vasaro or vase-maker. In the Collection of the late Mr. H. T. Hope. The *vro* at the end of the inscription has been deciphered *Urbino*, but it is probably intended for *vasaro*.

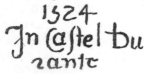

CASTEL DURANTE. On a plate; subject, a King distributing wine and bread to some soldiers; in front are four vases, and a larger one filled with loaves. Marquis d'Azeglio's Coll.

CASTEL DURANTE. Sebastiano Marforio, in whose workshop this piece was made on the 11th of October 1519, at Castel Durante. Inscribed on a large pharmacy vase, with scrolls, chimeræ, arabesques, &c. Bernal Collection, now in the British Museum; £23. There is one similar in the Victoria and Albert Museum.

CASTEL DURANTE. Inscribed in yellow colour on a dish; subject, Dido and Ascanius. Bernal Collection, £13. Also on one in the Campana Collection, dated 1525; subject, the Rape of Ganymede; and on another, subject, Marsyas. Sauvageot Collection.

1 5 2 6
jn castel
durante

CASTEL DURANTE or URBINO. An inscription on a pharmacy vase: In Castel Durante, near Urbino. In the Museum at Sèvres.

IN CASTELLO DURANTI.
APRESO A URBINO.
MIGLIE 7. 1555.

CASTEL DURANTE or URBINO. Inscribed on a pharmacy vase in the Marryat Collection.

A DE SEI D'MAGGIO
1550. AFARO IN
STVDI DURANTIAS.

CASTEL DURANTE or URBINO. Inscribed on a vase in the Hôtel de Cluny at Paris: Made of the earth of Castel Durante, near the city of Urbino.

fato in tera duranti
apreso ala cita d'urbino

CASTEL DURANTE. Francesco Durantino, vase-maker. On a cistern; subject after Giulio Romano.

FRANCESCO DURANTINO
VASARO. 1553.

CASTEL DURANTE. The Chevalier Piccolpasso, director of a botega for making pottery, circa 1550, wrote a treatise on the art of making and decorating maiolica, whilst this manufactory was under the patronage of Guidobaldo II. This manuscript has been secured by Sir J. C. Robinson for the library of the Victoria and Albert Museum. It is illustrated with pen-and-ink sketches of the mode of manufacturing the maiolica, and patterns of the ware made at Castel Durante. A translation, with copies of the drawings, has been published in Paris. M. Delange, in his translation of Passeri's work, speaks of a vase inscribed with Piccolpasso's name.

FATTO IN BOTEGA
DI PICCOLPASSO.

CASTEL DURANTE. A vase painted with grotesques, dated in front 1562, by Maestro Simono in Castello Durante; formerly in the possession of M. Cajani of Rome. Passeri mentions Maestro Simone da Colonello (see p. 80). It is figured in Delange's *Recueil*, pl. 75.

p mastro simono
in castelo durate

7

CASTEL DURANTE. This curious mark is on a dish decorated with trophies, in the Museum of the University of Bologna; the scroll is divided into two folds, on the upper one is inscribed *Pierro* or *Pietro da Castel (Durante)*; the lower portion has *fece* or *fecit*, with some illegible characters above.

CASTEL DURANTE. These marks are on a plate of this manufacture; subject, the Rape of Helen; from the Bernal Collection, now in the British Museum; cost £6.

IN CASTELLO DURANTO, 1541.

CASTEL DURANTE. On a pharmacy vase (Albarello), painted with trophies, grotesques, &c., and the bust of a man; the name is on a cartouche at back, on a blue ground. (Louvre, G. 244.)

CASTEL DURANTE or FABRIANO. Plate painted with a draped female on horseback, armed with shield and spear, in the act of charging a man seated on a rock and resting against his shield; Cupid above in a biga of doves. In brown *grisaille*. Reverse, strapwork and waved lines, and a monogram which is repeated on the woman's shield; perhaps the name of the person to whom it was given. Date circa 1540. Victoria and Albert Museum.

CASTEL DURANTE. This painter must have been engaged here in the seventeenth century, for the name of the place was changed to Urbania in 1635, in compliment to Pope Urban VIII.; it is on a plate, subject, the Triumph of Flora, &c. Campana Collection.

FATTA IN URBANIA NELLA BOTEGA DEL SIGNOR PIETRO PAPI, 1667.

CASTEL DURANTE. On a piece of maiolica; the mark is given by M. Jacquemart.

CASTEL DURANTE. These seven monograms or merchants' marks occur on pharmacy vases; they probably belong to the druggists for whom the vases were made, and not the painters or makers. The last of them is on a fine cylindrical pharmacy vase, with a large oval medallion of warriors in classical costume, and scroll border; at bottom is a negro's head, and at the top the annexed mark, probably a pontifical cipher of Pope Julius II. On the back is the early date of 1501. Bernal Collection, now in the British Museum. Mr. H. G. Bohn, in his *Monograms*, which forms a supplement to the priced catalogue of the Bernal sale, has ascribed this mark to P. INCHA AGRICOLA, and adduces as evidence of the existence of a painter of that name, No. 1949 in the Collection; but he has doubtless been misled by the erroneous reading of the inscription on that specimen given by the compiler of the catalogue (who was not *au fait* with the subject)— which is really the name of the place where it was made—thus *P. In chafaggiuolo*. This absurd error has been perpetuated by M. Jules Greslou, *Récherches sur la Céramique*, p. 196.

CASTEL DURANTE. On a picture of a landscape, mentioned by Mr. Marryat.

CASTEL DURANTE. On a maiolica pharmacy vase; subject, St. Martin dividing his cloak; marked in blue at the back. This is probably an owner's mark; it is surmounted by a crown.

GIOVANNI PERUZZI
DIPINSE 1693.

1698

CASTEL DURANTE. Piccolpasso in a manuscript (now in the library of the Victoria and Albert Museum, written in 1548) speaks of a certain

Guidō saluaggio

Guido di Savino of Castel Durante, who had carried to Antwerp the art of making fayence. This Savino has been confounded by M. A. Demmin with a certain Guido Salvaggio, through his misreading of an inscription on a plate in the Louvre, "Guidon Salvaggio," which, instead of being the signature of a painter, is only the description of the subject depicted, viz., a character of Ariosto's, *Guido the Savage*, shipwrecked in the *Isle des Femmes*.

PERUGIA. The name of this ancient city is in Greek Περουσια, in Latin *Perusia*, and formerly in Italian *Peroschia* or *Peroscia*; it is a populous city, the capital of Perugino, in the States of the Church. The inscription reads "Francesco Durantino, vase-maker, at the Mount Bagnole

Francesco Duratino Vasaro Amote Bagnole d Peroscia ‹1553‹

of Perugia," probably the same as that on page 81. It occurs on an oval cistern, painted with subjects after Giulio Romano. Fountaine Collection.

CASTEL DURANTE? On the back of a plate of blue enamel, with dark blue arabesques and masks, touched with white and yellow round the rim, and Europa in the centre; probably of the seventeenth century. Dr. Fortnum doubts the authenticity of this mark, but considers that if genuine it would belong to Faenza.

FAENZA.

Faenza was the most important, and probably the most ancient, of all the manufactories of maiolica in Italy.

The earliest piece which we have attributed to Faenza is the plate in the Hôtel de Cluny, which heads our list, dated 1475; then comes the tile inscribed Nicolaus Orsini, 1477, and the plate signed by Don Giorgio, 1485.

A most interesting specimen, from its bearing the name of the place as well as the date, is the enamelled tile-pavement of the St. Sebastian chapel in St. Petronia at Bologna, inscribed "BOLOGNIESUS. BETINI. FECIT: XABETA. BE. FAVENTCIE: CORNELIA; BE. FAVENTICIE: ZELITA. BE. FAVENTICIE: PETRUS. ANDRE. DE. FAVE.," and the date 1487.

There are two tablets of earthenware, covered with stanniferous enamel, white ground, with letters painted in black, in the Victoria and Albert Museum; one is inscribed "SIMONETTO. DI. CHORSO. DALL. ARENA. Pᴬ· M.D. XII.," above a shield of arms; the other is an oblong tablet with this inscription, "GIOVANNI. SALVETTI. Pᴬ· ET Cº· M.C.C.C.L.IIII. ET MICHELE. SVO. FIGL. (FIGLUOLO) Pᴬ· M.D.X.IIII." The inscription on these would show that they are Paduan or made for Paduans.

The Musée de Cluny possesses a pharmacy vase dated 1500, the companion to which has the name Faenza. In 1485 Tomasso Garzoni in the *Piazza Universale* praises the ware of Faenza as being so white and so brilliant.

In 1548 Piccolpasso, the director of a rival manufacture at Castel Durante, and who wrote about the time when Urbino and Gubbio produced their later works, gives the preference to the ware of Faenza.

The mark of a circle intersected by cross bars, with a small pellet or annulet in one of the quarters, has been found in connection with the signature of a Faenza fabrique (Casa Pirota), and it is therefore presumed that the pieces bearing it are from that manufactory (see p. 88).

Vincenzo Lazari speaks of a plate in the Museum of Bologna representing the Coronation of Charles V., bearing on the reverse "Fato in Faenza in Caxa Pirota." He also records that one Césare Cari, a potter, went from Faenza to Urbino.

Among the decorators of Faenza the same author notes Baldasara Manara, who signed his pieces frequently B.M. as well as his name at length. There is a celebrated painter who signs himself F.R., as noticed in the text; these pieces generally have on the reverse decorations in blue and orange. Another peculiarity among the painters of Faenza is a fine red colour employed by them; Piccolpasso says it is found especially in the workshop of Maestro Vergilio of Faenza, and Passeri describes the way to produce it. The backs of the pieces are usually ornamented with concentric circles or spiral lines in lapis blue on clear light blue, and when the reverse is white, the imbrications or zones are alternately blue and yellow.

The early pieces are archaic in character, the decorations are very ornamental, especially the grotesques or arabesques in *camaieu* on blue, or yellow ground, or alternately on the two colours. (Vide *Ker. Gall.*, enlarged edition, fig. 54.) The fabrique of Faenza does not appear to have adopted the yellow metallic lustre.

One of the finest specimens of Faenza known is the plate with grotesque figures, masks, cupids, trophies of arms, a satyr playing on a pipe, T R on a label in front of him and the motto *Auxillium meum de Domino*, with date 1508; the subject is taken from Albert Dürer, and Mr. George Salting had a print of the picture dated three years earlier than the plate. This is engraved in M. Delange's *Recueil de Faïences Italiennes*, and when sold at the Fountaine sale in 1884 was purchased for M. Adolphe de Rothschild for £920.

Mr. George Salting has left to the Victoria and Albert Museum a very fine vase of baluster form of about the same date with similar subjects, on a ground of dark blue and orange colour, which cost him over £1,100.

Besides the above the following are also in the Victoria and Albert Museum :—

A plateau with raised centre, the surface grounded in dark blue, with the coat of arms in the centre, around which is a band of dancing amorini and arabesque border, circa 1520. Soulages Collection; £80. A Faenza plate with arabesque border on blue, and medallions of profile heads, in the centre, amorini in a grotesque car, circa 1510; Bernal Collection, £36. A fruttiera; subject, the Gathering of Manna in the Wilderness, copied from an engraving by Agostino Veneziano, after Raffaelle; £100.

FAENZA. This inscription is round a maiolica plate, having in the centre the monogram of Christ in Gothic characters, surrounded by garlands in blue on white ground : Nicolaus de Ragnolis ad honorem Dei et Sanct. Michaelis, Fecit Fieri Ano 1475. In the Musée Cluny; one of the earliest dated pieces known.

NICOLAVS·DE·RASNOLIS
AD·HONOREM·DEI·ET
SANCT·MICHAELIS·
FECIT·FIERI·ANO·1475

FAENZA. On the rim of a maiolica plate; in the centre is represented Christ in the tomb, with emblems of the Passion. The name of Don Giorgio, 1485, has been

DON SIORSIO
1485

assumed to be that of Maestro Giorgio, before he went to Gubbio and was ennobled, but this is very doubtful. In the Sèvres Museum.

NICOLAUꝶ ORSINI
ⱮIIII77
ⱯƏI4 ƏI ꝶENⱯIU

FAENZA. The annexed inscription occurs on an oblong escalloped tile in the Sèvres Museum. At the top is "Nicolaus Orsini;" at the bottom, "1477. The 4th day of June," and between are the Orsini arms, supported by cupids. It is extremely interesting, being of so early a date.

Ⱦꝶ ꞇ
ⱥⱮSREⱭꝶI BꝶꝶU ꝑꝸ

FAENZA or CAFFAGGIOLO. Andrea di Bono. This name is written on a scroll in the centre of a circular maiolica plaque, dated 1491, bearing a shield with a lion rampant, and a small shield round its neck, enclosing a fleur-de-lis. Formerly in the Montferrand Collection, now in the Victoria and Albert Museum. (*Ker. Gall.*, enlarged edition, fig. 49.) Dr. Fortnum attributes this specimen to Caffaggiolo.

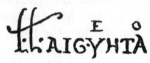

FAENZA. A very early plate, circa 1470, with the Virgin and Child painted on a dark blue ground, has on the back this mark in blue. Fountaine Collection, Narford. This curious signature has never yet been deciphered. It is figured in *Marryat*, p. 104, third edition.

IN FAENÇA

FAENZA. This mark is on the back of a small plate, with border of masks, cupids, and arabesques, in yellow on dark blue; in the centre Christ bound. Early sixteenth century. Henderson Collection.

FAENZA. On a plate; subject, Samson pulling down the pillars of the Temple; the back covered with coloured ornaments. Mentioned by Mr. Marryat.

F F ꝼꞌ
Ⱡ ⱬ F

FAENZA. The letter F of different forms probably indicates the Faenza manufacture. It occurs on plates with ornamented backs, in blue or yellow, of circles, foliage, imbrications, &c.

FAENZA. This mark is on a repoussé dish, with festoons of different colours, ornamented in arabesques; mentioned by Delange.

FATO IN FAEN3A
IN CAXA PIROTA

FAENZA. On the reverse of a plate in the Museum of the University of Bologna, representing the Coronation of Charles V. in that city in the year 1530, the probable date of the piece.

FAENZA. This inscription reads *FATE. IN. FAEnza. IOXEF. In. CAsa PIROTE*, 1525. Made in Faenza at the workshop of Pirote. The word Ioxef, which is also repeated on the interior of the plate, designates the subject, which is *Joseph's Cup*. In the possession of Baron Gustave de Rothschild.

FAENZA. On a plate painted in blue *camaieu*, an amorino in the centre, and border of dragons and trophies. Barker Collection.

FAENZA or PESARO. On a plateau, dark blue ground, in the centre a half-figure of a lady richly dressed, a banderole in front inscribed "SUSANNA BELLA P.V.," border of flowers, &c., circa 1500-10 on reverse, concentric lines of orange and blue, the mark in blue. Victoria and Albert Museum. Dr. Fortnum ascribes this piece to Pesaro.

FAENZA or PESARO. This device, similar to the preceding one, is in an orange-coloured pigment on the back of a fine dish, with full-length picture of St. John the Evangelist on the Island of Patmos, with chalice and serpent in the left hand and a book in the right hand. It is of course doubtful whether the device may be rightly considered a mark or only a decoration of the back of the plate. Formerly in the Nesbitt Collection; now in the collection of Mr. George Salting, in the Victoria and Albert Museum.

FAENZA. On the reverse of a fragment painted with allegorical subject by the artist, who signs F. R. The mark is a pink, similar to the rebus adopted by Benvenuto Tisio, called Garofalo, and the design for the piece may have been by that painter. In the Basilewski Collection.

FAENZA. On a plate with portrait of Laura, and arabesque border. This mark was formerly attributed to Pesaro.

FAENZA. On a pair of round candlesticks, with arabesques in pale blue painted on a dark blue ground. This mark and the preceding one are those of the Casa Pirota.

FAENZA. The same mark appears on a plate with a sunk centre, on which is painted a seated cupid with a hare, a duck, and a drum, surrounded by geometrical ornaments and a wreath of green leaves. The ground of the plate is pale blue. Both specimens are in Mr. George Salting's Collection in the Victoria and Albert Museum.

FAENZA. This is most probably another mark of the Casa Pirota. On a tazza painted with the Adoration of the Shepherds, with a border of deep blue ground painted with grotesques. In Mr. George Salting's Collection in the Victoria and Albert Museum.

FAENZA. This mark is on a plate cited by Brongniart.

FAENZA. On a large plateau, painted with the Judgment of Paris, surrounded by a border of arabesques on blue ground, dated 1527. Formerly in the Shandon (Napier) Collection. Now in Mr. George Salting's Collection in the Victoria and Albert Museum. The mark is only a portion of the somewhat elaborate decoration on the *back* of the plateau, which is given in facsimile in Dr. Fortnum's catalogue of the South Kensington Collection.

FAENZA. On a small shallow bowl representing the Saviour in a sarcophagus, border of cherubs'
heads, grotesques, &c., designed in white, and
shaded in yellow brown on dark blue ground. In
the British Museum.

This unknown mark of the wing of a bird is
on a maiolica tazza, inscribed "Nerone che fa
barare la matre." It is probably a Venetian
mark.

FAENZA or PADUA. An unknown mark on a
maiolica plate; subject, a woman bathing.

FAENZA or CAFFAGGIOLO. On a large dish; in
centre, St. Francis, encircled with rich arabesques
on orange ground, white borders, painted in blue
and yellow palmettes. These letters are on the
back. Dr. Fortnum ascribes this to Caffaggiolo.
Soltykoff Collection.

FAENZA. On a large dish, representing Christ
rising from the tomb; on each side are the Maries,
coloured on deep blue ground. On the tomb is
inscribed, "Cesaro Roman Imperatore Augusto,"
the date 1535, and S.P.Q.R. The portrait annexed
is on the lower part, and is introduced here to
show the curious characters which surround it.
Soltykoff Collection.

FAENZA or CAFFAGGIOLO. This monogram is
on the back of a bowl, with interlaced knots of
blue and orange; in front is a medallion of a
rosette, surrounded by yellow flutings, edged with
blue, in brilliant colours; circa 1520. Uzielli
Collection.

FAENZA. Marked in blue surrounded by rings,
on the back of a very rare plate, with deep blue
background, an allegorical subject of a Centaur
bound to a pillar by three cupids, with emblems
of love, war, music, &c. It is now mounted in
an inlaid marble frame of flowers and fruits.
Formerly Barker Collection.

FAENZA. This letter, B with a *paraphe*, is on the back of a plate, with flowers, &c. On the front are arabesques and scrolls *sopra azurro*, in the centre a cherub, and dated 1520. Perhaps the mark of Bettini, of Faenza.

FAENZA. On a dish about 13 inches in diameter, painted in trophies of arms on a blue ground. This was formerly in Mr. Addington's Collection, then in that of M. Spitzer, and is now in Mr. George Salting's in the Victoria and Albert Museum. Probably a mark of the Bettini family.

FAENZA. Maiolica plate of the sixteenth century, *sopra bianco* border, boy and wolf in the centre; marked in front. Formerly in the Collection of Marchese d'Azeglio. (See also the mark on next page with note.)

FAENZA. On the back of a plate surrounded by a border of foliage; on the front a border of fruit and flowers; on the sunk centre, supported by two amorini, a shield *azure* between three mullets, two and one *or*, an owl *azure* armed *or*. Formerly in Mr. H. A. Neck's Collection.

This passage occurs in the design (Solomon adoring the idols) of a plate in the celebrated service in the Correr Museum, Venice. It is probably copied direct from the design which was used by a maiolica painter, and has no significance in regard to the date or make of the dish itself. The Correr service, it is generally agreed, was painted by Nicola Pellipario at Castel Durante.

FAENZA. On a drug pot in the Franks Collection, British Museum, painted with the head of Camilla on a coloured medallion, trophies in grey and green; date, 1549.

FAENZA. On a fine plate, representing a fête in honour of Neptune, correctly drawn and elegant in style, with the arms of Sforza and Farnese. In the Campana Collection.

FAENZA. On a maiolica dish of uncertain manufacture, with a diapered border, and a figure in the centre. Dr. Fortnum has described a similar mark, but differing slightly, on page 500 of his South Kensington Museum Catalogue.

FAENZA. Painted by Baldasara Manara in 1536. This inscription is on the back of a circular plaque; subject, a Standard-Bearer of the Duke of Ferrara. British Museum.

MILLE CINQUE CENTO
TRENTASEI A DI TRI
DI LUIE
BALDESARA MANARA
FAENTIN FACIEBAT.

FAENZA. The signature of Baldasara Manara on the back of a plate, circa 1540; subject, Pyramus and Thisbe; formerly in the Collection of the Marquis d'Azeglio. Another, similar, but with the word *fan* (Faenza); subject, Time drawn by stags; in the Ashmolean Museum, Oxford (Fortnum Collection).

Baldasara
manara

Another signature of the same artist on a large plateau with a battle scene before a town; one of the horsemen bears a banner with a stag. There is also the motto "Ne supra crepitam abi" and the initials. A facsimile of this singular inscription is reproduced. In Mr. George Salting's Collection in the Victoria and Albert Museum.

N E
✠SVPRA✠CREPITAM✠
✠ABI✠
✠B✠M✠I FACIEBA

FAENZA. Plate, painted probably by Baldasara Manara, the initials of his name appearing with the date 1534. There are several pieces of this service extant; one is in the Geological Museum, Jermyn Street; another, formerly Bernal's, in the British Museum, cost £13 2s. 6d.; and a third is mentioned by Delange.

MDXX
XIIII
✠F✠ATNAN
ASIVS
✠B✠ ✠M✠

FAENZA. This monogram is on the back of a fine plate in the British Museum, ornamented in blue and orange; on the front is a landscape, with a diapered border, and figures playing on viols. The mark is much reduced in size. Formerly in the Bernal Collection, where it was sold for £43 1s. The signature T.B. appears to be the same as that on page 90, but minus the *paraphe*.

FAENZA or CASTEL DURANTE. A mark on the back of a square plaque, exquisitely painted with the Resurrection of Christ *en grisaille*, heightened with blue and yellow, after Dürer; circa 1520. Mentioned by Passeri; formerly in the Pourtales Collection; sold in Paris for £126 in 1865.

FAENZA. On a plate, painted with boys and animals on blue ground, arabesque borders, brilliant colours. Perhaps for Bettini.

FATO NELLA BOTEGA DI
MAESTRO VERGILLIO
DA FAENZA
NICOLO DA FANO.

FAENZA. On a plate, painted by Nicolo da Fano; subject, Apollo and Marsyas. Maestro Vergilio is mentioned by Passeri.

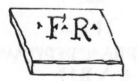

FAENZA. These initials are on the front of a large plaque, date about 1530, painted in rich deep blue, with green, yellow, and brown; subject, Christ bearing the Cross, and numerous figures, called "Lo Spasimo di Sicilia," after Raffaelle. Victoria and Albert Museum; cost £57 4s.

FAENZA. A mark by the same painter. On a plate; subject, St. Jerome; painted with a rich deep blue, like the preceding; formerly in the Narford Collection.

A beautiful plate, subject, Dido stabbing herself, with the same initials, was in Mr. Barker's Collection, afterwards in Madame Dyvon's possession, and is now in that of Mr. George Salting in the Victoria and Albert Museum. Another, with subject, the Holy Family, was in Mr. Addington's possession.

The following marks have long wanted a resting-place; they have wandered from Ferrara, Pesaro, Urbino, Venice, and have at length settled at Faenza.

This mark is on a tazza formerly belonging to the Marquis d'Azeglio; subject, St. Francis receiving the stigmata. Dr. Fortnum formerly attributed it to Urbino. M. Jacquemart reads the second monogram as Faenza, which is borne out, he says, by the mark given below. It is on a basin painted with arms; in the Sèvres Museum.

M. Jacquemart says, "En 1567 le navire *La Pensée* amenait à Rouen trois coffres bahuts *pleins de vaiselle blanche et peinte de Faenze.*" Of this pottery the Sèvres Museum possesses a cup, and another example, marked as in margin.

FAENZA. This mark, which M. Jacquemart thinks solves all difficulty in the appropriation of the monogram AF, is on a fine bowl, blue ground with white arabesques, arms in centre; he concludes that the A and F are the marks of the locality, the others those of the artist.

FAENZA or VENICE? This mark occurs on a moulded dish painted in outline with Mercury, and a border of flowers, in the Victoria and Albert Museum. Another moulded fruttiera in the British Museum has a similar mark. Possibly the mark of the Vergilio fabrique at Faenza, though attributed by Urbani de Gheltof to Venice.

FAENZA or URBINO. On a plate, with cavaliers, signed at the back (Francesco Durantino). Formerly in the Fountaine Collection, Narford.

FAENZA. On a dish, dated 1525; subject, Diana and Actæon, with a border of monsters, cupids and scrolls. Formerly Narford Collection.

FAENZA. The monogram AMR above the word Faenza, is on a maiolica dish of the sixteenth century.

FAENZA. This inscription of a painter's name appears on a superb plate now in the Museum of Sigmaringen; subject, the Descent from the Cross.

GIOVANO BRAMA
DI PALERMA
IN FAENZA
1546.

FAENZA. The first of these marks is on a maiolica plate with S.P.Q.R.; the second on a tazza cited by Brongniart, dated 1548. They are doubtless all marks of the same painter.

FAENZA. Both probably the same mark, one being reversed. The first is on a plate, with raised border and arabesques on a deep blue ground; the second on a metallic lustre portrait plate, "Pulisena." Uzielli Collection.

FAENZA. "Ennius Raynerius F.F. 1575." On a plate representing the Baptism of Christ, shields of arms, and I.B.R. The reverse is ornamented with yellow lines; *Gio Baptista R.* painted in blue; the name

Ennius raynerius F·F·1575

Gio: BAPTISTA·R

Ennius Raynerius in black. Campana Collection, in the Louvre. The F.F. following the name may be deciphered as *Faventino faciebat* or *Fecit Fieri;* probably *Faenza.*

FAENZA. Plate, on which is a portrait of a man with a white beard: around is written JOANNES. BAP. RUBBEUS; on the reverse is written twice, the name of Rainerius, with and without the Y. Campana Collection, in the Louvre. A third piece is in the Louvre; subject, Jesus and the Woman of Samaria, the latter part of the inscription only remaining.

FAENZA. On a very choice plate in the Fountaine Collection, satyrs and grotesques, and the motto, "Auxilium meum a Domino," figured by Delange, plate 23; the labels occur among the ornaments. In the sale of this Collection at Christie's, this superb plate realised £920.

This ancient centre of maiolica would naturally remain among the last to manufacture this description of ware; and there were several makers in the seventeenth century, but we know little of them. Some pharmacy vases of 1616 are signed "*Andrea Pantaleo pingit*"; and according to written documents Francesco Vicchij was proprietor of an important fabrique in 1639.

FAENZA. A beautiful square framed plaque representing the Entombment, after Mantegna's print, is dated MDXXIII. In Mr. George Salting's Collection in the Victoria and Albert Museum.

FAENZA. These monograms and date are on a circular plaque, in white enamel on deep blue ground; in the centre is the sacred monogram, Y.H.S. Victoria and Albert Museum. (*Ker. Gall.*, enlarged edition, fig. 51.)

Fortnum gives this mark from the reverse of a plate representing Samson pulling down the temple pillars. Formerly in the Marryat

Collection. It is ascribed by Argnani to the Atanasio fabrique in Faenza.

Given by Fortnum from a moulded tazza in the Kunstgewerbe Museum, Berlin. Faenza about 1550.

F.B.F.

On eighteenth century wares made by Francesco Ballanti. (Fortnum.)

FABBRICA
DI
R. B.
F.
1777.

Mark of the Benini Fabrique. (Fortnum.)

Zacharia Valaressi
1651 in Faenza.

On a white tazza in the Victoria and Albert Museum. (Fortnum.)

VERONA.

is mentioned by Piccolpasso as having considerable fabriques of maiolica in his time (about 1540), but this is the only piece we have been able to identify.

VERONA. The subject of this unique plate, from the manufactory of Verona, is Alexander liberating the wife and family of Darius; it bears a shield of arms, supported by flying amorini *or*, on a fess *ar.*, a lion passant, with a sceptre in his paw *az.*, in chief an eagle displayed *sa.*, the base paly *gu.* The interesting inscription on the reverse informs us that it was painted by Franco Giovani Batista, signed in contraction, and somewhat injured. The Rev. Mr. Berney, to whom the plate formerly belonged, thought it an original design by Batista Franco, which would confirm the statement of Nagler (*Künstler Lexicon*) that this artist did not die till 1580. The first three letters of the name have been read as *Giu* (Giuseppe), and not *Fco* (Franco), but it still remains a matter of opinion. Now in the Victoria and Albert Museum.

DIRUTA.

The maiolica of yellow lustre edged with blue, which was formerly attributed to Pesaro, has been recently classed among the wares made at the manufactory of Diruta, near Perugia, from the circumstance of a plate in the Pourtales Collection; subject, one of Ovid's Metamorphoses (No. 242), signed by El Frate of Diruta, 1541, being similarly decorated with the yellow lustre.

The plate in the Hôtel de Cluny, representing Diana and Actæon, after Mantegna, designed in blue, heightened with yellow lustre, marked with a C having a *paraphe*, is also attributed to this fabrique.

The earliest dated specimen, if this attribution be correct, is a relief of St. Sebastian within a niche, the saint painted in blue, the arcade of this peculiar yellow lustre; on the plinth is inscribed "A. DI. 14. DI. LVGLIO. 1501"—The 14th July 1501.

DIRUTA. These initials occur on a dish painted in metallic lustre, with the arms of Montefeltro; formerly in the Collection of the Comte de Niewerkerke.

DIRUTA. This mark is on a dish of blue *camaieu* with metallic lustre; subject, Diana at the Bath, finely designed. Sixteenth century. Musée de Cluny.

DIRUTA. On a plate painted with arabesques on blue ground. Formerly Narford Collection.

DIRUTA. D with a *paraphe*, painted with a subject from the *Orlando Furioso*. Formerly in Mrs. Palisser's Collection.

DIRUTA. D with a *paraphe*, and the initials G. S., on a plate; subject, two Lovers seated under a tree. Victoria and Albert Museum.

DIRUTA. The initials probably of Giorgio Vasajo, whose name occurs on a piece of ware belonging to Count Baglioni of Perugia.

DIRUTA. On a plate in the possession of Signor Raff. de Minicis of Fermo.

DIRUTA. Inscription on the back of a plate; subject, the Nuptials of Alexander and Roxana; formerly in the possession of Mr. A. Barker.

DIRUTA. On the reverse of a plate, painted in front with a Roman triumphal procession; on the pedestal of the arch is written ANT. LAFRERI. This name is considered to be that of the engraver or editor of the print from which this subject is copied, and has nothing to do with the painting on the maiolica. M. A. Jacquemart says there was an artist of this name established at Rome from 1550 to 1575, celebrated as editor of engravings. Several of Marc Antonio's engravings

FATTA IN DIRVTA
1525.

IN DERVTA
EL FRATE PENSE.

8

are signed by "*Antonius Lafreri Romœ Excud.*," others have "*Ant. Lafrerius Sequanus R.*" Campana Collection, in the Louvre.

1 5 3 7
fran^{co} Urbini.
T derula

.I 5 4 5.
in de rura
Frate fecit

El. Fh J. Durula
ph. 1541.

DIRUTA. On a very fine plate belonging to the Baron Salomon de Rothschild, representing Apollo pursuing Daphne; on the reverse the description of the subject is traced in blue over the letter P in golden lustre, perhaps the name of the artist or the person who lustred it. Perestino of Gubbio?

DIRUTA. A tazza in the Collection of Mme. la Comtesse de Cambis-Alais, representing Apollo with Cupid and Daphne and other incidents in the life of the god, bearing the painter's name, Francesco of Urbino.

DIRUTA. The mark of *Frate* on a plate; subject, Rodomont carrying off Isabella, from the *Orlando Furioso* of Ariosto. Louvre Collection.

On a plate in the Pourtales Collection, painted with one of Ovid's Metamorphoses, designed and shaded with blue, heightened with yellow metallic lustre. This and another in the Louvre, G. 575, "Birth of Adonis," also lustred, enables us to place many other pieces, unsigned, to Diruta.

DIRUTA. A mark on two pharmacy vases with portraits. This mark and the next are probably pharmacy numbers, and not potters' marks.

DIRUTA? This monogram is on a pharmacy vase or bottle; on one side a medallion with a male portrait and the monogram, the date 1579 on a cartouche above; on the other side a coat of arms with yellow arabesque tracery on dark blue ground.

D⁊

LVD

I 5 7 9

DIRUTA.   On a plate, the surface entirely covered with a composition of grotesque birds, foliage, mask, &c., outlined with blue on blue, green, and yellow ground; monogram and date on the reverse.   In the Victoria and Albert Museum.

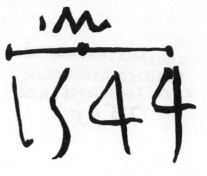

DIRUTA.   This mark of a recent manufactory of fayence (*maiolica fina*) is on a plate in the possession of M. Paul Gasnault of Paris.

FABRICA DI MAJOLICA
FINA DI GREGORIO
CASELLI IN DIRUTA 1771.

DIRUTA.   This mark is on the front of a plate of enamelled earthenware, with arabesques and monsters in white, shaded with olive green, on a dark blue ground.   Dated 1525.   Mr. George Salting's Collection in the Victoria and Albert Museum.

DIRUTA.   This mark is on a plateau of enamelled and lustred earthenware, painted with a scene taken from the fourth canto of *Orlando Furioso*.   Dated 1545.   Mr. George Salting's Collection in the Victoria and Albert Museum. Two examples of Diruta figure in *Ker. Gall.*, enlarged edition, figs. 55 and 56.

FABRIANO.

This manufactory is revealed to us by a magnificent tazza which was sent to the Paris Exhibition in 1867. The inside of the tazza is painted with a composition after Raffaelle: in a saintly crowd the Virgin and St. Anne are ascending the steps of a temple, advancing towards our Saviour, who is seated under the portico.   It is of a grand style, and well painted; underneath is written in blue "Fabriano, 1527."   It was purchased by Signor Castellani of Naples, and subsequently sold by auction on May 12, 1871, to Mons. Basilewski for £114.

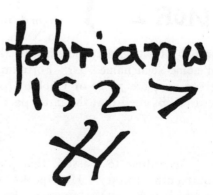

? BAGNARA.

.IOSILVESTRO DAGEI
OTRINCIDADERVTA:
FATTºIN BAGNIOREA
·I6 9 I

An inscription on a large dish, under a painting of the Holy Family; in the Victoria and Albert Museum. "Io Silvestro Dagli Otrinci da Diruta. Fatto in Bagniorea 1691."

RIMINI.

Piccolpasso mentions fabriques of maiolica here, but nothing is known of their early history, and the only records are the reverses of the pieces here given. M. Darcel observes a peculiarity in the landscapes, the trees being more natural, the trunks being in brown shaded black—not altogether black, as in the Urbino ware; the foliage is of a less glaring green, and hangs below the branches; the enamel has a more brilliant glaze. The dates on the pieces are 1535; one is quoted as late as 1635.

Jn arimin·

RIMINI. This mark is on a plate; subject, the Fall of Phaëton. In the British Museum.

IN RIMINO
1535.

RIMINI. On the back of a plate; subject, the Expulsion of Adam and Eve; Hôtel de Cluny; and on another, without date, mentioned by Delange.

FATO IN
ARIMINENSIS
1635.

RIMINI. On a plate mentioned by Delange.

ЛOE Σ

RIMINI. This mark in blue is on a bowl (No. 96) in the Louvre, which M. Darcel attributes to Rimini, from comparison with other signed pieces. The subject is God appearing to Noah. NOE refers to this; the Z and dead branch of a tree may possibly be the painter's rebus, Zaffarino, Żampillo, or some such name. Dr. Fortnum considers that this mark and the one given on page 73 as of Gubbio (forked L and branch) are the same. It will be observed that the latter part of the mark is very similar.

FORLI.

According to Passeri, this place had fabriques of maiolica in the fourteenth century. He speaks of a document of the year 1396, in which this passage occurs: "Pedrinus Ioannis a bocalibus de Forlivio olim et nunc habitator Pensauri"—"John of the potteries, formerly of

Forli, now at Pesaro;" and Piccolpasso, in the sixteenth century, speaks of the painted maiolica of Forli. Its contiguity to Faenza exercised a great influence on the decoration of the ware, and the patterns, both on the obverses and reverses, being similar, many of the pieces of this fabrique are attributed to Faenza. In the Victoria and Albert Museum is a kite-shaped plaque of the fifteenth century, with the arms of the family of Ordelaffi of Forli.

FORLI. A plate; subject, Crœsus, inscribed AURUM. SITIS. AURUM.

BIBE.; and another, the Murder of the Innocents, in Campana Collection; another, David and Goliath, circa 1530, in the Victoria and Albert Museum.

FORLI. There is a scodella, admirably painted in a yellow *grisaille* with an allegorical subject of many figures by the painter of the Forli tiles, in the Victoria and Albert Museum. The smaller mark is on the face of the pieces in the foreground, the larger is on the reverse. This rare example passed from the Castellani Collection to that of M. Basilewski, at the high price of £180, on the 12th of May, 1871.

FORLI. Leuchadius Solombrinus of Forli, painted in 1555. On a very fine plate, of the Marriage of Alexander and Roxana. From the Dellesette Collection, was in the possession of the late Mr. A. Barker.

LEOCHADIUS
SOLOBRINVS
PICSIT
FOROLIVIOMECE
M.D.L.V.

FORLI. This signature and date are on the reverse of a basin in the University Museum at Bologna, painted with the supper at which Mary Magdalen washes Jesus' feet. Leuchadius Solō-brinus pincksit M.D. 64. AN.D. (Anno Domini 1564). The inscription, with his name and approximate date on the preceding plate, enable us to assign this painter to Forli with some degree of certainty.

FORLI. On a fine plate; subject, Christ among the Doctors, painted in blue relieved with white, the edge filled with trophies of musical instruments; in the Victoria and Albert Museum, which, with another unimportant piece, cost £80. It reads "In la botega di Maestro Jeronimo da Forli." (*Ker. Gall.*, enlarged edition, fig. 57.)

A plate by the same artist, the centre painted in blue *camaieu*, with a crowded composition of uncertain signification, surrounded with a border of trophies on dark blue ground, and medallions with busts and inscriptions, was in the possession of Mr. S. Addington; and another fine specimen, a plate, painted with David and Goliath and similar border, dated June, 1507, belonged to the Marchese d'Azeglio, formerly in the Collection of Mr. Hailstone of Walton Hall.

FORLI. Tiles forming a pavement, painted with various coloured devices, coats of arms and portraits, among them one initialed P.R. and D.O. with the inscription "Ego·Pigit. Petrus. inmaginā. suā. et imagine. cāceleris. sue. Dionisi. Bertino Rio. 1513." From a villa at Pieve a Quinto, near Forli. In the Victoria and Albert Museum; £88. They are painted in an orange pigment, heightened with white, on a yellow ground, or on one of a nearly similar tint in *camaieu*, and are bordered with blue arabesque foliage. The tile represented in the vignette on the next page is supposed to bear the portrait of the painter, with his initials, P. R., and that of a *Cancelliere*, his chancellor or secretary, initialled D. O., with the inscription and date. Among other portraits on these tiles we have Niron; Chamilo; Sase; Charlomn; Stephanus; Nardinus; Cechus de Rubeis; a Doge with inscription Prencipus que Venecia; Ugolinus music; and the painter Melotius, pictor of Forli; also a Carolina and a Leta.

Dr. Fortnum (Catalogue of the Maiolica, South Kensington Museum) says, "There can be no doubt that this pavement is the handiwork of the painter who executed the large plate in blue *camaieu* of Christ disputing with the Doctors, signed by Maestro Jeronimo of Forli (4727-59), and the bowl (837-70), both in the South Kensington Museum; but the inscrip-

tion above given leaves us in doubt as to whether these examples were painted by the Maestro himself, or by one Pietro R." &c. There seem, however, to be some difficulties in the way of a satisfactory attribution, and how the writer of the catalogue arrives at the conclusion that P.R. means actually Pietro Rocca, the reader must refer to the Catalogue (page 557) to form his own judgment.

FORLI. This mark is on a maiolica plate, finely painted; quoted by M. A. Jacquemart.

VITERBO. A maiolica dish, dated 1544; subject, Diana and Actæon, with a border of arms and trophies; a man at the bottom is holding a scroll inscribed "Viterbo Diomed 1544." Victoria and Albert Museum. (*Ker. Gall.*, enlarged edition, fig. 58.)

VITERBO. On a plate in the Barberini Palace,
I. F. R. VITERBIEN.   at Rome. Subject, Hercules: probably seventeenth century. (De Mély.)

RAVENNA. A most interesting maiolica tazza of the commencement
of the sixteenth century was bequeathed to the Louvre by the Baron
J. Chas. Davillier, with the name of the place inscribed upon it in large
characters; inside is represented, in blue *camaieu*, Arion playing on the

lyre, supported on the waves by three dolphins, with a ship in the background from which he has been cast, and the city of Corinth. The subject
has been wrongly described as Amphion; it is from a painting of the
fifteenth century (figured in Delange's *Recueil*, pl. 46).

TREVISO. This inscription is at the bottom of
a deep plate or bowl, surrounded by arabesques,
on blue ground; on the interior is painted the
Sermon on the Mount, with the disciples asleep.
The legend surrounds a portrait supported by
cupids. Formerly in the Addington Collection.

An inferior incised ware was made at Treviso in the last century,
something of the same character as that made at La Fratta. A plate of
atrocious execution in this style is inscribed "Fabrica di boccaleria alla
campana in Treviso, Valentino Petro Storgato Bragaldo jo figlio fabricator. Jouane Giroto Liberal figlio fecie. Matteo Schiavon inciso e
delineator Anno dni. CIC. IC. CCLIX." (1759.)

PISA.

The city of Pisa was, about the middle of the sixteenth century, the
centre of a considerable trade in the exportation of Italian fayence into
Spain, and especially Valencia, in exchange for the golden metallic lustre
ware of that country. Antonio Beuter, about 1550, praises the fayence

of Pisa with those of Pesaro and Castelli, but we have only the specimen here noticed which can with certainty be attributed to it.

In the beginning of the sixteenth century, a Florentine artist carried into Spain the art of maiolica, and many bas-reliefs and azulejos have been noticed which are attributed to him by M. le Baron C. Davillier, some of which decorate the façade of the church of Santa Paula at Seville and Santa Anna at Triana. This artist is Niculoso Francesco of Pisa, whose works are in the style of Luca della Robbia. Large pictures, formed of a number of tiles fitting together, are signed by Niculoso, and dated 1504 and successive years.

PISA. A large vase, of fine form, with serpent handles, covered with arabesques on white ground, like the maiolica of Urbino. The word "Pisa" is written **PISA.** on a cartouche under one of the handles. Baron Alphonse de Rothschild's Collection.

CAFFAGGIOLO.

This manufactory was of early origin, and although it is not mentioned by Piccolpasso, its existence is revealed by the inscriptions on numerous plates; the name, spelt in various ways, is frequently given at length, accompanied by the cipher of a large P with a *paraphe* or bar through the lower part of the stem, and the upper loop of the letter curved over the stem in form of an S; sometimes the pieces bear the cipher only.

The most ancient dated pieces are two plates belonging to M. le Baron de Rothschild, one dated 1507, the other 1509, both decorated with grotesques in the style of Faenza, and remarkable for the red colour displayed in its tints.

Among the ornaments of this ware are frequently tablets bearing the letters S.P.Q.R. (Senatus Populus que Romanus) and S.P.Q.F. (Florentinus), and on several the mottoes *Semper* and *Glovis*, and the arms of Pope Leo X., who assumed the tiara in 1513.

The motto "Semper" was adopted by Pietro de' Medici in 1470, meaning that every action of his life should be done with the love of God. It was continued by Lorenzo the Magnificent.

The motto and device of a triangle, enclosing the six letters "Glovis," was adopted by Giuliano de' Medici, third son of Lorenzo, in 1516, which, read backwards, form "Si volge," *It turns*, meaning that Fortune, which had previously frowned upon him, had turned in his favour.

Another characteristic of this fabrique is the deep cobalt-blue backgrounds of many of the pieces, and the method in which it is coarsely but boldly applied by the brush, the marks of the brush being visible, although it adds greatly to the effect. The other colours used are a bright yellow, an orange of brilliant but opaque quality, a beautiful semi-transparent copper-green and bright opaque Indian red. In general characteristics Caffaggiolo is more akin to Siena, Forli, and Faenza than to other Italian fabriques.

The fabrique lasted probably throughout the sixteenth century, with various differences in orthography as regards the marks.

M. Darcel in his Catalogue of the Louvre Collection has, we think, been too liberal in his attribution of specimens to this fabrique; he includes thirty tiles from the Petrucci Palace at Siena, and a number of pharmacy vases, none of which bear the mark of the fabrique. The Louvre does not, in fact, appear to possess one signed piece of undoubted Caffaggiolo out of the sixty described.

There are several very fine pieces of this ware in the British and the Victoria and Albert Museums beside those mentioned in the text. A plateau with a triumphal procession in the style of Mantegna, painted in vivid colours on dark blue background, dated 1514, from the Montferrand Collection; cost £49 1s. 6d. Another is a plate with the St. George of Donatello, from the bronze statue on the church of "Or San Michele," Florence; Bernal Collection; cost £61 (*Ker. Gall.*, enlarged edition, fig. 59). The celebrated plate in the Soulages Collection, with a portrait of Pietro Perugino, with wide border of foliage and four medallions of birds, cost £200, but it is doubtful whether this latter specimen should be classed as Caffaggiolo.

CAFFAGGIOLO. This mark is on the celebrated plate from the Stowe and Bernal Collections, representing an artist in his studio painting a maiolica plate, whose progress a lady and gentleman, seated opposite, are intently watching. At the Stowe sale it bought £4, and at Mr. Bernal's it was purchased by the Victoria and Albert Museum for £120. Its present value is about £2000. (Vide *Ker. Gall.*, enlarged edition, colour plate, opposite p. 43.)

The same mark is on a large plateau painted in arabesques and grotesques on a blue ground, with a small central medallion representing Leda and Swan, with a minute label marked "Leda." This specimen was considered one of the finest in the Spitzer Collection, and realised at the Paris auction 48,000 francs, nearly £2,000. Now in Mr. George Salting's Collection at the Victoria and Albert Museum; it was previously in the Parpart Collection.

CAFFAGGIOLO. This inscription is found upon a deep plate, with a griffin in the centre, and arabesques, on deep blue ground. It was purchased at the Bernal sale by the Baron A. de Rothschild for £90. The compiler of the Bernal sale catalogue has made a ridiculous mistake, by reading it as the signature of a certain P. Incha Agricola. Such an error, unless pointed out, is necessarily calculated to mislead the more erudite inquirer, as will be seen by referring to page 83.

CAFFAGGIOLO. This mark, of a trident and an annulet, is on the back of a plate, painted with an imbricated pattern, blue and orange; on the front is a cupid, seated, playing a flageolet; the border of the plate is painted with masks and scrolls in orange, shaded with red, on a ground of dark blue, and the date 1531. In the sale of the Fountaine Collection it brought £120.

CAFFAGGIOLO. This inscription is interesting, combining the marks which appear frequently separate on pieces of this fabrique, enabling us thereby to identify them as made here. It is on an elegant plate, painted with arabesques, and a label with S.P.Q.R.; the back ornamented with ovals and stripes in blue and yellow. Formerly in Lord Hasting's Collection, Melton Constable, and is now in the Salting Collection.

CAFFAGGIOLO. On a plateau with arabesques and diaper ornaments, in white and yellow enamel on dark blue ground, in imitation of the Venetian enamels. There are two by the same hand, and marked alike with this trident, in the Victoria and Albert Museum. Date circa 1530.

CAFFAGGIOLO. Another mark of the trident, with " In Caffagguolo," occurs on a plateau painted with the triumph of a Roman General; the letters S.P.Q.R. are on a standard borne by a horseman, and also on four labels in the border. Formerly in the Spitzer Collection, now in that of Mr. George Salting in the Victoria and Albert Museum. The occurrence of the lettering with the trident would seem to show that we may take this mark as belonging to Caffaggiolo.

CAFFAGGIOLO. A plate, with Diana surprised in the bath by Actæon, has the annexed inscription in a cursive character. The name of the place is frequently misspelt in this way; and it is evident, from a comparison of the finish of the paintings of this fabrique, that inferior artists were also occasionally employed. Musée de Cluny.

IN GAFAGIZOTTO.

CAFFAGGIOLO. On a large dish, mentioned by Delange, in the Appendix to his translation of Passeri, dated 1570. The mark is not in facsimile.

IN CHAFAGGIOLO
FATO ADI 21 DI JUNIO
1570.

CAFFAGGIOLO. This monogram is upon a dish; subject, Coriolanus, with border of trophies, &c., and a tablet with S.P.Q.R.; dated 1546.

CAFFAGGIOLO. This occurs on a plate, with cupids in the centre, and a border of musical trophies, &c.

CAFFAGGIOLO. On a yellow lustre jug, with blue lines. The mark is below the handle. In the British Museum; from the Henderson Collection.

CAFFAGGIOLO. On a large dish, painted with the Carrying off of Helen from Troy, numerous figures, ships, boats, &c. Formerly Barker Collection. Another piece apparently by the same hand, in the Victoria and Albert Museum, is inscribed "*In Gafagiolo*," the interlaced S. and P. and the initials A. F.; cost £2 2s. The first two letters of the name of the place are evidently intended for *Ch*, which in Italian writing looks like a letter *g*.

CAFFAGGIOLO. Varieties of a mark, believed to be of this place, which occurs on a fine plate formerly belonging to Baron Gustave de Rothschild. It has in the centre a shield of arms and arabesque border, and is dated 1507. They appear to be a combination of the letters P. L. O., and it is the earliest dated piece of this botega we have met with.

CAFFAGGIOLO. This mark is on the back of a dish which has been ascribed to Caffaggiolo. The stroke of the loop of the P prolonged into an R and the bar across.

CAFFAGGIOLO. On a plateau painted with a portion of a triumphal procession after Mantegna; musicians, a jester, &c., precede two harnessed horses, at whose sides men carry golden vases; on dark blue background, the numeral I underneath. Reverse, concentric lines in blue, a mark, and the date 1514. In the Victoria and Albert Museum.

CAFFAGGIOLO. Galliano was probably a village or hamlet near this place. The inscription occurs on a plateau, painted with Mutius Scævola before Porsenna, and a border of dogs hunting wild animals in a woody

landscape; in the Ashmolean Museum, Oxford (Fortnum Collection). It is accompanied by the well-known monogram of S. and P. interlaced, a small G. and the initials A. F., and "In Galiano nell ano 1547." Fortnum Collection, Ashmolean Museum, Oxford.

CAFFAGGIOLO or FAENZA. On a dish of the first half of sixteenth century, painted with the Maccabees offering presents to Solomon. M. A. Darcel thinks this mark signifies Gaffagiolo. Louvre Collection. This letter is also on a plate in the same collection, G. 153, Hercules and Antæus. Dr. Fortnum attributes this dish to Faenza.

CAFFAGGIOLO. The large G is probably the initial of Giovanni Acole, 1509; it is placed on the interior of an inkstand composed of a group of figures representing *La Crèche*. The name at length, written in black, is here reduced to about a third of the actual size. Formerly in the Collection of Baron C. Davillier.

CAFFAGGIOLO. This mark (reduced) is on the large plateau of a procession of Pope Leo X., who is seated on a rich portable throne borne upon men's shoulders, preceded by an elephant surrounded by cardinals on mules, guards, &c.; on reverse, concentric lines of blue and the mark. In the Victoria and Albert Museum; £80. Leo X. was elected in 1513, when this plate was probably executed.

CAFFAGGIOLO. On a dish, with three-quarter portrait in costume of sixteenth century; on a scroll, "Antonia Bella Fiore Dequesate," so attributed by M. Darcel, but Dr. Fortnum disagrees with him. Louvre Collection.

CAFFAGGIOLO? or DIRUTA. On a piece of very early maiolica, given by M. A. Jacquemart.

CAFFAGGIOLO. A roughly sketched ? dolphin, on a dish painted in colours, probably at Caffaggiolo, and lustred at Gubbio. Subject, St. George, after Donatello. In Mr. F. A. White's Collection.

CAFFAGGIOLO or FAENZA. An a plate painted with an arabesque border. Ashmolean Museum (Fortnum Coll.)

CAFFAGGIOLO. This monogram is on two dishes in the Louvre, painted with a cornucopia and a vase of flowers in medallions, attributed by M. A. Darcel to this fabrique, but showing the decadence of the art.

CAFFAGGIOLO. These marks, which are probably only another form of those given on page 117 on the plate belonging to Baron Gustave de Rothschild, are given by M. A. Jacquemart as belonging to the first epoch of ornamental maiolica with vivid colouring. It has in the centre a shield of arms and arabesque border, and is dated 1507, the earliest dated piece of this botega we have met with.

CAFFAGGIOLO. This mark is on a very fine dish; subject, Judith and an attendant riding off, the latter holding the head of Holofernes. It was purchased by M. Spitzer from the Carrand Collection, and was one of the most keenly competed prizes at the Spitzer sale. Mr. George Salting bought it for 52,000 francs (£2,080). Now in the Victoria and Albert Museum.

CAFFAGGIOLO. On a very unusual plateau of white ground with bands of pale blue decoration, in which are musical instruments, arms, armour, and floral ornaments; also the arms of the family of Gonzaga Este. In Mr. George Salting's Collection in the Victoria and Albert Museum.

BORGO SAN SEPOLCHRO.

This name is upon the reverse of a plate, painted in blue on white ground, with a stag-hunt in a landscape; in the Victoria and Albert Museum; diameter $15\frac{1}{4}$ inches.

Gio. Battista Mercati of Citta Borgo San Sepolchro is spoken of by Lanzi as a painter of some note in the seventeenth century, and some of his works in the churches of Venice, Rome, and Leghorn are mentioned, but there is no evidence to fix the locality of this specimen.

GEO:BATA:MERCATI
1649

A curious lamp on a foot with long stem reveals the existence of this manufactory in the eighteenth century; it is mounted in silver. M. Rolet's name is also on a similar lamp found at Urbino.

Citta Borgo S Sepolcro a 6 Febraio 1771 Mart. Roletus fecit.

ST. QUIRICO.

ST. QUIRICO (Marches of Ancona.) This inscription, on a plaque in the Louvre, reveals the existence of a manufactory established by the Terchi family of Bassano, under the protection of Cardinal Chigi, about 1714. It represents the Striking of the Rock by Moses, and resembles the works of the Castelli fabrique; seventeenth century. Dr. Fortnum says, "Its productions were not sold, but given as presents by the Cardinal." Jacquemart says, "One Piezzentili, a painter, was the director appointed, having especially studied the works of Fontana." After him Bartolomeo Terchi from Siena succeeded, and Ferdinando Maria Campani of Siena also painted some of the ware.

Bar Terchi Romano in S. Quirico

SAN QUIRICO. This mark occurs on a basin painted with a group of Hercules seated between Venus and Vulcan, Cupid behind with an empty quiver. The letters S Q above the arms of the Chigi family without a shield, and below the date 1723; probably painted by B°. Terchi, who worked at this establishment for some time. Victoria and Albert Museum.

SIENA.

The earliest specimens known of this important manufactory are some wall or floor tiles of the commencement of the sixteenth century. These tiles are of fayence, covered with stanniferous enamel, and ornamented with polychrome designs of chimeræ, dragons, amorini, masks, birds, &c., in brilliant colours, especially orange and yellow on black ground, beautifully painted. They average about five inches square, but vary in shape and size, some being triangular, pentagonal, &c., to suit the geometrical designs of the wall or floor they covered. A series of several hundreds of these tiles is in the Victoria and Albert Museum, which came from the Petrucci Palace at Siena; some are dated 1509, and are painted with shields of arms and elegant arabesques. There are some in the Sauvageot and Campana Collections in the Louvre. A pavement of similar tiles, dated 1513, still exists *in situ* in a chapel of the Church of San Francisco at Siena; there is also a frieze of them in the Biblioteca of Siena.

These are attributed by Sir J. C. Robinson to Faenza, and by M. A. Darcel to Caffaggiolo, but they were most probably executed at Siena, where they are discovered in such quantities in the very buildings for which they were originally designed.

A circular plaque, of the same artist and date, is in the possession of Mr. Morland; the surface is entirely covered with a composition of beautiful arabesques in brilliant colours, relieved by a black ground; others were in the collections of Mrs. O. Coope and Sir A. W. Franks; a plate, apparently by the same hand, is mentioned below as once in the Henderson Collection. A plate with sunk centre and rich orange colour border, with blue and white arabesques, having in the centre the Virgin and two cherubs, was purchased by Mr. Bale at the Bernal sale for £41; it has on the back the initials I. P. It is now in Mr. George Salting's Collection in the Victoria and Albert Museum.

There is a beautiful plate with sunk centre of the Siena fabrique, formerly in the Marryat Collection, purchased for the Victoria and Albert Museum at £27, with a border of grotesques on orange ground; in the centre a full-length figure of St. James (the Great) in a landscape, inscribed "S. Jacobus M." Reverse, scale-work border in orange spotted blue, the letters I. P. in the centre; date about 1510. Dr. Fortnum is of opinion that the tiles and other pieces here noticed belong to Siena, as well as this example, which, from the mark I. P. and the assertion of Passeri that these initials represented *In Pesaro*, have generally caused all indiscriminately to be so attributed, although that mark was occasionally used by the Pesarese artists. Dr. Fortnum says, "A comparison of this specimen with the drug pot, dated 1501, in the Victoria and Albert Museum, the pavement tiles and the plate in the same collection, with St. Jerome, to which we have alluded below, and all with each other, leads to the belief that Maestro Benedetto of Siena was the producer of all these pieces."

On a plate, date 1542. Two others, with similar marks, both dated 1520, were in the Bernal Collection; one with St. Bartholomew is now in the British Museum; cost £41. The letters stand for Iachomo Pinxit.

SIENA. "Made in Siena by Maestro Benedetto," circa 1510-20. On the reverse of a plate, with foliated and interlaced ornament in blue *camaieu* on white; in the centre, St. Jerome in the desert. Victoria and Albert Museum; £10. (*Ker. Gall.*, enlarged edition, fig. 61.)

SIENA. Marked on the back of a very fine plate; subject, Mutius Scævola, with border of arabesques on blue, finely designed. From M. Rattier's Collection; purchased for £120, and formerly in the collection of Mr. Henderson. Now in the British Museum.

Enamelled statues of the school of Della Robbia were also produced at Siena. In the FRᴱ *BERNARDINUS DE SIENA. IN. B. S. Sᴬᵀᵁˢ* Louvre there is a bas-relief of the Entombment of this character; the inscription is unfortunately defaced, and the date cannot be read.

SIENA. Terenzio Romano. On a piece of maiolica in the Chamber of Arts, Berlin. TERENZIO ROMANO SIENA 1727.

9

BAR. THERESE 'ROMA.

SIENA. Bartolomeo Terenzio Romano. On a pair of plaques; subjects, Neptune and Europa, after Annibale Caracci. Eighteenth century. Montferrand Collection, now in the Victoria and Albert Museum. We suspect both these marks have been wrongly read, and are actually *Terche*, not Terenzio or "*Therefe*."

TERCHI.

SIENA. On a vase of the eighteenth century, with a painting after one of the old masters.

Bar Turc
Romano.

SIENA. Another variation of Bartolomeo Terchi's signature; on a plate in the Victoria and Albert Museum.

BAR. TERCHI. ROMANO.

SIENA. Bartolomeo Terchi Romano; on the companion vase to the preceding. It is probably the same artist as the Bartolomeo Terenzio Romano of Siena mentioned above; there being so great a similarity between the words *Terèfe* and *Terche*, as written at that time, some confusion may have arisen.

SIENA. Ferdinando Maria Campani of Siena, painted in 1733; he was called the Raffaelle of maiolica painters. On a plate in the British Museum, "God creating the stars," after Raffaelle.

FERDINAND CAMPANI
SIENA. 1736.

SIENA. Ferdinando Campani. On two plates; subjects, Galatea, after Annibale Caracci, and Juno soliciting Æolus to let loose the winds. Victoria and Albert Museum. (*Ker. Gall.*, enlarged edition, fig. 64.)

SIENA. This mark is on a fayence dish of the beginning of the eighteenth century, embossed and escalloped border, painted with blue scrolls and flowers. In the centre a bouquet. Perhaps the mark of Ferdinando Campani.

FERDINANDO MA. CAMPANI
DIPINSE IN SIENA.
1747.

SIENA. On a pair of plaques; subject, The Vintage. One in the Victoria and Albert Museum. (*Ker. Gall.*, enlarged edition, fig. 63.)

F. C.

SIENA. Ferdinando Campani. On a plate of the beginning of the eighteenth century, painted with arms and trophies *en grisaille*. Victoria and Albert Museum.

VENICE.

From the interesting researches of the Marquis Giuseppe Campori we are enabled to throw some light on the early fabriques of Venice in the later half of the fifteenth and the beginning of the sixteenth century.

In the archives of Modena we find that, in 1520, Titian, who was always in great favour with Alphonso I., Duke of Ferrara, was desired by this Prince to order a large quantity of Venetian glass from Murano, and some maiolica vases for the Duke's dispensary. Tebaldo, his agent, thus writes to his patron: " The 1st June 1520; by the captain of the vessel, Jean Tressa, I send your Excellence eleven grand vases, eleven of smaller size, and twenty little pieces of maiolica with their covers, ordered by Titian for your Excellency's dispensary."

The maiolica pavement in the vestry of St. Hélène, given by the Giustiniani family, and bearing their arms, about 1450-80, has been ascribed by some writers to Venetian potters, but neither Dr. Fortnum nor Signor Lazari subscribe to this view, and both authorities think that it was imported from Faenza.

The same doubt exists as to another, bearing the shield of arms of the Lando family, still existing in the church of St. Sebastian at Venice, which, with the date 1510, bears the monogram VTBL, enclosed in the letter Q in large capitals. Dr. Graesse also places this mark with those of Faenza.

In another letter, of the 25th May, 1567, Battista di Francesco, writing to the Duke of Ferrara for the loan of three hundred crowns, on condition of giving him his services, says that he is a master-potter, and makes very noble maiolica vases, of the best as well as inferior qualities; he lives at present at Murano, in the district of Venice, with his wife and children, and possesses a shop well stocked with vases and other productions of similar character, and having heard of the magnanimity and reputation of his Excellence from noblemen and gentlemen of Venice, he has a desire of serving him in his calling as a potter, and to fix his residence at Ferrara. He desires an answer addressed to M°. Battista di Francesco, maker of maiolica vases, Rio delli Verrieri, at Murano.

There were many manufactories of terra-cotta and earthenware in Venice in the fifteenth century, carried on by the guild of the *Boccaleri* (pitcher-makers) and *Scudaleri* (plate or dish makers), probably for domestic use alone. They had the exclusive privilege of manufacturing earthenware, and every effort was made by the State to protect this guild, and numerous decrees were issued to prevent the importation of foreign wares from the fifteenth down to the eighteenth century.

From the manuscript of Piccolpasso we know that the Durantine potter, Francesco or Cecco di Pieragnolo, established a kiln at Venice in 1545, and had taken with him his father-in-law, Gianantonio da Pesaro. Piccolpasso visited it in 1550, and describes the mills for grinding, also the patterns frequently made there, the arabesques, grotesques, landscapes, fruit, &c.

One of the earliest pieces, although undated, was probably made about the year 1540. It is the plateau described page 128; the inscription, there much reduced, reads, "In Venetia in cõtrada di St°. Polo in botega di M°. Ludovico," and beneath, a Maltese cross on a shield.

There are two other pieces of maiolica, evidently painted by the same Maestro Ludovico of Venice; one painted in blue *camaieu* with a mermaid, now in the Ashmolean Museum, Oxford (Fortnum Collection), has the inscription, "1540 adi. 16 del mexe de Otubre" (the 16th of the month of October); and the other, in the Victoria and Albert Museum, has "Adi. 13 Aprile 1543," followed by a word we cannot interpret, AO. LASDINR, and a dish by Jacomo da Pesaro, made at St. Barnaba in Venice, described page 118.

The next in order of date is the dish painted with the Destruction of Troy, in Mr. Fountaine's Collection, inscribed, "Fatto in Venezia, in Chastello, 1546," which tells us where the manufactory was situated.

In the Brunswick Museum another plate is noted, "1568, Zener Domenigo da Venecia feci in la botega al ponte sito del andar a San Polo"—Signor Domenico, of Venice, made in the fabrique at the bridge situate on the road to St. Polo; probably that which belonged to Maestro Ludovico. A specimen of maiolica, about the same date, bears the name of Io. Stefana Barcella, Veneziano; but he may, perhaps, although a Venetian, have worked in some other locality.

The next marks which attract our attention in order of date are very curious, and we shall see, in describing the pieces on which they occur, and the long intervals between their use, that they belong to a *locality* and not to a *painter*. The mark is a sort of fish-hook, in form of the letter C, and it is so intimately allied to the creeper, or grappling hook with three points, generally allowed to belong to Venice, that we are warranted (until further information is obtained) in placing it as a Venetian mark.

On a fountain in the Musée de Cluny, with masks and garlands of flowers, in relief, and painted with bouquets, we find this fish-hook introduced several times; and on a plate representing the Salutation is the same mark, with the date 1571, and another in the Berlin Museum bears the date 1622. The next time we meet with it is on a plate painted with six horses, belonging to M. Roger de Beauvoir, but in this instance it is accompanied by a name as well as the date,—L. Dionigi Marini, 1636, between two fish-hooks.

We now arrive at a description of maiolica of a totally different class to that we have been considering, and possessing so many peculiarities, that we are justified in assigning the pieces to one particular manufactory, the secret of producing it being lost on the death of the proprietor. The ware may be briefly described as follows:—It is very thin, and extremely light for the size, and is compact and as sonorous as if it were actually made of metal. The borders of the dishes are moulded into masks, flowers, festoons, fruit, &c., and the reliefs are thrown up from the back, like repoussé metal-work. On the back of these dishes may frequently be seen, three long marks, where it rested in the kiln, and leaves, cursively traced, in colour.

The marks on the back consist of letters or monograms, such as A F, A R, G, J G, &c., the meaning of which we are unable to discover; these letters are frequently combined with a sort of anchor, called by the French *grappin*, and by the English *grapnel* or *creeper*.[1]

M. Jules Labarte (*Histoire des Arts Industriels au Moyen Age et à l'Epoque de la Renaissance*) says, " A manufactory of maiolica at Venice in the seventeenth century produced some specimens inferior in point of art, but curious as records of keramic execution; these are dishes, the rims of which are generally loaded with fruits in relief, and the centres decorated with slight and very inferior painting. What renders this fayence singular is, that it is very thin, very light, and so sonorous as to be commonly mistaken for sheets of copper enamelled and *repoussé*. The Museum of Sèvres possesses very fine specimens. This manufacture was of short duration."

Signor Vicenzo Lazari attributed these pieces to an unknown manufacturer of the end of the seventeenth century, and M. Jacquemart is rather inclined to place them in the same century; but on due consideration we are still of opinion they were made by the Brothers Bertolini, the glass-makers of Murano.

The following account is extracted from Sir W. R. Drake's *Notes on Venetian Ceramics*, p. 25 :—

" In 1753 (not 1758, as erroneously stated by Lazari) a manufactory of maiolica was set up in Murano by the Brothers Gianandrea and Pietro Bertolini, who, previous to that date, had carried on in that island a privileged manufacture of painted and gilt enamel, imitating porcelain. In their petition to the Senate the Bertolini stated that they proposed to establish a new manufactory of maiolica in Murano, having, after many costly experiments, at last obtained such perfection in their work, that, as to *whiteness, lightness, and design* (candidezza, leggerezza, e pittura), they had nothing to envy in any other manufacture of the State, and they therefore proposed to open a shop in Venice to facilitate their sale. The petitioners alleged that their intentions were interfered with by the privileges which had been granted to Antonibon of Nove, and Salmazzo

---

[1] Johnson defines a creeper as " in naval language a sort of grapnel used for recovering things that may be cast overboard."

of Bassano, which exempting them from import and export duties, they were enabled to sell their maiolica at a lower price than the Bertolini could do, although the merits of their manufactures were in no way inferior."

A decree of the Senate of 14th April 1753, authorised them to open a shop in Venice, with exemption for ten years from import and export duties.

The Murano manufactory of maiolica did not succeed so well as the promoters anticipated, and it was probably discontinued about the year 1760. The concession was annulled by a decree of the 2nd April, 1763.

The marks, therefore, of a double anchor or creeper we may safely assign to this firm. The letters A F, so frequently found (as well as the others), are at present unintelligible, but may be the initials of the painters, interwoven with the trade-mark. There is one mark in particular which seems to call for a remark, viz., the A F and a Maltese cross between two palm branches saltire, surmounted by a coronet. A similar Maltese cross on a shield is on the dish of M°. Ludovico of Venice, made in the sixteenth century, two centuries earlier; we may also call attention to the same letters followed by V E for Venice.

1546

fatto in uenezia
in lchastello

VENICE. On a maiolica dish; subject, The Destruction of Troy, after Raphael. Formerly in the Narford Collection (figured in Delange's *Recueil*, plate 80). Fountaine sale, £325 10s.

VENICE. A large plateau, with sunk centre, having four medallions, bearing portrait heads of "SEMIRAMIS," "PORTIA," "ZENOBIA," "FULVIA,"

A di 13 Aprille, i 543

Ao LASDINR

between which are arabesques, foliated border. Reverse with the date 13th April, 1543, and a name as given above. In the Victoria and Albert Museum.

VENICE. On a dish 20 in. diameter, of pale grey ground, white ornamentation of lace-work, scrolls, &c., with four medallions of heads on the rim, inscribed LUCRETIA, OMERO, FAUSTINA, OVIDIO; in the centre are a fish and a mask, &c. This piece records the establishment of another Pesarese artist at Venice. Formerly in the possession of Mr. H. Durlacher.

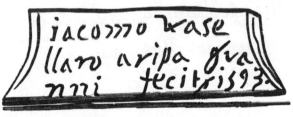

In Venetia—a Sto Barnaba.
In Botega dj. Mo Jacomo
Da Pesaro.
1542

VENICE. On a drug pot; pale blue ground, covered with leafage in a darker tint; on a central ribbon, "diafena nicol" in black letter, a shield of arms beneath; on a label behind is the inscription "Jacomo Vasellaro a ripa granni fecit 1593." Dr. Fortnum says this is a potter named Jacomo who worked on the Ripa Grande at Venice in 1593. This could hardly be that M°. Jacomo da Pesaro who was working fifty years before at St. Barnaba. In the Victoria and Albert Museum.

VENICE. On a plateau, circa 1540; light blue ground and arabesque border in blue; in centre an amorino carrying a vase of flowers. Victoria and Albert Museum. Another plate, supposed to be by the same artist, is in the Ashmolean Museum, Oxford (Fortnum Collection), dated 1540, painted with a mermaid, before alluded to.

In Venetia in cōtrada dj Sta Polo in botega dj M Ledovico

VENICE. This inscription is on the back of a dish; subject, Moses and Aaron entreating Pharaoh; with a rich border, and medallions of the first four months of the year. In the Brunswick Museum. This is probably the shop of Maestro Ludovico before named, and Domenigo, the painter attached to the establishment.

ZENER DOMENIGO
DA VENECIA
FECI IN LA BOTEGA
AL PONTE SITO DEL
ANDAR A SAN POLO.
1568.

is(7)i

C 1522

Dionigi Marini

1636

Io Stefano Barcella

Veneziano Rox

VENICE. On a plate, painted with the Salutation of the Virgin. Uzielli Collection. Dr. Fortnum doubts the correctness of this date, but we copied it while in the possession of the late Mr. Uzielli, and no imperfection in the glaze then existed; it was clearly 1571, and not 1671, as he suggests. The latter mark is on a plate in the Berlin Museum.

VENICE. The mark of Dionisi Marinus, and the date 1636. On a plate painted with six horses; in the Collection of M. Roger de Beauvoir.

VENICE. The mark of Io. Stefano Barcella, a Venetian painter only. The last word is perhaps intended for *pinxit*, although not very clear.

VENICE. This mark represents a *creeper* or grapnel, with the letters A F, and perhaps C C, interlaced. On dishes, with landscapes in brown, blue, yellow, and green, and arabesque borders executed in relief, of the eighteenth century, by Bertolini. Some specimens in the Sèvres Museum with this mark; another in the British Museum.

VENICE. Marked in dark red, on a piece of fayence formerly in the author's possession: a creeper with the letter R on the stem.

VENICE. This mark of a creeper is on a Venetian dish, eighteenth century, with shells and scrolls in relief on the border, outlined in brown and green; in the centre a landscape in brown, blue, yellow, and green; on the back are six leaves touched in brown. The same mark also occurs on a very fine dish painted with a classical subject. (*Ker. Gall.*, enlarged edition, fig. 67.)

VENICE. One of the fanciful marks of the Bertolini fabrique; in the centre of the flower are the letters A F in blue; it is on a fayence *plateau* of *octagonal* form previously in the Baron C. Davillier's Collection. It represents a pink (garofalo), and is perhaps a rebus of the painter's name, like that of Benvenuto Tisio (see *ante*, page 88).

VENICE. This mark is on a fayence plate of the eighteenth century, of the Bertolini fabrique, painted with a coat of arms, surrounded by amorini. The same device is on a plate in the British Museum; another of the same set having the double anchor or creeper.

VENICE. This monogram of C. S. L. is a mark on Venetian maiolica, quoted by M. A. Jacquemart.

VENICE or FAENZA. Another variation of the letters A F, so frequently seen on Venetian fayence, followed by V E for Venice. It occurs on a moulded dish, painted in outline with Mercury and a border of flowers. M. Jacquemart attributes similar marks to Faenza (see page 93).

VENICE. On a plate, similar in character to the preceding; subject, Judith and Holofernes, with an embossed border of scrolls and masks. In the Collection of the late Mr. Belward Ray.

VENICE, Venezia. This mark is frequently seen on old Venetian pottery, as well as porcelain.

VENICE (?). This shield, from its similarity to that shown above as being identified with this city, is thus placed. It occurs on a plate, painted in blue and white, with a coat of arms at top; very much like the pottery of Savona; circa 1700. Dr. Fortnum thinks that this mark belongs to Savona, Turin, or Padua, and not to Venice.

VENICE. On a specimen, coloured blue, of Judith and Holofernes, and coat of arms above; another is in the Victoria and Albert Museum.

VENICE or BASSANO. On an earthenware dish, rudely painted with landscape, embossed border; formerly in Captain Langford's Collection. Eighteenth century. Dr. Fortnum ascribes this to Bassano.

VENICE. On a Venetian dish, rudely painted in blue, yellow, and green, with brown outlines, a gadroon border in relief of these three colours, and in centre a castle, hare, and bird in yellow; date about 1750.

VENICE. Tazza, of enamelled earthenware, embossed with grotesques and a spread eagle in greyish blue, on a dark blue ground, sixteenth century. Mr. George Salting's Collection in the Victoria and Albert Museum.

BASSANO.

The first pottery at Bassano, near Venice, was, according to V. Lazari, founded by a certain Simone Marinoni, in the suburb called the Marchesane, about 1540, but it does not appear that his productions were of a very artistic character, for Lazari speaks of a plate dated 1555, representing St. Anthony, St. Francis, and St. Bonaventura, which was badly painted and failed both in the colours and in the glaze.

Towards the end of the sixteenth and the commencement of the seventeenth century, the same fabrique produced maiolica services, many of which have been preserved to our time; they bear the names of Bartolomeo and Antonio Terchi, two brothers from Rome, who appear to have travelled from one place to another, and painted or worked for a great number of establishments. The iron crown is not, however, the special attribute of Bassano; we find it on the maiolica of other towns. The manufacture appears to have ceased in the beginning of the seventeenth century, at least we have no record of its existence until a century afterwards.

Sir W. R. Drake (*Notes on Venetian Ceramics*) informs us that about 1728 a manufactory of *maiolica* and *latesini* (a term applied to the local maiolica) was carried on at Bassano by the Sisters Manardi, as appears from the petition of Giovanni Antonio Caffo, presented to the Senate in 1735, in which he states that he had been for many years engaged in their manufactory, and as the end of his time of service was about to expire, and he had a quantity of manufactured goods (of the value of more than 3000 ducats) on hand, besides many outstanding debts, he prayed he might be allowed to continue the manufactory, and to retain the workmen well skilled in the art, whom he had at very great cost obtained from foreign countries, and with that view permission should be granted to him to erect a furnace in the suburbs of Bassano for the manufacture of maiolica and latesini, similar not only to the manufactures of Lodi and Faenza, but also like those of Genoa, praying for exemption from duties, &c. Caffo's petition was remitted to the Board of Trade, who said that there was no necessity for requesting permission to erect a furnace for earthenware, as such a thing was never forbidden to any one, and referred to the proclamation of the 24th July, 1728, which invited the erection of furnaces, so as to prevent the great injury to the State by the large amount of money which constantly went to Milan, to the Romagna, and to Genoa, for the purchase of earthenware. They also stated that the favour of exemption from inland dues had already been granted to Giovanni Battista Antonibon of Nove, and to the Sisters Manardi of Bassano, and advised that his petition be complied with. This report was adopted by the Senate on the 3rd October, 1736.

Previous to 1753 Giovanni Maria Salmazzo had established at Bassano a manufactory of maiolica, in competition with Antonibon's establishment at Nove. At that time it would appear Antonibon's was the only fabrique for making maiolica in the Venetian dominions; this fact is alluded to in the report of the Board of Trade to the Senate of 17th August, 1756. The State had refused an application made by Antonibon for an exclusive right to make earthenware, but a decree in his favour had been made, prohibiting workmen quitting his establishment from taking service in any other for two years. Salmazzo complained in his petition to the Senate that the Antonibons having ruined two competitors, had endeavoured to ruin him; by bribing some of his workmen to " disobedience and mutiny," had compelled him to dismiss them, and they were immediately taken into Antonibon's service. The Board of Trade, after alluding to the high reputation which Antonibon's maiolica had gained, as also to the wealth he had acquired, advised the Senate to grant equal privileges to all, but declined to enter into the quarrels between them. The decree was made accordingly.

It is probable the *maiolica fina* of Salmazzo was continued for many years. We have seen many examples of this peculiar Italian fayence, which cannot be attributed to any other locale; some of these bear the initials G. S., which may be attributed to Giovanni Salmazzo.

G. S.   This mark of Giovanni Salmazzo, in gold, is on an *écuelle*, richly gilt and painted in medallions of figures in Italian landscapes, very much in the style of Nove fayence; in the possession of J. W. Crowe, Esq.

BASSANO. A plate, representing Lot and his Daughters leaving the city of Sodom; the name of the artist is given as in the margin. Seventeenth century. (Louvre.) Also on a small saucer of the seventeenth century, painted with a view of the gates of Bassano.

BASSANO. Bartolomeo Terchi. On the back of a maiolica vessel, with a landscape. Seventeenth century. In the Collection of M. Le Blanc.

Mark of Manardi, Bassano. (Fortnum.)

NOVE, NEAR BASSANO.

M. V. Lazari says that the fabrique in the village of Nove, near Bassano, which was established at the end of the seventeenth century, and advantageously known in Italy in the first years of the eighteenth century, was much more praised than that of Marinoni of Bassano. Of the fabrique of the Antonibons there are still preserved entire frames or panels of the finest and most ornamented maiolica, made in 1743-44.

The first notice we have, however, in the State records is in 1728. Sir W. R. Drake (*Notes on Venetian Ceramics*) has supplied us with the following information : —

In 1728 Giovanni Battista Antonibon established in the village of Nove, in the province of Bassano and near the town of that name, a manufactory of earthenware (*terraglie*), and on the 18th of April, 1732, the Senate granted him the privilege of opening a shop in Venice for the sale of his manufactures for two years, which on the 2nd of June, 1735, was extended for a further period of ten years. In 1741 the manufactory was in a prosperous state, and it was then carried on by Pasqual Antonibon, who, finding that the shop he had in Venice was not sufficient for the sale of his goods, petitioned for leave to open another, which was granted on the 6th of July, 1741. His father's name was still continued as proprietor, as shown in the piece referred to below.

The "Inquisitor alle arte," in his report to the Venetian Senate in 1766 concerning the Antonibons' manufactory of maiolica and earthenware, thus describes it: It consists of three large furnaces, one small

furnace, and two kilns (*furnasotti*, probably muffle-kilns); 120 workmen
of various provinces are employed in it, and his trade extends to the territories of the Friuli, Verona, Mantua, Trent, the Romagna, the Tyrol, and
other places. Persons from all parts flock to Nove to make purchases,
and they have also two shops in Venice, which are provided with a great
variety of specimens, always new, and whose whiteness (*candidezza*)
doubtless exceeds that of any other foreign manufactory. He would yet
have more extended his business, had not his attention and capital been
harassed by his experiments in waxed cloth (*tele cerate*) and porcelain.

In 1762 Pasqual took his son Giovanni Battista into partnership, and
they carried on their works for the manufacture of *maioliche fine* or fayence,
and *terraglia* or *terre de pipe*, as well as porcelain, together until 6th of
February, 1781, when they joined in partnership with Signor Parolini, still
continuing the fabrication "con sommo onore dell' arte," until the 6th of
February, 1802.

In February, 1802, the Antonibons let the fabrique on lease to Giovanni Baroni, and it was carried on by him for about twenty years by the
name of the "Fabbrica Baroni Nove," at first successfully, but it did not
continue long in a prosperous condition, and by degrees it was allowed to
go to decay, and in 1825 it was entirely abandoned by Baroni.

On the 1st May, 1825, Giovanni Battista Antonibon again took possession of the works, and, in partnership with his son Francesco,
resuscitated them, until their productions arrived at their former excellence
in *maiolica fina*, *terraglia*, and porcelain. In 1835 they discontinued
making porcelain, and confined their attention to fayence and *terraglia*,
making principally copies of the best productions of other European
fabriques. Rietti, a dealer at Venice, has the monopoly of the sale of
everything made at Nove, and the firm is still called, as in the last century,
"Pasqual Antonibon e figli, antica fabbrica, terraglie, maioliche fine, ed
ordinaire in Nove, di Bassano."

Alluding to the manufacture of the eighteenth century, Sir W. R.
Drake adds in a note, "Figures and groups, some of them of large size,
were manufactured by Antonibon out of a fine pipeclay (*terraglia*), and
are remarkable for their good modelling. Very fair imitations of this
manufacture are now made in the neighbourhood of Venice, and there sold
by the dealers as old specimens. The imitations lack the sharpness of
modelling, and are considerably heavier than the originals."

NOVE. The mark of Giovanni Battista
Antonibon of Nove. On a fayence tureen of
the middle of the eighteenth century, painted
in blue, with masks, flowers, and scrolls; the
shell-shaped handles and figure of Atlas on the
cover are mottled purple. (*Ker. Gall.*, enlarged edition, fig. 69.) The star forms part of

the ornament, which was adopted by him as a mark. In the Victoria
and Albert Museum. The letters signify, without doubt, Giovanni

Battista Antonio Bon : the B cannot be intended for Bassano, as the name of Nove is placed above. Antonibon has also written his name at length as Antonio Bon on a piece of porcelain which belonged to the Baron Davillier, *postea*, where it is described with others in the same Collection.

Mark of Giovanni Batt. Antonibon. (Genolini.)

Mark of the G. Baroni fabrique. (Genolini.)

Della fabrica di
Gio Batt^a Antonibon
nelle nove di Decen
1755.

NOVE. This mark of Antonibon's fabrique is on part of a fayence table service, painted in polychrome. *From the manufactory of Giovanni Battista Antonibon, the ninth of December* 1755.

Fab^a Baroni Nove.

NOVE, near Bassano. On a splendid presentation fayence vase, oviform, with square pierced handles and pierced neck, of *bleu du roi* ground with medallions painted in colours, of Alexander and the Family of Darius, and another classical subject after Le Brun ; small circular medallions between, of classical heads, two in each, elegant gilt scrolls and borders. This very effective vase, evidently a *chef d'œuvre* of the manufactory, is 2 ft. 5 in. high. The name is written on each side of the square pedestal ; date from 1802 to 1810 : by Giovanni Baroni, successor of Antonibon. It was purchased by a dealer at Venice and sent to Geneva, but not finding a customer, it was carried to Paris, where it was seen and secured by the late Mr. C. W. Reynolds.[1] (*Ker. Gall.*, enlarged edition, fig. 68.)

CANDIANA, 1620.

CANDIANA. The name of a manufactory, perhaps near Venice, where they enamelled earthenware with Turkish designs. There is one in the Sèvres Museum, signed as in the margin ; another is mentioned by Mr. J. C. Robinson, with the date 1637.

S. F. C.

CANDIANA was noted for its imitations of Turkish ware, with tulips, pinks, and other flowers ; usually of the first half of the seventeenth century. These letters are given by M. Jacquemart, found on a tazza of good form ; on a

---

[1] M. A. Jacquemart (*Histoire de la Céramique*, p. 584, Paris, 1873) has made a grand mistake in the reading of the inscription on the vase, which he says is "*Bracciano alle Nove*," repeated four times on the base, instead of "*Fab^a Baroni Nove*," thereby creating an ideal potter. He continues, "Il resterait à savoir si Bracciano etait le Directeur de l'établissement ou le peintre." Such mistakes cause a great deal of confusion, and this is the more inexcusable as he quotes our account in the last edition, where it is correctly given, but prefers reasoning upon his own false reading.

bandelette or scroll is written MS. DEGA, which probably refers to the person for whom it was made.

CANDIANA (?). Paolo Crosa. This name is on a cylindrical vase, blue ground, with yellow **PA. CROSA.** scrolls and white medallions, with flowers in imitation of Turkish. Seventeenth century. Formerly in the possession of the Marquis d'Azeglio.

This mark in blue is on a pair of hexagonal potiches, finely painted in blue *camaieu*, very much like Delft, formerly in Baron C. Davillier's Collection.

FLORENCE.

FLORENCE. Luca della Robbia, born A.D. 1400, commenced his career as a goldsmith, but afterwards became a sculptor, and attained considerable eminence in that profession. He subsequently adopted the device of covering his bas-reliefs of terra-cotta with a thick stanniferous enamel or glaze, which rendered them impervious to the action of the elements, consequently extremely durable. His early relievos consisted of scrolls, masks, birds, and designs of the Renaissance taste, which are usually white on blue ground; he subsequently coloured the fruit and flowers in natural tints, but white and blue appear to have been his favourite colours. There is a set of the Twelve Months painted in pale blue in *chiaroscuro*, with husbandmen engaged in seasonable operations for each month, on separate enamelled terra-cotta medallions, 12½ in. diameter. These medallions are ascribed to Luca della Robbia (Gigli Campana Collection), and are now in the Victoria and Albert Museum. (Cf. *Ker. Gall.*, enlarged edition, fig. 71.)

There is a very fine altar-piece of the later half of the fifteenth century, the Adoration of the Magi, in high relief, coloured with portraits of celebrated artists of the time of Luca della Robbia. In the Victoria and Albert Museum; height 7 ft. 8 in. (*Ker. Gall.*, enlarged edition, fig. 72.)

He died in 1481, and was succeeded by his nephew, Andrea della Robbia, born 1437, died 1528, who is known to have executed bas reliefs in 1515. After his death, his four sons, Giovanni, Luca, Ambrosio, and Girolamo, continued making the same description of coloured reliefs, but greatly inferior to those of their ancestor, the inventor. Girolamo went to France, and was employed by Francis I. in decorating the Château de Madrid, in the Bois de Boulogne, called ironically by Philibert Delorme, the architect, the "Château de Fayence," and died there about the year 1567.

This château abounded with enamelled terra-cottas; unfortunately none of them are preserved to our time. When this beautiful villa was demolished in 1762, the terra-cottas were sold to a pavior, who made them into cement. With Girolamo, the last of the della Robbias, departed also the secrets of the art. Sir J. C. Robinson (*Catalogue of the Soulages Collection*) says : " Generally speaking, the earlier works of Luca and those of Andrea after his (Luca's) death can be distinguished. The specimens which are only partially enamelled, *i.e.*, in which the nude details of the figures are left of the original colour or surface of the clay, appear to be of the earliest time, *i.e.*, the period of Luca himself. The pieces entirely covered with the white or white and blue enamels, were, however, doubtless after a time executed simultaneously. The former specimens were interesting as pointing to the origin of the ware. The flesh in these pieces was originally in every case painted of the natural colours in distemper, the draperies and accessories only being covered with the enamel glaze (in the then state of the keramic art it was impossible to produce flesh tints in enamel colours), and his invention consisted in applying the stanniferous enamel glaze to the terra-cotta sculpture, which had previously been executed in distemper." Luca della Robbia had many scholars and competitors; one of these pupils, Agostino da Duccio, has in his works a great analogy of style. There is a façade by this artist in the church of San Bernardino.

BL.1429
FACEBAT

FLORENCE. This mark is given by Dr. Graesse as on the back of a medallion of the Virgin and Child at the Museum of Sigmaringen, which is described in the Catalogue as Luca della Robbia; it is graved in the clay, but seems of very doubtful authenticity. The work is at least a century later, and has nothing of the character of Della Robbia.

LR=FA
1454

FLORENCE. Luca della Robbia (also from Dr. Graesse's book). This mark, graved in the moist clay before baking, is on a group of the Virgin and Child; formerly in Cardinal Fesch's Collection. [This mark and the preceding one are given with much misgiving. Dr. Fortnum considers both are "more than doubtful."]

F. F. FI.

FLORENCE. FIRENZE. We are not acquainted with the early marks on the maiolica made here. It is said to have been mostly in relief, like the Luca della Robbia. Fine Fayence of the eighteenth century is found with the letter F, which has been assigned to this city; but it has the honour of being the first, under the Medici, to have successfully imitated the Oriental porcelain as early as 1580. The mark is a doubtful one.

FLORENCE. A cock, the rebus mark of Cantigalli, of Florence, who make excellent imitations of old maiolica.

For further reference to Florentine wares, see
p. 49.

PADUA

Vincenzo Lazari informs us, that in a street which still retains the name of *Bocaleri* (makers of vases), a few years since were discovered traces of ancient potters' kilns, and some maiolica triangular wall tiles of blue and white alternately, of the end of the fifteenth or beginning of sixteenth century, among which was a plaque, 20 in. in diameter, of the Virgin and Child between S. Roch and S. Lucia in slight relief, surrounded by angels and a coat of arms. It is taken from a cartoon by Nicolo Pizzolo, a painter of Padua, pupil of Squarcione; on the summit of the throne is written NICOLETI, the name he usually adopted. It is now preserved in the Museum of that city.

A plate with figures after Carpaccio of the fifteenth century (*sgraffito*) is in the possession of the Baron Schwiter at Paris, which, although unsigned, was sold to him as an authentic work of Nicoleto of Padua.

This city is spoken of by Piccolpasso as possessing manufactories of maiolica in his time (1540), and several examples are here given.

There are some plates in the Victoria and Albert Museum: one, of foliated scroll-work and flowers on blue ground, with a camel in the centre, circa 1530; Bernal Collection; cost £6. Another, with arabesques on blue ground, a coat of arms in the centre, reverse marked with a cross, circa 1550; also from the Bernal Collection.

PADUA. On a maiolica plate; subject, Myrrha. Victoria and Albert Museum. (*Ker. Gall.*, enlarged edition, fig. 73.)

PADVA.
1548.

PADUA. On a plate; subject, Polyphemus and Galatea. Bernal Collection, now in the British Museum.

A. PADOA⊁
1564.

PADUA. On the back of a plate, painted with Adam and Eve, in the late Mr. A. Barker's Collection. The Paduan signatures are usually accompanied by a cross.

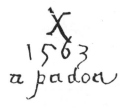

CASTELLI.

CASTELLI is a town or hamlet in the Abruzzi, north of the city of Naples. No time can be assigned for the commencement of the working in pottery, but it was one of the first to take advantage of the improvements of Luca della Robbia in the fifteenth century, and the maiolica of Castelli equalled, if it did not surpass, that of Pisa and Pesaro. Passeri quotes the testimony of a contemporary author to prove that both Pesaro and

Castelli were celebrated for the excellence and beauty of their manu-
factures of pottery. Antonio Beuter, a Spaniard, who wrote in 1540, says:
"Corebæus, according to Pliny, was the inventor of pottery in Athens.
He did not make them better, nor were the vases of Corinth of more
value, than the works of Pisa or Pesaro, or of Castelli in the Sicilian
valley of the Abruzzi, nor of other places, for fineness and beauty of work."
It is on the site of the ancient city of Atrium, and coins, fragments of
Greek pottery, and other remains have been frequently exhumed. The
traditions of other ages, the fine models of Greek art discovered in the
neighbourhood, the facility for making pottery—from having the requisite
clay, water, and wood, as well as its proximity to the sea for traffic—have
all contributed to the ceramic industry of Castelli. The manufacture of
pottery and porcelain was able to keep in activity thirty-five manufactories,
and to employ nearly all the population of the neighbourhood. No specimens of the maiolica of the fifteenth and sixteenth centuries can be now
identified. Few of the manufactories of Italy, which were so famous for
their maiolica, survived much beyond the beginning of the seventeenth
century; Castelli alone appears to have stood its ground, and towards
the end of the seventeenth century was as flourishing as ever in this
particular branch of industry. Francesco Saverio Grue, a man of letters
and science, became about this time director of the Neapolitan maiolica
fabrique at Castelli. The ware was ornamented with subjects of an
important nature, correctly designed and brilliantly coloured, to which also
was added the introduction of gilding the borders of the ware; sometimes
the landscapes were also touched with gold. His sons and brothers continued to add lustre to his name, and many distinguished artists proceeded
from his school, amongst whom may be noticed Gentile, Fuini, Capelleti,
and Giustiniani. The manufacture was patronised by the King, Carlo
Borbone, and his son Augusto, who emulating the Medici of Tuscany,
raised the ceramic art of the kingdom of Naples to great celebrity.

CASTELLI (?). This mark is given by Passeri, on a piece of the eighteenth century, and
was a crown used by Terchi. Dr. Fortnum thinks
it may be Bassano.

CASTELLI. Naples. On an earthenware plate
of the beginning of the eighteenth century,
painted in blue, with cupids and flowers. Dr.
Fortnum thinks it is more probably Savona.

CASTELLI (?). Naples. On a cup and
saucer, rudely designed, of a countryman under
an arcade.

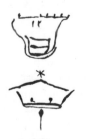

Fr. A. Grue eseprai
1677

CASTELLI. On a specimen in the Collection
of Signor Raff de Minicis of Fermo.

CASTELLI. This name is signed on a pair of circular plaques, 10 in. diameter, painted with the Holy Family, and a female in a bath; formerly in the Collection of Dr. H. W. Diamond.

iOĀNESGRVĀ FECIT.

CASTELLI. On a plaque; subject, the Adoration of the Magi; formerly in Mr. Marryat's Collection. Another, in the Collection of Signor Bonghi of Naples, is dated 1718.

D^r. Franc. Ant^o. Cav^r.
Grue P

CASTELLI. On a vase of the maiolica character; subject, Apollo and Marsyas; in Lord de Tabley's Collection.

Frac. Anis. Grue P.
Nopali, 1722.

CASTELLI. On a plaque, painted with a landscape and a bridge; on the keystone is a shield of arms, and at the foot of the bridge, on a wall, this tablet of the painter's name and date. In the late Mr. H. A. Neck's Collection.

CASTELLI. This mark is on the companion plate, painted with a landscape, in the late Mr. H. A. Neck's Collection.

DR Grue
pinxit.

CASTELLI. Saverio Grue, a maiolica painter of the eighteenth century, of classical subjects and mottoes.

S. Grue.

CASTELLI. Saverio Grue Pinxit. These initials are on plaques, illustrating mottoes—as "Perseverantia fructus," in Lord Hastings' Collection; another "Virtutis vere liberalitas," in Mr. Attree's Collection.

S. G. P.

CASTELLI. In the cabinet of M. le Comte de Montbrun there are two plaques painted with children and landscapes.

S. Grue P. Napou.
1749.

CASTELLI. The monogram of Saverio Grue, on a plaque with military figures, inscribed "Fortitude et Innocent," in the Sèvres Museum; also on a plate mentioned by M. A. Darcel, dated 1753.

$\mathfrak{H}$ p^t

CASTELLI. On a bowl and cover, painted with nude figures after Annibale Caracci; of the eighteenth century (Liborius died in 1776), in the Victoria and Albert Museum. (*Ker. Gall.*, enlarged edition, fig. 74.) This curious mark has the nondescript ornament at the beginning in a line with the name.

CASTELLI. The mark of Luigi or Liborius Grue, on some plates painted with landscapes and figures, heightened with gold; circa 1720.

CASTELLI. Gentili Pinxit. On a tile painted with a pastoral subject of the beginning of the eighteenth century. Signor Bonghi of Naples has a fine collection of examples of Bernardino Gentili or Gentile; one two feet high, representing the Martyrdom of St. Ursula, is richly coloured and heightened with gold. A plate, painted with a satyr surprising a nymph, and a border of cupids, &c., *en grisaille*, circa 1700, by Gentili, is in the Victoria and Albert Museum (No. 4345, 57). In the Museum Catalogue of 1868 this plate is so described, but Fortnum in his description in 1873, page 637, states that it is by L. Grue, and places its date seventy years later.

Another specimen, painted with the Crucifixion, is quoted by Jacquemart, bearing this inscription: "*Questo crocifisso del carmine lo fece Bernardino Gentile per sua divozione, 1670.*" He died in 1683.

CASTELLI. This minute signature is on a plaque painted with a landscape; in the foreground, among the ruins, is S. John with a lamb. Formerly in Mr. H. A. Neck's Collection.

CASTELLI. On a plaque; subject, the Triumph of Amphitrite. Louvre Collection.

CASTELLI. Another mark of Saverio Grue, given by Jacquemart; died in 1806.

CASTELLI. On a large and fine square plaque in the Berlin Museum.

CASTELLI. On a round plaque, painted with the Baptism of Christ, in the Berlin Museum.

CASTELLI (?). This mark is from a fine dish brought to England by Signor A. Castellani, painted with a battle, vigorously sketched, and a border of scrolls. The signature of the artist, Carlo Coccorese, is on a stone in the foreground; the date, 1734, is on the border; the D being omitted as usual at that time. On the horse trappings, two crossed C's crowned. Dr. Fortnum ascribes this piece to Naples.

This signature occurs on a piece in the possession of Monsignore Cajani. It is cleverly painted in the style of the Castelli or the later Sienese pieces, with a group of male and female satyrs gathering grapes.

CASTELLI (?). This artist is of the school of Gruc; signed on a plaque, painted with ruins in a landscape and a shepherdess leading a cow and sheep; in one corner is written the name *Luca Antonio Ciannico.*

PALERMO.

The Baron C. Davillier discovered this inscription on an albarello or drug vase, of good style, somewhat like the maiolica of Castel Durante.

FATTO IN
PALERMA
1606.

NAPLES.

Of the maiolica of the city of Naples we have no mention in the sixteenth century, nor have we met with any specimens of so early a date, although, as we have seen, Castelli in the kingdom of Naples is honourably mentioned, nay, even comparable to Athens, by Antonio Beuter, in 1540. M. A. Jacquemart says: "La confusion la plus absolue règne parmi les produits de l'ancien royaume de Naples," &c. He continues, "C'est encore à l'avenir qu'il faut laisser le soin d'éclairer ces questions. Quant à Naples, nous trouvons son nom sur des ouvrages *de la fin du seizième siècle,* empreints du style de l'epoque, et qu'il eût été facile de confondre avec les poteries du nord de l'Italie." He then describes three vases of colossal proportions, composed for decoration, only one of their sides being painted, caryatid handles, painted in blue *camaieu* with religious subjects; "la touche est hardie et spirituelle," &c.

As, however, there seems to be a diversity of opinion on the matter of dates upon these vases, we must give the result of our reference to two

Parisian ceramic authorities, and form our own opinions of their respective merits as reliable sources of information.

The works from which we quote are *Les Merveilles de la Céramique* (*Renaissance Italienne*), par Albert Jacquemart, Paris, 1868, p. 252, and *Guide de l'Amateur des Faïences et Porcelaines*, par Auguste Demmin, Paris, 1868.

NAPLES. A lofty vase, painted with the Sermon on the Mount, inscribed, according to M. Demmin, "Fran. Brand, Napoli, Casa Nova," with the initials B. G. crowned, as in the margin. M. A. Jacquemart gives a similar mark on the same vase, but he reads it thus: "Fran°° Brand, Napoli, Gesu Novo." The second vase, painted with the Last Supper, M. Demmin describes as being inscribed "Paulus Franciscus Brandi, 1684." M. Jacquemart, on the other hand, reads it thus: "Paulus Fran^{cus} Brandi, Pinx . . 68 ," and puts down the date as 1568.

The third and most important vase, the Miraculous Draught, causes the same difference of opinion. M. Demmin gives us a facsimile, which we reproduce in the margin. M. Jacquemart exclaims, "Un dernier vase positivement daté a été fait par un artiste du même atelier dont voici la signature, 'P. il Sig. Francho, Nepita, 1532.'"

We must, with this conflicting testimony before us, judge for ourselves, and looking at the style of the monograms, which assimilate with those of Savona, Venice, and others of the end of the seventeenth century, there can be little doubt these vases are of the same date, and clearly not of the sixteenth century; the description given shows the decadence of the art. There were four large vases of the same character in Mr. Barker's possession, which, although effective enough for the purpose of decoration, are as works of art below criticism.

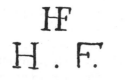

NAPLES. These initials frequently occur on plates of a maiolica pattern of the eighteenth century, which M. Brongniart places as Neopolitan. Dr. Fortnum (see Catalogue of Maiolica, South Kensington Museum, p. 632) says, "Some pieces of the last century, painted with figures, landscapes, &c., in very pale colours, and marked at the back with the letters H. F. or HF combined, are of Austrian and not of Italian origin"; but as he gives no reason for the remark, we prefer the attribution of M. Brongniart as we now place them.

F.D.V
N.

NAPLES. F. Del Vecchio; stamped on pieces of fayence in the Etruscan style, on a white and gold service of the eighteenth century.

NAPLES. Giustiniani. On vases, chiefly of Etruscan pattern; eighteenth century.

NAPLES. Giustiniani in Napoli. On Etruscan patterns, the mark impressed on the ware.

NAPLES. This mark is given by Brongniart as Neapolitan; it is on a maiolica plateau in the Sèvres Museum.

NAPLES. This mark is on a fayence jug, painted with flowers; eighteenth century.

NAPLES. M. Jacquemart refers all these with the enclosed crown to this city; those with the open crown to Bassano.

NAPLES. These two marks probably belong to the same artist, B. G., whose initials are quoted by Jacquemart as belonging to the sixteenth century; but there can, we think, be no doubt he has misread the inscriptions, and that they are actually of the end of the seventeenth century.

NAPLES. On a maiolica plate of the eighteenth century, with raised pattern on the border; subject in centre, a landscape, painted in blue.

NAPLES. Makers of modern pottery in imitation of the ancient Etruscan ware like that of Giustiniani. Specimens in the Victoria and Albert Museum.

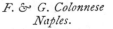

F. & G. Colonnese Naples.

M. Jacquemart says that when Charles III., King of Naples, established a manufactory of porcelain at Capo di Monte, near Naples, in 1736, fayence was also occasionally made, and describes a magnificent piece, "*Une fontaine de Sacristie*," modelled with the Dove of the Holy Spirit, cherubs issuing from clouds, &c., painted in colours and richly gilt, bearing the N. crowned and the words "*Capo di Monte.*"
"*Mo*lo."

LODI.

LODI. A large fayence dish, rudely painted with a fish, lemons, apples, &c., bears this mark in blue. The Lodi manufactory, established early in the seventeenth century, ceased towards the end of the eighteenth century. There are some specimens also in the Nevers Museum.

LODI. These two monograms of A.M. occur on separate pieces of Lodi fayence, one painted with blue, yellow, and red decorations; another with a cottage and peasant. One peculiarity of this ware is that there are three cockspur marks, each of three points, underneath. A piece belonging to M. Osmont of Paris is signed FERRET LODI; quoted by Jacquemart.

MONTELUPO.

The plates and dishes of coarse heavy earthenware, rudely painted with large caricature figures of soldiers and men in curious Italian costumes of the seventeenth and eighteenth centuries, in menacing and warlike attitudes, striding across the plates, holding swords, spears, and other weapons, are usually attributed to Montelupo, near Florence, but they also produced chocolate brown vases of a more artistic character in the style of Avignon. The manufactory is still in existence.

MONTELUPO, near Florence. The annexed mark is on a fluted tazza, painted with three standing cavaliers. Montferrand Collection, now in the Victoria and Albert Museum. (*Ker. Gall.*, enlarged edition, fig. *77*.)

MONTELUPO. So attributed by M. Jacquemart, but of doubtful attribution.

MONTELUPO. This curious inscription occurs on a fayence plateau with raised centre, painted with a coat of arms, from which radiate flutings filled in with grotesques, fleurs-de-lis, &c., in yellow, green, and blue. The reverse is dated 16th April 1663, Jacinto or Diacinto Monti of Montelupo. Victoria and Albert Museum.

MONTELUPO. This inscription occurs on a tazza of the decadence, painted in colours, with figures and foliage of ordinary and hard design, in the Sèvres Museum.

Dipinta Giovinale
Tereni da Montelupo.

MONTELUPO. On a plateau, with raised centre and radiated flutings, like the preceding. Victoria and Albert Museum.

ASCIANO.

ASCIANO, in Tuscany. On a plate, with coat of arms and blue and yellow leafage. (Fortnum.)

F. F. D.
FORTUNATUS PHILLIGELLUS
P. ASCIANI 1578 DIES
30 AUGUSTI.

ASCIANO. On a ewer, with moulded, wavy surface, snake handles, and painted shield of arms. British Museum.

F. P.
ASCIANI DIE XII MAIJ
1600.

MONTE, in the neighbourhood of Caffaggiolo. On a maiolica dish of Urbino character, sixteenth century; subject, the Rape of Helen, after Raphael. It is in the Hôtel de Cluny, and it is stated in the Catalogue to be the production of Monte Feltro, but the reason is not given.

SAN MINIATELLO, NEAR FLORENCE.

This very curious and interesting inscription has been sent by a correspondent. It occurs on an Italian maiolica plate, thus translated: This small plate was made in the workshop of Bechone of Nano at San Miniatello by Agostino di Mo. on the 5th of June 1581.

SI·FECE·QVESTO·PIATELO:
IN·BOTTECHA·DI·BECHONE
DEL·NANO·IN·SAMINIATELO
CHVESTO·T/·1TO·AGHOSTINO
DI·MO·A·DI·CINQE·DI·
GVGNIO· 1581·

MILAN.

MILAN. On a set of fayence plates with creamy glaze; subjects, figures, animals, and insects. Eighteenth century. Formerly in the possession of the Marchese d'Azeglio.

Milano

Milano
F⚓C

MILAN. On a dinner service; the tureen thus marked in red, painted with flowers in Oriental style, and coats of arms; the motto "Timidus ut Prudens;" eighteenth century; and on some pieces formerly in the possession of Lady Charlotte Schreiber. (*Ker. Gall.*, enlarged edition, figs. 79 and 80.) The initials are supposed to be those of "Felice Clerice," a name which occurs on a piece painted in the Chinese style, dated 1747.

Mil

MILAN. On two dishes and four plates, painted with Japanese patterns, of fine fayence. Eighteenth century. In the Museum of Sigmaringen.

F
Pasquale Rubatı
Mil.

MILAN. The name of this manufacturer appears at length on a jardinière in the Collection of M. Gasnault at Paris.

MILAN. This mark occurs on a fayence plate, purchased at Milan, from the Duke Litta's Collection, indicating *Fabrica Pasquale Rubati Milano;* formerly in the possession of Sir W. R. Drake.

F.
P. R.
Mil.ⁿᵒ

MILAN. The next mark of the same fabrique is on a fayence plate, painted with Chinese flowers, formerly in the Marchese d'Azeglio's Collection. Eighteenth century.

Mila°

MILAN. This mark is on a fine plate decorated with bouquets of flowers, blue and orange predominating, in the Bordeaux Museum.

M.ᵉ Trecchi

MILAN. From the similarity of style and colouring, this signature, hitherto unexplained, is attributed by Jacquemart to Milan. It occurs on one piece of a fine service, decorated in lake colours, like the Dresden gilt borders.

G. R.

ST. CHRYSTOPHE, near Milan, Lombardy. Manufacturer, Giulio Richard. On modern earthenware services; also on some early imitations, stamped with Wedgwood's name, in the Sèvres Museum. This national manufacture of pottery is still carried on by Giulio Richard & Co.

TURIN.

From the royal archives of Turin, M. le Marquis Campori has extracted some notices of the payments of money for maiolica, in which the name of Orazio Fontana occurs more than once, and he is styled Chief Potter of the Duke of Savoy, and he thinks Orazio was actually in the service of Emmanuel Philibert, but which M. Jacquemart observes could not be the case, as from the year 1565 he had opened at Urbino a fabrique, which he carried on until his death in 1571, and considers it an honorary title, showing the great esteem in which he was held by the Prince, by placing him above the potters he had called together to inaugurate the manufacture of maiolica at Turin. However, one fact is clear, that Savoy possessed at least one maiolica manufactory in 1564.

In the *Registre du Compte de la Trésorerie Générale* we read: " Item, two hundred scudi or crowns, of three lire each, paid to Maestro Orazio Fontana and to Maestro Antonio of Urbino, the price of certain earthenware vases brought to his Highness, as appears by his order, given at Nice the 6th January 1564."

" Item, the 15th August, paid to Antonio, potter, of Urbino, twenty crowns, of three lire each, to defray his expenses in accompanying the maiolica sent to his Highness in France."

" Item, 20th August 1564, two hundred crowns, of three lire each, paid to the very Reverend Signor Jerome della Rovere, Archbishop of Turin, on account of Maestro Orazio of Urbino, chief potter of his Highness, for two credences or cabinets of maiolica, which this master has delivered, as appears by a mandate given at Turin, the 23rd of April 1564."

Pungileoni mentions a certain Francesco Guagni who was in the Duke's service; he was a chemist, and endeavoured to discover the secret of porcelain at the Court of Savoy about 1577. The earliest specimen we have met with is the frutiera mentioned below. It was continued through the seventeenth and eighteenth centuries, although we have no particular information as to the names of the potters. In the eighteenth it was under royal patronage.

TURIN. On a fayence fruit dish with pierced sides of crossed bars, painted on the inside with a boy carrying two birds on a pole, marked underneath in blue; formerly in the Marchese d'Azeglio's Collection. (*Ker. Gall.*, enlarged edition, fig. 83.) In the Museo Civico, Turin.

TURIN. On a maiolica plateau, painted in blue on white, with horses, birds, and hares. Seventeenth century. Mark, a cross on a shield crowned, the arms of Turin. Formerly in the possession of the Marchese d'Azeglio; now in the Museo Civico, Turin.

Fabrica
Reale di
Torino
1737

TURIN. Maiolica of the eighteenth century; flowers painted in colours on white. This mark was on the back of the rim of a large dish in the Marchese d'Azeglio's Collection; in the centre at back is a monogram of F.R.T. for Fabrica Reale Torino; all the marks are in blue.

GRATAPAGLIA
FE:TAVR·

TURIN. On a large maiolica dish of the beginning of the eighteenth century, painted with Susanna and the Elders, formerly in the Marchese d'Azeglio's Collection; now in the Museo Civico, Turin.

VINEUF (Turin). There was a manufactory of fayence here, as well as porcelain, under the direction of M. D. Gioanetti, established about 1750.

TURIN. A mark of a shield, crowned, of the end of the seventeenth or commencement of the eighteenth century; quoted by M. Jacquemart.

TURIN. This shield, without a crown, is in blue on the back of a plate, painted with a cherub's head; of the same period.

TURIN (?). This mark is impressed on a pair of vases, 21½ in. high, of very light and resonant ware, with rich maroon-coloured glaze. The mark is a shield, with a large T and small B above, surmounted by a sort of mural crown. In the possession of Mr. Jackson of Hull. It is, however, doubtful whether the ware is Italian.

Laforest en
Savoye
1752.

LAFOREST, in Savoy. This mark is upon a finely painted specimen, quoted by M. Jacquemart, but nothing is known of the manufactory beyond this inscription and date.

Borgano.

On a service by Borgano about 1823. (Fortnum.)

Eredi Imoda.

Mark of Imoda.

Luigi Richard e C.

Mark of factory which made porcelain and fine earthenware in English fashion, 1846-63.

FERRARA.

From researches among the Ducal archives the Marquis Giuseppe Campori has discovered various allusions to the manufacture of pottery, reaching so far back as the end of the fifteenth century, which give us an insight into the history of the maiolica of Ferrara, its patrons and artists.

It seems that the art was imported into Ferrara by artists from Faenza. The first whose name is recorded is Fra Melchior, *Maestro di Lavori di Terra*, 1495. In 1501 payments were made to Maestro Biagio of Faenza (who had a shop in the Castel Nuovo), for various earthenware vessels and ornaments.

Alphonso I. became Duke of Ferrara in 1505, and being fond of chemistry, he had discovered the fine white enamel glaze *(bianco allattato)*, and in the following year Biagio is mentioned as being in his service. From this date until 1522 nothing further is recorded in the archives; but from another source we learn that in consequence of his war with Pope Julius II., being pressed for money, he deposited, for the purpose of raising the required sum, all the jewels of his wife Lucrezia Borgia, as well as his plate, and used earthenware vessels, *which were the products of his industry.*

In 1522 Antonio of Faenza was appointed potter, at twelve lire per month, with food and lodging, and he was succeeded by Catto of Faenza in 1525, who died in 1528. Some distinguished painters, to whom Ferrara owes its reputation, are vaguely mentioned in the archives. In 1524 twelve soldi were given to a painter named Camillo, for painting vases for the potter. The brothers Dossi (Battista and Dosso) were employed by Duke Alphonse to decorate his palace with pictures and frescoes, and they occasionally designed subjects for the potters. In 1528 two lire were given to Dosso Dossi for two days' work in tracing designs, and his brother Battista received one lire for models of handles for vases. To them may be attributed the *grotesche* or arabesques and Raffaelesque designs which were painted about this time, with the arms of Gonzaga and Este, for Francis II., Marquis of Mantua, who in 1490 married Isabella, daughter of Hercules I., Duke of Ferrara, the sister of Alphonso, probably made by the before-named Biagio of Faenza.

We have hitherto only spoken of the Fabrique called the Castel Nuovo, under the patronage of Alphonso I., but M. Campori adduces another, under the protection of Sigismond d'Este, brother of the Duke of Ferrara, where, installed in the Palace of Schifanoia, were the potter Biagio Biasini of Faenza from 1515 to 1524, and three painters, El Frate, Grosso, and Zaffarino.

M. Campori is of opinion that porcelain was invented by some person unknown to Ferrara in the time of Alphonso I., and quotes a letter addressed to the Duke by his ambassador at Venice, but it only refers to an imperfect, over-baked "écuelle de *porcelaine contrefaite*" presented to him, which, to our view, means only an imitation of real porcelain. From 1534 to 1559, during the reign of Hercules II., the son and successor of Alphonso, maiolica was little encouraged, and there is only one potter named in the archives, Petro Paolo Stanghi of Faenza. Alphonso II gave a fresh impulse to ceramics. The two names most frequently met with are those of Camillo of Urbino, and of Battista, his brother, both painters on maiolica. M. Campori gives cogent reasons that this Camillo was not a member of the Fontana family, as supposed by Pungileoni and others; he was accidentally killed in 1567 by the bursting of a cannon. In the person of Camillo we have another aspirant to the honour of being the inventor of porcelain. Bernardo Canigiani, ambassador of the Grand Duke of Florence, writing to his Court, says, "Camillo of Urbino, vase-maker and painter, and in some degree chemist to his Excellence, is the veritable inventor of porcelain." But this (like many similar assertions) only refers to experiments, and no pieces of this Ferrara porcelain are known, while those of Florence are found in many collections. When Alphonso II. married Margherita di Gonzaga, it is reasonable to suppose he would employ his own potters and artists to complete the maiolica marriage service for his household, specimens of which are well known, bearing on a shield his emblem, expressive of his devoted attachment—a burning heap of wood, and the motto *Ardet Æ* or *Eternum*. There are several pieces of this service in the Soulages Collection; others in the Louvre, &c.

Thomaz Masselli Ferrarien fec

FERRARA. On a large dish, painted with the Triumph of Bacchus, in lake colours, of the beginning of the eighteenth century. Montferrand Collection, now in the Victoria and Albert Museum. (*Ker. Gall.*, enlarged edition, fig. 84.)

GENOA AND SAVONA.

We have scanty information of the early manufacture of maiolica at Genoa. It is spoken of by Piccolpasso in 1548 as a great mart for this ware, as well as Venice. He gives us the prices charged and the principal

patterns, such as *foglie* or coloured leaves on white ground; *paesi*, landscapes; *rabesche*, arabesques, &c. Its early productions, like those of Venice, are confounded with others of the unsigned specimens, which are left solely to conjecture.

The marks formerly assigned to Genoa are now by general consent given to the Savona factories. The Savona ware is usually painted in a milky blue, and often with ornament in Chinese taste.

SAVONA. This mark in blue is underneath a fayence jug, painted with blue scrolls, leaves, and a bird, with double loop handles, of the beginning of the eighteenth century, mounted in silver. British Museum, from the Henderson Collection.

The mark reduced. Dr. Fortnum (Catalogue South Kensington Museum) says this mark is intended for a trumpet with the banner of Savoy, and is Savonese, not Genoese. See also p. 146, the trumpet mark.

SAVONA. This is on a bottle, painted in blue, with birds and ornaments; formerly in Mr. C. W. Reynolds' Collection. This mark is usually very large, and is probably that of Levantino. A similar beacon is still to be seen in the harbour of Genoa. (*Ker. Gall.*, enlarged edition, fig. 85.)

SAVONA. Maiolica of the middle of the eighteenth century. This mark, of a beacon, is on a vase from the Bernal Collection. It was placed by Brongniart as a mark of the Savona manufactory, but some have thought it more properly belongs to that of Genoa.

SAVONA. These marks, of a crown, with signs and initials of the painters beneath, are on coarse fayence dishes, with lake designs, purchased at Genoa; formerly in the Collection of the Marchese d'Azeglio. Other pieces of the same service were in the possession of Dr. Diamond, marked with the beacon.

SAVONA. This mark of a fish, here greatly reduced in size, is on a bottle, painted in blue *camaieu* with branches and animals, in the possession of M. Demmin. Probably the mark of Pescetto.

Probably SAVONA. On an Italian maiolica dish of the eighteenth century, with border moulded in relief, scrolls, &c., painted in blue *camaieu* with small birds, animals, &c.; in the centre, a man on horseback. The mark is much reduced.

ALBISSOLA. The manufacture of maiolica or fayence was carried on at Albissola, a village situate on the sea, near the town of Savona. This place has always possessed fabriques of fayence, the "faïence de Savone" being well known throughout Italy and France in the seventeenth century. It was a native of Albissola, Domenique Conrade, who introduced the art into Nevers.

In the parish church of Albissola there is a picture, two mètres high, formed of plaques of fayence joined together, representing in polychrome the Nativity; it is inscribed "*Fatto in Arbissola* (sic) *del* 1576 *per mano di Agostino . . . Gerolamo Urbinato lo dipinse*." The surname of the potter is obliterated and the words *Morto impenitente* substituted by the intolerance of the clergy. The painter's name is Girolamo of Urbino.

Mark of S. Rubatto of Sàvona. (Fortnum.)

A mark of Bartolomeo Guidobono. (Vignola.)

SAVONA. The Rev. Thomas Staniforth, of Storrs, Windermere, had two specimens with the letters G. A. G. and G. S., as in the margin,— perhaps the name of the artist, Gian. Antonio Guidobono, of Castel Nuovo, a maiolica painter at Savona in the beginning of the seventeenth century. His sons, Bartolomeo and Domenico, succeeded him.

SAVONA. The principal mark seems to be a shield of arms of the town. The first is from Brongniart; the second on a vase in the late Mr. Uzielli's Collection.

S.A.G.S.

SAVONA. These letters are on a cartouche, in the centre of a perforated dish, coarsely painted with scrolls in blue, yellow, and brown, by Guidobono. Seventeenth century. In the Victoria and Albert Museum. (*Ker. Gall.*, enlarged edition, fig. 86.) There was another important manufactory coeval with these, that of Gian Tomaso Torteroli, but we are not acquainted with his mark.

B C

SAVONA. On a dish with blue figures on a white ground.

AGOSTINO RATTI
SAVONA. 1720.

SAVONA. This name occurs on some maiolica of the eighteenth century, in the Chamber of Arts, Berlin.

B♦C
1743

SAVONA. This mark in blue is on the bottom of a fayence bottle.

SAVONA. This mark has the initials of Giro-lamo Salomone, a celebrated artist, who flourished in 1650.

SAVONA. This mark, a pentagram, is attri-buted to Salomone or Siccardi of Savona.

SAVONA. On a dish in M. Edouard Pascal's Collection, Paris.

SAVONA. On a fayence dish painted with sculpture and children, surrounded by arabesques. Montferrand Collection, No. 232.

SAVONA. This shield is on the back of a plate, painted with a hare leaping, formerly in Mr. Willet's Collection.

SAVONA. A mark given by M. A. Jacquemart, pro-bably that of Girolamo Salomone, with the sun placed above his initials; occasionally the sun alone is found as in the mark of the factory. See below.

SAVONA. Another mark, which is also attributed to Girolamo Salomone, with the sun in its splendour above a S.

SAVONA. This mark is given by Jacquemart as an uncertain mark of Naples, but it is believed on good authority, from the quality and decoration, to belong to Savona; it is called there the "Falcon mark," and is attributed by Dr. Fortnum to "Falco" of Savona.

SAVONA. This is called the "Tower mark," and may safely be attributed to Savona, the ware on which it occurs being evidently Savonese. On a saucer painted with figures.

SAVONA. The "Anchor mark" occurs on a plate painted in brown, with a cottage and small Callot sort of figures.

SAVONA. On a blue and white circular dish of Italian maiolica, with a raised pattern of shells on the border; three figures in the centre, of warriors, round these are six small compartments, with landscapes, figures, and animals; diameter 21½ in. The mark in blue much reduced. Rev. J. Sadler Gale, Bristol.

SAVONA. On a large plate, painted in blue, with a faun, woman, and cupids; in the possession of Dr. Belliol of Paris.

MBorrelli Inuent
Pinx: A:S 1735.

SAVONA. The name occurs on a cylindrical maiolica jar, painted on one side with a naval engagement, one of the ships on fire, and numerous boats and figures, yellow and blue colours predominating; signed at the right-hand corner. The name is repeated in large letters at the back: "Primum Opus M. Borrelli Mense Julij 1735." Formerly in the possession of the Marchese d'Azeglio.

N. G.

SAVONA. The initials N. G. surmounted by a coronet. On a dish in M. Edouard Pascal's Collection, Paris.

Jacques Borelly, Savonne,
1779, 24 Septembre.

SAVONA. Jacques Borrelly, of Marseilles, appears to have emigrated to Savona; other specimens are signed with his name Italianised, as *Giacomo Borelly.* This inscription is on a large vase decorated in green *camaieu.*

SAVONA. This mark, in black, with the *s* well formed, leads us to infer that the name was Boselli and not Borelli. It is on a *seau* painted with arms, and Baron Davillier had some other pieces with the name so spelt, as well as a plateau or Marseille fayence signed Boselli.

SAVONA. This mark, in blue, is on a fayence jug, mounted with silver, painted with blue *camaieu* birds and scrolls, similar to the preceding. It appears in this instance to represent a trumpet with a short flag, not a beacon, and having a cross upon it. Dr. Diamond, the former owner of the piece, referred it rather to Savona than Genoa, and Dr. Fortnum classes it as Chiodo. See also p. 142.

ESTE, a town between Padua and Ferrara. Little is known of the fayence manufactories of Este and Modena, and their productions are

ESTE.
G.

rare. This mark is impressed on a fayence boat-shaped ewer and basin, shell pattern, with rococo scrolls and ornaments in relief, of cream-coloured ware, circa 1770, formerly in Lady C. Schreiber's Collection.

ROME.

There is no authentic account of maiolica being made at Rome until the year 1600, of which year we find the two pharmacy vases described below; there are, however, re-cords of potters previous to this date. The style is of the Urbino grotesque decoration of the Fontana fabrique. These are in the Ashmolean Museum, Oxford (Fortnum Coll.), and Delange speaks of others with similar marks, which are probably the same, although there is a slight difference in the inscriptions on his "deux grands plats." There was a fabrique of white glazed earthenware established by a famous engraver, Giovanni Volpato, from Venice, in 1790, and a large sum of money was expended, there being at one time no less than twenty experienced artists employed in modelling the ware. They could not, however, compete with other wares made in England and France. He died in 1803, and the fabrique was carried on for a short time by his son Giuseppe; at his death, a few years after, his widow married Francesco Tinucci, the chief modeller, who conducted the business until 1818; it was discontinued in 1831. The early pieces bear the name of

G. VOLPATO ROMA, impressed in the clay. The first two marks are on the front of a pair of vases, with snake handles, painted with grotesques on a white ground, in the Ashmolean Museum, Oxford (Fortnum Coll.).

The third mark is on a large circular dish in the possession of Mrs. Lockwood, long resident in Rome; the central medallion subject is the Temptation of Adam by Eve, and is surrounded by a border of grotesques in the Urbino style on white ground.

LORETO.

In the Santa Casa at Loreto are still preserved upwards of 300 maiolica vases, mostly with covers, painted with designs from Raffaelle, Giulio, Romano, Michael Angelo, and others. They were made by order of Guidobaldo, Duke of Urbino: they represent scenes from the Old and New Testaments, Roman History, the Metamorphoses of Ovid, &c. They are not, as commonly said, by Raphael, but by Raffaelle Ciarla, a clever copyist on fayence of the works of the great masters. (*Valery*, vol. ii.) All these, which are arranged in two large rooms, came from the "Spezieria," or Medical Dispensary, attached to the Palace at Urbino.

The last Duke of Urbino, Francesco Maria II., in his dotage, had abdicated his duchy in favour of the Holy See, and dying in 1631, his heir, Ferdinand de' Medicis, removed the more ornamental pieces of maiolica to Florence. The vases from the Spezieria he presented to the shrine of Our Lady of Loreto, called the Santa Casa. This splendid collection of maiolica did not consist alone of vases for containing drugs, and it became the envy of more than one crowned head; the Grand Duke of Florence proposed to give in exchange for them silver vases of equal weight; Queen Christina was heard to say, that of all the treasures of Santa Casa, she esteemed them the most; and Louis XIV. is said to have offered for the four Evangelists and the Apostle Paul the same number of statuettes in solid gold.

CON·POL·DI·S·CASA. LORETO. "Con polvere di Santa Casa." (With the dust of the holy house.) This inscription is found upon small maiolica cups or bowls, beneath a representation of the Lady of Loreto and Infant Saviour, with a view of the sanctuary. These cups were made of clay, mixed with the dust shaken from the dress of the Virgin and walls of the sanctuary, and in this form preserved by the faithful. (*Ker. Gall.*, enlarged edition, fig. 88.) Occasionally some of the holy water from the shrine was sprinkled on the dust, thereby to impart a still greater sanctity. A cup in the Ashmolean Museum, Oxford, (Fortnum Coll.), is inscribed "Con pol et aqua di S. Casa" (With dust and water of the holy house). Sig. Raffaelle thinks they were made at Castel Durante for the establishment at Loreto. The seal of the convent was placed underneath in red wax.[1]

---

[1] Sometimes these cups are painted only with the Virgin and Child and the Santa Casa, the inscription being omitted, but they are soon recognised by their peculiar type.

The labour of conveying the stones of which the Santa Casa was built to Loreto and its construction was believed to have been due to supernatural aid, and that angels, not mortals, were the masons engaged in the work. Pilgrims flocked from distant parts to visit the shrine of our Lady of Loreto, and to that reverence for it was due the presentation of the vases of the Spezieria.

Sgraffiati or Incised Ware.

CITTA DI CASTELLO, PAVIA, LA FRATTA, &c.

This method of decorating earthenware appears to have been adopted in Italy as early as the twelfth and thirteenth centuries, examples of a coarse description having been found among plates intended for mural decoration in towers of churches in Pisa and other Italian cities of that period. The process consisted in covering the "biscuit" with a slip or *engobe* of white marl or clay mixed with water of the consistency of cream, and when dry this covering, after a slight baking, was scratched through with a sharp tool so as to display the design in the red ground underneath the slip. It was then covered with translucent lead glaze and tinted with green or yellow by the application of metallic oxides and re-fired. The *sgraffiati* of Citta di Castello are generally enamelled in yellow, green, and brown. There are three specimens in the Musée de Cluny. In the Louvre is a large cup ornamented in relief, on a triangular foot formed by three lions and two figures, graved at the bottom. In the Victoria and Albert Museum is a plateau of brown glazed earthenware, with a shield of arms in relief in the centre, encircled with scroll foliage; of the seventeenth century. A plateau in the British Museum, of incised pattern, with figures in costume of the end of the fifteenth century; a man holding a shield and a woman playing on a viol, near her a shield with armorial bearings; from the Bernal Collection; £48 2s. A plateau in the Victoria and Albert Museum, incised pattern of an amorino with griffins, within a rich arabesque border; on the reverse a stag; from the Bernal Collection; £40. Another plateau in the Victoria and Albert Museum has an incised group of a lady and two cavaliers in costume of the fifteenth century, and festoons of leaves; £40 10s. A large bowl, also in the Victoria and Albert Museum, of this *sgraffiato* ware, is supported by three seated lions, and an inkstand, in Earl Spencer's Collection, is supported by three winged lions. A *sgraffiato* ware plate, with arabesques, and in the centre an escutcheon of arms of the city of Perugia, circa 1530, is in the Victoria and Albert Museum. See *Ker. Gall.*, enlarged edition, figs. 89, 90, and 91.

Sgraffiati or *sgraffiato* wares were not confined to Italy, although it reached a high state of perfection in that country, but was a method of ornamenting pottery in France and England, and there is a fine specimen of French work of this kind in the Sèvres Museum, attributed to the fourteenth century. After the brown glazed ware had been introduced into England the *sgraffiato* method as described above came as a variation, and there are several specimens extant in our museums and private collections. In "Examples of Early English Pottery, Named and Dated," by J. E. Hodgkin, F.S.A., and Edith Hodgkin, several of these are described and illustrated. The earliest date mentioned is 1670, on a brown ware jug with an inscription; it is in the Norwich Museum. Another very curious specimen is a plate in the possession of Dr. Hugh Morris, with a rude device commemorating the birth of a double female child with the date (1680) across the middle of their bodies. Other specimens bear the following dates: 1692, 1697, 1703, 1705, 1708, 1711, 1726, 1730, 1736, 1740, 1752, 1755, 1764, 1766, 1770, 1779, 1781, 1791, and all bear names, mottoes, or legends inscribed.

CITTA DI CASTELLO. A plateau on a low foot of *sgraffiato* ware of quadrate interlaced ornament and mouldings, in cream colour on buff ground: in the centre a horse's head in purple colour; reverse plain with P. G. incised in the clay; about 1520. This is the only instance we know of a mark occurring on an early piece of this ware; the incision is in places filled in with the *engobe*, showing it is contemporary with the manufacture. In the Victoria and Albert Museum.

PRESBYTER ANTONIUS
MARIA CUTIUS PAPIENSIS
PROTHONOTARIUS
APOSTOLICVS FECIT
ANNO DOMINICÆ 1695.
PAPIÆ 1695.

PAVIA. This inscription is found on a peculiar sort of earthenware, of a brown glaze, decorated on both sides with leaves, scrolls, &c., slightly raised, on a hatched ground; the letters are incuse Roman capitals; in addition, these pieces have usually mottoes and emblems. One which was in the author's possession had a pear in the centre, and the motto "Fractos reficiens, non reficiar fractus"; this was dated 1693. One in the Victoria and Albert Museum, with the portrait of an ecclesiastic, has the motto "Timete Dominum" and "Libera me, Domine, ab homine malo et a lingua injusta." Another, in the Dellesette Collection, had "Solamente e Ingannato chi troppo si Fida, 1695." Another, in the Victoria and Albert Museum, has in the centre the portrait of an ecclesiastic, surrounded by a similar inscription, but dated 1694. These are probably the work of an amateur, Presbyter Antonius Maria Cutius of Pavia, who appears to have executed numerous examples. All the large pieces have inscriptions, which include his name.

PAVIA. Herr Jännike gives the following marks as those of the Pavia fabrique, but it is very unusual to find specimens marked.   These are marks of artists rather than those of any particular fabrique.

An inferior description of ware is still made at La Fratta: a modern basket-shaped pot, with bucket handle, in red glazed earthenware, recently made, is in the Victoria and Albert Museum.

UNCERTAIN MARKS.

M. le Marquis d'Azeglio possessed a fine covered vase with handles and foot, the subjects painted on it being historically interesting.   On a medallion in front is a Pope censing the Holy Virgin; above and below are written the following legends: "CLEMENS XI. VIRG. SINE LABE CON-CEPTÆ FESTUM CELEBRANDUM EDICIT."   "NEC SOLIS INSTAR SOLA REGNAT ILLUSTRATQUE"; on the reverse a man is pouring oil upon a flaming altar, and this inscription, "CLEMENS XI. PONTIFEX CREATUR—OLEM SUPER LAPIDEM RECTUM."   This piece is therefore commemorative of the fête of the Immaculate Conception founded by Pope Clement Albano, 1709-21.

ITALY.   This name is impressed on a fayence plate of the end of the eighteenth century, printed with a flying figure, inscribed beneath "Ganimede."

CARLO ALDROVANDI.

ITALY.   On the front of a plate; subject, St. Peter upon the water, and four Apostles in a boat.   Campana Collection, Louvre.

ITALY.   On a plate painted with a shield of arms, blue outlines and yellow metallic lustre. M. A. Darcel classes it with the Italo-Moresques. Louvre.

ITALY or SPAIN. This curious mark is on the back of a metallic lustre dish, 12½ in. diameter, border of scales and flowers in blue and yellow; I.H.S. in the centre.

ITALY. This mark of an uncertain manufactory of the middle of the sixteenth century, is given by M. A. Jacquemart; it occurs on the back of a portable spice-box of rectangular form with a handle at the back on each side of the handle is this ducal coronet, traversed by two palm branches and one of laurel, probably belonging to the Grand-Duke of Tuscany, Cosmo de' Medici, created 1569; it is decorated simply in pale blue and yellow The piece is made for two burettes, OLIO and ACETO, with four receptacles for ZUCHER, SALES, PEPE, and SPEZIO—*oil, vinegar, sugar, salt, pepper*, and *spices.*

ITALY. This uncertain mark is on the reverse of a plate formerly in Mr. Falcke's Collection.

ITALY. On a fine maiolica plate of Urbino character; subject, Alexander at the tomb of Achilles. Melton Collection.

ITALY. On a maiolica bowl, painted with arabesques of the seventeenth century, in the Sèvres Museum.

ITALY. This large asterisk or star is frequently met with on maiolica plates of the sixteenth century. Perhaps Faenza.

ITALY. On a small sunk-centre plate; painted with arms, and boys playing upon the bagpipes, vases, fruit, &c., on deep blue. Victoria and Albert Museum.

Uncertain. Fortnum Catalogue of the South Kensington Museum, Maiolica, p. 649.

Uncertain. Given by Dr. Fortnum, Catalogue, p. 652, without description or reference.

Fabrica di Bonpencier

Uncertain. Given by Dr. Fortnum, Catalogue, p. 651, without any description or reference, dated 1540, with initials, probably those of the potter.

1540

TÆ

Uncertain. Given by Dr. Fortnum, Catalogue, p. 651, without description or reference.

Ꝑ·P·1754

Uncertain These marks are found on an Italian maiolica plateau, dated 1547, with the potter's initials; the word refers to the subject painted upon it. From Fortnum's Catalogue of the Victoria and Albert Museum, p. 651; without description or reference. .

1547

E S I O N E

T Z

These initials and monogram of an unknown locality are on a plateau, apparently of the commencement of the seventeenth century, of Italian manufacture and decoration.

RĒ

·M·B·B

These initials are on a large plate in the British Museum, painted in dull blue *camaieu* with the decollation of St. John. It may perhaps be attributed to Urbino, a work of the later period.

·G·L·P·

I 6 6 7

A cup on a foot with fruit in relief.

B. S. 1780

Covered vases with ovolos in relief and twisted handles, · polychrome decoration with rococo medallions and garlands of flowers.

F.F.

Dishes and plates. Milan style, chrysanthemum pattern. Services of the same origin, famille rose style.

F. 5 F

Plate of fine fayence decoration in blue, yellow, and pale green.

G

A vase and cover, having floreated stalks in relief in natural colours.

Large gourds, citron, yellow ground, with floreated branches in relief in natural colours.

L 🦁 P

Pieces with reliefs, polychrome decoration, in which a brilliant green and red prevail. The colours and style indicate an Italian fabrique.

A·D·P· AC.

On a fountain decorated on the interior with bouquets, Moustiers style, and fishes swimming at the bottom; outside arabesque in polychrome.

P. G.
1638

Vases for drugs, blue ground with arabesques and brown trophies, medallions of arms.

P.R-NP
3

A service of fine fayence, decorated in violet *camaieu* with bouquets, birds and insects.

VH ƒ ſ-3-

A cabaret of rocaille form with reliefs; decoration of bouquets of tulips in blue heightened with gold.

W.
DA

Cache-pots with mask handles, decorated in blue with ornaments and bouquets.

SPAIN.

The Moorish occupation of Spain, however deplorable from the racial and religious standpoint, was not without its artistic advantages. For the Arabs, if not in themselves industrially fertile, have a vast appreciation of the fine arts, and did more to disseminate the knowledge of them than any race in mediæval times. To realise the truth of this, it is only necessary to compare the beautiful Hispano-Moresco pottery, with its intricate ornament in pale blue and golden lustre on a background of creamy white tin-enamel, with the tiles found at Veramin in Persia. The technique of the work is in both cases the same, and the actual ornament is essentially akin, and it is patent at once that the art, and in all probability the artificers themselves, had emanated from the same Eastern school.

It was Señor J. F. Riaño (*Industrial Arts of Spain*, South Kensington Museum Handbook, 1879) who noted the first mention of this Spanish-Moorish ware in contemporary writings. He quotes the Arab geographer Edrisi, who visited Calatayud, in Aragon, about 1154 A.D., and wrote, "Here the gold-coloured pottery is made which is exported to all countries." This clearly refers to a lustred pottery, though the earliest specimens in our possession were not made till the following century, viz., the Alhambra tiles, an example of which, decorated in golden lustre and blue on a tin-enamelled ground, is in the British Museum.[1]   The art spread widely in the south and east of Spain, and Malaga and Manises were celebrated centres of the industry in the fourteenth century.   Witness the words of Ibn Batutah quoted on page 156, and of Eximinez, who says, "But above all is the beauty of the gold pottery so splendidly painted at Manises."   The researches of Señor Don G. J. de Osma[2] among the archives of Valencia have recently thrown further light on the early history of the ware, and among other things he has established the fact that Eximinez wrote as early as 1383, not a century later, as was previously supposed.

The importance of Malaga as a centre of the art is further indicated by the use of the expression *obra de Malaga*, as a general term for lustred ware.   To quote one instance from Señor de Osma's notes.   In 1434 an account is mentioned of a certain "Çaat Naxen Moro de Mislata" for a quantity "de obra de Maleca daurata."   Mislata lies between Manises and Alacuas : the Moorish name of the potter is another point of interest.   The Hispano-Moresco style continued in use long after the expulsion of the Moors from Spain; indeed it has never been entirely abandoned, and at the present day good imitations of the old wares are made.   But there are marked differences between the earlier and later examples.   In the early wares the lustre is pale and filmy, and the accompanying light blue colour holds a predominating place in the decorative scheme.   As time went on the blue gradually gave place to the lustre, until the former almost disappeared in the sixteenth century.   The lustre, too, became more brassy and metallic in appearance, and lost much of its charm.   In the seventeenth century the art was in full decadence, and such examples as survive are coarse, and as a rule displeasing.   Needless to say, the designs have a conspicuous Moorish flavour even when they enshrine Spanish coats of arms and Spanish inscriptions.

Further information on the subject in general will be found in *Histoire des Faïence Hispano-Moresques à Reflets Métalliques*, Paris, 1861, by Baron J. C. Davillier; *Maiolica*, by Dr. C. D. E. Fortnum, 1896; *Hispano-Moresque Ware of the Fifteenth Century*, by A. Van de Put, 1904; and *Manuel d'Art Musulman*, by Gaston Migeon, Paris, 1907.

HISPANO-MORESCO. A very fine vase in the Henderson Collection (British Museum) bears this mark of a cross within a circle. In the quarters are the abbreviations which may be thus interpreted, "Illustrissimo Signore Cardinal D'Este. In urbe Romano," being part of a service painted for the Cardinal.

---

[1] See also *Keramic Gallery*, enlarged edition, fig 93.

[2] *Apuntes sobre ceramica morisca* por G. J. de Osma, Madrid, 1908.

HISPANO-MORESCO. These marks are on the backs of two small plates with sunk centres, painted in the centre with shields of arms, bearing a crowned eagle with open wings of blue, the rest of the surface diapered with leaves and interlaced tendrils of golden lustre. In the Fortnum Collection, Oxford.

HISPANO-MORESCO plate in the Campana Collection at the Louvre. Fifteenth century.

HISPANO-MORESCO. This mark is on the back of a small plate of metallic lustre with a sunk centre on which is the Sacred monogram, surrounded by floral ornaments in blue and lustred colours. In Mr. George Salting's Collection in the Victoria and Albert Museum.

HISPANO-MORESCO dish, covered with reddish gold lustre arabesques, circa 1480. In the centre is the annexed curious mark. Formerly in the possession of Lord Amherst of Hackney.

HISPANO-MORESCO (MALAGA). One of the finest examples of Hispano-Moresco lustred ware is the beautiful two-handled vase, about 22 inches high, which our Government bought from the Soulages Collection, and which is now in the Pottery Gallery in the Victoria and Albert Museum; it is labelled as the production of Malaga, and there is a woodcut of it in Litchfield's *Pottery and Porcelain*. (See *Ker. Gall.*, enlarged edition, fig. 92.)

A vase almost precisely similar, but having the additional attraction of the arms of the Medici family, was in the Magniac Collection, which was sold at Christie's in 1892. Messrs. Durlacher Brothers gave £703 10s. for this magnificent specimen, and it is now in the Collection of Mr. Du Cane Godman, F.R.S. The other collections of Hispano-Moresco pottery which were among the best known some years ago, those of M. Gavet and M. Pujol of Paris and M. Coloumbel of Asnières, have also been purchased by Messrs. Durlacher, and the finest pieces are now in the hands of English amateurs.

MALAGA. In the account of the travels of Ibn Batutah, who visited Granada about 1350 (translated by Defremery, Paris, 1858), we read, "On fabrique à Malaga la belle poterie ou porcelaine dorée que l'on exporte dans les contrées les plus éloignées." This traveller speaks of Granada itself, but says nothing of any manufacture of pottery there, and we may therefore take it for granted that Malaga was the grand centre of the fabrication in the kingdom of Granada. It is therefore probable that the celebrated and well-known vase of the Alhambra, the finest specimen of Moorish fayence known, as well as the most ancient, was made here.

The history of this vase is worthy of note. We learn from the *Promenades dans Grenada*, by Dr. Echeverria, that three vases full of treasure were discovered in a garden at Adarves, which was put in order and tastefully laid out by the Marquis de Mondejar in the sixteenth century with the gold contained in the vases, and to perpetuate the remembrance of this treasure-trove they were arranged in the garden; but the vases, being exposed to public view unprotected, sustained considerable injury by being rubbed and handled, and eventually one got broken, and every traveller who visited the garden took a piece as a souvenir, until all of it was gone. In 1785 two were yet preserved intact, but about the year 1820 another disappeared altogether, and of the three only one is now extant; it measures 4 ft. 7 in. in height, and was seen by the editor in 1889, at the famous Alhambra Palace at Granada. The colours of the decoration are a pure blue, surrounded or heightened with a gold lustre on white ground.

VALENCIA. Saguntum (now Murviedro), near Valencia, was noted in the time of the Romans for its manufacture of jasper red pottery, and is described by Pliny.

Lucio Marineo Siculo in 1517 (*Memorable Things of Spain*) says: "In Spain, earthenware vessels are made of various forms, and although they are excellent in many parts of Spain, the most appreciated are those of Valencia, which are very well worked and well gilt, and at Murcia much excellent pottery is made of the same kind, and at Morviedro and Toledo much is made, which is very thick, with white, green, and yellow, with gilding, and is employed for daily use; the kind most esteemed is glazed with white."

The Senate of Venice issued a decree in 1455 that no earthenware works of any kind should be introduced into the dominions of the Seigniory, either within or without the Gulf of the Adriatic; but an exception was especially made in favour of the crucibles *(correzoli)* and the *maiolica of Valencia*, which it was declared might be freely introduced. (*Drake's Notes on Venetian Ceramics.*) There is a large bowl and cover in the South Kensington Museum, painted with scroll diaper in gold lustre and blue, the cover surmounted by a cupola-shaped ornament in gold lustre, probably of Valencia manufacture; cost £80.

Valencia has from time immemorial been celebrated for its *azulejos* or enamelled tiles. There are many houses of the fifteenth and sixteenth centuries still existing in the ancient cities of Spain, the rooms being lined up to about 5 or 6 feet with tiles in borders and patterns of elegant geometrical designs and scrolls; the celebrity of this manufacture is maintained even to the present day. In the Chapter House of the Cathedral at Saragossa is an elegant example of flooring, the tiles averaging about 8 inches square, decorated with scrolls and medallions of landscapes and flowers: it is inscribed "Real[a] Fabricas de D[a] Maria Salvadora Disdier, Brit f[t] Año 1808." In 1788 Gournay mentions three fabriques of tiles at Valencia: Disdier, Cola, and Casanova. In the Sèvres Museum is a still later example, with landscapes and figures, with this inscription: "De la Real Fabrica de Azulejos de Valencia Año 1836." Fayence of every description was extensively made in the seventeenth and eighteenth centuries. (*Ker. Gall.*, enlarged edition, figs. 96 and 97.)

MANISES. Señor de Osma quotes an agreement dated 1404 naming two brothers, Mahomet Alcudo and Sahat Alcudo, Saracens, "Magistri operis terræ, habitantes en Manises." And many years later an English traveller named Talbot Dillon (*Travels through Spain*, London, 1780) says: "About two leagues from Valencia is a pretty village called Manises, composed of four streets. The inhabitants are mostly potters, making a fine fayence of copper colour, ornamented with gilding. The people of the country employ it both for ornament and domestic use."

MANISES. On a Spanish maiolica dish, ornamented with rich copper lustre approaching to **ruby, in** Oriental patterns on drab ground. In the centre **a hand and date**, here much reduced in size; on the back **Mº in large lustre** letters and annulets round. Formerly in Mr. Reynolds' Collection. The same mark, Mº on the back, and 1611 in front, is on a similar plate.

The lustred ware made here was held in great request by the Pope, cardinals, and princes. It has continued, although in a state of dilapidation and decay, until the present day, and is characterised in the latter times by the copper red tones of the lustres. (*Ker. Gall.*, enlarged edition, fig. 99.)

TALAVERA LA REYNA, near Toledo, was celebrated for fayence in the seventeenth and eighteenth centuries; in fact, the word *Talavera* was used to express all fayence, in the same manner as *fayence* in France and *delft* in England. (See *Ker. Gall.*, enlarged edition, fig. 104.)

Baretti, writing in 1760, says: "Talavera is a populous place and of much business; besides the silk there are several other manufactories; one in particular of earthenware is much esteemed throughout the country, and gives employment to some hundreds of people."

The fabrication of fayence at Talavera prospered down to the end of the last century; it is now fallen completely into decay, and only produces common earthenware. M. Charles Casati has written a *Note sur les Faïences de Talavera la Reyna*, but which adds little to our previous scanty knowledge; he states that he has met with a description of fayence in the vicinity of a different character to any other, the distinctive character being the light green tinge of the glaze; the designs are in bold outline, slightly coloured, bearing a certain analogy with the wares of Genoa and Savona, but less artistic. He also speaks of a ware similar to Delft which was produced here.

Talavera was one of the most important manufactories of pottery in Spain. In a MS. history of this place, dated 1560, quoted by M. Riaño, mention is made of "white, green, blue, and other coloured Talavera ware." In a report drawn up by order of Philip II. in 1576 it is stated that Talavera produced fine white glazed earthenware, tiles, and other pottery, which supplied the country, part of Portugal and India. In another MS. history of the year 1648 there are numerous details of the Talavera pottery, which "is as good as that of Pisa, and that a large number of *azulejos* were also made to adorn the fronts of altars, churches, gardens, alcoves, saloons, and bowers, and large and small specimens of all sorts. Two hundred workmen worked at eight different kilns; four other kilns were kept to make common earthenware. Red porous clay vases and drinking-cups were baked in two other kilns in a thousand different shapes, in imitation of birds and animals, and *brinquiños* for the use of ladies, so deliciously flavoured, that after drinking the water they contained, they eat the cup in which it was brought them." Madame D'Aulnois in her *Voyage d'Espagne* mentions the custom of ladies eating this fine porous clay. In another MS. history written about the same time it is said they made there "perfect imitations of Oriental china, and that this pottery was used all over Spain, and sent to India, France, Italy, Flanders, and other countries, and was esteemed everywhere for the perfection of the colouring and brilliancy of the glaze."

A specimen of the Talavera fayence of the later half of the eighteenth century is in the Sèvres Museum. It is a plate well-painted, with four subjects emblematical of the four divisions of the day; inscribed MANE. MERIDIES. VESPERA. NOX.; and in the centre "Soi de Juana Zamore A. 1786."

TOLEDO. In a MS. of 1648 the red earthen pottery (*bucaros*) of Toledo is spoken of. In Larruga's *Memorias Economicas*, written in 1787, he says that the manufacture of pottery continued in a brilliant state until 1720; that in 1731 they obtained certain privileges and regained the importance they had partially lost, but at the end of the century the pottery made there was very inferior. M. Riaño quotes a letter dated 1422 from Saragossa by Donna Juana de Aragon to the Abbess of St. Domingo el Real de Toledo, in which she gives orders for "yellow, black, white, and green tiles, which were made at Toledo," and mention is made also of painted tiles made there. Marinco Siculo in his *Memorable Things of Spain* devotes a chapter to the pottery of Toledo made there in the sixteenth century. In the Victoria and Albert Museum is the brim of a well of Toledo pottery, with a bold Cufic inscription in green on white ground, one of the most ancient specimens existing of this ware.

ALCOY, in Valencia, fabricated great quantities of fayence. Laborde says the ware was transported into Catalonia, Aragon, Murcia, and Castile; he adds, the inhabitants of Madrid purchase large quantities, probably for domestic purposes. We do not know its characteristics.

ONDA, in Valenvia, produced fayence for local use.

SEVILLE, in Andalusia, is cited by Laborde as possessing an important manufactory of fayence and long established. M. Jacquemart says he has met with ware which bears a great analogy with that of Savona, the predominating colours being orange and brown, in figures of good style, ruins and garlands of flowers. The mark of a S surmounting a star of five points, which has been attributed to Salomone of Savona, or one very similar, he thinks belongs to Seville. Some pieces of this character, in the possession of M. Arosa, are painted with figures dancing the fandango, some bulls being led to the arena, and with the arms of the Cathedral of Seville and a view of the Tour de l'Or.

SEVILLE. The Cartuja manufactory, M. Francesco de Aponte and Pickman & Co. Of recent manufacture, with a view of the Tour de l'Or and a lion, enclosed within a garter. On a specimen in the Harper Crewe Collection.

SEVILLE. Two marks of Pickman & Co. On separate pieces, made early in the last century. In the Harper Crewe Collection.

SEVILLE. There is a considerable manufacture at the present time at Seville, where they make *azulejos* or tiles of geometrical designs, the patterns being in slight relief, in exact reproduction of the original wall decorations at the Alhambra in Granada and the Alcazar in Seville. They also make decorative pottery of quaint forms but coarse quality. The Bull figures conspicuously as part of the decorations, and the colours are yellow, and green, and blue, in artistic combination. The pottery bears no *fabrique* mark, but some pieces have the word "Sevilla" and a date. Specimens purchased by the editor at Seville in 1889 are now in General Pitt-Rivers' museum at Rusholme, Dorset.

This mark at the bottom of a cup painted with Spanish arms; on the inside of the saucer, date 1728. In the Harper Crewe Collection.

ALCORA. There were some important pieces of fayence made at the Comte d'Aranda's manufactory (principally, perhaps, for presents) in the eighteenth century. Mr. Reynolds, the well-known collector, obtained from a palace in Spain twenty-four fayence plaques, with frames of rococo scrolls and masks in relief, the medallions and frames in one piece, some of large size. These were dispersed some years ago when the collection was sold. The paintings are very much in the style of Castelli ware, of mythological subjects, the Seasons, and Spanish costumes; one is inscribed, "Arquebuceros de Grassin. Infanteria." Another has on the back the word PERIS, probably the name of a painter. (*Ker. Gall.*, enlarged edition, fig. 102.)

ALCORA. "Fabrica de Aranda." This mark is on a lofty fayence fountain and cover, white glaze with a circular medallion on each side of ruins, painted in colours, and delicate scroll borders, the top in form of an animal's head.

This mark is on a pair of earthenware plaques with embossed frames of the time of Louis XV., painted in blue, with cupids after Boucher. Formerly in the Baron C. Davillier's Collection.

FABRICA REAL DEALCORA ANO 1735.

ALCORA. A Spanish fayence cup, painted with forget-me-nots, inscribed "DOMINICO SOY DE EL Pᴱ. Tᴿ. MARIANO RAIS," may be referred to this place.

A

In black, under a jug of Alcora fayence with a portrait, about 1750, and the inscription on a *banderolle,* "Soy de la Yllᵉ (ilustre) Sʳᵃ Dᵃ Fer-

A Z

nanda Condesa de Croix j'appartiens à l'illustre Sénora Dona Fernanda, Countesse de Croix." Formerly in Baron C. Davillier's Collection.

A very fine fayence cup, representing the family of Darius before Alexander, after Le Brun, is thus marked underneath. This painter's name

ALCORA ESPAÑA
Soliva.

is also found on Moustiers ware. Formerly in the possession of M. le Baron C. Davillier. (See notice on Alcora Porcelain.)

Herr Jännike gives the following marks of painters on Alcora fayence :

MOX *Mark of José de Zaragoza*	Soliua	Miguel	Vilarca
	Fᵒ	Grangel	GROS

TRIANA, near Seville. There were several fabriques here, one for the manufacture of the spires or ornaments of earthenware with which the edifices were crowned; another for *azulejos* or tiles, so much in use in Spain for walls and floors, and others for fayence. There is a very curious figure, in the costume of the eighteenth century, of a lady *en grande tenue,* forming a bottle; at the back is an inscription in Spanish; an authenticated specimen of Triana fayence. (*Ker. Gall.,* enlarged edition, fig. 100.)

VALLADOLID (Prov. of Leon). A correspondent in *Notes and Queries* (4th S. iv., Nov. 13, 1869) states that he has a Madonna in pottery, part of a *presipio.* It is very artistically moulded, drapery coloured and gilt, mantle fastened with a crystal. Inside, on the rim, is the word VEGA. He bought it at Seville as having been made at Valladolid, where many years ago a fabrique of pottery and porcelain existed.

The word VEGA refers to the person for whom it was made. A name somewhat similar, M. S., DEGA, occurs on a tazza which M. Jacquemart refers to Candiana.

SARGADELOS. The Royal Manufactory of MM. De la Riva & Co., on ware of modern manufacture, in the Harper Crewe Collection.

VILLA FELICE, in Aragon. Laborde notices the fact of a manufactory of fayence whose products were well known in the vicinity.

BARCELONA (Prov. of Catalonia). The Corporation of Potters existed in the thirteenth century. In 1314 a regulation was passed on the mark and stamp with which the masters were to seal their pieces, and the quality and other conditions which were to belong to them. From that time until the seventeenth century many other regulations have reached us relating to this corporation. Excellent lustred pottery was made at the end of the sixteenth century.

Pottery was made at MURCIA, MORVIEDRO, ZAMORA, DENIA, SARAGOSSA, GERONA, and many other towns of Spain. At BIAR (Valencia) alone there existed fourteen manufactories of earthenware in the sixteenth century.

At ANDUJAR, Ximenes Paton, writing in 1628, says: "The white unglazed earthenware of the towns of Andujar and Jaen is very remarkable for the curious manner in which they imitate different figures of animals, such as porcupines, fish, syrens, tortoises, &c." These models are continued at the present day.

SEGOVIA. The annexed mark of an ancient Roman building existing in this place is found on Spanish pottery, but is probably of recent date. It is stamped in the paste on a white leaf-shaped plate belonging to Sigª Doña Emilia Riaño, of Madrid.

PUENTE DE ARZOBISPO. Herr Jännike has given the accompanying mark as that of this fabrique.

PORTUGAL.

We have hitherto known but little of the fayence of Portugal, but the travels of M. Natalis Rondot and the Paris Exposition of 1867 have thrown some light upon the subject. There is no doubt that from the fifteenth or sixteenth century to the present time it has been extensively made, both in vessels for domestic use and in *azulejos* for the decoration of palaces and private houses.

Of the more modern period we know of many examples. In the hôtel of the Comte d'Almada au Raio are some *azulejos* commemorating the principal events of the revolution of 1640, which separated Portugal from Spain, battles, processions, &c.

The Church of St. Mamède at Evora is decorated with arabesque tiles, and the College of St. Jean l'Evangéliste has subjects on a large scale painted by Antonio d'Oliveira.

LISBON. The principal fabrique here was the Manufacture Royale de Rato, which supplied a great variety of wares, some on white ground with arabesques in colours, others in the style of Rouen. At the Paris Exposition of 1867 there was a vase in form of a negro's head, dishes and vessels with vegetables, fish, &c., in relief, candlesticks with dolphin stems, and escutcheons of busts of "Maria I. and Pedro III., Portugalliæ Regibus."

LISBON. This mark is found on an oval water-pot and cover, and on other specimens in the Sèvres Museum, presented in 1833. This pottery is made in the suburbs of Lisbon. There is also at CINTRA, a manufactory of pottery where statuettes are made; the glaze upon them is usually green, brown, or black.

CALDAS, PORTUGAL. Mafra, maker of modern imitations of Palissy ware; nineteenth century.

PORTO. There were several manufactories here; they made, among other things, pharmacy bottles painted with arms, &c. A plate in the Paris Exposition, painted with flowers and a fountain in the centre, had a medallion inscribed, "Na Real Fabrica do Cavaquinho." The fabrique of St. Antoine of Porto was also represented there by a lion similar to the animals of Luneville and other pieces.

PORTO (Oporto). Manufacture of M. Rocha Soares. Sometimes the mark is MIRAGAIA. PORTO., one word above the other, below a crown. The letters in the margin are on a teacup painted with landscapes in blue and violet in Oriental style. In the Sèvres Museum; date said to be about 1755.

M. P.

MIRAGAÏA.

COIMBRA also produced fayence. An inkstand and tea service of black glaze of very delicate fabric were exhibited at the Paris Exposition. Dr. Graesse gives the mark in the margin as that of this fabrique.

FABRICA DE MASSARELLOS. Dr. Graesse gives these marks, and other variations of the same letter, as the mark of this fabrique, the date of which he gives as from 1738 to 1833.

VIANA DE CASTELLO. Dr. Graesse gives these as the marks of this fabrique.

RATO. *Fabrica real.* Dr. Graesse gives these marks and other variations of F. R. (*Fabrica Rato*), in combination as a monogram and in single letters, as occurring in yellow and violet on specimens of this fabrique.

MALTA.

This mark impressed is on two modern triangular stone jars with incuse patterns. In the Sèvres Museum, presented in 1844.

NOTE.—As we have arranged the manufactories geographically rather than chronologically, we have considered it desirable, for the sake of reference, to keep the fayence of the seventeenth and eighteenth centuries of Italy and Spain under the general headings MAIOLICA, the terms *maiolica* and *fayence* being synonymous, the former applicable especially to Italy and Spain, the latter to France and Germany, thus separating earthenware into two principal divisions—pottery and porcelain.

PERSIAN, SYRIAN, AND TURKISH FAYENCE

HE fayence of the Near East forms a large, interesting, and supremely beautiful group, embracing the wares of Egypt, Syria, Persia, Turkey, and Asia Minor from early mediæval times onward. Historical considerations, backed by the results of excavation, indicate that this branch of the ceramic art is the lineal descendant of the old Egyptian pottery, and that it spread East and North from Egypt into Asia, taking in its course the natural variations due to locality and racial influence.

There are, however, certain features common to the group as a whole. The body of the ware is usually white with a loose sandy texture, and varies from an opaque friable earthenware to a translucent semi-porcelain, in accordance with the amount of vitreous matter which enters into its composition. It is white enough to afford a satisfactory background for painted decoration (usually executed in blue and brown), but a finer and cleaner surface was frequently added by means of a dressing of white clay. Over all is a clear glassy glaze, faintly greenish in tint, and so fluescent as to run down the sides of the ware and form in deep pools in the hollows. Sometimes, too, the body was coated with opaque tin-enamel of creamy white tone. This occurs principally on the early wares of the tenth to the fourteenth century, and is commoner on tiles than on rounded vessels. The tin-enamel is chiefly decorated with lustre pigment with or without touches of pale blue, though lustred ornament is by no means confined to the tin-enamelled wares. Indeed, it was one of the outstanding features of the Near Eastern fayence up to the seventeenth century, and the lustre itself is usually a golden brown with reflections varying from golden to deep ruby red. But the decorative varieties of the ware are legion. To mention but a few, we find single-coloured glazes—turquoise, deep blue, celadon green, brown, black, and brownish-purple—many of them evidently imitating Chinese porcelain glazes; deep blue grounds with lustred ornament; blue or dull white grounds decorated in a dry red and white colour, transparent green, and

165

leaf-gold; blue ornament on a white ground, often in Chinese taste; pierced, moulded, and carved ornament, the pierced designs sometimes filled in with clear glaze; black painting under a turquoise glaze; and finally, there is a large group with designs in brown and blue under a clear transparent glaze, which has been found principally in Egypt and Syria, though also in considerable quantity in Persia. This last is the ware which used to be miscalled Siculo-Arab, and now is known as Syro-Egyptian. The decoration, which is distinctively Eastern, consists of animals and birds (the hare and deer being common motives) surrounded by dense conventional foliage or arabesques. More rarely the heroes of Persian legend are represented on horse or foot, and ordinary personages, male and female, conventionally rendered with dumpy, rounded figures. Formal, geometrical designs and Arabic inscriptions are of common occurrence, and the intricacies of the decoration usually cover the entire surface of the ware with wonderfully rich effect. Where lustre was used over a tin-enamel the ornament was generally etched out of the lustred ground; but on the ordinary glaze the designs were as a rule painted direct in the lustre pigment. One of the latest and most beautiful classes of lustred ware was made at the end of the sixteenth century, in the reign of Shah Abbas. It is a translucent semi-porcelain with dark-brown lustre, showing rich ruby *reflet* on a ground of pure white, deep blue, or buff-brown. The distribution of the industry was wide and general, and though but a small fraction of its extent is as yet revealed, history and recent excavations show that there were large centres of manufacture at Fostat and Cairo in Egypt; Rakka and Damascus in Syria; Rey, Veramin, Sultanabad, Ispahan, and Kashan in Persia. The remains at Rakka, near Aleppo, date from the days of Haroun al Raschid, and the city was destroyed, like Rey and Sultanabad, in the thirteenth century by the Mongol invaders. (See *Ker. Gall.*, enlarged edition, figs. 544 to 555.)

GOMBROON WARE.—Gombroon, a port in the Persian Gulf, was a prominent trading station in the seventeenth century, and no doubt the fact that Persian wares were shipped from its harbour explains why "Gombroon ware" was at one time a general term for Persian pottery in England. The name has ceased to be general, but it has continued to be applied to a particular class of translucent Persian ware with pierced ornament filled in with clear glaze, like the "rice-grain" porcelain of China, and often with slight subsidiary decoration in blue and brown. Examples of this beautiful and delicate pottery as old as the tenth century exist, but they are extremely rare, and the better-known specimens date from the eighteenth and early nineteenth centuries.

Marks are most unusual in the early Persian wares, and though the potsherds dug up at Fostat in Egypt revealed a number of potters' signatures in Arabic, they are mostly of sixteenth century date. The Persian and Syrian blue and white pottery, which avowedly copied the Chinese from the sixteenth century onward, not uncommonly bears marks resembling Chinese seals, and modern Persian ware is frequently marked.

TURKISH FAYENCE forms a distinctive and singularly beautiful branch of the Near Eastern wares It is commonly called Rhodian ware, and though it was no doubt made in Rhodes among other places, it is found in all parts of the Empire of the Ottoman Turks. The body is of the same sandy texture as the Persian and Syrian pottery, and it is usually coated with a fine white surface clay. The ornament is painted in brilliant colours—chiefly blue, turquoise, green, and a peculiarly thick and upstanding red obtained from Armenian bol. Over all is a deep transparent glaze. The designs are of a boldness to match the brilliant colours; and though showing unmistakable Persian influence, they are distinguished by the naturalistic treatment of the flowers which form the favourite motives, such as the tulip, hyacinth, carnation, fritillary, cornflower, and lily. These flowers are thrown in bold sprays across the wares, or reserved in grounds of salmon pink, red, lavender, blue, green, or brown. Besides the floral motive, formal designs, diapers, animal, and very rarely human figures, coats of arms and ships sometimes occur, and the dishes are often bordered with a narrow band of cloud scrolls. The forms are chiefly of a useful nature, plates and dishes, covered bowls, jugs, tankard-shaped flower vases, ewers, sprinklers, lamps, and narghilis. Like the Persian pottery, the Turkish was used effectively in the form of tiles for the magnificent wall decoration of the mosques and public buildings. Large designs, made up in many sections, were used for this purpose, the whole closely resembling the carpets and textiles of contemporary workmanship. There must have been many centres of the manufacture of Turkish wares, but few are known as yet—viz., Nicæa, Kutahia, Demitoka, Rhodes, Lindus, and Damascus, and the various makes are not differentiated if we except those of Damascus and Kutahia. The Damascus ware is distinguished by the prevalence of a beautiful blue and the absence of the raised red; and the Damascus style inclined rather to the Persian and more conventional treatment of flowers. The Kutahian ware of the sixteenth century was closely akin to the Damascus, and many tiles, vases, and bowls painted in a lovely blue with Persian arabesques and rosette scrolls of rather Chinese appearance are assigned to this locality. In the Godman Collection there is an interesting jug with an Armenian inscription declaring it to be the work of Abraham of Kutahia in the sixteenth century. The best period of the Turkish pottery is that of the beautiful mosque lamp given by the late Dr. Fortnum to the British Museum and dated 1549. The ware seems to have rapidly degenerated, and to have been in full decline at the end of the following century, though the Anatolian factories in the neighbourhood of Kutahia were active until quite recently, and produced in the last two centuries quantities of not unpleasing domestic pottery, with thin white body and slight patterns of radiating leaf panels, scale diapers, &c., chiefly in blue, brown, and yellow. Good collections of the Near Eastern wares may be seen in the British and the Victoria and Albert Museums, and Mr. Godman has a wonderfully fine private collection at Horsham. Marks on Turkish wares, with the exception of the late Anatolian productions, are exceedingly rare. (See *Ker. Gall.*, enlarged edition, plate opposite p. 446, and figs. 556 to 560.)

Signature of Hatim in brown lustre, inside a covered bowl with three loop handles and a spout, painted outside with brown lustre on a ground of intense blue; translucent Persian ware; late sixteenth century. British Museum.

Mark on a saucer dish of similar ware painted in ruby lustre. British Museum.

Mark on a bowl of similar ware in the British Museum.

Arabic mark imitating a Chinese seal, on a saucer dish of similar ware. Seventeenth century. British Museum.

" The decorator of it, the poor Zarî, 1025 " (i.e., 1616 A.D.). The year is that of the Hegira. On a blue and white Persian ewer in Chinese style. British Museum.

Imitation of a Chinese seal, on a low vase of Persian ware painted in blue in Chinese style, the designs outlined in black. About 1600. British Museum.

Mark on a Persian blue and white dish. Seventeenth century. British Museum.

Mark on a Persian blue and white dish in Chinese style. Eighteenth century. British Museum.

On a blue and white Persian dish in the British Museum. "Belonging to Ahmed. Made by Muhammed Ali, 1232" (*i.e.*, 1816-17 A.D.).

On a "Gombroon" bowl, painted in blue, with passages of pierced or "rice-grain" ornament, in the British Museum. "Made by Muhammed Ali, 1234" (*i.e.* 1818-19 A.D.).

On a blue and white Persian saucer dish in the British Museum. Probably early nineteenth century. "Made by Muhammad ? Harbati."

Mark on a blue and white Persian bottle. Nineteenth century. British Museum.

Mark on a nineteenth century Persian bowl painted in blue and liver-coloured slip under the glaze. British Museum.

This is given by Mr. Marryat (p. 318, 3rd edition of his work), an ornate Greek cross on pieces of Turkish ware in Mr. L. Huth's Collection, and is thought to be the cross of the Order of Jerusalem at Rhodes.

A curious mark resembling that found on Caffaggiolo maiolica. It occurs on a covered flower vase of Turkish ware of the sixteenth century in the British Museum.

Mark in brown on a jug of Anatolian ware painted in blue, yellow, and thick red. Seventeenth or eighteenth century. British Museum.

Marks on a covered bowl of similar ware. British Museum.

Mark on a jug of similar ware. British Museum.

Mark on a cup of Anatolian ware. Eighteenth century. British Museum.

FAYENCE

France

N the *Archives de la Préfecture de la Nièvre* we find the following list of the manufactories of fayence established in the kingdom of France in the year 1790, which does not comprise the ordinary manufactures for common use, but only those of reputation, taken from a petition of the faïenciers of France to the National Assembly, stating their grievances in consequence of the injury done to their trade by the treaty of commerce between France and England, and the importation of English ware into France in immense quantities, also the increase in the price of lead and tin, which came principally from England. We have added within brackets the more recent divisions of departments, so far as the places can be identified.

Paris (Seine)	14	Varages (Var)	3	Bordeaux (Gironde)	8
Sçéaux (Seine)	1	Nismes (Gard)	2	Moyat	1
Bourg la Reine (Seine)	1	Saintes (Charente-In-		Rambervillier (Vosges)	1
Chantilly (Seine)	1	férieure)	2	Epinal (Vosges)	2
Melun (Seine-et-Marne)	1	Toulouse (Haute-Garonne)	2	St. Gnyé	1
Montereau (Seine-et-		Limoges (Haute-Vienne)	1	Toul (Meurthe)	1
Marne)	2	Dieu-le-fit (Drôme)	1	Dannière	1
Rouen (Seine Inférieure)	16	St. Vallier (Drôme)	1	Bechaume	1
Havre (Seine-Inférieure)	2	Marthe (Haute-Garonne)	2	Bois Depausse (Marne)	1
Bourvalles	1	Rennes (Ille-et-Vilaine)	1	Clemont } (Puy-de-Dôme)	5
Nevers (Nièvre)	12	Nantes (Loire-Inférieure)	1	Magonne }	
Marseilles (Bouches-du-		Quimper (Finistère)	2	Montaigu (Vendée)	1
Rhône)	11	Marinial (Haute-Garonne)	2	Vaucouleur (Meuse)	1
Lyon (Rhône)	3	Rénac (Ille-et-Vilaine)	1	Verneuil (Eure)	1
Tours (Indre-et-Loire)	1	Mones (Haute-Garonne)	1	Niderviller (Meurthe)	1
St. Omer (Pas-de-Calais)	1	Bazas (Gironde)	1	Haguenau (Bes-Rhin)	2
Aire (Pas-de-Calais)	1	Angoulême (Charente)	1	Thionville (Moselle)	1
Lille (Nord)	2	Bourg en Bresse (Aisne)	1	Ancy le Franc (Yonne)	1
Valenciennes (Nord)	1	Roanne (Loire)	1	Mont Louis (Seine)	2
Douay (Nord)	2	Poitiers (Vienne)	1	Boulogne (Pas-de-Calais)	1
Dijon (Côte-d'Or)	2	La Rochelle (Charente-		Laplume (Lot-et-Garonne)	1
Macon (Saône-et-Loire)	2	Inférieure)	1	Montauban (Tarn-et-Ga-	
Orleans (Loiret)	2	Langres (Haute-Marne)	1	ronne)	1
Aprey (sic) (Haute-Marne)	1	Besançon (Doubs)	3	Hardes	1
Grénoble (Isère)	2	St. Cenis (Aisne)	1	Bergerac (Dordogne)	2
Montpellier (Hérault)	2	Lunéville (Meurthe)	3	Espedel (Basses Pyrénées)	1
Moustier (Basses-Alpes)	5	St. Clement (Meurthe)	1		

SAINT-PORCHAIRE.

This is the latest title by which the beautiful fayence for many years known as "Henri Deux," and subsequently as "faïence d'Oiron," is to be henceforth called, if the views of M. Edmond Bonnaffé are generally accepted by collectors. The facts and deductions in his essay which was published in 1888 in the *Gazette des Beaux-Arts* appear to be correct, and he quotes from the official inventory taken after the death of François de la Tremouille at the Château of Thouars in 1542, wherein the following entry occurs: "Deux coppes de terre de Saint-Porchayre, et une grande boueste plate en carré de deux pieds de long, en laquelle a esté trouvé deux sallières de Saint-Porchayre." Again, thirty-five years later, in the inventory of some of the contents of the same château, taken after the death of the son of the above-named owner, the "deux sallières de Saint-Porchaire" are again mentioned.

Saint-Porchaire is situated a short distance from Bressieure (Deux Sèvres), in the same locality where all these fayences have been discovered. Pottery of some kind has been made in the district from time immemorial, and at the present day there still exist three fabriques of common fayence.

M. Bonnaffé has taken infinite pains to trace from the armorial bearings, which are part of the decoration of some of those coveted gems of the collector, the date of the earlier specimens, and he has divided them into earlier and later periods of design and manufacture, the latter pieces showing a deterioration from purity of design. As one of these bears the arms of the Vicomte de Beaumont, counsellor and chamberlain to Francis I., he contends that it must have been made previous to his death, which happened in 1528.[1]

As will be seen in the following notice, M. André Pottier, writing in 1839, knew of only 24 pieces, and subsequent writers gradually increased the number as fresh specimens were brought to light, until M. Delange in his *Recueil* described and illustrated 52 specimens, which with one more (in Russia) made a total of 53 when the previous edition of Chaffers was published. There are now extant 65 pieces, the latest discovery being a very remarkable ewer, found in 1887 at Bourges, at the house of a M. Rhodier, who had inherited it from his ancestors. It was purchased by M. Stein, the well-known Paris virtuoso, for about £3,000, and remained in his possession until purchased by Mr. J. Pierpont Morgan. It is well reproduced in M. Bonnaffé's essay, and is a charming little piece, only 27 centimetres (or about 9 inches) high, with a tiny figure of the Virgin under the spout, and the bands of inlaid enamel decoration of a dark black-brown of the kind generally found on the rare fayence.

The prices which these precious little pieces command are almost fabulous, and there is much jealousy on the part of French collectors to keep those which are in France from leaving the country, and to recover

---

[1] The establishment of the *faïence atelier* has been generally considered to be about 1524.

those which are lost. Thus Mr. George Salting had to give £1,500 for the tazza which M. Spitzer had bought at the Hamilton Palace sale, while the three specimens in the Fountaine Collection were all taken back to France when that sale took place in 1884, the candlestick which had cost Mr. Fountaine £1,000 a century ago realising the enormous sum of £3,675.

With these additional remarks on this celebrated fayence, the editor leaves the notice of Henri II., or Oiron, as Mr. Chaffers wrote it, because, save for M. Bonnaffé's later information and the fresh discovery of more specimens, his descriptions and statements apply to the ware, which, despite its new title, remains the same.

HENRI II. WARE.

OIRON (Deux Sèvres). 1520 to 1550. This elegant ware is of a distinct character and ornamentation to every other class of pottery. It is only by a recent discovery that we have been able to assign this manufacture to its original source. It was supposed by many that it was produced in France, and, from the devices and arms depicted thereon, that it was first ushered into existence under the fostering patronage of Francis I., and that it continued increasing in beauty and excellence during a portion of the reign of Henri II., until its extinction. In corroboration of this was adduced the circumstance that the emblems of these two princes alone are found upon it; a period, therefore, of about thirty years comprised the duration of this peculiar branch of manufacture. The marks in the margin are not those of the fabrique, but emblems found designed or painted on the ware.

It seems to have been the opinion of all the most able writers on the subject that it was made in Touraine. The first who promulgated it was M. André Pottier of Rouen, in Willemin's *Monuments Inédits*, &c., 1839. He says that of the *twenty-four* pieces then known, about one-half came from Touraine, and especially from *Thouars*. M. Brongniart, in *Traité des Arts Céramiques*, 1844, states that the majority of the *thirty-seven* pieces came from the south-west of France, from Saumur, Tours, and *Thouars*. M. Jules Labarte, in his Introduction to the De Bruge-Dumesnil Catalogue, 1847, also refers the greater number to Touraine and La Vendée. Le Comte Clément de Ris, of the Museum of the Louvre, in an article in the *Gazette des Beaux-Arts*, 1860, confirms the statement of M. Brongniart, that in all ten or twelve pieces have come direct from Tours, and that the original place of their production was betwixt Tours,

Saumur, and *Thouars*. A pamphlet, in form of a letter addressed to
M. Riocreux, Director of the Sèvres Museum, by M. Benjamin Fillon of
Poitiers, recently appeared in Paris, promising a solution of the mystery
which has hitherto enveloped the origin of this pottery. Our space will
not allow us to insert the letter entire, but we extract a few of the leading
points of discovery. It is headed "Les Faïences d'Oiron," and the writer
says that these wonders of curiosity, which have turned the heads of so
many amateurs, were actually fabricated at Oiron, near Thouars (Deux
Sèvres), with clay from the immediate neighbourhood.

Two artists assisted in the work—a potter named François Char-
pentier, and Jean Bernard, librarian and secretary of Hélène de Hangest
Genlis, widow of Artus Gouffier, a superior woman and cultivator of the
arts. After the decease of this lady in 1537, they both entered the
service of Claude Gouffier, her son, Grand Ecuyer de France, who had
inherited the tastes of his mother, and who, moreover, collected a vast
number of works of art (a catalogue of which, with the prices realised
after his decease, by auction sale, is still preserved) The librarian had,
whilst in the service of Hélène de Hangest, furnished designs for the ornamental binding of books and frontispieces, specimens of which are annexed
to M. Fillon's letter, etched by Octave de Rochebrune.

It has been noticed by Le Comte de Ris, in the *Gazette des Beaux-Arts*
(January, 1860), that a great resemblance exists betwixt the interlaced
ornaments of the Henri II. ware and the bookbindings of Grolier and
Maioli. M. Fillon (by the aid of the monograms, ciphers, and arms which
occur on this ware) has chronologically arranged them from the published
drawings, and comes to the conclusion that the earliest pieces were
executed under the direction of Hélène de Hangest herself, in the later
part of the reign of Francis I.; afterwards by her son Claude Gouffier,
and other hands, down to the accession of Charles IX. The arming of
the Protestants put an end to a fabrication which could no longer maintain
itself; for this reason, that its only object being to supply the *dressoirs*
and furnish the chapels of one family, their relations and personal friends,
and not for commercial purposes, it followed the fortune of its patrons in
a country menaced like Poitou with the horrors of a religious war. We
will briefly notice the monograms and initials placed upon the fayence of
Oiron, viz.: The sacred monogram; that of the Dauphin Henri; of Anne
of Montmorency; of Claude Gouffier, "composed of an H, in memory of
his mother, and a double C, which has been confounded with that of his
master." Mr. Magniac's ewer has the letter G repeated several times
round the body, which is the initial of Gouffier's name; and round the
foot of the candlestick which belonged to Mr. Fountaine may be observed
the letter H, repeated as a border, being the initial of his mother's name,
Hélène de Hangest. The arms upon this pottery are those of the King;
of the Dauphin; of Gilles de Laval, Seigneur de Bressieure; of the
Constable Anne of Montmorency; of François de la Trémouille, Vicomte
de Thouars; of another, unknown; and of William Gouffier. This last

occurs on a plate now in the Victoria and Albert Museum, which has in its centre an escutcheon, surrounded by fruit and cherubs' heads and flaming rays, all in relief; in the centre are the arms of William Gouffier, third son of Admiral de Bonnivet, when he was a Knight of Malta, that is to say, before he was raised to the episcopal chair of Beziers in 1547. The emblems are the salamander of Francis I. and the crescents of Henri II., which were never used by Diane de Poitiers, as is generally supposed. M. Fillon remarks that the cup which was shown to Bernard Palissy, and which he so much desired to imitate, was doubtless of the *faïence d'Oiron;* indeed, several of those pieces, with lizards, frogs, snakes, tortoises, &c., in relief, upon them, might have suggested his celebrated *figuline rustique.*

The distinguishing characteristics are, in the first place, the body or constituent part of this ware, which is very light and delicate, and of a pure white *terre de pipe,* of so fine a texture that it did not require, like the ordinary Italian fayence, any coating of opaque coloured glaze or enamel, but merely a thin transparent varnish Its fabrication appears to have required great care and diligence, for it is supposed, from the examination of a fractured vase in the Museum at Sèvres, that the foundation was first moulded by the hand, not turned in a lathe, quite plain, and without the least relief or ornament, the rough surface hatched with cross lines, and a thin outer crust, or *engobe,* of the same clay laid completely over the whole vessel; the ornaments were then cut out of the field (in the same manner as the *champ lévé* enamels) and coloured pastes introduced; the superfluous clay was removed by a sharp chisel, and the surface tooled to a uniform smoothness, it being subsequently baked and varnished. On carefully examining these specimens, it will be seen that all the furrows in which the coloured pastes have been inserted are depressed to a slight degree, as though they had sunk in the furnace, thus differing essentially from the painted earthenware, which would rather produce a low relief. A section of the broken vase before referred to is a convincing proof that the coloured pastes were actually encrusted, the sharp angles presenting too regular an appearance to have been caused by the mere absorption of colouring matter applied externally with a brush.

Secondly, the decorations are what is usually termed "*Renaissance,*" introduced by François I. in the commencement of the sixteenth century, and consist of interlaced scrolls and devices, tastefully arranged with great precision, partaking greatly of the early Moorish or Arabian character, the colours employed being usually yellow ochre and brown of different shades, with occasional touches of red, green, and yellow, on the raised figures. Independent of the beautiful encrustations, the vessel was also richly decorated with figures, marks, garlands, mouldings, &c., in high relief, modelled with great care, and harmonising well with the groundwork.

M. B. Fillon (*Art de Terre chez les Poitevins*) describes the pavement in the chapel of the château at Oiron. It is of square tiles, fitting together so as to form one pavement; each tile bears a letter, a monogram, or an escutcheon; each of these letters is painted in violet-brown on blue arabesques, and so disposed as to form the device of Claude Gouffier, HIC TERMINUS HAERET. The monograms are of the same colours as the letters, and are those of Claude Gouffier and of Henri II. before he was King of France. The arms are those of Gouffier quartered with Montmorency and Hangest-Genlis. The composition of the paste of these tiles having been analysed by M. Salvetat, is found to be identical with that of the Henri II. ware.

Two examples of this curious ware, the beautiful candlestick which with five other examples is now in the Victoria and Albert Museum, and the biberon formerly belonging to Mr. Andrew Fountaine, are represented in the *Keramic Gallery*, enlarged edition, figs. 107, 108. The biberon in Mr. J. Pierpont Morgan's collection is illustrated in the same publication, fig. 105.

M. B. Fillon instances various other pieces of a later period than those referred to in the subjoined list, of a much coarser character, and tells us in whose possession they now are, being principally in the immediate neighbourhood of Oiron and Thouars.

HENRI II. WARE. This mark occurs on a plateau in the Victoria and Albert Museum. It is scratched in the clay, under the glaze, and is an original mark or symbol of some kind or other, whether of the maker or not it is impossible now to determine. It is the only mark hitherto discovered on the ware.

SAINT-PORCHAIRE.

The following tables of Saint-Porchaire specimens, or, as it was then termed, Henri Deux ware, are printed in the present edition exactly as they were compiled by Mr. Chaffers in 1891, because although, as the Editor's Notes which follow will show, they are now incorrect by reason of several specimens having changed hands, still the tables will be interesting as a reference.

In the previous edition of Chaffers the 53 specimens then known were located as follows : 26 in England, 26 in France, and 1 in Russia. There are now, according to M. Bonnaffé, 65 specimens in existence, of which 5 are in Russia, in the Imperial Collection, the one No. 53 having been purchased by the Czar from Prince Galitzin, and three specimens, Nos. 27, 28, 29, after having been purchased by M. Basilewski, were also passed into the Imperial Collection, and are now on view in the Musée de l'Hermitage. Of the remainder, there are now rather more in France than in England, and since Mr. Chaffers compiled his list the following changes in ownership are known by the Editor to have taken place. At the Magniac sale, No. 1, the ewer from Odiot was sold for about £1500, and is now in the collection of the Rothschilds. At the Fountaine sale in 1884, No. 9, the candlestick, realised £3675; and No. 10, the biberon, £1060, both specimens purchased by M. Dutuit of Rouen; No. 11, the salt-cellar, *mortier à cire*, as it was termed, was bought by M. Mannheim of Paris for £1575. At the Spitzer sale in Paris, 1893, No. 14, the tazza, which at the Duke of Hamilton's sale in 1882 had cost £1218, was secured for England by Mr. George Salting for £1500; No. 15, a salt-cellar, was sold at the Hamilton Palace sale for £840; No. 16, the famous salt-cellar which has the salamander (Francis I. crest), which belonged to Mr. George Field, was sold at Christie's for about £500, and was in the possession of M. Stein of Paris until his death, when it was sold by auction in Paris (June 1899) and realised 49,000 francs, or, with the auctioneer's commission (which in France is payable by the purchaser), 50,000 francs or £2000. No. 20, the biberon, which belonged to Mr. Malcolm, was purchased by Messrs. Durlacher Bros., re-sold in Paris to M. Stein, and at the same sale brought £800, Mr. Fitzhenry being the purchaser in both cases. No. 47, the salt-cellar in Madame d'Yvon's Collection, was sold in 1892 at the Hôtel Druot for £1075, and is now in a Paris collection, probably that of one of the Rothschild family. Mr. J. Pierpont Morgan has purchased some of the above-named examples, which are on loan to the Victoria and Albert Museum.

The sums printed in the last column as "present values" by Mr. Chaffers have not been altered, but recent sales have shown that these figures are quite incorrect, and it is impossible to say how much one of these coveted specimens will bring in competition by wealthy collectors.

LIST OF SAINT-PORCHAIRE (HENRI II.) WARE.

COMPILED BY MR. CHAFFERS IN 1891.

IN ENGLAND.—26 PIECES.

	DESCRIPTION.	OWNER.	WHENCE OBTAINED.	COST.	Estimated VALUE.
				£	£
1	Large ewer........	H. Magniac, Esq.	Odiot Sale, 1842............................	96	1500
2	Large ewer........	Sir Anthony de Rothschild[1]	Strawberry Hill Col., 1842...............	20	1200
3	Large ewer........	,, ,, ,, ...	De Monville Coll............................	140	1200
4	Candlestick........	,, ,, ,, ...	Préaux Sale, 1850...........................	208	1000
5	Hanap..............	,, ,, ,, ...	De Bruge Sale, 1849........................	20	500
6	Tazza,...............	,, ,, ,, ...	Préaux Sale, 1850...........................	44	500
7	Cover of a cup...		Unknown......................................	...	150
8	Bouquetière.......	,, ,, ,, ...	Bought of a Curé at Tours...............	48	800
9	Candlestick........	Andrew Fountaine, Esq.......	Purchased a century ago..................	...	1000
10	Biberon.............	,, ,, ,, ...	,, ,, ,, ...	...	800
11	Salt-cellar..........	,, ,, ,, ...	,, ,, ,, ...	...	500
12	Biberon.............	Baron Lionel de Rothschild	Bought of Madame Delaunay...........	...	800
13	Salt-cellar..........	,, ,, ,, ...	Strawberry Hill, 1842.....................	21	300
14	Tazza...............	Duke of Hamilton.............	Préaux Sale, 1850, £52; Rattier, 1859	280	500
15	Salt-cellar..........	,, ,, ,, ...	Rattier Sale, 1859..........................	80	300
16	Salt-cellar..........	George Field, Esq............	Unknown......................................	...	300
17	Part of ewer.......	H. T. Hope, Esq..............	De Bruge Sale, 1849........................	16	300
18	Small ewer........	,, ,, ,, ...	,, ,, ,, ...	20	600
19	Small ewer........	M. T. Smith, Esq..............	Bought as Palissy..........................	...	600
20	Biberon.............	J. Malcolm, Esq..............	Pourtalès Sale, 1865.......................	1100	1100
21	Salt-cellar..........	Victoria and Albert Museum	Soltykoff, 1861 to Napier.................	268	300
22	Tazza and cover	,, ,, ,, ...	Préaux S., 1850, £62; Soltykoff, 1861	450	500
23	Tazza...............	,, ,, ,, ...	Bought at Poitiers for 50s., Delange...	180	180
24	Candlestick........	,, ,, ,, ...	Lassayette, £400; De Norzy Sale......	640	750
25	Salver..............	,, ,, ,, ...	Espoulart, 1857 for £140.................	180	400
26	Salt-cellar..........	,, ,, ,, ...	Addington Coll...............................	...	300

[1] The specimens named as belonging to Sir Anthony de Rothschild were at his death divided among members of the family, and the candlestick is now in the collection of Mr. Leopold de Rothschild.

13

LIST OF PORCHAIRE WARE.—*Continued.*

In France.—26 Pieces.

	DESCRIPTION.	OWNER.	WHENCE OBTAINED.	COST.	Estimated VALUE.
				£	£
27	Tazza................	Le Duc d'Uzes.................	Unknown........................	...	500
28	Cover of a cup....	,, ,, ...	,, ...	...	150
29	Pilgrim's bottle...	,, ,,	,,	...	800
30	Tazza and cover	M. Hutteau d'Origny..........	,,	...	500
31	Tazza and cover	Musée de Cluny.................	Bought by M. Thoré, in 1798 for.......	20	500
32	Salt-cellar..........	Baron Alph. de Rothschild...	Unknown.......................	...	300
33	Jug or canette.....	,, ,, ,, ...	Bought by Strauss for £600 sold for...	800	1000
34	Small ewer.........	,, ,, ,, ...	Préaux Sale, 1850.	44	500
35	Candlestick........	Baron Gust. de Rothschild...	Unknown.......................	...	1000
36	Hanap..............	,, ,, ,, ...	,,	...	500
37	Tazza................	Baron Jas. de Rothschild.....	South of France, 1860...................	480	500
38	Biberon.............	Museum of the Louvre........	Sauvageot, from Tours................	...	800
39	Salt-cellar..........	,, ,, ,, ...	Sauvageot, from M. Lehrié, 1824......	5	300
40	Salt-cellar..........	,, ,, ,, ...	Sauvageot, Troyes...................	...	300
41	Salt-cellar..........	,, ,, ,, ...	Sauvageot.	...	300
42	Tazza................	,, ,, ,, ...	Sauvageot, bought as Palissy	8	500
43	Salt-cellar..........	,, ,, ,, ...	Revoil Coll., 1828........	...	300
44	Tazza................	,, ,, ,, ...	,, ,, ,, ...	...	500
45	Tazza................	Sèvres Museum...................	Unknown........................	...	500
46	Cover of a cup...	,, ,,	,,	...	150
47	Salt-cellar..........	Madame d'Yvon...............	,,	...	300
48	Salt-cellar..........	Comte de Tusseau............	,,	...	300
49	Salt-cellar..........	,, ,,	,,	...	300
50	Salt-cellar..........	,, ,,	,,	...	300
51	Cover of a tazza..	M. B. Delessert.................	South of France, by Rutter.........	4	150
52	Biberon.............	Unknown.......................	Unknown........................	...	...

In Russia.—1 Piece.

53	Biberon ,............	Prince Galitzin..................	Préaux Sale, 1850............................	100	800

TOTAL KNOWN :—IN ENGLAND............. 26
IN FRANCE... 26 } 53 Pieces.
IN RUSSIA... 1

L. A.
1676.

THOUARS or OIRON (Deux Sèvres). The manufactory of fayence at Thouars, hitherto little known, has recently acquired great importance by the attribution of the Henri II. ware by M. B. Fillon to which we have before alluded. The fabrique was continued for making less important objects for more than a century. M. Fillon speaks of two tiles, one bearing the salamander of François I., the other the crescent of Henri II., still preserved over the doorway of the manor-house, which came from the chapel of the Château of Thouars. There are two lozenge-shaped tiles in the Louvre (G. 706, 707), which also came from the same château, bearing the arms of Marie de la Tour d'Auvergne of a later date. They are dated 1676, and have on the back the initials of the artist, L. A.; they are $9\frac{1}{2}$ in. by 8 in. There are also some specimens in the Sèvres Museum.

M. B. Fillon has given an emblematical figure found underneath a fayence vase, *l'oie de la plaine de Thouars*, which is probably and simply an allusion to the sovereignty of the Lords of Oiron.

LYONS, circa 1530. A document has recently been discovered in the Bibliothèque Impériale which reveals the existence of a manufactory of fayence here in the reign of François I., founded by an Italian artist of the name of Francesco of Pesaro. The charter alluded to contains a request from two other potters, Julien Gambyn and Domenge Tardessir, both natives of Faenza in Italy, to Henri II. It states, "Qu'ils ont la cognoissance et experience de faire les vaisselles de terre, façon de Venice." One of them, Julien Gambyn, had already practised his art at Lyons "soubs Jehan Francisque de Pesaro, tenant botique en icelle ville," and claims the privilege "et dresser train et mestier de la dite vaisselle, comme chose libre et de tout temps permise aux étrangers apportans en France moyen et pratique de quelque art ou mestier encores peu cogneu." Francesco of Pesaro opposes the application, and urges that "il a souffert de grandz frais durant vingt ans qu'il a exercé comme il fait de present." It goes on to say that, so far from having suffered, he has, by the monopoly so long enjoyed by him, greatly enriched himself. The two supplicants set forth their ability, and state that they are better cognisant of the art than Francesco himself. Henri II., by the advice of his Council, permits them to exercise the trade with the same liberty and facility as other artisans, and charges the Governor, M. D. Mandelot, to see that Francesco does not annoy them, under heavy penalties.

Another document, discovered among the "Actes Consulaires de la Ville de Lyon" (1556) informs us of the establishment of another manufactory "d'ouvrages et de vaisselle de terre," by a Genoese merchant named Sebastian Griffo, whereby certain privileges and immunities are granted him for two years, provided he resides continually in Lyons and brings thither workmen from Italy, because the said manufacture is new in the city and in the kingdom of France. He is desired to employ "des enfans de l'haulmosne" (charity children) to work in the said manufactory. Hence it will be seen that three manufactories of fayence were actually in operation simultaneously in the first half of the sixteenth century at Lyons. The products are unknown to us at the present day.

The foregoing extracts are taken from a pamphlet lately published by M. le Comte de la Ferrière-Percy, entitled *Une Fabrique de Faïence à Lyon sous le Règne de Henri II.*, and he suggests the probability of one of these being the source of the celebrated *faïence d'Henri II.;* but as regards the first two, alluded to as of the "façon de Venice," the expression does not certainly convey to us sufficient to identify the ware; and as to the third, from Genoa, in which *charity children* were to be employed,

we seem to be still further from solving the enigma as to its origin. However, the discovery of these documents opens a wide field for the researches
of the historian of French fayence, and, we doubt not, will be made
available in the pursuit.

The manufacture of fayence was continued, but we have very little
information of its more recent owners. From the documents collected by
M. Rolle, keeper of the records, we learn that on the 31st March, 1733,
Joseph Combe, originally of Moustiers, and manufacturer at Marseilles,
obtained, in conjunction with Jacques Marie Ravier of Lyons, a privilege
of ten years for carrying on "à la Guillotière une *manufacture royale* de
faïence." The undertaking proving unsuccessful, a woman obtained a
decree on the 22nd of April, 1738; her name was Françoise Blateran,
dame Lemasle, and she showed great courage and perseverance; so much
so, that in 1748 it was renewed for another term of ten years.

On the 22nd of April, 1766, another maker of fayence, le Sieur Patras,
obtained a decree.

I.P.S
A LYON   LYON. Dr. Graesse gives these marks as those of
1773   the Lyons fayence; the former is probably that of le
          Sieur Patras.
LYON
C.F

In the list of potters who petitioned the National Assembly in 1790,
we find three then existing there.

In 1800 there was a fabrique carried on by M. Merck, and in 1856
another by M. Chapeau Revol, specimens of which are in the Sèvres
Museum.

· EPERNAY. There was a manufactory here about 1650 to 1780. It
is an enamelled fayence, something like that of Avignon; the colour is
a chocolate brown. A large oval dish and cover, ornamented in relief,
with EPERNAY in raised letters on the top, is in the Sèvres Museum. This
fayence is frequently unmarked.

BEAUVAIS (Saveignies) was celebrated for the manufacture of decorative pottery in the fourteenth century, frequently mounted in silver. In
the inventory of Charles VI. (1309) we read of "Une godet de *terre de
Beauvais*, garny d'argent"; and again, in the *Comptes Royaux de France*
(1416), "Pour plusieurs voirres *godez de Beauvez*, et autres vaisselles
à boire, xxxs." Hence the old French proverb, "On fait des godés à Beauvais et des poêles à Villedieu" (Leroux de Lincy, *Proverbes Français*).
In 1500 Rabelais speaks of the "poteries azurées" of Beauvais. Palissy,
speaking of the potter's clay, says, "There is a kind at Savigny, in
Beauvoisis, which I think has not in France its like, for it endures a marvellous fire without being at all injured, and has this advantage also,
that it allows itself to be shaped more slenderly and delicately than any

of the others; and when it is extremely baked it takes little vitricative polish (*polissement vitricatif*), which proceeds from its own substance, and that causes that the vessels made with the said earth hold water quite as well as glass vessels."

Estienne (Robert) also speaks of the pottery of Beauvais in his work *De Vasculis Libellis*, edition of 1543, p. 22: ". . . Quemadmodum vulgus Italorum maiorica vasa appellat, quæ in altera ex insulis Balearibus fiunt, quam vulgus *maioricam* appellare solet, itidem et nos eadem ratione vasa Bellovaca dicemus *potz de Beauvays*."

There is a flat pilgrim's bottle in the Sèvres Museum with the arms of France; on each side are the fleur-de-lis and "Charles Roy" in Gothic letters. It was found in the Somme, and was probably made here in the time of Charles VIII. There is also in the same collection (Sèvres) a plate of red earthenware, covered with white *engobe*, red and green mottled glaze, the design graved through; in the centre a branch of three lilies, surrounded by square compartments, and on the border, inscribed in Gothic characters of the fifteenth century, these words, "Je suis planté pour raverdir, vive Truppet."

A plate of green enamel, with escutcheons of the arms of various provinces of France, between which are emblems of the Passion in relief, and a long inscription round in old black letter beginning "O vos omnes qui transitis per viam," &c., and ending with the date 1502, as in the margin. In the Soltykoff Collection, sold at the sale for £12. One of these escutcheons contains the arms of France; another of France quartered with Brittany; a third, France and Dauphiny; and a fourth, that in the margin, containing two stars and a stake, part of the arms of Beauvais, and the name *Masse*, probably the name of the artist.

The archives of Beauvais furnish us with several instances of presents of the pottery of Saveignies being made to royalty when passing through the city. On the 17th October 1434, a vase of Saveignies was presented to the French King. In 1520, Francis I., journeying to Arras through Beauvais with his Queen, they gave her "des bougies et des vases de Saveignies," and in 1536 they presented him with a "buffet de Saveignies." In January 1689, a like present was offered to the Queen of England when she passed through Beauvais in her flight from London to Saint Germain.

SAVEIGNIES (Oise). There are several more recent manufactories of *grès*, which were in existence towards the end of the last century, mentioned by M. Brongniart, specimens of which are in the Sèvres Museum: M. Laffineur, 1806; M. Delamarre, 1806; Madame Veuve Patte, 1806; and M. Bertin, 1833. There were two other manufactories of fayence carried on here by M. Gaudin and M. Michel towards the end of the last century. Specimens are in the Sèvres Museum, acquired in 1806.

BEAUVAIS (Oise). At Pont d'Allonne, near Beauvais, a fabrique of stoneware, salt glaze, was founded about 1842 by Messrs. Joye & Dumontier, but they did not equal that of Voisinlieu. Messrs. Clerc & Taupin, the present proprietors, have produced some artistic stoneware in Ziégler's style.

J Entoine

J'englefontaine

ENGLEFONTAINE. With the decorative pottery of Beauvais and Saveignies must be classed that of Englefontaine, of which there are some specimens in the Museum at Amiens. The forms of the jugs and vessels were not very graceful, and the mode of decoration a kind of *sgraffiato*, a lead glaze being employed. The mark is given by Herr Jännike in *Grundriss der Keramik*.

AVIGNON. This pottery is of a reddish brown, with a fine metalloid glaze, like bronze or tortoiseshell. The ewers and bottles are usually of elegant form, like those of Italy; they are sometimes perforated, sometimes with raised marks, &c., in yellow. The factory flourished from about 1650 to 1780; specimens are generally unmarked. There were potteries here early in the sixteenth century. M. P. Achard (archiviste of the department of Vaucluse) mentions several early potters whose names occur in the archives :—

> Maitre Calle Monteroux, poterius, 1500, au puits des Tournes.
> Maitre Veran Merlesius, potier, 1517, dans la paroisse St. Agricol.
> Maitre Guilhermus David, poterius, 1519.
> M. Petrus Bertet, 1539, Rue de la Pailhasserie.
> M. Johannes Roqueti, potier, 1551, Portalis Matheronis.
> M. Antoine Castan, potier, 1596, Rue St. Marc.
> M. Louis Fauquet, potier, 1715, Rue St. Sebastien.
> The Brothers Ruel and the Brothers Blanchard.
> In 1694 M. Montclergeon, and earlier, M. Vauceton.

An earthenware *cruche*, brown glaze and ornaments in relief, seventeenth century, sold at the Bernal sale for £10 10s., and a fine ewer in the Soltykoff sale brought £14. There are two good specimens in the Soulages Collection, Victoria and Albert Museum.

LHERAULE (Canton of Songeons) in the sixteenth and seventeenth centuries was the seat of an ancient pottery, contemporary, it is stated, with that of Palissy, but the productions bear no comparison. They are, like the later productions of Saveignies, of clay covered with enamel, of green or marone colour, with ornaments in yellow, red, or white. The pieces, in forms of statuettes of saints, crucifixes, and bénitiers, are rudely fashioned.

GOINCOURT (Oise), 1795. Near this place, in the environs of Beauvais, a manufacture of enamelled fayence called "*L'Italienne*" was established in 1795 by M. Michel. The statuettes and groups, virgins, saints, bishops, animals, &c., are frequently found in Picardy, but the manufacture has ceased many years.

Fayence of the end of the eighteenth century, a common description of ware painted with flowers, &c. The name stamped in the ware.

L'Italienne
or
L'ITALIENNE.

SAINT-PAUL (Oise). Fayence of the eighteenth and nineteenth centuries. Of ordinary quality, mostly designed with pricked paper (*à poncis*), bouquets, &c., in colours. Mark stamped in the clay.

S. PAUL.

SARREGUEMINES (Moselle). A manufactory of great importance, established about 1770 by Paul Utzchneider. This beautiful fayence is in imitation of porphyry, jasper, granite, and other hard marbles, sometimes cut and polished by the lathe, frequently with white raised figures on blue and other coloured grounds, very much in the style of Wedgwood, and red ware like the Japanese. There are many specimens in the Sèvres Museum. The name impressed on the ware.

Sarreguemines.

SARREGUEMINES. Messrs. Utzchneider & Co. still make fayence and porcelain of every description.

SAINT-SAMSON (Oise). A manufactory for crucibles, &c., in whitish paste. Paris Exposition, 1834.

E. L. B.

CHATILLON. The following notice occurs in the *Intelligenzblatt*, Leipzig, 1766: "Since everybody has sent silver services to the Paris mint, the manufacturers have invented all sorts of fayence and imitations of porcelain. It would be useful to visit the different fabriques to know the best sorts, and provide a stock of the best models. At Chatillon-sur-Oise there is a fayence manufactory; the ware resists heat and becomes red-hot rather than break; all sorts of vessels for actual use are made here; it is transported by the Canal de Briare on the Seine to Paris."

VOISINLIEU, near Beauvais (Oise). Established about 1839. Ziégler, a painter of considerable merit, having become unable on account of an injury to his sight to prosecute his profession, entered into partnership with a stoneware manufacturer, and by his devotion to the improvement of processes raised the quality of the productions, which became famous.

The large vase known as *Vase des Apôtres*, with figures in relief of the twelve Apostles, is considered to be his *chef-d'œuvre*, and has been said to be one of the finest of modern productions in ceramic art. He used a salt glaze of a brown colour, and his forms and style were pure and his paste hard and of good quality. This establishment having passed into the hands of

M. Mansart, increased at first very much, but soon declined, and ceased altogether about 1856.

CREIL. CREIL (Oise). Established in the last century by some English potters, and continued by Le Beuf, Milliet & Co., and M. de St. Criq & Co. The paste is a sort of demi-porcelain and opaque cream-coloured ware, like that of Wedgwood.

The word CREIL is impressed on the ware, and the initials, in cipher, of the agent, stencilled—Messrs. Stone, Coquerel et Le Gros, of Paris. There are in the Worcester Museum several plates with lightly printed views of the principal edifices of Paris. They are also sometimes painted with classical or allegorical figures in sepia.

MONTEREAU (Seine-et-Marne). On the 15th March 1775 we find the letters patent of the establishment of this fabrique, from which we give the following extract: "Sur la requête présentée par les Sieurs Clark, Shaw & Co., natifs d'Angleterre, contenant qu'ils ont commencé à établir à Montereau une fabrique de faïence anglaise, que les essais qu'ils ont faits des terres à pipes, argiles et glaises qui se trouvent dans les environs de cette ville leur ont trés-bien réussi pour la fabrication de la faïence anglaise dite *queen's ware;* que ces terres sont de nature à faire cette espèce de fayence beaucoup plus parfaite même que celle d'Angleterre puis qu'on peut lui donnez le plus grand degré de blancheur; qu'en conséquence les suppliants se proposent de monter en grand leur manufacture et de former à cet effet des ouvriers et apprentifs du pays qu'ils dresseront à ce travail afin de fournier au public de cette sorte de faïence qui est d'une composition plus parfaite et plus durable que toutes celles du royaume et qu'ils établiront à meilleur compte que toute ce qui s'y est fabriqué jusqu'à present; que les suppliants, que ont tous femmes et enfants et qui, avec deux autres ouvriers qu'ils sont encore ob'igés de faire venir d'Angleterre, forment ensemble le nombre de dix sept personnes, n'ont pu se déplacer sans beaucoup de frais; que d'ailleurs une entreprise de cette espèce, dont le capital formera par la suite un objet considérable, devant leur occasionner des dépenses infinies . . . ainsi que les pertes qu'ils ont déjà eues et qu'il aura encore à essuyer avant qu'ils puissent être bien au fait de gouverner le feu de bois, attendu qu'on ne brûle en Angleterre que de charbon de terre, etc. . . ." They therefore demanded various privileges, which were accorded, with permission to establish the works. A second arrêt of 15th March 1775 conceded to them from the first of January of the said year an allowance of 1200 francs a year for ten years. This English ware had a very extensive sale, and its introduction was a great blow to the manufacture of French fayence; it soon spread itself through the south of France, and was made especially at Toulouse and Sarreguemines. In the list of faienciers who petitioned the National

Assembly in 1790, two manufactories are alluded to at Montereau. It was afterwards carried on by M. de St. Criq about 1810, and subsequently by MM. Lebeuf and Thibaut, 1829, and specimens were marked with their initials, L. L. et T. Gratien Milliet was director about 1836. It was subsequently united to that at Creil.

COURBETON, near Montereau (Seine-et-Marne). A fabrique of *grès*, carried on by M. H. Mamet; specimens in the Sèvres Museum, acquired in 1839.

MENEÇY-VILLEROY. We are inclined to include this as a fabrique of fayence from having seen specimens marked D V with D. V., the same as on porcelain, the mark painted as well as impressed. M. A. Jacquemart quotes the existence of a water-pot painted in blue in the Rouenais style, with arms in pale blue, and underneath the words "Pinte de Ville-Roy, 1735"; also a plate in blue with arabesques in the same style, signed D. V.

CHOISY. Demi-porcelain or opaque cream-coloured ware was made here, very similar to that produced at Creil, and decorated with transfer prints. Porcelain was also made here.

   CHOISY. Herr Jännike gives   H B & Cⁱᵉ
both these marks, the initials H. B.   CHOISY
being those of H. Boulanger & Cie.   LE ROІ

ST. CLOUD, near Paris, 1690. This establishment was founded by Chicanneau père et fils, for the manufacture of fine fayence and porcelain, and in 1702 exclusive privileges were granted for twenty years to the heirs of Chicanneau, his son having the direction.

Abraham de Pradel in his Almanack of 1690 says, "Il y a *une* fayancerie à St. Cloud où l'on peut faire exécuter tels modèles que l'on veut," doubtless alluding to this establishment. In 1722 Henri Trou became director. This fayence is generally in blue *camaieu*, and similar to that of Rouen of the first period. The letter T which comes underneath the SᵗC is the initial of the director.

There are several pieces of fayence of this period preserved; one belonging to M. Fleury, a plate decorated in blue with elegant arabesques, and marked with Trou's initial, like that on the porcelain; another is in the Sèvres Museum, marked, and others without marks are also assigned to St. Cloud by the late M. Riocreux.

Before the discovery of the Moustiers manufacture, that ware was attributed to St. Cloud. In 1698 the fabrique was visited by Dr. Martin Lister, who gives an account of the porcelain made here, and in 1700 by the Duchess of Burgundy. The royal family took great interest in the works, and the Duke of Orleans, who had a laboratory of his own, suggested many improvements. There are specimens in the Sèvres Museum. (See also notice of St. Cloud Porcelain.)

PARIS (established about 1550). François Briot was a celebrated artist, modeller, goldsmith, and manufacturer of fayence. His works in gold and silver have disappeared with the other superb jewels described in the inventory of Henry II. in 1560, but some of his works are preserved to us in tin and in pottery. Briot was, although a goldsmith, what was termed a *potier d'estaigne*, and worked both in metal and in pottery; in fact, all the goldsmiths of the sixteenth century were necessarily acquainted with the potter's art of moulding in clay, for the purpose of reproducing their works in the richer metals. The two arts of the goldsmith and the potter were intimately connected together, the designs for important pieces of gold or silver plate being first modelled in terra-cotta or clay hardened by the fire. Those great artists, Luca della Robbia and Benvenuto Cellini, like most of the Italian artists, commenced their career by studying as goldsmiths, then, as their eminent talents developed themselves, they struck out into sculpture in marble or bronze. Andrea del Verrochio was a goldsmith, and in his studio or workshop was moulded the mind of Leonardo da Vinci. Pollajuolo, Ghirlandajo, and La Francia were at the same time goldsmiths and painters.

Benvenuto Cellini praises the extremely fine quality of the sand or extrait du rivage de l'Ile de la Sainte-Chapelle (la cité), which he says "a des propriétés que ne possédent point les autres sables." It was of this material that François Briot composed his fayence, some superb examples of which still remain to show his extraordinary talent. His enamelled earthenware vessels have been erroneously attributed to Bernard Palissy, but they are evidently a distinct manufacture, and were executed under the immediate superintendence of Briot himself in a rival establishment. The enamel of these pieces is more vitreous and transparent, the colours more brilliant and of a higher finish than any ever produced by Palissy, and resemble more nearly enamel or metal.

We are consequently compelled to differ from the opinion of M. Jacquemart, who says that "la pluralité des plats reproduits de Briot a tous les caractères des émaux et de la terre du potier des Tuilleries." A comparison of the salver of Sir E. M. Elton and others in this country with Palissy's productions will be a convincing proof of the difference of manufacture both in material and enamel.

The salver in the possession of Sir E. M. Elton, Bart., a circular earthenware dish, which is supposed to be the finest of its kind extant, enriched with very elaborate arabesque ornamentation in relief, is enamelled with the most brilliant colours; in the centre a figure of "Temperantia," surrounded by medallions of the four elements, terminal figures between, and round the border eight others impersonating the arts and sciences; diameter $16\frac{1}{4}$ in. In the Fountaine Collection at Narford was a ewer of enamelled earthenware to match this salver; the plateau is said to have been brought to England by an ancestor of the late possessor, who was a student at Padua, more than two hundred years ago.[1] M. Calixte de

---

[1] This beautiful ewer was sold by auction in the Fountaine sale, 1882, for £1365.

Tussau has a fine example of a plateau of similar design : at the feet of Temperantia is the monogram of François Briot, stamped with a separate mould, as shown in the margin. It may be observed that this stamp is not to be found on the salver of pewter as made origi- nally by Briot, and which would have appeared if it had been moulded together with the rest of the relief, but the letters FB are evidently stamped in the clay afterwards. Another in the Soltykoff Collection, sold for £400 to the Baron Sellière, was also finely enamelled ; the reverse, which was mottled in colour, had in the centre the letter F, the initial of François, engraved in the paste before it was fired. Another in the Soltykoff Collection, not so fine, sold for £200. There were also three smaller enamelled earthenware plates by Briot, representing the Earth and the Air personified, and the Judgment of Paris ; the last was sold for about £70. In the celebrated Forman Collection at Dorking is an earthenware plateau of the same pattern, but of less highly finished execution than that previously described ; it is probably the work of one of his successors.

PARIS (Pont-aux-Choux, 1740). *The Manufacture Royale de Terre d'Angleterre* was established opposite the *porte* of Pont-aux-Choux, at the corner of the Rue St. Sebastien. It was directed in 1749 by Edme, who in August of the same year married Marie Claude Serrurier, daughter of a draper of Nevers.

Heringle, who established a manufactory at Lille in 1758, states in his request that he had worked for seven consecutive years at this estab- lishment. We find it mentioned in *L'Almanach général des Marchands* of 1772 under the name of *Manufacture Royale des Terres de France, à l'imitation de celles d'Angleterre*. It was directed by M. Mignon, who undertook the manufacture of the choicest pieces to order, and forwarded them in the kingdom and abroad. It is mentioned in several other works of the period—*L'Indicateur Parisien* and in *Le Guide des Amateurs et des Étrangers par Thiery*. This pottery, which was also called *terre anglaise*, was probably an imitation of the cream-coloured or Queen's ware, so much in vogue at that time. However, the vases of this material were of con- siderable elegance, and were purchased by the King and the nobility, and esteemed worthy of being mounted in gilt bronze of the finest work. Many sculptors of great talent were engaged, especially Sigisbert Adam, the brother of Clodion. There is a glazed fayence bust of Louis XV. on a square pedestal of the *terre d'Angleterre*, made here about 1740, in the Sèvres Museum.

PARIS (Seine). Fayence of the end of the eighteenth century, called *fabrique générale de faïence de la République*. This mark is stamped in the paste on a plate painted with revolutionary emblems and motto. Not knowing how to produce the red, the *bonnet rouge* is painted yellow. This Olivier is probably the same as the maker of the earthenware stove in the Sèvres Museum representing the Bastille.

OLIVIER A PARIS.

PARIS. Fayence de Claude Révérend. This fayence, although exactly similar to that of Delft, is supposed to have been made in Paris by Révérend, who was for a long time established in Holland as a potter; and he obtained letters patent in 1664 to fabricate "fayence and imitation porcelain" in France. His fayence was called "*crucifères*." The pieces marked as in the margin are attributed to him, forming R A P (Révérend à Paris?), and they frequently bear French inscriptions. The decoration is polychrome and in blue, in imitation of the best pieces of Delft, with a firm white glaze and bright colours. There was a specimen in the Collection of the late Mr. C. W. Reynolds, and afterwards in the possession of his son, Captain Reynolds (marked in blue); and a splendid dish given to the Sèvres Museum by M. Sauvageot seems to have been specially made as a present to Colbert by Révérend to show his successful imitation of Oriental porcelain; it has in the centre the arms of Colbert. M. A. Jacquemart quotes a decree of the year 1664 granting to Claude Révérend the privilege of making fayence and imitating porcelain; the exact words are, "De faire la faïence et contrefaire la porcelaine aussi belle et plus que celle qui vient dès Indes Orientales," evidently one and the same thing; he goes on to say that this secret manufacture he had accomplished and brought to perfection in Holland, where the greater portion of his stock still remained, which he wished to transport into France. This is clearly a manufacture of fayence in imitation of porcelain, and not porcelain itself, as M. Jacquemart infers, which hypothesis is decidedly untenable. Claude Révérend does not say, "qu'il fait une porcelaine véritable, translucide et aussi belle que celle qui vient dès Indes Orientales," but "il contrefait une porcelaine aussi belle," &c., and not a word is said about its transparency or any other quality possessed by porcelain.

PARIS (Rue des Trois Couronnes). Established in 1833 by M. Pichenot for the manufacture of enamelled fayence, under the direction of a German named Loebnitz. In 1843 he patented his "*émail ingerçable.*" His widow ceded the manufactory to Jules Loebnitz, son of the director. It was remarkable for the great size of its products. In the Sèvres Museum is a large cistern of one piece, enamelled inside and out; large tiles and vases, from the Exposition of 1844; the pieces are marked 'Pichenot, 7 Rue des Trois Couronnes."

PARIS (7 Rue des Récollets). Ceramic painter. M. Hippolyte Pinart, painter of *faïence artistique*. He obtained a medal at the International Exhibition in 1862, where his talent was appreciated and his fayence found a ready sale.

PARIS (11 Rue de Sèvres). *Faïences artistiques*, A. Jean, manufacturer; imitations of maiolica, &c., established 1859. There were numerous specimens in the International Exhibition, 1862, for which he obtained a medal.

PARIS (Avenue des Parcs aux Princes, Bois de Boulogne). The Brothers Deck were first induced to imitate the Persian wares by M. Adalbert de Beaumont, a traveller and artist who collected innumerable designs and copies of detail and general effect. Since that time he took a practical chemist into partnership, M. Collinot, and erected a kiln for the production of his "*cloisonné*" wares in Arabian and Persian style, and traces his designs on the ware with aquafortis filled in with coloured enamels on flower-pots, vases, tiles, dishes, &c.

PARIS. Manufactory of *faïences d'art* by Théodore Deck, 1859, Magasin, 12 Rue Halévy. There were some specimens of his encrusted ware in the International Exhibition, 1862 which sold very freely to English amateurs, and he deservedly obtained a medal. This beautiful ware has coloured pastes inserted in patterns on the body of the ware, like the Henri II. ware, sometimes in Persian designs, and paintings of artistic subjects of great beauty and originality. Among the artists engaged at this fabrique may be noted Messrs. Anker, Ranvier, Legrain, Glück, Ehrman, Hirsch, Schubert and Benner, and Madame Escallier. There are several good representative specimens of Deck fayence in the Victoria and Albert Museum.

PARIS (Rue de la Roquette, Faubourg St. Antoine), 1675. In a memorial of Jean Binet, *ouvrier en faïence brune et blanche*, at this manufactory, presented in 1753 (*Mémoires de Mannory*, Paris, 1764), we have an account of some other potters who preceded him. The first was François Dezon in 1675, a maker of earthenware, who carried on the works with his sons. Genest was the name of his successor in 1730, who for twenty years was "*fabricant de faïence*" in the same house. In 1750 Genest sold the concern to Jean Binet.

PARIS (Rue de la Roquette). There is a medicine jar of the Rouen style in the Sèvres Museum, painted with arabesques and arms of the Orleans family; said to have been made by M. Digne in the middle of the eighteenth century. He was succeeded by M. Gauthier, who in 1830 sent some fayence services to the Museum.

PARIS (Rue de la Roquette). Fabrique de M. Tourasse, 1823.

PARIS (Rue de la Roquette). Fabrique de MM. Masson Frères, 1839. This fayence is praised by Brongniart on account of its brilliant blue enamel.

PARIS (Vaugirard). M. Pull, formerly a soldier, then a naturalist, undertook in 1856 the manufacture of pottery in the style of B. Palissy, and produced some clever imitations. He has copied "La Nourrice" and "Le Joueur de Viele," and also produced moulded

PULL

OR

Pull.

plates from the white metal salvers of François Briot (which Palissy himself had copied); these are so highly finished and so brilliantly enamelled that several connoisseurs have been deceived by them: one was sold at a shop in Paris to a rich banker for 6000 francs (£240). M. Lasteyrie says of this artist "que ses produits sont tellement bien imités, qu'il est devenu le désespoir des collectioneurs du Palissy." His mark is some-times in black enamel, sometimes in relief or incuse.

B. V.

PARIS. M. Victor Barbizet. Established 1850. Enamelled earthenware in imitation of B. Palissy, produced in great variety and at a low price; occasionally marked incuse with the letter B. V.

Lessore

PARIS. M. E. Lessore, a painter on fayence, formerly employed at Sèvres, which he left in 1850, and established himself at 16 Rue de l'Empereur, aux Batignolles. In 1859 he left and came to England, and was attached principally to the Wedgwood manufactory, but also painted for other firms. A dish by him, executed at Mintons', in imitation of maiolica, is in the Victoria and Albert Museum; purchased for £30. Some other imitations of decorations of unsaleable biscuit figures by him, in the style of Italian ware, have deceived collectors, a practice which ought not to be countenanced by respectable potters, and is no less derogatory to the artist. Lessore returned to France and resided at Fontainebleau, where he executed commissions for Wedgwood and Minton. See also notice of Lessore under "Wedgwood."

Vᵛᵉ· DUMAS
66 rue Fontaine-au-Roi.

PARIS. The potter Vogt, from Nuremberg, established himself at 66 Rue Fontaine au Roi about 1790, in the manufacture of stoves, &c. In 1834 he decorated tiles with encrusted or inlaid patterns of coloured clays covered with a plumbiferous glaze. Madame Veuve Dumas, his daughter, still continues making some beautiful pieces, many of which are marked with her name and address. M. Théodore Deck was for-merly manager of this fabrique, and there learned the art of nielloed earthenware.

I. D.

PARIS (Montrouge). M. Joseph Devers, an Italian by birth, formerly a painter, pupil of Ary Scheffer, commenced a fabrique of fayence here about 1847: terra-cotta vases and groups in the Della Robbia style, large medallions and all sorts of artistic pottery. In 1862 he received a medal from the International Exhibition for decorative pottery. There are specimens in the Victoria and Albert Museum, Nos. 23-64, 706-769.

PARIS (Rue de Charenton, 1766). In the *Intelligenzblatt* of Leipzig of this year we read: "Rue Charenton, Faubourg St. Antoine, vis à vis l'ancienne manufacture de velours, se trouve actuellement une manufacture de faïences bronzés qui va au feu; on fait toutes sortes de vaisselle."

PARIS (Rue Basfroy, près la Roquette, 1766). In the *Intelligenzblatt* of Leipzig of this year we find the following: "Rue Basfroy, près la Roquette, on fabrique dans la manufacture de M. Roussel des faïences qui sont intérieurement blanches et extérieurement de couleur olive. On elle faite toutes sortes de services complets. Cette faïence va au feu, est très légère et à meilleur compte que celle faite en terre de pipe Anglaise : la douzaine d'assiettes se vend de 3 à 5 livres."

PARIS. This talented artist has with great success turned his attention to painting on earthen- *M. Bouquet.* ware *au grand feu.* The subjects usually selected by M. Bouquet are landscapes and woodland scenery ; these are painted on plaques of coarse earthenware, similar to what we call Stourbridge clay, capable of bearing an intense heat, and at one baking the whole process is completed. Considerable chemical knowledge is essential for this kind of decoration, as but few colours will stand the great heat of the kiln, and skilful manipulation is required in painting on the treacherous surface of the clay, which must be executed offhand, without any possibility of retouching. The plaque is then placed in the furnace, a monotonous and almost indistinguishable sketch ; it is taken out a finished picture, rich in colour, artistic, and imperishable, not affected by the action of the atmosphere, and consequently suitable for exterior as well as interior decorations of houses and gardens.

SÈVRES (Seine-et-Oise). This mark is impressed on the back of two fayence plates of light fabrique, very much like the demi-porcelain plates made at Creil ; on them are also stencilled shields inscribed " Par brevet d'invention," surrounded by the words " Impression sous émail." The subjects are printed in brown, of Time and Cupid and " La Ceinture de Venus," &c.

SÈVRES. There were several manufactories of fayence here. A large and fine vase (style Louis XIV.) by a potter named Lambert, of about 1790, is in the Sèvres Museum, but it has no mark. Another manufacturer was M. Levasseur, about the end of the last century, and M. Clavareau, 1806 ; specimens in the Sèvres Museum.

AVON (Seine-et-Marne), near Fontainebleau. M. A. Jacquemart has accounted for another manufactory of pottery at this place, and quotes from the journal of Hérouard, Doctor of the Dauphin (Louis XIII). To this fabrique he refers the pieces marked B B, " La Nourrice," and small animals, as well as many others subsequent to Palissy. Hérouard says : " Le 24 Avril 1608, la Duchesse de Montpensier vient voir à Fontainebleau le petit Duc d'Orleans, second fils de Henry IV., et lui mène sa fille, agée d'environ trois ans. Le petit prince l'embrasse et lui donne une petite nourrice en potterie qu'il tenait." . . . " Le Mercredy, 8 Mai 1608, le Dauphin étant à Fontainebleau, la Princesse de Conti devait danser en ballet chez la reine, puis venir dans la chambre du Dauphin. On lui proposa de faire préparer une collation des petites pièces qu'il avait achetées à la poterie, il y consent. Après le ballet, qui est dansé à neuf heures du soir, le Dauphin mène Madame de Guise à sa collation, ils sont suivis de tous ceux qui avaient dansé le ballet, et de rire, et à faire des exclamations ; c'etaient des petits chiens, des renards, des bléreaux, des bœufs, des vaches, des escurieux, des anges jouant de la musette, de la flute, des vielleurs, des chiens couchés, des moutons, un assez grand chien au milieu de la table, et un dauphin au haut bout, un capucin au bas."

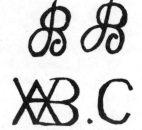

The two B's occur on works of secondary importance, as on a group of "La Samaritaine," two dogs and a snail, in the Sèvres Museum, and on "La Nourrice."

This mark, V A B. C, of an unknown potter, is found on a plate of agatised ware, representing the infant Bacchus, in the style of Palissy.

Clerici or Clerissy of Fontainebleau was also an imitator of Palissy in the first half of the seventeenth century. In March 1640 he had letters patent to found royal glassworks at Fontainebleau. M. Jacquemart thinks he must have been one of the principal artisans of the fabrique at Avon, patronised, as we have seen, by the Court.

At the Soltykoff sale in Paris in 1861 we remember to have seen two large dishes of enamelled fayence of the seventeenth century; they were of a bronze colour. In the centre was a shield of arms and the device "Sia laudato il santissimo sacramento," the letters in the inscription being reversed; the rest of the dish, including the border, was filled with rich arabesques, all in relief. It was of an unknown manufacture, somewhat similar to that of the Citta di Castello or La Fratta. The reverse of one of these dishes had the escutcheon of France and this inscription, "DU CHASTEAU DE FONTAINEBLEAU."

AVON LES FONTAINEBLEAU. Messrs. Godebski & Co., china manufacturers, of recent origin, and at No. 17 Rue Paradis-Poissonnière, Paris. This mark, used since 1874, registered as a trade-mark in London, 1876.

SAINTES, near Rochelle and other places. BERNARD PALISSY. This artist made a peculiar kind of ware, which has rendered his name celebrated over Europe. He was born at La Chapelle Biron, in Perigord, A.D. 1510; he was originally a painter on glass. In 1539 he married and established himself at Saintes. After many years of diligent research and patience under trying circumstances, including the reproaches of his wife—which might naturally be expected, for it is related he actually burned his tables and chairs to heat the furnace for his experiments in perfecting the pottery—he at length succeeded in discovering the enamel which decorates his ware. It is recorded of him that in his pleasant moments he used to say, in reference to his trade as a potter, that he had no property whatever except heaven and earth. His rustic pottery and other beautiful productions were soon appreciated, and he rose to opulence; he made large pieces, such as vases and statues, for Henri II. and his Court, to ornament their gardens and decorate their palaces and mansions. Being a Protestant, he was, after the Edict of 1559, taken under the protection of Catherine de' Medici, and settled in Paris, thus escaping the massacre of St. Bartholomew. In 1588, however, he was confined in the Bastille for his religious opinions, and lingered in those dungeons until his death, which happened in 1589. He had two nephews, Nicolas and Mathurin, who were associated with him in his ceramic productions, notably in the decoration of the grotto of the Tuilleries. His continuators were Jehan Chipault and Jehan Biot, in the sixteenth century, but they executed very inferior specimens. The natural objects found upon the Palissy ware are true in form and colour, being mostly modelled from nature; the shells are all copied from tertiary fossils found in the Paris basin; the fish are those of the Seine, and the reptiles and plants such as he found in the environs of Paris. We recognise one of Palissy's vases of the *figuline rustique* treasured up in the Collection of the Duke of Lorraine in 1633: "Un goublet antique de terre rustique."

A large round basin, representing Diana leaning on a stag, with dogs around her, after the celebrated relief in marble of Diane de Poitiers *en chasseresse*, by Jean Goujon, brought in the Soltykoff sale £292; another oval basin, with masks and flowers, £160; a pair of salt-cellars of two sirens, £80; and two statuettes of Mercury and a player on the bagpipes. £103. A very fine circular dish, with a lizard in the centre and rich border, was sold in the Bernal sale to Baron Gustave de Rothschild for £162; it was bought in a broken state in Paris for twelve francs, and after being restored was sold to Mr. Bernal for £4. There are several fine specimens in the Soulages Collection and in the Victoria and Albert Museum. (*Ker. Gall.*, enlarged edition, figs. 113, 114, 115, 116.)

SAINTES (Charente-Inférieure). This inscription is on a large hunting-bottle of white fayence, decorated in blue, with loops for suspension, painted with roses and tulips, and in the centre, within a wreath, on one side is the name ALEXANDRE BESCHET, and on the other the inscription in the margin, meaning the sign of the image of Notre Dame at Saintes, quoted by M. B. Fillon.

P. P

aLimage N.D.

a Saintes

1680

LA CHAPELLE DES POTS, near Saintes. It was here that Bernard Palissy learned the first elements of his trade; here also, after his death, an extensive manufacture of ware of a similar character was continued until the middle of the seventeenth century. A great variety of forms was produced, plates, dishes, bells in the shape of women with hooped petticoats, puzzle jugs, drinking-cups in form of the sabot, barrels, bénitiers, candlesticks, &c. Vast quantities of defective pieces and fragments of the ancient manufactory are dug up. At the present day common pottery is made here.

BRIZAMBOURG (Charente-Inférieure), near Saintes. There was another fabrique of fayence here (as appears from a document quoted at length by M. B. Fillon, *Art de Terre chez les Poitevins*, of the year 1600), in which we find that Enoch Dupas, *maistre faïancier de Brizambourg et y demeurant*, claimed from *Reni Arnaud, escuyer, seigneur de la Garenne*, la somme de six vingt escus (120 crowns) prix et rayson de vaisselles impressées de ses armes, moderée par le jugement à celle de soixante et quinze escus (75 crowns).

J.B

LA ROCHELLE (Charente-Inférieure). Herr Jännike gives these initials as those of J. Briqueville, who established a small pottery here about 1743.

MONTBERNAGE (Faubourg de Poitiers). About 1776 a fabrique was founded by M. Pasquier, who was associated with Felix Faucon, son of a printer at Poitiers. In the Sèvres Museum there is a plate, painted in blue, which bears the mark of two F's and a falcon in a cartouche, which is considered to refer to Faucon. It is probable that the latter remained sole director at Montbernage, and his associate Pasquier established himself at Poitiers.

A. MORREINE.w

Poitiers

1752

POITIERS (Vienne). A. Morreine was a modeller of figures in *terre de pipe*; his name is found traced with a point both before and after baking. This mark is on the figure of a monk praying.

Le Sieur Pasquier, *fabricant de faïence émaillée* at Poitiers, claimed in 1778 the protection of the Minister Bertin for the liberty to dig clay, which had been refused by the owners of the land.

faicte les 5 May
1642
par edme Briou.
dement a St Verain

ST. VERAIN. In the neighbourhood of Nevers there was a fabrique of *grès*. M. Rénault, of Luçon, has an inkstand with this inscription; it is covered with a thick enamel of a fine blue colour. The mark is traced before firing underneath the piece: Made the 5th of May, 1642, by Edme Briou, living at St. Verain.

NANTES (Loire-Inférieure). There was an ancient establishment for the manufacture of fayence of white enamel created by Jean Ferro, *gentilhomme verrier*, in 1588. Two other fayence-makers of the same town are mentioned in the archives of the Chamber of Nantes in 1654, named Charles Guermeur and Jacques Rolland. This ware was also white, sometimes with fleur-de-lis in relief, specimens of which are frequently met with in the neighbourhood.

I·R·PAIVADEAV·
1643

M. B. Fillon gives this mark, which is on the back of a plate, painted in blue *camaieu*, with four medallions of a lion, a stag, a serpent, and a horse, and in the centre the Massacre of the Innocents, copied from a print by Mark

Antonio, after Raphael, which he attributes to Nantes, and says it is very similar to that made by Clerissy of Moustiers, painted by Gaspard Viry.

On the 7th of March 1752, a fabrique of fayence was founded by M. Leroy de Montillée and a company, which was successfully carried on for some years, but having passed into the hands of M. Delabre in consequence of heavy losses sustained by him, it was sold in 1771 to Sieurs Perret and Fourmy, under whose management it again became prosperous and superior to what it had been under their predecessors; its products were in such high estimation that in 1774 it obtained the title of *Manufacture Royale de Nantes*. The original *arrêt* is given at length by M. B. Fillon (*Art de Terre chez les Poitevins*), and it accords to Joseph Perret and Mathurin Fourmy royal patronage and liberty for the servants to wear royal livery.

NEVERS (Nièvre). In the year 1590 the alchemist Gaston de Cleves dedicated a book to Louis of Gonzaga, Duke of Nevers; in the dedicatory epistle he extols this prince for having brought into his states expert artists and workmen in the arts of glassmaking, pottery, and enamel. The quotation from this scarce book is given by Marryat at some length : " Hinc vitrariæ figulinæ et encausticæ artis artifices egregii jusso tuo accersisti," &c. About this time the name of Scipio Gambyn is found in the parish registers as godfather in 1592; he is there described as " pothier." A relation of his, probably a son or brother, Julien Gambyn of Faenza, obtained authority to establish a manufactory of fayence at Lyons, but the earliest evidence of one at Nevers is that founded by Domenique Conrade, a gentleman of Savona, a native of Albissola, where the fayence of Savona, well known in Italy, 1560 to 1600, was made; in 1578 he obtained letters of naturalisation from Henri III., and about this time founded his fabrique at Nevers.

In a brevet according privileges to Antoine Conrade at a later period, by Louis XIV. and his mother the Queen Regent, it is stated, " Estant bien informé de son industrie et grande expérience à faire toutes sortes de vaisseaux de faïence, quel science rare et particulière était reservé secrettement de père et fils en la maison Domenique de Conrade."

In July 1602, Domenique Conrade's name first appears on the parish registers with the simple qualification of " Maistre potier demeurant à Nevers." His brothers, Baptiste and Augustin, are frequently mentioned from 1602 to 1613, and were doubtless associated with him.

Antoine Conrade of the second generation appears as " Faïencier de la maison du roi" in 1644. Domenique Conrade of the third generation is styled in the registers of 1650-72 " Maistre faïencier ordinaire de S. M."

Up to 1632 no other potters are spoken of, but in that year Barthélémy Bourcier founded a second manufactory.

In 1652 appeared successively two other fabriques, one by Nicolas Estienne at the " Ecce Homo," and the other by Pierre Custode and Esmé Godin at the sign " de l'Autruche."

From 1632 Pierre Custode is designated " Maistre potier en vaisselle de faïence," and he probably came from Savona with the Conrades, working under their direction until 1652, when he himself became a director.

At the beginning of the eighteenth century, in consequence of the success of the Conrades and Custodes, several other manufactories were started, and in 1743, by *un arrêt de conseil*, the number was restricted to eleven. Upon earnest solicitation in 1760 a twelfth was permitted by royal ordinance, which was in consequence called " La Royale."

The twelve fabriques were as follows : —

1.—1608. Fabrique des Conrades, 12 Rue Saint-Genest, founded by Domenique Conrade; successors, Garilland, Nicholas Hudes, and his widow Champroud.
2.—1652. Fabriques des Custodes, 11 Rue Saint-Genest, first called l'Autruche, founded by Pierre Custode and Esmé Godin, subsequently Enfert alone.
3.—1562. Fabrique l'Ecce Homo, 20 Rue Saint-Genest, founded by Nicolas Estienne, Louis Thonnelier de Membret, and Jean Chevalier Lestang.
4.—1632. Fabrique, 4 Rue de la Tartre, founded by Barthélémy Bourcier, succeeded by Dumont Champesle and Pierre Moreau.
5.—1760. Fabrique de Bethléem, 6 Rue de la Tartre, Messrs. Prou, Jolly, Levesque & Serizier.
6.—1760. Fabrique Halle, 12 Rue de la Tartre.
7.—1749. Fabrique Boizeau Deville, 14 Rue de la Tartre.
8.—1761. Fabrique Ollivier, 26 Rue de la Tartre.
9.—1716. Fabrique Gounot ou Merceret, 1 Rue de la Cathédral.
10.—1725. Fabrique de Prysie de Chazelle ou de Bonnaire, Place Mossé.
11.—1750 Fabrique du Bout-de-Monde, 10 Rue du Croux, by Perrony.
12.—1760. Fabrique la Royale, 13 Rue du Singe, Gautheron and Mottret.

In 1790 these were all in active operation, but shortly after this time, in consequence of the French Revolution and the treaty of commerce between France and England, by which the English potters had the opportunity of pouring in their earthenware at so cheap a rate that the French could not compete with them; added to this, the price of lead and tin, which came principally from England, was raised; all these disadvantages came so quickly upon the fabriques of the south of France that a panic ensued. In 1797 we read that at Nevers six had absolutely suspended their works, and the other six were reduced to half their number of workmen. On a subsequent page will be found a statement of the principal manufactories of France, which was attached to a petition from the fayenciers to the National Assembly.

Nevers has always been famed for the sand used in the manufacture of fayence. We are told in the *Encyclopédie Méthodique*, Paris, 1783, that Lille in Flanders, Saint-Cenis (Sinceny), Lyons, Nantes, and Rouen all obtained their sand from Nevers.

The fayences of the first epoch have been frequently confounded with Italian maiolica, but a little study will soon show the great points of difference. In the Nevers ware the figures are always yellow, either clear or opaque, on blue ground; the Italian figures are usually painted blue on yellow ground. At Nevers they never employed red or metallic lustre, and the outlines are always traced in manganese violet, never in purple or black; for example, on a plate painted in polychrome, with the four tens of a pack of cards, the clubs and spades are violet, the hearts and diamonds yellow. A particular sign on the monochromes of Nevers is the decoration on the reverse.

During the second epoch the ground was a peculiar lapis-lazuli blue, like the Persian, called *bleu de Perse*, spotted or painted with white, the vases and jugs being occasionally ornamented with masks and twisted handles, a decoration which was also imitated at Delft by an artist signing A. P. W.

The Chinese patterns are in light blue *en camaieu* on white, sometimes intermixed with a sort of brown lilac.

Those of the other periods, in the style of Rouen and Moustiers and the Saxon style, are well known; some also of the latter time have verses and inscriptions of a popular character, and revolutionary sentences, such as the following :—

　　"Aimons nous tous comme frères, 1793."
　　"Ah! ça ira."　　　　　　　　"La Liberté, 1791."
　　"Au bon laboureur François Simonin, l'an 4 de la liberté."
　　"Le malheur nous réunit" (a noble and a priest shaking hands).
　　"Aux mânes de Mirabeau, la partie reconnaissante, 1790."
　　"Le serment civique."　　　　"Vivre libre ou mourir."
　　"Je jure de maintenir de tout mon pouvoir la constitution."
　　"Dansons la carmagnole, vive la carmagnole, 1793."
　　"Vive le roi citoyen !"　　　　"Le lis ramenent la paix."
　　"Bourrons les aristocrates."　　"Indivisibilité de la République."
　　"Guerre aux tyrans et paix aux chaumières."

[The above were in the collection of M. Champfleury.]

　　"La Nation, la loi."　　　　"Vive la Constitution."
　　"Mirabeau n'est plus" (written on a tomb).
　　"Fraternité, egalité ou la mort."
　　"Vive la joye, la paix est faite."

There is a large punch-bowl or saladier, dated Nevers, 14th February 1758, decorated in polychrome, which is particularly rich with verses; the subject is "L'Arbre d'Amour"—six women at the foot of a tree, upon which are perched nine men, and on the top a cupid, "le trompeur." In the collection of the late Mr. C. W. Reynolds, and afterwards in the possession of his son, Captain Reynolds.

The classification of Nevers fayence by M. du Boroc de Segange is here given; each epoch comprehends three divisions—*polychrome, camaieu* (in monochrome), and *sculpture émaillée* :—

1st Epoch, 1600 to 1660.	Tradition italienne.
2nd Epoch, 1650 to 1750.	Goût chinois et japonais.
1630 to 1700.	Goût persan.
1640 to 1789.	Goût franco-nivernais.
3rd Epoch, 1700 to 1789.	Tradition de Rouen.
1730 to 1789.	Tradition de Moustiers.
4th Epoch, 1770 to 1789.	Goût de Saxe.
5th Epoch, 1789	Decadence de l'art.

M. du Broc de Segange, director of the Nevers Museum, in his book *La Faïence et les Faïenciers de Nevers*, Nevers, 1863, has thoroughly sifted all the available documents which could throw light on the early history of Nevers fayence. He has searched the parochial registers, and has thus been enabled to fix certain dates to the earliest specimens; he gives, in fact, a genealogical tree of every potter who has lived at Nevers, his date of birth, marriage, and decease. This work is illustrated with coloured engravings of the most celebrated specimens in the Nevers Museum, which collection already numbers more than five hundred pieces.

In the Musée de Cluny are two very fine ewers of the seventeenth century, with hunting and mythological subjects, Nos. 2147 and 2148; a ewer and basin, with the Triumph of Amphitrite, 2149 and 2150; also a very fine plate, 1235. At the Victoria and Albert Museum, a pilgrim's bottle of the first epoch, subject Apollo and Daphne, and a Bacchanalian scene, in polychrome on a blue ground, cost £15 4s. 6d.; and another bottle, with *bleu de Perse* glaze, enriched with white enamel flowers, £9.

A pair of very large Nevers ware pilgrim's bottles, with flowers and foliage in white, on metal plinths 16½ inches high, in the Bernal Collection, was purchased by the Earl of Craven for £53 6s.

N

NEVERS. This mark occurs on a plate, painted in blue, Chinese style, in the Nevers Museum, of the end of the seventeenth or beginning of the eighteenth century. M. du Broc de Segange attributes it to Nicolas Viode.

NEVERS. These marks were attributed by Brongniart to Senlis, but M. du Broc de Segange has rectified the meaning, and states them to be the monogram of Jacques Seigne, a celebrated fayencier of the eighteenth century. A mug, in form of a crown, with border of the vine painted in blue, is in the Sèvres Museum, and another in that of Cluny.

NEVERS. This mark is on a compotier, blue and orange; given by M. Brongniart.

NEVERS. This name of J. Boulard is on a statuette of the Virgin and Child, of fayence, painted in colours; at the bottom, in front, is written F. SIMON LEFEBVRE, and on the back the potter's name, who was a contemporary of the Conrades. In the possession of M. B. Fillon.

NEVERS. Domenique Conrade, the third of the name; from 1650 to 1672. He is styled in the parish register "Maistre Faïencier Ordinaire de S. M. le Roi." This signature is on a plate in the Sèvres Museum, painted in blue figures, with birds, figures, stags, &c.; in the centre a man on horseback riding over a bridge.

NEVERS. The initials of Henri Borne, on the back of a figure of St. Henry, $21\frac{1}{4}$ inches high; the companion statuette of St. Étienne, dedicated to his wife, is inscribed "E. Borne, 1689."

NEVERS. Jehan Custode, of the first epoch, 1602 to 1660, who painted at the age of twelve. On pieces in the Collection of M. André Pottier.

NEVERS. Jacques Bourdu, first epoch, 1602 to 1660. So attributed by M. du Broc de Segange.

NEVERS. Denis Lefebvre, 1636. So attributed by the same author, who has a specimen in his Collection. This mark is given by Jacquemart as occurring on a statue of the Virgin offering fruit to her Divine Son.

NEVERS. This mark is in white, in the centre of a *bleu de Perse* plate, painted with white scrolls and leaves. Franks Collection.

NEVERS. On a fayence jug, white ground, with small yellow and green flowers, blue-striped handle. Seventeenth century.

NEVERS. On a large plate, with ancient blue decoration and coarsely designed figures of a female draped figure, a countryman and his ass, a man on horseback, &c., is found this mark of three mullets (*trois molettes d'éperon*) or spur rowels, which are found on the shield of arms of the Conrades. The name of *Haly* is met with on plates painted in bouquets, having also olives, eggs, and fruit in relief, probably the work of Philippe Haly, son of the turner François Haly. The name of "F. Haly, 1734," is found on an equestrian figure of St. Hubert in the Museum at Varzy.

Claude Bigourat
1764.

NEVERS. Claude Bigourat and Jeanne Bigourat. Both occur on a bénitier, painted in blue *camaieu*, with their patron saints. Collection of M. du Broc de Segange.

F. R. 1734.

NEVERS. The signature of François Rodrigue (*dit* Duplessis) on a bénitier in blue *camaieu*, of the Virgin and Child. Collection of M. du Broc de Segange.

Borne
Pinxit
Anno
1738

NEVERS. Borne. On a dish with the Four Seasons. (*Ker. Gall.*, enlarged edition, figs. 117, 120.)

NEVERS. Until recently there was one manufactory of some commercial importance at Nevers, that of M. Montaignon, who succeeded M. H. Signoret (whose mark is in the margin), a manufacturer of pavements, encrusted tiles, garden ornaments, medallions, balustrades, flower-pots, bouquet-holders, decorated with deep blue on white ground, in the style of the old Nevers ware, and also of other polychromatic decoration.

M. MONTAIGNON. This manufacturer has adopted as his mark a rebus of his name, the tie (*taignon*) being coloured green and the letters in black; sometimes there is only "Mon" and the "tie."

MARZY, near Nevers (Nièvre). About the year 1850, M. Tite Henri Ristori, an Italian sculptor, founded a manufactory of fayence; the paste is almost of eggshell lightness and substance, and the vessels are very elegant in form and beautifully painted. At the Paris Exhibition the ware was much admired, and he obtained a first-class medal in 1856. In the Victoria and Albert Museum are ten pieces, bought at that time for £16 and £8; the others at less price.

TR
Marzy (Nievre)
1855

ROUEN (Seine-Inférieure). There was an establishment for the manufacture of pottery at Rouen early in the sixteenth century, which was

A ROUEN
1542.

evidently in great prosperity in 1542. There are two remarkable pictures which decorated the walls of the conservatory of Orleans House, Twickenham, when it was the mansion of H.R.H. the Duc d'Aumale; they formerly formed part of the pavement of the Château d'Ecouen, bearing the arms of Montmorency. These pictures are formed of a number of tiles placed in juxtaposition, representing the stories of Marcus Curtius and Mutius Scævola, and on them is written "A Rouen, 1542"; they each measure 5 feet 3 inches high by 6 feet 4 inches long.

M. E. Gosselin (*Glanes Historiques Normandes: les Potiers, Briquetiers, Tuilliers et Emailleurs de Terre de Rouen, XVième et XVIième Siècles*, Rouen, 1869) quotes several documents, wherein is named a certain Masseot Abaquesne who is styled "emailleur en terre." Masseot or Masso was at that time a sort of nickname for Thomas. In one of these acts, dated May 1545, Masso Abaquesne, "emailleur en terre," treats with an apothecary of Rouen to supply him with enamelled earthen utensils necessary for the "estat d'apothicairerie"; the order is for 346 dozen pots of all sorts, and as the potter is interdicted from supplying any other person during the delivery and for six weeks after, it is probable the apothecary purchased them for sale.

The next important document is of March 1548. It is the receipt for "cent escus d'or soleil" remitted to "Masseot Abaquesne, emailleur en terre, demeurant en la paroisse Notre Dame de Sotteville-lez-Rouen, par un notaire royal, au compte de hault et puissant Seigneur Messire le Connestable, grand maistre de France, pour certain nombre de carreaux de terre emaillée que le dit Abaquesne s'estoit soumis et obligé à faire au dit Sieur Connestable." The receipt is signed by Masso Abaquesne, by his wife Marion Durand (a cross), and their son Laurent.

In 1564, Masso Abaquesne being dead, his widow, Marion Durand, treats in her own name with the Abbé of a monastery in Normandy "pour la fourniture de quatre milliers de carreaux émaillés de couleurs d'azur, blanc, jaulne et vert, bon, loyal et marchand; suivant un patron paraphé et signé au prix de trente-six livres le mille."

In 1543 there is an act of the placement of an apprentice with Masseot Abaquesne, "qualifié de bourgeois et de marchand, moyennant la nourriture et le logement, en plus d'une somme de vingt quatre livres tournois." From this period until the middle of the seventeenth century no notices of the Rouen fayence have been discovered. The descriptions of pottery are very varied, and there were many establishments; among them we find a grant of privilege for fifty years, accorded to Nicolas Poirel,

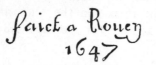

Sieur de Grandval, in 1646. The mark in the margin, "faict a Rouen, 1647," is attributed to him. It is on a circular plate in blue *camaieu;* in the centre is a female centaur, and a border of four octagonal medallions and flowers, in the Persian style (Collection Gouellain at Rouen). It is found also on a vase in the Collection of M. Pottier, of the same city. The fayence of Poirel de Grandval was in imitation of Delft, and he brought his workmen thence. Another grant of privilege was given to Edmé or Esmon Poterat of St. Sever, Sieur de St. Étienne, in 1673. According to a deed recently discovered by M. Pottier, he died in 1687, and was succeeded by his son, Louis Poterat, who had carried on a rival establishment at Rouen, and who was also one of the earliest makers of European porcelain.

Decrees were also granted to Le Vavasseur, Pavie, Malétra, Dionis Lecoq de Villeray, Picquet de la Houssiette, and de Barc de la Croizille. Gournay, in his *Almanach Général du Commerce,* mentions Belanger, Dubois, Flandrin Hugue, Valette, Dumont, Jourdain, La Houssiette, and Vavasseur; in the English style, M. Sturgeon. In none of these, however, do we find *Dieu* or *Gardin,* whose names appear on the ware.

The fabriques which have imitated more or less the Rouen style are Lille, Paris, Sinceny, Marans, Nantes, Moustiers, and Nevers, and they are in some instances very difficult to distinguish.

The following list of potters is taken from the notes of the late M. André Pottier, published by his executors.

RUE D'ELBEUF.

Edmé or Esmon Poterat, 1644; remplacé par M. de Villeray en 1722; puis Dionis en 1740.

Charles Thomas Antoine Mouchard, 1749.

Pierre Dumont, 1774.

Guillaume Heugue, 1774, associé à sa mère en 1775.

Michel Antoine Guillaume Heugue.

Seraphine Heugue.

Hubert Le Tellier, 1781.

Louis Jean Baptiste Picquet de la Houssiette, 1788.

Pierre Charles Le Page, 1798.

Guillaume Tharel, 1798.

Anne Jeanne Le Boullenger.

Nicholas L'Homme.

RUE DU PRE.

Louis Poterat, Sieur de St. Etienne, 1675.

Madelaine de Laval, veuve de St. Etienne, 1710.

Jean Bertin, 1720; Veuve Huet Bertin, 1740.

Nicolas Fouquay, 1720; successeur Girard de Raincourt, 1742.

Guillaume François Heugue, 1720, se transporte Rue St. Julien.

Michel Mathieu Vallet, père et fils; Mathieu Vallet; Mathieu Amablè Vallet; Pierre Alphonse Vallet, 1756.

Jean Baptiste François Augustin Heugue, 1774.

Marie Adelaide Julie Heugue, 1788.

Pierre Paul Jourdain, 1788

Claude Legrip, 1798.

RUE TOUS-VENTS.

Jean Guillibaud, 1720; Veuve Louë Guillibaud, 1740.

Jacques Nicolas Levavasseur, 1743; veuve, 1755.

Marie Thomas Philémon Levavasseur.

Amadée Lambert and Adrien Heugue.

RUE ST. SEVER.

Cauchois, 1712; André Pottier, successeur.

Jacques Nicolas de la Mettarie, 1719.

Pierre Jacques de la Mettarie.

Pierre Paul Caussy, 1720.

Pierre Guillaume Abraham Heugue, 1722.

Faupoint, 1722; Carré, 1722.

Jean Baptiste Antoine Flandrin, 1740.

Pierre Mouchard, 1746; associé en 1757 à Debarc de la Croisille; Gabriel Sas, successeur.

Jean Baptiste François Heugue, 1774.

Charles Framboisier et Veuve Framboisier, 1774.

Jean Nicolas Bellenger fils; Louis Cornu.

Jacques Charles Noël Dubois; Charles Guillaume Dubois.

Jean Baptiste Dupray; Jean Mathieu Vallet.

RUE ST. JULIEN.

Pinon, 1722; Maugard or Maugras, 1722.

Guillaume François Heugue, 1740, venant Rue du Pré.

François Henri Heugue, François Philippe Heugue.

Nicolas Louis François Macarel, 1740.

Pierre Michel Macarel, 1749.

Nicholas Roch Macarel, 1774.

Pierre Nicolas Robert Macarel.

Nicolas Maletra, 1740; Veuve Maletra, 1749.

Robert Thomas Pavie, 1754, mort en 1777.

William Sturgeon, 1770.

This list is far from being complete; among others we may note : Gabriel Fossé, established in 1739, succeeded by his widow. Bréard, about 1720. A decree of 7th July 1781 authorises Messrs. Macnemara, William Sturgeon, Simon de Suzay and Letellier to establish a *manufacture royale.* Specimens were made in 1783, but the opposition of other manufacturers stopped the enterprise. The number of fabriques was limited to eighteen; some of these had three kilns, so that the quantity produced need not be wondered at. Pierre Chapelle, whose pieces are hereafter mentioned, were signed in 1725, and made at the fabrique of Madame de Villeray; these are perhaps the finest known; he died in 1760, at the age of seventy-five. He had a brother, a son, and a nephew, who also painted on fayence. Claude Borne, 1736 to 1757; and many others.

We are inclined to think there was really no special mark of this fabrique. There was no rival and no competitor which would make it necessary to have a distinctive sign. It is true the fleur-de-lis was occasionally used, but the pieces so marked form the exception, and the monograms so frequently found on the Rouen ware are probably those of painters.

At the commencement of the eighteenth century, especially during the epoch of a ceramic painter named Guillebaud, about 1730, the Chinese style pervaded all the Rouen fayence, but it was transformed or travestied, and possessed a special physiognomy; the subjects were landscapes and buildings, with figures, fantastic birds, dragons, and marine animals, in blue, yellow, green, and red, bordered with the square Chinese ornaments. M. Jules Greslou places this (*sans grand certitude*) as the mark of M. Guillebaud; it is on a *porte huilier*, covered in floral arabesques in red and blue, finely painted.

Brument 1699.   A bowl, which has descended by inheritance to a family named Le Brument, of Rouen, has this signature; it is ornamented with designs of cartouches, scrolls, and leaves.

 When Louis XIV. sent his silver plate to the Mint to assist in defraying the expenses of the war, he had a service made at Rouen, which bears the mark of the fleur-de-lis.

 Another mark of a fleur-de-lis, quoted by M. Jacquemart.

 Some pieces were made in the forms of birds and animals, such as were served at table, as pheasants, hares, ducks, &c. Mr. H. G. Bohn had one specimen, of a turkey, marked as in the margin, with two batons crossed beneath.

G Æ   The mark of M. Guillebaud about 1730, decoration *à la corne*—Guillebaud à Rouen.

The paste of the Rouen fayence is heavier and thicker than that of Delft, but the designs and ornaments are in good taste, decorated in blue *camaieu* and in polychrome, some in the Nevers style, of white on blue ground, but of paler colour. It is the most artistic of all French fayences, by reason of the national character of its decorations; the pieces were often of large size, as fountains, vases, &c. There are many fine specimens in the Museum at Sèvres, some painted with arabesques, and armorial escutcheons, and the Victoria and Albert Museum is very rich in fine specimens of this decorative fayence, several of which are illustrated in the useful little hand-book to "French Pottery" published by the Education Department. The collections of M. Leveel of Paris, recently purchased for the Museum of the Hôtel de Cluny, and that of M. Pottier of Rouen, are also noted for their specimens of "Rouen." The letters on the ware are very numerous; some of them are given in the margin. In the Collection of M. Edouard Pascal are the following:—D V : P P : B B : P D : M D : D : L D : L : A D : H V : D Z : G : F D, &c. A salad bowl in the same Collection has the name of "Nicolas Gardin, 1759."

The mark of Nicolas Gardin about 1760, on a plate painted with trophies of torch, arrows and quiver, called fayence *au carquois*, scrolls on the border. Two fine polychrome plates, 20 inches diameter, in the Dejean Collection, Paris, for which he paid £60, painted with Judith and Holofernes, and Christ and the Woman of Samaria, have the signature of the potter ···*Leleu*. This mark is on a large octagonal plate, painted in red and blue border of arabesques; in the centre a basket of flowers.

ROUEN. On an earthenware tureen with a group of dead game in relief on the cover, but of inferior quality to the Rouen fayence generally; in the Victoria and Albert Museum. There is also a Rouen fayence ewer, painted with "St. Jeanne," and a landscape, dated 1737.

In the petition of the *faïenciers* to the National Assembly in 1790 there appear to have been sixteen fabriques of various kinds of fayence in active operation, being more than was allowed in any other city in France,—there being at Paris, 14; at Nevers, 12; at Marseilles, 11; Bordeaux, 6; Moustiers, 5.

There are some specimens of later Rouen fayence in the Sèvres Museum, from M. Letellier in 1809; M. de la Metterie in 1823, and M. Amadée Lambert in 1827; but we do not know when or by whom these establishments were founded.

There is a very fine specimen of Rouen ware of the beginning of the eighteenth century—a bust of Flora, on a long pedestal, the drapery and pedestal diapered with flowers and arabesques, height 7 feet 3 inches, presented by the late Duke of Hamilton to the Victoria and Albert Museum. (*Ker. Gall.*, enlarged edition, figs. 121-129.)

A·ROÜEN
·1725·
PEINt PAR
PiERRE
CHAPEttE

This mark, within a wreath, is on a celestial globe with the constellations in colours, supported on a pedestal, cherubs' heads on the four angles, and between the four elements.   The companion is the terrestrial globe, similar, but with the Four Seasons on the pedestal, and stand of four lions' heads and shoulders; about 4 feet high.   These very fine spheres were exhibited in Paris at the Exposition of 1867, painted by Pierre Chapelle in the fabrique of Madame de Villeray, Faubourg St. Sever at Rouen, and they decorated the vestibule of the Château de Choisy-le-Roi.

Collectors of Rouen, as of the other fayences of the French School, should be very wary of the imitations made in quantities in Paris, with which the market is flooded.   Genuine specimens are rare, and are only offered for sale at the dispersion of some famous collection.

To the school of Rouen belong the fayence of Paris, St. Cloud, Sinceny, Quimper, and Lille.

Herr Jännike gives the following signatures as occurring on specimens of Rouen fayence :—

Signature of Le Vavasseur   Signatures of Guillebaud   Signatures of Claude Borne.
in 1743.   in 1730.

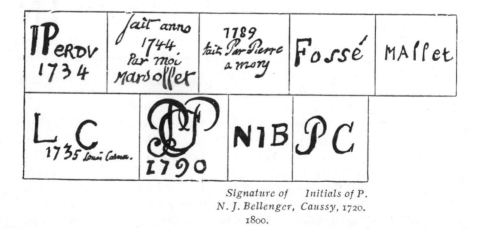

Signature of   Initials of P.
N. J. Bellenger,   Caussy, 1720.
1800.

P D P D — *P. Dumont 1722*	V D — *? Veuve Dubois 1800*	B D 2 BD B — *B. Dupray 1800*
M M — *Maugard 1723*	PR PR P1 — *? Rouen 1722*	MP MP — *P. Mouchard 1756*
S SP SG S GS2 SAS — *Gabriel Saint 1760*		H H H — *H. Heugue*
B B — *J. Bertin 1720*	Mv — *M. Vallet 1756*	L — *Lettellier 1781*

NIDERVILLER (Meurthe). Established about 1760 by Jean Louis, Baron de Beyerlé. The pottery is in the German style, in consequence of German potters being employed, and is remarkable for the richness and delicacy of its decoration; it is most frequently painted with flowers in bouquets and garlands. The buildings were constructed after his own plans, and being a good chemist, he brought the wares to great perfection. He was associated with a German named Anstatt or Anstette, and no expense was spared to ensure success; the fine fayence figures and groups are well modelled. About 1780, four years before his death, the estate was purchased by General Count Custine, and carried on by him under the direction of M. Lanfray, principally in the manufacture of porcelain.

It is probable that Custine became proprietor before this date, for a plate with the date 1774 bears the mark of two C's crossed, and in front the same monogram surrounded by palm branches, with the motto "Fais ce que tu dois, advienne ce qui pourra," evidently made for his own use. In the Collection of M. Meusnier.

The following document, quoted by M. A. Jacquemart (*Merveilles, &c.*, part iii. p. 78), seems to disprove the assertion of its German origin, the names being rather of a French character.

Etat Exact de Tous les Exempts de la Subvention qui sont actuellement dans ce Lieu de Niderviller, leurs Noms et Surnoms, et cela pour l'Année 1759.

Le Sieur François Anstette, controlleur de la manufacture, gagne environ trente sols par jour.

Le Sieur Jean Baptiste Malnat, directeur de la même manufacture, a cinq cens livres par an de gage.

Michel Martin, peintre, gagne environ vingt sols par jour.

Pierre Anstette, peintre, gagne environ vingt-quatre sols par jour.

Joseph Secger, peintre, gagne environ vingt sols par jour.
Fréderic Adolph Tiebauld, garçon peintre, gagne environ vingt-quatre sols par jour.
Martin Schettler, garçon peintre, gagne environ quinze sols par jour.
Augustin Herman, garçon peintre,　,,　　,,　　vingt　,,　　,,
Daniel Koope, garçon peintre,　　,,　　,,　douze　,,　　,,
Michel Anstette, garçon peintre,　　,,　　,,　vingt-quatre sole par jour.
Jean Pierre Raquette,　　　　　,,　　,,　dix-huit　,,　　,,
Nicolas Lutze, garçon peintre,　　,,　　,,　vingt　　,,　　,,
Deroy, garçon mouleur,　　　　,,　　,,　vingt　　,,　　,,
Charles Lemire, garçon sculteur,　,,　　,,　vingt-quatre ,,　　,,
Jean Thalbotier, garçon peintre　,,　　,,　vingt　　,,　　,,
Philip Arnold, garçon sculteur,　　,,　　,,　vingt　　,,　　,,
　　　Signed by the Mayor, Syndic, and échevin at Niderviller, 1759.

The sculptor Charles Sauvade *dit* Lemire, from the fabrique of Luné-ville, was the author of those charming statuettes to which Niderviller owes so much of its reputation. This artist had, during more than twenty years, the artistic direction of the fabrique. At first he was employed in the manufacture of fayence, and modelled some of those graceful figures which Cyflé had brought into fashion; he also made them in porcelain. Lemire remained at Niderviller until 1806 or 1808.

 NIDERVILLER. The monogram of M. de Beyerlet of Niderviller or Niderville.

 NIDERVILLER. General Custine succeeded Beyerlet. This mark was the first used under his direction.

 NIDERVILLER. Another mark of General Custine, on fine fayence as well as on porcelain,—the two C's with or without a count's coronet: used about 1792; he was beheaded in 1793. The two C's are also found on the German porcelain of Ludwigsburg, but surmounted by an Imperial crown with a cross at its apex. There are several specimens in the Sèvres Museum; and on jugs of white fayence with coloured designs. (*Ker. Gall.*, enlarged edition, figs. 148, 149, 150.)

NIDERVILLER. On an oval fayence dish painted with flowers, rococo border of yellow, blue, and lake, green leaves; marked in blue *au grande feu*.

Herr Jännike gives these additional marks of Niderviller pottery:—

BESANÇON (Doubs). M. Bulliard, fabricant, sent some services in 1809 to the Sèvres Museum of ordinary white and brown fayence.

D'ANNET (Château). Italian school; fine fayence. M. Brongniart gives this mark from an enamelled tile for pavements or walls, in the Sèvres Museum, from the Château d'Annet. Sixteenth century.

LUNÉVILLE (Meurthe). Established 1731. The most ancient fabrique of fayence was that established in one of the faubourgs at Willer by Jacques Chambrette towards the end of the reign of Leopold, to whom the Duke François III. accorded privileges by letters patent on the 10th of April and 14th June 1731. The proprietorship passed into the hands of Gabriel Chambrette, his son, and Charles Loyal, his son-in-law, as shown by the letters patent of the 17th of August 1758. These documents speak of them as being directors of the manufactory at Willer for making ordinary fayence and *terre de pipe*, and accord to it the title of the Royal Manufactory or *Manufacture Stanislas*. In 1778 it was sold to Messrs. Keller and Guérin; they make fayence of blue decorations like Nevers, and rose and green like that of old Strasbourg: it is still

K. & G.
LUNEVILLE.

carried on by the grandson of M. Keller. Schneider was a celebrated potter who worked at Lunéville. Large figures of lions, dogs, and other animals, sometimes of the natural size; pierced fruit baskets, like the German, &c., were made here in the eighteenth century. The name of the town is frequently printed at length, as on two large dogs in the Musée de Cluny. In 1790 there were three fabriques in active operation (*Ker. Gall.*, enlarged edition, figs. 141-144.)

BLOIS. There was a manufactory of fayence here in the seventeenth and eighteenth centuries. M Ulysse Besnard, director of the Blois Museum, informs us that it was of a superior quality, with pure white stanniferous glaze, decorated with

LEBARQUET.

enamel colours, equal to the most successful productions of Nevers and Rouen; some specimens are signed Lebarquet.

This mark, of recent date, occurs on each of a pair of candlesticks, painted with scrolls, masks, mermen, &c., in purple, orange, and green, in the Victoria and Albert Museum; it is engraved in the *Keramic Gallery*, enlarged edition, fig. 110; the numerals refer to the date, 1866.

BLOIS. Maiolica, decorated with arabesques in the style of the sixteenth century, with a crown above a fleur-de-lis; well painted on yellow ground.

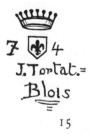

NANCY. On the 11th January 1774, the Sieur Nicolas Lelong was authorised to establish a fayence manufactory in the Faubourg de Saint-Pierre. This decree, dated 24th April 1774, was not the only one granted; for the *biscuit de Nancy* is frequently referred to.

RAMBERVILLERS (Vosges). This fayence manufactory is spoken of by Gournay, and is also in the list of 1791: "Ses faïences tiennent le feu, elles ont une blancheur et une beauté qui approchent de l'émail; on les orne de peintures fines." Carried on by M. Gerard.

ARBOIS (Jura), Franche-Comté. A manufactory of fayence existed here early in the eighteenth century. In the Sèvres Ceramic Museum there is a bowl with two flat handles, rudely painted with a cock, inscribed Joseph Laurent d'Arbois, 1746. The *Almanach de Gournay* in 1788 speaks of a fabrique here directed by a potter named Giroulet.

BELLEVUE, near Toul (Meurthe). A person named Lefrançois first established a manufacture of fayence here in 1758. On the 1st May 1771 he disposed of it to Charles Bayard and Francis Boyer, who by an *arrêt* of Council of 13th April 1773 were thereby authorised to carry it on; of which the following is an extract: "Sur la requête présentée au Roy, etc. . . . par Charles Bayard, ci-devant directeur de la manufacture royale de fayance et de terre de pipe à Lonéville et François Boyer, artists dans le genre de fayancerie, Sa Majesté a autorisée l'établissement formé à Bellevue, ban de Toul, géneralité de Metz, d'une manufacture de fayance et terre de pipe fine et commune, et leur a permis de continuer à y fabriquer, vendre, &c., pendant quinze ans," &c. Three months later another *arrêt* extended their privileges and permitted them to use the title of *Manufacture Royale de Bellevue*. Cyflé and other celebrated artists furnished some charming models; subsequently François Boyer was sole proprietor, and carried it on until 1806, when he was succeeded by M. Georges Aubry.

TOUL (Meurthe). A manufacture, we are informed by the *Almanach de Gournay*, was carried on here in 1788 by MM. Bayard, père et fils. It is therefore probable that Charles Bayard quitted Bellevue about that time. The objects produced here in fayence and *terre de pipe* are therein much extolled: groups, figures, busts, vases painted and gilt, medallions, &c., after the designs of the great masters. Herr Jännike gives a capital T. with a line above it as the mark of this fabrique, and J. Aubry *ainé* as the name of the potter or painter.

STRASBOURG (Bas-Rhin). The name of Hannong or Hanung has been associated with this important fabrique from its commencement to its close. The first potter of this name was a maker of stoves of green enamel, ornamented with subjects in relief, like those of Nuremberg. Towards 1709, Charles François Hannong created in the Rue du Foulon a manufactory of pipes; ten years later, a German fugitive, Jean-Henri Wackenfeld, came to Strasbourg and tried without success to found a porcelain manufactory. Charles Hannong, taking advantage of this circumstance, took Wackenfeld into his service in September

1721, and being well versed not only in the process of porcelain but also of fayence, this association proved successful in developing both.

In 1724, the works not being sufficiently large for the increasing business, a second fabrique was taken at Haguenau in the same department. Charles Hannong being advanced in years, relinquished the two manufactories into the hands of his two sons, Paul Antoine and Balthasar, who had long been associated with him, on payment of a certain annuity, by an agreement dated 22nd September 1732. The old man died 19th April 1739, ætatis seventy. In 1737, Balthasar having dissolved partnership with his brother, took for his share the establishment at Haguenau, leaving Paul Antoine alone at Strasbourg. The latter continued perfecting his productions, which had a very extensive sale. In 1744 Paul had discovered the art of applying gold to his fine white enamel, and profited by the occasion of a visit of Louis XV. to Strasbourg to present to him the first specimens.

This prosperity was not destined to last long, for Paul Hannong's successful attempts to make porcelain aroused the jealousy of the Royal fabrique, and in February 1754 a decree was issued prohibiting the manufacture and sale of porcelain in France, and he was compelled to remove to Frankenthal in the Palatinate. Pierre Antoine, one of the sons of Paul, took the fayence works at Strasbourg, on the death of his father in 1760, and the eldest son, Joseph Adam, inherited those at Frankenthal. Paul Adam Hannong died at Strasbourg, 31st May 1760, in the sixtieth year of his age; he was twice married, and had fifteen children. The two sons here named were his successors in the fabriques of Strasbourg and Haguenau. Not being a man of business like his father, and entering into speculations, Pierre Antoine sold to Sèvres the secret of making hard porcelain, and abandoned the direction of his works to the Widow Löwenfinck, and subsequently ceded them to his brother Joseph; and when the decree of 1766 permitted the fabrication of porcelain decorated in blue or *camaieu*, he made that and fayence simultaneously. Eventually difficulties arose relating to the payment of dues to the Receiver-General of the Bishopric of Strasbourg for funds advanced to the potter, which caused his ruin. The Prince-Bishop seized and sold the works, after having imprisoned the debtor, and, notwithstanding his strenuous efforts to re-establish his credit and his reputation, the unfortunate Joseph Hannong was obliged to flee into Germany, where he died. Thus the kilns of Strasbourg ceased work altogether in 1780. (*Tainturier.*)

The notice of Vincennes fayence, which was also produced by the Hannongs, should be referred to in connection with these remarks.

The ware is generally decorated with flowers in red, rose-colour, and green; a clock-case, in the Leveel Collection, Paris, has the name of the town at length.

STRASBOURG

STRASBOURG. Joseph Hannong. This monogram is on a pair of fayence bottle-stands (*port-huiliers*) in Captain Langford's Collection.

STRASBOURG. Hannong. On the figure of a bagpiper, of coarse white ware, artistically modelled; the mark is in pale blue. In the possession of the Rev. R. Waldo Sibthorpe.

STRASBOURG. This mark in blue is found upon the early pottery. Hannong's father was a tobacco-pipe maker.

The marks of the Hannongs are frequently accompanied by a number, and sometimes a letter indicating the pattern, to enable the merchants to give their orders to the manufacturers without making any mistake; a plan also adopted at Delft in many fabriques.

STRASBOURG. This monogram of Joseph Hannong is on a fine plate, with designs in blue, green, and yellow, somewhat similar to the fayence of Marseilles or Moustiers; marked in blue under the glaze.

There are some fine specimens of Strasbourg fayence in the Victoria and Albert Museum, notably a clock-case and bracket surmounted by a figure of Time, and a fountain representing Amphitrite on a shell drawn by a dolphin. These are illustrated in the useful little handbook of "French Pottery" published by the Education Department.

The following marks, chiefly initial letters or monograms of the different Hannongs, are given on the authority of Herr Jännike:—

Marks of Paul and Joseph Hannong.

The fayence of Strasbourg has been imitated in the South of France, especially at Marseilles. They are much alike, and frequently without marks, but may be known by this peculiarity: the fayence of Strasbourg has quite a plain surface where the colours have been laid on, whilst that of Marseilles has nearly always the colours in slight relief, and may be known by passing the hand over the decorated portions. German workmen were employed.

HAGUENAU. Established in 1724 by Charles Hannong, and continued by his son Balthasar in 1737. Paul Antoine Hannong subsequently had the works, and in 1752 he engaged the services of a certain H. E. V. Löwenfinck. On the death of Paul in 1760, the establishment became the property of Pierre Antoine Hannong, who took as a partner Xavier Hallez; it was eventually ceded to the Widow Anstett, and in 1786 the firm was Anstett fils, Barth & Vollet. It is now difficult, if not impossible, to separate the marks of Strasbourg and Haguenau, as the same marks were probably used at both factories.

VAUCOULEURS (Meuse). This fabrique was founded by Sieur Girault de Berinqueville by an order of council, December 16, 1738. The products were a very fine and well-worked fayence, richly decorated in the Chinese style of Strasbourg, with rock-work and flowers. There were some *potpourri* vases at the Paris Exposition, surmounted by flowers in relief and handles formed of groups of flowers. This fabrique is mentioned in the list of fayenciers in 1790 (p. 171).

MONTIGNY (Meuse), near Vaucouleurs. Two fabriques are alluded to in the letters patent of January 1743, which were registered in 1745, Mansuy-Pierrot and François Cartier, quoted at length in M. Jacquemart's *Merveilles*, &c., part iii. p. 88. Neither the marks nor the products are known.

LES ISLETTES (Meuse). This establishment, probably of still earlier date, was in 1737 under the direction of a M. Bernard, at which time Joseph Le Cerf, a painter of renown, decorated the ware; he afterwards went to Sinceny. We are not able to identify its earlier products. At the Paris Exposition some pretty specimens of recent work were exhibited by M. Maze Sencier.

MOUSTIERS (Basses-Alpes), Midi. Fine fayence, 1686 to 1800. We have no record of the origin of this important fabrique; but a manuscript read before the Academy of Marseilles in 1792, now preserved in the library of that city, gives us an insight to its history. It informs us that the fabrication of fayence in Provence commenced at Moustiers, and that the Spanish Government, wishing to improve their own manufacture, and knowing the importance of that already existing in Provence, the Comte d'Arenda, then Minister (1775 to 1784), engaged workmen from Moustiers and Marseilles to go to Denia, where, having expended a great deal of money in re-establishing the pottery and in making experiments to improve the colours, especially the blue, hitherto only known in France, it proved unsuccessful and was abandoned. One of the artists, of the name of Olery, returned to Moustiers and established himself there, where Clerissy had already made beautiful fayence, and was making a rapid fortune. With the knowledge he had acquired in the employment of colours and by introducing new forms, he soon surpassed Clerissy; but not being prudent, economical, or rich, his secrets became known, and he sank into mediocrity.

It is only within a few years that the fayence of Moustiers has become known to amateurs, and M. Brongniart makes no mention of it in his Treatise on Pottery published in 1844. It had been indiscriminately attributed to Rouen or Marseilles, and by some even to St. Cloud, but the researches of M. Riocreux of Sèvres, Messrs. Jacquemart and Le Blant, Dr. Bondil of Moustiers, M. Davillier, and others, have thrown considerable light upon its early history. According to M. Davillier, in the archives of Moustiers the name of Pierre Clerissy occurs in 1677 and 1685 without any mention of his profession, but in the year 1686 is found the baptism of Anne, daughter of Pierre Clerissy, "maitre fayansier." This is the earliest record of a manufactory here. In subsequent registers he is called "marchand faiencier," and on the 25th of August 1728 his death is recorded at the age of seventy-six. About the year 1686, therefore, at the age of thirty-four he probably founded this manufactory, which he directed for forty-two years. A second Pierre Clerissy, son or nephew of the first, born in 1704, having made a large fortune in the same business, was in 1743 ennobled by Louis XIV., under the title of Baron or Comte de Trévans. He associated himself with Joseph Fouqué, to whom the fabrique was eventually ceded between the year 1740 and 1750, and it has been continued uninterruptedly by members of the same family until 1850.

In the same archives for the year 1727, a certain Pol or Paul Roux is mentioned as "maitre faïencier" of this town; and in the year 1745 is the entry of the death of Marie, daughter of Joseph Olery, "maitre fabriquant en fayence."

We have, therefore, evidence of at least three manufactories of fayence existing in 1745. From the middle of the eighteenth century other fabricants, prompted by the prosperity of Clerissy, Olery, and Roux, came to establish themselves at Moustiers. In 1756 we are informed there were seven or eight, and in 1789, according to Dr. Bondil, these were increased to eleven : their names were Achard, Berbiguier et Féraud, Bondil père et fils, Combon et Antelmy, Ferrat frères, Fouqué père et fils, Guichard, Laugier et Chaix, Mille, Pelloquin et Berge, Yccard et Féraud.

M. l'Abbé Féraud, in a letter to M. Davillier, mentions also the Brothers Thion as possessing a very fine fabrique, and he adds that the Fouqués were the last who attempted to revive the manufacture of painted fayence. M. Fouqué, a descendant of the above, speaks also of another faïencier named Barbaroux.

The products of the Moustiers fabricants may be divided into three periods : —

1st Epoch. Towards the end of the seventeenth century; the subjects are hunting scenes, after Tempesta, Frans Floris, &c., painted in blue *en camaieu*, escutcheons of arms, champêtre scenes, and figures in the costume of Louis XIV., mythological and biblical subjects, with arabesque borders of the same colour. The outlines are sometimes lightly indicated in violet of manganese. These early specimens of Pierre Clerissy have no marks or signatures.

2nd Epoch. From the commencement of the eighteenth century to about 1745. The specimens of this period are better known to amateurs, and not so rare; they are also decorated in blue *camaieu* in the style of Jean Bérain and André Charles Boulle, with highly finished and graceful interlaced patterns, amongst which are cupids, satyrs, and nymphs, terminal figures, garlands of flowers, masks, &c., and canopies resting upon consoles or brackets, from which hang drapery, bordered or framed with foliage, and hatched spaces, mythological personages, vases of flowers, fountains, and other designs being frequently introduced : the centre subjects are classical or champêtre figures in costume of the time, sometimes coats-of-arms. Some of the fayence of this period is painted in cobalt blue in the Chinese style, which M. le Baron Davillier attributes to Pol Roux, and refers to a similar plate in the Sèvres Collection bearing the arms of *le grand Colbert.* The former he assigns to Clerissy. None of these bear the mark of the potter, but a few have the initials of the decorator.

3rd Epoch. From 1745 to 1789 the fayence is mostly painted in polychrome; some specimens are found in blue *camaieu*, but they are exceptions, and seldom in the Bérain style of arabesques; the colours are blue (which prevails), brown, yellow, green, and violet; on some, which are rarely met with, a red is introduced which sinks into the enamel in a furrow. The decorations on this ware are garlands of flowers, fruit, and foliage, finely painted, sometimes with mythological subjects, medallions enclosing cupids, busts of gods and goddesses, warriors, &c.

Other patterns of this period consist of grotesque figures or caricatures, sometimes in green and yellow, and sometimes *en grisaille* in the style of Callot; men with asses' ears playing upon their noses, which are shaped like trumpets; apes dressed in extravagant costume, riding upon impossible animals, chimeræ, &c. These are by Joseph Olery, and may be easily recognised, as they nearly always bear his trade mark, an O traversed by an L, the first two letters of his name, frequently accompanied by the initials of the decorator.

The population in 1789 was more than 3000, but at the present day it does not amount to above 1300, and there are only two manufactories of ordinary white fayence, that of M. Féraud and of Messrs. Jauffret & Mouton.

The outlines of the designs were transferred to the surface of the ware before it was painted, by means of paper patterns pricked with a fine needle and powdered with charcoal, so that the subject could be reproduced as often as required. Many of these pricked paper patterns are in the Sèvres Museum, and M. le Baron Davillier had about eighty more, some dated 1752 to 1756 (their authenticity is proved by the paper mark), the subjects too being of the same character as on the ware just described.

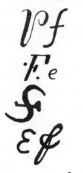

MOUSTIERS. These marks are found separately upon the blue *camaïeu* pieces; possibly the F may be intended for Fouqué, successor to Clerissy. A great many other letters are found upon this ware, but as we cannot tell with any degree of certainty whether they denote the potter's or painter's names, it is useless to reproduce them.

M·C·A 1756·J·A

MOUSTIERS. Another mark given by M. le Baron Davillier.

G.Viry f. a Monstiers.

chez Clerissy

MOUSTIERS. This is one of the earliest marks known, painted by Gaspard Viry for Pierre Clerissy. His name frequently occurs in the minutes about the year 1698, where he is styled painter; it occurs on a dish painted in blue, with a boar-hunt after Tempesta, with arabesque border, formerly in the possession of M. le Baron C. Davillier. The name of Jean Baptiste Viry, "peintre faillancier," also occurs on the register.

Soliua ca

Miguel Vilax

F o Grangel

CROS

MOUSTIERS. These names of painters, apparently Spanish, occur on some pieces painted in polychrome in the possession of M. Le Veel, M. E. Pascal, and other collectors. M. Davillier held that they formed part of a service which, according to tradition, was made for Madame de Pompadour about 1745, "au chiffre de dix mille livres," by Pierre Clerissy.

MOUSTIERS. (Olery.) Other specimens in which blue predominates, accompanied by other colours, as brown, yellow, green, and violet.

MOUSTIERS. The mark of Olery, being the first and last letter of his name. There is a basin, made on the occasion of the battle of Fontenoy in 1746, richly decorated in poly-chrome, with flowers, cupids, &c.; Victory in the centre, holding two flags; on one is written, "Ludovicum sequitur," on the other "Cum Ludovico delectatio," and a scroll held by cupids, with "Victoria." (Davillier Coll.)

MOUSTIERS. (Olery.) The first two marks are on a piece painted in blue *camaieu;* the other is sometimes found alone.

MOUSTIERS. (Olery.) With painter's initials, on a specimen in the Sèvres Museum.

MOUSTIERS. (Olery.) On a piece painted in blue *camaieu;* accompanied by painter's marks.

MOUSTIERS. (Olery.) On a very fine dish, painted in polychrome with a classical subject and elegant borders.

MOUSTIERS. Uncertain marks, probably subsequent to Olery. The monogram P.A. is the name of the potter, perhaps Achard; the other letters refer to the painter.

MOUSTIERS. This mark, with the name of the town on a flag, is on the interior of a plate representing a view of Moustiers. (Baron C. Davillier's Collection.)

ferrat moustiers   MOUSTIERS. Ferrat is the name of a manufacturer of this place about 1760, on an oval
dish with flowers in polychrome, in the Sèvres
Museum.   Ferrat Frères are mentioned by Dr. Bondil as potters still
carrying on business in 1789.

MOUSTIERS.   The name of Pierre Fournier
de Moustiers, 1775, in a circle, occurs on the
body of a gourd-shaped vessel, painted in
polychrome, with garlands of flowers, intended
probably for the name of the person for whom
it was made.

MOUSTIERS.   On a polychrome plate dated
1778, when the decoration was in its decadence.

MOUSTIERS.   The initials perhaps of Guichard the potter.   It is on a vessel with a
handle and spout, called in Provence *gargouline*,
painted with flowers; the mark is pounced in
the manner before described, applied by means
of paper pricked with a needle.

Thion à Moustiers.   MOUSTIERS.   A potter of the name of Thion
is mentioned by M. l'Abbé Féraud as having
a fine manufactory here.   This mark is on a
tureen of the eighteenth century, painted in colours; in the possession of
M. St. Leon, Paris.

Antoine Guichard,   MOUSTIERS.   A jug inscribed "Vive la paix,
de Moustiers, 1763,   1763."   In the collection of M. Champfleury.
le 10 X^{br} Guichard still carried on business in 1789.

There are several very good examples of Moustiers fayence, in the
shape of some plateaus, a barber's basin, plates, &c., in the Victoria and
Albert Museum, and some of these are described and illustrated in the
useful little handbook on "French Pottery" published by the Education
Department. (*Ker. Gall.*, enlarged edition, figs. 132-136.)

These marks are also given by Herr Jännike as occurring on Moustiers fayence; many are the initials of some of the artists mentioned above:—

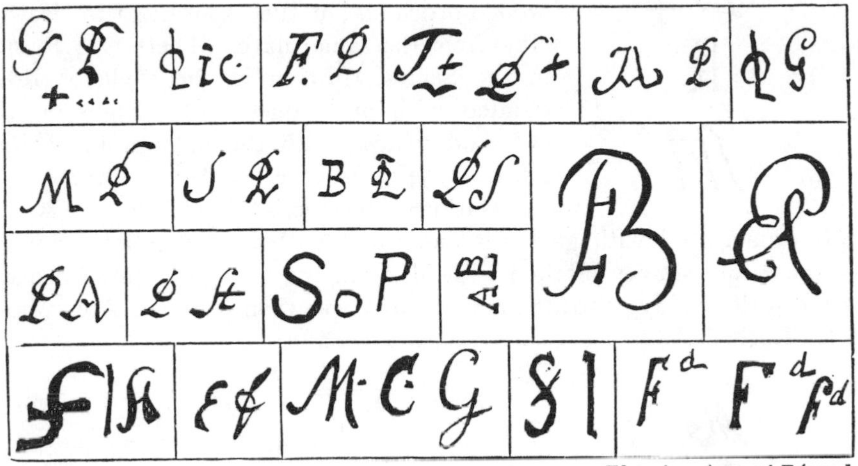

The signature of Féraud.

MOULINS (Allier). This mark occurs on an octagonal plate of the eighteenth century, painted with figures, flowers, and birds in the Chinese style of the Rouen school, styled *à la corne*. In the Sèvres Museum. There are some pieces of white fayence and stoneware of more recent date from the manufactory of M. Massieu, 1809, in the same museum.

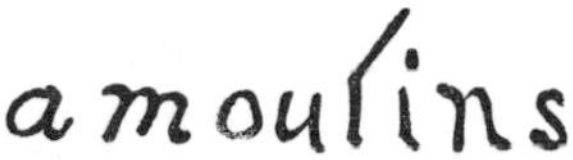

a moulins

MOULINS. There exists in the museum of this place a statue of St. Roch, much in the Nevers style; behind it is written the name of the modeller, *Chollet*, and underneath that of the painter, *Mogain;* on the pedestal are his initials and the date (*Jacquemart*).

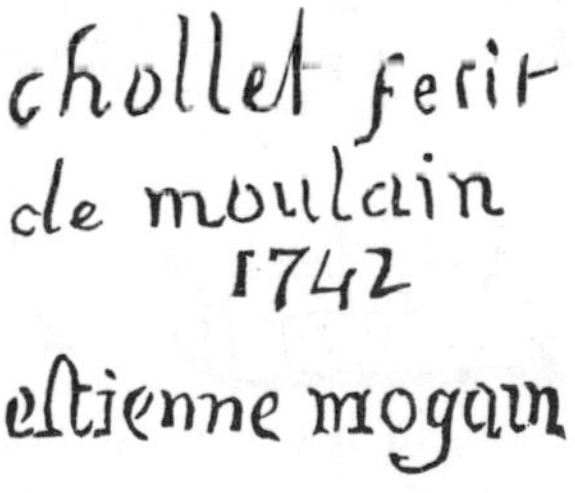

chollet ferit de moulain 1742

estienne mogain

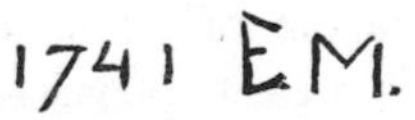

1741 EM.

POUPRES (Midi). There is a village near Moustiers of this name. This mark is found on the bottom of a fayence jug, painted with figures and flowers in purple and blue, *circa* 1750. Sèvres Museum.

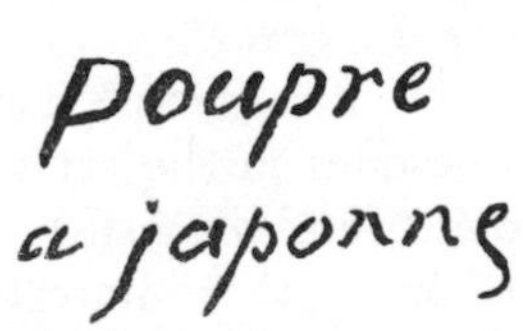

poupre a japonns

MARANS, near La Rochelle (Charente-In-férieure). The fayence manufactory at L'Ile d'Elle being closed, another was established at Marans about 1740 by M. Jean Pierre Roussencq from Bordeaux, but they continued to draw the clay from the same place. There is a fountain in the Sèvres Museum in the style of Rouen, painted with arabesques and designs in blue, red, and yellow, with the monogram of Rous-sencq, 1754. A vase of this fabrique is in M. Mathieu Meusnier's Collection; it is 3 ft. high, ornamented with garlands and acanthus leaves in relief. Some of the pieces are simply marked with M, as in the margin. Roussencq died on the 17th of May 1756; the manufactory was then removed from Marans to La Rochelle.

MONTAUBAN (Tarn-et-Garonne). In the list of fayenciers in France in 1790 (see p. 171) we find one manufactory cited. Herr Jännike gives a mark with a date 1778, the initials being those of D. Lestrade, and also a script M—"*M.*"

ARDUS (Tarn-et-Garonne). There existed a manufactory of fayence at Ardus, near Montauban, under the direction of a family named La Pierre. The ware produced was very coarse, in the style of Moustiers and Mar-seilles. M. Forestie, of Montauban, has published a work on the fayence of Montauban and Ardus; he has a large collection of the ware of the district, among which are two plates signed " D'Ardus, 1739."

Herr Jännike gives these two marks as the signatures of La Pierre and Quinquiry of this fabrique.

LA TOUR D'AIGUES (Avignon). This fabrique was, according to M. A. Jacque-mart (*Merveilles*, part iii. p. 155), created by the Baron de la Tour d'Aigues, M. de Bruni, in his own château. We do not know the date, except that it was previous to 1773, for in that year he applied for permission to join the fabrication of porcelain to that of fayence. A very curious piece made here is in the possession of M. Péchin, decorated in green *camaieu* with finely designed landscape and figures, inscribed underneath "*Fait à la Tour d'Aigues.*"

M. Ed. Pascal has also a charming oil and vinegar cruet-stand with arabesques in the style of Moustiers; it bears the mark of a tower, which we also find on a dish painted with flowers and bouquets in violet *camaieu*, and on another interesting piece belonging to M. Jules Ganonge of Nîmes :

it is an oblong dish, representing bubbling water in relief; in the centre is inserted a piece in form of a duck; the mark of *the tower* is in the middle of the dish, and inside is the date 1770. M. Bonnet of Apt has another specimen from this fabrique, presented by one of the Baron de Bruni's family. It was abandoned in 1793.

DIEU-LE-FIT (Drôme). A manufactory of glazed earthenware towards the end of the last century; the name occurs in the list of fayenciers who petitioned the National Assembly in 1790. In 1834 it belonged to M. Vignal, who sent specimens to the Exposition in Paris in that year; also in 1847. Sèvres Museum.

ST. CLEMENT (Meurthe). Established about 1750. There are some specimens in the Sèvres Museum, and others of later date, 1819 and 1823. In 1834, M. Cosson, the manufacturer, sent some fayence services to the Paris Exposition. There was an extensive manufactory here in the last century, co-existent with those of Niderviller and Lunéville, of a sort of pipeclay called *biscuit*, closely imitating china. In the *Chronique des Arts et de la Curiosité* was published in 1865 a list of the moulds which still exist at St. Clement—the Belisarius, the Shoemaker, the Paris Street-Criers, the Pleasant Lesson, the Leda, Venus and Adonis, &c. &c.

APT (Vaucluse), twelve leagues from Avignon. About the middle of the eighteenth century the fabrication of fayence commenced here, principally in imitation of jasper and brocatelle marble; it acquired considerable reputation. The manufacture of M. Bonnet was established about 1780, and is spoken of as imitating marbles; it is still carried on by his successor, producing vases of yellow clay with ornaments in relief. A vase made by M. Moulin in 1780 is in the Sèvres Museum, with ornaments in relief and festoons of various coloured pastes; in the same museum are some specimens by Veuve Arnoux in 1802. In 1806 the fabricants of Apt sent to the Exposition of National Industry at Paris specimens of their marbled ware. M. Reyraud was a potter there in 1830, and pieces marked R have been attributed to him. There is in the Victoria and Albert Museum (No. 378 —1869) a jug and cover of Apt ware in imitation of marble veined in brown and yellow, which bears the impressed mark of the Widow Arnoux. (*Ker. Gall.*, enlarged edition, fig. 109.)

GOULT. There was a small fabrique for fayence established at this place, which is not far from Apt, by M. de Doni, the *seigneur* of Goult. It existed from 1740 until about 1805, and its productions were similar in character to those of Moustiers. The marks as in the margin are given by Herr Jännike in his latest edition of *Grundriss der Keramik*.

VAL-SOUS-MEUDON (Seine-et-Oise). There was a manufactory of fayence here in the beginning of the eighteenth century, which existed

Claude Pelisie,
1726.

M. Sansont,
1738.

in 1818, but only produced latterly a common description of ware. A saladier or punch-bowl, belonging to M. Marne (formerly Mayor of this place), was made for his grandfather, who was locksmith to the King; it is painted in blue with a representation of a locksmith's shop and a man at the forge, inscribed "Claude Pelisie." Another plate in M. Michel Pascal's Collection is inscribed "M. Sansont, 1738." M. Lamasse of Meudon also has a specimen decorated in blue, similar to the Rouen ware.

VAL-SOUS-MEUDON. Manufactory of Messrs. Metenhoff & Mourot; stamped on plates, &c.

A specimen marked with the letter P and numeral 3 has been attributed by Dr. Graesse to the fabrique.

ARRAS (Pas-de-Calais). There are some specimens of glazed earthenware in the Sèvres Museum, produced by M. Fourneaux previous to 1809, but we do not know the date of its establishment.

DESVRE (Pas-de-Calais). A manufactory of pottery was established in the sixteenth century by Cæsar Boulonne at *Colombert*, a village near Boulogne. It was subsequently transferred to *Desvre*, and carried on by Dupré Poulaine up to 1732. The earliest specimens we have seen are painted in blue. One, formerly in Mr. C. W. Reynolds' Collection, has a portrait of a Bishop with mitre and crozier inscribed "S. NICOLAS P.P.N."; this is of the middle of the seventeenth century. Later pieces are painted with Chinese subjects, flowers and birds, in a coarse manner, the backs of the plates being brown, figures of pup-dogs, birds, &c.; a bird in the same collection has in front the initials D.P. for Dupré Poulaine (as in the margin); another has the name of the place, the colours employed on the polychrome pieces being claret of various shades, blue, yellow, and green. Mr. Reynolds obtained his specimens from the descendants of the family at Desvre. In 1764 Jean François Sta established a manufactory of fayence of a very common description, being an attempted imitation of that of Rouen. There were several other towns in the vicinity where fayence was made, but we have no reliable information respecting them.

Desvre.

BETHUNE (Pas-de-Calais). There is a specimen of fayence in the Sèvres Museum, acquired from the proprietor, M. Croizier, in 1809.

ST. OMER (Pas-de-Calais). After attempting to found at Dunkerque a fayence manufactory, but which at the request of Dorez of Lille was abandoned, the Sieur Saladin obtained authorisation to establish one at St. Omer. The terms of the *arrêt* are as follow: "Our well-beloved Louis Saladin, tradesman of Dunkerque, has informed us that he possesses the secret of making fayence as fine and good as that of Holland, and stoneware equal to that of England, and being informed that there is not in the vicinity any such establishment, he proposes to carry one on at St. Omer, it being fit for such an enterprise, from its canal and its prox- imity to the sea. We therefore permit Sieur Louis Saladin to establish in the town of St. Omer, or at the faubourg of the *Haut-pont*, a manufacture for twenty years, to the exclusion of all others within three leagues of the spot. Granted the 9th January 1751." In the Musée de Cluny there is a finely   *Saint-Omer* executed soup-tureen, in form of an open cabbage, and the button at top was a snail, coloured after   *1759.* nature; it was signed as in the margin. There was a manufactory still remaining in 1791 at the time of the petition against the English treaty of commerce.

HAVRE (Seine-Inférieure). There were two manufactories of fayence here in 1790, as appears from the petition to the National Assembly, and there are some specimens in the Sèvres Museum forwarded by the proprietors, viz., M. Delavigne in 1809 and M. Ledoux Wood in 1837.

SAINTE-FOY. This fabrique is noticed   *" Fait par moi* by M. A. Jacquemart (*Merveilles, &c.*, p. 35),   *Laroze fils, a Sainte-* but he hesitates where to place it, being of   *Foy."* opinion rather that it was near Dieppe. The inscription in the margin is on a gourd-shaped vase, painted with flowers and figures in the costume of the time of Louis XV.

AULNAY (Savoy). There was a fabrique of fayence here towards the end of the last century conducted by M. G. Muller; some pieces were sent to the Sèvres Museum in 1809.

FORGES-LES-EAUX (Seine-Inférieure). There was a manufactory here towards the end of the last century of English stoneware, which originated, according to Dr. Warmont (*Faïence de Sinceny*, p. 40), with some pupils from the establishment at Douai, worked by the Brothers Leigh from England. There are some specimens in the Sèvres Museum contributed by the following proprietors: M. Mutel & Co. in 1823, M. Ledoux Wood in 1823, and Messrs. Destrées & Damman in 1849.

DOUAI (Nord). Established 1782. Two brothers of the name of Leigh, from England, were engaged by M. George Bris of Douai to super- intend the manufacture of English stoneware and fayence; vast buildings were erected expressly and kilns constructed to carry on the pottery on a large scale in the Rue des Carmes (now a Normal School). This manu- factory, of which the products are much sought after by amateurs on account of their elegant forms, was the first of the kind established in

France; it was directed by Messrs. Houzé de l'Aulnoit & Co., who afterwards ceded it to a M. Halsfort. In 1788 Gournay mentions him as director, and M. Jacquemart tells us that it was to the competition of his stonewares and "cailloutages" that the potters of Saint-Amand attributed the decline of their manufactories. The chief workmen, who came originally from England, instructed pupils, who carried the new process to Montereau, Chantilly, Forges, and other places in France.

In the petition to the National Assembly in 1790 there were two potteries here, and a recent manufactory was conducted by Messrs. Vincent, Nachet & Co., of which specimens were sent to the Sèvres Museum in 1832.

ANGOULÊME (Charente). It was not actually in Angoulême, but, according to M. Jacquemart, in the Faubourg de l'Houveau, where the manufactory was situated, under the direction, in 1784, of *Veuve Sazerac, Desrocher & fils.* The Museum at Limoges possesses a curious lion holding a shield of the arms of France; round the base is placed, in Roman capitals, A ANGOULÊME DE LA FABRIQUE DE MADAME V. S. D. ET F. 28 AOUT; behind the shield is the date 1784. It was still at work in 1791, and was subsequently owned by M. Durandeau.

A manufactory of enamelled fayence by M. Glaumont is noticed in 1843. Sèvres Museum.

VENDEUVRE (Aube). A manufactory of earthenware, carried on by M. le Baron Pavée de Vendeuvre; there is a specimen in the Sèvres Museum, acquired in 1826.

MAUBEUGE (Nord). There was a manufactory of fayence here in 1809, the proprietor being M. Delannot; a specimen is in the Sèvres Museum.

HESDIN (Pas-de-Calais). There was a fabrique of fayence here in the beginning of this century, carried on by M. Pled; a specimen is in the Sèvres Museum, acquired in 1809.

BEAUMONT-LE-CHARTIF (Eure-et-Loire). A manufactory of fayence, by M. Lejeune, in 1827.

VALENCIENNES. About 1735, François Louis Dorez, son of Barthélémy, fayence-maker at Lille, founded in the town of Valenciennes a ceramic fabrique, which he directed until his death, which happened in 1739. It was continued successfully by his widow for a few years longer. In 1742 Charles Joseph Bernard succeeded, but his incapacity compromised the affair, and in 1743 Claude Dorez, another son of Barthélémy,

displaced him, and carried it on till 1748. Dr. Lejeal experiences some difficulty in distinguishing the works of Louis and Claude Dorez, but proposes, as the mark of the former, the cipher in the margin; an italic D is also attributed to one of the two; they occur on pieces of the Rouennaise character. There is such a close analogy between the fayence of Dorez, of Lille and Valenciennes, and that of Delft, Brussels, and Tournay, that it is difficult to determine their products.

Herr Jännike gives these marks as those of Valenciennes pottery during the directorship of Dorez.

From 1755 to 1757 another fabrique was started by Picard, which was also well encouraged. The last fayence-maker of Valenciennes was M. Becar, 1772-79.

ST. AMAND-LES-EAUX (Nord), near Valenciennes. This manufactory was founded about the year 1750, or a little earlier; the first notice we have of it is in that year. (See *Houdoy*, p. 61.)

In the *Calendrier du Gouvernement de Flandre, de Hainault et de Cambrésis* for the year 1775 we find: "Il y a à St. Amand deux belles manufactures de faïence qui égalent celles de Rouen, et une manufacture de porcelaine (le Sieur Fauquez fils, manufacturier)." In 1778 the Inspector of Manufactures reports the satisfactory state of the fayence fabrique of St. Amand. In the *Calendrier* for 1780 we read: "Il existe à St. Amand une belle manufacture de faïence, qui égale celle de Rouen, et qui est conduite par M. Fauquez fils."

In 1775 Fauquez married a sister of Lamoninary of Valenciennes; he occupied himself especially with the gilding of his ware; and his neighbours said he melted all his louis-d'ors and nearly ruined himself by his experiments.

On the 24th May 1785 M. Fauquez obtained permission to establish a porcelain manufactory at Valenciennes, but he continued to carry on the fayence manufactory at St. Amand simultaneously. In the Revolution of 1789 he emigrated, and his goods were confiscated.

In the year X. he attempted to revive the fabrique; and in the *Annonces* of the 15th April 1807 we read: "On prévient le public que la manufacture établie à St. Amand est remise en activité, on y fabrique de la faïence blanche, de la brune façon de Rouen," &c.

Fauquez went to reside at Tournay, where he died.

Three painters are named who were attached to this fabrique—Bastenaire-Daudenart, Desmurallc, a flower painter; but the most skilful was Louis Alexandre Gaudry, born at Tournay, died at St. Amand in 1820; he was a landscape-painter, and some pieces are marked with his signature or initial, J. or G. Joseph Sternig, a relation of Fauquez, was one of the artists who worked at St. Amand and at Valenciennes

M. le Dr. Lejeal (*Note sur une Marque de Faïence Contestée*) mentions a plate of fayence, beautifully painted with flowers, which belonged for eighty years to the same family, given by Fauquez himself. Bastenaire-Daudenart the painter acknowledged it to be the finest piece ever produced there. This piece bears the mysterious mark given below, which has hitherto caused so much discussion. (*Ker. Gall.*, enlarged edition, fig. 152.)

ST. AMAND (Nord). Dr. Lejeal, for the reason before named, so attributes this mark, which he says is an imitation of that of Sèvres, and

may be deciphered thus: the two F's interlaced and the two L's are the initials of Fauquez, and perhaps Lamoninary, his wife. This mark was thought by M. Houdoy to be Feburier of Lille, reading it like Dr. Lejeal as F. L. M. Riocreux, who considered specimens bearing this mark as belonging to the Department du Nord, suggested Picardy, Aire, or Aprey.

ST. AMAND. Another mark of this fabrique, in which the F's are more distinctly traced, and the letters at the side corroborate the opinion of Dr. Lejeal as the initials of the place.

ST. AMAND. Another mark, approaching nearer to that of Sèvres.

ST. AMAND. Another variety, so attributed by Jacquemart.

ST. AMAND. Another variety of the mark, with the initials of the name of the fabrique and makers.

This mark is also given by M. Ris-Paquot as found (in black) on St. Amand fayence.

St. Amand departeman du nor.

Herr Jännike gives this mark in cursive letters.

The following additional marks of St. Amand are given from Herr Jännike's large German work, *Grundriss der Keramik* :—

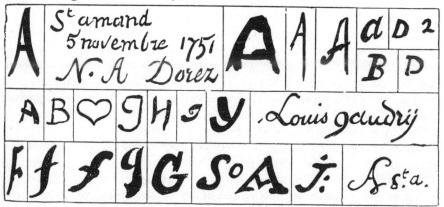

DANGU, near Gisors (Eure). From the documents brought to light by M. André Pottier we find that a fayence manufactory existed here, belonging to M. le Baron Dangu, who on the 11th July 1753 let it to Domenique Pelevé, a potter and painter, Adrian Levesque, modeller, and Jacques Vivien of Rouen. In default of payment of rent a seizure was made on the 24th January 1755, and in April 1757 the stock was sold publicly at the fabrique for the benefit of the Baron de Dangu and other creditors. Whether Pelevé or Pellevé continued it, or whether it passed into other hands, we do not know, but it was subsequently carried on; the fayence was in the style of Rouen and Sinceny. M. Gasnault has a pitcher inscribed " Jacques Vaillaux," and under the handle is written "Dangu, 1759."

AIRE. This town possessed a fayence manufactory, which was in activity from 1730 to 1755, founded by Sieur Prudhomme, but we know very little about it, except that it was still in existence in 1790, being mentioned among those who petitioned the National Assembly against the treaty of commerce between France and England. Gournay tells us that in 1788 it was the property of M. Dumez, who still retained it in 1791.

LIANGOURT (Oise). A manufactory of fayence, established under the patronage of M. le Duc de Rochefoucauld; a specimen in the Sèvres Museum, acquired in 1806.

MILHAC DE MONTRON (Dordogne). A manufactory of fayence, by M. Delanoue, in 1834; there is a specimen in the Sèvres Museum.

FOURNEAUX, near Melun. A manufactory of fayence: proprietor, M. Gabry, 1834.

LONGWY (Moselle). A manufactory of fayence: proprietor, M. Huart de Northomb, 1839.

ROUY, near Sinceny (Aisne), Picardy. A manufactory of fayence was established, 1790, by M. de Flavigny, Seigneur d'Amigny Rouy, who perished on the scaffold in 1793. It was sold by his widow to Joseph Bertin, who in 1804 was succeeded by his son Théodore: he enlarged the works, and this was the epoch *Rouy.* of its greatest prosperity. It employed five turners, five painters, three modellers, and a score of workmen. Being worked by the same workmen, and of the same clay, it much resembles the Sinceny fayence. Some few pieces have the name at length, as drinking-cups, &c. It was bought by the proprietors of Sinceny, and demolished in 1834.

D'OGNES or CHAUNY (Aisne), near Sinceny. There was, according to M. Jacquemart, a fabrique here established by M. Lecomte about 1737, which existed until 1774, in which year the works were destroyed by fire. The productions were similar to the fayence of Sinceny, and specimens marked C. H. have been attributed to this fabrique. Another factory, established about 1770 by M. de Fosselière, lasted only a short time, and little is known of its products. There is a flower-vase, painted in blue *camaieu* in the Chinese style, in the Sèvres Museum, presented by a descendant of one of the persons connected with the works.

SINCENY (Aisne), Picardy, formerly written St. Cenis, situated in the valley of the Oise, near Chauny. Established in 1733 by Jean Baptiste de Fayard, Gouverneur de Chauny et Seigneur de Sinceny. Dr. A. Warmont (*Recherches Historiques sur les Faïences de Sinceny, &c.*, Paris, 1864) divides the products of this manufactory into three periods:

> 1. Rouennaise, 1734-75.
> 2. Faïence au feu de réverbère, 1775-89.
> 3. Décadence de l'art, 1789-1864.

In 1737 letters patent were granted to M. de Sinceny, for the establishment of a manufacture of fayence at Sinceny, which sets forth that, having found in his park the various sorts of clay suitable for the purpose, and experiments having been made by himself and other potters, which had perfectly succeeded, and there being an almost inexhaustible supply of material; which fayence had already a great sale, and means of transport by the river Oise to Paris, Chauny, Moyen, Compiègne, &c., proposes to send it into the provinces of Picardy, Haynault, Champagne, and Burgundy, in which places there is not one manufactory of fayence, and having a good supply of wood for the kilns; permission was granted. The first director was Pierre Pellevé. In a recent South Kensington handbook on French Pottery, by Paul Gasnault and Edward Garnier, the date of Pierre Pellevé's directorate is given as about 1713. Two specimens of Sinceny fayence are in the Victoria and Albert Museum.

·S· pelleré   This mark, with the name of the director, Pellevé, is on a fayence jardinière in the collection of M. Pascal of Paris.

Among the painters were Pierre Jeannot (who placed his mark in the parish register as in the margin), Philippe Vincent, Coignard and his brother Antoine, Leopold Maleriat (who in 1780 was director), Alexandre Daussy, Julien Leloup, Pierre and Antoine Chapelle, Joseph Bedeaux, André Joseph le Comte, Pierre Bertrand, Frans. Joseph Ghail, and Joseph Lecerf. Bertrand's initials (as in the margin) are on a cup, in the Rouen style, in the Sèvres Museum; and that of Le Cerf, on a basket of the second period, painted in blue *camaieu*, inscribed "L. J. L. C. Pinxit 1776." The earliest pieces were painted in blue; the next in blue touched with red or green and yellow, and decorated with *lambrequins* (mantlings) *à la corne* (cornucopiæ), birds and butterflies, and Chinese figures, which,

from their frequent repetition in the same outlines, were doubtless stencilled by means of charcoal powder and pricked papers. Two early pieces, one dated 1734, and the other signed in blue with the S and two dots, like the first in the margin, are quoted by M. Warmont; the second mark, also blue, is on an *écuelle* in the Sèvres Museum; the third, which from its orthography is supposed to be about 1745, is in blue on an inkstand of white fayence. M. Warmont mentions large cider jugs of this period, small drinking-cups in the form of Bacchus astride a barrel, and a hand-warmer to hold hot water in the form of a book, on the back of which is written, "Liber Ludovici. Guilbert, 1758."
Some statuettes and figures were also produced about 1760 by a modeller named Richard; a statuette of St. Nicholas, and a group of three children, made for the Chapel of the Brotherhood of Faïenciers at Sinceny; small figures of soldiers on horse and foot for children to play with; a gardener, sweep, &c., of about the end of the eighteenth century.

About 1775 a great improvement was perceptible in the fayence of Sinceny; the paste was finer in quality, the colours more varied and brighter, in more exact imitation of the porcelain of Japan. This was accomplished by what is called *au feu de réverbère*, in contradistinction to the old process, *au grand feu*, the latter being only one baking, while in the other the ware was placed a second time in the kiln, and the pigments not exposed to so great a heat, allowing the employment of brighter colours. This new process was very costly, and required, as it were, a fresh apprenticeship, and the proprietors were compelled to procure hands from Lorraine, where it seems to have originated. They produced table services, decorated in polychrome with branches of roses, sometimes in green *camaieu;* delicate wicker-baskets; watch-stands, &c., painted with Chinese figures, rococo and other ornaments.
The mark *S. c. ij.* was used at this period; and an inkstand, painted with yellow roses, bears the inscription at length, as given herewith. M. Chambon was director about this time. M. Bose d'Antic, in a paper read before the Academy at Dijon (vide *Encyclopedie Méthodique*, Paris, 1783), says: "The fayence of St. Cenis, in Picardy, was formerly much sought after on account of its excellent quality, which has lately deteriorated, but now begins to re-establish its former reputation." From 1789 the fayence *au feu de réverbère* was discontinued, on account of its expensive character and the introduction of English ware at a lower price; but still both descriptions were occasionally made. The greater proportion of

the products of the Sinceny works were white fayence, with little or no decoration. The original manufactory, founded by M. de Fayard, was purchased in 1864 by M. Bruyère. (*Ker. Gall.*, enlarged edition, fig. 140.)

A manufactory was created at Bosquet-lez-Sinceny in 1824 by MM. Lecomte and Dantier, for making fayence; some of their products are marked "L. et D.;" and another at Sinceny by MM. Mandois (father and son), who marked their wares with the name at length, "*Mandois.*"

A recent manufactory of porcelain also exists here, carried on by MM. Moulin, father and son, the former an experienced fayence-maker and the latter a pupil of Sèvres. It is not extensive, but the articles produced are of excellent quality.

The following additional marks are given by Herr Jännike in his latest edition of *Grundriss der Keramik*, and some of them are the initials and marks of the artists mentioned above.

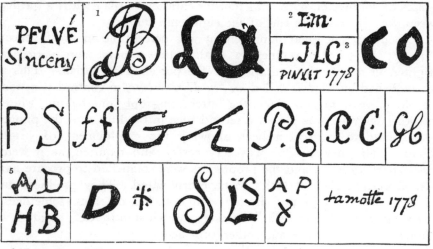

1 Monogram of Jos. Bedeau.   2 Initials of M. Melériat.   3 Initials of J. Lecerf.
4 Mark of Ghaïl.   5 Initials of A. Daussy.

BORDEAUX (Gironde), 1720. We have very little information about the manufactories of fayence which were established in this city, although it must have been one of its chief trades. In a document among the archives of Lille soliciting royal patronage for the celebrated manufactory of fayence of Jacques Feburier, he instances the *Manufacture Royale de Bordeaux*, founded by Jacques Hustin, which was in operation in 1729. There is a *seau* painted in polychrome with festoons and masks, in the Sèvres Museum, inscribed CARTUS. BURDIG. (Cartusia Burdigalensis), the Chartreuse or Convent of Bordeaux, which is in the style of the Rouen pottery, made apparently about 1740 or 1750. In the list of manufacturers in France in 1790 (p. 171) we find that no less than eight fabriques of fayence or porcelain were then existing at Bordeaux. A later manufactory established in 1829 by M. de St. Amand, associated with Messrs. Lahens and Rateau, which lasted a short time; it was re-established by M. D. Johnston, an Englishman, who marked his ware with the name of the town in full; he also made English porcelain.

L^R

BORDEAUX. A fabrique of pottery was carried on here by M. Boyer in 1830, and another by Madame Veuve Letourneau about the same time.

LIMOGES (Haute-Vienne). By a decree of the 8th of October 1737, Le Sieur Massié was authorised to establish at this town a fabrique of fayence; subsequently, on the discovery of kaolin at St. Yrieix, Massié associated himself with M. Fourneira and the brothers Grellet, and on December 30, 1773, another decree was obtained, authorising them to join the production of porcelain to that of fayence.

LIMOGES. J. Pouyat, manufacturer of modern earthenware services; some specimens are in the Sèvres Museum.

J. P
L

LIMOGES. On a dish in the Moustiers style (allegorical subject), Limoges Museum; time of Sieur Massié.

$\mathcal{M}_{1}$ + Limoges ◆
Le 18 ^{me} may
J74J

TAVERNES (Var), near Varages. A fabrique of fayence was established here about 1760 by M. Gaze, which ceased in 1780. One of his descendants has presented a specimen to the Sèvres Museum; it is a plate painted with bouquets of flowers in blue, something like the common ware of Varages; the mark is G, as in the margin.

#C‡
G.

MARTRES (Haute-Garonne), Languedoc. A manufacture of common fayence in imitation of Moustiers; a piece, painted with flowers in blue, yellow, green, and violet, and signed as in the margin on one side, inscribed Marie Thérèze Conte, on the other, is in the possession of M. Pujol of Toulouse.

faite à Martres,
18 Septembre,
1775.

MONTPELIER (Hérault), 1710. In a book published in this town in 1758 we are informed that there existed in the faubourgs "des manufactures d'un très belle fayence." This is confirmed by a document in the archives of Lille, in which Jacques Féburier, a fayencier, solicits royal patronage; he instances the Manufacture Royale de Montpelier, founded by Jacques Ollivier, as being at that time in operation, namely, in 1729. In 1718 M. Ollivier made an application to the Minister to be permitted to receive from abroad lead and tin for the use of his fabrique, which was granted, and he was allowed to introduce 200 quintals of lead, and fifty quintals of tin.

We also learn that in 1750 M. André Philip, from Marseilles, was established at Montpelier, and that he was succeeded by his sons Antoine and Valentine in the manufactory, which ceased in 1828. One of his grandchildren, Madame Gervais, perfectly remembers the royal arms over the door; she has presented to the Sèvres Museum some specimens of the ware, which are in imitation of the polychrome fayences of Moustiers and Marseilles.

Mr. Parkes in his *Chemical Essays* says, "There is also a considerable establishment for the manufacture of porcelain at Montpelier, a descriptive account of which, together with the process of making the peculiar glaze which was employed there, was published in the *Annales de Chimie*, tom. ii. p. 73." On referring to the paper, however, we find that it only relates to some experiments made by M. Chaptal on the clays of the neighbourhood to find suitable materials in the construction of a laboratory, and that he succeeded in making a sort of porcelain biscuit capable of resisting the fumes of hot acids, which appears to be similar to that previously discovered by Wedgwood, and a cheap sort of salt glaze; but there does not appear to have been a manufactory of porcelain at Montpelier.

 MONTPELIER. A manufactory of stoneware by Le Vouland. Crucibles, &c., were sent to the Paris Exposition in 1834.

MARIGNAC (Haute-Garonne). M. de Lafüe, *Seigneur du lieu*, established in 1737 a manufactory of fayence which was regularly authorised by the Council in March 1740, and continued at work for fourteen years, when it was given up from the difficulty of finding faithful workmen. In 1758 a M. Pons obtained privileges, and the manufacture was carried on by others until 1791, as shown in the list of fayenciers of that date (p. 171).

SAMADET (Landes), situated near St. Séver. This fabrique was worked in 1732 by virtue of a privilege accorded to M. l'Abbé de Roquépine, and was very successful, having been renewed twenty years afterwards. M. Jacquemart has discovered some authentic specimens of the Samadet fayence in the possession of M. Labeyrie; the ware is similar to that of Moustiers and Marseilles; the fabrication was continued to recent times. The Abbé de Rocquépine was succeeded by M. Dizes, who played an important part in the French Revolution and under the Empire. The Marquis de Poudens was the last proprietor.

VARAGES (Var), six leagues from Moustiers, 1730 to 1800. There was a manufacture of fayence early in the eighteenth century, founded by M. Bertrand before 1740, whose descendants still occupy the same premises, known as the "Fabrique de St. Jean," from having been built on the site of a church of that name. The following five fabriques were established at Varages in the last century, but ceased about the end of it :—

1. Bayol, dit Pin ; at a later period Grégoire Richeline.
2. Faber; later Bayol.
3. Clerissy, who was succeeded by Grosdidier.
4. Montagnac.
5. Laurent; later Guigou.

This fayence is coarsely painted in the same style as that of Moustiers, the outlines being frequently traced in black; also in the style of Strasbourg and Marseilles, in which the green, rose, and yellow prevail. There are still four manufactories here, making ordinary white fayence.

VARAGES. The mark of the fabrique was in the last century a cross traced in black, blue, or red, and the only one used; hence the ware was called "Faïence à la croix" at the famous fair of Beaucaire, where it was annually for sale.

VARAGES (?). On a French fayence plate, painted with a landscape and figures after Wouverman, crimson and green flower border, about 1770. Victoria and Albert Museum. The mark is in red. (*Ker. Gall.*, enlarged edition, fig. 137.)

VARAGES. Some specimens of fayence are in the Sèvres Museum, made by M. Brouchier in 1837.

VARAGES. Style of Moustiers; so attributed by Marryat.

MARSEILLES (Bouches-du-Rhône). The manufacture of fayence must have been in activity early in the seventeenth century in the South of France, especially in Marseilles, for in several of the laboratories are still seen the drug vases made at that time, and the Hospital of Narbonne is entirely furnished with them. M. le Baron Davillier possessed a plate which proves the existence of a pottery at Marseilles in the year 1697; it is inscribed "A. Clerissy à St. Jean du Dezert à Marseille, 1697," which is the name of a *quartier* adjoining the city. This is the earliest authenticated piece known with name and date.

M. A. Mortreuil, in his *Notice sur les Anciennes Industries Marseillaise* (not knowing the piece just alluded to), says, "Le plus ancien faïencier dont le nom soit connu à Marseille est un nommé Jean Delaresse, établi dès 1709. À cette époque la fabrication de la faïence ne devait pas avoir un grand développement; puisque cette même année deux barques venues de l'étranger, sans designation spéciale de provenance, importaient à Marseille huit mille douzaines de pièces de faïence. Mais un peu après le milieu de XVIII siècle, on comptait douze fabriques de poterie en activité, dont neuf de faïence émaillée" In the *Guide Marseillaise* we read their names were: Agnel et Sauze, près la porte de Rome; Antoine Bonnefoy, près la porte d'Aubagne; Boyer, à la Joliette; Fauchier, hors la porte d'Aix; Vve Fesquet, hors la porte Paradis; Vve Perrin et Abellard, Joseph Gaspard Robert, and Honoré Savy, hors la porte de Rome; Jean Baptiste Viry, aux allées de Meilham. Three other fabricants, Batelier, Eydoux, and Massuque, made only common pottery.

The Revolution of 1789 gave the same blow to the ceramic industry of Marseilles as to Moustiers. The twelve fabriques occupied 250 workmen; in 1805 there were only three, employing twenty hands; in 1809 only one, that of M. Sauze.

Of Jean Delaresse, before spoken of, no document concerning him, or specimen of fayence which can be attributed to him, has yet been discovered. From 1709 to 1749 nothing is known of the state of the fayence manufactories, but in the last-named year we hear of Honoré Savy being established at Marseilles. In 1765 he applied to the Minister for a privilege for making porcelain, which was refused him, as several similar applications had already been made. From one of these documents we learn that he had been "maître et fabricant de faïence depuis seize ans," and that he had found a green, superior to any other, and which he alone knew how to employ; this was called *le vert de Savy*.

On the 2nd of January 1762, a letter from M. Bertin of Versailles to M. de la Tour, Intendant de Provence à Aix, on the subject of the grievances and complaint made in the previous year by the *ouvriers faïenciers* of Marseilles says: "They complain of the great number of apprentices which the fabricants take, some as many as twenty-four, at a salary of five sols per day, *payés en faïence*, which mode of payment deteriorates the quality, and causes the workmen to emigrate to Genoa." In reply to his letter the Intendant says, "The fabrication being perfectly free, the number of apprentices cannot be limited, but they should in future be always paid in money." In the complaint of 1761 above referred to, they say that the importations of Genoese fayence into Languedoc and Provence, from whence they were spread over the rest of the kingdom, is absolutely ruinous to the manufacture of these two provinces, and to those of Marseilles.

Among the artists who went to Italy may be mentioned Jacques Borelly or Boselly, whose name is frequently found on the Marseillaise pottery; his Christian name is sometimes Italianised to *Giacomo Boselly*, and on two large vases, decorated in green *en camaieu*, we find "*Jacques Boselly, Savonne, 1779, 24 Septembre.*"

M. Rolet of Marseilles also emigrated to Urbino; his name is found on a fayence sliding lamp with silvered pillar in the Victoria and Albert Museum, bearing the following inscription: "*Fabrica di Maiolica fina di Monsieur Rolet in Urbino, à 20 Novembre 1772.*" These facts sufficiently explain the resemblance which exists between the fayences of Italy of the eighteenth century and those of Marseilles. There is, however, one peculiarity about the Marseillaise fayence which at once fixes its identity, and this is the three green leaves or marks on the backs of plates and dishes, so placed to hide the imperfections in the enamel, caused by the *pernettes*, or points of support on which they rest in the kiln.

In the *Journal des Fêtes données à Marseille en* 1777, on the occasion of the visit of the Comte de Provence (afterwards Louis XVIII.), we read that Monsieur went to the *fabrique de faïence* of Sieur Savy; all the workmen were at their posts, and the Prince was shown all the various operations of the manufacture, from the commencement to the final perfection of a piece. He was introduced into the grand gallery, where he saw an immensity of fayence of every description, which he much praised, and permitted Savy to place the manufacture under his protection, and to place in the gallery a statue of the Prince, which was to be forthwith made. It was styled "*Manufacture de Monsieur frère du Roi, hors de la porte de Rome*." It will be observed that no mention is made of porcelain, which, if Savy did make, must have been of quite secondary importance, and none has been identified as of his make. When the Comte de Provence, however, inspected the works of Joseph Gaspard Robert, he especially admired the porcelain, and a large vase, of which the design and modelling fixed his attention, and remarked, "Ceci mérite d'être vû," and paid the most flattering eulogiums to Sieur Robert. He noted with pleasure that a beautiful porcelain service, complete, was destined for England, and admired the execution of different porcelain flowers, which were as delicate as natural flowers.

Another celebrated manufactory was that of Veuve Perrin and Abellard, probably the most important as to the quality of fayence and great number of its products; they also made porcelain, but no specimens have been found. The fayences of this firm are more frequently imitated than any other.

In the petition of fayenciers in 1790 there were eleven manufactories then existing.

In the Victoria and Albert Museum are a pair of cups and covers of the eighteenth century, and a coffee-pot in embossed and painted earthenware. The fayence is the same character as that of Moustiers, and also of Strasbourg; the decorations are frequently in red or green, sometimes with Chinese designs, and in the style of Louis XV.

MARSEILLES. A. Clerissy, 1697. This cut represents the back of a plateau, 24 inches in diameter, representing in front a hunting scene after Tempesta—a lion attacked by three cavaliers, a fourth taking flight. It is painted in blue *en camaïeu*, clear violet outlines on bluish white enamel; the marly or rim, painted with bouquets and birds, in the Oriental style, something like Nevers ware of the sixteenth century. The mark in blue is much reduced, and the  initials of Clerissy's name cursively are traced round the under side of the rim. In the Collection of M. le Baron C. Davillier.

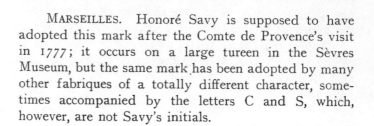

MARSEILLES. Honoré Savy is supposed to have adopted this mark after the Comte de Provence's visit in 1777; it occurs on a large tureen in the Sèvres Museum, but the same mark has been adopted by many other fabriques of a totally different character, sometimes accompanied by the letters C and S, which, however, are not Savy's initials.

MARSEILLES (Bouches-du-Rhône). This mark is found on fayence of the middle of the eighteenth century, attributed to Savy; on a plate painted with flowers.

MARSEILLES. On a pair of fayence vases painted in gold and colours, with two shields of arms. Formerly in Dr. Diamond's Collection.

MARSEILLES. This mark in brown is on a sucrier and cover, painted with green *camaieu* flowers in the colour called "*vert de Savy.*" Formerly in Dr. Diamond's Collection.

On a fayence oval dish, painted with flowers; the initials of J. Robert.

MARSEILLES. The mark of Joseph Gaspard Robert, on fayence, generally in black,—an R, with or without a dot, as found upon his porcelain. The first is upon a plate, painted with bouquet of roses in natural colours, in the Sèvres Museum. The same Collection includes a tureen, the cover having fish, well modelled. the decoration consisting of flowers, birds, and fish, in green shaded with black, with his name in full lengths, "Robert à Marseille." A certain sign by which some of his pieces may be known is the presence of gilding of remarkable finish and brilliancy. The *service aux insectes* and the *service aux poissons* were favourite patterns. The fabrique of Robert, according to M. Mortreuil, ceased to exist in 1793.[1]

[1] In the Mountferrand Collection (No. 538 and 539) were two plates, of octagonal form, of unglazed French fayence of the eighteenth century; on one was a landscape, and on the other the Grotto of Posilipo. These paintings were by an artist named Robert, who was a painter of landscapes and architecture, and considered one of the best of his time. During his later years, when he went to dine with a friend, he brought with him his plate, on which was a sketch in colour. These small paintings are generally of a greyish tint, and suffer from the advanced age of the artist. He was perhaps the same here spoken of.

MARSEILLES. Antoine Bonnefoy. M. Laurent Sauze, the last of the Marseillaise fabricants, has some specimens of his works so marked in yellow ochre.

MARSEILLES. Veuve Perrin. These marks are sometimes found on pieces which bear the initials of Veuve Perrin, but on many others also ; they may therefore be other marks of the fabricants of Marseilles. They are also found upon contemporary pieces of Milan.

MARSEILLES. Veuve Perrin. This mark generally in black, but sometimes in violet or brown. The first mark is on some plates with landscapes and cattle, formerly in the possession of the Marchese d'Azeglio; the second on a moutardier. Collectors should be on their guard against imitations made in Paris which bear this mark.

MARSEILLES. J. Fauchier. This mark, in blue, is on a large plateau with handles, of elegant form, painted with flowers and insects in natural colours, formerly in the possession of M. le Baron C. Davillier.

MARSEILLES. Jacques Boselly. On two fayence plates, painted with flowers, formerly in the Collection of the Marchese d'Azeglio. M. Demmin has in his possession a cup, decorated *à jour*, painted red and green, dated 1781.

Herr Jännike gives these additional marks on Marseilles fayence. The first is said to be the monogram of J. & G. Robert, and the third the initials of Savy; the fourth is perhaps another monogram of Robert's. (*Ker. Gall.*, enlarged edition, figs. 138, 139.)

AUBAGNE is in the Arrondissement of Marseilles. The *Tableau Général du Commerce de Gournay* for 1788 says, "Il y a à Aubagne seize fabriques de poterie, et deux de faïence fort bella, où l'on fait tout ce que l'on peut désirer dans ce genre. La consommation et l'exportation des unes et des autres se font aux Iles de l'Amérique, et à Aix, Marseille et Toulon." It is probable they were established some little time after those of Marseilles, as we have seen others spring up near the celebrated manufactories of Moustiers, and their products were in imitation, no doubt, of the rival fabriques with which they are now confounded.

MANERBE (Calvados), near Lisieux, in Normandy. There was a manufactory here in the second half of the sixteenth century. M. Raymond of Bordeaux, *Bulletin du Bouquiniste* (1ᵉʳ semestre, 6° année) quotes a passage from the 7th volume of *Ancienne Géographie :* "La vaisselle de terre de Manerbe, près de Lisieux, se rapporte à celle de Venise par sou artifice et sa beauté." The elegant glazed earthenware pinnacles which adorn the gables of the old mansions about Lisieux and other parts of Normandy were made here; they are about 5 or 6 feet long, with a series of small ornaments placed one upon another on an iron rod, and partake of the character of the *figulines rustiques* of Palissy, and have been frequently sold as such. Similar ornaments were made at Malicorne; a specimen is in the Nevers Museum (*Ker. Gall.*, enlarged edition, fig. 146.)

Dr. Graesse and Herr Jännike have both given this as the fabrique mark of Lisieux of the sixteenth century.

MALICORNE, near Pont-Valin (Sarthe). The glazed earthenware pinnacles for decorating the gables of old houses, similar to those of Manerbe, were also made here. There is a curious specimen, with grotesque figures, in the Collection of M. Champfleury of Paris; and in the Sèvres Museum is another. An *écuelle*, in the same museum, is classed as being made at Malicorne. This manufacture of *épis* or *estocs*, as the French term them, was carried on formerly at Infréville, Chatel-la-Lune, and Armentières, in Normandy.

SAINT-LONGE. SAINT-LONGES, near Mamers (Sarthe). M. E. Lamasse, of Meudon, near Paris, possesses a fountain 22 inches high, in the style of Louis XIV., oviform, with a landscape and garlands of fruit and flowers in relief, like the fayence of Lorraine; on the back is stamped "Saint-Longe."

AUXERRE (Yonne). Fayence of the ordinary style of the Nevers ware of the end of the eighteenth century. About 1798 there was a potter named *Boutet*, who signed his name in full. M. Chantrier, of Nevers, has some specimens.

AIEZY (Yonne). There are some specimens in the Nevers Museum, attributed to this place, of the end of the eighteenth century, in the ordinary Nevers style, without marks or monograms.

MEILLONAS (Ain). Gournay, in his *Almanach*, 1788, thus refers to this fabrique: "Manufacture de fayence fort estimée. Propriétaire, M. Marron, Seigneur de lieu." It was established between 1740 and 1750 by Madame la Baronne de Meillonas in her château, where she erected

 a furnace, and not only painted pieces herself for presentation, but employed other able artists. There are many specimens preserved in the vicinity, some of which are marked AR, as in the margin. They are usually decorated

with garlands of flowers and ribbons, and in the centre landscapes finely painted but generally unmarked. M. Jacquemart mentions some *jardinières charmantes* belonging to Mons.   *Pidoux* 1765
Voillard, signed as in the margin. M. Pidoux was a   *à Miliona*
painter of the establishment. It passed through different hands, and is now carried on by M. Joly.

COURCELLES (Sarthe). Established by a surgeon named Guimonneau-Forterie. There are some pieces signed by him, and dated 1762 and 1774, in the Collection at Mans, and a tureen on which is stamped "Par G. Forterie, chirurgien à Courcelles, 1783," and a siphon jug is inscribed "Forterie père, ancien chirurgien à Courcelles, 1789."

CLERMONT-FERRAND (Puy-de-Dôme). A
souvenir of this manufactory occurs on a large   *Clermont Ferrand*
ewer in the collection of M. Edouard Pascal
of Paris, inscribed as in the margin, orna-   *1734.*
mented with arabesques and an allegory of
Time, in blue *camaieu*, in the style of Moustiers fayence. It was conducted by a M. Chaudessolle in the Rue Fontgiève; its duration cannot be ascertained except by the pieces referred to. On a similar vessel of this fabrique is inscribed, "Convalescence de M. Rossignol, Intendant d'Auvergne, M. Cellier, Trésorier de l'Ordre, 26 Mars 1738."

CLERMONT-FERRAND. This inscription
occurs on the foot of a Rouen ware ewer,   m
blue *camaieu*, with scrolls and flowers, ex-   Clermont ferrand
hibited at the Paris Exposition, 1867, by   D'auvergne
Mons. Grange of Clermont.   21 jauier 1756

CLERMONT. There was a manufactory
here in the first half of the eighteenth cen-   **CLERMONT.**
tury. The ware was mottled brown, in imitation of tortoiseshell, and of Italian forms. Herr Jännike gives a cursive capital I as a mark of this fabrique.

SCEAUX-PENTHIÈVRE (Seine). In a decree dated June 1753 we read that, upon the request of Sieur Jacques de Chapelle, stating that he had established, about two years since, at the village of Sceaux, a manufactory of fayence, of which he alone possessed the secret; that the ware made there was appreciated by the public on account of its good qualities and properties; that the sale kept on increasing daily, and that a great number of workmen were engaged; he was consequently permitted to continue his trade. Nothing is said about making porcelain, but M. Riocreux quotes a document, or rather an interdiction from the Sèvres authorities, about 1752, that he was to confine himself to the manufacture of fayence, and it was not until Duc de Penthièvre became proprietor of the works that the making of porcelain was resumed. This ware is in the style of Strasbourg, the rose colour and green prevailing, painted with flowers and bouquets, but more carefully finished: landscapes on jardinères, &c.

After ten years' labour in bringing his fayence to a high state of perfection, he let his manufactory in June 1763 for a period of nine years to one of his painters, M. Jullien, who had worked for him since 1754. The latter took into partnership Charles Symphorien Jacques, a clever sculptor, turner, and modeller. It is difficult of explanation how Messrs. Jacques and Jullien, who had purchased of Babin the porcelain manufactory of Menecy under the protection of the Duc de Villeroy, could carry on at the same time two works of such different character and so far apart, but from existing documents this appears to have been actually the case.

On the 29th of April, 1772, the term having expired, M. Chapelle definitely sold his fabrique to Richard Glot, of Rue St. Denis, porte St. Sauveur. Glot was a clever sculptor, and in the purchase stipulated for all the secrets and processes of his predecessor as well as the materials. He greatly extended the works and multiplied the production of figures and groups, which were executed in the highest taste.

In 1775 Glot obtained the protection of the Duc de Penthièvre, High Admiral of France, and from that moment the fabrication of porcelain *pâte tendre* was taken up with great activity; but the fayence still continued in demand, and was considered the finest and best painted ware in France.

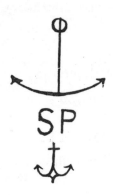

The mark S X was not used on the fayence, but was the usual mark on porcelain. The anchor was adopted by Glot in honour of the High Admiral traced in colour, surmounted occasionally by the word SCEAUX; the letters SP above the anchor stand for Sceaux-Penthièvre. The mark in the margin is on a covered vase in the Collection of M. Paul Gasnault, of Paris. The word Sceaux alone is sometimes found on fayence of the time of the Revolution. On the 14th July 1795 the works were sold to Pierre Antoine Carbaret, and the artistic character of the ware came to an end, and only vessels of utility were made. (*Ker. Gall.*, enlarged edition, fig. 152.)

RENNES (Ille-et-Vilaine). In the Abbey of St. Sulpice-la-Forêt are preserved some funeral tablets of fayence of the seventeenth century, supposed to have been made here; one of these bears the following inscription: "Cy gist le corps de défeunte janne Le Bouteiller, dame du Plecix coialu, decedée 29me Janvier l'an 1653, agée de 50 ans." At a recent Exposition in this city, Messrs. Aussant and André collected many curious pieces of fayence made in the vicinity; one was a jug of glazed earthenware, inscribed "*Fait à Rennes, Rue Hue, 1769.*" At a sale in the neighbourhood, M. Edouard Pascal obtained a piece with the same inscription, dated 1770. A white fayence group of Louis XV., with Hygeia on his left and Brittany personified on his right, surrounded by attributes, was exhibited, signed "*Bourgouin, 1764.*"

The first positive date recorded is the authorisation on the 11th July 1748, to Jean Forasassi, called Barbarino, a Florentine, to establish a fabrique of enamelled pottery in the Quartier des Capucins. This was carried on several years, and the other fabrique in Rue Hue was on a large scale.

In the *Almanach Général du Commerce* of Gournay, 1788, mention is made of the two manufactories of La Veuve Dulatty and Jollivet et Rennes. In the *Gazette des Beaux Arts*, vol. xv., several of the specimens are given by M. A. Jacquemart, which he thus describes: "La faïence de Rennes est bonne, son émail est pur et blanc: voilà deux qualités qui la mettent au niveau des œuvres de Nevers et du midi de la France. Cuite au grand feu, elle ne peut avoir, ni les délicatesses de Strasbourg, de Niderville et de Sceaux, ni les tons frais de la peinture à réverbère."

RENNES. The mark in the margin is given by Herr Jännike as the mark of this factory.
$$GDG\frac{2}{9}$$
$$1780$$

CASTILHON (Gard). Fayence in imitation of Moustiers was made here in the eighteenth century. A plate in the Collection of M. Edouard Pascal, painted with a grotesque personage, bouquets and garlands in green, heightened with manganese, is signed in full, "*Castilhon.*"

Castilhon.

APREY, near Langres (Haute-Marne). Established about 1750 by Lallemand, Baron d'Aprey, and it acquired some reputation. Ollivier at first directed the works, and afterwards became proprietor; under his direction an artist named Jary or Jarry gained great reputation as a painter of birds and flowers. About 1780 it was conducted by M. Vilhaut for the manufacture of a superior kind of fayence In a letter read before the Academy of Dijon by M. Bosc d'Antic on an improved method of making fayence, he fully describes the process adopted by M. Vilhaut at Aprey as being the best then existing; the paper is given *in extenso* in the *Encyclopédie Méthodique*, Paris, 1783, *sub voce* "Faïence." The early style is that of Strasbourg, with rose colour, green, and yellow predominating. One peculiarity of the Aprey fayence is, that its designs are rarely traced by a dark or black-coloured outline; it is still carried on by M. Louis Gérard. The mark in the margin (preceded by a potter's or painter's initial) is on some early specimens in the Sèvres Museum; other pieces are in the Collections of MM. Edouard Pascal and Mathieu Meusnier of Paris. (*Ker. Gall.*, enlarged edition, fig. 145.)

p. Ap

On a fayence *porte huilier*, painted with blue and lake borders, and edged with green; marked in black. The name is sometimes stamped on the ware.

c. aprey

LE CROISIC (Loire-Inférieure). A manufactory was established here in the sixteenth century by a Fleming named Gérard Demigennes. Horatio Borniola, an Italian, succeeded him in 1627, leaving it at his death to Jean Borniola and Beatrice his sister, wife of a person named Davys, but nothing is known of their productions.

17

AUCH (Gers). In 1758 Messrs. Ailemand, La Grange, Dumont & Co. solicited privileges for the establishment of a fayence manufactory in the garden of La Grange; their productions were sought for at the time and well spoken of, but no examples have been identified.

CHATEAUDUN (Eure-et-Loir). Jacquemart says that the Duke de Chevreuse had obtained a privilege for creating a fabrique of fayence in this town; in 1755 Pierre Bremont and Gabriel Jouvet were directors. It is mentioned by Gournay in 1788, but is not in the petition of fayenciers in 1790, given on p. 171.

M. MATHAUT (Aube). A fayence fabrique was established here, but its products are unknown to us. The letters-patent are dated 14th October 1749, and run thus: "The Sieur Gédéon-Claude Lepetit de Lavaux, Baron de Mathaut, a parish situate in Champagne, on the river Aube, having represented that he has found clay suitable for making fayence near the forest of Rians, and that such an establishment would be of great utility in the country, there being no factory of the same character within twenty-five leagues;" permission was accorded on the 26th May 1750, and a prohibition for ten years against any other within three leagues of Mathaut.

LE PUY (Haute-Loire). This fabrique of fayence was not exactly here, but first established at Orsilhac, then at Brives, by M. Lazerme about 1780. In 1783 the States-General of Languedoc agreed to accord a gratification *de six cents libres au Sieur Lazerme négociant du Puy*, "qui a établi à grands frais, dans son domaine de Orsilhac un fabrique de faïencerie, dont les ouvrages sont de la plus grande utilité cet établissement étant d'ailleurs unique dans le Velay." It is mentioned in 1785, in the *Almanach Général des Marchands*, &c., and in 1788 by Gournay.

BOURG-LA-REINE (Seine). The manufactory at Bourg-la-Reine was established in 1773, under the protection of the Comte d'Eu, by Messrs. Jacques & Julien; it was removed hither when the works at Menecy were closed.

BOURG-LA-REINE. There is a specimen of fayence in the Sèvres Museum, sent by the manufacturers, MM. Benoist and Mony, in the year 1819.

BOURG-LA-REINE. A fabrique of fayence is still carried on by M. Laurin, who uses the old mark placed upon the porcelain. Besides the white fayence for domestic use, more artistic pieces are produced, painted on the enamel after it has received a slight baking; it is principally in imitation of the Italian. The painter attached to the manufactory of Bourg-la-Reine was a pupil of Sèvres named Chapelet, who marked his decorations with a chaplet as here shown.

B la R   BOURG-LA-REINE. On a plate and jug of white fayence, in the Sèvres Museum.

BOURG-LA-REINE. This mark is more frequently found upon fayence than porcelain; it is in blue, on a specimen in the Sèvres Museum, and on a set of eight fayence plates, beautifully painted with exotic birds and trees, insects on the borders, much in the Chelsea style of painting of about 1750 to 1760.

CHAUMONT-SUR-LOIR (Loir-et-Cher). A château near Blois. Terracotta; 1760 to 1786. Jean Baptiste Nini was born in Lombardy about 1716; he at first established himself at Charité-sur-Loir, and about 1760 entered the service of M. Leray, possessor of the ancient château of Chaumont, as an engraver on glass and fayence in his manufactory there. There are some glasses extant engraved by him with extreme delicacy, and a great variety of terra-cotta portrait medallions of fine work, displaying great care in the execution of the details. His moulds in copper, graved with a burin, were bought in 1820 by a founder of Blois, and melted down into ingots. All his medallions, which are now getting scarce, are signed in small letters, graved in the soft paste: NINI or I. B. NINI, F., accompanied by the date; they are usually of two sizes, 6 inches and 9 inches in diameter. The most esteemed portraits are those of Louis XV., Louis XVI. Franklin (of whom there are six different sizes), some with the date in relief; Voltaire, Madame de la Reynière, Marie Thérèse, Empress Catherine II. of Russia, and about seventy others known, dated from 1762 to 1781, which will be found described at length in M. A. Villier's work on *I. B. Nini; ses Terres Cuites*, Blois, 1866. Several of these busts were reproduced by Wedgwood in his blue and white jasper, and Nini's name may be found upon some of them.

UZES (Gard). François Pichon, manufacturer. A specimen of fayence was presented by the maker in 1837 to the Sèvres Museum.

NÎMES (Gard). There is not much information about the fabrique at this place, but M. Jacquemart, in an article in the *Gazette des Beaux Arts*,[1] has told us that there was a street in Nîmes called "Rue de Faïence," which he thinks is proof that one or more factories existed there. Then Glot, writing in 1791, mentions two factories at Nîmes, but of the second there is no other information. M. Jacquemart mentions "*un petit sabot*" which was dated 1702 and bore an inscription, but then the date seems to be only verified by the memory of an owner, as the piece had been destroyed.

---

[1] "Les Poteries du Midi de la France, étude à propos d'un livre publié par M. C. J. Davillier," par Albert Jacquemart. The article discusses the following fabriques : Varages, Tavernes, Toulouse, Martres, Montpelier, Nîmes, Vauvert, Andruze, Castilhoun, Avignon, Goult, La Tour, d'Aigues, Meillonas, Clermont, Bordeaux, Rennes.

Nîmes.

P.B.C.

There is a specimen with the mark in the margin, the initials being those of MM. Plantier, Boncoirant et Cie., in the Sèvres Museum; and M. E. Pascal of Paris had a quaint jug formed of a man seated on a bench, with an inscription, in the patois of the locality, to the effect that a certain baker named Loubier, who was a friend of the fabricant, was of somewhat bibulous habits. The same collector also had plates with paintings of peasants in the costume of the country. The style was similar to that of Moustiers, Marseilles, and other French fayences, and the date was probably from about 1740-50, and not so early as M. Jacquemart thinks.

Rubelles.

A.D.T.

RUBELLES (near Melun). Fayence of opaque shaded enamel. The design is formed by the different thicknesses of the paste, in one or more colours. This was invented by M. le Baron de Bourgoing, and registered in 1856; he was associated with M. le Baron de Tremblay; it ceased in 1858. It has somewhat of the Palissy character; table services, chimney-pieces, &c.; sometimes marked A.D.T. or "Rubelles," both impressed on the ware.

VINCENNES (Seine), 1767. The existence of this manufacture is made known to us by a patent of 31st December 1767, from which it appears that M. Maurin des Aubiez was desirous to undertake a manufacture of fayence in the manner of Strasbourg, it being notorious that there did not exist in France any manufacture of fayence comparable in beauty and solidity to that of Strasbourg; being therefore desirous to establish one similar, he had purchased the secret, and brought to Paris a staff of workmen who had been engaged there, and had already expended 100,000 francs to arrive at that degree of perfection which it had now attained, specimens of which fayence had been submitted to and approved by the public. He also included in his request *the manufacture of porcelain*, and that he required a large and commodious building for the purpose, which he could not obtain without a great outlay of capital. It was accordingly decreed that the said Maurin des Aubiez should have accorded to him the possession for twenty years of the Château de Vincennes, in a square enclosure, which had formerly been employed for the ancient manufacture of porcelain, with a building and outhouses opposite, and a convenient residence for him and his family; permitting "the said Aubiez to make or cause to be made in our said château, fayence in the style of Strasbourg of every kind, as well as porcelain." Pierre Antoine Hannong appears to have been engaged as director of the "*Manufacture Royale de Porcelaine à Vincennes*," and the manufacture was carried on for four years until 1771, when Hannong petitioned for assistance, having got into difficulties in consequence of the undertakers having ceased to furnish funds necessary to carry on the works, and which had unfortunately altogether ceased; the petition also stated that he had taken a smaller establishment at Vincennes on his own account, but in a few months this also failed. From a document in the archives at Sèvres, Hannong himself applied at first for the privilege which was accorded subsequently to Maurin des Aubiez, but he was refused; he, however, made fayence, and was signalled at Sèvres as endeavouring to make porcelain and to entice away the workmen from the Royal Manufactory. In 1766 an order was given to interdict his works, but from some high patronage he was allowed to continue under certain restrictions.

The marks used by Hannong on his porcelain are supposed to be the same as those he afterwards used at the Faubourg St. Lazare, here given in the margin. There are some pieces attributed to this manufactory in the Sèvres Museum: one of these is a high teapot decorated in rose-coloured *camaieu;* the monogram is P. H. in blue. (*See also notice of Strasbourg,* pp. 210-213.)

ORLÉANS (Loiret). According to M. A. Jacquemart, the first establishment of which we have any record is that authorised by a Council of the 13th March 1753 in favour of Sieur Jacques Étienne Dessaux de Romilly, privileged for twenty years to make "une faïence de terre blanche purifiée;" it was called the *Manufacture Royale.* In 1755 Sieur Leroy directed the works, and was succeeded in 1757 by Charles Claude Gérault Deraubert; this fabrique produced glazed statuettes tinted something like the Italian.

Only one piece has come under the notice of M. Jacquemart which bears the mark indicated in the *arrêt*, an O crowned in blue (see margin); it is a Chinaman seated, holding in his hands two branches of a tree, unfortunately broken, but forming part of a candlestick, like Dresden; these were executed by Jean Louis, who came from Strasbourg and Sceaux; this was soon converted into a porcelain manufactory. In 1760 fayence was still made at Orléans, especially large figures from 4 to 8 feet high, of which Bernard Huet was the author; his name is sometimes found written retrograde TƎVH. The *Almanach de Orléans*, 1776, does not mention the fabrique of Gérault, Rue de Bourdonblanc, but only those of Mezière, père et fils, in the Rue de la Grille, and aux Dames de la Croix; two years later Fédèle made fayence in Rue du Dévidet; in 1790 there were two in existence, but in 1797 all had disappeared, and the Widow Baubreuil erected a fayence manufactory in imitation of the English ware.

ORLÉANS (Loiret). Enamelled fayence, about 1780. Another manufactory of fayence was **ORLEANS** carried on about the same time by a potter named Barré. There was a fabrique of stoneware carried on by M. Laurent Gilbert in 1834, and another of fayence and marble ware by M. Gaumont in 1830; specimens of these are in the Sèvres Museum.

TOULOUSE. A manufactory of fayence was established here early in the eighteenth century; the ware is very much in the style of the early Rouen. There is a large hunting-bottle with eight loops in four rows at the sides for suspension, painted with blue flowers, and round the neck the annexed inscription, which belonged to Captain Reynolds,

LAU rens + Basso +

A Toulouza

Le 14ᵃ maÿ 1756.

son of the well-known collector, Mr. C. W. Reynolds. In 1790 there were two manufactories, as appears by the petition of the fayenciers to the National Assembly in that year, but we have no particulars respecting them. M. Vinot of Paris has some pieces painted with arabesques and the word *Toulouse* in full.

TOULOUSE (Haute-Garonne). Established 1820. Fouqué, Arnoux & Co.; on enamelled fayence, both white and coloured. They still make all sorts of ware, from terra-cotta to fine porcelain, the works being conducted by M. Fouqué.

QUIMPER (Finistère), near Brest. In a document deposited at Sèvres mention is made of a fayence manufactory in the style of Rouen established here about 1690. In a recent exposition of ancient fayence at Rennes, in Brittany, there was a large plate of this manufacture, dated 1700, similar to that of Rouen and Moustiers, painted with emblems and bordered with scrolls, on blue ground.

QUIMPER. A manufactory of glazed stoneware, grey and brown, by De la Hubaudière, 1809. It has the appearance of being much earlier in date; the mark stamped.

QUIMPER. Another manufactory of stoneware, by Messrs. Elowry and Porcher, 1840.

QUIMPER. Fayence thus marked (La Hubaudière & Co.) may be considered as modern, the mark having been adopted to prevent the sale of the products for those of old Rouen fayence. A manufactory of pottery was established at Quimper a long time previous to the purchase of the works by La Hubaudière et Cie., M. Pierre Caussy, a native of Rouen, being the founder, who marked his pieces with a C. They were similar to old Rouen fayence, but are distinguishable by the paste being coarser, the enamel more grey, and a manganese violet being used to trace the outlines of design.

QUIMPER-CORENTIN (Finistère). On fayence of the eighteenth century, early part, something in the style of Rouen; flowers, common quality.

MONTET (Saone-et-Loire). A manufactory near Charolles, directed by M. Laurjorais; stamped on white stoneware. Paris Exposition, 1819 and 1830.

TOURS. Established about 1770 by Thomas Sailly at the Faubourg St. Pierre-des-Corps, for the manufacture of fayence and glazed earthenware; after his death in 1782 it was carried on by his son, Noel Sailly. Porcelain was also made here in the same year.

TOURS. On a fayence pilgrim's bottle, painted with the arms of France, crowned; the centre is pierced through; the name is probably that of the person for whom it was made. Sèvres Museum.

fait a tours le
21 Main 1782
Lovis❖ LiAVTE

TOURS (Indre-et-Loire). Established in 1842 by Charles Avisseau for the reproduction of pottery in the style of Bernard Palissy, which he successfully imitated; he died in 1861, and was succeeded by his son, M. E. Avisseau. In the International Exhibition of 1862 three specimens were exhibited, for which he deservedly received a medal; two were imitations of the Henry II. ware; the third, a group of a stork and snake, which, for truthfulness to nature, surpassed any work of Palissy. M. Landais of Tours, the nephew of M. Avisseau, is also a successful imitator of Palissy: there are several specimens in the Victoria and Albert Museum, which were exhibited in Paris in 1855.

avisseau
atour
1855

TOURS. Some of F. M. Landais' pieces bear his name at full length: others have simply his monogram, as in the margin.

LANGEAIS (Indre-et-Loire). M. Ch. de Boissimon & Cie. On a pair of vases and baskets of fayence with open work and coloured fruit and flowers in relief.

> CH. de BOISSIMON et Cie.
> a LANGEAIS INDRE & LOIRE.

CASEMÈNE, near Besançon. The mark of a manufactory, stamped, founded by Laflèche-Paillard at the beginning of this century, and lasted but a short time.

GIEN
Geoffroi

GIEN. A manufacture of maiolica was established here about 1864 in imitation of that of Italy of the sixteenth and seventeenth centuries, and other varieties of early wares, but latterly the quality of its productions have become of a very ordinary and uninteresting character.

PREMIÈRES (Côte-d'Or), near Dijon, established in 1783 by a brickmaker named Lavel or Laval, who was instructed in the making of fayence by an Italian monk named Leonardi, then travelling through the country. His grandson, Dr. Lavalle, still continues the work in a more artistic style; the modern marks are sometimes pencilled in this character, or stencilled.

PREMIÈRES (Côte-d'Or). Monogram of Dr. J. Lavalle, on a fayence plate, painted with Cupid holding a cornucopia of flowers.

PREMIÈRES (Côte-d'Or). Initials of Dr. J. Lavalle, on a plate painted in blue *camaieu*, with trees and flowers; the mark within an ornamented circle.

PREMIÈRES (Côte-d'Or). There was another fabrique of fayence carried on by M. Pignant, who in 1826 sent specimens to the Sèvres Museum.

MUSIGNY (Côte-d'Or). Established about 1790 by M. Bosc, for the fabrication of *grès;* mentioned by M. Brongniart.

VAUDANCOURT (Marne). A manufactory of *grès* by M. A. Bodelet in 1836 is mentioned by M. Brongniart.

GIEY-SUR-ANJOU (Haute-Marne). A manufactory of *grès* and porcelain, carried on by M. Guignet, of which specimens are in the Sèvres Museum, acquired in 1827 and 1831.

FRANCE—UNCERTAIN MARKS.

From "Les Merveilles de la Céramique," by A. Jacquemart.

These marks are on a plate in the Marseilles style.

On a table fountain in the Rouen style. Dr. Justus Brinckmann says that this mark is that of a fayence factory of Dorotheenthal, near Arnstadt, established about 1720, and which lasted until 1780. A potter named Johan Christoph Alex worked there from 1724-26.

ALEX 1724

On a fountain in blue *camaieu* with arabesques. Poitiers.

J: Alliot

On a *bénitier* with twisted columns, three yellow fleurs-de-lis at the top, pierced panels, the bowl decorated in polychrome.

C D
CABRI
1762

On a bas-relief of the Crucifixion, fine enamel border of arabesques in blue.

Jr Jamart
1696

On a plate in blue *camaieu* in the Nevers style.

Jean:gony

This mark is on a barrel fixed on its stand, surmounted by Bacchus on horseback, blue and yellow circles, blue decoration outlined in black. This is probably another of the numerous marks of Rouen fayence.

+ L e g e r +
L e i e u n e +
+ 1730 +

On a *canette* in the Rouennaise style, with Chinese figures, brilliant colours.

NicoLasH.V
1738

On an earthenware plate: on the border ornaments in brown and dull green; in the centre a family are reciting the *Bénédicité* (1629).

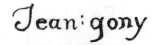

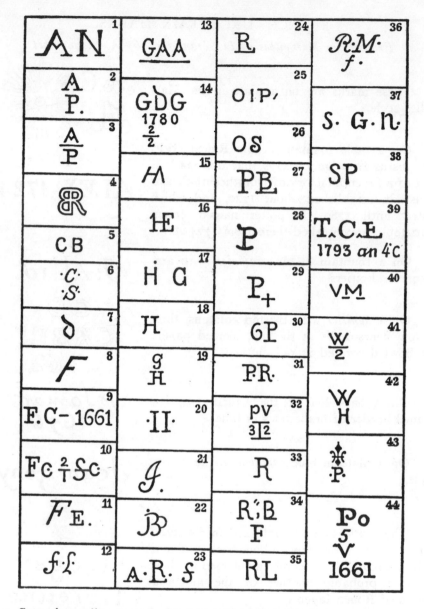

1. Cream-jug, yellow ground with a medallion painted in blue.

2. Large vase of *terre de pipe,* raised in blue, the cover surmounted by a pine-apple and four leaves.

3. Style meridional. Service *à marques variées.*

4. Fayence, yellow ground with medallions of coloured flowers.

5. Sauce-boat, polychrome flowers.

6. Tankard of Italian form, serpent handle, blue decoration like Nevers.

7. Dish with bouquets of flowers—Strasbourg style.

8. Plates of red clay and heavy decoration of flowers in the style of Rennes, but with bright red.

9. Large dish, like Marseilles.

10. Fayence mug, birds and flowers—Rouen style.

11. Plate, very white enamel and flowers—Marseilles style.

12. Portions of a service of fine fayence, rococo reliefs, finely painted with landscapes and flowers; the rose-coloured tone by its freshness resembles Niderviller.

13. Tureen, bouquets of flowers—Marseilles style.

14. Covered cup and saucer, Pompadour style, light manganese colour.

15. Dish with bouquets of flowers, polychrome style—Franco-Hollandais.

16. Baskets painted with forget-me-not and other small flowers, like the South of France style, royal arms in the centre.

17. Perfume-burner, painted in colours with flowers.

18. On fayence, with leafy handles and buttons, painted with flowers in bright colours.

19. Plates, heavy and thick, polychrome Chinese subjects.

20. Dish with garlands and grotesques, in the Moustiers style.

21. Christ at the pillar, coarse design, in blue on white enamel.

22. Plates painted in blue shaded with grotesques and flowers.

23. Dish in Strasbourg style, with finely painted flowers. The F incuse.

24. Dishes with mythological subjects—Moustiers style; since attributed to Bernburg : see new notice.

25. Pieces of fine fayence with reliefs.

26. Soup-tureen—Moustiers style; decoration of bouquets; since attributed to Anspach.

27. Fayence vase of complicated pattern, flowers, masks, &c., in relief.

28. Milk-jug, painted with flowers.

29. Small tureen, surmounted by an apple, painted with flowers—style of Strasbourg and Marseilles.

30. Thick and heavy fayence, sometimes in blue and sometimes in pale colours with flowers.

31. Jardinières with bouquets in pale violet, butterflies, &c.

32. Compotier, four-lobed, blue decoration, the border in the Chinese style; bouquet in centre, Marseilles style.

33. Thick plates, painted, with flowers and fruit in bright yellow.

34. Plate with polychrome decoration in the Marseilles style.

35. Plate escalloped, with flowers in the style of Lorraine.

36. Small cistern of thick fayence, polychrome decoration of grotesques in pale colours, imitation of Moustiers.

37. Service in fine fayence, meridional, in the centre subjects in *camaïeu*—Le Départ pour la Chasse, Le Retour, Don Quichotte, Josué arrêtant le Soleil; rococo borders in blue and pale green, touched with manganese.

38. Very fine fayence, beautifully painted with arabesque borders and bouquets of flowers, as good as porcelain.

39. Fayence mug decorated with characters of the Italian comedies.

40. Plateau, rococo style, garlands, arabesques, and bouquets.

41. Tureen, surmounted by a branch with fruit and leaves, coloured, decorated with flowers in the style of Rouen.

42. Compotiers, pierced and gadrooned with bouquets, like Strasbourg.

43. Cruet-frame, representing a vessel sailing on the sea.

44. A plateau of coloured masks, and border of reddish-brown enamelled flowers, &c.

Russia, Sweden, and Denmark.

BOUT the year 1700 the Czar Peter the Great, during his stay at Saardam, induced some potters of Delft to emigrate to St. Petersburg, where he established them. Some fine stoves were made here, but we have little information on the subject, except the following notice in the *Connaissances Politiques* of Beausobre, published at Riga, 1773: "There is also among the porcelain manufactories at St. Petersburg a fabrique of fayence, on the other side of the Neva, where they make every description of vessels in large quantities, of correct design and in good taste. They have a magazine at St. Petersburg, where table services may be had complete for 24 or 30 roubles, and even at lower prices. A private gentleman of Revel has also established at his own cost, near this city, a fabrique of fayence, and has obtained potters and painters from Germany."

RÖRSTRAND AND STOCKHOLM.

On the 20th May 1725, Baron Pierre Adlerfelt, the Swedish Minister at Copenhagen, requested permission for the potter Jean Wolf to found a porcelain manufactory in Sweden, which was accorded, and 200 silver dollars were sent in July of the same year for travelling expenses and 200 rixdollars to buy 200 pounds of cobalt blue from Saxony, and to bring specimens of the porcelain which he had made at Copenhagen. Wolf estimated the necessary capital at 7000 rixdollars specie, or 28,000 rixdollars,[1] and he stated that at Copenhagen 48,000 rixdollars had been granted for a similar establishment; after which Wolf was "remercié et congédié." On the 15th of September Wolf paid a second visit, accompanied by André Nicolas Ferdinand, and they exhibited several specimens of their art, viz., "a statuette, a plateau on four feet, vases, and other objects all made of white clay, well and neatly executed, painted in blue, also some moulds, called *hirda*, made of the English tin and metal of Prince Robert." This was before the use of plaster-of-Paris or gypsum moulds had become known.

---

[1] A rixdollar specie, equivalent to four rixdollars, was divided into three silver dollars or nine copper dollars.

On the 13th June 1726, a society of twenty members was formed of the leading men, among whom were Messrs. Caméen, Bunge, Gyllengrip, &c., and the State of Stockholm granted the use of a building in that part of the city called Stora Rörstrand (Great Rörstrand) for the manufacture of porcelain (fayence). Wolf was dismissed in 1728. He was succeeded by Christophe Conrad Hünger, who had worked at Meissen as gilder and enameller, and afterwards at Vienna, from which place he probably came into Sweden; he is described as one of the first master-potters in Europe, and was made chief of the manufactory; but he did not succeed in gaining the confidence of the society, for he left in 1733, after which Wolf's associate, André Nicholas Ferdinand, was appointed, who retained the post until 1739. Jean George Taglieb, also a German, was his successor, but he did not please his employers, and left in 1741, when a Swede named André Fahlstrom became master and director, and under his auspices the manufactory began to develop itself, but it was several years before satisfactory results were obtained. On the 4th February 1729, letters patent were granted giving an exclusive privilege for twenty years, and exemption from all duties of the articles employed in the manufacture, and permission to import and sell wholesale and retail the products at all fairs and in all towns of the kingdom free from the octroi and other taxes. The directors promised to produce ware equal in all respects to that of Delft, and in sufficient quantity to supply the wants of all the kingdom; after expending large sums of money it was, however, many years before the simplest products could be successfully made.

Christophe Conrad Hünger, who was dismissed in 1733, in 1741 addressed the deputation of commerce and manufactures for the privilege of making the *véritable porcelaine* of a clay which he said he had found in Dalecarlia, "et de faire des pots aux drogues et des formes aux pains de sucre," employing another clay of a brownish-red colour dug up near the city, presenting at the same time specimens, which they found "translucide, assez beaux et étincelant comme la vraie porcelaine quand on le battait avec le briquet." In consequence of a supposed interference with the interests of the Rörstrand manufactory of fayence and its privileges granted in 1735, his offer was rejected, but he obtained the right of making on his own account for twelve years the drug pots and sugar-loaf moulds; but receiving no encouragement, want of funds compelled him to leave Sweden, to which country he never returned.

A deputation was appointed in July 1743 to inspect the Rörstrand manufactory and report upon its administration, which was far from satisfactory. They found there neither master nor book-keeper, the building had become ruinous within and without, and immediate repairs were necessary; finishing their remarks with the observation: "Everything leads us to believe that the works are conducted without energy and proper surveillance." In 1753 a decisive alteration was affected, both in the condition of the fabrique and the quality of its productions.

A new society was formed in January of that year, composed of eighteen members, but the one who exercised the greatest influence was Elias Magnus Ingman, afterwards ennobled by the name of Nordenstople; he died 23 January 1773, sole possessor of the Rörstrand fabrique. Under his zealous patronage it was greatly extended, as shown by the following analysis: In 1731 were produced finished pieces of the value of 700 copper dollars; in 1734, about 5000; in 1740, 37,000 dollars; in 1753, 53,000; and in 1755 it was increased to more than 76,000 silver dollars (or 200,000 copper); and in 1765, to nearly 100,000 silver dollars (or 300,000 copper), employing 128 workmen. Ingman or Nordenstople, just previous to his decease, sold the Rörstrand works to his son, Elias Magnus Nordenstople, proprietor of the Marieberg fabrique, which he had acquired by purchase; shortly after this the fabrication of fayence with a stanniferous glaze was discontinued, and what was called *porcelain de silex*, or English stoneware, substituted, being covered with a translucid plumbiferous glaze. The heirs of Nordenstople sold the fabrique in 1797 to B. R. Geyer, and it has since then changed hands several times.

During the first period, from the date of its foundation in 1726-59, the products were chiefly imitations of Oriental and Delft ware, sometimes, but rarely, of French fayence; the forms were simple, occasionally ornamented in relief, but usually in blue *camaieu*. The master-potters were Jean Wolf, 1726-28; Christophe Conrad Hünger, 1728-33; André Nicholas Ferdinand, 1733-39; and André Fahlstrom, 1741-60. Two Swedish painters whose initials are frequently found on the early fayence were Daniel Hillberg and Carl Herweghr.

The second period, 1760-82 or '83, when the fayence with stanniferous glaze was abandoned, the ware was of fine quality, the forms and decorations being copied principally from that of Strasbourg and Marseilles, the fruit, flowers, and leaves in relief, the colours being nearly always applied upon the glaze in the rococo style. The master-potters of this period were Jonas Taman after André Fahlstrom's death, 1760; Eric Fahlstrom, 1761; Jacob Orhn or Orn, 1761-82; and Philippe André Schirmer, who attended solely to the English stoneware. Among the painters were two who distinguished themselves, Henri Sten and André Stenman; the former came to Rörstrand in 1755, and in 1767 went to Marieberg; Stenman introduced the art of printing on fayence, and afterwards carried out his inventions at Marieberg.

The marks and signatures of the first period, when Rörstrand had no rival, were *Stockholm*, or sometimes *St.* or *S.* only, accompanied by the date of fabrication, the price, and the initial of the painter, traced in blue, underneath each piece; on a plate painted with flowers, in the Sèvres Museum. The mark in the margin bears the initials of the painter, André Fahlstrom.

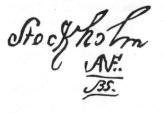

The next mark has the date 22nd August 1751, and the painter's initials, Daniel Hillberg; this mark in blue is on a punch-bowl of enamelled fayence; on the inside is written "Alla wakra flickors skäl"—"Here's a health to all good lasses." Later, after the foundation of the fabrique of Marieberg, and apparently to distinguish the products, the mark was changed to *Rörstrand*, or an abbreviation of the word, retaining the other marks, traced in brown, black, or blue. During the transition we find both *Stockholm* and *Rörstrand*, the name of the capital as well as that of the fabrique, as in the margin, dated 14th August 1759.

A mark of Rörstrand, written at length, and dated 25th June 1765; given by Strähle in his account of the Rörstrand fabrique.

RÖRSTRAND, dated 4th December 1769, on a fayence tureen, scroll borders, edged with green, yellow, and purple, and bouquets of flowers; in the Sèvres Museum.

These marks are found impressed on ware in imitation of Wedgwood and other English fabriques; about 1780.

RORSTRAND & Rorstrand.

MARIEBERG.

The first idea of establishing a manufacture of fayence and porcelain here originated with Jean Eberhard Louis Ehrenreich, dentist to King Adolphe Frederick in 1758. Marieberg consisted of a few small houses in the mountains near Stockholm. In the spring of 1758, Ehrenreich requested of the King, after presenting spemimens of his fayence and porcelain, the privilege of producing "differentes espèces de porcelaines fines et ordinaires, vraies et fausses, ainsi que des grès cérames," soliciting an indemnity of 10,000 silver dollars. A society was formed and the privilege granted on the 28th May 1759. The principal supporter of this new enterprise was the Baron Charles Frederick Scheffer, afterwards Count, a rich and influential person. The Marieberg property was bought in his name. Among the rest were the brothers Benoit and Pierre Bergius, George Henri Conradi, Henry König, Jean Westerman, afterwards Liljencrantz, &c. The building was erected in October 1758, and in the following April Ehrenreich commenced his works, but in May the whole fabrique was destroyed by fire. In September the new fabrique was completed, and in April 1760 operations were commenced afresh. Ehrenreich engaged Jean Buchwald as master-potter in 1761, which post he held until 1765. One hundred and thirty workmen were employed, and in the following year the number was increased to two hundred and fifty. The fabrique went on prosperously until 1766, when Ehrenreich abandoned the directory, for reasons unknown to us, and in the following year he went to Stralsund. He was succeeded by Pierre Berthevin, who had been employed in France in a fabrique of *porcelaine tendre*, but whether this means fayence or the veritable porcelain it is difficult to determine. The fabrication decreased considerably, and in 1769, Berthevin quitted Marieberg, returning to France. Henri Sten succeeded as director, which situation he retained until 1782, when the fabrique was sold to Major Nordenstople. In 1784 a German named Philippe André Schirmer displaced Henri Sten; Dortie, a Frenchman, 1778-82, assisted in the production of true porcelain, but as this new fabrication did not produce any revenue it was renounced.

In 1788 many of the shares of the works had been sold at Stockholm, and Baron Liljencrantz becoming nearly sole proprietor, he sold the whole to Major Nordenstople of Rörstrand in July 1782. After his decease in 1783, his heirs continued the manufacture a few years, principally of English fayence, and it altogether ceased in 1788 to 1789. An eminent painter named Henri Frantzen was engaged here from 1761 until his death in 1781; his works are usually signed F.; he had two sons, Jean-Otho and Francis-Henry Frantzen, who also painted at Marieberg. Under Berthevin the art of printing on fayence was successfully introduced by André Stenman, who came from Rörstrand in 1766, bringing with him the secrets of his art.

The fayence of Ehrenreich has a clear white glaze. A journal of the 27th September 1762 advertises that "the fabrique of Marieberg exposes for sale in the magazin at Stockholm various sorts of *fayence porcelaines*, blue, white *Marseille*, enamelled plates, tureens, dinner, tea and coffee services, and objects of decoration and ornament;" the prevailing style is *rococo*, imitating Strasbourg and Marseilles, and the painting was over the glaze. Sometimes statuettes are found representing characters in the French comedies, Scapin, &c.

The earliest dated pieces of fayence are 1763; the latest we have met with are 1780; the English pottery subsequently made is sometimes stamped with the name at length.

MARIEBERG. This mark is on an enamelled fayence tureen, like Strasbourg. The three crowns are the arms of Sweden, M. B. for Marieberg, E. Ehrenreich the director, and F. the initial of the painter Frantzen; the other letters and figures denote the date 24th November 1764, and the price.

MARIEBERG. Another mark with the three crowns, the initials of Berthevin, and of the name of the place.

MARIEBERG. Enamelled fayence like Delft, with Berthevin the director's initial, dated 14th October 1768.

MARIEBERG. A mark of the 14th September 1770, with the initial of Sten, who was for many years a distinguished painter at Rörstrand, and succeeded Berthevin as director here about the year 1769.

STRALSUND.

STRALSUND. This manufactory of fayence was established early in the eighteenth century, for it is recorded that one Jean Paskovitz, who had been engaged at Rörstrand, where he only remained a month, went to Stralsund on the 20th May 1731. According to Count Bielke, who furnishes no date, it was founded by M. Von Giese, a counsellor of commerce, who obtained his materials from the island of Hiddenso, near the Isle Rugen, but its early history is unknown, as well as its products. Ehrenreich, who quitted Marieberg in 1766, went in 1767 to Stralsund, accompanied by some workmen of Marieberg and Rörstrand, to work at this manufactory; but it received a severe shock in 1770 by the explosion of a powder-mill, which destroyed a great portion of this fabrique; it was carried on with varying success until 1786, when it ceased altogether from want of funds.

Stralsund is now a Prussian town, but as it belonged to Sweden at the time of its pottery factory here noticed, it has been included in this section of the book.

Count Bielke possesses many specimens of Stralsund fayence, which are very similar to those of Marieberg. The ware bears the mark of the arms of the town, viz., three radiating lines under a crown; sometimes the capital E, the first letter of Ehrenreich's name, follows, accompanied by the date.

STRALSUND. This mark is on a specimen in the Gasnault Collection; it has underneath the signature of an artist who also painted at Rörstrand—*Carl Herveghr.*

18

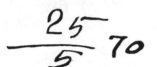

STRALSUND. The arms of the town, three radiating lines under a crown, followed by E for Ehrenreich, and date 25th May 1770, with the price.

Note.—This mark, which comprises all these seven characters, and the next, of January 1768, are placed in one line, not in two as here given.

STRALSUND. A similar mark with Ehrenreich's initial, dated 20th January, 1768. On a tureen painted with flowers, in the Sèvres Museum.

STRALSUND. These marks in black occur on a potpourri vase, painted with a landscape, in the Hamburg Museum, and are said to indicate the date and initials of the potter: Ehrenreich Wahlbom, April 21, 1774.

GUSTAFSBERG, near Stockholm; a modern factory where are produced imitations of Wedgwood's jasper ware.

HELSINBERG (Scandinavia). A manufactory of stoneware was established about the year 1770, and produced a good quality of ware for domestic purposes; at a later period moulded ornaments for the external decorations of edifices were also made.

HELSINBERG.

The following additional marks in blue under the glaze are given on the authority of the official catalogue of German and Scandinavian fayences

of the eighteenth century in the Hamburg Museum. The curator, Dr. Brinckmann, has informed the editor that the arrow-like mark is intended to represent three leaves of the box (German, Rux), a fayence factory having been established in 1752 by a potter named Johann Baptist Rux, at the village of Schretzheim, near Ellwangen, in Würtemberg. See also Schretzheim.

Notices of Rendsburg and of Killinghusen, two other Holstein fayence factories, will be found on pp. 296, 297.

COPENHAGEN.   In the account of the Rörstrand fabrique, Strähle states that on the 20th May 1725 the Baron Pierre Adlerfelt, Swedish Minister at Copenhagen, sent Jean Wolf from the Copenhagen fayence manufactory to form a similar establishment at Stockholm.   Wolf, estimating the probable cost, stated that at Copenhagen the sum of 48,000 rixdollars had been expended in its construction.

COPENHAGEN.   Wolf was succeeded by Johan Pfau in 1727, under whose direction only blue and white ware was produced, and he was followed by Christian Gierlor, who subsequently became proprietor of the factory.   The following marks occur in blue under the glaze on some

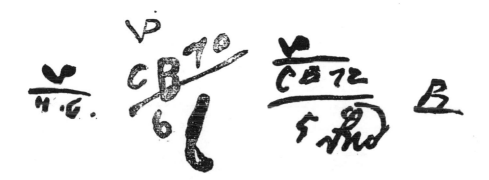

portions of table services in the Hamburg Museum, and are attributed to Pfau's period, the monogram ⱽᴾ being I. P., for Johan Pfau.   The B is only a painter's initial.

COPENHAGEN. A second fayence factory was established in 1753 by Jacob Fortling at Kastrup, in the island of Amager. He was granted a concession in 1755, but was not allowed to produce blue and white, a privilege reserved to the older factory. Fortling died in 1761 and the manufactory ceased in 1770.   " $\mathcal{J}$ "
Tureens formed as animals, geese, cocks, and other similar models are attributed to Fortling's time.   His mark is said to have been a cursive F.

REVAL (in the Baltic province of Russia).   Here in 1780 a chemist named Karl Christian Fick established a fayence manufactory which only

lasted until his death in 1782. The productions are similar in character
to these of Rörstrand : —

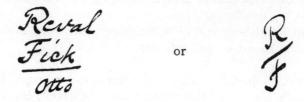

     or

No previous notice of this factory has appeared in any book on the
subject, and the Editor is indebted to Dr. Brinckmann of the Hamburg
Museum for the above information.

FAYENCE

1holland, 13elgium, and Germany

AYENCE with stanniferous enamel was known from the earliest times. Theophilus (*Diversarum Artium Schedula*) devotes a chapter to the art of painting earthenware vessels with various vitrified colours, and a commentator on his work relates the fact of this glaze (of which he gives the composition) having been used at Schelestadt, in Alsatia, as early as 1278. In the *Annales Dominicanorum Colmariens* (1283), *Urstis. Script. rerum Germ.*, v. ii. p. 10, we read: "Obiit figulus Stelztatt qui primus in Alsatia vitra vasa fictilia vestiebat." M. Piot (*Cabinet de l'Amateur*) cites, as a proof that the stanniferous enamel was well known in the commencement of the fourteenth century, a receipt given in the *Margarita Preciosa*, a treatise written in 1330: "Videmus, cum plumbum et stannum fuerunt calcinata et combusta quod post ad ignum congruum convertuntur in vitrum, sicut faciunt qui vitrificant vasa figuli;" and it is not stated to be an invention or a novelty but merely as a fact known to the potters of that time. Hence it is evident that the art of covering earthenware vessels with an opaque enamel made of lead and tin was used long before Lucca della Robbia's time, and that he merely applied it to sculpture in terra-cotta, which had previously been executed in distemper. The Moors of Spain applied this enamel to their pottery in the twelfth and thirteenth centuries; the Arabs before them, even in the eighth century, were acquainted with it, and the *azulejos*, or tiles of the Alhambra, of the thirteenth century, are well known; while some even go so far as to assert that the tiles discovered at Nineveh are enamelled in like manner, and not merely glazed. The instances, therefore, given by M. Demmin of similar enamelled fayences existing at Leipzig and Breslau of the twelfth and thirteenth centuries, show that it actually was adopted about that time in various parts of Germany, but does not prove that it was invented there; but he is entitled to as much consideration as others who attribute its invention to Italy.

HANAU. Quality unknown. *Circa* 1650. In a MS. of 1707, in an inventory of a Nuremberg mansion, are mentioned "Zween weiss und bloue Hanauer Krug mit Zinn beschlagen;" and in the *Handbuch der Erfindungen von Busch* we read that towards the middle of the seventeenth century two Dutch merchants established a fayence fabrique at Hanau, which was purchased at the commencement of the eighteenth century by Simon von Alphen.

Specimens marked with *H*, also with a monogram V A, said to be that of Von Alphen, and with the name "Hanau," have been attributed to this fabrique.

TEYLINGEN.   This place has become celebrated in ceramic history from its association with the unfortunate Jacqueline, Countess of Hainault and Holland, and the manufacture of a sort of earthenware jug called the *Jacoba Kannetje*. This princess, born about 1400, became wife of John, Duke of Brabant, and, after many severe trials, abdicated in 1433, and retired to the Château de Teylingen, about five hours' journey from Rotterdam. While here, according to the tradition, she employed her leisure in superintending the manufacture of stone pots or cruches, and is said to have thrown many of them into the fosse of the château as souvenirs to posterity, that in after-ages they might be considered works of antiquity; for this reason these particular cruches found in the fosse, and others similar, are called *Jacoba Kannetjes*. Such is the legend in Holland, which is in some degree verified by the actual discovery of a vast quantity of them on the spot, proving at least that there was a manufactory. However, it is probable the same description of pottery was made for common use simultaneously in other parts of Holland and in Germany. This manufacture therefore goes back to the commencement of the fifteenth century. Some archæologists are of opinion that these vessels were placed before the guests at table, used only once, and, when empty, thrown into the moat of the castle. This stoneware is of a cheap character and common quality, of coarse grain, and not enamelled or coloured, but still hard and impermeable; the forms of these cruches are generally globular, with a small handle and a foot, the body and neck being marked by circles or rings with the lathe, and the foot escalloped as if pinched by a finger or thumb; they are otherwise plain and without any ornamentation. Some idea of them may be formed by referring to Nos. 1, 8, and 11 on p. 29 found in London. The *Jacoba Kannetje* figured by Marryat in his "History of Pottery" is a superb *Raeren* ware canette of the sixteenth century, with designs and ornaments in relief. Nothing less resembles the real *Jacoba* than the specimen there given, which is nearly two centuries later in date of manufacture.

UTRECHT. Fayence with stanniferous enamel. A manufactory of tiles, "carreaux de revêtement," decorated in blue or violet, *en camaieu*, was founded in the eighteenth century, and carried on by the following proprietors in succession :—

1760.—The founder, Albertus Prince.
1798.—Hendrik Jacob Kraane-Pook and Gerrit Bruyn.
1823.—Hendrik Jacob Paul Bruyn and Pieter Ambrose Bert.
1824.—Baudewyn and Jacob Van der Mandere.
1839.—Baudewyn, Jacob Van der Mandere, David Hendrick and Franciscus Marinus
         Royaards.
1844.—The Brothers Royaards and Hendrick Camerlingh.

The manufactory was closed in 1855, having been worked with two kilns and about fifty workmen; they imitated the ancient tiles of Delft, and having no mark, these are often sold for real Delft. There are still two manufactories at the Hallsteig Barrier, one belonging to M. Ravenstein, the other to M. Schillemans, for making tiles in imitation of Delft.

OVERTOOM. A manufactory of fine fayence was established in 1754 in the parish of Amstelveen, near Amsterdam, in a theatre where French performances were formerly given; the Barons Van Haeren and Van Palland were the proprietors, Ariel Blankers, director, and Wollen Tusnig, modeller. The constructions were called Blankenburg, after the director's name. The fayence, though rather heavy, was of a fine white enamel, very hard, and of good forms; besides table and tea services, they made some pretty groups of birds, modelled from nature, statuettes, vases, &c. These are now very scarce, as the works were limited; they were closed in 1764, having lasted only ten years; no mark is known. The machinery and materials were bought by the Count Von Gronsfeld, who removed the manufactory to Weesp.

HOUDA (North Holland). Gaberil Vengobechea. This mark, stamped, is on fayence plates with coarsely painted violet scrolls; there are three triple cockspur marks round the border underneath.

Gaberil Vengobechea
Houda.

HAMBURG. The name of this artist occurs on a four-sided tea-caddy, artistically painted in blue, with figures of lovers and rococo scrolls, gilt borders; formerly in Mr. H. G. Bohn's Collection. This interesting specimen is the only one we have met with made at Hamburg; our first impression was that the

Johann Otto Leſſel
Sculpſit: et Pinxit.

Hamburg Menſis
Januarij Anno 1756

vessel was made at Delft and painted at Hamburg, but the words *sculpsit et pinxit* clearly prove that it was both made and painted at Hamburg.

BAILLEUL (Nord), or BEILEN, in Holland. The inscription has been read differently, but the Dutch town is probably intended. M. A. Jacquemart attributes to this place a soup-tureen in the Musée de Cluny. Gournay in his *Almanach Général du Commerce* says: "The fayence of this locality equals in beauty that of Rouen, and has the advantage of bearing the most violent heat, and is sold at a moderate price, the workmanship being cheap." We have not met with this variety, but the tureen, M. Jacquemart says, is decidedly of French fayence, not German;

Ghemaeckte tot Belle
C. Jacobus Hennekens
anno 1717,
and inside
Belle C.I.H.

it is decorated with shields of arms and Dutch inscriptions; the cover has lions and heraldic emblems in relief, and is inscribed "Ghemaeckte tot Belle C. Jacobus Hennekens anno 1717;" made at Bailleul. This piece was read by Demmin *(Guide de l'Amateur de Faïence)* "*Ghemaeckt tot Beile*," and attributed by him to Beilen, near Assan, Holland.

AMSTERDAM or ARNHEIM.   A German Jew of Breslau, named Hartog, known by the adopted name of Hartog Van Laun (maker of the planetarium described by Professor Van Swinden, and purchased by the Society Felix Meritis in Amsterdam), in conjunction with another named Brandeis, established a manufactory of fayence about 1780 at "Flacke-feld, near the Gate of Weesp, at Amsterdam." It ceased about 1785. The ware is heavy, not very artistic, and usually in blue *camaieu* decorations. A piece given by a son of Brandeis to M. Demmin bears this mark.

M. Brandeis has still at his residence, 419 Rapenburger Straat, several pieces of the ware made here. A fruit-dish, painted in lilac *camaieu* with peasants dancing, has this mark of chanticleer proclaiming the dawn. (*Ker. Gall.*, enlarged edition, fig. 177.) [Sir A. W. Franks and some other authorities are of opinion that the fayence here described should be classed as Arnheim.]

Note.—There is a considerable manufactory of modern artistic majolica at Florence, known as the "Canta Galli," which has a similar mark, that of the singing cock, which must not be confounded with the Arnheim fayence.

ROTTERDAM.   According to Jännike there was a fabrique here, but very little seems to be known about it. In the Collection of M. Ollin of Brussels there is a set of four figures in Watteau costume representing the seasons of the year, marked " J. Aalmes pi a Rotterdam," and also a specimen marked " Aalmes 1731."

DELFT.   The ancient town of Delft is situated between the Hague and Rotterdam, and few names are better known, especially to the collectors of pottery.

In the sixteenth century Delft was celebrated throughout Europe for its excellent beer, which was attributed in a great degree to the quality of the water. There were nearly three hundred breweries along the sides of the canal; all these were destroyed in the great fire which devastated the town in 1536; but owing to the consideration shown to them by Charles V., in relieving the brewers from all taxes on the materials they employed for twenty years, they were quickly reinstated, and in fifty years the trade became more flourishing than ever. The opulence of the brewers of Delft was proverbial.

It was destined, however, to give way to an industry of a more artistic character, but how the change was effected must remain a mystery.

The brewers, with the trades in connection, such as coopers, boatmen, &c., numbered more than one-third of the entire population. In the commencement of the seventeenth century the celebrated breweries of Delft were gradually discontinued, and by 1640 they had all closed, one after the other.

Bleswick (*Beschryvinge der Stadt Delft*, &c., Delft, 1667) styles the Delft ware *Delfsche porceleyn*, by which term it was always known, being the nearest approach to the Oriental or true porcelain made at the time he wrote, and usually imitating the Japanese designs. The intercourse with Japan was carried on solely by the Dutch vessels, which constantly arrived from Decima to the East India Company's depôt at Delft, the cargoes being largely supplemented by quantities of Japanese wares; thence they were dispersed throughout Europe. The cities of Delft and Rotterdam each contributed a sixth of the capital of this celebrated company. The brilliant actions of the Dutch mariners have been extolled by many writers of the seventeenth and eighteenth centuries. The exploits of one of their vessels, called *The Devil of Delft*, are mentioned by Dudley Carl on; this vessel engaged and captured a vast amount of treasure from the Spanish galleons. *Les Delices de Pays Bas*, 1679, relates that Admiral Piet Hein, a native of Delft, captured in one year "sept millions deux cent mille livres d'argent, trois millions six cent mille livres de marchandises, quatre millions en canons et autre equipages. Cette année là, les associés de la compagnicre çurent cinq cents pour cent de leur misc, et encore n'eurent-ils que la moitié des trésors capturés."

It is to the end of the sixteenth century that the first attempts to make fayence can be traced, and in the commencement of the seventeenth century the industry assumed a commercial aspect. Hence the origin of Delft fayence may be fixed about 1600. Bleswick says: "C'est à l'epoque où les brasseries si renommés de Delft declinèrent et disparurent que les faïenceries commencèrent à fleurir."

This brings us to the consideration of the origin of the manufacture of fayence at Delft. All the books which treat of the industries of the Netherlands are silent as to the fayence of Delft before 1650, and it is not until 1667 that Bleswick mentions it, and he evidently considered it of small importance, for out of nine hundred pages he only devotes to it about fourteen lines. The *Delices de Pays Bas*, in 1678, is also silent as to the importance of this manufacture.

M. Havard, *Histoire de la Fayence de Delft*, to whom we are indebted for the most complete history yet written, and whose instructive and beautifully illustrated work is now before us, has thrown considerable light upon its hitherto obscure origin, and by his perseverance has furnished us with a biography of all the ceramists of Delft. He has, moreover, corrected many errors and exaggerations which have been advanced without due consideration or authority, and which rest entirely on the crude and imaginative remarks of persons unqualified to reason with discretion or prudence, yet arbitrary and partial in the highest degree.

M. Havard refutes the absurd pretensions and gross errors of an author who endeavours to assign to the fifteenth century the introduction of fayence into Delft. The proofs M. Demmin adduces (*Guide de l'Amateur de Faïence*, &c.) are two pieces of Delft fayence: one represents a horse fully caparisoned and saddled, painted in colours; on this he finds the letters I. H. F., and under them the number 1480, which he mistakes for a date; for there is nothing in the piece indicating an earlier period than the eighteenth century, and the Arabic numerals, which he erroneously imagines were used in the fifteenth century, are merely the ordinal number of a fabrique called "The Fortune," I. H. F. signifying *In het Fortuyn*, where the practice was to mark their pieces in that way. A mark of the same fabrique has the number 1185; according to this method of reasoning, he might have fixed it at the twelfth century.

Great exaggerations have been made by authors as regards the population of Delft; it was for a century and a half the most important manufacturing town in Europe. In the year 1680, when at its greatest prosperity the population did not exceed 24,000, and the number of persons employed in the fayence fabriques was not more than 1500 or 2000 at most, and the number of fabriques did not exceed thirty. In 1659 and 1664 the official documents in the archives only mention twenty-three. In 1780 they were reduced to half that number, and in 1794 to ten. In 1808 there were only seven: the Lampetkan, the Porceleyne Fles, Bloempot, Klaauw, the Greekse A, Drie Klokken, and the Roos. By degrees these also disappeared, the Lampetkan in 1810, the Bloempot in 1816, the Greekse A and the others a few years later

We may here also allude to the erroneous statements of prices paid to decorators of fayence. M. Havard says: "Everybody has read the gross exaggerations of the prices paid to these clever artists. It will be seen by the following document it was by *sous*, and not *florins*, that the decoration of various objects was computed; and in the same ratio we need not be surprised at the low prices named in their tariff. A very fine polychrome bottle belonging to M. Fetis of Brussels is inscribed "G. N. H. 7st."; this, which at the present day would realise perhaps as many pounds, was actually sold for seven stivers, that is, seven Dutch sous, equal to fourteen sous of the present day. An order is quoted from a dealer at Tournay to Zacharias Dextra, of the *Drie Astonnen*, in 1758, whose fine works are well known, thus: For decorated pieces the prices were as follows per dozen:

	Sols.
6 douzaines de grand plat fon bleu et en couleur des nouveaux dessains à	50
6 douzaines dito moien plat bleu et en couleur à .	40
2 douzaines salladier a cartiez den bleux à .	50
2 douzaines salladier a cartiez den bleux à .	34
100 douzaines de tasse à caffée bleux est en couleur rouge .	8

In an early register preserved at Delft, the only person whose name appears as *Plateelbacker* (master-potter) is an entry on the 1st September

1584 of the marriage of Herman Pietersz, fayence-maker, widower, born at Haarlem, with Anna Cornelisz. He had doubtless learned his trade at Haarlem, where many potters then resided, making a coarse description of pottery (so indeed was all that was made in the sixteenth century), viz., a red ware covered with lead glaze. The true Delft fayence of yellow biscuit, with stanniferous enamel, which constitutes real Delft, was not known until the seventeenth century.

The source from which M. Havard derives his information as to the names of the *Plateelbackers*, or master-potters who had passed their examination and received a diploma, is from the *Meesterboek* of the Gild of St. Luc, in which their names are enrolled. It forms two volumes, and was recently discovered in the Royal Library at the Hague, and contains entries from 1611 to 1715. In addition to this there is a list of marks deposited in 1680 by a decree of the magistrates of Delft; a list of master-potters made in 1759, and a register of potters' marks deposited in 1764, all of which are in the archives at Delft. Our diligent author, M. Havard, has also searched the registers of births and marriages in Delft from 1575 to 1808, contained in more than 150 volumes, to complete his biography of all the ceramists of Delft.

This *Meesterboek* of St. Luc commenced in 1613, and the first eight names mentioned are: 1st. Herman Pietersz, 2nd. Pauwels Bouseth, 3rd. Cornelis Rochus Van der Hoek, 4th. Egbert Huygens, 5th. Michiel Noutsz, 6th. Thomas Jansz, 7th. Abraham Davitsz, and 8th. Symon Thonisz.

It was doubtless between 1596 and 1611, the epoch in which the Gild of St. Luc was founded, that the origin of the fayence of Delft may be traced, and that Herman Pietersz was the great promoter of it.

In the *Recueil Delft* no mention is made of *Plateelbackers*. In 1596 there is a list of all the professions allowed and exercised within the walls of Delft, but in that no mention is made of makers of fayence. The *Meesterboek* of St. Luc must, therefore, be our starting-point of information.

The Gild of St. Luc consisted of eight bodies of artists and workmen, grouped together in rather a heterogeneous manner: 1. Painters of every kind, whether in oil or water, pencil, or otherwise, no distinction apparently being made between the artist and the whitewasher or house-painter; 2. The painters and engravers upon glass, glassmakers, and glaziers; 3. The fayence-makers and painters upon fayence; 4. Upholsterers and makers of tapestry; 5. Sculptors in wood, stone, and all other substances; 6. Sheath or case makers, who at this time were real artists; 7. Art painters and librarians; and, lastly, 8. Dealers in paintings and engravings. All the trades which involved the arts of design were here represented

The Gild had absolute power over every article produced by these trades; no person could execute or cause to be executed any object appertaining to them without the authority of the Syndics, and every infraction of their rules was visited by a fine of ten florins and forfeiture of the object executed. Any unauthorised person attempting to work at any of these trades, even putting in a pane of glass, for instance, was subject to a fine of twelve florins and confiscation. Nobody could sell a painting, a glass, or a piece of fayence, without being a member of the corporation. Before becoming a master-potter every person had to serve an apprenticeship of six years, and at the end of every two years the contract had to be renewed until the full term was completed, which involved a fresh payment. This course being accomplished, the apprentice had to submit proofs of his capability in order to pass his examination. In fayence, the painter, *Plateelschilder*, and the thrower, *Plateeldrayer*, were required, before obtaining their diplomas, the former to decorate a dozen large dishes, and a fruit-dish entirely covered with ornament; the latter to throw upon the wheel an ewer, *siroopot*, a salad-bowl, and a salt-cellar with a hollow foot out of a single piece of clay, in the presence of two deacons of the craft, and was locked up in a room while at work; then both thrower and painter had to form and paint a pile of thirty small plates. If not approved, they had to serve a year and six weeks longer before they could again offer themselves for election. The *droits de maîtrise* were heavy for the period: for a native of Delft 6 florins, for a stranger 12 florins, for the son of a potter 3 florins. M. Havard relates that Jan Van der Meer and Pieter de Hooch, the two celebrated painters of the Dutch school, not being able to pay the charge, were forced to solicit the indulgence of the Burgomaster, and to pay by instalments, their friends becoming surety.

There were several good points in the management of the Gild. A school of design was established, which all the apprentices were obliged to frequent, and annual meetings for the distribution of prizes to the most efficient. As early as the middle of the seventeenth century each trade raised a fund for mutual help to the sick and needy, and almshouses for those incapable of work.

In 1764 an edict was issued compelling all master-potters to send in to the Gild of St. Luc a description of their sign, with the mark they were accustomed to place upon their wares, and prohibiting any persons, under a fine of six hundred florins, from counterfeiting the marks of other potters. These were entered in a register which is still preserved, and this was until recently the only official document known relating to the history of the *Plateelbackers* of Delft, except a short list of marks sent by some potters in 1680 to protect themselves from counterfeits.

Scarcely any of the most talented ceramists who took the lead in this movement were natives of Delft; neither Albrecht de Keizer, who was the first Syndic of the trade, nor Abraham de Kooge, nor Frytom, nor Fictoors, nor Kleynoven were natives. Among the families which form a sort of dynasty of potters there are not more than five or six of Delft origin—the Mesch, de Milde, Kam, Brouwer, and one or two others. The two Cleffius were from Amsterdam; the Hoppestein, the Eenhoorn, and the Pynacker families did not belong to Delft, and in becoming master-potters were obliged to acquire the right of citizenship; and in

1680, of the seven potters who depcsited their marks to protect themselves from counterfeits, only two were natives of Delft.

There is a difficulty in tracing the genealogy of many of the potters. M. Havard says : "In those times, indeed, the workmen, the labourers, and others of low condition, were not accustomed to retain their family name distinct; they restricted themselves, according to the custom of the fifteenth and sixteenth centuries, to making their Christian names precede that of their father." Thus, in the case of Herman Pietersz, founder or promoter of the Gild of St. Luc in 1611, Herman being the son of Peter, was called Herman Pieterszoon, or Pietersz by abbreviation. The son of Herman christened Gerrit, was styled Gerrit Hermanz; and his children, Herman and Annetje, were styled, for the same reason, Herman Gerrits- zoon and Annetje Gerritsdochter, that is the son or daughter of Gerrit, and by abbreviation Herman and Annetje Gerritsz. But if good fortune arrived, or there was some motive for distinguishing themselves from the common, they adopted a surname, which was chosen from their profession, from physical or moral qualities, a colour or a talent, or they appended to their prenomen the place of their birth or their property. In looking over the *Meesterboek*, out of thirty names which first occur, we shall scarcely find six which are anything else than direct patronymic indica- tions. In artistic professions, on the other hand, the surname was generally used; so that in the registers of St. Luc the names of painters, librarians, glass and tapestry makers, have a sort of aristocratic appear- ance, while the modest potters seem to be disinherited.

In the middle of the seventeenth century all this was changed. The trade had increased, and prosperity was at its height; Delft fayence became celebrated, and orders were received from all countries. It was then that the master-potters became great and influential and took upon themselves some distinctive surname. Thus Jacob Wemmertsz added the high-sounding name of Hoppestein; Pieter Pansz styled himself Van Kessel; Jacob Jacobszoon became Dukerton; and so on of twenty others. Some sonorous appellation was chosen when fortune or reputation made them distinguished. In 1650, when Quiering Aldersz married and was elected master-potter, he was content to use that name alone; but when he became Syndic in 1659, he was transformed into M. Van Kleynoven.

The early ceramists of the seventeenth century are peculiar from the immense number of figures crowded into their compositions. One signed by TOMES JANSZ (1590-1611), representing the Last Judgment, in the Collection of M. Loudon of the Hague, is so intricate that M. Havard in his work could find no means of reproducing the four hundred figures which compose the picture and its elaborate border. Two others by the son of HERMAN PIETERSZ (Gerrit Hermanszoon, 1614) are nearly as intricate. One is a charge of cavalry, in the Slaes Collection, dated 1634; the other, a kermesse, dated 1640, is in the Evenepoel Collection. Some, however, are of a more quiet and harmonious character, and not so crowded, being mythological subjects after the paintings of Goltsius.

About 1650 a great change was made in the decoration of fayence, and painters of greater merit, as well as potters of a higher character, entered upon the scene, whose names we will briefly introduce to our readers, omitting for want of space those whose works are not so well known. The dates immediately following the names indicate their admission to the Gild of St. Luc as licensed potters.

ABRAHAM DE KOOGE, 1632, was a painter in oil, but he also painted on fayence. He produced those splendid plaques of landscapes in blue *camaieu*, which have never been surpassed. Examples of them are in the Loudon and Evenepoel Collections.

ALBRECHT CORNELIS DE KEIZER, 1642, was the first to imitate the designs on the Japanese porcelain, but he did not confine his talent to this particular style. His works are of very high finish, and usually painted in blue. A lofty *vase à jacinthe*, of elegant form, of his second period, *cir.* 1660, representing a garden scene and figures, and round the top a frieze of cupids, 2 feet 10 inches high, is an heirloom in the possession of Walter Moseley, Esq., of Buildwas Park, Shrewsbury. His son, CORNELIS DE KEIZER, and his sons-in-law, JACOB and ADRIAN PYNACKER, were equally eminent in carrying out his wonderful imitations of the Japanese porcelain.

FREDERICK VAN FRYTOM, 1658, an excellent artist, preferred blue *camaieu* to polychrome. A plaque representing an extensive landscape with figures is preserved in the Royal Hague Museum.

WOUTER VAN EENHOORN, established in 1658, and his sons, SAMUEL and LAMBARTUS, who succeeded him, devoted themselves to polychrome, in which they excelled.

The KAMS, numbering five fine artists, were accustomed more especially to paint in blue with Japanese subjects.

PIET VIZEER, 1752, emulated the choice polychromes of Lambartus Van Eenhoorn. No potter, in fact, ever managed his colours so admirably *au grand feu*, nor infused so much vigour and intensity into his works.

GYSBRECHT VERHAAST, 1760, was a careful artist, and composed some fine tableaux upon a beautiful enamel. He painted Dutch scenes after Teniers and Brouwer.

The two DEXTRAS, ZACHARIAH, 1720, and JAN THEUNIS, 1769, both imitated the Dresden decoration, and excelled in fountains, tureens, and other important pieces, in polychrome and gilding.

Four members of a patrician family of Delft, the VAN DER HOEVES, were elected as *Plateelbackers* in the Gild of St. Luc—CORNELIS ROCHUSZ VAN DER HOEVE, one of the founders, in 1611; JAN GERRITZ, admitted in 1649; and the two CORNELIS in 1662 and 1698. This family bore in their arms three violins sable on a field argent. M. Havard suggests that these four ceramists desired to leave to posterity tangible emblems of their shield, which seems probable, as the only four genuine violins knows are by different hands and of successive dates.

AUGUSTIJN REYGENS or REYGENSBURG, 1663. His productions were decorated with the beautiful red and gold so much in vogue; ALBRECHT DE KEYSER and JAN KULICK, who possessed the secret, being connected with him in the manufacture.

ARIJ JAN DE MILDE, 1658, was the maker of the red ware teapots then so much in use. They were of the Japanese form, and were also made at the manufactory of L. VAN EENHOORN, stamped with "The Unicorn," a rebus on his name; by M. GOUDA, of "The Roman," and others, and subsequently copied by the ELERS of Bradwell. BÖTTGER of Meissen produced similar articles about 1710.

LOUIS FICTOOR, 1689, was established at "the Dubbelde Schenkkan." His beautiful products soon attracted attention; his elegant bottles and jugs were frequently ribbed and richly decorated in colours with Oriental designs

LIST OF POTTERS.

With dates of election to the Gild of St. Luc, and reference to the annexed Table of Marks.

1. Gerrit Hermansz, 1614.
2. Isaac Junius, 1640.
3. Albrecht de Keizer, 1642.
4. Jan Gerrits Van der Hoeve, 1649.
5. Meynaert Garrebrantsz, 1616.
6. Quiring Alders Kleynoven, 1655.
7. Frederick Van Frytom, 1658.
8. Jan Sicktis Van den Houk, 1659.
9. Jan Ariens Van Hammen, 1661.
10. Augustijn Reygens, 1663.
11. Jan Jans Kulick, 1662.
12. Jacob Cornelisz (Vanden Burg), 1662.
13. Willem Kleftijus, 1663.
14. Arij Jans de Milde, 1658.
15. Piet Vizeer, 1752.
16. Gysbert Verhaast, 1760.
17. Arend de Haak, 1780.
18. Dirk Van Schie, 1679.
19. Pieter Poulisse, 1690.
20. Lucas Van Dale, 1692.
21. Cornelis Van der Kloot, 1695.
22. Jan Baan, 1660.
23. Jan Decker, 1698.
24. Arij Cornelis Brouwer, 1699.
25. Leonardus of Amsterdam, 1721.
26. Paulus Van der Stroom, 1725.

DE METALE POT

This manufactory was founded in 1631 by P. J. Van Kessel which soon became flourishing and assumed great importance.

27. Jeronimus Pieters Van Kessel, 1655.
28. Lambertus Cleffius, 1678.
29. Lambartus Van Eenhoorn, 1691.
30. Factory Mark.

DE GRIEKSE A *(The Greek A)*.

Founded in 1645 by G. L. Kruyk.

31. Gisbrecht Lambrecht Kruyk, 1645.
32. Samuel Van Eenhoorn, 1674.
33. Adrianus Kocks, 1687.

34. Jan Van der Heul, 1701.
35. Jan Theunis Dextra, 1759.
36. Jacobus Halder, 1675.

DE DUBBELDE SCHENKKAN. *(The Double Bottle)*.

Established by Samuel Pererius Van Berenvelt, 1648.

37. Factory mark (initials).
38. Amerensie Van Kessel, 1675.
39. Louis Fictoor, 1689.
40. Hendrik de Koning, 1721.

T'HART *(The Stag)*.

Founded in 1661 by Joris Mesch.

41. Factory mark.
42. Matheus Van Boegart, 1734.
43. Hendrick Van Middeldyk, 1764.

DE PAAW, 1651 *(The Peacock)*.

Founded by C. J. Meschert and others.

44. Usual mark of the factory.

T'OUDE MORIAANS HOFFT *(The Old Moor's Head)*.

Founded in 1648 by Abram de Kooge.

45. Rochus Jacobs Hoppestein, 1680.
46. Antoni Kruisweg, 1740.
47. Geertruij Verstelle, 1764.

DE KLAEW *(The Claw)*.

Founded in 1662 by Cornelis Van der Hoeve—the mark is intended for the claw of a bird. Its productions, mostly in blue, had an extensive sale. Continued by the Schoenhoves from 1668 to 1705, when it passed to Pieter Oosterwick ; in 1740 to Kornelis Van Dyk.

48. Lambertus Sanderus, 1764.

DE BOOT (*The Boat*).

Established in 1667 by Harmen Groothuysen.

49. Dirk Van der Kest, 1698.
50. Johannes den Appel, 1759.

DE DRIE KLOKKEN (*The Three Bells*).

Established by Simon Mesch in 1671.

51. The usual mark of the factory of the three bells.

DE ROMEYN (*The Roman*).

Established in 1671 by Martinus Gouda.

52. Reinier Hey, 1696.
53. Factory mark of Japanese characters.
54. Factory mark of Japanese characters.
56. Petrus Van Marum, 1759.
57. Johannes Van der Kloot, 1764.

DE 3 PORCELEYNE FLESSIES (*Three Porcelain Bottles*).

No. 10 shows the sign. Established in 1668 by Albrecht de Keizer, whose mark was AK in a monogram (Table, No. 3).

58. A tripartite mark of Cornelis de Keizer (CK in monogram) and his two sons-in-law, Jacob and Adrian Pynacker deposited in the Gild in 1680.
59. Adrian Pynacker alone, 1690. It passed eventually to Hugo Brouwer in 1764.

DE DRIE ASTONNEN (*The Three Ash Barrels*).

Established 1674 by Gerrit Pieters Kam.

60. G. Pieters Kam.
61. Factory mark.
62. Zachariah Dextra, 1720.
63. Hendrick Van Hoorn, 1759.

DE PORCELEYNE SCHOTEL (*The Porcelain Plate*).

Established about 1700.

64. Johannes Pennis, 1725.
65. Jan Van Duijn, 1760.

DE ROOS (*The Rose*).

Established 1675 by Arendt Cosijn. The products of this factory are justly celebrated for richness of colour and elegant forms.

66. Factory mark.
67. Factory mark.
68. Dirck Van der Does, 1759.

DE PORCELEYNE BIJL (*The Porcelain Hatchet*).

In 1679 Huibrecht Brouwer was established here. The products of this factory are well known and very varied. The mark of a hatchet was invariably used, those of the potters being rarely added.

Joris Van Torenburg, 1697.   Initials.
Justus Brouwer, 1759.   Initials.
Hugo Brouwer, 1776.   Initials.
69. The factory mark.

DE PORCELEYNE FLES (*The Porcelain Bottle*).

Founded by Jacobus Pynacker about 1680.

70. Johannes Knotter, 1698.
71. Pieter Van Doorne, 1759.
    Dirk Harlees, 1795.

DE STAR (*The Star*).

Established by Theodorus Witsenburg in 1690.

72. Factory mark.
73. Cornelis de Berg.
74. Jan Aalmes, 1731.

75. Justus de Berg, 1759.
76. Albertus Kiell, 1763.

T'FORTUIN (*Fortune*).

Founded in 1691 by Lucas Van Dale.

77. Factory mark.
78. Factory mark.
79. Factory mark.
80. Paul Van der Briel, 1740.
81. Paul Van der Briel, 1740.

DE VERGULDE BLOMPOT (*The Golden Flower-Pot*).

Established in 1693 by P. Van der Strom.

82. Factory mark.
83. Matheus Van Bogaert.
84. Pieter Verburg.

DE TWEE WILDMANS (*The Two Savages*).

Established 1713.

85. William Van Beek, 1758.

DE TWEE SCHEPJES (*The Two Ships*).

86. Anthony Pennis, 1759.

T'JONGUE MORIAAN'S HOFFT (*The Young Moor's Head*).

87. Johannes Verhagen, 1728.

DE LAMPETKAN (*The Ewer*).

88. Gerrit Brouwer, 1756.
89. Abram Van der Keel, 1780.

Discontinued about 1813.

TABLE OF AUTHENTICATED POTTERS' MARKS.

1 16G(34 DEN 2M	19 +702. P	36 A I:H	54 (F Y 4 Z)	73 C B ✿
2 Jinius 16 1657	20 L V	37 D.S.K.	56 P:V:M	74 Aalmes 1731
3 AK	21 C VK 1729	38 AK	57 B.	75 ❋ I:B
4 VH C	22 I: BAAN	39 E	58 DSA	76 A:K ❋
5 M HVCZS 1618	23 Jan Decker 1698	40 HDK 1721	59 AK or AK	77 Fortuyn
6 A	24 AB	41 THART	60 GK	78 J P F 183
7 F·V FRYTOM	25 Leonardus 1727	42 MVB 1757	61 astonne 3	79 IHF 1480
8 J V H	26 P.V.D.S. A:1754.	43 HVMD	62 Z:DEX	80 PVB
9 H 12 30		44 DAV or paun	63 HV hoorn	
10 AR	27 IVK	45	64 P	81 B
11 I K	28 E	R.$.	65 Duyn	82 Clompot
12 I:C 22½	29 VK	46 AK	66 R	83 MVB 1757
13 WK 4	30 NP or MP	47 G:V:S	67 Roos	84 VB
14	31 G K	48 L.S	68 D V D.D	85 W:V:B
15 P:Visser	32 E	49 D.VK boot 1700	69 PPP	86 P or A
16 G Verhaast	33 AK	50 J DA	70 K S	87 IVH 1728
17 AREND DE HAAK	34 JVDH	51	71 PD	88 G B
18 D.V.schic	35 A ITD	52 Reinier	72 ❋	89 Lpetkan a VD Reel 1791
		53 三保		

TABLE OF POTTERS' MARKS ON FAYENCE.

In the accompanying list of potters, and the table of their marks on fayence, there are many meriting more notice than the bare mention of their names. We will briefly point out several artists who have distinguished themselves, and are not previously noticed in our preliminary remarks, but whose works are diligently sought for by discriminating collectors.

No. 1.—Gerrit Hermansz. The pieces attributed to him all usually painted with battles and historical subjects, crowded with figures, in blue *camaieu*.

No. 2.—Isaack Junius, originally a painter in oil, painted subsequently on fayence. Two of his plaques represent, in blue, the tomb of Guillaume le Taciturne, Prince of Orange, the first Stadtholder after the War of Independence, who was assassinated in 1584—whose tomb was visited in the year 1884, being the tercentenary of the expulsion of the Spanish from the Netherlands.

Nos. 66 and 67.—Arendt Cosijn, of the fabrique "*à la Rose*," is celebrated for his vases, which may be ranked among the choicest products of Delft, being delicately and artistically decorated.

No. 69.—The products of "The Hatchet" are very varied and well known; usually painted in blue. The whale and herring fisheries, and subjects of an industrial character, frequently occur.

Nos. 35 and 62.—The two Dextras, Zachariah of the "Drie Astonnen" and Jan Theunis of the "Griekse A," both imitated the Dresden decoration on large pieces, as fountains, tureens, and vases.

No. 19.—Pieter Poulisse, the manager of Adrian Pynacker's fabrique, introduced the vivid red and gold in his paintings with great effect. A superb piece, with pastoral scenes, is in the Loudon Collection.

No. 28.—Lambertus Cleffius, of the "Metal Pot." *The Haarlem Gazette*, of 1678, announces that he had discovered the secret of imitating Oriental Porcelain successfully.

No. 52.—Reinier Hey, of the "Roman," was a very talented artist. A plaque painted with shipping, after Van der Velde, is in the Loudon Collection.

No. 89.—The "Lampetkan," or Ewer, with its last potter, Abraham Van der Keel, is noticeable as the last of the celebrated fabriques of Delft, being demolished about 1813.

This is the end of the list of potters at Delft as officially known to us by the archives, and by a reference to the books of the Gild of St. Luc. The marks which follow are upon specimens of Delft in the Dutch style that have come under our observation, and can of course be considerably increased in number.

At the present time there is a factory at Delft where reproductions of the old Delft fayence are made, and a staff of some 200 hands was employed when the Editor visited it in 1895. The mark is sometimes the name of the firm, THOOVT & LABOUCHERE, impressed in a circle, and also that reproduced in the margin. The reproductions are chiefly those of blue decoration on a white ground.

SIXTEENTH AND SEVENTEENTH CENTURIES.

Unknown; marked in blue. Chinese designs in blue.

D.V.X.I

Unknown; marked in blue. Chinese designs in blue.

AX

Unknown; marked in gold; early gilding.

D

Unknown; marked in gold.

I ♂

DELFT. Mark unknown; the date 1629; painted in polychrome in the Oriental style.

16 S 2 9

AF

DELFT. On oblong and octagonal plates, painted in blue *camaieu*, in the Chinese style.

IE

On a square canister, the ground painted with blue flowers, figures and interiors; on the sides Justice and Plenty in blue *camaieu*.

I·D·P

1698

Unknown. Japanese designs in colours.

H.S.i
R

Cornelius Zachtleven, born at Rotterdam 1612, died 1690. M. de Vilestreux of the Hague has two oval plaques with polychrome borders; subjects sketched in violet *en camaieu*, of two men in the style of Teniers, one holding a scroll, on which is Zachtleven's name.

C. Zachtleven Fa.
1650.

Unknown. On plates, &c., in imitation of Faenza ware.

Unknown. Plaques; blue *en camaieu*, coloured borders.

J.V.L
1773

Unknown; marked in blue. On a plaque, in imitation of a cage of canary birds.

A*DB*   Unknown. Canettes, with figures and foliage,
ANNO   flowers, &c.
1774

C.D.G.   Unknown. On a triangular plateau; blue Chinese designs.

G⊃G   Unknown. On oblong and octagonal plates; painted in blue *camaieu*.
1779

D.M   Unknown. On shaped pieces; blue monochrome.

I.G.V   Unknown. On shaped pieces; blue monochrome.
1768

W.D.   On a crocus-pot, in form of a fish; blue designs.

BP   On a canette or jug, in blue *camaieu*.

I G   On a canette or jug, in blue *camaieu*.

D   On a tureen and plate; blue dragons; Chinese patterns.

M.Q.   On a plate of blue decoration, of the Decadence period.

R.T.C   On a butter-dish, forming a bundle of asparagus on a plate.

A.I.1663.   On a plaque in blue *en camaieu:* The Last Supper.

S M. 1725,   On a canette *(stortenbeker)*, in blue *en camaieu*, with *Looft Godt boven alle*—"Love God above all."

$$\frac{D}{18}$$
      On a plate painted in blue *en camaieu*.

W   On a dish, with figures in blue, coats of arms and cupids, coloured border.

↑VR↗   On a dish painted in colours.

H.   On a canette or jug, painted in blue *en camaieu*.

On a dish with festooned border, also on a tea-service.

BFS

On a dish, blue: Flight into Egypt.

HvS
1781

On compotiers, in form of fruits and on plates, in blue *camaieu* and Chinese patterns.

$VI⊟✳$

On a small bust of William III., King of England and Stadtholder of Holland, with an ermine mantle and a crown on his head, well modelled, decorated in blue *camaieu*.

K

On a plaque painted in blue *camaieu*, representing an inundation at Scheveningen, inscribed 15th November 1775, "*De Overstroming voor Scheveningen.*" In the Queen of Holland's possession.

I Kuwzt
1775

AALMES, ceramic painter. A plateau, belonging to a cabaret, painted with a Dutch drinking-scene, is marked thus. In the Collection of M. de Vilestreux, at the Hague. This mark is attributed by Jännike to Rotterdam (*q.v.*).

A almes
1731

This mark is found on fayence jugs covered with imitation Chinese lacquer.

This monogram and date was on a vase and cover in the Montferrand Collection, No. 240; the cover was surmounted by a lion, and the vase enriched with arabesques.

AP
1719
8
16

JOHN THEOBALD FRANTZ. On a large plaque, with a bust of St. Peter, painted in blue. Victoria and Albert Museum. The mark at the back in blue. Dr. Justus Brinckmann says that this potter was a German, and probably the brother or father of Johan Philipp Frantz who worked at the Dorotheenthal factory until 1722 and previously at Brunswick.

Heindering Waanders
1781.

HEINDERING WAANDERS was a potter at Delft; his name occurs on a money-box, painted in blue *camaieu*, with ornaments in yellow, signed on the foot; in the Collection of M. Demmin.

R
R÷I
1765

On a plate, decorated, with Chinese landscapes in blue. In Victoria and Albert Museum.

HDX
13
̅II̅

On a coffee-pot, with Chinese figures outlined in blue, embossed with rococo scrolls, *circa* 1760; formerly in the possession of Mr. Hailstone, Walton Hall.

R

On plates, painted with flowers in yellow and green.

DRX
5

Mark in blue, on a small shaped teapot, with red and blue decorations of a Chinese character, part of which are in slight relief. Formerly in the Editor's possession.

AK

Mark in red, on a small oval bowl and cover, fluted, with decorations of blue, red, and gold. Formerly in the Editor's possession.

It is impossible to give a complete list of the marks on Delft fayence, owing to the fact that workmen, potters, and artists signed individual pieces, and they are too many to enumerate. Illustrations of Delft specimens in the Victoria and Albert Museum. (See *Ker. Gall.*, enlarged edition, figs. 172-176.)

BELGIUM.

BRUSSELS. We have the evidence of the *Journal de Commerce* of March 1761 that at least one ceramic manufactory of importance then existed: "Philippe Mombaers, manufacturier de fayence de S. A. Roy¹., fabrique à Bruxelles toutes sortes de fayances, consistant en plats d'épargnes, terrines ovales et rondes en forme de choux, melons, artichots, asperges, pigeons, coqs, dindons, poules, anguilles, pots à beurre, saucières, cafetières, fontaines, saladiers, assiettes, paniers à fruits, services de table, &c. Cette manufacture est préférable à celle de Delft et de Rouen, n'est point chère et est parfaitement bien assortie. Le tout a l'épreuve du feu." Many of these have doubtless been attributed to Delft and other now better-known fabriques. Beside Philippe Mombaers, there was at Brussels a Widow Mombaers and a Widow Artoisonnez; of the latter there is a fine example in the style of Rouen, now preserved in the Sèvres Museum.

The following marks, found on specimens of Flemish fayence, have been attributed to Brussels; they are taken from Jännike's *Grundriss der Keramik.*

Note.—Dr. Justus Brinckmann considers that the second mark given in this group, *i.e.*, the C. B. under a crown, is a German and not a Belgian mark. He attributes it to Friedberg, in Bavaria. The same authority also challenges the three marks of " K " with hay-fork, in the last row of marks, which he attributes to Abtsbessingen, near Sondershausen, established about 1750. The K. stands for Kiel, the name of a fayence painter (T. G. Kiel), who sometimes signed his work with this initial and sometimes with his full name, as on a specimen dated 1756.

This mark is also given by Jännike as that of a fabrique of a potter named Kuhn at Etterbeck lez Bruxelles, but it is probably the monogram of the painter, Ebenstein, whose work and whose mark are noticed under the heading of Brussels Porcelain *(q.v.).*

LIÈGE. We only know of the existence of this fabrique by the mention of it by Gournay in his Almanack of 1788: "Le vernis de cette faïence est beau, blanc, et peu sujet à s'écailler. Entrepreneur M. Bousmar." He was, perhaps, a son of M. Boussemart of Lille, who died in 1778.

ANDENNES (Namur). A. D. Vander.Waert. Services; the mark impressed. Sèvres Museum, presented in 1809.

ANDENNES (Namur). B. Lammens & Co., impressed on fine enamelled fayence tea-services. Presented to the Sèvres Museum in 1809.

TOURNAY. There was a manufactory of fayence existing here before the year 1696; allusion is made to it in a document among the archives of Lille. Jacques Feburier petitions for permission to establish a fabrique of ware "*à la façon d'Hollande*," and of much finer quality than that of Tournay. M. Jacquemart says that when Fénélon was intrusted with the education of the Duke of Burgundy, the intendants or comptrollers were called upon to furnish memoirs of their districts, that the Prince might become acquainted with the complete organisation of the kingdom. The intendant or Lord-Lieutenant of Hainault thus expresses his opinion about ceramics: "But the fayence is not of the first order, although made of the same earth as that made in Holland, which they draw from the village of Bruyelle, a league from Tournay." He continues: "La commodité que les fayanciers de Tournay ont d'avoir cette terre est très grande et devrait les exciter à perfectionner leurs ouvrages. Cependant les Hollandais viennent chercher cette terre pour en fabriquer leurs fayances qu'ils envoient ensuite vendre dans tous les pays conquis." Who then was the manufacturer that called forth these reproaches? M. Lejeal tells us that it was Pierre Joseph Fauquez, already established at St. Amand, and who, after his death in 1741, was buried in the church of Notre Dame at Tournay, his native town, where he had also a fabrique, which his son, Pierre François Joseph, inherited. On the conclusion of the peace at Aix-la-Chapelle, Fauquez junior established himself at St. Amand and ceded the Tournay fabrique to Peterynck of Lille, who raised it to the highest rank among ceramic establishments. The marks used by Fauquez and Peterynck on their fayence are not at present identified, and it is very difficult to distinguish between the French and Dutch fabrications.

TOURNAY (?). This mark is on a large dish of fine fayence painted in bright blue *camaieu*, figures in the centre and ornaments in the Flemish style.

TOURNAY (?). On a fayence cruet-frame, with marks, and finely decorated in bright colours with Chinese landscapes; the initial is, perhaps, that of Peterynck.

TOURNAY. A fayence compotier of similar decoration, with a better-defined mark.

LUXEMBOURG. Established at Sept Fontaines in 1767 by the Brothers Boch, who previously were manufacturers of common pottery at Audun-le-Tiche, in France, commenced about 1730. In 1767, encouraged by the Government, they founded this important fabrique, which has been continued to the present day with great success; besides this at Luxembourg, the Messrs. Boch carry on the ancient manufactory of Tournay and others in Germany.

LUXEMBOURG. This mark is impressed on a mug of cream-coloured or Queen's ware, formerly in Mr. W. Chaffers' Collection.

TERVUEREN, near Brussels. A manufactory of fayence was established here about 1720, under the protection of the Duke Charles IV. of Lorraine, Austrian Governor of the Pays Bas. An authentic specimen is in the Museum of the Porte de Halle at Brussels—a vase ornamented with garlands of flowers in relief and the arms of Charles of Lorraine, marked under the foot as in the margin.

$$\overline{\underset{\text{C.P.}}{\text{C C C}}}$$

BRUGES. Towards the end of the eighteenth century a manufactory of fayence was established by Henry Pulinx, examples of which are now rare. M. Em. Dullaert, the present proprietor, in the Rue de Vieux Bourg at Bruges, possesses some specimens, and has forwarded us the photograph of a tureen of fayence, painted in colours, with grapes, melons, &c., which has the founder's monogram, H. P., as in the margin.

HP

This mark is also given by Jännike as one adopted by H. Pulinx of Bruges.

LILLE. There are documents in the municipal archives of Lille which prove the existence of a manufactory here in the year 1696. It was founded by Jacques Feburier of Tournay and Jean Bossu of Ghent, the first a modeller of twelve years' experience, the second a painter of fayence for twenty years. By the petition they promise to make ware *à la façon d'Hollande,* and of much finer quality than that made at Tournay. Jacques Feburier died in 1729, and the manufactory was carried on by the Veuve Feburier and her son-in-law, François Boussemart; it was at this time in a very flourishing state, and they were anxious to obtain royal patronage. We quote the following extract, as it alludes to two other royal establishments, of which we have as yet no further information. The document commences by stating that the manufactory is "sans contredit la plus importante du royaume," and "ils ont lieu d'espérer que sa Majesté ne leur refusera pas la grace de l'ériger en manufacture royale, comme elle a érigé celle établie à Bordeaux par Jacques Hustin et celle fondée à Montpellier par Jacques Ollivier." In 1732 we find they had three kilns for baking fayence, making every year 1,287,600 pieces. In 1776 M. Boussemart's manufactory employed sixty workmen, and at his death in 1778 he was succeeded by M. Petit.

The second important manufactory of fayence was established in 1711 by Barthélémy Dorez and his nephew, Pierre Pelissier, for the manufacture of fayence and porcelain. It continued in active work for nearly a century, but the products, like those of Feburier and Boussemart, cannot be identified, owing to the absence of the marks of the fabriques. The decorations were principally in the style of Delft, Chinese patterns, and frequently similar to those of the South of France. The manufactory was carried on by the children of Barthélémy Dorez, Claude and François Louids, who subsequently left Lille to establish a *fabrique de faïence* at Valenciennes. About 1748, a grandson, Nicolas Alexis Dorez, was proprietor; between 1750 and 1755 it became the property of Messrs. Hereng & Boussemart, and in 1786 it was ceded to Hubert François Lefèbvre, who continued the works until about 1801.

A third fayence manufactory was founded in 1740 by a Mons. Wamps, a maker of Dutch tiles; after his death Jacques Masquelier became director of the works, and was proprietor in 1752; he obtained on the 10th of May 1755 permission to add to his works the fabrication of fayence "à la manière de Rouen et des pays étrangères." This appears to have been carried on in the same family until 1827, when it altogether ceased.

A fourth was established in 1774 by M. Chanou, who made "ouvrages de terres brunes appelés terres de St. Esprit à la façon d'Angleterre et du Languedoc," but we do not know how long it lasted.

A fifth appears by another document to have been established for the manufacture of fayence stoves by a person named Heringle in 1758; he was a native of Strasbourg, and had worked seven consecutive years at the "Manufacture Royale de la terre d'Angleterre à Paris."

A sixth manufactory was originated by an Englishman named William Clarke in 1773, for earthenware *façon d'Angleterre*. The document states that he was "natif de Newascle [Newcastle] en Angleterre, disant qu'il posséde le secret d'une espèce de faïence que ne se fait qu'en Angleterre, qui est à peu près aussi belle que la porcelaine, et que a la propriété de resister au feu sans se féler, que la terre de cette fayence se trouve dans le royaume même à portée de cette province." Authorisation was accorded in March 1773.

The monogram of François Boussemart (without the word Lille) is on the back of a very remarkable dish of Lille fayence in the Victoria and Albert Museum.

A mark of Boussemart, composed of the initials F. B. L., and accompanied by the name of the place at full length; on some plates, decorated in the Rouen style, in the Patrice Salin Collection, Paris.

LILLE. This mark, in a coloured wreath crowned, the letters in black, is on the back of a fayence plate painted with rococo scrolls and flowers, and a banderole, supported by two cupids, inscribed "Maître Daligne," in the Sèvres Museum and in Baron Davillier's Collection; it probably emanates from the Royal Manufactory founded by Feburier, and was painted by Boussemart for M. Daligne; it is very similar to the Rouen ware. Collectors should be very suspicious of specimens bearing this mark; it has been frequently imitated by Paris fabricants, especially on plaques painted in Dutch landscapes.

LILLE. Nicolas Alexis Dorez, grandson of the founder, Barthélémy. The name occurs underneath a large vase, intended as a present to an association of lace-makers; it is of elegant form, with twisted handles: in the front, surrounded by scrolls, is a medallion representing a woman seated, making lace on a pillow, a child by her side. In M. Jules Houdoy's possession.

N : A
DOREZ
1748.

LILLE. This mark is on a tea-service with polychrome decoration, in the possession of M. Leveel of Paris; marked under the cover, and probably belongs to the manufactory of M. Masquelier.

Lille, 1768.

LILLE. The name of a printer who worked in the manufactory of Masquelier; it occurs on a bowl of similar decoration in M. Houdoy's possession.

CAMBRAY.

LILLE. Jacques Feburier. These marks occur on a portrait altar in the Sèvres Museum, decorated in blue *camaieu*, altogether in the Dutch style. The name of the Borne family as ceramists seems to have been well known; it occurs both at Rouen and Nevers.

Fecit IACOBUS FEBVRIER
Insulis in Flandria,
Anno 1716.

Pinxit MARIA STEPHANUS
BORNE Anno 1716.

LILLE. This mark is on a plate painted in blue *camaieu* in the style of Rouen. The initials are of François Boussemart, son-in-law of Jacques Feburier, and his successor.

This mark, probably of a painter, is underneath the F. B. given above.

LILLE. Another mark on a plate of blue *camaieu*, of the Rouen design, attributed to Boussemart.

LILLE. These marks are attributed to Masquelier, son-in-law and successor to Lefèbvre; on a plate, painted in blue *camaieu.*

LILLE. On an earthenware salt-cellar, painted with a blue bird in the centre and flowers, marked underneath in blue, and attributed to this manufactory.

These additional marks are attributed by Jännike to Lille, as well as various forms of Dorez's initials, and those of Joannes Franciscus Jacqrie, "pinxit Lille," also of Petit, the successor of Boussemart.

LILLE. A Delft ware painted female figure of the eighteenth century, in Oriental costume, seated on four bales of merchandise (one of them having the name of I. SPEDER, the others the initials only), was bought at Lille, and believed to have been made there.

MANUFACTURE UNKNOWN. Sixteenth century. Terra-cotta without glaze, Dutch or Flemish. We must not omit to mention some ornamental red terra-cotta bricks used formerly in the construction of the large chimney-pieces of the sixteenth and seventeenth centuries.

The ornamentation is in relief on one side only, of subjects from Scripture history, and armorial bearings, chiefly of Dutch and Flemish origin; Renaissance ornaments, and designs for borders, of continuous patterns. Three of these, formerly in the author's possession, selected from upwards of a hundred, which came from an old house at Ipswich, called Cardinal Wolsey's Palace, have the story of Susanna, soldiers marching, and medallions of classical busts; these measure—length $5\frac{1}{2}$ by $3\frac{3}{4}$, and are $2\frac{1}{2}$ inches thick. Two others, in M. Demmin's Collection, are dated 1578 and 1598, and bear the arms of Philip II., son of Charles V., from a palace he occupied near Bruges. In the Cluny Museum is one similar, semicircular, bearing the arms of Holland, Zetland, and Friesland, dated 1575.

There is a Flemish Renaissance chimney-piece in the Victoria and Albert Museum, which cost £110; it came from an old house at Antwerp: the back of the fireplace is constructed of 168 bricks, with various Scriptural subjects in relief; on the top is a large triangular-headed brick with the arms of Charles V., the motto "PLUS OLTRE," and the date 1532.

[It will be observed that although Lille has been a French town (Département du Nord) since its restoration by the Austrians in 1713, the

Editor has allowed the notices to remain under the same classification as
in the previous edition.   It was in the earliest stages of its ceramic history
a Flemish town.]

GERMANY.

BAYREUTH (a town in Bavaria).   There was a manufactory of pottery
here in the sixteenth century of a brown stoneware, with Renaissance
medallions, arabesques, &c., in relief.   At a later period fine fayence was
produced, usually painted in blue *camaieu;* the designs are delicately
traced with a brush, as fine as if with a pen, on a fine paste; the forms
are canettes, jardinières, &c.   This mark is on a
large vase, with handles, in the Sèvres Museum;
the monograms beneath are perhaps those of the
decorator named Knötter.   On other specimens
are the marks N.F. and BK. C., &c., but fre-
quently without any marks.   Two spice-plates, numbered 3007 and 3008,
in the Hôtel de Cluny, marked K.; a large plaque of this manufacture,
46 inches long by 27½ inches wide, is in the Collection of M. Meusnier,
at Paris, and a great many pieces in blue *camaieu* are at the Château de
la Favorite, near Baden; a bottle at the Museum of Sigmaringen is
dated 1524.

BAYREUTH.   There are some specimens of fayence
of the eighteenth century with this mark in the Sèvres
Museum, which M. Brongniart bought at Nuremberg; and
considered to be of this manufacture.

BAYREUTH.   On a fayence plate with flowers in blue
camaieu; sometimes the letter C is found instead of H.

BAYREUTH.   The following additional marks in blue under the glaze
found on specimens of Bayreuth fayence are given on the authority of the
official catalogue of German and Scandinavian fayences of the eighteenth
century in the Hamburg Museum (pp. 147-148):—

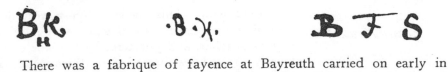

There was a fabrique of fayence at Bayreuth carried on early in
this century by M. Schmidt, some of the products being in imitation of

Wedgwood. There are five specimens in the Sèvres Museum bearing the counterfeit mark of "Wedgwood."

H   HOLITSCH (Hungary). On a plate painted with flowers in brilliant colours, reputed to be of this fabrique.

NUREMBERG. The celebrated Veit Hirschvogel of Schelestadt was born at Nuremberg in 1441, and died in 1525, contemporary with Luca della Robbia, the Florentine, who was born in 1400 and died in 1481. The painted glass of four windows in the church of St. Sebald at Nuremberg, representing the Margrave Frederick of Anspach and Bayreuth, with his wife and children, was executed by Veit Hirschvogel in 1515. He was succeeded by his sons and continuators in the manufacture of pottery. In the Berlin Ceramic Museum, M. Kolbe (the director of the Royal Porcelain Manufactory) has recently placed a jug of Hirschvogel of the year 1470. This authentic specimen was purchased at the Minutoli sale for eighty-three thalers; it is something like the Italian maiolica, but easily distinguished by the bright colours and fine quality of the enamel. It is ornamented in relief with the Crucifixion; beneath are three niches, containing statuettes of Faith, Hope, and Charity, painted in colours, amongst which the green predominates, as usual in the German school. In the Dresden Museum is a pitcher of green glaze, with a Scripture subject in relief, of excellent moulding, by Hirschvogel, dated 1473. The chimney-pieces and tiles of the early Nuremberg make are frequently met with; there is a large collection also in the Berlin Museum, from the Minutoli sale, of the fourteenth, fifteenth, and sixteenth centuries. The finest chimney-piece known is one still existing in its original position in the Château de Salzburg, of the fifteenth century, for which, it is said, an English amateur recently offered the sum of 36,000 francs, or nearly £1500! In the Hôtel de Cluny is a bas-relief, of the seventeenth century, of green enamel, with busts of Julius Cæsar, Charlemagne, and other worthies, and a group of St. George, and a relief of Wolffgang, Grand-Master of the Teutonic Order. In the Sauvageot Collection in the Louvre are some tiles of the fifteenth century. In the Victoria and Albert Museum is a fine cruche, with raised figures of Adam and Eve, enamelled with blue, yellow, green, white, and manganese, by Veit Hirschvogel, of the fifteenth century; and another by his successors.

1550

NUREMBERG. This mark is on a very fine stove, with portraits in relief, in black and gold, quoted by M. Demmin.

Hans Kraut

1578.

NUREMBERG. This name is on a very fine stove of green earthenware plaques with religious subjects in relief, and pilasters; by the side of the stove is a raised seat ascended by three steps. In the Victoria and Albert Museum.

NUREMBERG. On a fayence dish, with blue scrolls, yellow and pink leaf medallions; in the centre is the Ascension, with soldiers and rocky landscape. Glüer is probably the name of the artist.

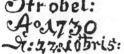

NUREMBERG. This mark of Strobel, 22, 10 bris (December) 1730, occurs on a large dish, painted in blue, with arabesque borders, birds and fruit in the centre. In the Sèvres Museum.

NUREMBERG. There are two plates of the eighteenth century in the Sèvres Museum, one in imitation of Faenza, the other an allegory of Luther; they are marked as in the margin. There is also a large bell, which still has a fine ring, decorated in blue *camaieu*, with the arms of Nuremberg, and an inscription in German: "The town of Nuremberg of the Holy Roman Empire," and the signature of the potter, "Strobel." The mark here given is not a facsimile.

G. F. Greber
Anno 1729.
Nuremberg.

Stadt Nuremberg
1724.
Strobel.

NUREMBERG. A service painted with coats of arms, made in 1741, gives us the name of a potter written at full length on one of the pieces, the others having his initials only, as shown in the margin. M. A. Jacquemart thinks it probable, from the frequent recurrence of his initials, that he was an eminent potter at whose establishment Strobel painted. Some of the pieces marked K bear also the initials of the city, as here shown.

NUREMBERG. This name is on a jug of white enamel painted with scrolls and large flowers, attributed to this city by M. Jacquemart.

These additional marks are given by Jännike as those of potters and artists who made and decorated fayence at Nuremberg :—

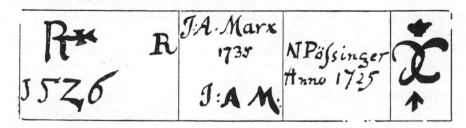

NUREMBERG. This mark is also given as that of a modern fabrique established by J. von Schwarz in 1880.

Reference should be made to the note on the former attribution of a *porcelain* factory to Nuremberg in the chapter "Bavaria."

NUREMBERG. The following four additional marks in blue under the glaze, are given on the authority of the official catalogue of German and Scandinavian fayence of the eighteenth century (p. 147) in the Hamburg Museum :—

Matthias
Rosa
im. Anspach

O S

ANSPACH (Bavaria). The existence here of a fayence manufactory is revealed by a very fine *surtout de table*, or tray to put on a table, with elegant mouldings, decorated in blue *camaieu* scrolls in the style of Rouen. The inscription leaves no doubt either of the place or name of the potter. (*Jacquemart.*)

ANSPACH. This mark has been recently identified as that of a potter named Oswald, who worked at Anspach about 1730.

BADEN. About 1799 Charles Stanislas Hannong, grandson of Balthasar, whom the Republic of France had condemned to exile, founded a fabrique of fayence and terra-de-pipe.

STREHLA, and other places in the valley of the Elbe. Earthenware, both of lead and tin glazes. This place has been known for its manufacture of pottery of all sorts for many centuries. A pulpit of enamelled earthenware still exists in Strehla; it is supported by a life-size figure of Moses, and ornamented with eight plaques of religious subjects and the four Evangelists; at the bottom is inscribed: "Im Jahre Christi Geburth 1565 ist diese Kanzel Gott zu Ehren gewacht durch Michael Tatzen, Topfer und Bildschnitzern zu Strehla, meines alters im 24 Jahr."

LEIPZIG. In the Convent of St. Paul, which was built in 1207, there was a frieze of large bricks or tiles, covered with stanniferous enamel, representing, in high relief, heads of Saints and the Apostles, 15 by 20 inches square, 2½ inches thick. On the demolition of the convent some of these were taken to the Museum at Dresden, the others sold. They are of Byzantine character, and evidently of the twelfth or thirteenth century, showing the early use of this enamel in Germany. The enamel is green, shaded gradually with black, very thick and durable; the hair, beard, and eyes are coloured, the ground also enamelled. (*Demmin.*)

BRESLAU, capital of Silesia (Prussia). Earthenware, with stanniferous enamel, of the thirteenth century. In the Kreuzkirche (Church of the Cross), built in 1280, is the monument of Henry IV. of Silesia, the founder, erected after his death in 1290. On a sarcophagus reposes the full-length life-size figure of the Duke; the head is natural and full of expression; he is clad in a coat of mail ornamented with Silesian eagles, and partly covered with an ermine mantle, on his brow a ducal coronet, and he holds a shield of his arms. All the details are minutely portrayed; the colours of the enamel clear and bright, the red is brilliant, and the green, which predominates, is of the same shade as that of Nuremberg. Round it is the Latin inscription: "Hen. quartus mille tria C. minus X. obiit ille egregiis annis Silesiæ Cracov. Sandomiriæ Dux nocte Joannis." The artist is unknown. M. Demmin cites these instances at Leipzig and Breslau as incontestable proofs of the knowledge of the Germans in the art of enamelled earthenware sculpture on a grand scale nearly two centuries earlier than it was known to the Italians.

AUGSBURG. Some recent excavations in the gardens of the ancient Convent of Carmelites have brought to light a quantity of small terracotta figures, mostly broken and imperfect. It is supposed they were made here in the beginning of the fifteenth century (1420-60); they are curious from the variety of costumes of all classes—equestrian figures, warriors, artisans, the Virgin and Infant Saviour, &c.—all finely modelled. Many of these are in the Berlin Museum.

In the Hôtel de Ville at Augsburg are three very large monumental stoves, covered with a black stanniferous glaze, ornamented with figures in high relief, the work of Adam Vogt, 1620, signed by him; he was born at Landsberg.

OBERDORF (Frontière Barvaroise). Hans Seltzmann, potter. A very fine stove of stanniferous enamel, of Gothic design, green ground and yellow ornaments, is in an ante-chamber of the Hoch Schloss of Fuessen, in Bavaria, bearing the following inscription: "Dieser Ofen wol gestalt wuurd gemacht de man zallt 1514 jaar, bey Hansen Seltzmann Vogt zu Oberdorf." (This stove, so well designed, was made by Hans Seltzmann, Mayor of Oberdorf, in the year 1514.)

MEMMINGEN (near Kaufbern, in Bavaria). Earthenware and fayence, with stanniferous enamel. Some very fine stoves were made at this place, sometimes moulded, sometimes modelled, of the sixteenth and seventeenth centuries, of which many museums contain specimens. The fayence plates and dishes are usually in blue camaïeu, of Renaissance patterns, with wide borders similar to the Italian, for which they are sometimes taken; some have coats of arms. The fayence of the last century is of common quality, with coloured flowers, in the style of that of Marseilles.

BUNZLAU (Silesia). Grès, or stoneware, was made here in the sixteenth and seventeenth centuries. The products of the last century are distinguished by ornaments in relief, flowers, coats of arms, &c., sometimes gilt. At the present time a great trade is carried on in the manufacture of chocolate and coffee-pots, usually of brown glaze lined with white. The late King Frederick William IV. of Prussia always used this in preference to more costly ware. In the town-hall of Bunzlau there is preserved a great coffee-pot hooped like a barrel, nearly 15 feet high, made in the last century. The manufactory is still continued by Lepper and Küttner, principally for vessels of domestic use.

HARBURG (on the Elbe, opposite Hamburg). Johan Schaper was born towards the end of the sixteenth century, and flourished here from 1620 to 1670, the date of his ·decease. His exquisite paintings of landscapes and figures are usually in Indian-ink, or brown *en grisaille*, the colours being fixed by heat; his name is frequently found minutely written, so as to be scarcely perceptible without a magnifying-glass. His fayence mugs are generally of white stanniferous enamel, painted in brown, shaded, the lights being scratched in with a point, carefully and delicately drawn; he also painted on glass in the same style, of which there are several examples in the Victoria and Albert Museum. (*Ker. Gall.*, enlarged edition, fig. 167.)

Ioh Schaper.   HARBURG (Hanover). German jug, painted in grey *camaieu*, with a landscape signed by the painter (Marryat Collection). In the Victoria and Albert Museum. The monogram I.S. interlaced is sometimes found on Schaper's works.

Dr. Justus Brinckmann, of the Hamburg Museum, informs the Editor that no factory existed at this place, but that it was the birthplace of Schaper, who painted fayence; the jug was therefore probably made elsewhere, and only decorated by the artist. (*Ker. Gall.*, enlarged edition, fig. 167.)

FULDA. The mark in the margin, which is in black, occurs on a vase in the Hamburg Museum, and is attributed to Fulda, the work of a potter named Friedrich von Löwenfink, and dates from the eighteenth century.

GENNEP (Luxembourg). There are three fayence plates of the eighteenth century, with stanniferous glaze, in the possession of Mr. Swaab of the Hague; they are 24 inches in diameter, of yellow, brown, and green enamel; one represents the Sacrifice of Abraham, dated 1712; another the Holy Family; and a third La Vierge de Kevelar (near Clèves). These last two are inscribed with the subject, and the name of the potter, "Antonius Bernardus von Vehlen, 1770-71."

SCHERZHEIM or SCHRETZHEIM (near Elvangen, in Würtemberg). The Wintergursts, father and son, were celebrated potters here, and made fayence with stanniferous enamel from the beginning of the seventeenth century to about 1810. It is from this manufactory that the table-services, of which each piece represents an animal or vegetable, were made. At the Château de la Favorite, at Baden, parts of a service may be seen in the form of a ham, head of a wild boar, &c.

The marks in the margin are given by Jännike as those of Schretzheim. (See also notes on the preceding page.)

PROSKAU (Prussia). M. Jacquemart gives us this mark, which is stamped in the clay, on a cup and saucer of glazed brown ware with silvered ornaments in relief, and the arms of the Grand-Duke of Mecklenburg and inscriptions, dated 12th December 1817, and the name. Dr. Justus Brinckmann says that this stamped mark of "Proskau" is only found on the brown stoneware made at Proskau at the beginning of the nineteenth century.

G. Manjack fecit
PROSKAU.

A manufactory of fayence was established at Proskau, in Silesia (Germany), in 1763, the mark being a cursive P., and later on two initials, D. P., which were those of Dietrischstein Proskau, the dominion of Proskau being in the Principality of Dietrischstein. Later still a roman P. was used. The fayence made here in 1788 is somewhat similar to our Leeds ware, which has sometimes printed decorations bearing the name of the engraver, one Endler.

GÖGGINGEN (Bavaria). Established circa 1750. Fayence with stanniferous enamel. It is usually decorated in blue with flowers, leaves, and ornaments, something in the style of Moustiers, signed at length; several examples in the Collection of the Historic Society at Augsburg. The mark in the margin is on a specimen painted with arabesques in blue, and a genius supporting a medallion; below are the initials of the artist. In M. Pascal's Collection.

KÜNERSBERG. This name in full is met with on fayence. In the Collections of M. Gasnault and M. E. Pascal of Paris are some specimens painted with flowers, &c., in violet *camaieu*.

KÜNERSBERG. A mark so attributed by M. Jacquemart.

Note.—Künersberg was formerly erroneously included in the Scandinavian potteries, but it should be under German, Bavaria. The factory was established in 1744 by Jacob von Küner.

POPPLESDORF (near Bonn). M. L. Wessel, manufacturer of fayence and porcelain; mark stamped. An anchor is sometimes found on the fayence of Mettlach (Prussia) with the name in full.

HÖCHST, near Mayence, Principality of Nassau; founded by Gelz of Frankfort in the beginning of the eighteenth century. Its products are of an artistic character, the figures exquisitely modelled and painted. The mark is a wheel of six spokes, taken from the arms of the Archbishop of Mayence, protector of the fabrique. The arms of the Electoral See being, *gules*, a wheel with six spokes, *argent*, first assumed by Archbishop Wittigis, who was the son of a wheelwright.

HÖCHST. An artist of the name of Zeschinger sometimes signed his name at length, but more frequently his initials only. Other letters are found accompanying the wheel, but in such an important manufactory there were doubtless many other artists whose names are unknown to us.

HÖCHST. The original manufactory was destroyed by General Custine, and it altogether ceased in 1794; subsequently the moulds were purchased and removed to Damm near Aschaffenburg, and the mark adopted was the wheel and letter D. There are some figures of characters from Schiller's plays with this mark, and many other statuettes of considerable merit. The Collector should refer to the notice of Höchst porcelain.

MAYENCE (?). Found on fayence pieces of the eighteenth century, painted with flowers, fine colouring.

DIRMSTEIN. Nothing seems to have been known of a factory at Dirmstein, which is not far from Ludwigsburg, and was called the Bishop of Worms' Fayence Factory, until a pamphlet was written on the subject by Ernst Zais, published in 1895. The mark was that given in the margin, and there is a specimen in the Museum at Turin. Figures with this mark were also in the Marquis d'Azeglio's Collection, but it was not known to what fabrique to ascribe them, and the mark was classed as "German unknown" in previous editions of Chaffers. According to Herr Zais, the factory was established by a potter who came from Höchst, and in 1774 it was flourishing, the directors being named Vogelmann and Graef. The productions were a fine fayence something like that of Höchst, a stoneware not unlike that made in England. In 1783 the financial position was critical, in 1785 it was struggling, and its doors were closed in 1788. Tea and coffee services, groups, and figures were made.

LOUISBOURG, in Würtemberg. Previous to the arrival of Ringler, who established the fabrique of porcelain, fayence was made here. M. A. Jacquemart describes a piece of elegant form, violet marbled ground, which had a medallion, the eagle of Germany, and an escutcheon with two C's crossed and beneath the date 1726.

ARNSTADT (Gotha). Established about the middle of the eighteenth century, where porcelain was also subsequently made. This inscription is on a fayence jug, painted in blue *camaieu*, with St. George and the Dragon, coloured flowers on sides, purple and green check border at top. Formerly in the Collection of the Rev. T. Staniforth, and now in the British Museum.

Pinxit F.G. Fliegel
Arnstadt d: 9 Maÿ
·1775·

M. Jacquemart (*Merveilles*, &c., part iii. p. 207) quotes a piece in the possession of M. Paul Gasnault, finely painted with fruit and flowers, inscribed, as he says, "Pinxit F. G. Fliegel, St. Georgen Amsee R. 3 Noffember 1764," which he attributes to SAINT GEORGES in Bavaria; but by comparison with the mark in the margin it is clearly Arnstadt at the sign of St. George, which subject is also depicted on Mr. Staniforth's jug, the unintelligible word *Amsee* being probably an erroneous reading of Arnstadt.

ARNSTADT (Gotha). This mark of two pipes crossed has been assigned to this place by Marryat.

ALTROLHAU, near Carlsbad. A manufactory conducted by A. Nowotny; the mark impressed. Some specimens presented to the Sèvres Museum.

MORAVIA (Frain). Besides the usual stamp, the ornamented pieces have an anchor, ribbon, and leaves in colour.

MARBURG (Hesse). There was a pottery here in the sixteenth century, which has been continued to the present day. The later specimens are terra-cotta with lead glaze, having patterns of coloured earths laid on in relief or encrusted, which, although very effective, are produced at a very cheap rate. Conrad Amenhauser, the potter, has issued some pretty models.

FRANKENTHAL. Paul Hannong, driven from Strasbourg in February 1754, in consequence of the Sèvres monopoly and his persecution on account of the knowledge he possessed of making the true porcelain, founded a manufactory here, which became very successful, especially for porcelain, but fayence was also made. Carl Theodor, the Elector, having conceded him a large fabrique and a grant of money, and subsequently purchased the factory. When the Frankenthal fayence was marked, it bore the monogram *C. T.* (Carl Theodor) as on the porcelain.

FÜNFKIRCHEN (Hungary). In the Paris Exhibition of 1878 there were some decorative pieces of fayence sent by a manufacturer named W. Zsolnay. Some of the forms were quaint and the decorations in arabesques, brilliant, the body soft and glaze good; the mark in blue representing the façades of five churches (Fünfkirchen).

FLÖRSHEIM, on the Main. In the National Museum at Munich there are specimens of fayence attributed to Flörsheim, where a potter named Christoph Mackenhauer carried on the business, at first in his own name, and later under the style of Mackenhauer & Company, until 1825, when, on the death of both partners, a daughter, one Caroline Schmidt, a widow, continued the works for some time. The marks are given in the margin.

The mark of a ship in full sail is also given of a modern fabrique established by W. Dienst in 1880.

ZELL, near Klagenfurt, in the Austrian Alps. A fabrique is said to have been established here by F. Lenz about 1820, and candlesticks and table-services in the Empire style, of a ware something like Wedgwood or Leeds ware, have Zell impressed in the paste. The two marks in the margin are also given by Jännike as those of modern productions at this place by Haager Hörth & Co., and of C. Schaaf, 1845.

NEUHALDENSLEBEN (Hanover). Modern imitations of maiolica have been made here within the last few years, and the marks, being the devices

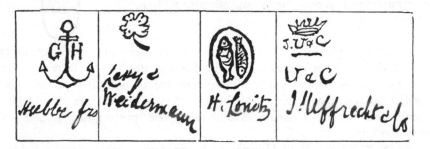

the different firms have adopted, are given, not because the productions have much importance from the collector's point of view, but because without an explanation they are puzzling to localise.

SCHLIERBACH. Jännike mentions a fabrique of earthenware established about 1831, where table-services were made, decorated with flowers in relief, signed Wächtersbach, and marked with a shield as in the margin.

BONN.   The same author gives this mark as that of a fabrique here, which he tells us was established by a potter named Clemens August from Frankfort.

BERNBURG (Western Germany).   Nothing was known of any fayence factory here until quite recently.   An article on the subject appeared in *Der Cicerone* from the pen of Max Sauerlandt, giving illustrations of a few specimens which he attributes to a fayence factory at this place, commencing about 1725.   According to his story, a potter named Johann Kaspar Ripp or Rib, born in 1681, married in Frankfort 1702, and remained there until 1706, when he worked at Anspach some time previous to 1710, since a dish there bears his name, place, and date.   He was a wanderer, apparently resembling our English Billingsby of Derby, and in

Supposed to be Ripp's Signature.   Monogram of Duke Victor Frederick.

1712 was in Nuremberg, and concerned in the foundation of a fayence factory there.   When he was at Zerbst, another town in the western part of Germany, he stated that he had learnt fayence making in Holland, and Mr. Sauerlandt traces him from Hanau to Bernburg in 1720, where, according to some evidence which has satisfied him, he started a factory. The specimens illustrated in *Der Cicerone* have every appearance of the old blue and white Delft; they are said to be well and closely potted, and give a ring similar to porcelain, and one of the marks is the monogram of the Duke Victor Frederick, who was Duke of Anhalt at the time.

Ripp is also believed to have started a factory at Zerbst about the same time, and this is said to have been in existence as late as 1861.

A specimen of fayence in the Hamburg Museum, which is mentioned in Chaffers' previous editions as having an uncertain Delft mark, is now attributed to Bernburg.   Specimens are also in the Museums of Berlin and Leipzig.

SOME MINOR FACTORIES.

The following marks on German fayence are also given in Herr Jännike's *Grundriss der Keramik*.   They are quite unimportant fabriques, and in many cases the productions are of little merit; but as the marks occasionally form the subject of inquiry, the Editor has thought it better to add them with such information with regard to potters' or proprietors' names and the dates given by Jännike.

KÖNIGSTEDTEN.
(J. C. Frede.)

HORNBERG.
Horn frères, 1880.

RÜCKINGEN.

OFFENBACH, 1739.
(Lay.)

AMBERG.
Modern fabrique.
(E. Kick.)

GRUNSTADT.
Bardollo frères.

RHEINSBERG.
(F. Hildebrandt.)

WITTEBURG.

DANTZIG.

SCHWEIDNITZ.
(M. Krause.)

ANNABURG.
(A. Heckmann.)

LESUM. (Vielstick,
1755-94.)
(There is a specimen
of this fayence
(marked) in the
Hamburg Mu-
seum. *See also
notice of Au-
mund on the
following page.*)

VORDAMM.
(A. Francke.)

RENDSBURG (Holstein). The Hamburg Museum Collection contains
a specimen with the word Rendsburg, and a signature of Duve, painter,

the marks being in grey, and also specimens marked as in the margin. Dr. Brinckmann says that this factory was established by C. F. G. Clar and T. Lorentzen, two merchants, the pottery resembling Leeds ware. The initials in the mark are R. F. No. 1, standing for Rendsburg Fabrick, No. 1.

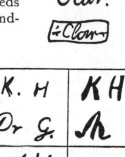

KELLINGHUSEN (Holstein). The Hamburg Museum contains specimens of fayence bearing these marks. Dr. Brinckmann, the curator, has supplied the editor with some particulars of this fayence factory. Killinghusen is a small town in Holstein where four different fayenciers worked. In 1765 Sebastian Heinrich Kirch, who had formerly made fayence at Jever, is said to have been the technical leader, and on his disappearance the work was continued by Carsten Behrens, and after his death in 1782 was carried on by his heirs until 1825 Three other manufactures followed, one owned by the brothers Geppel, one by Jacob Stemann, junior, which lasted until 1840. They produced useful and decorative ware for the country houses on both banks of the Elbe.

K. H	KH
Dr G.	M
K·H·	K4H
P. A	M

GROHN.   Modern fabrique.   .   .   .   .

NEUFRIEDSTEIN.

DORNHEIM.
(Kock and Fischer.)

GRÄFENRODA.
Modern fabrique.
(A. Schneider.)

EISENACH.
(A. Saeltzer.)

AUMUND, near Vegesack (unter-Weser). This factory was established by three merchants, Joh. Christoph Mülhausen, Diderich ter-Hellen, and Wilhelm ter-Hellen in 1750. Their master potter, who directed the works, was T. E. Vielstick, from Brunswick. The mark M. T. T. stands for Mülhausen, Ter-Hellen, Ter-Hellen. Vielstick afterwards set up another factory at Lesum, which continued until 1794. The mark of this potter will be found on p. 296.

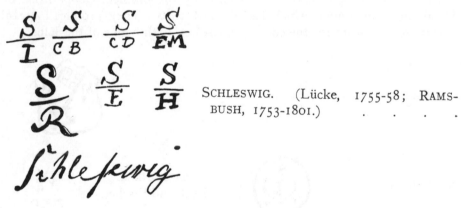

SCHWERIN. This was the capital of the Grand Duchy of Mecklenburg. The fayence factory was founded by a potter named Appelstadt about 1760, whose initial letter A forms part of the mark in the margin. Tureens, vases, bowls, were produced, generally painted in blue.

MINDEN. The letter M is sometimes found on Minden fayence, but it more often bears the mark in the margin of three crescents or half-moons from the coat of arms of the Hanstein family to whom the factory belonged.

JEVER.

SCHLESWIG. (Lücke, 1755-58; RAMSBUSH, 1753-1801.)   .   .   .   .

The fayence factories of Kiel, Stockelsdorf, and Eckernförde were in previous editions of Chaffers classified under Scandinavia and Denmark. They are now included in the German chapter to which they properly belong. Of these Kiel is by far the most important, but at all three some of the best German fayence was produced in the eighteenth century, particularly the ware decorated by what are known as "muffle" colours, that is, those which will not bear the high temperature of an ordinary kiln.

KIEL. A manufactory of fayence was in existence at Kiel, on the shores of the Baltic, towards the latter half of the last century, under the direction of M. Buchwald; one of the principal painters being Abraham Leihamer. Jean Buchwald had been engaged as master-potter under Ehrenreich at Marieberg, 1761 to 1765; a few years after, probably in

1767 or 1768, he became director of the Kiel fabrique; we see by his signed and dated pieces that he was at Kiel in 1768 and 1769. The ware made here was very similar to that of Strasbourg, with coloured scroll border. (*Ker. Gall.*, enlarged edition, fig. 170.)

KIEL. This mark is on a fayence vase and cover, painted with peasants and rural scenery; similar to the Strasbourg style. Dr. Justus Brinckmann says that the initial T in the margin is that of a potter named Taenich, who first established a manufactory of fayence at Kiel in 1758. From 1764 to 1768 he marked specimens with his full name, "Johann Samuel Friedrich Taenich." He was in 1759 first painter under Hannong at the Frankenthal porcelain factory, and later, from 1770-74, was director of a fayence factory of Hubertsburg, in Saxony, and became proprietor of the fayence works at Mosbach, in the Bavarian Palatinate. Nothing is known of him after 1779.

KIEL. On a fayence vase, circa 1770, globular, with raised borders, edged with brownish green and sprigs of flowers, and flowers in full relief on the cover; marked in red. This, and some other pieces of Copenhagen fayence, were brought from the Baltic.

KIEL. This mark, with the initials of Buchwald, the director, and Leihamer, the painter or maker, is found on some fine *camaieu* paintings of bright green, heightened with black and touched with gold; the date is 1769.

KIEL. The mark in the margin is on a bowl with a cover in form of a mitre, probably used for "bishop," a sort of punch or spiced wine: it is painted with ladies and gentlemen seated at a table drinking *bishop* out of a bowl of the same form; on the reverse, soldiers skirmishing. This fine specimen, which was formerly in a private English collection, is now in the Hamburg Museum, which contains other specimens marked with various painters' initials.

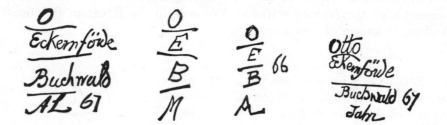

STOCKELSDORF (Holstein). Under this heading Herr Jännike gives two additional forms of Leihamer's signature, with that of Buchwald as director. The Hamburg Museum contains several specimens of this faience with these marks in black, and a milk-pot bears an abbreviation of the name of the place "Stoff." Some fine figure painting was executed here and magnificent stoves were made, painted in colours and gilded.

ECKERNFÖRDE. Another fabrique of which Buchwald was director is mentioned by Jännike, and the marks here given would seem to show that Leihamer also worked here, the A. L. being most probably his signature, as in the preceding notice of Stockelsdorf. There are several

specimens of this fayence bearing these marks in the Hamburg Museum. Dr. Brinckmann says that this fayence factory was established in 1766 by Johann Nicholas Otte, or Otto, under Buchwald's direction. After Otte's death Buchwald, together with Leihamer, migrated to Kiel. Jahn, whose name sometimes occurs on specimens, was an excellent flower painter at Eckernförde.

GERMANY. The mark of a small factory established at Friedberg, in Bavaria, about 1754. C. B. means Chur-Bayera. The works have been started by the order of the Elector of Bavaria, Maximilian Joseph III. (See note on page 279.)

GERMANY—UNCERTAIN MARKS.

A. F.
1687.

GERMANY. Unknown mark. On a fayence plate in the Collection of M. Perillieu of Paris.

m.9.l.
1762

GERMANY. Unknown mark. On a fayence scent vase in the Saxon style, painted in colours.

On an inkstand in form of a fortress, painted with polychrome arabesques in the Renaissance style.

A·B
1638

On a mug of white enamel, painted with arms. Dr. Brinckmann thinks this must be Anspach fayence, as Valentin Bontemp is known to have painted at that pottery as early as 1735.

On a plate, escalloped edge, the border of foliage and landscapes; in the centre a female seated in a landscape with ruins. In the style of Marseilles.

LBurg.
1792.

On vases decorated on white enamel, with arabesque borders and polychrome medallions, in which red and blue predominate.

GHEDT
W:I:M
1750

On a plate, escalloped edge painted with a Chinese subject treated in the style of Louis XIV.—a lady and Chinese attendant.

F.B.G.F.
1779

On a mug, with polychrome decoration in crude colours, outlined with black.

G·C·P.
1750

On a fayence plate, rudely painted with a quaint subject.

On a small pitcher, twisted handle, in the form of S, with blue figures, garlands and birds of a good style. Dr. Justus Brinckmann informs the editor that a fayence painter of this name (N. Possinger) worked at Nuremberg in 1725.

TABLE OF UNKNOWN GERMAN POTTERS' MARKS.

1 AB	**9** ·H.H	**19** M	**28** T.
2 A/P/MR	**10** HE HA	**20** M/6	**29** T DR
	11 P. / So	**21** R / N·	**30** V H / 3
3 B/S	**12** HL	**22** oFF	**31** W
4 DP / 83x	**13** ·HS·	**23** PH.	**32** (flower)
5 F	**14** .K.	**24** K / M / 67	**33** b.
	15 HK	**25** R·M / E	**34** x a
6 F·	**16** HV XX		**35** NO
7 H	**17** S·	**26** S·K	**36** : HN XX
8 H·	**18** L.	**27** KB.B	**37** WS

1. Dish, escalloped, rococo relief on the border, grapes and fruit, in which manganese colour prevails.

2. Basket, plaited and pierced, glossy white enamel, at the bottom a polychrome bouquet of flowers—like Marieberg.

3. Cup ornamented on the outside with bouquets and garlands of flowers in relief, and coloured.

4. Candlestick, greyish enamel, decorated in polychrome.

5. Tureen, the cover surmounted by fruit and leaves, blue decoration, Rouenais style.

6. Pilgrim's bottle, blue ornaments and flowers of German fabrique.

7. Pot-pourri, with garlands of flowers in relief and coloured.

8. Trembleuse cup and saucer, yellow ground, with medallions of flowers.

9. Plateau, with grotesques in green *camaieu*. Moustiers style.

10. Bottles of fayence, green enamel decorated in blue.

11. Vegetable dishes, with flower knobs and polychrome flowers.

12. Jugs of fine fayence, Chinese decoration, rose-colour heightened with gold. German or Italian.

13. Large dish, blue ground, with playing-cards placed irregularly.

14. Fayence of very fine paste, decorated with highly finished figures, in pale colours.

15. Plates, with Rouenais decoration. Dr. Justus Brinckmann informs the editor that this monogram is found on fayence made at Cassel, where a factory existed in 1680. From 1717 to 1724 T. H. Koch worked there, and this monogram of HK is found on fayence of Cassel dated 1719. The identical monogram is also known to occur on some Strasbourg fayence of about 1725, so it is probable Koch went from Cassel to Strasbourg.

16. Jugs, painted with flowers in pale yellow and manganese.

17. Large dish, blue decoration; in centre a landscape.

18. Plate, blue decoration. German.

19. Jug, painted with a landscape in blue.

20. Tureen, on the cover a lemon with leaves. Painted with bouquets of flowers.

21. Tureen, with a branch on the top, painted with flowers. Nuremberg?

22. Dish, escalloped edge and a German inscription between two palm branches.

23. Small dish, with border of plaited branches; in the centre a flower. Baireuth?

24. Large dish, decorated in shaded violet with a large rose, flowers and butterflies. Perhaps Sweden.

25. Cup, with bouquets of flowers. Strasbourg or Sweden?

26. Cream-jug in light fayence, decorated cursively with bouquets, manganese prevailing.

27. Pieces of fayence, decorated in blue-black *camaieu* with bouquets. Probably Stockholm. A somewhat similar mark is attributed to Boussemart of Lille.

28. Large basket-dish. Nuremberg style.

29. Compotiers, with polychrome bouquets, highly finished. Saxon style.

30. Night-lamp, decorated with bouquets, detached in sombre tones of colour.

31. Canette, with polychrome decoration.

32. Plates, decorated in the Strasbourg style, white enamel reliefs.

33. Saucer, painted in the Strasbourg style.

34. Pieces with polychrome decoration, heightened with white.

35. A flask, painted in the Oriental style.

36. A punch-bowl, similar to the Marseilles decoration.

37. A dish, with German characters and flowers.

SWITZERLAND.

Comparatively little has been written about Swiss fayence hitherto, but the opening of the New Swiss National Museum at Zurich will no doubt give a considerable impulse to the study and collection of these interesting productions.

There were numerous local potteries in the German, French, and Italian districts of what is now known generally as Switzerland, and it is only by careful comparison and attention to matters of detail that the specimens can be hypothecated to their respective localities, because Swiss fayence is rarely marked.

The Editor is indebted for much of the information contained in the following notices to Sir Henry Angst, H.B.M. Consul at Zurich, and also director of the Swiss National Museum mentioned above.

ZURICH. Pottery was made here as well as porcelain, and the manufactory was conducted by M. Nœgeli, who in 1830 sent some specimens to the Sèvres Museum. M. Jacquemart mentions a pretty covered urn or pot-pourri jar, enriched with reliefs and decorated with polychrome bouquets fairly outlined, which has the mark in the margin; he also mentions the use of the ordinary barred Z.

WINTERTHUR (Zurich district). Painted stoves of fayence were made here from about the end of the sixteenth century to the beginning of the eighteenth century. In the seventeenth century there were at one time over twenty potteries in this little town. Besides stoves, great quantities of vessels for ordinary daily use were made, large plates and dishes, having the arms of the family painted in the centre, also allegorical, biblical, and other subjects, the chief colours employed being blue, green, yellow, and pale red. The trade was carried on by families as a tradition, and those of Phau, Graf, and Erkardt are among the best known which have been handed down to us. Inkstands, jugs of many forms, are still to be found in collections of Swiss pottery. Winterthur pottery is never marked, but on the stoves there is generally a name and date. M. Jacquemart mentions that the Winterthur potters were partial to monumental designs, fortresses flanked by towers, embattled castles covered with rich arabesques in the Renaissance style; one in the Pascal Collection is signed A. B. and dated 1638; another bears the date only, 26th September 1689; the latter is a stove designed as a fortress, its approaches filled with soldiers.

BERNE. There were several potteries during the seventeenth and eighteenth centuries in this district; among others those of :—

(a) SIMENTHAL. White glaze, painting in colours over the glaze. Manufactured in the Bernese Oberland.

(b) LANGNAU. Yellowish ground, outlines engraved in the ground, the colours laid on under a transparent glaze, manufactured principally in the Emmenthal.

(c) HEIMBERG. White or dark brown ground, the outlines of the design engraved like the pottery of Langnau.

There are no marks for any of these fabriques. M. Jacquemart mentions some stoves, or "furnaces," as they have been called, which M. Gasnault considers came from the borders of Lake Constance and the Vorarlberg, and a charming little model of a stove which he purchased from the descendant of a manufacturer; it is signed E. I. F. 1772, and is the work of Emmanuel Früting of Berne, born 1745, died 1798.

Schaphuÿsen.
Genrit Euers.

SCHAFFHAUSEN. There was a manufactory here in the beginning of the sixteenth century. This mark is on a dish, of brown ground, with white and blue figures, representing the Flagellation, and a German inscription with the name of the potter, Genrit Evers, and in another part his initials,

G. E.; it is in the Musée de Cluny. There is a date on the piece, but unfortunately the figure denoting the century is partly obliterated. It is probably 1695, from the costume; it is certainly not later, but has been quoted by some as 1495, which reading is quite erroneous.

MUNSTER (Lucerne). Pieces attributed to a pottery here are marked with M, according to Sir H. Angst.

LENZBURG (Aargovie). Sir H. Angst considers that some specimens of Swiss pottery marked L. B should be attributed to a pottery at this place.

STECKBORN. M. Jacquemart mentions a stove at the château of Sigmaringen, decorated with painted figures in eighteenth century costumes, signed Daniel Hafner, Steckborn.

THOUNE, or THUN. There appears to have been a fabrique of considerable extent at Thoune, or Thun, near the lake of that name in the canton of Berne, but we do not know the date of its foundation. It does not appear, however, to have existed more than some thirty or forty years, to judge from the specimens we have seen. The ware is a reproduction of highly glazed *sgraffito* ware. Specimens marked as in the margin are in the possession of Mr. Henry Graham of the *Aberdeen Free Press*, and the Editor has seen some with the name " Thoune " only.

GRÈS.

Stoneware with transparent glaze is called in France GRÈS or GRÈS ÇERAME, and in Germany STEINGUT; but the term *Grès de Flandres* is most frequently used in alluding to it. The classification of the stoneware vases of the sixteenth and seventeenth centuries has never hitherto been seriously attempted, but the whole series of the *grès çerame* has been placed under one unsatisfactory heading, GRÈS DE FLANDRES. From the compact and almost imperishable nature of the material, and its capability of receiving impressions of subjects in relief, more or less artistic, by means of moulds, at a comparatively cheap rate, these stoneware vases have been preserved to our time in considerable quantities. It must be borne in mind that these vessels are not always made in the year indicated, for the moulds were used successively through a series of years, and it is no uncommon occurrence to find two different dates on the same specimen.

An attempt has been recently made to localise the places of manufacture, which has been generally adopted on the Continent, and we are bound, in the absence of more reliable information, to lay before our readers the result of researches made on the probable sites of the fabriques in the Netherlands and the Rhenish Provinces.

At the Exhibitions of Brussels and Dusseldorf in 1880, a grand display of vases of the *grès çerame* was collected from all available sources, including some of the finest from the Victoria and. Albert Museum. Mons. H. Schuermans of Liège, at the request of the President, wrote a descriptive account of these vessels, he having previously made a catalogue of the numerous specimens in the Museum of the Porte-du-Halle at Brussels.

From unwearied investigations in excavations on the sites of disused fabriques and from written records, aided by a careful comparison of examples in various public and private collections, M. Schuermans may be considered a competent authority. He has ventured to promulgate an entirely new classification, based not only on his personal researches, but upon the discoveries of M. Schmitz at Raeren in 1874 and of M. Dornbusch of Cologne in 1873, with others who have paid especial attention to the subject. His arrangement of localities where the fabriques of *grès* existed has been generally adopted by collectors and directors of museums abroad.

The usual designation of this stoneware was formerly *Grès Flamand* or *Grès de Flandres*, but the appellation has been considered incorrect, inasmuch as there were several fabriques of similar stoneware on the borders of the Rhine. Flanders, as at present constituted, could not have produced this particular *grès*, for in the valley of the Scheldt the necessary materials for its manufacture are not to be found. But in the sixteenth century, when this industry flourished, Flanders comprised geographically all the Low Countries (Pays Bas), including that portion now ceded to France. All these fabriques, therefore, whether in Brabant or Limburg, or in the counties of Hainault and Namur, were at that time considered Flemish.

It is proved by documents, as well as by discoveries of débris of pottery and the remains of kilns, that stoneware was made at Verviers, Dinant, Namur, Buffioulx, Chatelet, and other places, many doubtless being of inferior quality, all of which are situated in the valleys of the Sambre and the Meuse. The most important factory, however, was at Raeren, near Aix-la-Chapelle. The Rhenish Provinces of Germany furnish us with numerous fabriques, the more important being at Frechen in the vicinity of Cologne, Siegburg, opposite Bonn, Grenzhausen and Höhr near Coblentz. A peculiar variety of stoneware was made at Creussen, near Baireuth in Bavaria.

It is worthy of note that the earliest and most important collections of this *grès*, made in the beginning of last century, were purchased at Ghent, notably those of M. d'Huyvetter, M. Verhelst, the Comte de Renesse, and M. Minard; the last was presented to the city of Ghent. M. Schuermans has consequently arrived at the conclusion that some of the finest examples of the *grès çerame* were fabricated in the Netherlands, especially at Raeren, where numerous kilns have been found and vast quantities of fragments of *grès* exhumed.

RAEREN is in the ancient Duchy of Limburg, about two leagues from Aix-la-Chapelle. Until the treaty of 1814 Raeren was part of the Pays Bas. When this industry commenced is unknown, but it certainly flourished throughout the sixteenth century. The vases made here were usually of cylindro-spheroidal form, with a central band containing subjects in low relief (and frequently inscriptions), such as dances of peasants, shields of arms of states, princes, and nobles, illustrations from the Old and New Testaments, especially the history of Susanna. This was a favourite subject in Flanders, and these were probably made expressly for that country. It is seen on the fine chimney-piece at Bruges, and on the terra-cotta bricks found in the old houses of Ghent and Bruges, the inscriptions on these vases being in pure Flemish, differing materially from the Low German on others made in the Rhenish Provinces. The necks are ornamented with medallions, and the ground-work with Renaissance strap-work, guilloche borders, &c., the colours being usually brown, sometimes greyish-white with reliefs in blue. Some of the vases are of annular shape, called *Ringkrüge*, with portraits in relief, and frequently bearing the marks of the Raeren potters. The most celebrated makers were the Mennickens, especially Baldem (Baldwin), Jan Emens, Engel Kran, &c., whose names are found in ancient documents, and are still borne by many of the present inhabitants of the locality. The most important example of the Raeren stoneware is the noble ewer formerly in the D'Huyvetter Collection, now preserved in the Victoria and Albert Museum, which clearly indicates the origin of this particular *grès de Flandres*. The spout is in form of a lion's head, and a similar ornament is at the bottom of the handle; on the central band are represented in relief personifications of the seven virtues and the seven liberal arts; below these are the following inscriptions: WAN . GOT . WIL . SO . IST . MEIN . ZILL . MESTER . BALDEM . MENNICKEN . POTTENBECKER . WONEDE . ZO . DEN . RORREN . IN . LEIDEN . GEDOLT . 1577. (*I submit to God's will. Master Baldem Mennicken, potter, dwelling at Rorren. Patience under suffering.*) On each side is a circular medallion of the arms of England, inscribed WAPEN . VON . ENGELLENT . AO . 77. It has also the following abbreviations, found on many other Raeren vases: H.S. (*Hungrigen speisen*); D.DR. (*Durstigen dräncken*); N.K. (*Nackten kleiden*); GEF.T. (*Gefangenen trosten*), &c. A canette of pyramidal form, with incuse flowers and a medallion in front of figures in relief, has the name of IAN . BALDEMS 1596. Another cruche, with the history of Susanna in relief, bears the maker's name, ENGEL. KRAN. A° 1584; and a canette, with the history of Esther, maker FANT. GENAT. All these are in the Victoria and Albert Museum.

The celebrated Collection of M. d'Huyvetter of Ghent was dispersed after his death. Many of the best pieces were bought by M. Weckherlin of Brussels; others found their way into public museums. There is a good collection in the Museum at the Porte-du-Halle, Brussels, especially a candelabrum, dated 1550, one of the earliest dates we have met with.

The Vicaire Schmitz, emulating the example of M. Dornbusch, who discovered the white stoneware of Siegburg, commenced the excavations. at Raeren about the year 1872, and continued his explorations until 1874. He was rewarded by finding large quantities of this identical *grès*, of precisely the same types, bearing dates from 1560 to 1620, and the remains. of numerous kilns at Raeren and its immediate environs. Among the more highly finished vases of the sixteenth century were also exhumed others of a more remote period, similar to the legendary *Jacoba Kannetje*, of a very rude character.

It is supposed that the decadence of this industry at Raeren took place in or about 1618, the commencement of the Thirty Years' War, which put an end to the exportation of this ware to Germany, where it had found so ready a sale.

Editor's Note to 13th Edition.—The valuable monograph recently published on this subject from the pen of Otto von Falke gives us many particulars hitherto unknown about this German stoneware. The craft seems to have commenced in Raeren as early as 1500, and the potters occupied themselves with making imitations of the small Gothic cans and funnel-shaped beakers under the influence of Cologne and also of Siegburg. In 1570 we first get a dated specimen from the hands of Jan Emens, the most celebrated maker of this stoneware, and there is a canette in the Victoria and Albert Museum, and another in the Louvre, bearing the date 1594, also some signed J E M. Then we have jugs and tankards signed by pupils of his, P. E., the initials of Pieter Emens, and potters named Kalb and Kalfs, with signatures E. E. and G. E., all on work in the style of Jan Emens with dates 1578 and later.

About the middle of the seventeenth century the craft seems to have declined, and nothing of importance was produced.

In the latter part of the nineteenth century a revival was attempted by Hubert Schiffer, who has made some good brown stoneware.

FRECHEN. The fabrication of *grès* in this locality probably commenced at the epoch when the municipality of Cologne, in order to avoid the frequent fires which occurred within its walls, interdicted the stoneware potters from continuing their industry therein, and it was then carried on in the vicinity.

From the commencement of the sixteenth century, or perhaps earlier, the *grès* of Frechen took an artistic character. The jugs and vases are mostly spherical, bearing frequently a central band with Gothic letters and moral sentiments, sometimes alphabets, and on the belly medallions. or other detached ornaments. Towards the end of the sixteenth century arms were introduced in rosettes, with spots of blue enamel on brown ground. The brown stoneware jugs so well known from their frequent ocurrence in excavations in the metropolis were probably made for general use at Frechen, as we learn from the petition of William Simpson to Queen Elizabeth, before alluded to (p. 44). These vessels had bearded heads under the spouts, which we were able to identify as the *Bellarmin* so frequently alluded to in old plays; but jugs of a similar ware were also made, called *Bartmann*, the mask being more elongated; the variation, however, is more easily recognised than described.

SIEGBURG. The fabrication of *grès* is very ancient in this locality. The oldest (thirteenth and fourteenth centuries) are often in brownish-grey with pinched feet like the Jacoba Kannetje. In the sixteenth century, however, the ware assumed a more artistic character, and a fine whitish-grey clay was the material used, sometimes styled *terre de pipe*. The usual forms are cylindrical canettes, called in Germany *Snel*, with handles and long oblique spouts rising from the central bands, attached to the neck by a scroll or flat piece of clay. These are known as *Toot-kruik Schnabelkrug*, &c. The ornamentation in low relief consists of elaborate Renaissance arabesques, with masks, coats of arms, &c.

Editor's Note to the 13th Edition.—Herr Otto von Falke's contribution to the History of German Stoneware recently published (1908; see Bibliography, and already quoted above) informs us that the most important fabriques of this Siegburg *grès* was that of the family of Knütgens, of whom there were three master potters, Anno, Peter, and Christian. The work of Anno is the best, being inspired by the late Gothic. The Knütgen family were not only potters, but they were wealthy citizens, and filled many important municipal offices. Some of their jugs bear as part of the decorations the arms of Julich-Clere-Berg, the reigning Duke of their time. They are generally of the light-coloured stoneware, almost the colour of the putty, and the forms are generally those funnel-shaped tankards smaller at the top than the bottom, and relief work well executed, but there is not much originality or variety of design. Some are marked with initials L. W., and dates are from 1570-80. Some fine stoneware tankards marked with initials F. T. are attributed to a workman in the employment of the first Knütgen. His best work is the famous Lazurus tankard in the Munich Museum, which he has signed four times : the date is 1569. Another monogram, H. H., marks the work of Hans Hilgens, who lived and worked at Siegburg from 1569-96, and this is one of the best known of the marks on German stoneware. Other makers who have left some of their work marked with initials are Flack, Omian, Simons, and also potters signing C. M. and L. W. After 1600 very little was produced, and when the town was destroyed in 1632 by the Swedes, the craft seems to have disappeared.

In 1873 M. Dornbusch commenced his researches in order to discover the origin of the *grès*, and exhumed a quantity of debris of an ancient Rhenish fabrique at Siegburg, opposite Bonn, on the Sieg, the other side of the Rhine. Following up his discoveries of this peculiar ware, he consulted the archives, and found documents proving that a large manufactory formerly existed there, which had previously been erroneously adjudged to the category of *grès de Flandres*. His experiences were published at Cologne in the *Annales de la Société Historique du Bas-Rhin*.

The white earth of Siegburg has been used in the present century by a potter of the locality named P. Löwenich, and the vessels may be confounded by some inexperienced persons with the old, being of good finish.

GRENZHAUSEN (Nassau), near Coblentz, and HöHR, are both situated in the country called *Kannenbackerlandchen*, and to these localities are attributed the *grès* of a fine quality which is in imitation of the more ancient stoneware of Raeren, for which it is easily mistaken. Some of the vessels made here bear the initials G.R., which refer to Guillaume III.

of Orange-Nassau, King of England. A keg or barrel of greyish-blue, of
the incontestable Nassau fabrique, bears the letters G.R., with portraits of
William III. and Mary of York, his Queen, with the device " AN . ONSEN .
HOLLANSSEN . TUYN . SOO . BLOEIN . ORANIE . APELLEN . EN . ROOSEN."
(In our Dutch garden thus flourish the oranges and roses.) These were
made for the English market.

From some documents recently published by W. Müller (*Das-Nas-
sauische Krug und Kannerbackerland und seiner Industrie*) it is shown that
the Counts of Wied and Isenburg sent to Siegburg and other places for
potters, to give a fresh impulse to the ceramic industry of Grenzhausen.

The decoration of a more recent date consists of a fine blue enamel
on grey, with *champlévé* or incused ornaments on engine-turned ground in
leaves, flowers, rosettes, &c.

The fabrication of *grès* has still more recently been revived in Nassau,
imitating the ancient *grès* of the locality.

CREUSSEN, near Baireuth, in Bavaria. The ceramic industry of this
locality was of longer duration than those we have before spoken of.
Many of these vessels have a simple dark-brown glaze, but the greater
part are covered with brilliant colours and painted enamel inscriptions.
The varieties are called in Germany *Trauerkrüge* or mourning jugs, being
ornamented with guilloches and bands in white and black, sometimes
partly gilt; *Planeten-, Jagd-*, and *Apostel-krüge*, in allusion to the subjects,
planetary, the chase, and our Saviour and the Apostles; sometimes oviform, but usually cylindrical, in all shades of the prismatic colours.

The following anecdote shows the German characteristic of these
Apostle-jugs, which were so popular in that country; it is from a comic
poem called the *Jobsiade*, by Kortüm of Mulheim, published in 1784. The
student Jobs presents himself for examination, and in answer to the question, "What is a bishop?" he replies, "An excellent liquor composed
of wine, sugar, spices, and orange-juice." Then to the next question,
"What is an apostle?" he says, "An apostle is a large jug, which will
contain a sufficient quantity of wine or beer, from which at banquets, or
in the country, the students quaff when thirsty." The manufacture was
discontinued about the beginning of the last century. One of these
tankards in the Museum at Brussels bears the date 1710. It may be
observed, as a caution, that a great number of these mugs have come from
the manufactory of an uniform brown colour, the ornaments and figures
not enamelled in colours; these have been subsequently painted in oil
colours by dealers; but the fraud is easily detected by scraping them with
a knife, which will remove the paint, while the enamel resists.

LAUENSTEIN, near Coblentz. Established about 1760. The *grès* or
stoneware of grey and blue, ornamented with flowers and other ornaments
in incused patterns graved on the surface, is still made in large quantities,
and is carried by the Rhine boats to the markets in Holland, where it
meets with a ready sale. There were also manufactories of *grès* in the
vicinity of Coblentz, at Neiderfell, Langerwche, and Vallendar, still exist-

ing towards the end of the eighteenth century, specimens of which are in the Sèvres Museum, acquired in 1809.

METTLACH (Rhenish Prussia). A modern fabrique by MM. Villeroy and Boch, *grès* with *platinée* ornaments, examples of which are in the Sèvres Museum.

Herr Jännike gives these marks as those of this fabrique:—

REGENSBURG (Ratisbon). *Grès* or stoneware was made here at an early period. The first specimens were of a brown common earth, made of clay from Abensburg, with ornaments and mythological subjects: the ware was subsequently much improved. Jerome Hoppfer, an engraver of the sixteenth century, who lived here, signed his *grès* with the initials I.H. There are some specimens in the Berlin Museum, and two large vases, dated 1715, in the Historischen Verrein at Ratisbon. In the eighteenth century earthenware was made here of both lead glaze and stanniferous enamel.

DRYHAUSEN, near Marieburg, in Hesse. There were manufactories here from the fifteenth to the nineteenth century for the *grès* or stoneware, but we have no particulars respecting them. The Hessian wares were largely imported into England in the sixteenth, seventeenth, and eighteenth centuries.

HUBERTSBERG, in Saxony (1784). The Count Marcolini established a manufactory of earthenware with salt glaze in the character of English pottery, where Wedgwood was also imitated.

These marks are also given by Jännike as those used at this fabrique.

Several illustrations of these *grès* jugs will be found in *Ker. Gall.*, enlarged edition, figs. 159-165.

GRES—UNKNOWN MARKS.

F. T. 1559. A jug of white stoneware, 13 inches high; subject, The Prodigal Son; Nuremberg Museum, and M. Milani's Collection, Frankfort (*see* Edit. note to 13th edit., p. 309).

H^{V}G. A canette, with three coats of arms and arabesques; Victoria and Albert Museum, £5.

N E M 1589 A jug, with portraits of the Kings and Queens of France, Hungary, and Prussia; and another, in the Sauvageot Collection, bearing the same mark.

B. V. 1574. A canette, with medallions of David, Venus, Lot, and the Crucifixion, in the Victoria and Albert Museum.

K? R. 1598. Jug, with medallions of dancing figures and German inscription; Louvre Collection, No. 416.

L. W. 1573. A jug of conical form, with medallions and bands, months of the year, &c.; Louvre Collection, No. 402 (*see* Edit. note to 13th edit., p. 309).

M. G. 1586. A gourd, with long neck, of white ware, in the Weckherlin Collection.

L. W. In the Sauvageot Collection and Victoria and Albert Museum (*see* Edit. note to 13th edit., p. 309).

W. T. Drinking-cup, in the form of a book; Sauvageot Collection (*see* Edit. note to 13th edit., p. 309).

R.V.H Blue and grey jug, of the seventeenth century; Sauvageot Collection.

M. O. Blue and grey jug, with medallions of the Electors of Saxony; Sauvageot Collection.

I. E. These initials, which are those of Jan Emens, are found on some of the finest pieces in the Weckherlin Collection; also on a canette, dated 1594, in the Victoia and Albert Museum; a cruche, same date; and one in the Louvre, No. 411.

I. R. 1588. With the arms of Saxony, of brown ware; Weckherlin Collection.

M. G. 1586. A gourd, with long neck, of white ware in the Weckherlin Collection.

B. M. The initials of Baldem Mennicken, sixteenth century; Louvre Collection, No. 415.

A vase, in blue and grey, with three handles; sixteenth century; Louvre Collection, No. 425.

On a jug, of the sixteenth century; Louvre Collection, No. 455.

Cruche, with masks and arabesques, and medallions of the arms of the Electors; Sauvageot Collection, No. 417.

H. W.

Enamelled fayence tea and coffee services of the eighteenth century, marked with three anchors the manufacture of M. L. Cremer.

ORIENTAL POTTERY AND PORCELAIN

China

POTTERY

THOUGH the traditions of the potter's art in China go back to fabulous times, the earliest Chinese pottery with attractions that appeal to the Western collector is the green-glazed ware of the Han dynasty (206 B.C.-220 A.D.). A considerable quantity of this has reached Europe in recent years from the ancient tombs of Northern China, which the construction of railways has incidentally laid bare. This mortuary pottery is not only of great antiquarian interest, in that it represents the familiar objects of everyday life during the Han dynasty, but it is also exceedingly attractive owing to the skill and vigour with which these representations have been modelled, and the beauty of the green glaze to which long years of burial have imparted wonderful iridescent tints The tomb of a substantial person at this period was furnished with clever models of his house, his farm buildings, his implements, and even his family, his retinue, and his domestic animals, besides a complete outfit of crockery, including majestic wine jars, incense-burners, and more ordinary kitchen utensils. In many cases these models are so skilfully idealised that they have assumed a highly ornamental character without losing the truthfulness of their natural forms, and the handsome wine vases and jars are enriched with ornamental friezes in low relief, in which hunting scenes, wild animals, and mythological creatures are figured with great vivacity and artistic feeling. The ware itself is a red or grey pottery, varying from comparative softness to the hardness of stoneware, and the objects, though sometimes unglazed, are usually covered with a green glaze, which has become in most cases iridescent and crackled. In some instances the glaze is of a brownish yellow colour, and occasionally it is mottled with dark purplish brown, while the use of white clay or slip in ornamentation is not unknown. How long this class of pottery continued in use is not yet ascertained, but there is reason to think that it was made as late as the T'ang dynasty (618-906 A.D.).

Of the other kinds of pottery made in China during the first centuries of our era there is little definite knowledge. A single mention of "one lac-black earthenware dish" occurs in the T'ao Shuo[1] as found in the tomb of the Empress Tao, consort of Wu Ti (140-85 B.C.). Two large vases in the British Museum, of ovoid shape, with constricted mouth and four loop-handles on the shoulders, have a red stoneware body with a mottled golden bronze glaze covering the upper part only. There is reason to believe that they were made before the sixth century of our era. Chinese literature speaks of green ware imitating green glass as made during the Sui dynasty (581-617 A.D.), but its precise nature is left in doubt, and the theory that it was a forerunner of the later celadon is purely conjectural.

During the T'ang dynasty (618-906 A.D.) great progress was made in every branch of the fine arts in China, and though little is known as yet of the pottery of the period, there is every reason to suppose that it shared in the general advance. To this time may be fairly assigned certain beautifully modelled human and animal figures, formed in a soft white clay as fine as pipe-clay, sometimes coated with a thin glaze of yellowish tint, and sometimes left unglazed, and painted with black and red pigments. There are vases, too, with ovoid bodies and small necks, flanked with a pair of high dragon handles, which probably belonged to the sepulchral furniture of this period. These are generally of dense grey-white stoneware, with a wash of white clay and glaze, sometimes pale yellow, sometimes boldly splashed with brownish yellow, green, and manganese purple. This dappled glaze, the forerunner of the tiger-skin and tortoiseshell glazes, is found on pottery stored in the Shoso-in at Nara, in Japan, which is not later in date than the eighth century of our era. In the British Museum there is a vase with dull purplish black glaze, and two tea-bowls with metallic reddish brown glaze, remotely resembling Samian ware, which were found in a tomb, reasonably supposed to be of the T'ang period. Other specimens attributed to this period have a fine white semi-porcelain body with pale green glaze, and a grey-white body with surface wash of white clay and a creamy white glaze, which recall the descriptions in Chinese literature of the celebrated Yüeh and Hsing wares. The one made at Yüeh Chou in Chekiang, and the other at Hsing Chou, in Chihli, are contrasted as resembling, the latter silver or snow, the former ice or jade. The Ta-yi kilns in Szech'üan were celebrated in the poetry of the period for a ware white as snow and resonant as jade. It is probable that some of these wares represent the earliest kinds of porcelain, but that is a point to which we shall refer later, keeping for the present to the history of pottery. The reign of Shih Tsung (954-9 A.D.), of the After Chou dynasty, is celebrated in history for a ware with glaze which was "blue as the sky after rain," usually known as Ch'ai ware; but as it was made for a short time only, and for Imperial

[1] *Description of Chinese Pottery and Porcelain, being a translation of the T'ao Shuo.* By S. W. Bushell, 1910; p. 96.

use, no actual specimens are at present known to exist. A lineal descendant of this was the almost equally nebulous Ju ware which was made for the northern Sung Emperors at Ju-chou for a brief period. The principal Sung wares are the Ju, Ko, Kuan, Ting, Lung-ch'üan and Chün wares. They are usually classed as porcelain by the Chinese, though in many cases they are but a fine stoneware, often of red-brown body, and in the case of the Chün varying from semi-porcelain to soft brick red and buff earthenware. The feature of all these Sung wares was the glaze, and though fineness of grain and good potting were highly esteemed, it seems to have been a matter of no moment whether the body of the ware were white or dark in colour. The colours of the Ju and Kuan glazes seem to have been as a rule various tones of pale blue or green, though some of the latter are described as deep green and ash-grey. The Ko wares are described as pale blue or green, rice-white, and ash-grey, and they were distinguished as a rule by a crackled surface. The Lung-ch'üan wares have been identified with the well-known celadon, the body of which is a greyish white porcellanous stoneware and the glaze a thick, smooth, and semi-transparent covering, varying in tint from olive to pale grey-green, or sea green. The Ting wares comprise a great variety, from a fine, white and often translucent porcelain with smooth white glaze of faintly creamy tint to a buff stoneware, with yellowish glaze minutely crackled. The finer kind was known as Pai Ting or white Ting ware, and the coarser as Tu Ting or earthy Ting ware; the former was very highly valued. Both the celadon and the Ting wares are often orna- mented with designs, boldly carved, finely traced with a point or pressed on a mould, floral patterns, flying phœnixes, fish or mandarin ducks being favourite forms of ornament.

The Ting ware was originally made at Ting-chou, in Chihli, under the Northern Sung (960-1127 A.D.), but it has been copied with varying success in many other parts of China, and its manufacture continues to this day. Similarly the Lung-ch'üan celadon was made near the township of that name in the province of Chekiang, during the Sung dynasty, but the manufacture was removed to Ch'u-chou-fu under the Ming; and though it seems to have disappeared from this locality in the seventeenth century, the celadon glaze is still made at Ching-tê-chên and Canton, and in many places in Japan.

The Chün wares, so called from Chün-chou in Honan, are noted for a variety of thick, variegated and opalescent glazes. The colours are described by the Chinese as (1) rose-crimson; (2) pyrus-japonica pink; (3) aubergine purple; (4) plum-coloured blue; (5) mule's liver mingled with horse's lung; (6) sky-blue; (7) rice coloured (*mi-sê*); (8) dark purple; (9) furnace transmutations.

The more usual tints are pale lavender or dove-grey, often broken with one or more accidental patches of contrasting colour, usually purple or crimson. Among the rarest and richest are the dappled crimson and crushed strawberry reds. But of all these Sung wares there are many varieties which space will not permit to be discussed here. Few of them bear marks, the principal exception being the Chün wares, which are often incised with a numeral (see p. 359).

There were many lesser factories operating during the Sung dynasty, most of which were engaged in imitating the products of the greater factories already mentioned. The two best known are the pottery at Chien-an (afterwards at Chien-yang) in the province of Fukien, where a dark-bodied ware was made with thick black glaze, mottled and streaked with golden brown,[1] and the factories at Tz'ŭ-chou in Chihli, where a creamy white ware of Tu Ting type has been made from Sung times to this day. The latter ware is distinguished by skilful painting in black-brown slip or pigment and maroon slip, and more recently, in red, green, and blue. The older paintings are often in a sketchy and impressionist style, but vigorous and bold. They are sometimes signed. The creamy glaze is sometimes combined with dark brown or black, and there are some examples in which the ornament is achieved by the graffiato process, i.e., covering the ware with a wash of clay which contrasts in colour with the body, and carving or engraving the ornament through this outer coating.

Imperial factories were established in Chang-nan-chên in the province of Kiangsi in the Sung dynasty, and the name of the town was changed to Ching-tê-chên during the Ching-tê period (A.D. 1004-7) of that era. The district had been noted for pottery as early as the Han dynasty, and it eventually became the ceramic metropolis of China; but, as its fame is chiefly associated with porcelain, we shall return to it later.

The use of glazed pottery for architectural ornaments was appreciated in China from very early times. Roof-tiles with disks at one end ornamented with dragons and other devices in sunk relief were used as borders, while elaborate mouldings, finials, and dragon gargoyles, besides spirited figures modelled in full relief, are found on old and modern temples. Perhaps the most celebrated structure in which the potter played a prominent part was the so-called porcelain pagoda of Nanking. It was commenced by the Ming Emperor Yung-lo (1403-24), completed in 1430, and destroyed during the Taiping rebellion in 1853. White porcelain bricks were used in the construction of the lowest story, the rest was faced with glazed earthenware. The manufacture of this architural pottery must have formed a considerable industry in various parts of China during the Ming dynasty; and the potteries did not confine themselves to tile-work and temple ornaments, but produced ornamental figures, incense-burners, vases, besides the more ordinary crockery with the same materials. These, like the architectural fittings, usually have a hard buff pottery body, with rich glazes of green, yellow, manganese purple, and turquoise blue, singly, or in tasteful combinations of two or more of these colours. Extensive potteries near Peking still manufacture pottery of this kind, and successfully imitate the old turquoise and purple porcelains which are so highly prized by collectors.

---

[1] The "hare's fur" or "partridge" cups, so highly prized by the tea-drinkers in Japan, were originally made here.

The province of Kuang-tung has been celebrated for pottery since the Sung dynasty, the districts of Amoy and Yang-chiang being specially concerned in the industry. Perhaps the best known production of this province is the "Canton stoneware," a hard grey or red-brown ware with thick mottled glaze, in which blue, grey, brown, and green contend for the mastery. This class of ware dates from the Ming dynasty, and is still made in large quantities at Yang-chiang. Every kind of ornamental and useful ceramic object is made here, from roof-tiles to ginger jars; and green, turquoise, yellow, purple, and brown glazes are used as at the Peking potteries. The age of these Canton wares is often very difficult to determine. A good celadon glaze is also used, and among the most striking productions of the Canton potteries are well-modelled figures of deities and mythical personages, with the flesh in brown unglazed ware, and the draperies richly covered with celadon green or variegated glazes. The Canton wares are not infrequently marked with potters' names.

Pottery of a very distinctive type is made at Yi-hsing-hsien in the prefecture of Chang-chou-fu, province of Kiangsu, where the industry has flourished since the reign of Chêng Tê (1506-1521). These potteries, which were founded by Kung Ch'un, are noted for a fine stoneware, varying in hardness and colour, the latter being most commonly red, but sometimes drab or buff. All kinds of objects were made, but the ware is best known in Europe from the teapots which were largely imported by the Portuguese and Dutch in the seventeenth and eighteenth centuries, and were imitated in Holland by De Milde and De Calve, and in England by Dwight and Elers. The vessels are usually unglazed: they are often ornamented with small applied reliefs, or moulded in fanciful forms, the teapots and water-droppers resembling lotus seedpods, finger citrons, pomegranates, bamboo joints, phœnixes, ducks, and what not. Glazes, however, were sometimes used, for we read of a celebrated potter named Ou, who flourished in the reign of Wan-li (1573-1619), imitating the old Kuan and Chün glazes on Yi-hsing ware. Later on, and particularly since the eighteenth century, opaque enamels have been used to decorate the ware. Potters' names are commonly found impressed with a seal on the Yi-hsing wares (see p. 375).

PORCELAIN.

The exact period when porcelain was first made is still a matter of doubt, though its Chinese origin is beyond dispute. The theory that it dates back as far as the Han dynasty (206 B.C.-220 A.D.) seems to rest chiefly on the assertion that the word *tz'ŭ*, which is now used for denoting porcelain, was invented at that time. But the word *tz'ŭ* is freely applied to dark-coloured and opaque wares which would be classed in Europe as stoneware, and it may just as well have been coined in the Han dynasty to distinguish vitrified stoneware from soft earthenware. In fact the Chinese cannot be said to possess any word which is used in the restricted modern sense of our word *porcelain*. The terms in general use in Chinese literature are *t'ao*, *yao*, and *tz'ŭ*, of which the first two literally mean a "kiln," and can apply equally well to any kind of ware baked in a kiln. Indeed the word *yao*, which is said to have come into use first in the T'ang dynasty (618-906 A.D.), is most commonly used in the comprehensive sense of "ware," and is applied indifferently to opaque stoneware such as Chün yao, and to the translucent porcelain of the Ming dynasty such as Yung yao (Yung Lo porcelain) and Hsüan yao (Hsüan Tê porcelain). Much more convincing evidence is provided by literary references in the T'ang dynasty, *e.g.*, to the wares of T'ao Yü in the seventh century, which are described as "imitation jade," and to the Hsing Chou and Yüeh Chou wares, which are compared to snow and ice, silver and jade, and to the white bowls from the Ta Yi kilns in Szech'üan, which "surpassed hoar frost and snow." A still more interesting reference is quoted by Dr. Bushell[1] to the words of the Arab traveller Soleyman: "There is in China a very fine clay with which they make vases which are transparent as glass: water is seen through them. These vases are made of clay."[2]

It is practically certain, then, that translucent porcelain was made in China in the T'ang dynasty, if not earlier, but the matter is of academic interest, for at present we possess no examples which can be reasonably dated earlier than the Sung dynasty (960-1267 A.D.). As for our own word *porcelain*, it is only within the last two centuries that it has come to be used definitely for the white, translucent, and highly vitrified ware which we distinguish from both earthenware and stoneware. Its derivation is probably from *porcellana*, a cowry shell, and it was formerly applied to shell-like substances, of which porcelain was one. It was, for instance, used for cups and ornaments made of strips of mother-of-pearl shell, and Marco Polo (in the fourteenth century) employed it in this sense as well as in reference to Chinese porcelain. For a long time it was applied to fine white earthenwares, such as Damascus ware, maiolica and Delft, and even to the red stoneware teapots imported from China in the seventeenth century and imitated in Holland by De Milde and others, and in England by Dwight and Elers.

CHING-TÊ-CHÊN.

Before passing to the discussion of the various kinds of Chinese porcelain, it will not be out of place to give a brief description of the great ceramic centre, Ching-tê-Chên, the Stoke-upon-Trent of China. As already stated, it was established as early as the sixth century, and was then known as Chang-nan-chên; but its great importance dates from the time of the imperial patronage accorded to it in the Ching Tê period, when it was called Ching-tê-chên, or the borough of Ching Tê; this was in

[1] Introduction to his translation of the *T'ao Shuo*, p. xiv.

[2] *Relation des Voyages fait par les Arabes et les Persans dans l'Inde et à la Chine dans le IXe siècle de l'Ere chrétienne*, traduit par M. Reinaud, Paris 1845.

A.D. 1004. The Père d'Entrecolles, a Jesuit, who went into China to establish missions in many of the provinces, collected some valuable details of the manufacture of porcelain. These he fully describes in a letter to Père Orry in Paris in 1712, accompanied by specimens of the two principal ingredients, *kaolin*[1] and *petuntse*. He visited the Imperial Manufactory, and gives the following interesting account: "Ching-tê-chên wants only to be surrounded by walls to deserve the name of a city, and will bear comparison with the largest and most populous cities of China. There are eighteen thousand families, and more than a million of souls: it is situated on the bank of a fine river. The expense of procuring materials is very considerable, for everything consumed here has to be brought a great distance—even the wood for the furnaces has to be taken a hundred leagues; provisions also are very dear, yet numerous poor families find employment who could not subsist in the neighbouring towns; the young and the old, the lame and the blind, all find work at which they can earn a livelihood by grinding colours or otherwise." "Formerly," says the *History of Fou-liang*, "there were only three hundred furnaces, now there are nearly three thousand." Ching-tê-chên is situated in a vast plain, surrounded by high mountains from which issue two rivers, flowing into each other, and form a wide open basin; here are seen two or three rows of boats, tied together stem and stern; these are employed either in ascending the river for materials, or in descending it to take the porcelain to Jao-chou.

Lord Macartney, ambassador to the Emperor of China in 1792-94, says that not far from the route taken by the English on their way to Canton there was an unwalled city called Ching-tê-chên, where three thousand furnaces for the baking of porcelain existed, all lighted at the same time, which at night presented the appearance of a town on fire.

THE MANUFACTURE OF THE PORCELAIN.

The hills which encircle Ching-tê-chên abound in the minerals necessary for the potter's craft. The chief of these materials are the China-clay and China-stone, which form the principal constituents of true porcelain. China-clay is called by the Chinese Kao-lin, from a mountain of that name, but there were many sources of supply in the neighbourhood and many qualities of the mineral. During the Ming dynasty the finest kaolin was mined at Ma-tsang, but that source gave out towards the end of the dynasty. Another valued kind was the red kaolin from the property of Fang, on the east of Ching-tê-chên, which ceased to be excavated before the nineteenth century. Though red in the raw condition, it burned to white, as did also the coarse yellowish kaolin found in the east of the city.

---

[1] *Kaolin* is the name of a native earth found in China answering to our *China clay*; *petuntse* is a siliceous stone found also in China, answering to our Cornish granite or *China stone*. The word *kaolin* is said to be derived from *kaoling* (lofty ridge), the name of a hill where some of the material is found.

The miners harnessed the mountain torrents for their crushing and refining operations, and sent the prepared material in boats or by land to Ching-tê-chên. Kaolin is an infusible substance, and its function is to give strength and solidity to the porcelain, or, as the Chinese say, to form the bones of the ware. The second material, China-stone, is fusible at a high temperature, and melts into a clear glass. Mixed with the kaolin, its function is to bind together the opaque particles of the latter by melting round them in the furnace and to give the ware the translucency which characterises porcelain. It is the flesh which clothes the bones of the porcelain body. It is also used, softened with a little lime, to form the transparent glaze. The China-stone is likewise mined and washed and crushed in the mountains, and sent to Ching-tê-chên in the form of briquettes stamped with the maker's name. From this circumstance it got the name of petuntse, which means white (*pai*) briquettes (*tun*) for porcelain (*tz'ŭ*).

A third material is sometimes used in place of kaolin. This is the soapy rock or steatite (called by the Chinese hua-shih), similar to that used in England by the old Worcester potters. It was a relatively expensive mineral in China, and was only used for a special ware which is differentiated in the West by the misleading name of "soft-paste," and to which further reference will be made. The peculiar virtue of the hua-shih was to give the body a smooth and waxen surface like vellum, susceptible to very delicate painting; and some of the potters obtained a very similar result by the less expensive process of dipping the ordinary porcelain body into a wash of steatite which left a thin coat on the surface. The steatitic body is opaque, and at the same time surprisingly light to handle. The use of hua-shih and the varying nature of the kaolin will account for many of the more or less marked differences which are observable in Chinese porcelains; but in some cases where certain coloured glazes were required, a mixed body almost resembling earthenware seems to have been preferred by the potters.

The general principles of the manufacture of porcelain are the same in China as elsewhere, with the prominent exception that in the ordinary wares the body and glaze are baked together at one single firing, whereas in other countries it is usual to slightly harden the body in a light preliminary firing before the glaze is applied. As many processes of decoration have to be applied before glazing, it is clear that the greatest care and skill must be required of the Chinese potter in handling the ware in the relatively soft and plastic condition in which it remains until it is put into the furnace.

THE DECORATION OF THE PORCELAIN.

In a book on marks and monograms it is not necessary to dwell at length on the details of manufacture, but it may be of interest to describe briefly a few of the Chinese methods of ornamentation. These are

22

apparently of a very simple nature, such as the use of coloured glazes, painting in underglaze colours and overglaze enamels, carving, engraving, pressing in moulds, and applying reliefs and embossments to the body, and the astonishingly beautiful results of these processes on old Chinese porcelain are due to the artistic feeling and the wonderful manipulative skill of the Chinese potters.

The colours which bedeck the porcelain surface are due to small doses of certain metallic oxides incorporated in the glazing material, or applied to the finished white glaze in the form of vitrifiable enamels. The oldest colours were all incorporated in the glaze, and it was not till later periods that these were gradually reinforced by enamel colours. Oxides of copper, manganese, cobalt, iron, and antimony are responsible for most of the glaze colours, and a great variety of hues was obtained from these few minerals by altering the conditions in which they were fired and by blending them in various ways.

The most prolific of these minerals is copper, from which were obtained the ancient turquoise, crimson and mottled glazes of Sung wares, the leaf-green glazes and enamels of later periods, besides the pure turquoise, and the many tints of underglaze red, including *sang de bœuf*, peach bloom, and maroon.

Manganese is responsible for the many shades of purple, violet, and aubergine, and in part for the black glazes.

Cobalt, which is closely allied to manganese, produced the many shades of blue, including the pigment with which the "blue and white" porcelain is painted.

Iron oxide is the base of the celadon green, and metallic brown glazes, and some of the blacks; as an overglaze enamel it produces the rich coral and Indian reds.

When the oxides are mixed with the glaze itself their colour is developed in the full heat of the kiln, and such colours are known as high-fired colours or *couleurs du grand feu*. Between these and the low-fired enamels are certain intermediate colours called by the French *couleurs du demigrand feu*, and fired in the cooler parts of the kiln. These include turquoise, violet or aubergine purple, leaf-green and yellow. They are mixed with a softer medium than the ordinary glaze, though, like it, they are applied direct to the porcelain body. It will be observed that these glazes are always covered with a fine network of almost imperceptible cracks, an accidental crackle quite distinct from the well-known crackled glaze of which we shall speak presently. The colours of the *demigrand feu* were largely used in the Ming dynasty before the pure enamel colours came into common use.

True enamel colours are painted on the finished ware, the colouring oxides being mixed with a glassy flux to make them adhere to the glaze, and fired at a comparatively low temperature in a small enamelling kiln; they are called low-fired enamels or *couleurs du petit feu*. In the Ming dynasty they were limited to green, yellow, manganese purple, coral-red, and brown-black, though there are indications that a tentative use was also made of an overglaze blue enamel which was not fully established till the early part of the present dynasty. The green, yellow, purple, and blue of this early period were transparent enamels, and it was not till the beginning of the eighteenth century that opaque enamel colours came into use. The eighteenth century witnessed a great development in the use of enamels; the rose-reds and carmines derived from gold were now employed on Chinese porcelain, and many new tints were obtained by blending the enamels and tempering them with arsenical white. Gold and silver are also fixed at a low temperature, and rank with the low-fired colours, though the use of gilding was perfectly understood in the early reigns of the Ming dynasty.

Though the enamel colours are generally painted on the porcelain in regular patterns with a brush, they were not infrequently applied in the manner of a glaze to cover considerable areas, and even the entire surface of the ware. In this case they are usually washed on over the white glaze, but in some cases they are applied direct to the porcelain body which has been already fired and is in the condition known as *biscuit* (*i.e.* unglazed porcelain). This was especially the case with the old transparent greens, manganese purple, and yellow, and one of the rarest and most highly prized kinds of porcelain is decorated in this way, *i.e.* enamelled on the biscuit (*émaillé sur biscuit*).

To leave enamel colours, and return for a moment to the subject of glazes, there are several methods of applying the glaze, whether coloured or uncoloured, to the porcelain body. It may be applied by "dipping," i.e. submerging the vessel in a tub of liquid glazing material, or by painting the glaze on to the ware with a brush, or by blowing the glaze-liquid from the end of a bamboo tube over which a piece of gauze has been tightly stretched. In some cases the colour itself was powdered on to the ware by the last method and the glaze added afterwards, which accounts for the peculiar stippled appearance of certain coloured glazes such as the so-called "powder blue" and certain reds.

In the firing of porcelain or pottery a considerable contraction of the material takes place, and in order to obtain a perfectly smooth and even surface both the body of the ware and the glaze must have the same contraction. If the glaze contracts a fraction more than the body, it will split up into a number of cracks; and if, on the other hand, the body contracts more than the glaze, the glaze will be forced up into lumps and inequalities. Both these faults the Chinese learned to turn to good account. By a nice adjustment of the materials, they were able on the one hand to give the surface of the glazed porcelain a slightly lumpy and undulating appearance, which added greatly to the play of light and shade. This effect they compared to "chicken skin" or "millet-like elevations in the glaze," and it has been named in Europe "orange peel" glaze. Conversely they were able to make the beautiful crackled glazes which have been the despair of Western potters. It is said that this was effected by the use of a small admixture of steatite; but whatever the method was, the Chinese obtained a complete mastery of the process, and could regulate the size of the crackle at will. Thus we find in the same vase clearly defined bands of crackle in varying sizes and shapes. It was a common custom to emphasise the lines of this intentional crackle with red or black pigment. One Chinese account states that they did this by taking the ware before it had quite cooled and while the cracks were still slightly gaping, and rubbing the surface with pigment : when the porcelain had cooled and the cracks closed up tight, the surface was washed, and there appeared a delicate network of red or black veins. This is said to have been done at the Chi-chou factories, in Kiang-si, as early as the Sung dynasty. In some cases the crackled vases were washed over with a coloured, but uncrackled and transparent, enamel.

Another surprising glaze effect which started from an accident, and was actually regarded at first as a technical failure, was the *flambé* or transmutation glaze (*yao pien*). It was one of the varieties of Chün-chou glazes of the Sung dynasty; and though it was frequently produced from that time onwards, it was not till the Yung Chêng period (1723-35) that the potters brought it under complete control. The glaze seems to be composed of a mass of contending colours, in which green, blue, grey, crimson, and purple struggle for the mastery. These varied effects are mostly, if not entirely, due to the behaviour of copper oxide in a kiln in which the atmosphere, changed by the admission of pungent smoke followed by currents of pure air, becomes at one moment reducing and at another oxidising. Another and an easier method of producing these variegated effects was practised later in the eighteenth century, viz. applying patches of coloured glazes, and letting them run one over the other. The Chinese *flambé* glazes were long a puzzle to Western potters, but they have now been completely mastered both in England and abroad.

Painting in enamel colours over the finished glaze has already been described. Underglaze painting is applied in the usual way, but to the raw body of the ware before the glaze is added. Consequently it is only possible in this case to use a limited number of colours which will stand the full heat of the porcelain kiln. Until quite recent times these colours were limited to blue, red or maroon, and more rarely brown-black. Slips (*i.e.* liquid clays) were occasionally painted on with a brush, but this was practically confined to white in the case of porcelain, though on certain stonewares we find red-brown or maroon applied in this manner. Singularly beautiful effects were obtained by delicate traceries of a pure white slip (formed of steatite or gypsum) under the greenish-white porcelain glaze as early as the Yung Lo period (1403-24). A kindred, but rather coarser, method was to apply thin shavings and strips of the body-clay, and model them with a wet brush into the required design; this was usually covered with glaze, but sometimes left standing up in "biscuit," in effective contrast with the surrounding glaze.

Relief ornaments formed separately in moulds and "luted on" (*i.e.*

stuck on with liquid clay) to the surface of the ware were used on pottery as early as the Han dynasty, and the use of moulds for impressing the whole surface of the vessel was known in early times. The green celadon and the white Ting wares of the Sung and Yuan dynasties were elaborately ornamented in this way. But some of the most beautiful and most esteemed decoration from the Sung dynasty downwards has been accomplished by free-hand carving of the surface or by etching with fine point. A more delicate operation was the carving of openwork designs and lattice work, in which the knife passed clean through the thin porcelain wall, cutting away the ground of the pattern. This was done while the ware was still unfired and relatively soft, and the utmost manipulative skill was required for the work. Vessels treated in this fashion were provided with an inner shell if intended for holding liquid, but incense and pot-pourri vases, and boxes for holding fighting crickets and the like, were naturally suited for this kind of decoration. Sometimes the carving in openwork was combined with dainty reliefs in biscuit, as on certain rare and beautiful covered bowls on which are medallions with tiny figures or flowers in biscuit reliefs with passages of pierced fretwork between. One of these in the Morgan Collection in New York has the date mark of the T'ien Ch'i period (1621-27). Another effective decoration was achieved by cutting out a pattern in small sections à jour, and allowing the glaze to run into the perforations and fill them with transparent glass, so that, while the vessel was still capable of holding liquids, the design showed up as a transparency against the light. This method was sometimes combined with the use of enamel colours, and it has been successfully employed in recent times in Japan, where the decoration is known as "fire fly" ornament. It is usually known in England as "rice-grain" decoration, following the French à grains de riz, from the size and shape of the excisions. It is interesting to observe that the "rice-grain" decoration was used in Persia, Syria, and Egypt as early as the eleventh century, though it does not seem to have been introduced into China before the eighteenth century. In fact, most of the Chinese examples date from the beginning of the nineteenth century. Another very beautiful and kindred decoration is "lace work," in which intricate scroll patterns were deeply incised in the ware, and covered over with a transparent glaze usually of pale celadon green tint.

Painting in liquid white clay or "slip" on a white or coloured ground was in common use in China from early times. The material used was steatite or gypsum, which showed up in dead white lines against the faint greenish tint of the ordinary porcelain glaze. On the coffee-brown, blue, dark lavender and celadon green glazes these white traceries stand out in bold contrast.[1]

---

[1] The following passage relating to the manufacture at the end of the seventeenth century is of considerable interest. We find a notice of porcelain in the travels of Ysbranti Ides, ambassador to China from Peter the Great in 1692. He states that "the finest, richest, and most valuable china is not exported, or at least very rarely, particularly a yellow ware, which is destined for the Imperial use, and is prohibited to all other persons. They have a kind of crimson ware, which is very fine and dear, because great quantities of it are spoiled in the baking. They have another sort, of a shining white purfled with red, which is produced by blowing the colour through a gauze, so that both the

EARLY PORCELAINS

If we may judge from the few existing specimens of Sung dynasty wares, the quality of translucency, which we regard as essential in porcelain, was not held of much account in the Sung period. Indeed, it is only in the ivory white wares of the Ting class that we meet with any indication of translucency, and that only where the sides of the vessel are particularly thin. We gather, however, that during the Yuan dynasty a more translucent ware was generally manufactured, and that the white Imperial bowls with engraved designs and marked with the characters *Shu fu* (see p. 364) formed the connecting link between the Ting wares of the Sung and the beautiful egg-shell porcelain bowls of the Ming dynasty. The Shu-fu bowls were fired upside down like the Sung Ting wares, and consequently had a raw mouth-rim which was generally concealed beneath a metal band, but like the Ming bowls they were of translucent white porcelain.

MING PORCELAINS.

In the Ming dynasty (1368-1634 A.D.) great progress was made in the manufacture of porcelain; and as early as the reign of Yung Lo (1403-24) bowls were made of a thinness and delicacy which were never surpassed in China. This was the so-called "bodiless" (*t'o t'ai*) porcelain, so attentuated that it seemed to consist of glaze alone. It was decorated with designs delicately etched in the paste or traced in white slip under the glaze, and so faint as to be only visible when held against the light like a water-mark in paper. A fine example bearing the mark of the Yung Lo period in archaic characters (see p. 351) is in the British Museum. The manufacture of these fine white bowls continued to the end of the Ming dynasty, though at certain periods a slightly thicker ware (*pan t'o t'ai* or half bodiless) seems to have been preferred.

Though it is probable that painting in blue on the porcelain body before glazing was attempted as early as the Sung dynasty, and further developed during the succeeding Yuan dynasty, we know of no examples older than the Ming. Chinese writers speak of this class of decoration, commonly called "blue and white," as fully established even in the earliest Ming reigns. The blue colour was obtained from oxide of cobalt, and in

inside and out are equally beautified with crimson spots no bigger than pins' points, and this must be excessively dear, since for one piece that succeeds a hundred are spoiled. They have a china purfled in the same manner with gold; also a kind of china which looks like mosaic work, or as if it had been cracked in a thousand places and set together again without cement. There is another kind of violet-coloured china, with patterns composed of green specks, which are made by blowing the colours at once through a frame pierced full of holes, and this operation succeeds so rarely, that a very small basin is worth two or three hundred pounds. Specimens of white porcelain are found engraved or painted with designs in the very body of the paste in such a manner as to be only seen when held up to the light, in the same manner as the watermark upon a sheet of paper, or become visible when the vase is filled with liquid, when the imperial dragon, animals, birds, or fish are distinguished, having no traces whatever on the surface."

addition to the native supplies of this material a superior mineral was imported from the West under various names, of which the most suggestive is *hui hui chi'ng* (Mohammedan blue), implying that it came from Arab sources. As blue painting had been in general use in Persia and Egypt for several centuries, it is probable that the imported cobalt was derived from these countries. The Mohammedan blue was deep but brilliant, and of a slightly violet tone. It was brought to China in the reign of Yung Lo (1403-24) by the celebrated Eunuch Chêng-ho, and was used in the reign of Hsüan Tê (1426-35), which was particularly noted for the quality of its blue and white porcelain. The supply seems to have temporarily failed during the Ch'êng Hua period (1465-87), but to have been renewed in the reign of Ch'êng Tê (1506-21), only to cease altogether during the Wan Li period (1573-1619). This fine blue was never very plentifully supplied, and we may be sure that it was only used in the finer wares. For the rest the commoner blue would be employed, which will account for the dull and impure quality of some of the Ming blue and white. A distinguishing feature of Ming blue and white porcelain, as compared with several wares of the present dynasty, is in the execution of the painting, the designs being clearly outlined and afterwards filled in with flat washes of colour.

Another underglaze colour which was used alone or in combination with the blue in painted decoration, was a red derived from oxide of copper. In tint it varies from vivid blood-red to dull maroon, and the porcelains of the Hsüan Tê period (1426-35) were noted for the successful development of this colour. Indeed its brilliance was so great during this reign, that it was called *pao shih hung* (precious stone red), and it was believed that pounded rubies were actually used in its production. Another descriptive name for it was *yu li hung* (red within the glaze), which serves to distinguish it from the less esteemed *fan hung*, a red derived from oxide of iron, which was applied over the glaze. The latter when of a rich coral tint is very beautiful, and was effectively employed as a ground colour on which to trace delicate patterns in gold. This red and gold ornament was a feature of Yung Lo porcelains, and a few good examples are shown in the British Museum, *i.e.* small bowls with blue and white designs inside and red and gold outside. The style was admired in Japan, where it was called *Kin-ran-de*, and was adopted by the celebrated potter Zengoro Hozen, who received the art name of Eiraku, the Japanese rendering of Yung Lo, in testimony of the Chinese origin of the style.

Another feature of the Ming porcelain is the use of coloured glazes—violet, turquoise, yellow, and aubergine purple—of the *demi-grand feu* over elaborate designs carved and pierced in the porcelain body. The colours are kept apart by carved or raised outlines of the ornament. Large wine jars, barrel-shaped garden seats, flower pots, figures of sages, sometimes within elaborate rockwork grottoes, and numerous other objects, mostly of considerable size, are seen in this kind of porcelain. An unmistakable reference to this class of ware is found in the T'ao Shuo among the productions of the Hsüan Tê period, viz., "barrel seats decorated with floral designs carved in openwork filled in with colours."[1]

A further development was the use of these coloured glazes to fill in lightly incised designs in a coloured ground, leading up to the final abandonment of the carved or etched outlines in favour of black outlines painted on the biscuit and washed over with transparent green, yellow, and purple enamels.

The precise period in which painting in enamel colours over the white glaze first came into being has long been a matter of dispute. Chinese writers place it very early in the Ming dynasty; and though the famous chicken wine-cups[2] of the reign of Ch'êng Hua (A.D. 1465-87) exist for us only in literature, there seems no good reason to doubt that the Ch'êng Hua period was noted for finely enamelled porcelain. Authentic examples of Chia Ching (1522-66) porcelain painted in on-glaze enamels are to be seen in most good collections, but the bulk of existing Ming enamelled wares belong to the reign of Wan Li (1573-1619). They are painted in green, yellow, aubergine, and coral red, with occasional touches of black, in addition to underglaze blue, a combination generally known as the "five-colour" scheme. The Chinese name for it is *Wan Li wu tsai* (Wan Li five colours), but the expression *wu tsai*, though literally rendered "five colours," has the general significance of "enamels." It is not to be supposed that this kind of decoration ceased with the Ming dynasty. Indeed it was freely used in the present dynasty in the reign of K'ang Hsi (1666-1722) and a particularly close imitation of the Wan Li enamelled porcelain was largely made in the reign of Yung Chêng (1722-35).

Single-colour glazes were freely used on Ming porcelains, red, various shades of blue, metallic brown, and celadon green of the *grand feu,* turquoise, yellow and aubergine-purple of the *demi-grand feu,* besides various crackles, of which stone-grey and greyish green are the commonest. Mottled or *flambé* glazes are also found; but they do not seem to have been deliberately made until the reign of Yung Chêng in the present dynasty, and we must regard the earlier examples as more or less fortuitous effects.

There can be no doubt that the Ming potters were capable of producing porcelain of the utmost refinement; but the specimens which have survived the dangers of transport, and the chances of the three hundred and sixty years which have elapsed since the end of the Ming dynasty, are mostly of heavy build, and often of rather clumsy form. Many of

---

[1] *Description of Chinese Pottery and Porcelain, being a Translation of the T'ao Shuo,* by S. W. Bushell; 1910, p. 138.

[2] *Chinese Pottery and Porcelain,* op. cit., p. 141. "The wine-cups of Ch'êng Hua porcelain comprise many different patterns and designs, but all are remarkable for artistic drawing, for the combination of the colours both dark and pale, and for the translucent purity and strength of the material. The 'Chicken Cups' are decorated above *moutan* ponies, below with a hen and chicken instinct with life and movement."

them are clearly export wares, and the fact that they have been recovered
to a great extent from India and Persia, and the near East, will explain
the solidity of their make.   But for all their thickness, the paste is as
a rule remarkably white, and of an almost unctuous fineness of grain;
and the decoration is bold and effective, even when roughly executed.   It
should be added that most of the Ming porcelains in Western collections
belong to the later reigns, and that examples older than the sixteenth
century are excessively rare, though the early date-marks, especially those
of the Hsüan Tê and Ch'êng Hua periods, have been systematically
inscribed on blue and white and enamelled wares for the last three
hundred years.

K'ANG HSI PORCELAINS.

The short reigns with which the Ming dynasty ended, and the present
Chi'ng dynasty began, were too troubled to favour the growth of peaceful
arts, and the first reign of importance in the ceramic history of the
present dynasty was that of K'ang Hsi, which lasted a full cycle from
1662 to 1722.

The Imperial factories at Ching-tê-chên came under the care of the
celebrated Lang Ting-tso, and an epoch of great brilliance began.   The
bulk of the finest porcelains in our great collections dates from the K'ang
Hsi period.   To Lang himself are attributed the noble *sang de bœuf*, or
ox-blood red glazes, and the cognate and equally prized " peach-bloom "
red and apple-green.   The *sang de bœuf* red and the apple-green are
always crackled, though the cracks are often so fine that they are only
apparent on close inspection; and the two colours appear frequently in
the same piece.   The finest peach bloom too is frequently broken by passages
of apple-green, which give it an additional beauty and value.

Single-coloured porcelains of great variety were made at this time,
all distinguished by conspicuous excellence of colour and form.   The pure
white wares were of the utmost refinement, whether plain, or decorated
with delicately incised or etched designs, slip-traceries, reliefs, or open
work.

The large group of porcelains decorated with washes of transparent
green, aubergine and yellow, applied direct to the biscuit, and often over
patterns traced in black outline, which we have already mentioned among
the Ming wares, must be assigned principally to the K'ang Hsi period.
This is particularly applicable to those finely modelled figures of sages and
deities, with white biscuit faces and coloured draperies, which command
such extravagant prices to-day.   Under this heading too should be ranged
the sumptuous vases of the *famille noire* or *famille jaune*, with designs,
usually floral, reserved in grounds of black or brownish-yellow; the designs
themselves were usually filled in with green and aubergine in the
latter class, and green, aubergine and yellow in the former.   On a few
rare specimens the designs are reserved in a transparent leaf-green

ground.   The black of this so-called *famille noire* has an iridescent greenish sheen, which distinguishes it from all other blacks.   It is produced by coating the surface with a dull black pigment, and then washing it over with a thin transparent green enamel.

The blue and white porcelain of the K'ang Hsi period is justly admired for its technical superiority over all other kinds of blue and white, and for its supreme decorative qualities.   As might be expected, it varies widely in quality and value, but even the inferior specimens of this period have a charm not to be found in the later wares.   The native cobalt was used for the manufacture of the blue colour, but no pains were spared in selecting and refining the mineral, the finest cobalt being set apart and mixed with the commoner kinds in proportions varying according to the class of ware to be decorated.   The best blue and white porcelain has a body of the purest material, and is carefully painted with blue of a deep but brilliant sapphire tone, without that tinge of purple which is observable in later and earlier blues.   The glaze which covers it is clear and limpid like fresh spring water, though like almost all Chinese porcelain glazes it has a faint greenish tinge, recalling the film inside an egg.   The colour is never flat or still, but is laid on in graded depths which give it the life and fire of a precious stone.   The designs are innumerable, formal arabesques or bronze ornaments with ogre faces peering out from the intricacies of the pattern, passages of diaper and mosaic, the flowers of the four seasons, elaborate court, hunting, battle and historical scenes, figures of tall graceful ladies, and a hundred other motives.   Among the best known are the arabesques with ogre heads, the tiger-lily design covering the entire surface with a sinuous pattern of formal lilies, the radiating "aster" pattern, the "Love Chase," in which a man and girl on horseback are depicted hunting a hare, and the isolated figures of tall girls called by the Dutch *lange lijsen* or "long Elizas."   In some of the most prized examples the pattern is reserved in white on a blue ground, as in the tall vases with magnolia branches thrown up against washes of deep blue, and the "hawthorn jars" with sprays of white prunus blossom in a sapphire blue ground, netted over with lines resembling the cracks in ice.   Another highly prized class of blue and white is the so-called "soft paste," to which we have already referred (p. 321).   It is characterised by an opaque, and sometimes earthy-looking body, and soft-looking glaze usually more or less crackled, and varying in tone from a dead white to a pale buff.   The painting differs from that of the ordinary blue and white, in that it is applied in fine brush strokes like miniature work instead of broad washes.   There is no doubt that this "soft paste" (which is really extremely hard, and has nothing whatever in common with the European soft pastes of Sèvres, Chelsea, &c.), was made in the Ming dynasty, but the bulk of existing specimens date from the K'ang Hsi and succeeding periods.

Painting in under-glaze red, which seems to have fallen into disuse during the latter part of the Ming period, was revived in the reigns of

K'ang Hsi and Yung Chêng. It is often combined with blue painting. Another colour used in combination with under-glaze blue was the Nanking yellow, and a pale variety of the lustrous brown known as *café au lait* and *feuille morte*.

Blue and white painting is not usually found surrounded by any coloured grounds except the powder-blue and coffee-brown, and occasionally yellow and coral red.

The enamelled porcelains of the K'ang Hsi period form another large and important class. They are a continuation of the late Ming "five-colour" ware, and from the predominance of greens in various shades they are often grouped under the title *famille verte*. The enamels are always of the transparent kind, and include several shades of green, aubergine purple, brownish yellow, Indian red, green-black, and a beautiful enamel blue, which distinguishes the K'ang Hsi palette from the Ming. It is true that a tentative use of this blue enamel is found in rare examples of Wan Li period, but it was not successfully developed till the K'ang Hsi period, when it gradually supplanted the under-glaze blue in the "five-colour" scheme. The painting of the K'ang Hsi *famille verte* porcelain is characterised at once by breadth of treatment and refinement, and it stands as a happy mean between the bold but somewhat crude painting of the late Ming enamelled wares and the more minute and effeminate style which succeeded it in the reigns of Yung Chêng and Ch'ien Lung. In the finest specimens the enamels are pure and brilliant, and, standing out in palpable relief, give the ware a richly jewelled appearance. In combination with ground colours, the *famille verte* enamels are used with great effect, as in panels inserted in a ground of powder blue, or over the powder blue itself, or on a crackled green, grey, or lustrous brown glaze. (See *Ker. Gall.*, enlarged edition, fig. 524.)

Much of the *famille verte* porcelain of this period has strong affinities in its decoration with the Japanese Arita wares, and one group, painted chiefly in underglaze blue and coral red, appears to be a direct imitation of the "old Imari" porcelain. The last years of the long reign K'ang Hsi witnessed the beginnings of a radical change in the enamelled wares. An opaque rose-pink enamel derived from gold first came into use at this time, and it was followed in the next reign by a series of opaque enamels which gradually ousted the transparent colours of the *famille verte*. The earliest specimens of the *famille rose*, as the new enamelled ware is called, are distinguished by a dull and rather impure carmine, opaque white, and yellow side by side with the transparent enamels which had not yet been abandoned.

YUNG CHÊNG PERIOD (1723-35).

But in the succeeding reign of Yung Chêng (1723-35) the *famille rose* colours were perfected and the many shades of ruby and rose reds were combined with opaque blues, yellows, and whites, and mixed colours of various tones. This new colour scheme is seen to perfection on the Canton "eggshell" porcelains, which were sent in the white state from Ching-tê-chên and enamelled by the skilful workers in the Canton *ateliers*.   The exquisite "ruby back" dishes of thin porcelain of the finest quality, decorated on the front with pheasants, poultry, and symbolical flowers, or with Chinese interiors and graceful ladies and children, surrounded by richly diapered borders, are the finest specimens of this class.   Some of these Canton plates have as many as seven different patterns on the sides and rim, and are known as the "seven border" plates. The enamels are almost all of the opaque kind, but are laid on thickly and stand out in relief from the porcelain surface.   (See *Ker. Gall.*, enlarged edition, figs. 527-9.)

In several other groups of Yung Chêng enamelled wares, however, the traditions of the *famille verte* still survived.   One of these was a whole-hearted imitation of the Wan Li "five coloured" porcelain, and so close were the copies that many of them are classed as Ming wares in our collections.   Another group marks more clearly than anything the passing of the *famille verte*.   Transparent green, yellow and aubergine are still used, but in thin, broken washes picking out the details of a design outlined in underglaze blue.   The effect is soft and harmonious, but contrasts feebly with the bold passages of colour in the K'ang Hsi *famille verte*.

A characteristic ornament of this time is a branch of some flowering shrub or tree prettily thrown across the white porcelain surface, and usually accompanied by one or two birds.   The blue and white porcelain seems to lose its virility after the K'ang Hsi period, and the strong vibrating masses of colour give place to minutely pencilled patterns.

But the reign of Yung Chêng is chiefly celebrated for its fine single-colour porcelains and for beautiful imitations of the old Sung glazes. Specimens of Ju, Kuan, Ko, Lung-ch'üan and Chün wares were sent from the Imperial collections to be imitated at Ching-tê-chên and many of these copies are only to be recognised by the superior fineness of the porcelain body on which the Sung types of glazes are displayed. Many of the Sung wares, it will be remembered, had dark-coloured bodies which emerged at the base rim, and showed to a lesser degree at the mouth where the glaze was thin.   This peculiarity, usually described as "the brown mouth and iron foot" of the Sung wares, was copied by coating the mouth and foot of the white Yung Chêng porcelain with a brown ferruginous earth.   This artificial dressing is usually quite obvious, and serves to identify the Yung Chêng copies.   It is safe to say that most of the finer single-colour glazes and crackles of avowedly Sung type in our collections were made at this time.   The splashed and mottled or transmutation glazes, called by the French *flambé*, which had hitherto been largely accidental, were now able to be produced at will. The direction of the Imperial factories was in the hands of Nien Hsi Yao, the successor of Lang Ting Tso, at the beginning of the Yung Chêng period; and in 1720 T'ang Ying was appointed assistant director.   The

latter, who assumed sole charge from 1736 to 1749, was the most brilliant
of all the directors of the Imperial factories, and under his care the industry reached its highest development. All that had been done in previous
reigns was copied at will, and many new decorative effects were discovered.

CH'IEN LUNG PERIOD (1736-95).

The Emperor Ch'ien Lung, who reigned from 1736-95, took a personal
interest in the art. He collected old porcelains, and wrote odes to be
inscribed on the new. The potters at this time boasted that there was
nothing they could not imitate in porcelain. Natural stones such as jade
and agate, shells, lacquer, grained wood, rhinoceros' horn, and in metal
work, bronze, iron and copper were copied with bewildering exactitude.
Wonderful imitations of patinated bronze are among their most remarkable glazes, and glazes imitating the colour of tea-dust and iron rust are
reputed to have been invented at this time, though there are some much
older glaze-effects which can scarcely be distinguished from them. A more
hybrid production was the porcelain *lacquée burgautée*, in which the white
porcelain was coated with black lacquer inlaid with designs in mother-of-pearl.

Meanwhile in the enamelled ware the transition from the *famille verte*
to the *famille rose* colour scheme, which had been progressing in the Yung
Chêng period, was completed. Opaque colours and rose tints held undis-
puted sway. A colour which does not seem to have been used over large
areas till late in the Ch'ien Lung period is an opaque bluish green which
came to be freely used as a ground colour for the insides of bowls and
vases. Encrusted floral designs in rather high relief and sometimes a
climbing vine with squirrel-like animals on the branches, are not uncommon
on the vases of this time. Thin "eggshell" painted with panels containing
groups of stately personages in official robes, the panels framed in rich
brocaded diapers, belong to the Ch'ien Lung period. These are commonly
known as "Mandarin" vases. On many of the wares a dark coral red is
conspicuous, and is often used with overpowering effect.

Speaking broadly, the Ch'ien Lung porcelains display marvellous
technical qualities, but the decoration is rather laboured and minute, and
of an effeminate delicacy which contrasts with the breadth and freedom
of the earlier styles.

THE NINETEENTH CENTURY.

With the abdication of Ch'ien Lung, in 1795, terminated what was
perhaps the most brilliant period in Chinese ceramic history. It had
extended through the three reigns of K'ang Hsi, Yung Chêng, and Ch'ien
Lung, with a duration of about a hundred and thirty years. There was no
immediate falling-off in the quality of the ware at the commencement of
the reign of Chia Ch'ing (1796-1810), but from the beginning of the
nineteenth century began a gradual but sure decline. From this time
onwards, the potters seem to have been content with working over the old

ground, and in the absence of progress their skill gradually evaporated. Many pretty porcelains, however, were produced in the Chia Ch'ing and the succeeding Tao Kuang period (1821-50), and some of the enamelled wares are not without a certain delicacy and charm. Among these the so-called "Peking" or "medallion" bowls hold a high place. Inside they are usually painted in underglaze blue, while the exterior is richly adorned with ruby, blue, yellow, lavender, or French grey enamels, broken by small medallions with enamelled or blue designs. The coloured grounds are often delicately engraved with scroll diapers, a form of ornament known as "graviata." Another effective ornament of this period consists of a floral design or branches of bamboo reserved in white in a coral-red background.

In the reign of Hsien Fêng (1851-61) the factories at Ching-tê-chên were pillaged during the Tai-ping rebellion, and the industry has scarcely yet recovered from this crushing blow. During the last reign Kuang Hsü (1875-1909), and the present, a considerable revival has taken place, the late Empress-Dowager having been an active patron of the porcelain industry, and some of the modern wares, notably those with single-colour glazes of the *sang-de-bœuf* class, are sufficiently well made to pass as antique. But the collector will observe a lack of refinement in the material and of accuracy in form in the modern wares, and in the case of the *sang-de-bœuf* red and *flambés* the glaze on recently made specimens almost always runs down uncontrolled beneath the base rim, which consequently has to be ground flat. But if the unwary collector is liable to be deceived by modern Chinese reproductions, he is perhaps still more in danger from the clever Japanese imitations which cover almost the entire field of old Chinese wares, and nothing but wide experience and a well-trained eye will save him from falling a victim to the best of these.

EXPORT PORCELAINS.

To return to the older wares, there are several large and interesting groups of porcelain especially made for export to the nearer East or to Europe. The export trade in porcelain dates from the Middle Ages, when it was carried by caravans or by Arab and Chinese ocean traders to the East Indies, India, Ceylon, Arabia, Egypt, and Persia, to be farther transported to Europe and North Africa. The earliest export wares were the strongly made celadon bowls and dishes. Blue and white porcelain followed in due course, and in the last half of the Ming dynasty the trade must have assumed large dimensions. Persia seems to have been a good customer, and wares ornamented in almost pure Persian taste form a considerable class by themselves. In these the blue is often of a dark indigo tint, which seems to have been admired by the Persian connoisseurs. Other specimens of the Ming blue and white found in the near East have a pale blue of silvery grey tint on a thin crisp porcelain, which has a peculiar delicacy much admired by the Chinese themselves. Of the enamelled wares, the Wan Li "five-colour" porcelains are also found in Persia and India, and a contemporary ware in which a lustrous coral red and green give the predominant notes. A thick coarse porcelain, crudely painted with Indian red and bluish green, was largely exported to the East Indies, where it is constantly met with to this day. The Dutch and other East India Companies, which established trade between Europe and China from the seventeenth century, imported vast quantities of Oriental porcelain. At first this consisted chiefly of blue and white as far as China was concerned (the enamelled wares being chiefly drawn from Japanese sources). Next came the Batavian ware, so called from the Dutch entrepôt in Java, a porcelain decorated with coffee brown glaze broken by panels painted in blue or early *famille rose* enamels. The practice of ordering whole table services from China began at least as early as the year 1702, for there is a plate in the British Museum, with the typical armorial decoration, bearing that date; and from that time onward dinner services were a regular article of commerce for the Canton merchants. Coats-of-arms were sent out to be copied, and these at first appeared surrounded by Chinese ornament; but, as the century advanced, a gradual invasion of European styles took place, and the armorial services returned with borders in the Meissen, Sèvres, and even Derby styles. This is the ware which was till lately supposed to have been made, or at least decorated, at Lowestoft, a great and wholly undeserved compliment to the small Suffolk factory. Nor was the European influence confined to this class of porcelain. The Jesuits, in the seventeenth century, had supplied religious designs to be executed on the blue and white porcelain, and later we find European engravings and mezzotints, both sacred and profane, rendered in sepia or Chinese wares. (See *Ker. Gall.*, enlarged edition, fig. 530.) Another class of porcelain shows the reverse procedure, the ware being shipped to Europe in the white, and decorated at the European factories and by private enamellers. Not a little of this work was done at Chelsea, or at least by artists whose painting may be also recognised on Chelsea porcelain. Unfortunately the European decorators were not content to paint the white Chinese porcelain, but they must needs take the beautiful "blue and white," if the decorations were slight enough to admit of it, and load the white spaces with clumsy enamelled designs. This hideous profanation has been dubbed with the appropriately ugly name of "clobbering." It was rife in Holland as early as the first years of the eighteenth century, and has been practised in England as late as the middle of the nineteenth. Wares so disfigured were sometimes marked by the clobberer with a garbled Chinese seal in red.

Though the bulk of our specimens of Chinese porcelain was made at Ching-tê-chên, there is no doubt that minor provincial factories supplied local requirements and sent their surplus goods into the export market. The rough and coarse wares which were distributed among the East Indies were probably to a large extent the output of Southern Chinese factories, and there are a few specimens of Ming blue and white of fair quality in the British Museum which may be attributed on good grounds to provincial potteries. One is a wide-mouthed bottle which bears the inscription *Fu fan chih tsao* (made on the boundaries of Fukien), figured on p. 376; and the other a figure of Shou Lao, which is reputed to be Wên-chou ware, and was apparently made at Wên-chou-Fu in the province of Chekiang. At Chapu, in the same province, there is record of a factory making blue and white wares in the eighteenth century.

But the best known provincial porcelain factories were situated at Tê-hua, in the province of Fukien. Founded at the beginning of the Ming dynasty, according to the *T'ao Lu*, they continue active to the present day. They are the source of the well-known *blanc de Chine*, a beautiful ivory white porcelain, highly translucent, with smooth glossy glaze which blends closely with the body and varies in colour from a rich cream to milky white. The wares are usually of an ornamental character, figures of deities, sages, and historical personages (the most common subject being Kuan Yin, Goddess of Mercy), vases, wine and libation cups, incense-burners and brush-pots. They frequently bear moulded or engraved ornament and inscriptions in Grass character, besides occasional stamped marks.

PORCELAIN SHAPES.

Nowhere have the ornamental and useful qualities of porcelain been more fully recognised than in China, and the shapes which it has assumed are innumerable. Though not so largely used for ritual purposes as its rival bronze, porcelain was not uncommonly employed in the manufacture of the temple sets which include an incense-burner, two pricket candlesticks, and two flower vases. There were also square vases for holding divination rods, wine ewers, libation cups and bowls. The incense-burning apparatus included an incense-burner, usually of tripod form with two square handles, with or without a pierced cover, an incense-box with cover, and a low round jar for holding ashes, a spoon-like shovel, and a pair of tongs. Less conventional incense-burners took the form of various ornaments and figures of deities, sages, or animals, in which the open mouth or nostrils frequently served as an outlet for the fumes. Akin to these are the joss-stick-holders, usually in the shape of a conventional lion, before which is a small tube to hold the incense-stick. The forms of ritual vessels were almost always copied from ancient bronzes. Indeed a very large proportion of the more ornamental porcelain forms derived from bronze models, the more ordinary shapes being dictated by the requirements of use and by the exigencies of the potter's wheel.

Objects for domestic use included oblong pillows which could be filled with hot or cold water, basins and ewers, deep flower-pots, and shallow bulb bowls, flower vases of every form, including hanging vases and wall vases with flat backs, hat-holders, plaques for inlaying in screens, tiles, tables, go-boards, barrel-shaped seats, fish bowls, besides large wine and meat jars with or without covers, wine ewers, teapots, tea bowls, with or without covers, wine cups, sometimes on high stems, rice bowls and bowls for various foods, saucer-shaped dishes of all sizes, bottles and perfume sprinklers with long tapering necks, round cake-boxes, and square boxes for various uses. The special furniture of the scholar's table included brush handles, brush rests, often in the shape of a conventional range of hills, cylindrical pots for washing the brushes, ink slabs with a rough unglazed space for grinding the ink, a small screen to fend off the splashes of the ink when it was being prepared, water-droppers, usually of fantastic and often very beautiful forms, rests for the writer's wrist, colour boxes, small boxes for seal-vermilion, seals usually surmounted by lion or dragon figures, paper-weights and miniature vases to hold a single flower.

Among the articles for special use were the cylindrical or square vases for holding arrows, often fitted with an elaborate railed stand: boxes with delicately perforated sides for holding fighting crickets: lanterns with openwork sides, and snuff or scent bottles of innumerable forms, and usually lavishly decorated. Many of the snuff bottles are masterpieces in miniature.

The purely ornamental wares include vases of every conceivable form —oval, globular, square-bodied, beaker, baluster, club-shaped, or with fantastic forms of fungus, bat, peach, gourd, melon, &c.—and of all sizes, from tiny vessels fit to hold a single orchid, to the tall "ground vases" five or six feet high. There are besides a great quantity of figures and statuettes, chiefly of deities, Taoist sages, philosophers and historical characters, or of sacred creatures, such as the conventional lion (often called the dog of Fo (Buddha) because he is placed as a guard at the entrance of Buddhist temples), and the kylin, the tortoise, phœnix, and stork. The most familiar figures are those of Shou Lao, God of Longevity, with bald protuberant forehead, and carrying a peach or ju-i sceptre, and often accompanied by a stag or stork: Kuan Ti, the bearded God of War, usually seated and holding a sword: Kuan Yin, the Goddess of Mercy, often with a child in her arms, and strangely recalling figures of the Virgin: Tung Fang-so, with the three peaches which he stole from Hsi Wang Mu: the Eight Taoist Immortals: the jolly pair of laughing boyish gods, Twin Genii of Mirth and Harmony (Ho Ho Êrh hsien): Ho Shang (the Japanese Hotei), a smiling fat personage with bare pendulous abdomen, supposed to represent the Maitreya Buddha: and figures of Manjusri on a lion, Samantabhadra on an elephant, and Buddha himself in various postures. There are besides a vast number of objects of special form made for export to foreign countries—ewers with long spouts, narghili and water pipes for Persia and India; jars for the Dyaks, and deep bowls with pagoda-covers for the Siamese; besides the special European goods, such as coffee pots, tea and coffee cups with handles and saucers, flat-rimmed plates, vegetable dishes, salt-cellars, milk jugs, &c., pairs of vases, *garnitures de cheminée*, consisting of three covered vases and two beakers—anything, in fact, that the European merchants were minded to order.

SUBJECTS OF DECORATION.

The ornament on Chinese porcelain is borrowed from many sources, chief among which are stone and wood carvings, brocaded textiles, bronzes and water-colour paintings on silk and paper. Most of the carved and moulded designs of the early wares—phœnixes flying among flowers, archaic dragons, fishes in relief, fret borders, arabesques, and ogre heads, &c.—may be traced to the ancient bronzes. Textiles provided the richly diapered border patterns, and many of the beautiful floral designs of the blue and white and enamelled wares. The figures, nature studies, and landscapes were no doubt chiefly copied from pictures, and even from standard drawing books. Appropriate subjects were supplied by religion, history and literature. Of the three Chinese cults, that of Confucius is represented by deified mortals, such as the founder himself, K'uei Hsing, the demon-faced god of literature, who stands on a dragon, and Kuan Yü, a hero of the romantic times of the three Kingdoms, who was afterwards canonised as Kuan Ti, the God of War. The twenty paragons of Filial Piety also serve to illustrate the spirit of Confucianism. Buddhism, which gained a foothold in China in the first century of our era, is illustrated by pictures of Buddha and the Bodhisattvas, Manjusri on a lion, Samantabhadra on an elephant, and Avalokita (Kuan Yin), the eighteen Arhats or Buddhist Apostles, the Deva Kings, and the canonised animals, such as the dragon, phœnix, lion, elephant, horse, and hare. But by far the most prolific source of inspiration was found in the Taoist cult, founded by Lao Tzŭ, the contemporary of Confucius, in the sixth century B.C. The worship of longevity and the pursuit of the elixir of life were the prominent features of the Taoist cult, and the foremost deity is Shou Lao, God of Longevity, who lives on Mount Pêng Lai in the Isles of the Blest, surrounded by those who have discovered the elixir and attained immortality. The eight Taoist Immortals, usually represented in pairs, each with fixed attributes, are Chung-li Ch'üan with his fan or fly whisk: Lü Tung-pin with a sword: Li T'ieh-Kuai with pilgrim's gourd and staff: Ts'ao Kuo-ch'iu with castanets: Lan Ts'ai-ho with basket of flowers: Chang Kuo Lao with bamboo tubes and rods: Han Hsiang Tzŭ with a flute: and Ho Hsien Ku with a lotus. There are, too, the three star gods of Happiness, Rank, and Longevity: Fu Hsing, who carries a babe and a peach: Lu Hsing, in official robes and carrying a ju-i staff with fungus-shaped head: Shou Hsing, with a scroll attached to a long staff and a peach. The Queen of the Genii is Hsi Wang Mu, in whose home in the K'un-lun Mountains the sacred peach tree of long life grows. Fable says that she visited the Han Emperor Wu Ti with an attendant carrying a tray of peaches, three of which were stolen by Tung Fang So, who gained thereby a longevity of three thousand years. The Twin Genii of Mirth and Harmony also belong to the Taoist cult. There is besides a host of worthies (Hsien jên), such as Wang Chi, who is represented watching two sages playing chess in the mountains; Hou Hsien

Shêng, with his three-legged toad, and others too many to enumerate. In the animal world the hare is sacred as the animal who lives in the moon, where he pounds the elixir of life with pestle and mortar, while the tortoise and the stork are emblems of longevity. The subjects taken from profane history consist principally of battle scenes and incidents from the romantic story of the Three Kingdoms, court scenes, groups of mandarins and their attendants, and incidents in the life of famous historical personages such as Chiang-tzǔ Ya, minister of Prince Si Po, who is depicted fishing on a promontory; the poet Li T'ai-po, reclining in drunken repose by a wine jar, or beside his adored lotuses, or being waited upon at court by the Emperor and his Ministers; and T'ao Yuan-ming, or Chü Tz'ǔ-t'ung, the lovers of the chrysanthemum.

The Seven Worthies of the Bamboo Grove form another favourite group, as do also the frequenters of the Orchid Pavilion; and the Virtuous Heroines are a not uncommon subject. Ideal figures of tall, graceful girls (*mei jên*) usually appear in isolated panels, and domestic scenes with ladies and playing children are sympathetically rendered. And the Four Liberal Accomplishments—writing, painting, music, and chess—are illustrated by appropriate groups.

The commonest animal subjects are the mythical creatures such as the dragon, the imperial monster usually represented as guarding the sacred pearl and surrounded by cloud scrolls and flames. He appears enveloped in the clouds or rising from sea waves, and on imperial wares of the present and the last dynasties he is always depicted with five claws. Another dragon is the *ch'ih-lung*, an archaic lizard-like creature with divided tail. Next to the dragon comes the phœnix, or *fêng-huang*, a bird of auspicious appearance, which has the head of a pheasant, beak of a swallow, long neck, gorgeous plumage, and long streaming tail. It is the especial emblem of the Empress. Scarcely less familiar is the lion, a conventional creature, not unlike a Peking spaniel, and usually depicted in twos or threes sporting with a ball of brocade, from which it draws out long streamers in its teeth or paws. The kylin is another common subject for decoration, a mythical creature of composite form, with the body and legs of a deer, horned head of a dragon, and bushy tail. He is a creature of good omen like the phœnix, and should be distinguished from the strange tribe of chimæras known as *hai shou*, or sea monsters, by the Chinese. Of the more ordinary creatures, the monkey and the horse are most commonly depicted on porcelain, the eight celebrated horses of the Emperor Mu Wang being a favourite theme, and the dragon-horse skimming over sea waves occurs frequently on Ming porcelain.

Landscapes form another frequent motive, and aquatic scenes. A common border is formed of curling waves dashing against rocks, or wavy water on which plum blossoms are carried, or watery depths with fishes swimming among aquatic plants. Fish are depicted with great skill by both Chinese and Japanese, the favourite species being the carp, an emblem of perseverance, and consequently of literary success. The carp is represented leaping up waterfalls, and the story runs that when the carp succeeds in making the ascent of the Yellow River in the third moon of the year, and passing the falls at the *Lung Mên* (Dragon Gate), he turns into a dragon, a myth which is frequently represented in porcelain.

Birds, trees and flowers provide a host of motives, all exquisitely rendered by the Chinese painter. Cranes among lotuses, mandarin ducks swimming in pairs (an emblem of conjugal love), and gorgeous pheasants on rockery are perhaps the most effective designs, though the smaller birds are prettily depicted with their appropriate trees and shrubs. A bird singing on a rock, or a solemn eagle on a mountain peak are especially common on a very attractive group of Ming blue and white porcelain, painted in pale silvery blue on a thin crisp ware. Insects, too, are used to fill up smaller spaces, and occasionally they form a primary motive, as on certain specimens of the Ming ware just described, where a large cicada on a rock fills the foreground of a landscape panel.

But of all the subjects of porcelain decoration none, perhaps, are so frequently or so skilfully used as flowers, shrubs and trees. They are usually depicted in combinations which have a meaning to the Chinese. Thus the pine, bamboo and winter-flowering plum *(sung, chu, mei)* are the three faithful friends, and are associated with Confucius, Buddha, and Lao Tzŭ. Or again, the prunus, tree peony, lotus and chrysanthemum are the flowers of the four seasons, representing winter, spring, summer and autumn respectively. The pine and the bamboo are also emblems of longevity, the peony of riches and honour, and the lotus has a Buddhistic significance. The peach is a Taoist emblem of long life, and both blossom and fruit form a common motive. Wild orchids, rushes and flowering grasses are freely used, and a garden scene with flowering plants and fantastic rockeries is a favourite decoration Sometimes the entire surface of a vase is covered with a mass of blossoms of different kinds, a decoration known as "the hundred flowers." Among fruits the peach, pomegranate and finger citron typify the three abundances of years, sons and happiness; and three plums are an attribute of Lao Tzŭ. The gourd too is an emblem of longevity, and the gourd vine, like that of the melon and the grape, lends itself to continuous scroll design. Another emblem of longevity is the *ling-chih* fungus, commonly depicted with grass growing through it. The head of this fungus seems to supply the shape for the end of the *ju-i* sceptre of longevity, and it appears in endless repetition in a common border pattern.

SYMBOLS IN DECORATION.

Pure Chinese ornament is rarely devoid of emblematic meaning, but there is a large number of sacred and semi-sacred symbols which are interwoven in the decoration, and sometimes used in place of a mark under the porcelain. Of these the *Yin-yang* and the *Pa Kua* are perhaps the most conspicuous. The *Yin-yang*, in form a circle bisected by a curved line, symbolises the dualism of nature. The *Pa Kua* consists of eight trigrams or sets of three parallel lines, one set undivided and the rest divided in different ways. They illustrate a mystic system by which all the phenomena of nature are explained. There are besides the eight musical instruments and the twelve ornaments embroidered on the ancient sacrificial robes, the eight Happy Omens from the foot of Buddha, viz. (1) the wheel of the law, sometimes replaced by a bell; (2) the conch-shell of victory; (3) the umbrella of state; (4) the tasselled canopy; (5) the lotus flower; (6) the vase, containing a *ju-i* sceptre or a peacock's feather; (7) the pair of fishes; (8) the angular knot. To these are added the Seven Gems of the Universal Monarch:—(1) the golden wheel; (2) the "jade-like girl"; (3) the horse; (4) the white elephant, which carries the jewel of the law; (5) the minister; (6) the general; and (7) the bundle of jewelled wands which fulfil every wish. Another symbol of universal occurrence is the *swastika*, which is used sometimes by the Chinese as a synonym for the word *wan* (ten thousand), and seems to express a wish for long life. It

is often worked in to ornamental diapers or frets, which resemble the well-known "key pattern." The attributes of the Taoist Immortals are also employed as symbols, and there is the comprehensive group known as the Hundred Antiques *(Po Ku)*, which seems to include emblems of all kinds, both sacred and profane. It includes the eight Precious Things *(Pa pao)*, viz. the sphere or pearl, the cash, the open lozenge, the solid lozenge, the musical stone, the pair of books, the pair of rhinoceros horns and the artemisia leaf, all of which are usually decked with ribbons. Others are the tripod censer, the fan and staff, wine jar, water pot, *ju-i* sceptre, coral branch, &c. Groups of these symbols are commonly used to fill panels in porcelain decoration. The Chinese word for a bat has the same sound as *Fu* (happiness), and for this reason the bat is used as an emblem of happiness, and five bats symbolising the five happinesses frequently occur on porcelain.

The art of calligraphy ranks in China with painting and drawing, and well-written inscriptions are regarded as integral parts of decorative ornament. Hence the frequency of lines of poetry (usually in five or seven characters), dedicatory and complimentary inscriptions, &c., besides the ornamental forms of such beneficent words as *Shou* (longevity), *Fu* (happiness), and *Lu* (rank).

THE EIGHT PRECIOUS THINGS (*Pa pao*)

 The jewel (*chu*).

The "cash" (*ch'ien*).

 The lozenge (*fang shéng*).

The painting (*hua*).

 The musical stone (*ch'ing*).

The pair of books (*shu*).

 The pair of horn cups (*chüeh*).

 The artemisia leaf (*ai yeh*).

SYMBOLS, Etc., USED AS MARKS

 The conch-shell.

 Tripod vase.

 The tripod vase.

 Tripod vase.

 The lotus flower.

 Flower symbol.

 The lotus flower.

 Flower symbol.

 The lotus flower.

 Flower symbol.

The pair of fishes

Swastika or fyl-fot symbol, Chinese *wan* (tenthousand) symbolising longevity.

The knot.

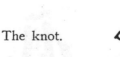 The knot.

Fu, the sacred axe.

Fungus *(ling chih)*, emblem of longevity.

Fungus *(ling chih)*, emblem of longevity.

Fungus *(ling chih)*, emblem of longevity.

Head of a *ju-i* staff of longevity (derived from the fungus).

A fly.

A gourd inscribed *shihfu* (manifest happiness).

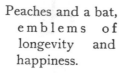

Peaches and a bat, emblems of longevity and happiness.

Stork (emblem of longevity), with the mark of the Dresden Collection below. The Dresden Collection was formed by Augustus the Strong, about 1694-1705.

Stork on a late Ming blue and white plate in the Max Rosenheim Collection, exhibited at the Burlington Fine Arts Club in 1910.

The hare of the moon, a sacred animal of the Taoist cult.

Rabbit on late Ming porcelain in the Franks Collection.

A brush *(pi)*, a cake of ink *(ting)*, and a longevity sceptre *(ju-i)*, forming the rebus *pi ting ju-i* = "May things be fixed as you wish," on eighteenth century porcelain in the Franks Collection.

Unknown mark on a blue and white bowl found in Siam.

Marks on Chinese porcelain and pottery are classified as (1) marks indicating date, (2) "Hall" marks, (3) marks of commendation which include expressions of praise of the ware itself, or of good wishes for its possessor, and (4) potters' marks which include the name of the maker or the place of manufacture, or both. The transliteration of Chinese characters followed throughout, is that used by Sir Thomas Wade in his transliteration of the Mandarin dialect, and adopted by Professor Giles and other compilers of standard dictionaries.

Marks are painted in underglaze blue or in enamel colours on the glaze, or stamped with a seal in the body of the ware, or more rarely etched with a fine point. They are usually written either in the ordinary script (*ch'iai shu*) or in the angular seal character (*chuan tzŭ*), more rarely in archaic script or in the cursive hand known as "grass" writing (*tsao shu*). The usual place for the mark is under the base, where it is commonly enclosed in a double ring, but sometimes it is placed in the decoration, or on the mouth-rim of the vessel. Marks on imperial wares are carefully pencilled, but on the ordinary trade goods they are often so freely and carelessly written as to be scarcely recognisable.

DATE MARKS

Indications of date are expressed by (*a*) the "reign name" of the Emperor, or (*b*) by cyclical dates.

(*a*) The Emperor, whose personal name ceased to be used when he ascended the dragon throne, selected a title by which he wished his reign to be known. This is the *nien hao* or period name which appears in porcelain marks,[1] and is by far the commonest form of date mark.

Before the eighteenth century the *nien hao* was almost invariably written in the ordinary script (the Yung Lo mark on p. 351 being quite exceptional), but from the reign of Yung Chêng (1723-36) onward, it occurs frequently in the angular seal character. Date marks in seal character before this reign should be regarded with suspicion.

It is stated in the *T'ao Lu*, that in the year 1677, the prefect of Ching-tê-chên issued an order forbidding the potters to inscribe the Emperor's name or depict the deeds of distinguished men on porcelain, lest they should be dishonoured by the breaking of the porcelain. It is unlikely that this prohibition remained in force for any length of time, but its existence may account to some extent for the frequent use of symbols in place of the mark on K'ang Hsi wares, and also partly for the fact that the double ring under the base of many pieces has been left blank.

The reader is cautioned against placing too much reliance on the dates implied in the year-period marks. When they occur on Imperial wares they can be trusted implicitly; but in the private factories which catered for the general public, the *nien hao* of dead Emperors were used

---

[1] After his death the Emperor was also known in history by an honorific title under which he was deified. This is called *miao hao*.

with bewildering freedom. This is especially the case with the *nien hao* of the early Ming Emperors such as Hsüan Tê and Ch'êng Hua which are perhaps the commonest date marks on modern wares.

The complete *nien hao* consists of six characters, usually written in two columns of three each and read downwards, starting with the right hand column. The first character is *ta* (great), the second gives the name of the dynasty, the third and fourth the reign-name of the Emperor, the fifth is the word 年 *nien* (year or period), and the sixth a word meaning *made* usually *chih* 製 but sometimes *tsao* 造 . To take an example, the *nien hao* of Ch'êng Hua (1465-87) is

1	2	3	4	5	6
Ta	*Ming*	*Ch'êng*	*Hua*	*Nien*	*Chih*
6		3	4	5	1	2

= made (in the) Ch'êng Hua period (of the) great Ming (dynasty).

Sometimes the first two characters are omitted, and the mark is written in two columns of two characters, thus—

Ch'êng Hua nien chih = made in the Ch'êng Hua period.

On rare occasions we find the word *yü* (imperial) substituted for *nien*, as—

Yung Chêng yü chih = made by order of the Emperor Yung Chêng.

Occasionally the characters of the mark are strung out in a single line read from the right.

In the following lists of *nien hao* of the Sung and Yuan Emperors, the name of the dynasty and the words *nien chih* are omitted for brevity's sake. The same applies to the minor reigns of the Ming and the present dynasties, but in the case of the reigns which were celebrated for their wares, or of which the names occur on known examples of porcelain or pottery, the date marks are given in full as they appear in actual specimens.

CHINESE DYNASTIES

FROM 206 B.C. TO THE PRESENT TIME.

	漢	Han . . 206 B.C.	西	魏	Western Wei 535-557 A.D.	元	Yuan . 1280 A.D.		
後	漢	Hou After } Han . 25 A.D.	東	魏	Eastern Wei 534-543	明	Ming . 1368		
蜀	漢	Shu Minor } Han 221	北	齊	Northern Ch'i } 550-577	清	Ch'ing . 1644		
	魏	Wei	北	周	Northern Chou } 557-581				
	吳	Wu		隋	Sui . . . 589				
西	晉	Hsi Western } Chin 265		唐	T'ang . . 618				
東	晉	Tung Eastern } Chin 317	後	梁	After Liang . 907				
劉	宋	Liu Sung . . 42	後	唐	,, T'ang . 923				
齊		Ch'i . . 479	後	晉	,, Chin . 936				
梁		Liang . 502	後	漢	,, Han . 947				
陳		Ch'ên . 557	後	周	,, Chou . 951				
北	魏	Pei Northern } Wei 386-532		宋	,, Sung . 960				
			南	宋	Nan Southern } Sung 1127				

The Three Kingdoms

NIEN HAO OR REIGN NAMES

SUNG DYNASTY, 960-1279 A.D.

建隆	*Chien Lung* .	960
乾德	*Ch'ien Tê* . .	963
開寶	*K'ai Pao* . .	968
太平國	*T'ai P'ing* .	} 976
興國	*Hsing Kuo*	
雍熙	*Yung Hsi* . .	984
端拱	*Tuan Kung* .	988
淳化	*Shun Hua* . .	990
至道	*Chih Tao* . .	995
咸平	*Hsien P'ing* .	998
景德	*Ching Tê* . .	1004
大中	*Ta Chung* . .	} 1008
祥符	*Hsiang Fu* .	
天禧	*T'ien Hsi* . .	1017
乾興	*Ch'ien Hsing* .	1022

天明 祐	*T'ien Shêng* .	1023
明道	*Ming Tao* . .	1032
景祐	*Ching Yu* . .	1034
寶元	*Pao Yüan* . .	1038
康定	*K'ang Ting* .	1040
慶歷	*Ch'ing Li* . .	1041
皇和	*Huang Yu* . .	1049
至和	*Chih Ho* . .	1054
嘉祐	*Chia Yu* . .	1056
冶平	*Chih P'ing* .	1064
熙寧	*Hsi Ning* . .	1068
元豐	*Yüan Fêng* .	1078
元祐	*Yüan Yu* . .	1086
紹聖	*Shao Shêng* .	1094
元符	*Yüan Fu* . .	1098

建	中	*Chien Chung*	
靖	國	*Ching Kuo*	1101
崇	寧	*Tsung Ning* . 1102	
大	觀	*Ta Kuan* . . 1107	
政	和	*Chêng Ho* . . 1111	
重	和	*Chung Ho* . . 1118	
宣	和	*Hsüan Ho* . . 1119	
靖	康	*Ching K'ang* . 1126	
建	炎	*Chien Yen* . . 1127	
紹	興	*Shao Hsing* . 1131	
隆	興	*Lung Hsing* . 1163	
乾	道	*Ch'ien Tao* . 1165	
淳	熙	*Shun Hsi* . . 1174	
紹	熙	*Shao Hsi* . . 1190	
慶	元	*Ch'ing Yüan* . 1195	

嘉	泰	*Chia T'ai* . . 1201	
開	禧	*K'ai Hsi* . . 1205	
嘉	定	*Chia Ting* . . 1208	
寶	慶	*Pao Ch'ing* . 1225	
紹	定	*Shao Ting* . . 1228	
端	平	*Tuan P'ing* . 1234	
嘉	熙	*Chia Hsi* . . 1237	
淳	祐	*Shun Yu* . . 1241	
寶	祐	*Pao Yu* . . 1253	
開	慶	*K'ai Ch'ing* . 1259	
景	定	*Ching Ting* . 1260	
咸	淳	*Hsien Shun* . 1265	
德	祐	*Tê Yu* . . 1275	
景	炎	*Ching Yen* . 1276	
祥	興	*Hsiang Hsing* 1278	

YUAN DYNASTY (1280-1367).

中	統	Chung T'ung . 1260		泰	定	Tai Ting . . 1324
至	元	Chih Yüan . 1264		致	和	Chih Ho . . 1328
元	貞	Yüan Chêng . 1295		天	曆	T'ien Li . . 1329
大	德	Ta Tê . . 1297		天	曆	T'ien Li . . 1330
至	大	Chih Ta . . 1308		至	順	Chih Shun . 1330
皇	慶	Huang Ch'ing 1312		元	統	Yüan T'ung . 1333
延	祐	Yen Yu . . 1314		至	元	Chih Yüan . . 1335
至	治	Chih Chih . . 1321		至	正	Chih Chêng . 1341

Unimportant Nien Hao of the Ming Dynasty.

建	文	Chien Wên . 1399-1402		景	泰	Ching T'ai 1450-56
洪	熙	Hung Hsi . 1425		天	順	T'ien Shun 1457-64
正	統	Chêng T'ung 1436-49		泰	昌	Tai Ch'ang . 1620

Unimportant Nien Hao of the Ch'ing Dynasty.

天	命	T'ien Ming 1616-26	天	聰	T'ien Tsung 1627-35
崇	德	Ts'ung Tê 1636-43			

SUNG DYNASTY.

Ta Sung Ching Tê nien chih.
In seal characters.
(1004-1007)

Ta Sung Yüan Fêng nien chih
(1078-1085).

MING DYNASTY.

Hung Wu nien chih
(1368-1398).

The same in seal characters.

Yung Lo nien chih
(1403-1424).

The same in archaic characters.

Ta Ming Hsüan Tê nien chih
(1426-1435).

Ta Ming Hsüan Tê nien chih.
In seal characters.

Ta Ming Ch'êng Hua nien chih
(1465-1487).

Ch'êng Hua nien chih
(1465-1487).

The same in seal characters.

Ta Ming Hung Chih nien chih
(1488-1505).

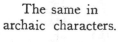

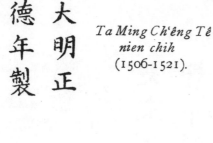

德年製　大明正　*Ta Ming Ch'êng Tê*
　　　　　　　　　nien chih
　　　　　　　　　(1506-1521).

曆年製　大明萬　*Ta Ming Wan Li*
　　　　　　　　nien chih
　　　　　　　　(1573-1619).

靖年製　大明嘉　*Ta Ming Chia*
　　　　　　　Ching nien chih
　　　　　　　(1522-1566).

啟年製　大明天　*Ta Ming T'ien*
　　　　　　　Ch'i nien chih
　　　　　　　(1620-1627).

慶年製　大明隆　*Ta Ming Lung*
　　　　　　　Ch'ing nien chih
　　　　　　　(1567-1572).

年製　崇楨　*Ch'ung Chên nien*
　　　　　　chih
　　　　　　(1628-1643).

CH'ING DYNASTY.

治年製　大清順　*Ta Ch'ing Shun*
　　　　　　　Chih nien chih
　　　　　　　(1644-1661).

熙年製　大清康　*Ta Ch'ing K'ang*
　　　　　　　Hsi nien chih
　　　　　　　(1662-1722).

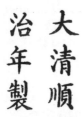

The same in seal
characters.

The same in seal
characters.

大清雍正年製

Ta Ch'ing Yung Chêng nien chih (1723-1735).

The same in seal characters.

大清乾隆年製

Ta Ch'ing Ch'ien Lung nien chih (1736-1795).

The same in seal characters.

嘉慶年製

Chia Ch'ing nien chih (1796-1820).

Ta Ch'ing Chia Ch'ing nien chih. In seal characters. (1796-1820).

大清道光年製

Ta Ch'ing Tao Kuang nien chih (1821-1850).

Ta Ch'ing Tao Kuang nien chih. In seal characters. (1821-1850).

大清咸豐年製

Ta Ch'ing Hsien Fêng nien chih (1851-1861).

The same in seal characters.

大清同治年製

Ta Ch'ing Tung Chih nien chih (1862-1874).

The same in seal characters.

大清光緒年製

Ta Ch'ing Kuang Hsü nien chih (1875-1909).

The same in seal characters.

MISCELLANEOUS DATE MARKS.

Wu Fêng êrh nien = second year of Wu Fêng (*i.e.* B.C. 57). Incised on an unglazed pottery jar in the British Museum.

Mark copied from a coin of Wang Mang (A.D. 9-23) inscribed *pu ch'üan* stamped on an unglazed pottery scoop in Mr. William C. Alexander's Collection. Exhibited at the Burlington Fine Arts Club in 1910.

大明天　啟元年

Ta ming t'ien ch'i yüan nien = first year of T'ien Ch'i of the great Ming dynasty (1621 A.D.).

Ch'ien lung nien chih = made in the Ch'ien Lung period (1736-95); a short form of the seal mark on p. 353.

Ta Ch'ing Ch'ien lung fang ku = imitation of antique (made in) the Ch'ien Lung period of the great Ch'ing dynasty (1736-95) (Bushell).

(b) CYCLICAL DATES.

Another Chinese method for computing time is the system of sixty year cycles, which is supposed to have begun 2637 B.C., the first cycle in our era being the forty-fifth and starting with the year Four. Each year of the sixty 's named in two characters which consist of one of the Ten Stems preceding one of the Twelve Branches. A table of the Stems and Branches is given below. The Ten Stems are divided into five pairs which correspond with the five Chinese elements—wood, fire, earth, metal, and water. The Twelve Branches are also used to represent the twelve Zodiacal signs—the rat, ox, tiger, hare, dragon, serpent, horse, sheep, monkey, cock, dog, and boar—as well as the twelve divisions of the day and the points of the compass. Taking the first stem and combining it with the first branch, the second stem with the second branch, and so on, it will be seen that the combinations are not complete until the sixty has been reached, the least common multiple of ten and twelve. A complete table of cyclical years since 4 A.D. is given on the next page.

Stems.		Elements.			Branches.	Zodiacal Signs.	
1. 甲	Chia	Corresponding to	木 Mu (wood)		子	Tzŭ	rat
2. 乙	i				丑	Ch'ou	ox
3. 丙	Ping	” ”	火 Huo (fire)		寅	Yin	tiger
4. 丁	Ting				卯	Mao	hare
5. 戊	Wu	” ”	土 T'u (earth)		辰	Shên	dragon
6. 己	Chi				巳	Ssŭ	serpent
7. 庚	Kêng	” ”	金 Chin (metal)		午	Wu	horse
8. 辛	Hsin				未	Wei	sheep
9. 壬	Jên	” ”	水 Shui (water)		申	Shên	monkey
10. 癸	Kuei				酉	Yu	cock
11.					戌	Hsü	dog
12.					亥	Hai	boar

TABLE OF CYCLICAL DATES FROM A.D. 4.

Left half

Cyclical Signs		CYCLE BEGINNING				
		4	64			
		304	364	124	184	244
		604	664	424	484	544
		904	964	724	784	844
		1204	1264	1024	1084	1144
		1504	1564	1324	1384	1444
		1804	1864	1624	1684	1744
甲	子	04	64	24	84	44
乙	丑	05	65	25	85	45
丙	寅	06	66	26	86	46
丁	卯	07	67	27	87	47
戊	辰	08	68	28	88	48
己	巳	09	69	29	89	49
庚	午	10	70	30	90	50
辛	未	11	71	31	91	51
壬	申	12	72	32	92	52
癸	酉	13	73	33	93	53
甲	戌	14	74	34	94	54
乙	亥	15	75	35	95	55
丙	子	16	76	36	96	56
丁	丑	17	77	37	97	57
戊	寅	18	78	38	98	58
己	卯	19	79	39	99	59
庚	辰	20	80	40	100	60
辛	巳	21	81	41	101	61
壬	午	22	82	42	102	62
癸	未	23	83	43	103	63
甲	申	24	84	44	104	64
乙	酉	25	85	45	105	65
丙	戌	26	86	46	106	66
丁	亥	27	87	47	107	67
戊	子	28	88	48	108	68
己	丑	29	89	49	109	69
庚	寅	30	90	50	110	70
辛	卯	31	91	51	111	71
壬	辰	32	92	52	112	72
癸	巳	33	93	53	113	73

Right half

Cyclical Signs		CYCLE BEGINNING				
		4	64			
		304	364	124	184	244
		604	664	424	784	544
		904	964	724	784	844
		1204	1264	1024	1084	1144
		1504	1564	1324	1384	1444
		1804	1864	1624	1684	1744
甲	午	34	94	54	14	74
乙	未	35	95	55	15	75
丙	申	36	96	56	16	76
丁	酉	37	97	57	17	77
戊	戌	38	98	58	18	78
己	亥	39	99	59	19	79
庚	子	40	100	60	20	80
辛	丑	41	101	61	21	81
壬	寅	42	102	62	22	82
癸	卯	43	103	63	23	83
甲	辰	44	104	64	24	84
乙	巳	45	105	65	25	85
丙	午	46	106	66	26	86
丁	未	47	107	67	27	87
戊	申	48	108	68	28	88
己	酉	49	109	69	29	89
庚	戌	50	110	70	30	90
辛	亥	51	111	71	31	91
壬	子	52	112	72	32	92
癸	丑	53	113	73	33	93
甲	寅	54	114	74	34	94
乙	卯	55	115	75	35	95
丙	辰	56	116	76	36	96
丁	巳	57	117	77	37	97
戊	午	58	118	78	38	98
己	未	59	119	79	39	99
庚	申	60	120	80	40	100
辛	酉	61	121	81	41	101
壬	戌	62	122	82	42	102
癸	亥	63	123	83	43	103

Like the *nien hao*, the cyclical dates usually end with the words *nien chih* or *nien tsao* (both meaning "made in the year ——"), but as the number of the cycle is usually omitted, the exact date can only be guessed from the style of the ware on which the mark occurs, or from some other circumstance, as in the annexed mark, *Yu hsin ch'ou nien chih* ("made in the hsin ch'ou year recurring"). The *hsin ch'ou* year recurred in the long reign of K'ang Hsi in 1661[1] and 1721, and we may reasonably conclude that the date indicated is the year 1721. Occasionally the *nien hao* is given as well as the cyclical year, and then the exact date is easily computed.

The same characters are used in computing cyclical dates in Japan.

Ping hsü nien chih = Made in the *ping hsü* year, which may refer to the year 1886, 1826, 1766, 1706, 1646, &c.

Ta ming ch'êng hua yüan nien i yu = The *i yu*, first year of the Ch'êng Hua (period) of the Great Ming (dynasty), *i.e.* 1465 A.D.

For other marks containing cyclical dates, see pages 373 and 374.

In rare instances the number of the year of a reign, with even the number of the month and day, is given in both Chinese and Japanese date marks, and for this reason the following table of numerals is appended. The characters are the same in both Chinese and Japanese.

---

[1] The *nien hao* of the Chinese emperor is reckoned officially from the beginning of the year following the death of his predecessor. Thus the K'ang Hsi period dates from 1662, though the emperor actually began his reign in 1661.

NUMERALS.

Fig.	Common Form.	Short Form.	Long Form.	Chinese.	Japanese.
1.	一		弌	*I*	*Ichi*
2.	二		弍	*Êrh*	*Ni*
3.	三		弎	*San*	*San*
4.	四		肆	*Ssŭ*	*Shi*
5.	五		伍	*Wu*	*Go*
6.	六		陸	*Liu*	*Roku*
7.	七		柒	*Ch'i*	*Shichi*
8.	八		捌	*Pa*	*Hachi*
9.	九		玖	*Chiu*	*Ku*
10.	十		什	*Shih*	*Ju*

Another Japanese rendering of the numerals is: 1, *Hitotsu*, or *hi*. 2, *Futatsu* or *fu*. 3, *Mitsu* or *mi*. 4, *Yotsu* or *yo*. 5, *Itsutsu* or *itsu*. 6, *Mutsu* or *mu*. 7, *Nanatsu* or *nana*. 8, *Yatsu* or *ya*. 9, *Kokonotsu* or *kokono*.

Numbers between ten and twenty are expressed by placing the numerals in excess of ten after the character for ten, and multiples of ten by placing the requisite numeral before the character for ten, as in the following instances :—

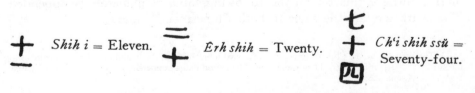

十一 *Shih i* = Eleven.   二十 *Êrh shih* = Twenty.   七十四 *Ch'i shih ssŭ* = Seventy-four.

NUMERALS USED AS MARKS.

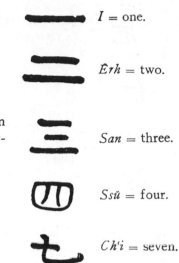

I = one.

$\hat{E}rh$ = two.

Numerals incised on Chün-chou porcelain of the Sung dynasty, exhibited at the Burlington Fine Arts Club in 1910.

San = three.

$Ss\check{u}$ = four.

$Ch'i$ = seven.

(2) HALL MARKS.

Hall marks are so called because they contain the word *t'ang* (a hall), or some equivalent, such as *chai* (a studio), *fang* (a retreat), &c.; and they may refer to the potter's shed, the painter's studio, the dealer's shop, the house of a noble, or the palace or pavilion of an emperor. The absence of any preposition leaves it doubtful whether the mark refers to the place *where* or the place *for which* the object is made, and the general sense alone decides the translation. Such marks usually consist of four characters, the first two giving the name of the hall, the third the word *t'ang* (hall), and the fourth the word *chih* or *tsao* (made). The last word is occasionally omitted, and sometimes the mark is lengthened to six characters or more by addition of descriptive words or phrases. The key-word to these marks is

T'ang (a hall), for which is sometimes substituted one of the following :—

Chai (a studio).

Fang (a retreat).

Hsüan (a terrace).

 Chü (a retreat), and more rarely *chuang* (a workshop), and *t'ing* (a retreat).

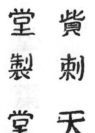

The *T'ao Shuo* (see Bushell, op. cit., p. 110) mentions a white Ting ware vase of the Sung dynasty with the characters in the margin obliquely inscribed upon it. The mark reads *Jên ho kuan* = Hall of Generous Harmony.

Yang ho t'ang chih = Made at (or for) the hall for the cultivation of harmony. On a saucer painted in blue and red under the glaze in the Franks Coll. Early eighteenth century.

Yü t'ang chia ch'i = Beautiful vessel of the Jade hall. On late Ming porcelain, blue and white, and blue and red underglaze.

Ch'i yü t'ang chih = Made at the hall of rare jade. On two blue and white saucers of the K'ang Hsi period (1662-1722) in the Franks Coll.

Tzü tz'ü t'ang chih = Made at the hall of the purple thorn. Given by Bushell and Jacquemart.

T'ien ch'ang t'ang chih = Made at the hall of heaven-sent prosperity. Given by Bushell and Jacquemart.

Yung lo t'ang chih = Made at the hall of perpetual enjoyment. On a snuff-bottle painted in blue and red under the glaze. Early eighteenth century. Franks Coll.

永樂
堂製

Ts'ai hua t'ang chih = Made at the hall of brilliant painting. On a saucer with Buddhistic ornament in enamels. Early nineteenth century. Franks Coll.

彩華
堂製

Ts'ai hsiu t'ang chih = Made at the hall of brilliant decoration. On a nineteenth century blue and white bowl in the Franks Coll.

彩秀
堂製

Ts'ai jun t'ang chih = Made at the hall of brilliant colours. In red on a saucer dish painted in enamels over a blue outline. Early nineteenth century. Franks Coll.

彩潤
堂製

Ching wei t'ang chih = Made for the hall of respectful awe. On a white dish with "rice-grain" decoration in the Franks Coll. Late eighteenth century. Supposed to be a palace mark.

敬畏
堂製

Tê hsing t'ang chih = Made for the hall of fragrant virtue. On a blue and white bowl of the Wan Li period (1573-1619), painted with the eight horses of Mu Wang. Franks Coll.

德馨
堂製

Lu yi t'ang = Hall of waving bamboos. On enamelled porcelain of various periods in the present dynasty.

綠猗堂

Yü hai t'ang chih = Made at the hall of ocean jade. In black, on a set of trays enamelled in colours on the biscuit. Early eighteenth century. Franks Coll.

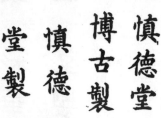

(1) *Shun tê t'ang chih* = Made for the hall for the cultivation of virtue; (2) *Shun tê t'ang po ku chih* = Antique made for the hall for the cultivation of virtue. A palace mark on blue and white, and enamelled porcelains made in the early nineteenth century.

Chü shun mei yü t'ang chih = Made at the Chü shun hall of beautiful jade. On a late seventeenth century blue and white saucer dish in the Franks Coll.

I yu t'ang chih = Made at the hall of (?) prosperity and profit. On a pipe painted in blue and white, with graceful girl figures. K'ang Hsi period (1662-1722). Franks Coll.

Ta shu t'ang chih = Made at the big tree hall. In black on an enamelled bowl of the Ch'ien Lung period (1736-95) in the Franks Coll.

Lin yü t'ang chih = Made at the hall of abundant jade. On a blue and white bowl, K'ang Hsi period (1662-1722), in the Franks Coll.

Ching lien t'ang fang ku chih = Imitation of antiques made at the Ching-lien hall. On a nineteenth century blue and white bowl decorated with floral sprays. Franks Coll.

Ssŭ kan ts'ao t'ang = Straw pavilion on the river bank. Given by Bushell.

Fêng hsien t'ang = Hall for the worship of ancestors. Given by Bushell.

Fu ch'ing t'ang chih = Made at the hall of happiness and good fortune. Given by Bushell as on a specimen in the Walters Coll.

Ching ssŭ t'ang chih = Made for the hall of classic lore. On a wine cup of the Yung Chêng period (1723-35), in the Walters Coll. Given by Bushell. *Ching ssŭ* (lit., Box containing the classics) is a phrase connoting deep scholarship.

Lu chu shan fang chên tsung = Precious treasure of the green bamboo mountain lodge. (Bushell.)

Tan ning chai chih = Made in the studio of peace and tranquillity. On a colour dish with lotus scroll in blue and white. Nineteenth century. Franks Coll.

Chan ching chai chih = Made in the studio of deep peace. On a yellow-ground bowl. Early nineteenth century. In the Collection of General Sir R. Biddulph.

Ssŭ pu chai chih = Made for the pavilion for meditation for the correction of faults. On a nineteenth century enamelled bowl in the Franks Coll.

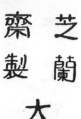

Chih lan chai chih = Made at the epidendrum studio. On a seventeenth century bowl with blue and white decoration, enclosing medallions with figures of Buddha. Franks Coll.

Ta ya chai = Pavilion of grand culture. A palace mark of the late Empress Dowager. On an enamelled bowl in the Franks Coll.

Yu chai = Quiet studio. Studio name of a painter on an enamelled "egg-shell" cup, about 1724. Franks Coll.

Tsui yüeh hsüan chih = Made on the terrace of the drunken moon. On an early nineteenth century enamelled bowl in the Franks Coll.

Ku yüeh hsüan chih = Made by Ku Yüeh-hsüan (ancient moon terrace). Mark on glassy porcelain finely enamelled. Mid-eighteenth century. (Bushell.)

Chu shih chü = The red rocks retreat. (Bushell.)

Wan shih chü = The myriad rocks retreat. (Bushell.)

Shu ch'ang, i.e. Made for the *shu ch'ang kuan*—a college in the Han-lin University at Peking. (Bushell.)

Shu fu, a phrase meaning "Imperial palace," said to have been engraved inside white bowls in the Yuan dynasty. Found occasionally on modern wares, *e.g.* a bowl with engraved decoration and bluish-green glaze in the Franks Coll.

(3) MARKS OF COMMENDATION

(A number of symbols are given on pages 341-4.)

Three of the many fantastic "seal" forms of the character *shou* (longevity). A blue and white vase in the Franks Coll. is decorated entirely with the numerous varieties of the word known as the "hundred *shou*."

Another fanciful form of *shou*, known as the "spider mark," and found on blue and white porcelain made about the year 1700 for export.

Lu = Emolument. Frequently inscribed on porcelain with the two companion blessings, *shou* (longevity), and *fu* (happiness). The last named occurs in a four-character mark below (*wan fu yu t'ung*), and another character *fu* (riches) occurs on other marks given below.

Seal form of *lu* (emolument), on a blue and white dish of the K'ang Hsi period (1662-1722), in Mr. F. A. White's Collection.

Dr. Bushell suggested that this mark is a variation of *Fu shou* = Happiness and longevity. It occurs in Chinese blue and white, and also on Japanese (Kaga) enamelled ware.

Wan fu yu t'ung = May infinite happiness embrace your affairs. On two sixteenth century bowls in the British Museum, one decorated in blue and white inside and gilt coral red outside.

Fu kuei ch'ang ch'un = Riches, honour, and enduring spring. Found on several sixteenth century specimens, chiefly blue and white, in the British Museum.

Mark in the form of a "cash" coin, reading *Ch'ang ming fu kuei* = Long life, riches, and honour. On a blue and white bowl, with sixteenth century mount, in the Franks Coll.

In the square *Tê hua ch'ang ch'un* = Virtue, culture, and enduring spring, surrounded by the characters *Wan li nien tsao* = Made in the Wan Li period (1573-1619). On a pair of dishes painted in dark but vivid blue, in the Franks Coll.

Yung ch'ing ch'ang ch'un = Eternal prosperity and enduring spring. On late Ming porcelains.

Two marks reading *Wan shou wu chiang* = A myriad ages without ending. The second is in seal character.

T'ien kuan tz'ŭ fu = May the powers of heaven grant happiness.

天官吉祥狀元文章
賜福如意

Chi hsiang ju i = Good fortune and fulfilment of wishes! (Bushell.)

Chuang yuan chi ti = May you obtain the degree of Chuang-yuan. On a brush-pot. (Bushell.) The degree of Chuang-yuan is the highest attainable by State examinations.

及弟山斗

Wên chang shan t'ou = Scholarship lofty as the hills and the Great Bear. On a blue and white brush-pot, with six scholars seated at a table and a long inscription. K'ang Hsi period (1662-1722). Franks Coll.

Tan kuei = Red olive; a symbol of literary honours. On a Ming bowl, blue and white inside, and coral red with gilt lotus scroll outside. Franks Coll.

丹桂永盛慶

Yung shêng = Ever full. On a blue and white wine cup in the Walters Coll., Baltimore. (Bushell.)

Ch'ing = Congratulations. (Bushell.)

Ta = Great.

大

Ta chi = Great luck.

大吉

胎
玉
Tai yü = Body like jade. The word jade *(yü)* 玉 occurs by itself or in numerous combinations as a mark,

e.g. 真 玉 *Chên yü* = veritable jade. 玩 玉 *Wan yü* = trinket jade. 西 玉 *Hsi yü* = western jade.

These marks are chiefly on blue and white of the K'ang Hsi period (1662-1722).

集
錦
Chi chin = Massed brocade. On blue and white porcelain in Mr. F. A. White's Coll. K'ang Hsi period (1662-1722).

宝
勝
Pao shêng = Inexpressibly precious. On a blue and white bowl with dragon continued over the rim on to the reverse. Early eighteenth century. Franks Coll.

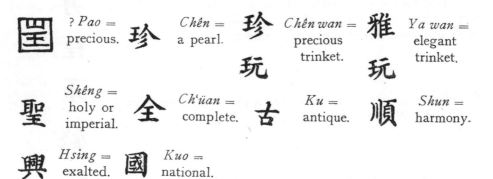

圁 ? *Pao* = precious. 珍 *Chên* = a pearl. 珍 玩 *Chên wan* = precious trinket. 雅 玩 *Ya wan* = elegant trinket.

聖 *Shêng* = holy or imperial. 全 *Ch'üan* = complete. 古 *Ku* = antique. 順 *Shun* = harmony.

興 *Hsing* = exalted. 國 *Kuo* = national.

Marks found on small blue and white pieces of the K'ang Hsi period (1662-1722).

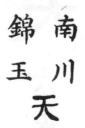

錦 南
玉 川
天

Nan ch'uan chên yü = Elegant jade of Nan ch'uan. On a blue and white saucer of the K'ang Hsi period (1662-1722), in the Franks Coll. Dr. Bushell explained that Nan ch'uan (south (of) the river) is a name given to the town of Ching-tê-chên.

T'ien = Heaven. On blue and white porcelain. Supposed to be an abbreviation of the reign name *T'ien ch'i* (1621-27), but this is extremely doubtful.

Kung = Workmanship. On a blue and white barrel-shaped sprinkler in Lord Altamont's Collection. K'ang Hsi period (1662-1722).

Fa = Issued (? for sale). On a blue and white bowl of fine quality in the Franks Coll. K'ang Hsi period (1662-1722).

Kao = High (in value). Incised on the base of a Chün ware vase of the Sung dynasty, in Mr. William C. Alexander's Collection.

Pao yung = Precious (vessel) for use. On a Ko ware bowl of the Sung dynasty in Mr. G. Eumorfopoulos' Collection. This and the last mark were figured in the Catalogue of early Chinese wares exhibited at the Burlington Fine Arts Club in 1910.

Chih = Made (to order). On an early eighteenth century enamelled plate in the Franks Collection.

Fu kuei chia ch'i = Fine vessel for the rich and honourable. On late Ming porcelain.

I shêng = Harmonious prosperity. On a saucer dish of Canton stoneware, with mottled brown and grey glaze. Franks Collection. Probably eighteenth century.

友
來

鼎
之
珍

鼎
之
珍

珍
玩

如
玉

玲
藏

深
珍
甤

奇
石
寶

奇
玉
宝

博
古

奇
珍

漢
溪
若

Yu lai = Arrival of friends. On a seventeenth century blue and white dish in the Franks Collection.

Ch'i shih pao ting chih chên = A gem among precious vessels of rare stone. On a bowl enamelled in colours in the Franks Collection. Seventeenth century.

Ch'i yü pao ting chih chên = A gem among precious vessels of rare jade. On blue and white porcelain of the seventeenth century, in the Franks Collection.

Po ku chên wan = A jewelled trinket of antique art. On blue and white porcelain of the K'ang Hsi period, in the Franks Collection.

Ch'i chên ju yü = A gem rare as jade. On blue and white porcelain of the K'ang Hsi period, in Mr. F. A. White's Collection.

Jo shên chên tsang = To be treasured as very precious (lit. Like a deep gem). On porcelain of various periods, the present mark being in seal characters.

Huo ch'i jo shên chên tsang = To be treasured like a deep gem of the boiling stream. Probably an allusion to the jade found in mountain torrents. On blue and white porcelain of good quality in the Franks Collection.

Ts'ang lang lü shui = Green water of the boundless ocean. On a blue and white saucer-dish of the sixteenth century in the Franks Collection.

滄浪在川愛蓮 綠水知樂珍賞

Tsai ch'uan chih lo = Rejoicing in the stream. On a saucer painted with red fish among water plants. Yung Chêng period (1723-35). Franks Collection.

Ai lien chên shang = Precious reward for the lover of the lotus. On a saucer painted with water lilies of the Yung Chêng period. Franks Collection.

Kuan lien fang chih = Made for the look-lily boat (a lake excursion boat). On a tazza of blue and white porcelain of the Ch'ien Lung period (1736-95) in the Franks Collection.

製舫蓮觀

Shêng yu ya chi = The elegant collection of holy friends. On blue and white cups painted with graceful ladies, in the Franks Collection. Late seventeenth century.

雅集聖友師府

Shuai fu kung yung = For the public use in the general's hall. On a blue and white bowl painted with dragons in the Franks Collection. Wan Li period (1573-1619).

公用

Nei yung chih ch'i = Vessel for use within the house. Incised on the base of a Ming vase, with turquoise ground, and engraved bands of ornament coloured yellow and aubergine, in Mr. S. E. Kennedy's Collection.

之器內用

酒 *Chiu* = wine. 棗湯 *Tsao t'ang* = decoction of dates. 薑湯 *Chiang t'ang* = decoction of jujubes.

These three inscriptions are said in the *Ching-tê-chên T'ao Lu* to occur inside Imperial altar cups of the Chia Ching period (1522-66).

Hsieh chu chu jên tsao = Made for the lord of the Hsieh bamboos. The minister of the fabulous Huang Ti cut bamboos for musical instruments in the Hsieh Valley. On an early nineteenth century enamelled bowl in the Franks Collection.

Hsü = Dawn. On blue and white porcelain of the K'ang Hsi period (1662-1722), in Mr. F. A. White's Collection.

A private seal. (Bushell.)

G.

Mark resembling the letter **G.** On a pair of bottles with formal floral scrolls painted in fine blue. K'ang Hsi period. In Mr. F. A. White's Collection.

One of many illegible seals, known as "shop marks," which occurs on Chinese porcelain of all periods.

Another formal seal from early eighteenth century porcelain, adopted by the Old Worcester Porcelain Company as their "square mark."

(4) NAMES OF POTTERS OR POTTERIES.

The name of the potter rarely appears in Chinese porcelain marks, though it is far more common on earthenware and stoneware. The reason is probably that in the large porcelain factories, where a minute division of labour was observed, no particular individual could fairly receive credit for the finished piece. But it must be remembered that the "hall marks" often contains the "studio name" of the decorator, and consequently ranks as a signature.

Hu yin tao jên = The Taoist hidden in a pot. An art-name adopted by Hao Shih-chiu who is described in the *T'ao Lu* as a very skilful potter of the reign of Wan Li (1573-1619).

Wan li ting yu ch'ên wên ching su = Ch'ên Wên ching modelled it in clay in the *ting yu* year of Wan Li (*i.e.* 1597). Incised on a seated figure of buff stoneware with marbled ornament in the Collection of Mr. G. Eumorfopoulos.

T'ien Ch'i i ch'ou nien chin shih chih = Made by Chin-shih in the *i ch'ou* year of T'ien Ch'i (*i.e.* 1625). Incised on a Canton stoneware dish with mottled glaze in Sir Arthur Church's Collection.

Wang shih ch'ih ming = Mr. Wang Ch'ih-ming. Impressed on a pillow of creamy ware painted in black in Mr. G. Eumorfopoulos' Collection. Probably Tz'ŭ-chou ware, late Ming period. The last three specimens were exhibited at the Burlington Fine Arts Club in 1910.

Chang chia tsao = Made by Chang-chia. Impressed on a pillow of similar ware to the last, and in the same collection.

Wang pu t'ing tso = Made by Wang Pu-t'ing. Impressed on a box with beautifully carved reliefs and an opaque yellow glaze in the Veitch Collection, Birmingham Art Gallery. Early nineteenth or late eighteenth century.

Wang ping jung tso = Made by Wang Ping-jung. On a similar specimen in the Hamburg Museum.

Wu shên nien liang chi shu = Painting of Liang-chi in the *wu shên* year. On a coffee-pot with enamelled rosettes in a brick red ground, in the Franks Coll. The cyclical date *(wu shên)* no doubt refers in this case to the year 1808.

Kuang liang chi tsao = Made by Kuang Liang-chi. Stamped on a brown biscuit figure of Ho Shang in the Dresden Collection: late seventeenth century.

Chiang ming kao tsao = Made by Chiang Ming-kao. Stamped in an ornamental framework on a white biscuit Buddhist figure in the Franks Collection. Early eighteenth century.

Chia ch'ing san nien ssŭ ming chi jih wang shêng kao chih = Made by Wang Shêng-kao at the end of the fourth month of the third year of Chia Ch'ing (*i.e.* 1798). Painted in blue beneath a bowl with "rice-grain" decoration, in the Franks Coll.

Lin ch'ang fa tsao = Made by Lin Ch'ang-fa. On a blue and white dish of the early nineteenth century in the Franks Coll.

Shang su. A name on an eighteenth century vase with brownish yellow glaze and ornament in bronze style in the Franks Coll.

Koming hsiang chih = Made by Ko Ming-hsiang. Stamped on Canton stoneware of the eighteenth century.

Ko yüan hsiang chih = Made by Ko Yüan-hsiang. On similar ware.

Huang yün chi = Recorded by Huang-yün. On a Canton stoneware figure of a cat, with red *flambé* glaze, in the Franks Coll. Nineteenth century.

Li Ta-lai. A potter's name on a Canton stoneware jar in the Franks Coll. About 1800.

T'ai-yüan. A potter's name on similar ware.

Yüeh-ch'ang. A potter's name on similar ware.

Yi hsing. Yi hsing hsien in the province of Kiangsu, where the fine pottery teapots &c. in red, buff, and drab ware are made. On an opium pipe-bowl in the Franks Coll., and made by Ching Yüan-yu; see below.

Mêng-ch'ên and *Hui* (on the right), names of an old Yi-hsing potter impressed on modern teapots in the British Museum.

Chin yüan yu chi = Recorded by Chin Yüan-yu. Stamped on an opium pipe bowl in the Franks Coll. Yi-hsing ware, with enamelled decoration.

 Yu lan pi chih = Secret manufacture of Yu-lan. Stamped on a light red stoneware teapot with engraved decoration, in the Franks Coll Eighteenth century Yi-hsing ware.

 Ch'ên ming yüan chih = Made by Ch'ên Ming-yüan. Stamped on a drab stoneware teapot with blue-speckled surface in the Franks Coll. Early eighteenth century Yi-hsing ware.

Hsiu lung tê chi = Recorded by Hsiu Lung-tê. On a red stoneware teapot in the Franks Coll. Early eighteenth century Yi-hsing ware.

 *Fu fan chih tsao* = Made on the borders of Fukien (the province). On a Ming blue and white bottle in the Franks Coll.

 Kuan yao nei tsao = Made in the Government kiln. In red on a bowl with yellow ground in the Franks Coll. Early nineteenth century.

In preparing the sections on Chinese and Japanese wares, the following works have been consulted :—

Catalogue of a Collection of Oriental Porcelain and Pottery, by A. W. Franks, 1879.
Oriental Ceramic Art, by S. W. Bushell, 1899.
Chinese Art, vol. ii. Victoria and Albert Museum Handbook, by S. W. Bushell, 1906.
Porcelain, Oriental, Continental, and British, by R. L. Hobson, 1909.
Marks on Pottery and Porcelain, Burton and Hobson, 1909.
Japan and China, vol. ix., by Capt. F. Brinkley, 1904.
Catalogue of Japanese Pottery, in the Museum of Fine Arts, Boston, by E. S. Morse, 1901.
Japanese Pottery, South Kensington Museum Art Handbook, 1880.

Japan

HE native name of Japan is Nippon, or Dai Nippon, Great Nippon, *i.e.* the Land of the Rising Sun.

It may be desirable to give a brief account of the form of government in Japan, the more especially as important recent changes have been made, altering the constitution very materially. The sovereign power was lodged in a supreme head or ruler, but the greater part of the country was subject to vassal princes or *Daimios*, who paid tribute or rendered military service to the lord paramount. Every office was hereditary, descending from father to son. There was a single race of sovereigns, reputed to have descended from the gods, who governed the empire through successive centuries down to A.D. 1195, when the late singular government arose, the then commander of the army usurping the greater part of the secular power, leaving the lawful sovereign little more than spiritual power. The spiritual sovereign was known by the title of Mikado, and his court by that of the Däiri, or assembly of native princes. The temporal or actual sovereign was called the Siogun or Shogun. Both sovereigns had their separate courts and capitals, the spiritual chief residing in Miako, the temporal chief in Yedo. The Mikado, although nominally supreme, had not a particle of temporal power, being literally shut up in Miako, in his little principality of Kioto, with the revenues of which and presents sent him by the Siogun he was compelled to rest satisfied.

DAI-NI-PON.

The laws of *Gongen-Sama*, the great founder of the dynasty (1593-1606), denounced as high treason, with death for the penalty, any one harbouring a foreigner within the dominions of the Siogun; all who had been cast ashore or made the attempt were either killed or imprisoned, and no Japanese was allowed to leave his island home.

After the expulsion of the Spaniards and Portuguese from Japan and the first massacre in A.D. 1590 of upwards of 20,000 Christians, followed in A.D. 1637 by a second, in which 37,000 were put to death in one day, the following decree was passed, which isolated Japan from the rest of the world, and which was fully acted up to for more than two centuries : "No Japanese ship or boat whatever, nor any native person, shall presume to go out of the country. Whosoever acts contrary to this shall die, and the ship, with the crew and goods abroad, shall be sequestered till further orders. All Japanese who return from abroad shall be put to death. Whoever discovers a Christian priest shall have a reward of 500 schuets (£381), and for every Christian in proportion. All persons who propagate the doctrine of the Christians or bear this scandalous name shall be imprisoned. The whole race of the Portuguese and whoever belongs to them shall be banished to Macao. Whoever presumes to bring a letter from abroad or to return after he has been banished shall die with all his family, also whoever presumes to intercede for him shall be put to death. No nobleman nor any soldier shall be suffered to purchase anything of a foreigner."

The Dutch, a few years after the expulsion of the Portuguese, succeeded in obtaining the confidence of the Japanese, and were permitted to reside on an island called Deshima, near the port of Nagasaki, in the province of Hizen, where they erected a factory, and had an exclusive right of trading there, which was carried on surreptitiously and to a limited extent with the Japanese, and by their non-interference with the religion of the people they retained the privilege for more than two hundred years.

In 1868, however, this anomalous state of things was altered, a revolution broke out, and the office and power of the Siogun were abolished. He had been usually but erroneously called by a Chinese title, the *Taicoon* or *Tycoon* (which dates only from 1858), but the Mikado was in 1868 restored to his ancient supremacy. He is regarded as a source of power and property. "There is no single thing existing in the land which is not the Emperor's; the water in which the child is washed at its birth, and the earth in which it is buried, are all his. The rice we eat, the money we use, the clothes we wear, the cap we put on, the staff which supports us, are all the produce of the Emperor's land. He is the father and mother of the empire."

Under the influence of these principles a marvellous national movement has taken place. The Daimios, or territorial princes, who, under the Siogun, exercised almost absolute sway within their territories, have almost unanimously surrendered their lands and titles to the Mikado, from whom they are to hold their possessions henceforth in dependency, and are no longer to be styled Daimios, but simply *Kazoku* (nobles). The majority of these had voluntarily given in their adhesion in 1869, being reappointed *Chiji*, or governors of their respective provinces.

The Mikado received in great state the Duke of Edinburgh at Yedo, the first known instance of the reception of a foreign prince (except Chinese).

The first great collection of Japanese art seen in the Western world was at the International Exhibition at Paris in 1867, sent over by the Tycoon the year preceding his deposition, which was dispersed piecemeal to visitors. To this succeeded the Japanese Court at Vienna in 1873, which contained superb pieces of the rarest and finest work in porcelain, enamel, and lacquer principally examples of modern manufacture. Among the lacquer-work at Vienna may be especially noted two cabinets, valued by the Japanese Commissioners at £938 and £730 each; these and other fine specimens were recalled to form a National Art Museum in Japan. Many choice pieces were, however, secured for private collections in this country from these exhibitions. The International Exhibition at Phila-delphia in 1876 was, in a historical point of view, of far greater interest, from the fact of more ancient examples being exhibited; and as the chief intent of making such a collection became evident to the intelligent anti-quaries of Japan, very careful catalogues were prepared, and we are consequently enabled to assign localities and approximate dates to the ancient as well as the more recent examples.

The system of Japanese writing is directly the reverse of ours; they, like the Chinese, write from top to bottom, and from right to left in per-pendicular lines, and their books begin where ours end. They have three modes or systems of writing : the first consists of Chinese characters; and although no approach to fusion has ever taken place between the two nations, yet the Japanese did adopt at some distant period the Chinese system of writing; but the difference of the language, although it carries the same impression to the mind, is expressed in other sounds. The second and third consist of two alphabets known as the *Katagana* and *Hiragana*, phonetic systems adopted at a later period, but not altogether displacing the first; thus it is not uncommon in books to find the three systems written on the same page.

The Sinto is the original religion of the Japanese, and Tensio Dai Sin is the supreme of all the gods of the Japanese, and patron and protector of the Empire. On this are engrafted the two religions derived from China—Buddhism and Confucianism.

The Japanese use no other furniture in their rooms than rugs or mats, and a pillow or padded rest for their heads, lacquered or inlaid cabinets with porcelain vases, &c., among the wealthy; but beds, tables, and chairs are superfluities. The greatest Daimio holds these as encumbrances and altogether insufferable, being only fit for foreigners.

The travelling equipage of the Japanese Diplomatic Mission, in their visit to the several Powers of Europe in 1862, numbering thirty-five in all, including the envoys, ministers, subordinate officers, secretaries, doctors, accountants, cooks, barbers, and servants, with baggage and provisions, &c., to match, consisted of fifty crockery teapots, 5000 cham-pagne bottles of soy, a service of five porcelain cups for every individual, with saucers innumerable to serve as plates, &c. There were also fifty *hibachi*, or vessels for burning charcoal, to warm the rooms, and heat water or other liquids.

It will be remarked in examining the Japanese Historical Collection in the Victoria and Albert Museum how many of the examples of ancient pottery are destined for the preservation and use of tea; they are mostly of coarse manufacture and rudely ornamented, but they were evidently prized for their antiquity and fitness for the purpose, real or imaginary. In this we must allow the Japanese to be the best judges of their qualities, for it is scarcely competent for Europeans to express an opinion, having, comparatively, at so recent a period become acquainted with the beverage. These jars or bottles are frequently covered with ivory lids, sometimes of wood, and are used to contain the tea-leaf, either freshly cropped and dried or ground. Jars for ground tea were made at Seto in Owari in the fourteenth century, and there are many others of the seventeenth century.

Old Bizen tea-vases were in demand, as were also "Raku" ware, tea-bowls from Kioto; others of "Shigaraki" ware (province of Omi) were used for keeping rice-seed to be steeped in water; ash bowls for cere-monious tea-parties of "Hitasuki" ware, and "Takatori" tea-bowls of the sixteenth and seventeenth centuries. For drinking the spirit called Sake, "Soma yaki" cups were used. Many other varieties will be noticed in speaking of the productions of the provinces under their respective headings. These common and slightly ornamented wares were used principally by the tea-clubs formed for drinking powdered tea. The ceremonies connected with this usage were numerous. The vessels were to be of a coarse and archaic character; the tea used was the finest green, ground to powder and frothed up with a brush or whisk made of bamboo; it was passed round in a bowl made for the purpose, of rude pottery, and various solemn forms had to be adhered to—even the size of the room was prescribed. The Raku ware was much in vogue among the tea-clubs.

In every branch of her industrial arts Japan is deeply indebted to her neighbours on the mainland, and pottery is no exception. The history of Japanese ceramics shows that at every stage of their development the influence of China or Corea was apparent. The earliest examples which we possess, excavated from burial mounds, and dating from the third century B.C. to the seventh century A.D., are precisely the same as those found in Corea, and this fact serves to explain the tradition that a Corean in the first century of our era introduced the art into Japan. Further improvements in the eighth century are, again, attributed to a Corean monk named Gyogi, who is reputed to have gone from place to place teaching his art. Many of the traditions which have clustered round his name are purely fictitious, and the statement that he introduced the potter's wheel in Japan was disproved by the discovery of wheel-made ware in the old burial mounds.

The early pottery was mostly red or grey, unglazed, and varying in hardness from soft terra-cotta to stoneware: needless to say it was un-marked. The introduction of tea from China brought with it a demand for more refined wares, and we see the Japanese turning for aid to China. A potter named Kato Shirozaemon (commonly named Toshiro) visited China in 1223, and learned the secret of applying thick rich glazes from

the Sung potters. On his return, after a search for suitable clays, he
found what he required at Seto, in the province of Owari, and settled there
in 1227, his family continuing the work for many generations. The
energies of the potters were now largely devoted to supplying the vessels
required in the ceremonial drinking of tea, and in these we find Corean
influences strongly in evidence. The yellowish white bowls, the inlaid
and marbled wares of Corea, were accepted as models by the tea-drinkers.
The Karatsu factories were founded by Coreans, the Raku ware was
invented by a Corean in the sixteenth century, the famous Satsuma potteries were started by captive Corean families, who have preserved
their individuality to this day. But it was to China that the Japanese
turned for knowledge of the manufacture of porcelain. Gorodayu Go-
Shonzui journeyed to Ching-tê-Chên in 1510, and spent five years there
among the porcelain factories. He returned with a perfect knowledge of
the manufacture of blue and white porcelain; but when the stock of
Chinese materials which he brought with him was exhausted, he was
unable to discover native sources of supply. Indeed, nearly a century
elapsed before the abundant native materials were discovered on Mount
Izumi-yama in the province of Hizen, by a Corean named Risampei. From
this time the manufacture of porcelain was established in Japan. The
next important step was the discovery of the use of enamel colours
for the decoration of the ware. It is said that this was first learnt by
the Corean potters in Hizen, but it is certain that two Japanese potters,
Kakiemon and Tokuemon, were responsible for the development of this
beautiful decoration; and tradition attributes their enlightenment to
Chinese sources, a thing in itself highly probable. From Hizen the secrets
of porcelain making and enamel painting gradually spread, and a revolution was worked in Japanese pottery by Ninsei in Kioto, who first
applied painted enamels to glazed pottery. He was followed by a host
of Kioto potters, and the Awata district of Kioto became for ever famous
for its enamelled fayence.

But if the inspiration in so many cases came to Japan from China and
Corea, there was no lack of native talent to take up the ideas and develop
them on original lines. The Japanese are a nation of potters, and as
they work in families and small groups, each setting a particular mark or
seal on its wares, the variety of fabriques is enormous and bewildering.
In this they differ from the Chinese, who seem to have combined to work
in large factories, and whose names rarely appear on their productions.
Japanese porcelain, on the other hand, was rarely marked with potters'
names before the nineteenth century. It was purely imitative of the
Chinese, and the marks which do occur are usually Chinese *nien-hao*, or
date marks, symbols or words of commendation. The porcelain itself
differs slightly from the Chinese in make, being always submitted to a
preliminary firing, after which the glaze is applied and melted in a second
firing. In appearance the Japanese porcelain, if we except one or two of
the finer makes, such as Hirado and Nabeshima, is, as a rule, coarser and

greyer than the Chinese, the glaze is not so smooth and oily, and the bottoms of dishes are frequently scarred with "spur marks," *i.e.* holes made by the points of the supports on which the ware stood in the kiln. There are of course many other points of difference in the colour and style of decoration, but these vary with the individual wares.

The subjects selected by the Japanese artists in decorating their wares are generally birds and flowers, artistically and naturally drawn, enclosed in medallions, of various forms, and never adhering to the principles adopted by Europeans of centres surrounded by circles and well-balanced lateral ornaments, making the two halves of a subject correspond. These notions of taste are completely set at defiance; the borders even of the same medallion are of irregular form, sometimes divided in halves or quarters, and set in the sides, corners, or edges of a piece, in what we might call the most admired disorder; their flowers are natural, and without the stiffness we are accustomed to see. On the other hand, the human figure is always treated in a conventionalised type. Among birds we find represented the stork, pheasant, falcon hawk, poultry, &c., and especially a species of beautiful duck with richly coloured plumage, called *kinmodsui.* The flowers and plants are numerous, but the favourites are the *Paulownia imperialis* and the chrysanthemum, both being imperial emblems; the camelia, the lotus, the bamboo, the pine-tree, the *sakura* or flowering cherry, the *butan* or pæony, the wisteria, the peach, the wild vine, gourds, the fungus, &c. Small animals are frequently introduced, such as dogs, cats, foxes, monkeys, and rabbits,[1] and a great variety of fishes and insects. Among them the *doogame,* or common tortoise, the *minogame,* or tortoise with a feathery tail, the *tako,* or cuttlefish, are conspicuous. A favourite object in landscapes is the sacred mountain Fusiyama (an extinct volcano), represented as seen from Yedo. Among the chimerical birds the principal is the *hōō* or bird of paradise, with a peacock's tail and rich plumage, whose appearance upon earth denotes some extraordinary event, as the birth of a prince or accession of an emperor. The *rio* or dragon, whose dwelling is in the depths of the sea, is a huge, long, four-footed snake, scaly all over the body like a crocodile, with sharp prickles along its back, the head monstrous and terrible; it has but three claws on each foot, whereby it is distinguished from the Chinese imperial dragon which has five claws. In some of the Japanese Emperor's furniture, hangings, &c., this dragon is represented holding a round jewel or pearl in the right fore-claw.

The *kirin* of Japan (akin to the *kylin* of China) is a winged quadruped of incredible swiftness, with two soft horns standing before the breast and bent backwards, with the body of a horse and feet of a deer. To the *kirin* is attributed extreme good-nature, and it takes especial care in walking not to trample on any plant, nor to injure the most inconsiderable worm that might chance to be in its way.

---

[1] The Japanese are particularly successful in portraying the expression of birds and monkeys, especially the latter, with distorted limbs, humorous positions, and comical faces.

A few of the deities, demi-gods, &c., are here given:—

Fukurokuju, the god of knowledge, seated on a stork.

Dai-ko-ku, the god of plenty, whose hammer has the miraculous property of turning everything it strikes into something precious.

Jiu-ro-jin, "oldest of men," the god of good luck and happiness, attended by a deer.

Hotei, the god of happiness, holding a wine-cup

Yebisu, the fisher-god of Japan.

Bishamon, god of military glory, dressed as a warrior and holding a spear and a small pagoda.

Benten, the madonna or guardian goddess of the mountain Fusiyama, sometimes seated playing on a lyre.

Kami-nari, the thunder-demon, sitting on a cloud with a drum on his back.

Kintoku, a sort of infant Hercules, who at three years of age was able to hold a powerful bull by the horns.

Daruma, a follower of Buddha, who by long meditation in a squatting position lost his legs from paralysis and sheer decay.

Shoki, the strong man, who is represented fighting with a demon.

These are frequently represented on Japanese pottery and porcelain, but there were many other household gods *(Kami)*, and every house possessed a *kami-dana* or "shelf for the gods," on which were placed shrines, lighted up during the period of family devotions, morning and evening,—the god of the kitchen, the Shinto gods *(Kami)*, the *Hotoké* or Buddhist deities, the god of punishment and revenge *(Fudo-son)*, and patrons of all sorts of personages, &c. Among the emblems the most commonly used are those of *Longevity, Happiness*, &c. The word *shou* (Japanese *ju*), "Longevity," is the most frequent, and is represented in endless variety. A set of a hundred forms of this character is on the roll in the British Museum.

THE CRESTS OF THE MIKADO.

1. The Mikado has two crests; the first Imperial ensign is called the *Guikmon* or *Kiku*, representing the back or under side of the chrysanthemum flower, and has been used since it was first adopted by the founder of the family, who ascended the throne of Japan 667 B.C.

2. The second crest represents the *Kiri* or *Paulownia imperialis*, with its leaves and flowers. It is the official ensign, the mark of power, seen on coins, and was seen on the bread and cakes served at the receptions of the Dutch Ambassadors.

These two marks, together or separate, are frequently seen on porcelain vases and other objects for Imperial use, sometimes accompanied by the three-clawed dragon, or the chimerical bird *Hō-ō*.

These arms or crests of the Mikado and the Daimios are unchangeable; the names of the inheritors may vary according to the mutations assumed by the family or its title, but the crest remains the same. Their retainers have these cognisances worked on the backs or sleeves of their tunics, and the crests are frequently found on porcelain enamels, and lacquer-work made specially for the use of the nobles.

THE CRESTS OF THE SIOGUNS.

1. The crest of Minamoto Yoritomo, the founder of the Minamoto family, and the first who usurped the temporal sovereignty of Japan, 1185-1202. This crest continued in use until 1586.

Hide Yoshi, surnamed Taikosama, was Siogun in 1586, but the period only lasted until 1593.

2. The crest of Jyéyas, surnamed Gonghensama, the head of the Tokoungawa family, 1593-1606.

The fifteen succeeding Sioguns were of the same family.

This *Minamoto* crest of three mauve or marsh-mallow leaves was used until the extinction of their power in 1868.

THE CREST OF THE REGENT OR GOTAIRO.

3. The crest of Ikamon-no-kami, the Prince of Hikoné. The late Regent was assassinated in 1860. The office of Regent was assumed whenever a minor filled the Siogun's throne. He resided at Yedo. Sir Rutherford Alcock says, "Over the gates, in copper enamel, is the crest of the noble owner (an orange on a branch with three leaves), the chief of the house of Ikamon, in whom is vested the hereditary office of Regent."

THE CRESTS OF THE THREE GREATEST DAIMIOS.

4. The Prince of Kaga.

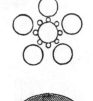

5. The Prince of Satsuma (viceroy of the island of Kiu-Siu).

6. The Prince of Shendi. A mirror case of lacquer-work bears this crest. In Mr. J. L. Bowes' Collection.

DAIMIOS OR PRINCES OF SECONDARY RANK.

There are as many as 278 Daimios, each having his crest; we give only some of the more important of them

7. Nagato.

9. Bizen.

8. Aki.

10. Harima.

11. Kuroda.

17. Sataké.

12. Shimosa.

18. Suwò.

13. Wakasa.

19. Sinano.

14. Tanga.

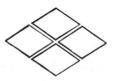

20. Nambu.

15. Ossumi.

21. Chikugo.

16. Yamashiro.

22. Akita.

23. Kuwana.

26. Owazima, or Owajima.

24. Asiu.

27. Prince of Hizen.

25. Hikoné.

28. Prince of Kaga.

JAPANESE PERIODS.

The Japanese system of dates is somewhat like the Chinese *Nien-hao*, and is written in the same characters, *Ch'iao Shu*, differing only in the names of the periods, which are assumed by the Emperors when they ascend the throne. In Japan these periods were more frequently changed in each Mikado's reign. They are called *Nengo*, and complete lists may be found in Kæmpfer's "Japan," in Hoffman's "Grammar," and another has been privately printed by Mr. E. Satow. The *Nengo* is composed of two, seldom of more characters, which must be taken from a particular table, selected specially for this purpose, consisting of sixty-eight characters.

The ordinal numbers used by the Japanese are similar to the Chinese, but differently pronounced in each country. (See page 355.)

Note.—Inscriptions in the Chinese character are frequently found on Japanese wares.

"NENGO" OR JAPANESE PERIODS.

	A.D.			A.D.
德中授和中四永長享吉安德德正禄正正仁明亨德應龜正永禄 建文天弘元德明應正永嘉文宝亨康長寛文應文長延明文永大亨 Ken-tok	1370.	永治禄龜正禄長和永保安應曆治文寶和亨禄永德保文保享延 天弘永元天文慶元寛正慶承明萬寛延天貞元寶正享元寛延寛 Di-yei	1532.
Bun-tin	1372.	Ko-dsi	1555.
Ten-du	1375.	Yei rok	1558.
Ko-wa	1380.	Gen-ki	1570.
Gen-tin	1380.	Ten-show	1573.
Mei-tok the IV.	1393.	Bun-rok	1592.
O yei	1394.	Kei-chiyo	1596.
Show-tiyo	1428.	Gen-wa	1615.
Yei-kiyo	1429.	Kwan-jei	1624.
Ka-kitsu	1441.	Show-ho	1644.
Bun-an	1444.	Kei-an	1648.
Ko-tok	1449.	Show-o	1652.
Kiyo-tok	1452.	Mei-reki	1655.
Ko-show	1455.	Man-dsi	1658.
Chiyo-rok	1457.	Kwan-bun	1661.
Kwan-show	1460.	Yem-po	1673.
Bun-show	1466.	Ten-wa	1681.
O-nin	1467.	Tei-kiyo	1684.
Bun-mei	1469.	Gen-rok	1688.
Tiyo-kiyo	1487.	Ho-yei	1704.
En-tok	1489.	Show-tok	1711.
Mei-o	1492.	Kiyo-ho	1717.
Bun-ki	1501.	Gen-bun	1736.
Yei-show	1504.	Kwan-po	1741.
Dai-jei	1521.	Yen-kiyo	1744.
Kiyo-rok	1528.	Kwan-yen	1748.

		A.D.				A.D.
曆 寶	*Ho-reki*	. . 1751.		化 弘	*Koo-kwa*	. . 1844.
和 明	*Mei-wa*	. . 1764.		永 嘉	*Ka-yei*	. . 1848.
永 安	*An-jei*	. . 1772.		政 安	*An-sei*	. . 1854.
明 天	*Ten-mei*	. 1781.		延 萬	*Man-en*	. 1860.
政 寬	*Kwan-sei*	. . 1789.		久 文	*Bun-kiu*	. . 1861.
和 享	*Kiyo-wa*	. . 1801.		治 元	*Gen-dzi*	. . 1864.
化 文	*Bun-kwa*	. . 1804.		應 慶	*Kei-oo*	. . . 1865.
政 文	*Bun-sei*	. . 1818.		治 明	*Mei-ji*, 1868 to present	
保 天	*Ten-foo*	. . 1830.			time.	

EXAMPLES OF DATES.

Gen-ki nen-sei. "Made in the period Gen-ki," A.D. 1570 to 1573. On a bowl painted in colours and gilding, with flowers and panels of figures, &c. Franks Collection.

Ten-show. "Seventh year," corresponding with A.D. 1579.

Show-o. "Second year," corresponding with A.D. 1653.

Yem-po nen-sei. "Made in the period Yem-po," A.D. 1673 to 1681. On specimens of Nabeshima porcelain, made at Iwayagawa, province of Hizen. Franks Collection, Two circular trays painted with fans, blossoms, &c.

Bun-kua nen-sei. "Made in the period Bun-kua," A.D. 1804 to 1818. On porcelain painted blue, from Hizen, a square vase painted with figures. Franks Collection.

Mei-ji-nen To-yen-sei. "Made by To-yen in the Mei-ji period," 1868 to the present time. On a blue and white porcelain saucer with phœnixes, &c. Franks Collection.

JAPANESE WARES.

ARRANGED IN PROVINCES AND TOWNS, WITH THE NAMES OF THE PRINCIPAL FABRICS AND POTTERS THEREIN.

Notes.

The references are principally to the Catalogue of the Japanese Historical Collection of Pottery and Porcelain exhibited at Philadelphia in 1867, now preserved at the Victoria and Albert Museum, descriptive tablets being affixed with corresponding numbers. These are alluded to as *Jap. Hist. Coll.*

We may here again remark that the Japanese word *Yaki* is a general term, used indifferently to signify pottery or porcelain, and has misled many, by comprehending the word in its latter sense. Hence Dr. Hoffmann, and after him M. A. Jacquemart, formed erroneous opinions as to the origin of porcelain-making in Corea as well as Japan.

PROVINCES.

		PAGE			PAGE
	Yamashiro	391		Tambà	413
	Yamato	400	5.	Izumo	413
1.	Izumi	401		Iwami	413
	Settsu	401		Harima	414
	Isé	402	6.	Bizen	415
	Owari	404		Nagato	416
2.	Totomi	407	7.	Awaji (Island)	416
	Kii	407		Omi	408
	Musashi	408		Chikuzen	417
3.	Mino	411	8.	Higo	417
	Echizen	411		Hizen	418
4.	Kaga	411		Satsuma	420

DENOMINATION OF WARES (YAKI).

	PAGE		PAGE
Akahada	400	Gobosatsu	394
Akashi	415	Gosuke	411
Arita	419	Hagi	416
Asahi	392	Hansuke	406
Awata	394	Himeji	414
Bairin	408	Hirado	420
Banko	402	Hoko	425
Benshi	410	Hokuhan	406
Bizan	395	Hoju	425
Dohachi	397	Horaku	405
Eiraku	399	Hozan	395
Fujina	413	Hozen	398
Fukagawa	421	Hyochi yen	410
Fukami	422	Imado	409
Fushimi	392	Imbe	415
Fuyeki	403	Inuyama	405
Gempin	404	Kagura	400

DENOMINATION OF WARES—(continued).

	PAGE		PAGE
Kahin Shiriu	399	Oribe	404
Kairaku yen	399	Ota	410
Kakiemon	419	Otokoyama	407
Kameyama	424	Otowa	397
Kaneshige	414	Owari	405
Kanzan	399	Raku	396
Karatsu	418	Rakuzan	413
Kawamoto	406	Rantei	398
Kentei	397	Rujozen	398
Kenya	409	Same	424
Kenzan	394	Sampei	416
Kikko	402	Sanrakuyen	407
Kinshosha	410	Sarayama	424
Kioto	391	Seifu Yohei	399
Kishiu	407	Seta	408
Kitei	398	Seto	404
Kiyochika	415	Shiba	409
Koto	424	Shidoro	407
Kozan	395	Shigaraki	408
Kutani	412	Shino	404
Kuwana	403	Shippo Kuwaisha	406
K'wa-bo	416	Shuhei	397
Kyomizu	396	Shuntai	405
Maiko	414	Soma	414
Makuzu	399	Tai hei	395
Mikawaji	420	Taizan	395
Mikuni	411	Takatori	417
Mimpei	416	Tanzan	395
Mimato	401	Tatsumonji	424
Mishima	417	Toshiro	404
Mokubei	397	Toyosuke	405
Mokume	403	Toyo-ura	416
Mompei	408	Tozan	412, 414
Nabeshima	420	Tsuji	421
Nagasaki	420	Unyei	413
Nagoya	406	Yatsushiro	417
Nakajima	425	Yedo Banko	410
Naosaku	413	Yenzan	414
Nemboku an Kiso	421	Yohei	402
Ninsei	393	Yokkaichi	402
Niraku	419	Yoshida	415
Ofuke	404	Yusetsu	402
Ohi-machi	413	Zengoro	398
Okawaji	420	Zeze	408
Okazaki	400	Zoroku	400
Onike	394	Zoshuntei Sampo	421

YAMASHIRO.

This province is situated in the northern central part of Japan, and is one of those appropriated for the support and maintenance of the Imperial Court.

KIO or KIYOTO, a principality in the province of Yamashiro, was formerly called MIACO, which in Japanese signifies a city, and was so called by way of pre-eminence, being the residence of the Daïri or hereditary ecclesiastical Emperor and his court, and on this account reckoned the capital of the whole Empire, but since the removal of the Court to Yedo it has been officially called Kioto.

KIOTO.

Miaco, which was in Kæmpfer's time called the Imperial City, is thus spoken of by him in his *History of Japan*, 1727: "Miaco is the great magazine of all Japanese manufacturers and commodities, and the chief mercantile town in the Empire. There is scarcely a house in this large capital where there is not something made or sold. Here they refine copper, coin money, print books, weave the rich stuffs with gold and silver flowers. The best and scarcest dyes, the most artful carvings, all sorts of musical instruments, pictures, japanned cabinets, all sorts of things wrought in gold or other metals, the finest tempered steel, sword-blades and other arms, are made here in the greatest perfection, also the richest dresses, and other things too numerous to be mentioned. In short, there is nothing that can be thought of but what may be found at Miaco, and nothing, though never so neatly wrought, can be imported from abroad, but what some artist or other in this capital will undertake to imitate. Considering this, it is no wonder that the manufacturers of Miaco are become so famous throughout the Empire as to be easily preferred to all others, though perhaps inferior in some particulars, only because they have the name of being made at Miaco," now called Kioto.

FUSHIMI-YAKI. Fushimi-mura, in the province of Yamashiro, was a town where pottery was made at a remote period. In or about 1620 a man named Koemon commenced to make human figures with plastic clay, which is continued to the present time as a trade by the people. The figures are made in a clay mould, each part separately, then joined together and painted, but not glazed. In the Japanese Historical Collection, No. 258, is a group of Fukurokuju, God of Longevity, with an attendant, moulded in whitish clay, made at Fushimi in imitation of the figures produced by Koemon, and signed with that artist's name in 1840. On the back of the figure is the inscription given in the margin. In the same neighbourhood, at a village called Fuka-kusa, unglazed vessels are made for religious festivals.

ASAHI-YAKI. This factory was founded 1644-47, and is situated in Uji, province of Yamashiro. The word *Asa-hi* is derived from its colour, and means "the morning light," similar to a famous Corean bowl used for ground tea.

Kobori-masa-kazu, a founder of one branch of the tea-ceremony, gave a seal to mark the works.

Tamara-yaki was founded about the same time.

Uji is the centre of tea-cultivation in Japan.

The ware is a dull red or buff stoneware with greyish glaze, usually thin, uneven and patchy. The manufacture ceased about 1730, but was revived in 1852 by Chobei, a descendant of the original Asahi potters. Mark as in margin.

NINSEI-YAKI. Nomura Seisuke, native of the village of Ninwaji, is one of the most celebrated Japanese potters. He took the studio name of

Ninsei, a composition of the first syllables of Ninwaji and Seisuke. Through a potter named Kurobei, he learned the secret of enamelling on pottery as practised in Hizen, and he began to make enamelled fayence about 1655. He seems to have moved from place to place, working in the Omuro district (at Seikan and Ottowa), at Awata, Iwakura and Mizoro. It is claimed for him that he improved the technique of the local wares, paying great attention to the fineness of the body, and uniformity in the crackle of the glaze; that he shook off foreign influences and developed the naturalistic style of decoration which is the characteristic of Japanese fayence; and that he introduced the art of enamelling on fayence, as an improvement on the painting in brown pigment which has been hitherto the recognised method of displaying pictorial designs on pottery. His wares are very hard, with brick red or yellowish grey body; the glaze has a uniform and circular crackle, and his enamels are at once soft and rich in effect.

His usual mark, impressed with a stamp, is *Ninsei;* but he used several others, such as —

 *sei* (for Nin*sei*)   *Ninsei,* in a seal with the upper part like a looped curtain (*maku-in*)

Genuine examples of his work are almost unknown in Europe, but there is no lack of more or less accurate copies bearing his mark.

A host of potters followed the lead of Ninsei, and numbers of kilns were erected in the neighbourhood of Kioto. Each has a different name and a different mark, but their typical production, a creamy or grey stoneware with crackled glaze and enamelled decoration, is known by the general name of Awata ware.

Another Kioto potter of fame almost equal to Ninsei was Ogata Sansei, elder brother of the celebrated artist Korin. He is known by various studio names, the commonest of which is Kenzan. He was a master of all forms of decoration, but preferred to paint his simple, bold designs in dark brown on the creamy fayence, and his wares, both in their vigorous, impressionist style and general colouring strongly recall the Chinese Tz'ŭ-chou wares of the Sung dynasty. Kenzan was born in 1660, and died in 1743; his descendants carried on the traditions of his art, and there is a specimen in the British Museum signed *Sandai Kenzan* (Kenzan of the third generation). Kenzan worked at Awata, and for a time at Iriya, in Yedo. Among his favourite designs are a branch of blossoming prunus, a floral scroll, a flight of geese, lightly sketched flowers and trees, and vigorous landscape.

KEN-ZAN-YAKI. A bowl of drab glazed ware, crackled, painted with snow-covered pines in enamel colours and traces of gilding—imitation of ware by Ogata Shinsho at Awata, east of Kioto. This mark in black ("Ken-Zan") is on the bottom, A.D. 1730. *Jap. Hist. Coll.*, 270.

KEN-ZAN-YAKI. A fire-pan of buff glazed ware, painted with flowers and an inscription, in which is the square mark here given; on the bottom is the other mark, "Ken-Zan," made at Kyomizu in Kioto, A.D. 1750. *Jap. Hist. Coll.*, 271.

Sandai Kenzan Saku = Made by Kenzan of the third generation. Incised on a pottery netsuké with brown glaze, in the form of a monkey. British Museum.

Other Marks of Awata Potters are :—

AWATA.

Onike = Honourable pond : a reference to the pond at Mizoro, near Kioto. On a yellow-glazed tea bowl, roughly painted with birds and water plants. Franks Collection.

Gobosatsu. A mark found on Awata wares, ranging in date from the end of the seventeenth to the middle of the nineteenth century. (Morse).

Hozan, the art name given to Yasubei at the beginning of the eighteenth century, and used by his descendants, who have made an immense variety of pottery at Awata.

Hozan, another form of the same.

Tai hei, an additional mark used by one of the Hozan family. On a peach-shaped vessel, painted in natural colours, in the Franks Collection, and dated 1865.

Kinkozan, a name given to a member of the Kagiya family in 1756, and used by his family since. Found on typical Awata fayence of high quality.

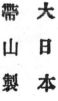

Dai Ni-pon Tai-zan sei = Made by Taizan in Great Japan. The name Taizan was first adopted by Tokuro Yohei about 1720, and has been used by the family ever since.

Bizan, the art-name of Hasegawa Kumenosuke, who joined with Taizan in 1820. The mark continues in the family.

Tanzan. The art-name of Yoshitaro, a prolific Awata potter of the second half of the nineteenth century.

Kozan. On Awata fayence about 1820.

RAKU

RAKU
(abbreviated form).

SEINEI : mark of
Raku Tanniu,
c. 1840.

RAKU-YAKI. A Corean named Ameya settled in Kioto about 1525. He introduced the manufacture of Raku ware, and his wife Teinin continued it after his death. Their son Chojiro attracted the patronage of Senno Rikiu, the master of tea ceremonies, who gave him the studio name of Tanaka. The famous Taiko Hideyoshi honoured the ware by presenting a gold seal in 1588 to Chojiro. This seal was engraved with the character *Raku* (enjoyment), a mark which has been used by Chojiro and his descendants ever since.

The Raku ware is a soft buff pottery, fired at a low temperature, and capable of being made in small private kilns. It has been in fact largely made by amateurs. The chief feature is the glaze, which is thick like treacle, waxen, and semi-opaque. The first Raku glaze was black, but in Chojiro's time a light red or salmon colour was introduced; in the seventeenth century a crackled straw-yellow glaze was made, and black pitted with red. In the eighteenth century green and cream white were added to the list, and gilding and splashed glazes also appeared.

The popularity of the Raku ware is due to the fact that its thick smooth glaze was specially suited for tea-bowls, and its simple and archaic appearance appealed to the taste of the masters of tea ceremonies. It was imitated by many potters and amateurs in various places in Japan, and numerous marks on Raku wares will be recorded in their several positions.

KYOMIZU.

KYOMIZU-YAKI. Kyomizu is a district of Kioto, but the term Kyomizu-yaki has come to include almost every kind of Kioto pottery except the Awata class. It also includes porcelain, which was introduced into this district about 1760. Among the best known Kyomizu marks are those of Rokubei (*d.* 1759), who decorated fayence in the naturalistic style. His son Rokubei Seisai opened a factory in 1811; he also made porcelain. He was succeeded in 1860 by his son Sho-un.

DOHACHI. Mark of Takahashi Dohachi, who set up at Awata about 1750, and died 1804.

A second Dohachi worked at Kyomizu from 1811 and two more of the family succeeded, carrying on the business to the present day. The second Dohachi decorated his wares with birds, flowers, landscapes, &c., taken from nature, and his style found many followers.

Dai Ni-pon Do-hachi tsukuru = Made by Dohachi in Great Japan.

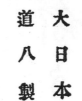

MOKUBEI, a skilful potter and clever copyist (*b.* 1767, *d.* 1833). He imitated Kochi-yaki (a Chinese Ming pottery decorated with coloured glazes, green, purple, yellow, and turquoise over raised designs), and made ivory white, celadon, and enamelled porcelains.

Mokubei.

Ko ki kwan Moku-bei tsukuru = Made by Mokubei, the connoisseur of antique vessels. (Morse).

SHUHEI, about 1800, made beautiful enamelled porcelain and gilt designs on red ground *(Kinrande)*.

Ogata Shuhei. On a beautifully enamelled porcelain bowl in the British Museum. Early nineteenth century.

KENTEI, about 1800; unglazed fayence with designs in gold or enamels. He was followed by his son of the same name.

Otowa. Mark of Otowaya Sozaemon, whose art-name was Kentei, and who lived at the end of the eighteenth century. He made a light buff pottery of fine grain, unglazed, but painted in enamels and gold. He was succeeded by a second Kentei.

Ken, for Kentei.

RANTEI (= phœnix hall) is the studio name of a Kyomizu potter of the early nineteenth century. He made, among other wares, blue and white porcelain and celadon.

KITEI (= tortoise hall) is the studio name of Wake Heikichi, an eighteenth century potter, whose descendant of the third generation made a reputation for blue and white porcelain. The latter began in the Bunsei period (1818-29), and his son carries on his work, using the family mark.

Ki tei (tortoise house). On a box in the form of a pomegranate made of thick porcelain faintly enamelled. Franks Collection.

The ZENGORO family, which includes Tenkaichi Soshiro (*c.* 1640), the fourth generation, and Ryozen, the tenth generation, whose son was the celebrated Zengoro Hozen, better known by one of his studio names, Eiraku. He studied at Awata, and made both porcelain and fayence; and his wares included imitations of Kochiyaki, celadons, blue and white porcelain, and porcelain with red ground decorated with gilt designs and broken by panels of blue and white.

He was invited to Wakayama, capital of Kishiu, by Prince Harunori in 1827, where he had a kiln in the royal park and made the *Kairaku-yen* ware, decorated with coloured glazes, chiefly turquoise, yellow, and aubergine purple. He received here the two seals *Eiraku* and *Kahin Shiriu*.

He afterwards worked at Kaseyama, near Nara, in Setsu, in 1840, and in the same year at Omuro, in Kioto. In 1850 he moved to Otsu, on Lake Biwa, and died in 1855.

His son, Eiraku Wazen, succeeded him, and his grandson, Eiraku Tokuzen, has carried on the industry in the present century.

Riyo-zen. Stamped on a stoneware incense-burner with purple glaze, in the Franks Coll.

Hozen. Mark of Zengoro Hozen, art-named Eiraku.

Eiraku. Stamped on a porcelain canister painted in dark brown, with silver and gold, in the Franks Coll.

Dai Ni-pon Eiraku tsukuru = Made by Eiraku in Great Japan: on a porcelain bowl painted in red and green, with figure subjects, in the Franks Coll.

Kairaku yen sei = Made in the Kairaku garden. On a canister with pattern in relief filled in with purple and turquoise glazes, in the Franks Coll.

Kahin Shiriu. Stamped on a quatrefoil bowl of coarse porcelain, with artistic designs in red, green, and gold, in the Franks Coll.

SEIFU YOHEI, a pupil of the second Dohachi, opened a factory in 1844, and copied Chinese blue and white porcelain with success. His son, who succeeded him in 1861, made enamelled porcelain, and a third Seifu who followed in 1878, is one of the best modern Kioto potters.

KANZAN DENSHICHI, porcelain-maker of Kioto: he is celebrated for his decoration in gold and bronze on red ground, imitation damascene work in gold and silver and iron, beautifully executed in flowers and ornaments, which appear as if inlaid in a style called "Zogan," originated by himself; he also copies the Yeiraku ware, and coats some of his porcelain with *cloisonné* enamel. This family have a kiln at Kyomizu, near Kioto.

KAN-ZAN-YAKI. *Dai Ni-pon Kanzan-sei* (the mark of Kanzan-Denshichi of Kyomizu), in blue under a porcelain bowl coated with *cloisonné* enamel, yellow figured ground, with compartments of flowers.

MAKUZU. A potter named Chozo (studio name Kosai) who set up in Makuzu-ga-hara, Kioto, early in the nineteenth century, was a successful maker of blue and white porcelain. He was given the names of Roku-roku-rin, Kozan, and Makuzu. His grandson in 1860 took the name of Miyagawa Kozan, and nine years later he removed to Ota.

Makuzu Kozan tsukuru = Made by Makuzu Kozan. Impressed in a gourd-shaped seal on a vase with crackled creamy glaze painted in colours with gilding, with a rocky landscape and figures. Franks Coll.

ZOROKU, mark of a Kioto potter who made fayence and celadon porcelain, 1849-1878. He was succeeded by his son of the same name.

ZOROKU, another form of the mark.

OKAZAKI ware made by Bunzaburo in the village of Okazaki as late as 1870. A Raku ware, and usually marked *Kagura.*

Kagura. Stamped on a shell-shaped box of Raku ware with yellow glaze, in the Franks Coll.

YAMATO.

AKAHADA-YAKI. Ware made at Koriyama and named after the mountain Akahada yama. In the seventeenth century tea ware was made here with opaque pinkish grey glaze resembling the Hagi ware. The work ceased at the end of the century, but was revived in 1761, when a buff lustreless glazed ware was made and decorated with variegated and monochrome glazes or minute enamelling.

AKAHADA-YAKI. (Aka-hada, "Raw flesh.") Examples —A brazier of buff ware with white crackled glaze resting on three feet, a seal stamp impressed on the bottom, a specimen of the "Akahada" ware made in the county of Soishimo at Koriyama, A.D. 1840, *Jap. Hist. Coll.,* 231 ; and an incense-box of buff ware in form of a pot-bellied dwarf, glazed brown drapery ; the same ware made also at Koriyama, 1840. *Jap. Hist. Coll.*

AKAHADA-YAMA. On a stoneware tea-bowl with olive-brown glaze, impressed inside with figures and trees, marked with the name of the fabric ; followed by a circular seal, *Boku-haku,* the maker at Koriyama. Franks Collection.

IZUMI.

MINATO-YAKI. There were potteries in this province in remote times, and the half-fabulous Giyogi is said to have worked here in the eighth century. At the end of the seventeenth century, Ueda Kichizaemon was a potter of repute who worked at Sakai, and introduced a thin mottled glaze of yellow tint, and sometimes of claret colour. In the Bunsei period (1828-29), Kichizaemon, fifth of that name, copied Raku ware and the Chinese "Kochi-yaki." His wares have green, yellow, claret, amber-brown, and salmon glazes, on a fine hard light grey body, and closely resemble Awaji ware (*q.v.*).

MINATO-YAKI. A teapot and a nautilus cup, the former in form of a tortoise, the tail forming a handle and the head a spout, of glazed pottery, bears this seal, which reads *Sen-shui*, the province called also Idsumi: *Sakai*, the name of the place; *moto*, original; *Minato-yaki*, Minato ware; *Kichi-ye-mon*, the maker's name. Franks Collection.

SETTSU.

OSAKA, which has been termed the Venice of Japan, is in the central portion of Japan, in the province of Settsu, adjacent to Yamashiro, and is the centre of trade in Japan. Hiogo is the shipping port of Osaka, lying about thirty miles distant on the banks of a river, both being now open to foreign trade. The ancient name of Osaka was "Naniwa." A teapot of trefoil shape of grey stoneware with ornaments in white slip has at the back an inscription, "Nani-wa cha-mise Matsu-no-o." "The Matsu-no-o (Old Fir-tree) Tea-house at Naniwa." Franks Collection. Osaka is cele-brated for its beautiful egg-shell porcelain and other descriptions of china: the former is made extensively. The mountain of Fusiyama, venerated by the Japanese, is seen from Osaka as well as from Yedo, and is fre-quently represented on their ware.[1] Sunsets, birds, trees, &c., are lightly sketched on it, and touches of a beautiful cobalt blue show above all other colours. Those delicate cups, covered with minutely plaited wicker, and sometimes with lacquer, are from Osaka.

Sir Rutherford Alcock, when visiting the shops at Osaka, having in view the purchase of objects for the International Exhibition (1862), says: "Of bronzes I saw little to compare with the choice there is in Yedo and at Yokohama, where foreigners create a large demand. In a lacquer-ware shop we found only a very indifferent show, and the prices were altogether fabulous. We were more fortunate in our search after pottery and porcelain, and priced and appropriated a perfect wealth of

---

[1] Kæmpfer describes it as "mons excelsus et singularis," which in beauty perhaps has not its equal, for which poets cannot find words, nor painters skill or colours sufficient to represent the mountain as the Japanese think it deserves.

'Palissy' pottery with raised fishes and fruit. Certainly this was the only harvest I was enabled to secure; many of the objects were unique in kind, and nothing like them could be found in Yedo or Nagasaki. Some very perfect eggshell was also picked up here, remarkably fine and surprisingly cheap."

Osaka as well as Kioto, being both in the vicinity of royal palaces, were the chief places of manufacture for the choicest examples of all descriptions of art-work, including porcelain, lacquer enamels, bronzes, embroidery, &c., being made for the use of the Emperors and princes.

At Sanda in this province a kiln was erected in 1690 on the Arita system by the Prince of Settsu, to imitate the Chinese celadon, in which it was successful.

 RAKU-YAKI. A figure of fine ware, painted and glazed, representing Fukurokuju, seated on the ground holding a fan in his left hand, was made by Kik-ko, of the city of Osaka, A.D. 1860. His work is finer and more delicate than other Raku ware, but is not favoured by the tea-clubs so much as commoner ware. *Jap. Hist. Coll.*, 256. Mark as in margin, *Kik ko*.

ISE.

BANKO-YAKI. Numanami Gozaemon, a rich merchant living at Kuwana (1736-95), studied the art of the Kioto potters and started a private factory, where very clever imitations of Raku, Korean, Ninsei, and Kenzan wares were made, besides many original works. He was induced by the Shogun to move to Yedo about 1786, and settled for a time at Kommemura. He learned the methods of the Chinese enamellers and copied the green and red decorations of the Wan Li period. In addition, he used coloured glazes with success, and imitated Kochi-yaki. His ware is known as Ko-Banko, and the marks used by him are *Banko* and *Fuyeki*.

About 1830 a potter named Mori Yusetsu, whose father, a waste-paper buyer, accidentally discovered Banko's recipes, revived the use of the old Banko seal. Yusetsu's ware is chiefly fayence, and some of it is decorated in the Ko-Banko style, and passes for the original ware; but it is chiefly unglazed, thin and hard, and skilfully modelled with ornaments in relief. Yusetsu made much use of interior moulds, if he was not actually the inventor of them, as some accounts imply, and his ware shows finger-marks on the outside where the pressure was applied.

His brother Yohei seems to have adopted the name of Fuyeki, and used that mark.

A large number of factories in the nineteenth century adopted Yusetsu's style, and their productions are often lumped together as Banko ware. The potters of Yokkaichi are specially prolific in this class of ware since 1868.

Three forms of the mark *Ban-ko*.

Ni-pon Yu-setsu, stamped on a Banko teapot of trans-lucent ware in white and brown.   Franks Coll.

Banko Fuyeki, on Yohei's ware.   (Morse.)

ISÉ-BANKO-YAKI.   Red biscuit ware, with two handles and four feet, round the neck dragons in relief in white on one side enamelled flowers, on the other an inscription cut through the red glaze.   On the bottom are the stamps impressed *Nippon Banko*, and in the oval *Shibata tsukuru* (made by Shibata). A.D. 1875. *Jap. Hist. Coll.*, 322.

ISÉ-BANKO-YAKI.   A teapot and cover of biscuit ware, with pale green crackled glaze, painted with flowers in enamel.   "Isé Banko" ware, made in the province of Isé.   The same mark is impressed on the side, the space not being enamelled. A.D. 1875. *Jap. Hist. Coll.*, 320.

KUWANA-YAKI.   M. Nakayama of Kuwana, in this province, is a maker of Banko ware; a dish with crayfish, crabs, &c., cleverly modelled. *Jap. Hist. Coll.*

YOKKA-ICHI-YAKI.   A porcelain cup or small bowl, cream colour, painted and gilt inside and out, with groups of figures; made at Yokka-ichi in the province of Isé in 1780. *Jap. Hist. Coll.*

MOKUME YAKI.   Shitome-Sohei, a potter of Yokka-ichi, makes porce-lain, earthen and stone ware, the last called "Banko-yaki," after the inventor—pieces of various colours potted by hand, not thrown or moulded; also vases and other specimens, in which two or more coloured clays are blended together throughout the body, producing a singular mottled or marbled effect, called "Mokume" ware; in some pieces white porcelain clay is inserted by perforation of the body, inscriptions being thus inlaid so as to show through the entire thickness of the vessel; tea wares of extreme thinness, the handles being made movable on a pivot; the enamel colours on white slip are stated to be a peculiarity of this factory.

BANKO-YAKI.   Y-Mori of Yokka-ichi makes earthenware dishes cleverly decorated with flowers.   He is the successor to the inventor of Banko-yaki, who was his ancestor, and whose name he continues; he was the master of Shitomei Sohei.

OWARI.

SETO-YAKI. This ware is made at Seto in the province of Owari; its origin is unknown. It is, however, stated that in the period of Yengi (A.D. 927) a sort of pottery was offered to the Emperor, but none is preserved. Great progress was made by Kato Shirozayemon, who went to China in 1223, and studied there for five years, on his return he went to Hizen, and thence to Yamashiro, and attempted to make his ware; also at Owari and Mino, but did not succeed. Having found suitable clay at Seto, he erected a kiln called Heishi-kama. The articles made from the clay he brought from China are called by the tea-clubs *Karamono*, "China ware," while that from Seto clay is called *Ko-seto*, "Old Seto." These are a kind of stoneware called by the Japanese *Shaki*. His works are scarce and valuable. Kato-Shirozayemon was abbreviated to "Toshiro."

The feature of the Ko-seto ware is its glazes, which are black, amber-brown, chocolate and yellowish grey, generally variegated and streaked, two or more glazes being superposed on the same piece. A crackled yellow glaze was used in combination with others as early as the time of the second Toshiro (1250-1300), but it does not seem to have been used alone before the fifteenth century. From the seventeenth century onwards this yellow Seto (Ki-seto) ware was largely produced. The Kato family continue to make their wares in modern times.

SHINO-YAKI, first made by Shino Ienobu about 1480, is a coarse ware with thick crackled white or grey glaze, sometimes roughly painted in dark brown.

GEN (for Gempin).

GEMPIN-YAKI, made by a Chinese refugee who settled at Nogoya in 1659, is either an unglazed pottery with impressed or incised ornament, or a greyish-white glazed ware with rough painting in impure blue.

ORIBE-YAKI is a name given to all the wares made at Narumi, where a factory was started by Furuta Oribe (1573-92). The manufacture continues to this day. The ware is usually coated with glazes of sugary white, buff, sage green, and salmon-pink colour, singly or in combination. It is also sketchily painted in dark brown.

OFUKE or MIFUKAI-YAKI was made at Akazu first in the seventeenth century, but the potters were soon moved to Nagoya. The ware is noted for its "vitreous, semi-translucid Owari glaze, over which are run broad bands of brown ochre, splashed with a glaze like Avanturine lacquer, and between them streaks of green and violet." The mark "fuke" found in Ofuke ware, is given by Morse.

FUKE.

SHUNTAI-YAKI is another Akazu ware dating from the seventeenth century. It has usually splashed glazes, grey crackle streaked with blue, showing tinges of violet and buff.

SHUNTAI.

INUYAMA-YAKI was first made at Inaki in 1752, but the factory was moved in 1810 to Maruyama. It is a grey stoneware, with colourless or grey translucent glaze, painted in red-brown slip, russet red and green enamels, with black lines and white slips. The mark *Inuyama* has the same characters as *Kenzan*.

INUYAMA.

TOYOSUKE-YAKI, made by Toyosuke at the Horaku factory in Nagoya about 1820. It is a fayence with crackled greenish grey glaze, the vessels usually painted inside in black with splashes of green, and lacquered outside with black lacquer, decorated with gold, silver, or red designs. Marks Horaku and Toyosuke.

HORAKU

TOYOSUKE.

OWARI (second only to Hizen) is the province where the most important manufactories of porcelain are carried on; one of the principal manufactories being probably at Okasaki, noted for its fine white porcelain.

OWARI.

Hepburn says, "At Sedo, a town in Owari, much porcelain is made. *Sedo-mono* signifies crockery generally, being derived from *Sedo*, the name of the place, and *mono*, articles or things." It was noted for its fine blue and white porcelain *(Sometsuke)*. Large and massive porcelain greenhouse pots and vases for exotic trees and plants are made in Owari, with fine cobalt blue deep borders and flowers, which being under the glaze, is impervious to the effects of the atmosphere.

Eggshell porcelain is produced in great perfection at OKASAKI in this province, as well as the exquisite vases and plateaux with *cloisonné* enamel ornamentation on the porcelain body, some in coloured lacs, others in pastes like enamelled metal.

川本
枡吉

KAWA-MOTO MASU-
KICHI.

奇陶軒
北半製

大日本
瀬戸製

七寶會社

SHIPPO KUWAISHA.

大日本
半介製

In 1801 a potter named Kato-Tamikichi went to Arita in Hizen to study porcelain-making, and returned after five years to Seto in Owari, where he succeeded in making *Sometsuke*, or porcelain decorated in blue under the glaze, which has kept on improving up to the present day. The best makers at the present day are Kawamoto-Hansuke and Masu-kichi, the latter especially in producing large pieces in plates and table-tops from five to ten feet in diameter, and lofty vases. *Jap. Hist. Coll.*, 169-174.

SETO-YAKI. *Ki-to-ken Hoku-han-sei.* "Made by Hokuhan at the Kito (Curious Pottery) House." On a blue and white porcelain dish, with river scene and gentleman and lady in a boat, with verses above and inside. Franks Collection.

SETO-YAKI. Reading, *Dai Nipon Seto sei*, "Made at Seto in Great Japan." On a porcelain bowl covered externally with *cloisonné* enamel; on the inside is a landscape painted in blue and gold and coloured pendants, the outside consists of three medallions, one of which represents the famous volcanic mountain Fusiyama and diapers on turquoise ground. Franks Collection.

NAGOYA-YAKI. The Shippo Kuwaisha of Nagoya in Owari is a company which made porcelain coated with *cloisonné* enamel. In the Philadelphia Exhibition of 1876 it was commended for some ingenious designs.

In some of this Nagoya work silver cloisons are also employed, and inlaid portions of the same metal. One vase, ornamented with marine animals, as the octopus, prawn, &c., is mentioned as a most remarkable specimen of skill in carrying out a difficult design in this not very tractable material by the Shippo Kuwaisha. Hansuke of Seto at Philadelphia Exhibition, 1876, was commended for his decorative porcelain, for good potting and delicate decoration.

SETO-YAKI. *Dai Nipon Hansuke sei.* "Made by Hansuke of Great Japan." On a pair of porcelain cups coated with *cloisonné* enamel in medallions and diapers on a lilac ground. A.D. 1876. Franks Collection.

TOTOMI.

SHIDORO-YAKI. This ware was first made about 1644-47 in a village called Shidoro-mura, in the province of Totomi, where the manufacture of tea-materials, &c., is still continued.

SHIDORO.

SHIDORO-YAKI. In the Japanese Historical Collection is a koro or brazier of red ware, glazed, in form of an elephant, made at Shidoro-mura, in the province of Totomi, A.D. 1760. *Jap. Hist. Coll.*, 210.

KII OR KISHIU.

KISHIU-YAKI. This factory is situated at Waka-yama, province of Kii, and is stated to have been founded 200 years ago. Since the before-named Eiraku-Zengoro went there by order of the Prince of Kii for the purpose of promoting the art, great progress has taken place. In the Japanese Historical Collection is a porcelain vase, $15\frac{1}{2}$ inches high, with impressed ornament, the interspaces coloured purple, the whole covered with a crackled glaze; a specimen of "Kishiu" ware, made at Waka-yama, in this province, A.D. about 1830: it bears this mark, *Kai-raku yen-sei*, "Made at the Kairaku (Mingled Enjoyment) House." The mark stamped. *Jap. Hist. Coll.*, 289.

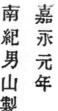

KISHIU-YAKI *Ka-yei guan nen nan-ki Otoko-yama sei.* "Made at Otoko-yama in Southern Kii, in the first year of Ka-yei," corresponding with A.D. 1848. On Japanese porcelain, with designs outlined in relief, slightly crackled, dark violet ground and floral pattern. It is called "Kishiu" ware. Franks Collection.

SANRAKUYEN-YAKI. A dish with a cover, resembling Kishiu porcelain, of flattened spherical form, with moulded flower ornament, one of the forms of Jiu ("Long life"), glazed turquoise and purple. A specimen of *San-raku-yen* ("Three enjoyments") ware of the nineteenth century. *Jap. Hist. Coll.*, 586. This ware was made in a private kiln at Tokio.

JIU.

San raku yen sei = Made at San-raku (Three enjoyments) garden. On a porcelain fruit-dish covered with purple glaze with spots of turquoise. Franks Coll.

OMI.

SHIGARAKI-YAKI, made at the village of Nagano-mura. The earliest productions, dating perhaps from the thirteenth century, are rough pottery now called Ko-Shigaraki. In the sixteenth century the renowned tea-drinker Sho-o interested himself in the factory, and popularised the tea ware, which had a hard greyish buff body with red brown smear, and a little grey-green glaze. This is called Sho-o Shigaraki, and some of its varieties are streaked with black or spotted with white, or rough with embedded quartz. Other celebrated *cha-jin* (tea-drinkers) gave their names to other kinds of Shigaraki ware, *e.g.* Senno Rikui (end of sixteenth century), who favoured a greyish crackled ware resembling old Corean; and Soton, who favoured a white ware with crackled buff glaze, about 1630.

SETA.

MOMPEIZAN.

ZEZE-YAKI, made at Zeze, near Lake Biwa, from the seventeenth century. There are two kinds: (1) *Oe-yaki*, resembling the Seta and Takatori wares, with golden brown, russet and purplish glazes, and (2) *Seta-yaki*, made first in the seventeenth century, and revived in 1801 by Ikeda Mompei. It has splashed glazes with red, green, buff, and blue tints. The second Mompei made also a fayence like that of Awata. Marks, Mompei and Mompeizan.

Other modern Zeze wares imitate Kochi-yaki and Kyomizu wares.

BAIRIN. Mark of Bairin at Beppo, about 1800. (Morse.)

IGA.

IGA-YAKI was made at Marubashira, and dates back to the fourteenth century, when it was of the Seto type; but the later productions of the factories are scarcely distinguishable from the neighbouring Shigaraki wares.

MUSASHI (PROVINCE).

TOKIO (Yedo) is on the east coast of Nippon, and Yokohama, its shipping port, is about sixteen miles distant. Yedo was formerly the residence of the Shogun, or, as he was subsequently called, the Tycoon, the temporal Emperor of Japan; but since the revolution and downfall of the Tycoon it has become the seat of Government and residence of the Mikado, and it may therefore now be called the capital of Japan. Tokio is a suburb of Yedo, where the principal commerce is carried on, and is a great mart for all Japanese produce. The collection of Japanese art at the Alexandra Palace was selected and consigned to England from a large depôt called

Kiriu-Kosho Kuwaisha, "The First Japanese Manufactory and Trading Company at Tokio," and there is now established a school of art styled "The Association of Painters of Porcelain at Tokio." We see by the invoice that a great portion of the pottery, porcelain, and other wares from the manufacturing districts were sent there to be decorated.

The shops at Yokohama, being so much frequented by foreigners, are plentifully stored with all sorts of porcelain, lacquer-work, enamels, bronzes, embroideries, &c., at moderate prices, and are eagerly purchased by those who cannot detect the difference between the showy, coarse work and the fine, highly finished rarities. These inferior articles are exposed on the lower floor, and can be reproduced in any quantity to meet the demand. The choicest are kept in the upper rooms in lac and inlaid cabinets. The oldest examples are, as a rule, much superior in point of excellence; they are highly prized, and even sought for by the wealthy natives themselves. The prices asked for them would frighten any but an experienced collector; they are not in common demand, and cannot be multiplied. Lately many fine examples, which had remained as heirlooms in the possession of the Daimios, have been sent to the shops at Yokohama for sale.

SHIBA-YAKI. A factory near Tokio produces the elegant eggshell cups decorated in gold and colours, sometimes enveloped in minute wicker-work, which are known as *Shiba-yaki*. A set of Saki cups, in the Franks Collection, of eggshell porcelain, painted and gilt, with busts of Japanese ladies, has on each the artist's signature, *Shogetsu-ro-jin*, "The Old Man Shogetsu," and a seal signifying "seventy-two years old," of Shiba ware, made at Tokio, No. 1118.

Another eggshell set, with landscapes, artist's name, *Getsu-ho*, and three others with the name *Shun-zan*.

IMADO-YAKI. In the northern part of Tokio, called Imado-machi, are numerous kilns for making an inferior pottery for domestic vessels, tiles, &c. A mottled ware of black and white clay and a kind of fayence with a glaze like the Raku ware, was made here a few years ago.

No. 259 is a brazier of black glazed earthenware, the bottom engraved with a seal, carried by a red silk sling; made at Imado in the northern district of Tokio, 1840. *Jap. Hist. Coll.*

RAKU-YAKI. In the Middle Ages a lacquerer in Kioto named Haritsu made a splendid lacquer encrusted with flowers and insects in a Raku ware, made by himself. This form of decoration was followed by a native of Kioto named Miura-Kenya, who went to Tokio about twenty years since,

KENYA.

and still retains the Raku factory in Asakusa in the north of Tokio. A bowl of thick brown ware, partly covered with a rich green glaze, the rest of the surface filled with flowers, which have the appearance of being inlaid. His works are close imitations of Nature. The traditions of Haritsu have been followed by Benshi and Kenzan of Kioto. *Jap. Hist. Coll.*, 251.

RAKU-YAKI. On the bank of the river Sumida-gawa in Tokio lives a potter named Kozawa Benshi, who was much interested in making the Raku ware. In latter years he modelled figures in terra-cotta from designs in children's picture-books, with the help only of the spatula and knife, and resuscitated the art practised by Miura-Kenya, who is still living at a very advanced age. In the Philadelphia Exhibition of 1876 his terra-cottas were commended for great force of expression and singular skill in conveying the meaning of the groups of figures. A tray of red and black lacquer, inlaid with small earthenware shells and a young crab; made by Kozawa Benshi in Tokio, A.D. 1850. *Jap. Hist. Coll.*, 252.

YEDO BANKO-YAKI was made by Numanami Gozaemon during his stay at Yedo about 1786 (see p. 402).

OTA-YAKI. The kiln at Ota, near Yokohama, was established after the opening of the harbour, by a merchant of Yokohama named Suzaki Yasubeye, for the purpose of imitating the Satsuma ware. He brought from Kiyomidsu a porcelain-maker named Kozan. The imitation was so successful as to materially reduce the value of the original Satsuma.

香　眞
山　葛
造　窯
瓢　日
池、本
園　東
画　京

MAKUZU-YAKI. *Ma-kuzu-yo Ko-zan-tzo* = Made by Kozan at the Makuzu kiln. Found on porcelain with details in relief in biscuit. One of the Kozan family from Makuzugahara, near Kioto, went to Ota, near Yokohama, A.D. 1875. Franks Collection. See also p. 399.

TOKIO, JAPAN. *Ni-pon To-kio Hyo-chi-yen gua* = Painted at the Hyochi garden, Tokio, Japan. On a pair of flower vases of Arita porcelain made by Tsuji, and decorated at Tokio in 1875, in colours with gilding. *Jap. Hist. Coll.*, 367.

ニッポン ニ 東京
錦
窯
舍
精
製

TOKIO, JAPAN. *Ni-pon Tokio Kinshosha sei tsukuru* = Carefully made by the Kinsho Company at Tokio, Japan. On a porcelain vase painted in enamel colours, with gorgeous birds and flowers. Late nineteenth century. British Museum.

MINO.

MINO-YAKI. This ware was made at several villages in the province of Mino, especially at Tajimimura. During the seventeenth century the Emperor encouraged the manufacture; it was confined to earthenware until 1810, since which time the real porcelain, called *Shin-sei*, "new thing," was made. There are still 110 kilns making porcelain decorated with cobalt under the glaze. Eggshell porcelain has been made at the Ichi-no-kura factory since 1830.

MINO-YAKI. A pair of porcelain flower vases with reticulated ornament painted in blue, with handles in form of fishes, made by Kato Gosuke of Tajimimura, in this province, A.D. 1875, are in the *Jap. Hist. Coll.*, 184. Mark, *Ni-pon Mino Kuni Ka-to Go-suke sei* = Made by Kato Gosoke in the province of Mino, Japan.

MINO-YAKI. *To giyoku yen sei* = Made in the Togi-yoku (jade pottery) garden. On a pair of covered tea bowls of blue and white porcelain. Late nineteenth century. Franks Collection.

ECHIZEN.

MI-KUNI-YAKI. "Three Kingdoms," the name of a place in the province of Echizen. This mark is on an oblong stand, containing a small pot of grey stoneware; the upper part is covered with a deep green glaze, red border, the sides pierced and edges gilt. Marked in red. Franks Collection.

MI-KUNI.

KAGA.

The materials for making porcelain were discovered in the hills near the village of Kutani-mura about 1650, but the manufacture was not carried to success until the return of Goto Saijiro in 1664 from Arita, whither he had been sent to learn the secrets of the Hizen potters. Three distinct types of porcelain were made in the province of Kaga :—

.(1) *Ao-Kutani*, so called from the predominance of a green *(ao)* enamel, which was associated with yellow, purple and soft "Prussian" blue. These enamels were translucent like the Chinese *famille verte* colours, and were either applied in broad washes over designs outlined in black on the biscuit, or were simply used for painting diapers, scrolls or floral designs on the biscuit or over a white glaze.

(2) *Arita Kutani*, decorated in the Arita style with enamels, silver and gold, and a limited use of underglaze blue.

(3) *Ko Kutani*, or old Kutani, in which a soft Indian red predominated, though usually broken by medallions of enamelled decoration.

The typical Kutani colour is a soft, opaque and subdued red, sometimes verging on russet brown. The ware itself varied widely, from stoneware through semi-porcelain to fine porcelain, and the glaze was usually dull and lustreless, sometimes crackled in parts.

About 1750 the Kutani factories ceased their activity, but in 1779 a revival took place in the Nomi district under Honda Teikichi, a native of Hizen. His kiln was near Wakasugi, and he favoured the Arita style of decoration. He died in 1822, but other potters continued the work in the district, and we hear of kilns erected at Tsuchi-yama, Wake-mura, Yamata-mura, Rendaiji, Motoe and other villages between 1820-60.

Meanwhile another revival took place at Kutani in 1809, under Yoshida Danemon, who moved after two years to Yamashiro-mura. The Ao Kutani methods were followed until 1840, when Iida Hachiroemon made a speciality of gold designs on a red ground (the *Akaji kinga* style), which became the typical Kaga style. In 1858 Zengoro Wazen, son of the celebrated Eiraku, came to Kutani, and worked there for six years. From 1863-69 a severe depression almost crushed out the industry, but it has recently taken a new lease of life, and *Akaji-kinga* and *Ao Kutani* methods are freely used.

KUTANI.

Up to 1850 practically the only marks used on Kaga wares were the name of Kutani or the word *fuku* (happiness); since that date the names of potters and the full mark *Dai Nippon Kutani tsukuru* (= Made at Kutani in Great Japan) have been placed on the wares.

The Kaga ware made by Hachiroemon and his pupils (and called Hachiroe) is a soft creamy ware with crackled glaze. Arita porcelain has been sometimes sent to the Kaga factories to be decorated.

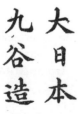

KAGA-YAKI. *Dai Ni-pon Ku-tani tsukuru* = Made at Kutani in Great Japan. On a porcelain cup painted in black and red, with gilding: a water-lily inside. Franks Collection.

KAGA-YAKI. *Tozan no in* = Seal of Tozan. On a pair of flower vases with wide mouths and ring handles: porcelain painted in red with gilding, made by Kichizô Uchiumi at Kutani, and bearing the seal in the margin in red on the bottom: made in 1875. *Jap. Hist. Coll.*, 314.

OHI-MACHI-YAKI. Pottery of the Raku type was made at Ohi-machi, near Kanazawa, on the boundary of Kaga. The factory was founded in 1666 by Haji Chozaemon, and the typical ware is a soft buff pottery with amber-brown and greyish green glazes.

Another Raku ware, but of white tone and often enamelled, was made at Eda-machi, Kanazawa, in 1827 by one Gembei and his successors.

OHI-YAKI. A coarse brown glazed earthenware is made in this province called "Raku" ware, at Ohi-machi. Specimens of A.D. 1790 and 1820 are in the *Jap. Hist. Coll.*, 249, 250.

OHI.

TAMBA.

The Tamba ware made at Onohara in the seventeenth century, and afterwards at Tachikui, is chiefly tea ware for the tea ceremonies, and is coated with glazes of the old Seto type.

In the nineteenth century a light grey ware with *pâte sur pâte* and enamelled decoration was made at Sasa-yama. The potter Naosaku (about 1840) placed his mark on this kind of ware.

NAOSAKU.

IZUMO.

The factory at Rakuzan was founded by Gombei (about 1676-1720), who made tea ware in the Hagi, and sometimes in the Seto style.

The Fujina factory, established by Funaki Yajibei in 1764 and patronised by Prince Fumai, produced a variety of earthenwares with Seto glazes, spangled glaze like "avanturine" lacquer, soft yellow glaze decorated in red, green and gold, and a greyish fayence with elaborate ornament in enamel colour. The Fujina factories closed about 1868, but were reopened in 1875 by Jakuzan.

RAKU-ZAN.

Unyei. Stamped on a pair of pricket candlesticks of grey ware with pale celadon green glaze. Fujina ware about 1830. *Jap. Hist. Coll.*, 225.

IWAMI.

SOMA-YAKI. A factory was started in 1655 at Naka-mura by Toshiro, a retainer of the Prince of Soma. A grey stoneware was made either unglazed or speckled with brown under a translucent colourless glaze. The principal ornament on the Soma wares is a prancing, tethered horse, painted in brown or blue or in white slip. This is the crest of Soma, and the original design for the pottery is said to have been drawn by Kano Naonobu. Other Soma wares have splashes of *flambé* glaze, *e.g.* red streaked with bluish grey, brown, purple and green: grey surface with brown marbling (*Mokume* ware): granulated glaze with surface like shark-skin *(Same-yaki)*. The sides of the tea bowls are almost always deeply indented.

SOMA-YAKI. This badge of the Prince of Soma is found in relief on many pieces of Soma ware, accompanied by the stamp of Soma, given below, on pieces decorated with horses, &c.

SOMA-YAKI. A square basket, with a horse prancing in the centre tied to a stake, in relief, outlined in a brown, open-work border. Mark *Soma*. Victoria and Albert Museum, presented by Sir A. W. Franks.

SOMA-YAKI. Yen-Zan, a maker's name, stamped on cup of Soma ware. Franks Collection.

SOMA-YAKI. Kane-Shige, a maker's name, stamped on cups of this ware, accompanying the Soma mark. Franks Collection.

HARIMA.

MAIKO.

MAIKO-YAKI—made in the Akashi district—is a grey stoneware with brown specks and translucent glaze, strongly resembling Soma ware. The factory was started by Mikuni Kyuhachi in 1820.

AKASHI.

TOZAN-YAKI. A porcelain made at Himeji with clay found on Mount Tozan in the nineteenth century. It was chiefly of the blue and white variety, though a celadon glaze was also used. The manufacture has ceased to be of interest since 1868.

TOZAN-YAKI. A specimen of "Tozan" porcelain made at Himeji, painted in blue with landscapes and ornamental details. Marked underneath *Himeji sei* (Made at Himeji). A.D. 1820. Franks Collection.

TOZAN-YAKI. A pair of porcelain vases of "Tozan" ware painted with flowers in blue, with a blue mark underneath. *Jap. Hist. Coll.*, 366. Sir A. W. Franks has a porcelain bottle of pale green celadon glaze with two fish handles, inscribed "Made at Himeji."

TOZAN.

BIZEN.

Kilns were erected in the neighbourhood of Imbe as early as the end of the fourteenth century, and a rough reddish-brown stoneware was made, with little or no glaze, the surface often rough with blisters and inequalities. About 1583, after a visit from the Taiko, great activity prevailed, and vessels were made for the tea ceremonies. From this time the Bizen potters have been celebrated for their finely modelled wares, and especially for figures and statuettes. The early wares are called *Ko Bizen*, and a general term for Bizen pottery is *Imbe Yaki*. The characteristic Bizen ware is a reddish-brown stoneware, with a thin skin of lustrous translucent glaze which shows a greyish tint where it has run thick, and is sometimes splashed or spotted with an opaque greenish grey. The finest period for Bizen figures was in the eighteenth century, but the potters still preserve their skill in modelling. Two rare classes of Bizen are *Ao Bizen*, which has a slatey blue tint, and the *Shira Bizen*, which is almost white and is sometimes decorated with red and gold.

Among the Bizen marks are crescents representing the new and the waning moon, and a cherry blossom, besides a variety of strokes or dashes which were used as kiln marks. These kiln marks were used in other districts as well to distinguish the wares of individual potters when they made use of public kilns.

Dai Ni-pon Im be to — Imbe pottery of Great Japan. On a square bottle of dark red stoneware with incised diaper ornament, nineteenth century. British Museum.

Kiyo-chika. On a brown stoneware ornament formed of a group of Chinese lions (Kara-shishi), in the British Museum. Nineteenth century.

Yoshida tsukuru = Made by Yoshida. On a cake box of chocolate-brown stoneware, with incised branches of pine, bamboo and plum. Bizen ware about 1840. *Jap. Hist. Coll.*, 195.

K'wa-bo. Stamped on a brown stoneware group of the gods Hotei and Daikoku in the Franks Collection. Eighteenth century.

NAGATO.

HAGI-YAKI was first made at Matsumoto in the sixteenth century by a Corean named Rikei, who took the name of Koraizaemon. The ware was in Corean style, and had a greyish crackled glaze with salmon clouding. The foot rim usually had a triangular nick.

In the seventeenth century a factory was opened at Matsumoto by a potter named Kinsetsu, who made Raku ware in addition to the old Hagi types, pale green and lavender glazes, variegated greyish or cream-white glazes, and painted ware. The thick, streaky lavender glazes often resemble very closely the Chinese Yuan wares.

TOYO-URA-YAMA.

TOYO-URA-YAKI. Founded about 1720 for the manufacture of terra-cotta ash-bowls for tea ceremonies. The kiln is situated at the foot of a hill called Toyo-ura-yama in the province of Nagato. No. 236 is a specimen made in 1846. The Japanese Historical Collection contains a terra-cotta ash-bowl, mottled black, incurved rim, of A.D. 1846, made at Toyo-ura. A pot and cover of porcelain, crackled inside, outside of dark green lacquer, with decorations of a dragon, fishes, and phœnixes in gold, made at Toyo-ura, is in the Franks Collection.

AWAJI.

The factory at Igano Mura in the island of Awaji was started by Kashiu Mimpei about 1830. After some years of experiment he succeeded in making a fine ware with coloured glazes—yellow, green, &c.—after the style of the Chinese Kochi-Yaki. Mimpei had studied at Kioto, and in 1834 he persuaded Ogata Shuhei to come from that city and help him. In 1838 he made a greyish white glaze, and in the next year a lustrous black. He also made fine tortoiseshell *(bekko-de)* and tiger-skin glazes.

In 1862 Mimpei retired, and the work was carried on by his son, assisted by his nephew Sampei. Another factory was opened at Samoto. Awaji ware has a hard white body, varying from stoneware to porcelain. The glazes are peculiarly smooth and wax-like. Fayence of the Awata type was also made there with crackled glaze and enamelled decoration.

MIMPEI.

No. 284 (Japanese Historical Collection) is a flower-vase of yellow glazed porcelain, representing a green bamboo stem, made by Kashiu Mimpei, A.D. 1830. Height 12 inches. No. 286, a cup by Mimpei, of yellow glazed porcelain, partly facetted, bears the Ch'êng Hua mark, made in 1830. *Jap. Hist. Coll.*

賀　日
集　本
三　淡
平　路

SAMPEI-YAKI. Porcelain tea-service, painted in enamel colours with flowers and fruit. On the bottom in gold the maker's name, Kashiu Sampei, in the island of Awaji, A.D. 1875; reading, " *Ni-pon Awaji Ka-shiu Sampei.*" *Jap. Hist. Coll.*, 288.

CHIKUZEN.

Potteries existed in this province in the ninth century, but their importance dates from the sixteenth century, when two Coreans, Shinkuro and Hachizo, were settled there and worked in Corean style. In the seventeenth century multiple glazes in the Seto fashion were introduced, and became the feature of the ware which is known as *Takatori-yaki.* The factory appears to have been moved frequently in search of supplies of clay, but it seems to have been fixed in 1708 at Sobara Mura.

The TAKATORI glazes include coffee-brown, chocolate-brown, tea-dust green, rich purplish black, bluish grey *flambé*, and translucent brown and green.

Takatoriyo = Takatori pottery (Morse).

Taka for Takatori.

HIGO.

YATSUSHIRO-YAKI was first made by a Corean who had previously worked at Agano, in Buzen, taking the name of Agano Kizo. About 1630 he was moved to the neighbourhood of Yatsushiro, and set up his kiln at Koda, or, according to others, at Shirno Toyohara. His wares are of two distinct kinds, one with mahogany-coloured and splashed glazes of the Seto type, and the other (the typical Yatsushiro ware) a grey stoneware with ornament inlaid in white, and sometimes black, in Corean style. Other factories were opened, and the work has been continued to modern times, most of the beautiful vases and bowls with delicate inlaid patterns in a soft grey ground being nineteenth century work.

The Corean inlaid patterns imitated on Yatsushiro ware include (1) the stork and cloud pattern *(un-kaku-de)*; (2) streaky white ornament showing the marks of the brush *(hakime)*; and (3) a pattern of "cord marks" called *Mishima* style from its resemblance to the lines of closely written characters on the celebrated "Mishima Almanack."

28

YATSU-SHIRO-YAKI. In the Japanese Collection, No. 304, is a vase of grey porcelain with crackled glaze, incised with water-plants and a band of fret pattern filled in with white; on the bottom is this stamp in the Katakana character. "Yatsu-Shiro" ware, A.D. 1800, in the province of Higo.

YATSU-SHIRO-YAKI. A jar of grey-coloured porcelain, with an incised pattern of closely arranged parallel lines filled in with white; Yatsu-Shiro ware, in the province of Higo, A.D. 1720. Height 16 inches. *Jap. Hist. Coll.*, 302.

MISHIMA-YAKI. A brownish glazed earthenware bottle marked with white lines; a specimen of Mishima ware. *Jap. Hist. Coll.*, 591.

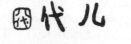 *Yatsu-shiro*, in two forms (Morse).

 Ya = Yatsushiro.

 Gen.

HIZEN (ISLAND OF KIUSHIU).

KARATSU-YAKI. The first factories at Karatsu date back to the eleventh century. They are said to have been founded by Koreans, and their productions, Corean in style, are known as *Oku-gorai*. The work was continued by native potters, and in the thirteenth century a rough ware was made in the Seto style, and known as Seto Karatsu or Ko-Karatsu. At the end of the sixteenth century a further importation of Corean potters took place, and a ware known as Chosen-Karatsu was made, a hard dark ware, with mahogany glaze and passages of dark cream colour. In the middle of the seventeenth century, splashed or *flambé* glazes were used, chiefly mahogany brown, with streaks of bluish white, or clouds of blue and green. Another class of ware, grey or greyish brown, was painted with archaic designs in reddish brown or black under the glaze, and known as *e-gorai* or "painted Corean." In the eighteenth century inlaid ornament like that of Yatsushiro was used, and granular glazes in white or grey. Most of the ware seems to have been archaic in style, and suited for the tea ceremonies; but in recent years skilful figures were made by Nakazato Keizo, who ceased work in 1895.

Shichi ju ni sai Ni-raku saku. Made by Niraku at the age of seventy-two. Mark scratched underneath a water jar of pale reddish-brown stoneware, with pale brown glaze, mottled with deep brown and green; incised ornament, filled with white slip. Karatsu ware, about 1800. *Jap. Hist. Coll.,* 168.

ARITA-YAKI. The province of Hizen is chiefly celebrated for porcelain factories located in the neighbourhood of Arita. It has already been mentioned that the first porcelain made in Japan was manufactured by Gorodayu-go-Shonsui with Chinese materials, but that the native materials were first discovered in Hizen,

ARITA.

on Izumi-yama, by a Corean named Risampei in the first decade of the seventeenth century. This marks the true beginning of Japanese porcelain. It has also been mentioned how Kakiemon, an Arita potter, developed, if he did not introduce, the use of enamel colours for decorating the surface, having learnt his secrets from a Chinaman.

KAKIEMON WARE. The porcelain associated with the name of Kakiemon is the most beautiful enamelled porcelain made in Japan. It has at its best fine milk-white body and glaze, and is delicately painted in brilliant translucent enamels, a bright blue, turquoise green, soft red of orange tint, and pale primrose yellow. The designs are simple and restrained, but disposed with perfect grace—a single spray of some flowery plant, a blossoming prunus bough and a tiger, a boy or a brace of quails beside a banded hedge, a pheasant on a rock, or a few single blossoms, passages of red diaper or borders of broken flowers—leaving ample play to the fine white surface of the ware. This is the "fine old Japan" which served as a model for Meissen, Mennecy, Chelsea, Bow, Worcester, and numerous other European porcelain factories in the eighteenth century.

It is impossible that all the Kakiemon ware can have passed through the hands of one individual potter. The name is doubtless used to cover all the porcelains decorated in a style which he popularised. Indeed the quality of the Kakiemon ware varies widely, and at times the glaze is greyish, coarse, and partially crackled.

IMARI-YAKI. Another class of "Old Japan" is known from the seaport of Imari, its place of export. It was, however, made inland in the Arita district, though it must have been chiefly destined for export to Europe, the designs being unsuited to Japanese taste. Imari ware, freely imported by the Dutch in the seventeenth century, was a strong, coarse porcelain with greyish bubbly glaze, heavily decorated in a dark impure underglaze blue, combined with overglaze red and gold. Enamel colours were also used—green, manganese, yellow, and rarely black. The designs are crowded and roughly executed, but the general effect is often highly decorative. Baskets of flowers, irregular panels of landscapes or growing plants, and passage of diaper and bold flowering sprays are common motives. The forms of the ware—large dishes, plates, tea-cups and saucers, sets of covered vases and beakers—are clearly designed for Western trade.

In the eighteenth century a more Japanese style of decoration was adopted; the ware was purer, the painting more careful, and Japanese crests (particularly the chrysanthemum badge), delicate wistaria designs, phœnixes, and occasionally figures occur in the decoration. There was naturally Arita porcelain made solely for Japanese use, but this rarely found its way out of the country before the end of last century. It consisted chiefly of incense burners, sake-cup stands, covered bowls, tea bowls, and other native forms, of small size and simple decoration.

Other Arita wares besides the enamelled class consist of blue and white, celadon green, ruri (dark blue), lustrous brown, violet purple, embossed and pierced and sometimes engraved wares. About 1868, when the country was again opened to commerce with Europe, a quantity of heavily lacquered Arita ware was shipped from Nagasaki. It is often described as Nagasaki ware, and consists of large vases or bottles with bag-shaped or beaker-shaped mouths, such as are seen in the windows of tea-merchants' shops.

OKAWAJI OR NABESHIMA-YAKI. A kiln was opened in 1660 at Okawaji, a village eight miles from Arita, to make porcelain for the Prince of Nabeshima, who removed the best workmen from the neighbouring potteries of Hirose and Ichinoe. Towards the end of the eighteenth century the feudal patronage relaxed, and the ware degenerated. The early Nabeshima porcelain was not made for the market but for the prince's use. It was a fine white ware with lustrous glaze, and its decoration was either in delicate enamel colours in the Kakiemon style, in a soft light underglaze blue, or in the characteristic Nabeshima style, i.e., with naturalistic branches of blossoming cherry, maple leaves floating on water, and flowering sprays in underglaze blue with touches of enamel. A feature of the Nabeshima wares is a border of strokes like the teeth of a comb (called *Kushide* or comb pattern) on the exterior of the foot rim. A fine celadon was also made at Okawaji.

MIKAWAJI OR HIRADO-YAKI. The discovery of porcelain stone at Amakusa in 1712 led to the commencement of the manufacture at Mikawaji, but it was not till the factory was taken over in 1751 by Matsura, the Prince of Hirado, that porcelain was successfully made. Between this latter date and 1843 one of the finest Japanese porcelains was made at Mikawaji for the sole use of the Prince of Hirado. It is a milk white ware fine as pipe-clay, and with a pure glaze of velvety lustre. The decoration is usually in a beautiful pale, pure blue, and the designs are commonly landscapes, figures, trees, and flowers. A

HIRADO SEI
(Made at Hirado).

favourite pattern consisted of boys playing under a pine tree, the number of the boys varying from seven to three, according to the quality of the ware. Besides this very beautiful moulded, carved, and pierced decoration were used, and good figures were modelled, either in pure white or with details picked out in coloured glazes—brown, blue, and black—in the biscuit. In the last part of the nineteenth century the Hirado potters have manufactured for the general market.

Potters' names do not appear on the private wares made for the Hizen princes, nor indeed on any of the Arita porcelains before the nineteenth century, but it is not unusual to find copies of Chinese *nien hao*, and marks of commendation or words of good omen in place of a mark.

Zoshun-tei Sam-po sei = Made by Sampo at the Zoshun hall. On a pair of fish-shaped porcelain dishes, painted in underglaze blue, and enamels (chiefly red) with gilding. Arita; middle nineteenth century. Franks Coll.

Hicho-zan Shimpo tsukuru = Made by Hichozan Shimpo. In red on a covered bowl of Arita "egg-shell" porcelain painted in enamel colours with groups of flowers. Nineteenth century. British Museum.

Nemboku an Kiso tsukuru = Made by Nembokuan Kiso. On beaker-shaped vase of late nineteenth century Arita porcelain, painted in underglaze blue and maroon. British Museum.

Nichi Hi-zen Fuka-gawa sei = Made by Fukagawa of Nichi Hizen. On a pair of flower vases of Okawaji porcelain with crackled celadon green glaze richly enamelled and gilt: date about 1875. *Jap. Hist. Coll.*, 355.

Hi-zen Tsuji sei = Made by Tsuji in Hizen. On a coffee pot of fine porcelain decorated in black, green and red, with gilding, about 1875. *Jap. Hist. Coll.*, 344.

老
三
製

Fuka-mi sei = Made by Fukami. On a pair of flower vases of Arita porcelain, with ornament in low relief and a pale yellow ground: made in 1875 by Suminosoke Fukami. *Jap. Hist. Coll.*, 343.

於
香
蘭
社

西
山
製

MIKAWAJI-YAKI. These marks are on a porcelain vase decorated with enamel colours and gold; on one side an unglazed panel with a lion in relief; on the bottom are the marks in the margin impressed in the circle incuse: the other marks are painted red. Made at Mikawaji, in the province of Hizen, A.D. 1875. The circular inscription commences from the lowest point towards the left: *Dai Nipon Mikawaji-sei*, "Made at Mikawaji in Great Japan." *Jap. Hist. Coll.*, 361.

MARKS OF COMMENDATION, &c., FOUND CHIEFLY ON EARLY PORCELAIN.

Ho = Precious. In gold on a blue ground beneath a porcelain saucer dish painted in colours with gilding, with four radiating medallions with baskets of flowers in a deep blue ground. Arita, about 1700. Franks Coll.

Ho tei no takaru = A gem among precious vessels (in Chinese, *Pao ting chih chên*). On an octagonal porcelain bowl painted in blue with touches of colour and gilding: landscapes inside and eight views outside. Arita, eighteenth century. Franks Coll.

Ka = happiness. On a porcelain saucer painted in blue with foreign figures in a landscape. Arita, eighteenth century. Franks Coll.

Kin = gold. On a pair of porcelain basins painted in colours with a peach bough, and eight compartments with floral designs. Arita, early eighteenth century. Franks Coll.

Fuku = happiness. On a pair of shallow porcelain bowls painted in colours with gilding, with medallions of plants in a red ground. Arita, about 1700. Franks Coll.

KUTANI-YAKI. A deep dish of Kutani porcelain, 16½ in. diameter, is in the Japanese Historical Collection, No. 309, the centre painted with firs and bamboos in green and purple on a yellow ground; the hollow with trellis and wave ornament in the same colours, thick rich glaze; painted mark at the bottom, meaning *Fuku*, "Happiness," frequently found on this ware; the date ascribed to it is seventeenth century.

A flower in red on two porcelain plates, painted in colours with gilding with a vase, rockwork, flowers, and phœnixes. Arita, seventeenth century. Franks Collection.

Fu ki cho shun = Riches, honour, and enduring spring (Chinese *fu kuei ch'ang ch'un*). A common mark on early Arita and other porcelains

Tai min nen sei = Made in the Great Ming dynasty. On a saucer dish painted in colours with a landscape and two deer. Arita, seventeenth century. Franks Coll.

Sem-mio nen sei = Made in the period Semmio; perhaps a garbled form of the Chinese mark *Ta ming Hsiian Tê nien chih*. On blue and white porcelain of recent date in Mr. F. A. White's Collection and in the Franks Collection.

Bun mei kai kua = Enlightenment and civilisation. On a bowl encrusted with cloisonné enamel. Seto about 1860. Franks Collection.

The fungus mark on Arita porcelain of the early eighteenth century, painted in underglaze blue, enamels and gilding. Imitated at Worcester. Franks Coll.

KAMEYAMA-YAKI. A factory opened in 1803 at Kameyama, in the neighbourhood of Nagasaki, made good porcelain with Amakusa materials. It was decorated in blue and white in the Chinese style, and some of it closely resembles Ming blue and white. The blue is dark with a tinge of mauve. The enterprise was abandoned in 1864; an attempt to revive it in 1872 resulted in failure. Mark, *Kameyama tsukuru* = made at Kameyama.

Other important porcelain factories existed at Wakayama, in Kishiu, where Zengoro Hozen, better known as Eiraku, worked from 1827-1844 (see p. 398). His wares are painted in enamels, or decorated with coloured glazes on the biscuit, and bear the marks *Kairakuyen*, *Kahin Shiriu* and *Eiraku*.

Similar wares were made at Otokoyama from 1847-1866 and marked *Nanki Otokoyama*, at Ota, and also at a private factory in Tokio which used the mark *San-rakuyen*. Fine blue and white enamelled porcelain was made near Hikone on the shore of the Lake Biwa, in the province of Omi. It is marked *Koto* (east of the lake).

KOTO.

Eggshell porcelain of wonderful tenuity has been made by the Japanese since about 1840. It was first made at the Hirado factories, and afterwards at Tokio (*Shiba-Yaki*), Seto and Mino.

Porcelain is also made in the province of Satsuma. An abortive attempt is recorded in the seventeenth century, but the manufacture was established at Tatsumonji in 1779. Another factory was started at Sarayama. Enamelled decoration was used till about 1868, since when only coarse blue and white has been made.

SATSUMA.

In 1596 Shimazu Yoshihiro, Prince of Satsuma, brought back from Corea a number of skilled potters whom he settled in his fief. They seem to have been divided into two principal groups, the one working at Chosa, where the prince had a castle, and the other in Sasshiu. The kilns were subsequently moved, but the Chosa group united at Tatsumonji in 1650, and the Sasshiu group moved to the Nawashiro district in 1603, and a little later founded a second kiln at Tadeno.

The early Satsuma wares include a great variety: in Corean taste, with reddish-brown body, translucent glaze, and inlaid "Mishima" ornament; grey granulated glazes like the *Same-Yaki* (shark-skin ware); *flambé* glaze with greenish-blue markings like Canton stoneware; "iron-rust" glaze with splashes of *flambé*; black glaze; black with gold specks; tea-green glaze over russet-brown; mixed glazes, green, grey and brown in Seto style, and "tortoiseshell" glaze.

Another kind has dark-brown archaic patterns painted under a translucent glaze on a stone-grey ware. This is known as *Sunkoroku*. But the most familiar and the most attractive Satsuma ware is a fine hard stoneware with crackled glaze, at first a greyish-white, and afterwards of a mellow ivory tint. This was first made in the Nawashiro district in the seventeenth century, and it seems to have been derived from the Chinese Ting class of pottery. Early attempts were made to decorate this ware with enamel colours, but it was not till the end of the eighteenth century that any quantity of it was successfully painted. The best period covers the first half of the nineteenth century when the finest ivory-white fayence with evenly crackled surface was sparingly decorated in Indian red, green, blue, purple, black, and yellow enamels with gilding and silvering. The ornaments were slight and beautifully executed. In more recent times the surface of the ware has been completely covered with minutely painted ornament. This is chiefly done at Tokio, and the work is intended for the Western markets. The modern ware is greyer and coarser. It should be added that a great quantity of Kioto fayence is passed off as Satsuma, and that a factory at Ota, Yokohama, was started to produce wholesale imitations of Satsuma ware.

日本
薩摩中嶋製

Ni-pon Satsu-ma Naka-jima sei = Made by Naka-jima of Satsuma in Japan. On a pair of flower-vases of crackled creamy fayence painted in colours with gilding, about 1875. *Jap. Hist. Coll.*, 296.

薩製

Satsu sei = Made in Satsu(ma). On Tachino ware about 1830 (Morse).

岗古

Hoju. On Satsuma ware about 1800 (Morse).

芳光

Hoko. On Satsuma ware about 1860 (Morse).

EUROPEAN PORCELAIN

PORCELAIN has this distinguishing characteristic: when held up to a strong light, it appears *translucent*, unlike pottery or fayence, which is *opaque*. The *pâte dure*, or true porcelain, is of the whiteness of milk, and feels to the touch of a hard and cold nature, and is somewhat heavier than soft paste; underneath the plates and other pieces, the rims or projecting rings upon which they rest, are left unpolished or without glaze.

The properties of porcelain may be thus defined:—

Hard.—The finest and most valuable have these essential and indispensable properties: the component earths are combined in such relative proportions that proper baking renders the mass translucent, fine, hard, dense, durable, and sonorous when struck with a hard body; a white colour, approaching the tint of milk; a grain fine and close; texture compact, intermediate between the closeness of glass and the obvious porosity of the best flint ware; fracture semi-vitreous, and will sustain without injury sudden alternations of high and low temperature; the presence of an alkaline component possessing the quality of a flux relative to the others, most economically brings all of them into a state approximating to fusion, and in the kinds varies the translucency, which foreigners try by every method to decrease, and the English manufacturers seek to increase, while preserving the fine close grain. The biscuit must be adapted to readily absorb water without injury. This is covered with a glaze, clear, white, transparent, indestructible by acids or alkalies or temperature, beautifully fine to the touch, smooth, and appearing soft like velvet, rather than lustrous or glossy like satin. When first applied to the ware the water readily permeates, and on the surface the thin coating of components quickly dries into a solid shell, uniformly thick in all parts, and sufficiently firm to bear handling without being rubbed off during removal into the seggars.

The *pâte tendre* has the appearance of an unctuous white enamel like cream, it is also to the touch of a soft soapy nature; it is less dense, yet sonorous, translucent, granular, and a very fine porous fracture, harder and less brittle than glass, and will sustain considerable alternations of temperature. Not being able to sustain so great a degree of heat in the kiln, it is consequently softer than the other. As a rule, all painting upon porcelain, or enamel painting and artistic work of every description in colours, as well as gilding, are executed *upon the glaze*, and *not* upon the biscuit. An exception, however, to this rule is the well-known *blue painted;* this and the *blue printed* are placed upon the biscuit *under the glaze.*

The *bleu du roi* (or, as it is termed in England, *Mazarin blue*) of Sèvres, Worcester, Derby, and some few Staffordshire china factories, is also under the glaze. The colour is PAINTED upon the biscuit ware, after which it is glazed and fired in the gloss-oven; it is afterwards painted in colours and gilt, and submitted to a further fire in the muffle kiln.

All ground colours (except the *bleu du roi*, and possibly one or two others) are upon the glaze, certainly on Staffordshire china and earthenware, many of the ground colours being too delicate to withstand the intense heat of the gloss-oven.

The method of *ground laying* is as follows *on glazed ware:* The artist lays even all the proper parts of the ware, with a pencil of suitable size, and a preparation of linseed oil, turpentine, and red lead, as a flux; he then with a lock of cotton or wool, applies the powder of the enamel colour, carefully adjusting the coating, so that all the parts may be equally covered; this is then baked or fired in what is called a *hard* kiln, the heat not being so intense as the gloss-oven, but much greater than required for gold and enamel colours; it is afterwards painted and receives another firing; this ground is therefore *laid*, and not *painted*, as in the *bleu du roi.*

It may be observed that Mr. Spode produced some specimens of *rose du Barry* on the biscuit with success, but great loss ensued, and it was discontinued.

Colours.—The best colours now used in the art have these components :—

REDS—Oxides of gold and iron.
PURPLES—Oxides of cobalt, chromium, tin, and calcium.
PINKS—Oxides of chromium, calcium, and tin.
BROWNS—Oxides of chromium, iron, and manganese.
BLUES—Oxides of cobalt and silica. *Mat blue*—Oxides of cobalt, lime, and zinc.
YELLOW AND ORANGE—Oxides of lead, silver, and antimony.
GREENS—*Yellow* or *emerald*—Oxides of chromium and silicon. *Blue* or *celeste*—Oxides of chromium, cobalt, silicon, and zinc. *Green edge*—Oxides of copper and chromium.
BLACK—Oxides of cobalt, nickel, manganese, iron, and chromium.[1]

The amateur must be upon his guard in collecting porcelain, and not place too much reliance on the marks which he may find upon the ware. When the mark is not indented on the paste or baked with the porcelain when at its greatest heat, usually in blue (*au grand feu*), it gives no guarantee for its genuineness : the mark was nearly always affixed before glazing. It is necessary, in forming a correct judgment of the authenticity of a piece of valuable china, such as Sèvres, that many things be

---

[1] Shaw's *Chemistry of Pottery.*

taken into consideration. First, above all, it is most important to be satisfied whether the porcelain be of hard or soft paste, and whether such descriptions of paste were made at the particular epoch represented by the mark; then, if the decoration be in keeping with the style adopted at the time indicated, the colours, the finish, the manner of decoration, and various other *indicia* must also be taken into account.

The reader will find a most valuable reference to representative specimens of Continental porcelain fabriques in the ten cases of some 500 specimens collected by the late Sir A. W. Franks, K.C.B., and bequeathed to the Bethnal Green Museum pending their accommodation later on in the British Museum. The specimens have been collected on account of their marks and monograms, and in the notices of the different ceramic factories given in the following pages, many of them will be found quoted. They comprise chiefly Italian, Spanish, German, French, and Dutch factories.

As regards public collections of specimens of English ceramics, that formed by Lady Charlotte Schreiber in the Victoria and Albert Museum, is frequently referred to in the notices of those fabriques. There is also a good collection of English porcelain in the British Museum, which is well arranged and labelled for public information.

The references to private collections have been corrected so far as it is possible to do so, and specimens which have passed from the ownerships referred to in the previous edition, have been in many cases traced to their present possessors.

Italy

FLORENCE

A PRIVATE manufactory of porcelain (*soft paste*) was established here as early as 1580, under the auspices of Francesco I. (de' Medici), Grand Duke of Tuscany. He established a laboratory, where experiments were made; the manufactory was in the Boboli Gardens. He has the glory of being the first maker of artificial porcelain in Europe whose productions are known to us; not, it is true, so hard as that of China,—that is to say, composed of *kaolin* and *petuntse*, but softer and translucid, which is one of the principal tests of porcelain. Vasari speaks of the translucid pottery of the Grand-Duke Francis; he tells us that he called to his assistance the celebrated Bernard Buontalenti, and that in a short time he made porcelain vases as fine as the most ancient and the most perfect; he also relates that Alphonso II., Duke of Ferrara, profiting by the talents of Giulio d'Urbino, applied himself to this industry.

M. Jacquemart[1] gives a receipt for making the porcelain of the Grand-Duke Francis, taken from a manuscript discovered in the Bibliotheca Magliabechiana, compiled by some person in the Duke's employ. The fabrication of this porcelain was abandoned after the death of its inventor. In the *Diarie de Carte* of the year 1613, at Florence, it is said that at a ball there, tickets were issued made of the *porcellana regia*, on one side of which were the arms of the Medici, and on the other a scimitar. It is called the Medici porcelain, some of the specimens having the arms of that family painted upon them. With the exception of the unknown production of an ancient potter at Venice, and what may have been made by the Duke of Ferrara, this was the first porcelain made in Europe, and is now very scarce, not more than about thirty-six pieces being known. The mark is painted in blue, and represents the Cathedral of Florence. The first we have here given is on the bottom of a large

---

[1] *Histoire de la Porcelaine*, Paris, 1860.

bowl, painted with small blue flowers on white ground, of very compact

potting, now in the Victoria and Albert Museum; the second mark is on a plate of the same fabrique, which, with an elegantly formed ewer of the same porcelain, was given to the British Museum by Mr. C. D. E. Fortnum. (*Ker. Gall.*, enlarged edition, figs. 184, 5, 6). The same mark is on a ewer in the Ashmolean Museum, Oxford (Fortnum Collection).

A charming little ewer of this fabrique, the body ovoid with scroll handles springing from the neck and meeting over the mouth, the spout in the form of an inverted lily, painted with floral sprays and arabesques in blue on white ground, 8 inches high and bearing the same mark, was sold at Christie's in July 1896 for the large price of £304 10s., Messrs. Durlacher Bros. being the purchasers. It is now in the Collection bequeathed by Mr. George Salting to the Victoria and Albert Museum.

The discovery and identification of this porcelain is due to Dr. Foresi of Florence, further corroborated by MM. Piot and Jacquemart of Paris. Its history, with description and figures of all the then known pieces, is to be found in Baron J. C. Davillier's *Les Origines de la Porcelaine en Europe*, 4to, Paris, 1882.

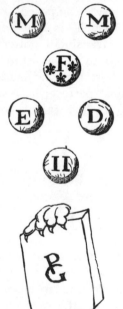

FLORENCE. The arms of the Medici family. On a vase in the Collection of M. Gustave de Rothschild, and other pieces; the six pellets, one bearing the three fleurs-de-lis, having initial letters which may be thus read—"*Franciscus Medici Magnus Etruriæ Dux Secundus.*"

FLORENCE. A fine and interesting piece was in the Collection of the late Signor Alessandro Castellani; it is a shallow basin, in the centre of which is the figure of St. Mark, with the lion, painted in the usual blue pigment, and in a manner which stamps it as the work of a master's pencil. The monogram, composed of the letters G. P., is painted on the volume held beneath the lion's paw; and on the reverse of the basin is the usual mark of the Cathedral. It has been suggested that the monogram may be that of Rafaelle's great pupil, Giulio Pippi *detto* Romano; but, unfortunately for this hypothesis, Giulio Romano died in 1546, whereas the Medici Porcelain does not appear to have been perfected before 1580. (*Fortnum's Catalogue*, p. lxvii. of Introduction.) The figure of St. Mark is after a design by Geo. Penz.

LIST OF PIECES OF FLORENTINE PORCELAIN OF THE SIXTEENTH CENTURY.

1. Vase, with handle over the top, painted with ara-
  besques, and in front the arms of the Medici. *Baron Gustave de Rothschild.*
2. Large dish, painted with historical subject. *The same.*
3. Another piece. *The same.*
4. Another piece *Queen of Portugal.*
5. Another piece. *The same.*
6. Large bowl painted in blue with flowers. *Victoria and Albert Museum.*
7. Plate, in blue with flowers. *The same.*
8. Oil and vinegar cruet. *The same.*
9. Plateau, with arabesques. *Sèvres Museum.*
10. Plate in the same style. *The same.*
11. Large square bottle, with the arms of Spain. *The same.*
12. The companion bottle, dated 1581. *The same.*
13. Another piece (a fragment?). *The same.*
14. Hunting-bottle, in Persian style. *Baron Alphonse de Rothschild.*
15. Hunting-bottle, with rings. *Baron C. Davillier.*
16. Small jug. *M. Arondel.*
17. A flacon. *The same.*
18. A large flacon of flattened circular form. *Unknown.*
19. Basin, with St. Mark and the lion in the centre. *M. A. Castellani.*
20. Plate with blue flowers. *Right Hon. W. E. Gladstone.*
21. Plate with blue flowers. *Mr. C. D. E. Fortnum.*
22. Plate with blue flowers. *M. Florest, Florence.*
23. Plate with blue flowers. *The same.*
24. Bocaletto, Persian decoration. *Baron de Monville.*
25. Another piece. *Unknown.*
26. Small ewer, described on previous page.

Dr. A. Foresi, of Florence, who claims the discovery of the documents in the Magliabecchi Library, and by whose research twelve of the pieces above described were brought to light and appropriated, has also become possessed of a trial piece, made, he thinks, in the time of Cosmo I. It is a porcelain hunting-bottle with Oriental decoration similar to No. 15, with mask loops for the cord to pass through; under the foot is written *Prova*, as in the margin. This piece he considers was also the Medici porcelain.

DOCCIA.

DOCCIA. This manufactory was founded in 1735 by the Marchese Carlo Ginori, contemporaneously with the Imperial Manufactory of Sèvres. At this early date he commenced making experiments at Doccia, a villa of the family a short distance from Florence, in the vicinity of Sesto. The Marquis Charles, at his own expense, sent a ship to the East Indies to obtain samples of the materials used in the composition of Chinese porcelain, and in 1737 he secured the services of Carlo Wandhelien, a chemist, who became director of the works, and its first productions became articles of commerce. In 1757 Carlo Ginori died, and was succeeded by his son, the Senator Lorenzo, who enlarged the works, constructed more improved furnaces, increased the number of workmen, and gave it the architectural appearance it now presents: he was consequently enabled to produce statues, vases, and other objects of large dimensions. These improvements were continued and increased by his son and successor Carlo Leopoldo, who established a museum for models of the most celebrated sculptors, ancient and modern, and a school of design, which may be seen by the improved character of the borders and ornaments, as well as the high finish of the ware of this period. After his death, and during the minority of his eldest son, the direction of the manufactory was confided to the Marchese Pier Francesco Rinuccini, and afterwards to the Marchesa Marianna Ginori, the mother of a more recent owner of the fabrique, Lorenzo Ginori Lisci, the great-grandson of the founder. The early moulds of the Capo di Monte porcelain were transferred to Doccia when that manufactory was discontinued in 1821; the consequence is, that Europe is inundated at the present day with false examples of Capo di Monte porcelain, and which can be purchased to any extent at the Doccia fabrique; the mark being also imitated, tends to throw discredit on everything emanating from it.

It may be observed that in all those countries where similar manufactures were established, they were either of short duration, or were indebted for their prosperity to the patronage and royal munificence of the sovereigns in whose states they were situated, and afterwards became their property. Doccia, on the contrary, sustained itself by the exertions alone of the Ginori family, who first originated it; the sole encouragement it obtained from the Tuscan Government was the prerogative of being the only fabrique of the kind in the state, which prerogative ceased in 1812.

During the last thirty-five years or so the fabrication of the imitative Capo di Monte ware of the eighteenth century, in coloured *mezzo-relievo*, has been brought to great perfection, as well as the imitation of the maiolica of Xanto, and Maestro Giorgio, of the sixteenth century, by the invention and introduction of the metallic lustres in the colouring. These important results were obtained and perfected by Giusto Giusti, a pupil of the Doccia school, to whom honourable mention was accorded in the London Exhibition in 1851, as well as in that of Paris in 1855: he died suddenly in 1858.

The Doccia manufactory is particularly distinguished by the variety of its productions, and successful imitations of the maiolica of the sixteenth century, of the Capo di Monte porcelain bas-reliefs, the reproduction of Luca della Robbia, and Chinese and Japanese porcelain.

The principal artists from 1770 to 1800 are given by Mr. Marryat :—

Rigaci, *miniatures.*	A. M. Fanciullacci, *chemist.*
Antonio Valleresi, *flowers.*	Giov. Bat. Fanciullacci, *miniatures.*
Angiolo Fiaschi, *figures.*	Antonio Smeraldi, *figures and landscapes.*
Carlo Ristori, *landscapes.*	Giov. Giusti, *flowers and landscapes.*
Gasparo Bruschi, *modeller.*	Giusep. Ettel, *modeller.*
Giusep. Bruschi, *modeller.*	Gaet. Lici, *modeller.*

Pietro Fanciullacci, *painter and chemist.*

DOCCIA. This mark, in red, is on a porcelain *écuelle*, the dish painted in the centre with a shield on a cross of the order of St. Stephen, quartered with the Ginori arms (three stars *argent* on a bend *or*), supported by an eagle  on each side, and festoons of flowers; the borders are elaborately painted with flowers in a very effective manner; the cover has a floral monogram, composed of a large *M*, *G*, *L*, and a *C*, the last in blue, being probably that of the *Marchesa Marianna Ginori Lisci;* the *C* may be intended for her husband, *Carlo* Leopoldo Ginori. Formerly in the Collection of the Marchese d'Azeglio.

DOCCIA. The initials of Pietro Fanciullacci, a chemist as well as a painter, on a porcelain sugar-basin and cover, painted with peasants and landscapes, formerly in the possession of the Marchese d'Azeglio.

DOCCIA. *Hard and soft paste.* This mark is a star, being part of the Ginori arms; it is in gold on the richest specimens, but is more generally found in red, on a cup and saucer, painted with Florentine arms and medallions of landscapes. The same mark is also found on the Nove porcelain, and occasionally on that of Venice. Specimens bearing this mark are also found with Italian views, and lettered descriptions of the same: Mr. J. Loraine Baldwin had one with the description "Sepulcro digli Orazi," and "Sepulcro di Virgilio," written underneath each view, and this is a typical specimen of the fabrique of La Doccia. The same mark occurs on a very rich specimen, perhaps the finest in the Franks Collection—a fan-shaped jardinière in an oval-shaped stand, exquisitely painted with panels having subjects of ladies and military officers, the panels divided by pilasters richly gilt on blue ground. There was a similar set of three jardinières in the Reynolds Collection. (See *Ker. Gall.*, enlarged edition, fig. 206.)

It is impossible to distinguish between Doccia and Le Nove, and while the Editor has included the above specimens in the former fabrique, Sir A. W. Franks has classed them amongst the latter.

DOCCIA.   The same star, but with more points; marked in red, on a fine specimen, with landscapes and festoons, gilt border; formerly in Mr. Bohn's Collection.

 DOCCIA.   Another mark, of a double triangle; stamped in gold on the best pieces.

GINORI.   DOCCIA.   The name of the Marchese Ginori is sometimes impressed, which is occasionally abbreviated, and only GIN. used.   This is a comparatively modern production.

CA N.S.   DOCCIA.   Porcelain.   This mark is on a tea-service, painted with nymphs and satyrs.   A teacup and saucer in the Franks Collection, has in addition CA impressed; another has P.G.   There is another which was formerly in Mr. Napier of Shandon's Collection, and in that of the Marchese d'Azeglio.   The same mark occurs on a milkpot, painted with Carnival figures and garden scene.   These letters (N.S.) are proved satisfactorily to belong to the Doccia fabrique; we have seen a complete *déjeûner* service so marked, many of the pieces bearing in addition the name GINORI.   These initials are attributed to Nicolo Sebastino.   On a specimen in the Franks Collection these letters are accompanied by a cross.

 DOCCIA.   These marks, a mullet and double triangle, or a modification of the preceding, are in blue or gold on superior quality of porcelain.

There are also in the Franks Collection some oval medallion portraits, white on blue ground, in imitation of Wedgwood's jasper ware, which Sir A. W. Franks attributes to Doccia.

The present proprietorship of the Ginori factory is vested in a limited company trading under the title of "S. C. Richard Ginori," and a great number of hands are employed at works a short distance from Florence. At the International Exhibition of Turin, 1911, this company received the Grand Prix for an important exhibit of their porcelain, which was of the best quality and excellent decoration.   The mark "Richard Ginori," in gold, is only applied to the porcelain decorated at the works.

CAPO DI MONTE.

CAPO DI MONTE.   *Soft paste.*   This manufactory was founded by Charles III. in 1736.   It is considered of native origin, as the art, which was kept so profound a secret in Dresden, could, at that early period, have scarcely had time to be introduced here, the character of its productions being also so essentially different. The King himself took great interest in it, and is said to have worked occasionally in the manufactory. Starrien Porter, in a letter to Mr. Pitt (Lord Chatham), dated April 8, 1760, speaking of this factory, says, "The King is particularly fond of his china factory at Capo di Monte; . . . during the fairs held annually in the square before the palace at Naples, there is a shop or stall solely for the sale of his china, and a note was matutinally brought to the King of the articles sold, together with the names of the purchasers, on whom he looked favourably." On obtaining the crown of Spain, he took with him twenty-two persons to form his establishment at Madrid.

The beautiful services and groups in coloured relief are of the second period, *circa* 1760. These are generally unmarked, but a peculiarity which distinguishes the old from the more recent reproductions is the "stippled" mode of rendering the flesh tints; this can be seen more clearly when the specimens are examined under a magnifying glass.

The earliest mark is a fleur-de-lis, generally roughly painted in blue, as in the margin. These marks have been hitherto considered as denoting the ware made at Madrid only, but the fleur-de-lis was used both at Capo di Monte and Madrid. In so placing these, we are guided by the opinions of several gentlemen well qualified to judge, and who, from long residence in Italy, have come to that conclusion. The first mark here given has, indeed, been always appropriated to Capo di Monte, and, upon comparing it with those which follow, the similarity will be admitted; it is really a badly formed fleur-de-lis. The manufactory was abandoned in 1821. (*Ker. Gall.*, enlarged edition, figs. 190-3.)

NAPLES. Second period, under the patronage of Ferdinand IV., 1759. These marks stand for Naples, surmounted by a crown; they are in red or blue, and sometimes only impressed in the moist clay. (*Ker. Gall.*, enlarged edition, figs. 194-7.)

NAPLES. This mark of the initials of King Ferdinand under a crown is in blue on a cabaret with classical figures in relief. On a cup and saucer with a painting of Mount Vesuvius in Sir A. W. Franks' Collection. See also mark below.

NAPLES. This mark occurs on services in the Etruscan style; the initials stand for Ferdinandus Rex; used about 1780. A service with this mark, painted with copies of frescoes and antiquities of Herculaneum, inscribed "*Museo Ercolano*." A book in the library of Sir Charles Price gives a description of a service of 180 pieces, presented by the King of the Two Sicilies to George III. in 1787. The preface, by the Director Venuti, states that the subjects are all copied from Greek and Etruscan specimens in the Royal Museum. This service is still in existence at Windsor; it is of white ground with a red and black border, the subjects painted on the flat surface.

NAPLES. A vase, with flowers in relief, edged with blue and red; the mark in blue (for *Fabbrica Reale*). On a delicate cream-coloured cup, of soft paste. Sometimes the cipher is found without the crown.

Giordano.

NAPLES. This name, probably of a modeller, occurs indented on a fine statuette.

𝒜piello

NAPLES. This modeller's name is scratched under the glaze of a pair of soft-paste china figures of male and female peasants.

Giovine in Napoli.

NAPLES. The name of a painter marked in red.

𝓑𝓖.

NAPLES. This monogram is deeply impressed on some Neapolitan china plates, inscribed "*Il Pescatore*" and "*Donna dell' Isola di Procida*," painted with costume figures, the views being in the Bay of Naples; probably Giustiniani. This mark should rightly have been included among those of fayence, as Sir A. W. Franks, who knows the plates, informed the Editor while the earlier portion of the book was in the press that they are fayence and not porcelain. Collectors should refer to a notice of imitations of Capo di Monte, in the chapter on "Misleading Marks" at the end of the book.

MILAN, 1665. In the *Philosophical Transactions* for the year 1665 we read the following: "Notice was lately given by an inquisitive Parisian to a friend of his in London, that by an acquaintance he had been informed that Signor Septalio, a Canon in Milan, had the secret of making as good porcelain as is made in China itself, and transparent, adding that he had seen him make some. This, as it deserves, so it will be further inquired after, if God permit."

MILAN.   The "Manufacture Nationale de J. Richard & Cie," for porcelain as well as fayence, is successfully carried on.   Their ordinary mark is in black initials; they have obtained several medals at the recent expositions.

Note.—This is the same company as S. C. Richard Ginori, noticed under the heading of Ginori; the company's headquarters are at Milan, hence the confusion in its being entered under this head.

TREVISO.   There was a manufactory of soft porcelain here, probably established towards the end of the last century; carried on by the Brothers Giuseppe and Andrea Fontebasso.   Sir W. R. Drake had in his Collection a coffee-cup of soft porcelain inscribed, "*Fabbrica di Giuseppe ed Andrea Fratelli Fontebasso in Treviso, Gaetano Negrisole Dipinse,* 1831."

TREVISO.   On a porcelain coffee-cup and saucer, the cup painted with a garden scene, with a man and woman holding flowers, the former holding a bird, the latter a cage; at bottom "*Gesner Id. xiii.;*" the saucer gilt only, and marked underneath "*Treviso,*" in blue; the other is red.   (*Ker. Gall.,* enlarged edition, fig. 199.)

G.A.F.F.

Treviso.

TREVISO.   Fratelli Fontebasso, marked in gold on a porcelain *écuelle,* blue ground, with gold fret borders and oval medallions of Italian buildings, landscapes, and figures.   A charming specimen, formerly in the possession of the Rev. T. Staniforth.   Now in the Franks Collection.

F.F.

Treviso. 1799

TURIN.   VINOVO.   This manufactory was established about 1770. Vittorio Amedeo Gioanetti was born in Turin in 1729; he was a professor of medicine, and took his degree as doctor in 1751, and a public testimonial was accorded to him in 1757; he was subsequently elected professor of chemistry in the Royal University, and was a successful experimentalist.   It was about 1770 that he established a manufactory of porcelain at Vinovo or Vineuf; attempts had been previously made, but they were unsuccessful, and it was not until Gioanetti applied himself to the manufacture that it succeeded perfectly.   In the *Discorso sulla Fabbrica de Porcellana stabilita in Vinovo,* Turin, 1859, will be found a description of the various earths and clays of Piedmont as described by Gioanetti himself; it was noted for its fine grain and the whiteness of the glaze, as well as the colours employed.   The cross alone in brown is on a cup and saucer, painted with the arms of Sardinia and gilt borders, in Sir A. W. Franks' Collection.

$+$

TURIN.   VINOVO or VINEUF.   Sir Augustus Franks, in his *Catalogue of Continental Porcelain,* tells us that in 1766 G. V. Brodel, a manufacturer at Vische, started porcelain works at Vinovo, near Turin, with the help of Pierre Antoine Hannong of Strasbourg, but this venture being unsuccessful came to an end, and was then taken in hand by the Dr. Gioanetti mentioned in a subsequent paragraph. This transfer of the industry took place about 1730, and the Doctor died in 1815.

The porcelain is of a peculiar composition, containing silicate of magnesia, and has been termed by Brongniart a hybrid paste.

Specimens bearing this mark have been erroneously ascribed to Bristol, but the paste is quite distinct.

TURIN. VINOVO. Sometimes only a cross, and the letter V, for Vinovo. In the Franks Collection there is a statuette in white (the Assumption of the Virgin), the figure kneeling on a globe; inside the pedestal there is a monogram M.I.A., probably Maria. The mark as in the margin is in grey under glaze.

TURIN. VINOVO. The letters stand for Dr. Gioanetti, Vineuf. These marks are usually graved in the paste, but sometimes coloured. This mark also occurs on a bowl and cover, white with the royal arms of Savoy in gold and the initials V. A. (*Ker. Gall.*, enlarged edition, fig. 200), also on a cup and saucer in the Franks Collection. The cup, decorated with the arms of the King of Sardinia in gold, has also AI scratched in the paste.

M. le Baron C. Davillier had some Vinovo porcelain cups with this mark in black; they are decorated with flowers.

TURIN. VINOVO. A custard cup and cover, gilded knob and border with sprigs of blue cornflowers, with the mark in the margin painted in reddish-brown over glaze, is in the collection of Mr. Frank Hurlbutt.

TURIN. These marks of a cross and a crescent are on an oblong china tray, painted with roses and detached flowers, formerly in the Baldwin, but now in the Franks Collection.

These three marks are upon an oval plateau, painted with flowers and attributes of the chase in the Sèvres style; the first is in black, the second incuse in the paste, and the third in rose colour. This painter's name occurs on another cup, green ground with medallions of flowers richly gilt, "*Ca. pinx.*" in rose colour, and the cross, V, and D.G. (as given above) in blue. In the Baron Davillier's Collection.

VICENZA. There was a manufactory of porcelain here, but we have no particulars respecting it. This mark is stamped on a dessert plate, and by some connoisseurs referred to this place.

VENICE.

The discovery of the *true* porcelain at Dresden (so called from being hard like the Oriental), which was brought to considerable perfection about 1715, on the discovery of the kaolin at Aue near Schneeberg, caused an intense excitement all over Europe, and the sovereigns of the chief states bestirred themselves to promote and encourage the art of making porcelain by every means in their power.

Vienna was one of the first to obtain the secret, which soon spread over Germany. Venice was not long in following the example: porcelain of soft paste was made here probably about 1720. The first proclamation we have any record of was made in 1728, offering facilities and privileges to any person who would undertake such works, and all subjects or foreigners who desired to introduce into the city of Venice manufactories of fine earth or porcelain and maiolica, in use in the East or West, were invited to compete.

At the date of this proclamation a porcelain manufactory did actually exist in Venice, but the exact time of its establishment is not known.[1]

Mr. Rawdon Brown (quoted by Drake, *Notes on Venetian Porcelain*) tells us the "Casa Eccel^{ma} Vezzi" was founded by Francesco Vezzi, who was born October 9, 1651. He and his brother Giuseppe were goldsmiths, and had made large fortunes by their trade. In 1716 these two "Merchants of Venice" offered the state 100,000 ducats for the honour of being ennobled, and in the same year they were elected and declared Venetian noblemen. Francesco turned his attention to the manufacture of porcelain. "Early in 1723 he had given up the goldsmith's trade, and was no longer under the protection of the 'golden dragon' which guarded the entrance to his shop: emerging from the plebeian rank of smelter and banker, he suddenly became a gentleman and a competitor with kings in an artistic and refined trade. Thirty thousand ducats was the sum invested by Francesco Vezzi in a porcelain company, amongst whose shareholders were Luca Mantovani and others, including, 'there is reason to believe, Carlo Ruzini, who reigned Doge from 1732 to 1735."

Francesco Vezzi died on the 4th May 1740; the site of his manufactory was at St. Nicolo in Venice.

Sir W. R. Drake informs us that "in September 1740 we find Luca Mantovani (his partners Doge Ruzini having died in 1735, and Francesco Vezzi in 1740) paying an annual rent of 100 ducats to the Brothers Ruzini (the Doge's heirs) not only for rent, but also for the

---

[1] A soft-paste porcelain cup, painted with coats of arms, dated 1726, is quoted below.

goodwill of the furnace at St. Nicolo, which had existed (probably for earthenware) since 1515. How long after Vezzi's death the manufactory of porcelain was carried on does not appear, but, judging from the statements made to the Senate in 1765, it did not long survive him, and the secret of his process for making porcelain had evidently not been disclosed."

There is evidence that in 1735 the Vezzi manufactory had been successfully established in the state, and had succeeded in producing porcelain, the specimens of which were referred to as being on a par with the productions of the principal fabriques of Europe. It is also known that the cause ascribed for that manufactory not being permanent, but sinking "into inactivity and decay," was the fact that it was dependent on the purchase of porcelain paste in foreign countries. Materials for making porcelain were to be obtained in the Venetian dominions, but not such as to produce the *hard* or Oriental porcelain; they therefore procured it from Saxony, and probably also some of the workmen, which will account for the fact that the "Casa Eccellentissima Vezzi" produced both *hard* and soft paste porcelain.

To the Vezzi manufactory we must refer all the pieces marked in red or blue with VEN^A. or other contractions of the word VENEZIA; they are painted with masquerades, grotesque Chinese figures, and decorations in relief, flowers, birds, arabesques, and geometrical patterns in colours, statuettes, &c., especially in the Venetian red, which pervades all the decorations, the handles, borders, and moulding being sometimes covered with silver or platina, producing the effect of oxidised metal mountings. Another striking peculiarity in the decoration of porcelain of this period is a border of black or coloured diaper-work, formed by crossed lines and in the interstices small gilt points or crosses, bordered by scrolls in the style of Louis XV. These specimens are mostly of hard paste in form of bowls, plates, tureens, &c., and by some connoisseurs have been taken for Dresden; but they are doubtless of Venetian make and decoration; being unmarked, our only means of judging is by comparison. One fact is, however, clear, which has hitherto been doubted by some, viz., *that both hard and soft paste were made, not only by the Vezzi, the Hewelckes, and Cozzi at Venice, but by the Antonibons at Nove.*

We are again indebted to Sir W. R. Drake for our information respecting the following manufacturers:—

After the Vezzi manufactory had ceased to exist, we have no documents to prove that any efforts were made to introduce the manufacture of porcelain into Venice until December 1757, when a petition was presented to the Venetian College by Frederick Hewelcke[1] & Co., who stated that the sale, introduced and directed by them in Dresden, of Saxon porcelain, had been carried on in a very flourishing manner, but that in consequence of the then existing war (the Seven Years' War, which

---

[1] The name in the several documents is spelt in various ways—Hewelcke, Hewelike, Hewecken, and Hebelechi.

commenced in 1756) they had been obliged to abandon Saxony, and to seek in a foreign country a peaceful refuge, convenient for the exercise of their art. They prayed that exclusive permission for twenty years might be accorded to them to manufacture in some convenient spot Saxon porcelain (*porcellana di Sassonia*) of every kind, form, and figure with exemptions from taxes, for the exercise of their art during that period. The "Co." appears to have consisted of Maria Dorothea, the wife of Nathaniel Friedrich Hewelcke, who, with her husband, in 1758 presented a joint petition more in detail, asking for rigorous penalties to prevent persons in their employ taking service elsewhere, or giving any information, in order that the secret of their manufacture should not become known, &c.

The report of the Board of Trade states that Hewelcke was a man well furnished with means and capital, and one of the conditions recommended was, that the *concessionnaires*, the Hewelckes, should countermark the bottom of their works with the letter V, denoting Venice.

On the 18th March 1758, the Senate granted to the Hewelckes the privileges they had requested. In what part of the Venetian dominions they established their manufactory does not appear, but when Antonibon Nove's application was presented in 1762, they sent a specimen of their porcelain which they had made in Venice.

There is in the Franks Collection a large portrait medallion recording the artist Fortunato Tolerazzi Fece Venesia 1763," and there is also a letter V below the bust, which Sir A. W. Franks thinks was placed there in compliance with a special injunction to mark the pieces "*Con la lettera V dinotante Venezia*," and this piece was produced about the time when the direction of the works by Hewelcke and his wife ceased.

The privileges accorded to Antonibon in 1793 caused a great competition between the rival porcelain-makers, which the Board of Trade in their recommendation styled *la fortunata emulazione*. So it may have been to the state, but to the Hewelckes it seems to have proved eventually *unfortunate*, and at the termination of that war which had brought them to Venice in 1793 they returned to their native country.

In 1765 the Senate granted to Giminiano Cozzi, in the Contrada di San Giobbe, Venice, protection and pecuniary assistance in carrying out a manufacture of porcelain. Cozzi's first efforts were directed to imitate the Oriental ware; he states in his petition that he founded his anticipations of commercial success mainly on the fact that he had discovered at Tretto, in Vicentina, in the Venetian territory, clay suitable for the manufacture.

The "Inquisitore alle Arti" reported upon Cozzi's fabrique thus: "Concerning the manufactory of Japanese porcelain (*porcellana ad uso del Giappon*), it was commenced only in 1765; your Excellencies were eyewitnesses of its rapid progress, and therefore deservedly protected and

assisted him. He now works with three furnaces, and has erected a
fourth, a very large one, for the manufacture of dishes. He has constantly in his employ forty-five workmen, including the six apprentices,
whom he has undertaken to educate, and from the date of his privilege in
August 1765, down to the middle of December 1766, has disposed of
16,000 ducats' worth of manufactured goods, &c.; so that it may be fairly
inferred that he will yet continue to make greater progress both in quantity
and quality." This prophecy was fulfilled, and a very large trade was
carried on for nearly fifty years. The pieces produced at Cozzi's
manufactory were marked with an anchor in red, blue, or gold, and are
still frequently met with, although specimens of his best products have
become scarce; they consist of statuettes in biscuit, in glazed white porcelain, and of coloured groups, vases, &c. The gilding on Cozzi's porcelain
is especially fine, the pure gold of the sequin having been used in its
decoration. We have imitations of the porcelain of other countries,
Saxony, Sèvres, Chelsea, and Derby; the imitations of the Oriental are
astonishing. The Marchese d'Azeglio possessed some examples of the
coloured groups, as well as the glazed white figures; in fact, specimens of
nearly all the varieties of Venetian porcelain we have been describing were
to be found in his historically interesting collection.

Cozzi's manufactory ceased in 1812. Since that date there does not
appear to have been any porcelain made in Venice, but at Nove they still
continued making porcelain for more than twenty years later. Lady
Charlotte Schreiber had a splendid set of five porcelain vases of the Cozzi
period, the centre being 17 inches high, the others $13\frac{1}{2}$, beautifully painted
with bouquets of flowers, mask handles with festoons of fruit in relief; all
these pieces are marked with the red anchor. (*Ker. Gall.*, enlarged edition,
fig. 190.) Lady Schreiber had also several cleverly modelled statuettes
of this white glazed porcelain which, until Sir William Drake's "Notes"
were published, had been catalogued and sold as White Capo di Monte;
these were sold at Christie's in 1890, and were purchased by the Editor,
in whose possession they are now. There are also some good specimens
in the Franks Collection.

1765
Venesia
Fabª Geminiano
COZZI

This mark is on a coffee-pot, with cover
decorated in pale colours with flowers and gold.
Franks Collection.

Venª

VENICE. The mark of the "Casa Eccelmª
Vezzi," from *circa* 1720 to 1740. This mark
is found painted in red; sometimes stamped, as
on a cup and saucer, with raised ornaments and the arms of Benedict XIII.
(Orsini), who was Pope about 1730; in the Franks Collection. A
similar mark is on a cup and saucer, painted with the Ottoboni arms, and
the initials G O or P O interlaced, formerly in the possession of the
Marchese d'Azeglio.

VENICE. This mark, engraved and coloured red, is on a porcelain cup and saucer, painted in colour, with a large shield of arms of four quarterings (not heraldic), formerly in the possession of the Marchese d'Azeglio; it is the earliest dated piece of Venetian porcelain known, made by Vezzi at St. Nicolo.

Venᵃ.A.G.1726.

VENICE. These letters, marked in gold on a specimen in Captain Reynolds' Collection.

Vᵃ.

VENICE. These marks are on some cups, with VENEZIA in red, painted with flowers and ornaments in the Persian style; soft paste. The meaning of the letters C P is unknown; the characters underneath are the price—Lire nuove 3, and Lira 1, 10 soldi. Formerly in M. le Baron C. Davillier's Collection.

C .P.

N.3.

C .P

a L 1:10

VENICE. This fanciful mark of the Vezzi period, in blue, is on a porcelain saucer, the cup having VENᵃ in smaller characters, painted with blue birds and leaves, partly gilt. A cup and saucer with similar mark was in the possession of the Marchese d'Azeglio, another in the Franks Collection.

VENICE. This is another singular mark of the "Casa Eccellᵃ Vezzi"; the V formed of flourishes in the shape of three cranes' heads and that of a lion, in allusion to the lion of St. Mark; it occurs in red on a porcelain cup and saucer.

VENICE. These letters incised on a quadrangular compotier, painted with grotesque animals and the Mark Venᵃ. In the possession of Sir Kingston James.

A f

C *f*   VENICE. These marks are scratched in the paste on
C   teapots of the Vezzi period. In the possession of Sir
A   Kingston James.

M *f*   VENICE. Other marks found on this porcelain of the
N *f*   same period. In Sir Kingston James's Collection.

Lodovico Ortolani Veneto VENICE. The signature of Ludovico Orto-
dipinse nella Fabrica di   lani, a Venetian, painted at the porcelain manu-
Porcelana, in Venetia   factory in Venice. This was the Vezzi fabrique,
circa 1740; it occurs on a saucer, painted in
lake *camaieu*, with a lady seated holding a
bunch of grapes, and a tazza and cupid (symbolical of Autumn), border
of leaves, scrolls, and birds. (*Ker. Gall.*, enlarged edition, fig. 201.) Now
in the Franks Collection.

Jacobus Helchis fecit.   VENICE. The mark of a painter of the
Vezzi petriod, on an *écuelle* painted in Indian-
ink, with a naked boy looking through a telescope, and extensive landscape, rococo border, etched in lines as from an engraving. In Mrs. Beresford Melville's Collection, and a similar one in the Franks Collection.
Both were formerly in the Reynolds Collection. Sir A. W. Franks
considered these specimens to be either Early Meissen or Vienna.

VENICE. The mark of a painter (Giovanni Marcone)
of the Cozzi fabrique, *circa* 1789, on a cup and saucer
painted in colours with classical subjects and female
figures; another plate has a similar subject, with border
of festoons, flowers, and birds. Marcone appears to
have painted both at Nove and Venice.

VENICE. On a soft-paste cup, painted with flowers,
in M. le Baron C. Davillier's Collection; the letters are
in black, the anchor in red.

It is not unusual to find services decorated with the heraldic shield of
the noble Venetian families, in addition to figures or sprigs and bouquets
of flowers; these services were given as dower presents to Venetian brides.
One such tea-service in its original leather case (also embossed with the
arms of the Semitiecoli family) was in the Cavendish-Bentinck Collection
dispersed some years ago.

VENICE. (Cozzi period.) Another variety of the
anchor, painted red. Mr. Arthur Verschoyle has also
some good specimen cups, saucers, and vases with the
anchor mark.

This inscription in red over glaze is on a coffee-pot and cover, painted in pale colours with groups of flowers, is a very unusual mark of the Cozzi Venetian factory which Sir A. W. Franks says was started in 1754. The mark generally found on this porcelain is the anchor in red.

1765
Venezia
Fabᵃ·Gaminiano
Cozzi

VENICE. This mark, in red, is on a porcelain cup, painted in the Chinese style with flowers; the saucer, of the same pattern, has the Venetian red anchor underneath the letters instead of the star. Formerly in the possession of the Marchese d'Azeglio.

A·G·

*

VENICE or GERMAN. These two marks are on two porcelain cups and saucers, formerly in the collection of Mr. C. W. Reynolds, now in the possession of Miss Emily C. Preston. This can scarcely be an Italian mark from the dotting of the I., and is in all probability German.

A.E.W.
I W

N.B.—The establishment of Messrs. Bertolini at Murano was, as we have seen, an important manufactory of maiolica, as well as of glass. It has also been supposed that they produced porcelain; but the following notes will prove that none was ever made there. They certainly produced very clever imitations of porcelain in opaque white glass called *smalta*, which have been frequently mistaken for porcelain, and this was apparently all they ever attempted. Early in the eighteenth century they obtained a decree for the sole manufacture of what they called *canna macizza* and *smalto*, both of which were enamelled glass, painted and gilt. Another decree, dated 1738, permits them to construct four additional *crucibles* for the same manufacture. In a petition for a decree for ten years, in 1753, the Brothers Bertolini state that they had invented the manufacture of painted and gilt enamel, in imitation of porcelain ("che oltre aver essi inventato le manifatture di smalto dipinte e dorate a somiglianza di porcellane"). These imitations are not uncommon. Captain Reynolds had a small vase, 14 inches high, painted with Mercury and Minerva, and a cup and saucer with the arms of Doge Tiepolo, both of which have the mark "Venᵃ," as on porcelain. Sir W. R. Drake (to whom we are indebted for this information) says the Abbé Zaneti, curator of the Murano Museum, showed him specimens of Bertolini's *smalto*, or painted and gilt enamel, with Japanese designs; and after every possible inquiry and search in Murano by the Abbé and other competent authorities, "it may be taken for granted that the Bertolini did not at any time make porcelain."

NOVE.

The manufacture of porcelain at Nove may be traced back as far as the 12th of January 1752, at which time Pasqual Antonibon brought from Dresden a certain Sigismond Fischer to construct a furnace for making porcelain in the Saxon style.

From this time forward he continued his experiments, and must have made great progress in the art, for in February 1761 he had three furnaces, of which one was for Saxon *(ad uso Sassonia)*, the other two for French porcelain *(ad uso Francia)*. It was about this time that Pasqual Antonibon possessed, in addition to his ceramic works, a fabrique of waxed cloth *(tele cerate)*, in which he had invested a large capital: it was not, however, a successful speculation; but it did not disconcert his other establishments; they continued prospering, and his porcelain kept on always advancing to perfection.[1]

In 1762 Antonibon submitted to the Board of Trade specimens of his porcelain, and petitioned that the patent rights which had been conceded to Hewelcke should be extended to him. At that time, the report states, Antonibon had at Nove a manufactory, rich in buildings, machinery, and tools; the capital embarked in it was estimated at 80,000 ducats, and he gave employment to 150 men and their families, in addition to 100 people employed in his retail business, carried on at his three shops in Venice, so great was the sale of his products. This extensive manufactory was, however, principally for maiolica.

On the 7th April 1763 a decree was made in his favour, and he appears to have set earnestly to work in his manufacture of porcelain. His competitor, Hewelcke, shortly after deserted Venice; but he had a more formidable rival in Giminiano Cozzi, who obtained a decree for making porcelain in 1765, in which Pasqual Antonibon's manufacture is noticed, the Senate declaring it to be the duty of the magistrate to make such arrangements as would lead to an amicable understanding between the rival manufacturers and their workmen.[2]

Pasqual Antonibon and his son Giovanni Battista continued the fabrication of porcelain until the 6th of February 1781, when they entered into partnership with Signor Parolini, always continuing the same manufacture, *con sommo onore dell' arte*, until the 6th of February 1802; it was then leased to Giovanni Baroni, and he produced some very charming pieces, both in form and decoration; but in a few years, from being badly conducted, it began to fall off, and by degrees it went to decay and was abandoned. The "Fabbrica Baroni," however, lingered on for more than twenty years.

On May 21, 1825, the old firm of "Pasquale Antonibon & Sons" resumed the works, the actual proprietors being Gio. Batt. Antonibon and his son Francesco. They continued making porcelain until 1835, but all their efforts to sustain it were ineffectual; they could not compete with the porcelain manufactories of France and Germany, so they were compelled to abandon the manufacture,[3] since which time to the present they confine their attention to *terraglia (terre de pipe), majoliche fine (fayence)*, and *ordinarie* (ordinary wares), which have a fine glaze and rank amongst the best modern Italian fayence. At the Italian Exhibition at South Kensington in 1888 the Antonibon exhibit was awarded a special mention by the jury, of which the Editor was a member.

We have been favoured with the following interesting communication

---

[1] Letter of Francesco Antonibon, dated August 1869, to Lady Charlotte Schreiber.

[2] Drake's notes on Venetian Ceramics, p. 33.

[3] Letter from Francesco Antonibon, one of the present proprietors, to Lady Charlotte Schreiber, who has kindly placed it at our disposal. It forms a complete history of the Nove porcelain.

from the Baron Charles Davillier, which we give in his own words. Describing a dish in his collection, he says :—

"Le sujet se divine; à droite Venise, caractérisée par le bonnet ducal, le lion de S. Marc et les roseaux de la lagune; une femme debout à droite est ornée de la couronne murale; c'est sans doute la ville de Bassano; elle présente à Venise une jeune femme agenouillée que soutient le Temps, et qui offre à Venise des vases, plats, tasses, &c., produits de sa fabrique. Sur un des vases est une armoirie (une fasce rouge sur fond blanc), peut-être celle de Bassano, un plat porte le monogramme ci-contre de Giov. Battª Antonibon. Violà donc une pièce certaine de cette fabrique.

"Une assiette évidemment de la même main représentant Hercule qui terasse Nessus et enlace Déjanire : sur la bordure, le même mono-gramme, et jaune ombré de brun, comme ci-contre. Ces deux pièces, meilleures comme dessin que celles de la céramique du temps, rappellant, par le style et par la couleur, les compositions de Tiepolo, alors en si grande vogue. Passons à une troisième pièce : c'est."

NOVE. The mark on the porcelain of Antonibon is usually a star of six rays in blue or red, sometimes in gold. Lady Charlotte Schreiber had a specimen on which the star is impressed, and another star by its side painted in red, also a vase and cover painted in lake *camaieu* of St. Roche, with N stamped in the clay. (*Ker. Gall.*, enlarged edition, fig. 209.) A cup, formerly in the Reynolds Collection, has a red star and the letter P, probably for Parolini. A star is sometimes found on the porcelain of Venice, but rarely.

NOVE. This curious mark of Antonibon's manufactory is on the centre of a set of three *éventail* jardi-nières of porcelain, beautifully painted with mythological and classical subjects, and garden scenes, elaborately gilt borders, and the arms of Doge Tiepolo. The comet is uncommon; the painter's name is Giovanni Marconi. (*Ker. Gall.*, enlarged edition, fig. 206.)

The star, in blue, is on a fine jardinière similar to the above, which was also formerly in the Reynolds Collection. It was apparently painted by the same artist, Giovanni Marconi. Franks Collection.

This mark in gold, the star of six points with monogram J. Z., is on a cup and saucer painted in colours with gilding, formerly in the Reynolds Collection. Franks Collection.

NOVE. This mark is on a teapot, like Doccia ware, ornamented with raised flowers and painted bouquets: it is the name of the place, in raised letters repeated as in the margin. Formerly in the possession of Right Hon. W. E. Gladstone; sometimes the word "Nove" is written in red and sometimes incised in the paste.

NOVE. These two marks are also found; the latter is pencilled on a porcelain jardinière and stand, with green and gold bands, painted with bouquets, marked in gold. Victoria and Albert Museum; cost £12.

NOVE. The mark of Giovanni Baroni, successor of Antonibon, 1802-25. On a very fine vase and pedestal, 2 feet 5 inches high, painted with a subject representing Alexander the Great and the family of Darius, and a classical subject after Le Brun. Formerly in Mr. C. W. Reynolds' Collection.

NOVE. Giovanni Baroni. On a very fine porcelain vase, oviform, with coloured painting round the body of merchants of European nations, merchandise, and shipping, with handles in form of female figures. (*Ker. Gall.*, enlarged edition, fig. 207.)

NOVE. Another mark attributed to this manufactory. Two finely decorated vases of the old Le Nove porcelain, but unmarked, which were formerly in the Reynolds Collection, are now in two Collections known to the Editor, those of Lord Abercromby and Mr. Arthur Verschoyle.

ESTE, between Padua and Ferrara. Porcelain was made at this town as well as fayence, and of a high character. We have seen many examples quite equal to anything produced at Doccio, which it much resembles. Lady Charlotte Schreiber had a pair of statuettes on square pedestals, modelled with great feeling and grace, one of the Virgin standing on the horns of the moon, trampling on a serpent, an apple at her feet, inscribed in front IMMACULATA, on the back ESTE, incuse; and the other of St. John holding a cup containing a serpent and a book inscribed S. JOANNES; on the back ESTE + 1783; height with pedestals, 15½ inches.

Giovanni Pietro Varion, a Frenchman, who had previously been a modeller in Antonibon's fabrique at Nove, left there about 1765 with his wife, Fiorina Fabris, and directed his steps to Bologna, but it does not appear that his patron, who desired to establish him there, was successful, or carried it on to any great extent. In 1776 and 1777 Varion made several attempts to introduce the manufacture into Modena without success. (See MODENA.)

In 1780 Varion and his wife returned to Este. Girolama Franchini, a clever artist, goldsmith, and engraver, associated himself with Varion, and erected a fabrique to make porcelain. They produced several important pieces; a stupendous group of Parnassus is mentioned as being much admired in the shop of Franchini at Este, as well as several pastoral and mythological groups of porcelain, which were distinguished by their extreme whiteness.

After Varion's death his widow continued making porcelain, as shown in a decree of 27th August 1781: "Per dieci anni avvenire calcolabili dal di della pubblicazion della presente, oltre la fabbrica Cozzi, e le altre due già esistenti l'una in villa delle Nove della dita Antonibon; e l'altra in Este di d. Fiorina Fabris r. del fù Gio. Pietro Varion, non potranno erigersi nuove fabbriche di porcellane in Venezia e nello Stato."

By this document it is clear that the Widow Fabris had the exclusive right, and probably retained the secret of making porcelain.

By a decree of the Senate, 29th March 1781, it appears that Antonio Costa and Fiorina Fabris were associated in a manufacture of terraglia, in imitation of the English ware made by Wedgwood. We have no notice of Gio. Battista, but he may probably have been the son of Fiorini Fabris above named.

ESTE. This mark is on a large porcelain vase of scroll form, painted with flowers, and ornamented at the bottom and on the pedestal with leaves and flowers in low relief, with scroll handles; 16 inches high; dated about 1780.

Giovanni Battista Brunello, some years before 1765, had a manufactory of maiolica at Este, the productions being of an artistic character and much esteemed. It is said that several artists from Antonibon at Nove assisted him; among them were Gio. Maria Ortolani, M. Antonio Verziera, and a certain Reato, the first of whom for seventeen years studied under Antonibon. Brunello copied the English pottery, "le terraglie inglesi" of Wedgwood, which had been brought to such perfection in 1759 at Burslem that it was sought after throughout Europe. Giovanni Battista Brunello died about 1780, leaving his son Domenico to continue his industry, who desired to add to his fabrique the important manufacture of porcelain, which had taken root at the fabrique of Franchini, to which we shall presently allude, and had been introduced by M. Varion and his wife, Fiorina Fabris. In consequence of the second privilege accorded to Franchini in 1785, Brunello's trade diminished; he consequently tried in 1787 to obtain a faculty to make *mezze porcellane*, which differed slightly from the porcelain of Fabris and that of Cozzi of Venice. Although he met with great opposition, he succeeded, by the employment of other materials, in gaining his point, and made both terraglia and porcelain.

The fabrique of the terraglia of Brunello was in 1810 ceded to Domenico Apostoli, under the direction of Domenico Contiero, formerly modeller to Franchini, and in 1833 it reverted to Pietro Apostoli, a clever artist, who produced vases ornamented in relief of a bright red and brown maiolica, coloured like tortoise-shell, &c.

ESTE. These initials of Domenico Brunello are incised on a white porcelain teapot, with a band of key-pattern in relief round the body, the cover surmounted by a bird. In the possession of Sir Kingston James.

ESTE. Girolami Franchini having discovered in the mountains around Este and Vicenza a suitable earth, obtained in March 1782 a privilege for making terraglia after the English fashion, and established a fabrique at Este. In 1785 a second privilege was granted, annulling the decree made in 1771 accorded to Costa and Fabris for making terraglia, in which, by the introduction of new materials, he had much improved the ware. The Franchini fabrique after the death of Girolamo was continued by his son Domenico, who excelled in white maiolica as well as in porcelain. Sometimes the word ESTE is found accompanied by a date.

MODENA. In the year 1776, Gio. Pietro Varion of Paris, fabricator of porcelain, encouraged by the Marchese Paolucci, Minister of Duke Francesco III., made several attempts to introduce the manufacture of porcelain into Modena, but through the malicious opposition of the makers of porcelain at Venice he was unsuccessful. He is thus described in a memorial of 1776: Pietro Varion, native of Paris, at present residing in Este, manufacturer of porcelain after the manner of France, Florence, and Vienna, is desirous of coming to settle in Modena to introduce the fabrication of porcelain, &c. To prove his ability, he exhibited various groups, similar to that he had made for the hereditary Princess of Modena. In the following year he had made another vain attempt.

About five years after (1782), Giovanni Oxan, a native of Franconia, sent the Duke the following brief petition:—

"Ser^{ma.} Altezza—Gio. Oxan desiderando di stabilirsi negli Stati di V.A. ed in essi introdurre la di lui arte di fabbricare la porcellana esercita finora in quelli di Parma,[1] supplica di poter ció eseguire.—GIO. OXAN."

This was followed by a memorial to the Consiglio di Economia, with specimens and a specification of the necessary expenditure in the erection of a porcelain fabrique; but it was of no avail. The next day the Duke made known his determination in the following brief answer:—

---

[1] This is the first notice we have met with of the existence of a manufacture of porcelain in Parma.

"Semprechè non trovi chi voglia intraprendere simile commercio incomba pure agli altri suoi affari."

ROME. A manufacture of biscuit porcelain was introduced here by the celebrated engraver, Giovanni Volpatto of Venice, in the year 1790. Great care was taken in the execution of groups and statuettes from the antique, and fine modern models, after Canova, &c.; at one time no less than twenty experienced artists were employed in modelling. Large furnaces were erected and a considerable sum of money expended in experiments, but the manufacture could not compete with the French wares. In 1803 Giovanni Volpato died, and shortly after his son Giuseppe also died, leaving a widow and six sons. She subsequently married Francesco Tinucci, the chief modeller of the biscuit figures, who superintended the manufactory till 1818, when her eldest son succeeded to the works; but in 1820 they declined. The Pope wishing its re-establishment, it was continued until 1831, when Angelo Volpato died and was succeeded by his younger brother, Giuseppe; but the works soon ceased. Few pieces bear the mark, but occasionally they were stamped G. VOLPATO ROMA, on biscuit statuettes after Canova and the antique.

Spain and Portugal

MADRID.—BUEN RETIRO.

HEN Charles III. of Spain reigned in Naples, he established in 1736, at Capo di Monte, the celebrated porcelain manufactory. The King, it is said, took great interest in it, and worked occasionally there. Don Eugenio Larruga, in his *Memorias Politicas y Economicas*, vol. iv., Madrid, 1789, says that "it was the King's intention to imitate the porcelain manufactured at Meissen, and that in order to discover the secret process employed there, he engaged Don Louis Schepers, descended from a Belgian family, established many years in Italy and Spain." We do not find this statement confirmed by any other author: the evidence against it is, however, that neither the paste, the modelling, nor the painting of Capo di Monte porcelain are like old Dresden—one of the reasons why the manufactory at Naples is considered of native origin. The protection which Charles III. bestowed on the works at Capo di Monte ended on his coming from Naples, after the death of his brother Ferdinand VI., to take possession of the crown of Spain. He then determined to establish a manufactory at Madrid, where the process of the Italian fabrique might be continued, and which would likewise be an object of his attention and protection. The documents we have been able to examine in the Archives of the Royal Palace at Madrid, at Alcala, in the Ministry of Finance, and elsewhere, which now for the first time have been published by any Spanish or foreign writer, prove the interest which Charles II. took in establishing the manufactory of Buen Retiro.

Before the King left Naples, he ordered that the following letter should be written to the Secretary of State at Madrid :—

"In the same manner the workman and the utensils used at the royal manufactory of porcelain of Capo di Monte are to be embarked from Naples direct to Alicant, in the vessels prepared for that purpose, in order to continue from there the journey to Madrid. The necessary conveyances are to be provided, and the expenses to be charged to his Majesty's account."—*Letter from the Marquis of Squilace to his Excellency Don Ricardo Wall, Naples*, Sept. 11, 1759.

Charles III. landed at Barcelona on the 17th of October of the same year, and continued his journey by Catalonia and Aragon to Madrid, and neither the entertainments which he had to attend nor the business of all kinds which pressed upon him made him forget his plan of establishing the porcelain manufactory.

In a letter from the Marquis of Squilace to the Secretary of State, Wall, dated Saragossa, November 11, 1759, he tells him that the King had heard of the arrival at Madrid of some of the workmen of Capo di Monte, and gives orders that the necessary assistance should be afforded them, and if the director, Don Juan Thomas Bonicelli, had applied for money, the sum considered necessary should be given. Two days afterwards Wall answered Squilace, saying :—

"I will give the orders and help the workmen who are to establish the manufactory, and let them have every facility to examine the different sorts of earths and places which may suit them, and the director, Bonicelli, shall have the money given him that he may require for the purpose."

In a minute of Wall's addressed to the Minister of Finance, the Count of Valparaiso, on the 22nd of November, and in several other documents, it appears that, by the King's orders, 300 ducats of gold were given to Giuseppe Gricci, "modeller of the manufactory," in the absence of Bonicelli, who had not yet arrived at Madrid.

The King stayed at Saragossa for more than a month, owing to the illness of his wife and children, and was not able to continue his journey until the beginning of December. The King, however, ordered Squilace to write to Wall on the 21st of November, saying the King had been informed that a place was found near Madrid where the works could be established, but that he did not know the exact locality; that his Majesty was anxious to be made acquainted without delay, and the plans were to be sent immediately. Wall answers on the 24th of November that Giuseppe Gricci had undertaken to draw a plan of the spot chosen for the porcelain manufactory. There are still documents existing which relate to the same subject, discussed by the King and his Ministers during his stay at Saragossa.

Charles III. reached Madrid on the 9th of December, and before his arrival the Count of Valparaiso had paid 100 doblones of gold more to the modeller, Giuseppe Gricci, who wrote from the Batuecas on the 5th, asking for "altro cento dopie per potere compire a quanto necessita questa Reale Fabbrica." The director, Don Juan Thomas Bonicelli, must have arrived at the same time, and probably treated of these matters with the King, for there are two communications of his, dated the 14th of December, both addressed to Wall. In one he says, his Majesty had deigned to gratify with an aid of costs the workmen employed in the building, and begs the sum should be given to him; and in the other, he includes a list of the workmen belonging to the royal manufactory, "who have arrived from Naples, with the salaries they have earned until the present time, that in sight of them the necessary arrangements should be made of what they are to receive according to his Majesty's orders."

This list is most important, and we give it at full length, for it tells us the names of the artists and workmen who came from Naples to establish the manufactory of Buen Retiro.

LIST OF THE PERSONS EMPLOYED AT THE ROYAL MANUFACTORY WHO HAVE LATELY ARRIVED FROM NAPLES.

CAYETANO SCHEPERS, Chief Composer.
PABLO FORNI.
JOSEPH GRICCI, Principal Modeller.
CARLOS GRICCI, his Son.
ESTEBAN GRICCI, Modeller.
CAYETANO FUMO, Modeller.
BASILIO FUMO, Modeller.
JOSEPH FUMO, Modeller.
CARLOS FUMO, Modeller.
MACEDONIO FUMO, Modeller.

JOSEPH SANTORUM, Modeller.
JUAN BESCIA, Modeller.
BAUTISTA DE BAUTISTA, Modeller.
ANTONIO MORELLY, Modeller.
SALVADOR NOFRI, Modeller.
PHELIPE ESPLORES, Modeller.
AMBROSIO DE GIORGI, Modeller.
PEDRO ANTONIO DI GIORGI, Modeller.
PABLO FRATE, Modeller.

Workmen employed in the Kilns:—

JENARO BONINCASA.
NICOLAS ROCIO.
PASQUAL ROCCO.
JUAN FRATE.
BALDO DE BENEDITIS.

NINCENZO FRATE.
MATHEO MAYNI.
GIORCHINO AMABLE.
JOSEPH ESCLAVO.
ANTONIO AQUAVIVA ESCLAVO.

Workmen who pound the Colours:—

FRANCISCO CONTE.
NICOLAS CONTE.
ANGELO LIONELLI.

JOSEPH CARAMELLO.
JOACHIM PATAROTI, Carver in pietrodure.

Workmen employed at the Wheel:—

JOSEPH GROSSI.
NICOLAS BOTINO.

JUAN REMINI, Gold-beater.
PEDRO CHEVALIER, Mounter.

Painters:—

JOSEPH DE LA TORRE.
JUAN BAUTISTA DE LA TORRE.
NICOLAS DE LA TORRE.
RAPHAEL DE LA TORRE.
FERNANDO SORRENTINI.
MARIANO NANI.
JENARO BOLTRI.
NICOLAS DONADIO.

ANTONIO PROVINCIALE.
JOSEPH DEL COCO.
CARLOS REMISSI.
FRANCISCO SIMINI.
XAVIER BRANCACIO.
JOSEPH ESCLAVO, a Black.
FRANCISCO ESCLAVO, a Black.

Ten days after the King's arrival, on the 19th of December 1759, Don Carlos Antonio de Borbon, his Majesty's architect, presented to him the plans and design of the building required for the manufactory. The place selected was near the Hermitage of St. Anthony, inside the royal gardens of the Buen Retiro, which had been chosen for the purpose.

The architect presented his estimate with the plans of the building, but I have been unable to find among the papers in the archives at Madrid the original document. The copy exists, and states that "the walls were to be brick and mortar, the foundations of granite, a row of stones two feet high on the walls, vaults to serve as roofs to all the rooms," &c. Ponz tells us in his *Viage por España*, vol. vi. p. 108, that the building was "large and of regular architecture."

The sum asked for the building was 179,130 reals, and 217 arrobas of lead for water-pipes. On the margin of the plan there is a copy of the King's approval on the 28th December, who gives orders that it should be executed without delay, and there are copies of communications which were written on the same day, ordering the money to be given to the architect.

Don Carlos Antonio de Borbon was a black slave, who, according to Larruga (*Memorias*, vol. iv. p. 213), had been captured with five other blacks by the seaman Barcelo during the reign of the King's predecessor (Ferdinand VI.) The Queen-mother sent them to Naples, and Charles III. gave them an artistic education. Don Carlos Antonio devoted himself to architecture, and came to Spain with the King's household.

In January 1760, another architect, Don Carlos Witte, was ordered to make ready a paper-mill, which had been abandoned in the royal gardens of St. Fernando, near Madrid, that it might likewise be used for the manufacture of china. On the 22nd of May the work was finished; the money spent on the building was 6226 reals. There are estimates, signed and approved of by the architect Borbon, for fresh outlays for the building in the Retiro, amounting to 145,000 reals and 46,168 reals. On the 4th of July of the same year (1760), Squilace sent orders to Wall, in the King's name, to build a house for the manager of the works near the Hermitage of St. Anthony. Larruga tells us that "the King spent in establishing this manufactory eleven millions and a half of reals (£115,000), with a cost of two millions of reals a year to keep it up (£20,000).

William Clarke, in his *Letters Concerning the Spanish Nation*, written at Madrid during the years 1760 and 1761, London, 1763, says, p. 262: "At Madrid is lately set up a manufacture of porcelain in the gardens of the King's palace at the Retiro, wrought by artificers brought from Saxony;" and there are documents existing at the Royal Archives at Madrid, of the years 1760 and 1761, proving that they had begun to work at the manufactory. The workmen employed there were to be attended by the doctors of the King's household, and they enjoyed several legal privileges. In Townsend's *Journey through Spain in* 1786 *and* 1787, London, 1792, he says, in vol. ii. p. 278 :—

"I tried to obtain admission to the china manufacture, which is likewise administered on the King's account, but his Majesty's injunctions are so severe, that I could neither get introduced to see it, nor meet with any one who had ever been able to procure that favour for himself. I was the less mortified upon this occasion, because, from the specimens which I have seen, both in the palace at Madrid and in the provinces, it resembles the manufacture of Sèvres, which I have formerly visited in a tour through France."

Another traveller in Spain confirms how strict the orders were that no one should be allowed to visit the works—*Nouveau Voyage en Espagne, ou Tableau de l'Etat actuel de cette Monarchie*, Paris, chez Regnault, 1789, vol. i. p. 233 :—

"Le monarque actuel a établi dans leur intérieur une fabrique de porcelaine, dont l'entrée est jusqu'à present interdite à tout le monde. On veut sans doute que ses essais se perfectionment dans le silence avant de les exposer aux yeux des curieux. Ses productions ne peuvent encore se voir que dans les palais des souverains ou dans quelques cours d'Italie, auxquelles il les envoie en presens."

I have only been able to find mention of a permission granted in 1800 to Citoyen Alquier, envoy of the French Republic, who is recommended most earnestly to the director to visit the manufactory.

We cannot find any document proving the precise date when porcelain began to be manufactured at the Retiro. It may probably be found in one of the archives of the state, as well as details referring to the designers and cost of the most important pieces preserved in the royal palaces at Madrid. The rapidity with which the workmen were installed leads us to suppose no time was lost. Clarke, who writes in 1761, says the works were begun, and in 1764 there were already pupils of the manufactory who attended the classes of design at the Academy of St. Fernando. In a document at the archives of the Ministry of Finance, there is a memorandum asking the Academy to send an account of what is due for these pupils. Larruga, in his *Memorias*, tells us that as soon as the building was finished they began to make china under the direction of Don Cayetano Schepers, but all that was done during the time he was superintendent failed, much to his astonishment, as he employed the same process and the same workmen that he had done in Naples, where all had turned out successfully. Schepers attributed this to the squabbles between the Spanish and Italian workmen. Nothing important was made at the manufactory during Cayetano's direction. At the Ministry of Finance there is a series of documents, from 1783 until the end of the century, which proves that Sebastian Schepers, a son of Cayetano, was making experiments to make porcelain with different clays of the country. He complains constantly of the obstacles which meet him at every step. There is an interesting document at the Ministry of Finance, which Don Sebastian presents in 1797, giving an account of the different methods employed in other countries in the manufacture of china.

In the meanwhile, the porcelain made at the manufactory during the first thirty years was kept for the exclusive use of the royal family of Spain, or to be sent as presents to foreign courts. Nothing was put for sale until January 1789, after Charles III.'s death, which occurred in 1788, when Charles IV. determined that the china manufactured at the Buen Retiro should be sold to the public.

The director at that time was Don Domingo Bonicelli, a son of Don Juan Bonicelli. Don Domingo was commissioned to look for a suitable place where the things could be exhibited for sale inside the Retiro itself, and a wareroom was prepared, which had been occupied by the Swiss guard, near the Hermitage of St. John. Don Manuel Machuca y Vargas, an architect, arranged it for the sum of 35,000 reals (£350). In order to facilitate the sale, another room was taken at Madrid, in the Calle del Turco, which is mentioned in *Noticias Varias y Curiosas de Madrid*, published by Valero Chicarro in 1792 and 1793. This establishment cannot have given great commercial results, for in 1800 the director of the manufactory, Don Cristobal de Torrijos, begs the Government to close the warehouse in the Calle de Turco, and leave only the one at the Retiro open to the public, giving as a reason that "the objects manufactured were simply for ornament, and could only be bought by very rich persons," and those who could afford to buy them would not mind going as far as the Retiro to fetch them. In Southey's *Letters from Spain*, London, 1797, p. 118, he says :—

"The old palace of Buen Retiro is converted into a royal porcelain manufactory; the prices are extravagantly high, but they have arrived to great excellence in the manufacture. The false taste of the people is displayed in all the vases I saw there, which, though made from Roman models, are all terminated by porcelain flowers."

In the manufactory of Buen Retiro several kinds of china have been made, *hard* and *soft* paste, white china, glazed and unglazed, or painted and modelled in the same style as at Capo di Monte. There are many specimens existing like Wedgwood, white on blue ground, and they also made flowers, coloured, and of biscuit, groups and single figures of biscuit, as well as painted and glazed porcelain. The most remarkable specimens existing of this manufactory are those modelled in the Neapolitan style. Even in Spain the specimens of this china are very scarce, and it is only at the royal palace at Madrid, and at Aranjuez, the Escorial, and La Granja, that an idea can be formed of the perfection to which the manufacture had arrived. The finest and most important specimens existing are two rooms, the one at Madrid and the other at Aranjuez, in which the walls are entirely covered with large china plaques, painted and modelled in high relief with figures, flowers, and fruits, and fine large ornamentation. The room at Aranjuez seems the one first made, and is signed "José Gricchi," the principal modeller of the manufactory at the time it was established in 1759. Antonio Conca in his *Descrizione Odeporica della Spagna in cui Spezialmente si da Notizia della cose spettanti alle Belle Arti*, Parma, 1793, vol. i. p. 310, says, "Il Gabinetto abbellito di porcellana della Fabbrica del Retiro ha meritato le lodi de curiosi viaggiatori." He also tells us, p. 119, "Un altro Gabinetto vien chiamato della Cina pel suo principal ornato di bei putti, di bassi relievi, e di altre opere di porcellana della nuova Real Fabbrica del Retiro." Ponz describes the room at Madrid in the first volume of his *Viage de España*, Madrid, 1782: "The room is covered with large plaques of porcelain, made at the manufactory of the Retiro. In some are represented figures of children, copied from good models, and between each compartment looking-glasses are let in." Ponz says of the room at Aranjuez, "The porcelain room you have already seen, and known how fine it is, and how remarkable are the pieces of which it is made. It was begun and finished in the manufactory that his Majesty has at the Retiro." There is every reason to suppose that a great deal must have been thought of these rooms at the time.

Ever since Charles III. had established the manufactory in 1769 until 1803, they had followed the system adopted at Capo di Monte, in all that had relation to the paste, glaze, and other manipulations of this artistic industry. At the beginning of the century, however, this system was considered imperfect, and the idea occurred to the persons in charge of the establishment to imitate the porcelain made at Sèvres. Don Bartolomé Sureda, a native of Mallorca, went to Paris, where he endeavoured to learn the manner in which the Sèvres manufactory was worked, which he did, as he tells us, after endless contrarieties and troubles. On his return to Spain in 1803 he was appointed director of the manufactory of Buen Retiro, and he began a series of experiments with the different kinds of earth which were to be found in Spain, in order to imitate the paste and brilliancy of decoration of Sèvres.

For the preparation of the important pieces which were to be decorated, two workmen were engaged from Paris, M. J. Victor Perche and M. Vivien, who agreed to do all that was required in this sort of work. M. Perche's contract began in October 1803, and was renewed until 1809, when it ended. The wife of Perche, Donna Maria Juana Ferandini, agreed also to glaze the porcelain that should be given her by the director.

They were not satisfied at the Retiro manufactory with copying the porcelain of Naples and Sèvres, for they also made very fine imitations of Wedgwood and other of the principal manufactories of Europe. The finest specimens, as before stated, and which give the best idea of the excellence of the manufactory, can only be seen in Spain. The two rooms at Aranjuez and Madrid, and a magnificent clock and four large vases with porcelain flowers, which decorate one of the state rooms of the palace, are the finest things which exist in Buen Retiro. These vases are placed in the four corners of the rooms. Each of them, including the base and porcelain flowers, is about two mètres high. The clock is decorated with large biscuit figures, and admirably modelled. It was made for the King's use, to decorate the room in which it is still placed.

There are several vases at the royal palaces at Madrid, Aranjuez, and the Retiro, of Buen Retiro china. They are very often without covers, and sometimes have bouquets of porcelain or muslin flowers, and bronze gilt handles. Among them are some imitating Wedgwood, although the blue is not so pure or the biscuit-work so fine as the English. In some cases gold is added to the blue, and a very common mark at the base is R. F. D. PORCELANA D. S. M. C.

Among the private collections worth noting at Madrid containing specimens of Buen Retiro china are those of Count de Valencia and M. Ignace Bauer. The first of these gentlemen has collected together a number of groups and single figures, which form a very interesting collection; M. Bauer has four fine figures of children, the largest I have ever seen, measuring 32 inches in height. Two of them represent the seasons, Spring and Winter; the other two are black figures, evidently representing Africa and America. M. Bauer has also a group of Christ and an Apostle, made of white glazed china, modelled in the Italian style, about 26 inches high, and several other interesting specimens of the manufactory.

As we have stated before, the porcelain made at the Retiro was not exposed for sale for the first thirty years of the manufacture, and in the latter period the sale cannot have been great, for the establishment in the Calle del Turco was closed, as the one at the Retiro was considered enough to meet the demands of the public. This is one of the reasons why, even in Spain, this china is very rare.

We have not been able to find any details of the room at Madrid, or the fine clock and vases at the palace, but consider these to have been made in the later period of the manufactory. At the archives of the Ministry of Finance there are many papers relating to a dinner service which was made in 1798 for Charles IV., and presented to him on his birthday, and a dessert centrepiece which was made for the King at the same time. Some of the accounts are extant of the cost of these things, which were presented from 1797 until 1800. This centrepiece is probably the same which still exists in Casa del Labrador at Aranjuez. The cost of these pieces of porcelain must have been exorbitant. Some of the monthly accounts are in existence which were sent to the Ministry of Finance of the principal things made at the Retiro from 1807 to 1808.

When the French made their entry into Madrid, in the spring of 1808, they took possession of the royal manufactory. In July of the same year it continued in the hands of French soldiers, and during their stay they forced open the doors of the chemical laboratory and stole several of the things it contained. The director, Sureda, informs the Minister of Finance of what had occurred in a despatch which is among the papers at Alcala. The Minister wrote to General Belliard, begging him to put a stop to these excesses and return the stolen things. The manufactory went on working during the reign of Joseph I. In *Travels through Spain and Part of Portugal*, London, 1808, p. 23, it said —

"The gardens of the Buen Retiro are open to the public. In the neighbourhood of these the royal porcelain manufacture is carried on in a large white building."

Lord Blayney, in his *Narrative of a Journey through Spain and France in* 1810-14, London, 1814, says—

"Several royal manufactories were established within the walls (of the Retiro), particularly of tapestry and porcelain, which were established by Charles III., but have declined since his death, and have now entirely ceased."

Richard Ford tells us in his *Handbook for Travellers in Spain*, p. 680, that:

"Everything was destroyed by the invaders, who turned the manufactory into a fortification, which surrendered, with 200 cannon, August 14, 1812, to the Duke of Wellington. Ferdinand VII., on his restoration, recreated *La China,* removing the workshops and warerooms to the Moncloa."

At the Museo Arqueologico at Madrid there is a large collection of models, which were removed from the Moncloa after the china-works there had ceased.

This is all the information we have been able to collect concerning the royal porcelain manufacture of Buen Retiro. Some marks, not hitherto published, are annexed; and we give a list of the artists who worked at the manufactory, which will help collectors to classify the specimens of this china belonging to them.

LIST OF THE DIRECTORS AND ARTISTS WHO WERE EMPLOYED IN THE ROYAL MANUFACTURE OF PORCELAIN OF THE BUEN RETIRO FROM ITS FOUNDATION IN 1759 UNTIL 1808.

DIRECTORS.

BONICELLI (Juan Thomas), Principal Director at the establishment of the manufactory in 1759.

BONICELLI (Domingo). In 1786 he was Director; in 1796 he solicits his retirement, and probably died soon after.

CHRISTOBAL DE TORRIJOS, appointed Director in 1797, after the death of Don Domingo Bonicelli.

SUREDA (Bartolomé), Director in 1804, and continues in 1808.

PRINCIPAL MODELLERS AND SUPERINTENDENTS.

Possessing the Secrets of the Fabrication (*Secretistas*).

SCHEPERS (Cayetano), first Modeller in 1759.

GRICCI (Carlos), son of Joseph Gricci; came to Spain in 1759; he appears in a list of artists employed in 1764; he died in 1795.

GRICCI (Felipe), 1785; in 1802 he was first Modeller.

FORNI (Antonio), second Modeller in 1802.

SCULPTORS.

AGREDA (Esteban), born at Logroño, 1759; he obtained several prizes at the Academy of San Fernando; employed in 1797, and continued there in 1808.

AVILA (Ceferino de), employed from 1799, and continued there in 1808.

AVILA (Juan de), 1778, and continued there in 1808.

BAUTISTA (Bautista de), 1759.

BAUTISTA (Cayetano), 1785.

BAUTISTA (Juan Lopez), employed from 1799 to 1808.

BENEDICTIS (Cayetano), 1785 to 1802.

BENINCASA (Miguel), 1778, and continues in 1808.

BENINCASA (Vicente), 1785.

BERGAR (Alonso), 1764.

BESCIA (Juan), 1759.

BORBON (Genaro), 1784, and continues in 1808.

BORBON (Geronimo), 1802.

CARAVIELO (Miguel), 1785.

CHAVES (Alonso), born at Madrid in 1741; in 1760 was appointed Modeller; and in 1763 obtained second prize at the Academy, and a first prize in 1766.

CHAVES (Justo), 1785.

ESPLORES (Felipe), 1759.

ESTEBE (Antonio), 1778, and continues there in 1808.

FLORES (Josef), 1785.

FORNI (Pablo), 1759.

FRANCHOLY (Angel), 1776 to 1808.

FRANCHOLY (José), 1804, and continues there in 1808.

FRANCHOLY (Luis), 1785.

FRATE (Carlos), 1785, and continues in 1802.

FRATE (Fernando), 1785 to 1802.

FRATE (Josef), 1785.

FRATE (Pablo), from 1759 to 1785.

FRATES (Bernardo), 1773 to 1808.

FRATES (Francisco), 1764 to 1808.

FRATES (Juan), from 1794 to 1808.

FRATES (Mateo), from 1797, and continues in 1808.

FRATES (Mateo), born in Madrid in 1788; gained a first prize at the Academy in 1850; in 1829 was appointed Director of the china establishment at the Moncloa.

FUMO (Basilio), in 1759 he was Director of the china manufactory; in 1779 was appointed a member of the Academy of San Fernando; died in 1797.

FUMO (Bernabé), 1802.

FUMO (Carlos), 1759.

FUMO (Cayetano), 1759.

FUMO (Felipe), 1785, and continues in 1802.

FUMO (Joseph), 1759; died in 1799.

FUMO (Macedonio), 1759, and continues in 1764.

GIORGI (Ambrosio de), 1759.

GIORGI (Antonio), 1795 to 1808.

SCULPTORS—*(continued)*.

GIORGI (Carlos), 1785 to 1808.

GIORGI (P. Antonio), 1760 to 1808.

GIORGI (Pedro Antonio de), 1759, and continues in 1785.

GRICCHI (Joseph), 1759; in 1766 he was appointed honorary director of the Academy of San Fernando; he died in 1769.

GRICCI (Estéban), 1759.

GUIJARRO (Dionisio), 1798 to 1808.

LLORENTE (Manuel), 1764 and 1785.

MORELLY (Antonio), 1759 to 1785.

NOFRI (Salvador), 1759, and continues in 1785.

NOFRI (Justo), 1778 to 1808.

NOFRI or NOFERI (Juan), 1802.

OCHOGAVIA (Manuel), 1764; born in Galicia in 1744; in 1760 he won a second prize of sculpture at the Academy, and in 1763 a first prize.

PALMERANI (Angel), 1799 to 1808.

PALMERANI (Domingo), 1795 to 1808.

PENABA (Joseph), 1793, and continues in 1808.

ROCCO (Vicenti), 1791, and continues in 1808.

ROCCO (Bartolomé), 1763 to 1808.

RODRIGUEZ (Antonio), 1797 to 1808.

SANCHO (Dionisio), 1788; born at Cienpozuelos in 1762; won a prize at the Academy in 1793; was appointed a member of the Academy, 1796; in 1810 he went to Mexico, where he died 1829.

SANTORUM (Joseph), 1759.

SORRENTINI (Fernando), 1785 to 1808.

SORRENTINI (Francisco), 1802.

SORRENTINI (Rafael), 1785.

VALENTIN (José), 1779 to 1808.

VALENTIN (Miguel), 1785.

PAINTERS.

ALONSO (Francisco), 1764.

BOLTRI (Genaro), 1756; born in Naples in 1730; in 1759 he came to Madrid with Charles III's household, and worked at the Retiro; died in Madrid in 1788.

BRANCASIO (Xavier), 1759.

BRANCACHO (Domingo), 1762 to 1803.

BRANGA (Ignacio de), 1800; painter of figures; he continues there in 1808.

CAMARON (Josef), 1802; born at Segorbe in 1760; in 1776 he won a prize of painting at Valencia; he was pensioned to Rome, and appointed painter in ordinary to the King.

CASTILLO (Fernando del), born at Madrid in 1740; he was appointed painter at the manufactory, and worked there until his death in 1777.

COCO (Joseph del), 1759.

CRUZ (Mariano de la), 1807 to 1808.

DOMEN (Carlos), 1785.

DONADIO (Nicolas), 1759.

GIORGI (Miguel), 1761 to 1802.

GIORGI (Pedro Antonio), 1802.

MARTINEZ (Antonio), 1764.

MARTINEZ (Pedro), 1796 to 1808.

NANI (Mariano), 1759; his wife received a pension from 1804, probably the year of his death.

PESHORN (Jorge), 1788, and continues working in 1802.

PROVINCIALE (Antonio), 1759 and 1785.

QUIROS (Juan Jose), 1802.

REMINI (Carlos), 1759.

ROMERO (Juan Bautista), 1800; flowers and fruit; appears in the lists of 1802.

RUBIO (Joseph), 1799 to 1808.

SEMINI (Francisco), 1759.

SORIANO (Joaquim), 1799; landscape painter in 1800; continues in 1808.

SORRENTINI (Fernando), 1759.

SORRENTINI (Gabriel), 1769 to 1808.

SORRENTINI (Josef), 1756, probably from Capo di Monte; in 1802 he begs for a retiring pension.

SORRENTINI (Manuel), 1785, and continued in 1802.

SORRENTINI (Pablo), 1764 to 1808.

TORRE (Francisco de la), 1779 and 1808.

TORRE (Francisco de la), 1796, and continues in 1808.

TORRE (Josef de la), 1785 and 1802; probably a son of Joseph de la Torre who came to Spain in 1759.

TORRE (Joseph de la), 1759.

TORRE (Juan Bautista de la), 1759 and 1785.

TORRE (Julian de la), 1802.

TORRE (Nicholas de la), 1759, and in 1802 solicits his retiring pension.

TORRE (Raphael de la), 1759.

VELASQUEZ (Castor), 1807, and continued in 1808; born at Madrid in 1768, and obtained a prize at the Academy in 1787.

VARIOUS ARTISTS EMPLOYED IN THE MANUFACTORY.

ARGREDA (Manuel), sculptor, and brother of Esteban Agreda; he superintended the making of biscuit china; born at Haro in 1773; won prizes at the Academy, and was employed at the manufactory from 1805 to 1808.

BAUTISTA (Francisco), appears in 1802 as maker of porcelain flowers.

BAUTISTA (Juan), employed to make porcelain flowers from 1785, and continues in 1808.

BAUTISTA (Sebastian), appears in 1802 as maker of porcelain flowers.

CHEVALIER (Pedro), mounter of snuff-boxes from 1759, and continued to work at the manufactory in 1763.

ESCALERA (Josef), mounter of snuff-boxes from 1781, and continues at the manufactory in 1808.

PERCHE (Jaime Victor), French workman, brought from Paris to prepare porcelain, from 1803 to 1809.

VIVIEN, French workman brought from Paris to prepare porcelain, from 1803 to 1809.

MARKS USED AT THE MANUFACTORY OF BUEN RETIRO.

The usual mark in blue, also on two fine lofty vases, with subjects from "Don Quixote"; belonging to Don J. F. Riaño.

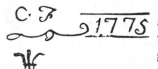

CAYETANO or CARLOS FUMO. The initials and date are graved in the clay under the glaze; the fleur-de-lis is pencilled in blue. On a fine group of two children playing with a goat. In the possession of Don J. F. Riaño.

This mark is graved in the clay under the glaze on a group, modelled by Salvador Nofri; belonging to Count de Valencia.

OCHOGAVIA (?). Graved in the soft clay, on a pair of figures representing the months of October and November, which have also the fleur-de-lis in blue. They were purchased from a private Collection in Malaga by the Editor in 1889.

1798, SORRENTINI (?). These marks are pencilled in red on a pink cup and saucer, with landscapes painted *en grisaille;* belonging to Don J. F. Riaño.

PEDRO ANTONIO GEORGI (?). The initials P. G. are gilt, the M crowned in red, the V and M graved in the clay; on a cup and saucer, buff colour; belonging to Don J. F. Riaño.

PROVINCIALE (?). The letters Po are graved in clay, the fleur-de-lis in blue, on two saucers, beautifully painted with children; belonging to Don J. F. Riaño.

CHARLES III. On two jardinières; the interlaced C's graved in the clay, the fleur-de-lis in blue.

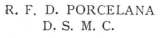

On two vases imitating Wedgwood's blue and white jasper, with white biscuit flowers thirty to fifty centimètres high; in the possession of the Marquis of Salamanca.

The signature of Joseph Gricchi referred to in the list of sculptors given on p. 461.

The royal manufactory and everything connected with it was destroyed by the French in 1812, and the place converted into a fortification, which surrendered, with 200 cannon, on the 14th August 1812 to the Iron Duke; it was subsequently blown up by Lord Hill when the misconduct or perfidy of Ballasteros compelled him to evacuate Madrid. It has been one of the calumnies against the English that all the finest specimens of china were destroyed by them from jealousy, whereas the French destroyed everything and converted the manufactory into a Bastile, which, and not the china, was destroyed by the English. Ferdinand VII., on his restoration, recreating *La China*, removing what was left to La Mancha, once a villa of the Alva family on the Manzanares.

BUEN RETIRO. The mark, painted in red, on a porcelain cup and saucer, brown ground, painted with flowers and fruit; in the Victoria and Albert Museum.

BUEN RETIRO. The fleur-de-lis was used as a mark at Madrid as well as at Capo di Monte. It is sometimes placed above the letters O.F.L. as here shown. Mrs. Beresford Melville has a pair of small figures of peasants, one with the ordinary fleur-de-lis in blue, and the other (the male figure) with the fleur-de-lis as in the margin,

but stamped in the paste. The mark is very scarce. There are in the Franks Collection several excellent specimens of Buen Retiro.

This mark in blue over-glaze is on a cup painted in colours. The initials F. G. are probably those of Felipe Gricci, the superintendent of the works, and the cypher which is incised in the paste is presumably the same letters combined. Franks Collection.

This mark, the fleur-de-lis in relief, is on one of a pair of flower-holders, in the form of negroes holding on their backs conical-shaped shells with the bases ornamented by marine shells. One of the pair has the mark in relief, the other has it painted in blue. Franks Collection.

BUEN RETIRO. This monogram of Charles III. is found on the Buen Retiro porcelain, without the crown. The authenticity of this mark has been questioned, but it occurs *incised* in the paste in addition to the fleur-de-lis in blue on a bowl and plate of undoubted genuineness. The decoration is simple; grotesque mask handles to the bowl, and oval medallions of pink landscapes; plate inferior quality of paste to the bowl. Formerly in Lady C. Schreiber's Collection.

BUEN RETIRO. This mark is on a very fine vase, 19 inches high. From the family of one of the directors. The upper and lower parts are painted with landscapes, the centre is of mottled lake ground.

BUEN RETIRO. On a soft paste cup and saucer, delicately painted in figures; the fleur-de-lis is blue, and gold letters.[1] (See specimens in *Ker. Gall.*, enlarged edition, figs. 210, 213.)

ALCORA. The Comte de Laborde, in his *View of Spain*, as recently as 1808, says, "On ne fait de porcelain (en Espagne) qu'a Alcora et à Madrid; celle d'Alcora est très commune, on en fait très peu." In confirmation of this assertion, M. Charles Davillier, when on a visit to Spain, saw an engraving of a furnace for baking porcelain with this inscription: "Modele de four pour la porselene naturelle, fait par Haly pour M. le Comte d'Aranda. Alcoro, 29 Juin, 1756." It is also noticed by Don Antonio Ponz, *Viage de España*, in 1793.

ALCORA. Two large plaques of very fine fayence, which have been classed as porcelain of the later half of the eighteenth century, from the Comte d'Aranda's manufactory, both very well painted, were formerly in Mr. C. W. Reynolds' Collection: one represents Christ bearing His cross, in colours; the other, painted in sepia, of costumes of three Spanish provinces, with figures at a fountain; is now in the Victoria and Albert Museum. (*Ker. Gall.*, enlarged edition, fig. 214.)

Alcora porcelain is frequently unmarked, and therefore specimens are often assigned to other fabriques. During a journey through Spain in 1889 the Editor purchased in Madrid a service of some twenty-five or thirty pieces of simple decoration, sprigs of roses and other flowers on a cream-coloured ground. Many of these specimens are marked with A, sometimes in black, sometimes in a brownish-red colour, and a few of them have the A incised in the paste as well. The service has been separated, and the cups and plates are in various private collections. Occasionally, and on the best quality specimens, one finds the A in gold.

MONCLOA, near Madrid. A porcelain fabrique was established in 1827, under the superintendence of M. Sureda, who was formerly director of that of Buen Retiro. M. Frederick Langlois, from the porcelain

---

[1] The information given in the above notice of the factory of Buen Retiro is partly quoted from the historical notes of Don Juan Facundo Riaño of Madrid, whose collection has been already referred to.

manufactory of Bayeux, was director of this royal fabrique from 1845 to 1848.

OPORTO (Vista Allegre). *Hard paste.* Estab-lished about 1790; directed by M. Pinto Basto; it is marked in gold or colours; the letters are frequently seen without a crown. A cup and saucer, turquoise with white and gold flowers, marked VA in gold, is in the Victoria and Albert Museum. The manufacture of porcelain is still carried on at Vista Allegre by Messrs. Ferreira, Pinto, and Filhos.

An octagonal plate, with the VA in gold and the triangle incised, with flowers in the centre border, is in the Franks Collection.

GERONA, on the road from Barcelona to Perpignan. The shield of arms of Cordova and the word " Gerona " beneath, is on a tea-service formerly in the Reynolds, Bohn, and Baldwin Collections. The arms are sur-mounted by a female stabbing herself, holding a flag inscribed with "*Antes la muerte que consentir vivir p*r (para) *un tirano.*" Sir A. W. Franks, who is acquainted with these specimens, considers them to be Oriental porcelain, and the device in the margin not a fabrique mark, but part of the decoration of the service.

LISBON. The following examples were in the Schreiber Collection :—

A white biscuit plaque, representing the erection of the statue of Joseph I. of Portugal, in "Black Horse" Square, Lisbon, and the machinery employed for the purpose; at the back is a long inscription in Portuguese, stating that the machinery was the invention of Brigadier Bartholomeu da Costa, "the first who made porcelain in Portugal," and who discovered it at the same time in which he conceived and continued the work of casting the royal statue; the execution of the plaque itself would appear to be due to Joao Figueireido, of the Royal Military Arsenal, in the year 1775.

A circular plaque of the equestrian statue of Joseph I. of Portugal, in white on a grey ground, dated "Lisboa, anno 1775." Inscribed on the back in Portuguese, "Porcelain discovered by Bartholomeu da Costa in 1773."

Small medallion portraits, in imitation of Wedgwood, of Maria I. of Portugal and of her husband. The former described on the back, in Portuguese, as the work of Joao Figueireido, Lisbon, 1782; the latter dated Lisbon, 1783.

There are in the Franks Collection two very small oval medallion portraits of this character, evidently made for the purpose of mounting in gold as brooches or bracelets.

Saxony

MEISSEN, COMMONLY CALLED DRESDEN.

 MANUFACTORY was established at Meissen, on the Elbe, about twelve miles from Dresden, by Augustus II., King of Poland and Elector of Saxony, for the manufacture of hard paste or true porcelain. The experiments of Tschirnhaus and Böttger commenced about 1706; to the latter is attributed the invention of hard paste. His first attempt produced a red ware, like jasper, which was cut and polished by the lapidary and gilt by the gold-smith; it was made from a kind of brown clay found at Meissen. This red ware, made by Böttger, was a fine stoneware, having the opacity, grain, and toughness of pottery. A square Böttger-ware coffee-pot, cut and polished, with flowers and the head of a boy, is in the Victoria and Albert Museum; another is in the Franks Collection, which is rich in varied specimens of this curious and interesting ware.[1] An improvement upon this was a brownish-red ware with a good glaze, on which were placed designs in gold and silver leaf, like the Japanese. In 1708 Tschirnhaus died, and shortly after Böttger succeeded in discovering the mode of making white porcelain by the accidental detection of the *kaolin* necessary for the purpose. The story is thus told : John Schnorr, a rich ironmaster of the Erzgebirge, in the year 1711, riding on horseback, at Aue, near Schneeberg, observed that his horse's feet stuck continually into a soft white clay which impeded his progress. Hair-powder for wigs, made principally from wheat-flour, was at that time in general use, and an exam-ination of this earth suggested its substitution for the more expensive material, which was sold in large quantities at Dresden, Leipzig, and other places. Böttger used it, among others, and finding it much heavier, desired to find out the deleterious ingredients, and analysed it, when, to his great surprise, this ingenious chemist found in it the identical properties of the *kaolin*, which alone he required to complete his immortal discovery of true porcelain. This white earth was known in commerce by the name of *Schnorrische weisse Erde von Aue.*

---

[1] The Franks Collection at time of writing (1911) is in the Bethnal Green Museum, but when the new buildings at the British Museum are completed, it is intended to transfer this collection to Bloomsbury.

In consequence of this important discovery, Augustus II. proceeded to establish the great manufactory at Meissen, of which Böttger was appointed director in 1710. In 1715 he succeeded in making a fine and perfectly white porcelain. The first attempts to paint upon this white body were very imperfect, consisting either of a blue colour under the glaze, or imitations of Oriental china. It has been stated that, up to the period of Böttger's death, which happened in 1719, only white porcelain had then been made in Saxony; yet the success of this manufacture occasioned attempts at imitation in France, and porcelain works were established at St. Cloud, and in the Faubourg St. Antoine, at Paris.

Under the directorship of J. G. Höroldt, or Herold, the manufactory developed considerably, and it is during the period of his directorship from 1720 until about 1740 that paintings of a superior character, improved gilding, and the beautiful ground colours—maroon, apple-green, canary-yellow, and a pale mauve—were introduced, which we find on vases and on the fine table services which were produced about this time. On the tea services one finds these ground colours on the *under* sides of the saucers, a method of decoration copied doubtless from the Chinese, and which we find in the eggshell plates known among collectors as "ruby-backed." About 1731 the services of an eminent sculptor, Johann Joachim Kändler, were obtained, and the modelling of groups, figures, vases, and animals which can be attributed to him are now the most highly valued of all the old Meissen productions. The famous crinoline groups as they are termed, the harlequin figures, and the bold lifelike models of animals and birds of this period are exceedingly valuable.

After about 1740 the taste in China assimilated the more rococo designs affected by French fashions, and the figures and groups are in the form of Arcadian shepherds and shepherdesses, courtiers, musicians, peasants, mendicants, pedlars, and cupids in fancy costumes, elegant and dainty, but wanting in the vigour and strength of Kändler's art. The table services, too, which formerly had been decorated either in Chinese subjects or in the style of Vernet, were now à la Watteau, painted in conversations, courting scenes, and generally more frivolous and effeminate. It is considered by connoisseurs that the cream of the Meissen productions were made between 1731 and about 1760.

Another period may be said to have commenced in 1763 when a slight variation of the mark was adopted by placing a dot between the hilts of the swords, and during the period of this mark it is said that the King took a personal interest in the directorship of the works. This is therefore sometimes called King's period, but the collector's term is *Saxe au point*.

The greatest prosperity of the factory was the period which followed the Seven Years' War, say, from 1763 to 1774, and was marked by an alteration of style in forms and models introduced by the employment of a noted sculptor from Paris, François Acier, who introduced the French style prevalent at Sèvres. There is said to have been considerable friction between Acier and Kändler, which was overcome by allowing each to select the half of designs for new models. Kändler died in 1775, and Acier retired on a pension in 1781, but about this time the taste had again changed from the rococo of Louis XV. to the more severe lines of Louis XVI. taste, and we therefore find in the groups of the later half of the Marcolini period that, instead of the scroll-shaped bases to figures and groups, there are round-moulded stands ornamented by pearlings or flutings. A painter named Dietrich, who had formerly worked at Dresden, exercised a marked influence upon the Meissen factory.

He was not, as has been stated by several writers, a director of the factory, but was appointed Head of the (then) new Art School. He was born in 1712 and died in 1774, so that his time synchronises with the best productions at Meissen.

In 1774 Count Camillo Marcolini was appointed director, and again the mark was slightly altered by replacing the dot between the sword hilts by a star; sometimes this star is accompanied by a number, generally the figure "4." The Marcolini period continued until 1814, and was marked by careful, painstaking work, but lacking the freshness and vigour of the Kändler period, or the charm and delicacy of the time which immediately succeeded it. The old clay pits had become exhausted long ere this time, and the material which was now procured lacked the brilliant whiteness of the old china clay. In Marcolini's time a favourite decoration was a rich bleu de roi or royal blue, with the subject still in the Watteau style, but also in the manner of Angelica Kauffmann, carefully painted. Figures with lacework decoration were also produced in considerable quantities, a clever effect being rendered by placing real net which had been dipped in a solution of china clay on the figure. In the kiln the lace net was destroyed and left a "negative" of china lace which is very effective, and has often puzzled amateurs as to its method of production. A. M. von Oppel succeeded Marcolini, and in 1839 his place was taken by M. Kühn, and the establishment became known as Koniglich Sächsische Porzellan Manufactur. Subsequently to the Marcolini time we have Meissen or, as it is commonly but erroneously called, "Dresden" china of the modern period, with which the collector is not concerned.

NOTES ON MEISSEN (DRESDEN) CHINA.

A Dresden china figure of a Dutch skipper, or court fool, of stout build, with a pointed hat, has in front the initials I. F. and the date 1736; formerly in Lady Charlotte Schreiber's Collection, but now in the private collection of Mr. James Ward Usher of Lincoln (see *Ker. Gall.*, enlarged edition, fig. 216). Another figure from the same model has I. F. 1752 on the breast of the figure; it is marked in blue underneath with the crossed swords, and was in the Staniforth Collection. There is a similar figure in the Franks Collection, but the date is 1741, the letters I. F. being the same.

Several important groups of this period, including one in which Count

Bruhl is being frightened by a mouse, portrait figures of Augustus Rex and lady in costume (the Countess de Kosel), and others, formed part of the large collection of Dresden groups and figures made by Lady Firbank, which was sold at Christie's in 1906. The largest and most valuable collection of Dresden groups and figures in England is that which was some years ago on loan to the Bethnal Green Museum by the Hon. W. F. B. Massey-Mainwaring. While the ninth edition of "Chaffers" was going through the press (May 1899) this fine collection of old Dresden china was purchased by private treaty, and resold *en bloc* for the sum of £30,000 to Mr. King of 138 Piccadilly.

"The Dresden porcelain reached its highest development under the administration of the famous Count Bruhl, the same in whose wardrobe Frederick the Great, when he took Dresden, found 1500 wigs, with suits of clothes and snuff-boxes to match. His taste for magnificence made itself felt at Meissen, and we owe to him the most beautiful specimens it produced" (*Chambers's Journal*, 1857).

Among the pieces produced about this time by or under the direction of Kändler may be especially noticed Count Bruhl's tailor and his wife riding upon goats with all the implements of their trade. To Kändler are also attributed the groups and figures forming, when placed together, "The Carnival of Venice," composed of *Le Bœuf Gras* escorted by upwards of a hundred different figurines in the forms of cupids, representing the various professions and trades, as a Lawyer, Doctor, Apothecary, Councillor, Knife-grinder, Gardener, Barber, &c., two carts, each drawn by four horses, full of masked personages, and the centre formed by a large clock with rococo scrolls. These were all of coloured porcelain and independent of each other, being united or separated at pleasure. A complete set is of course exceedingly rare.

Kändler modelled men and animals of the natural size, also peacocks, herons, pelicans, and all sorts of birds. In the rich collection of Lord Hastings at Melton Constable there was a whole menagerie which issued from the Dresden manufactory about this time. Kändler made the twelve Apostles, life size, and worked for five years, from 1751 to 1756, on a colossal equestrian statue of Augustus III., but it never was completed, in consequence of the invasion of Frederick the Great, and the members of the "Porcelain King," as he was called, were dispersed, nothing now remaining but the head. The china was at that time much esteemed, as we find by a note in the *Gentleman's Magazine* for May 16, 1763: "This day a service of Dresden porcelain was sold at Mr. Uhthoff's sale, in Philpot Lane, for £115."

In the *London Magazine* of May 1753 we read: "This fabrick, which brings annually great sums of money into the country, is daily increasing in reputation, and is carried to all the courts of Europe; even the Turks come from Constantinople to purchase it, and the rarest pieces that are made are carried thither to embellish the Grand Seignior's and his great officers' houses and seraglios.

"The table services may be had from 100 to 1000 guineas and upwards, according to the quantity, size, and nature of the painting they are composed of.

"Those most commonly bought are about the value of 160 or 300 guineas. The plates are from 8 shillings to 24, and the terrines, dishes, bowls, &c., according to the bigness, &c. The sets of porcelain for tea, coffee, or chocolate, may be had from 15 to 60 guineas. There is one particular kind from which they will abate nothing of 100 guineas the set; this is a double porcelain, not made at once, but a second layer added to the first form, resembling a honeycomb on the outside, which is of a pale brown colour, the letts or cavities being all painted as well as the bottoms of the inside of the cups and dishes. This, as all other sorts, may be had painted with landscapes and figures, birds, insects, fruits, flowers, the first being the dearer, the latter the best executed, being almost equal to nature in beauty and liveliness of the colours. The grounds of all these different sorts of porcelain are various, some being painted on white, others in pink, some in compartments, others without. The spaces between are sometimes of a white, yellow, or pea-green colour, or the whole ground is white with running flowers. This sort, and the pea-green in compartments, are the newest made, and in the most elegant taste.

"The single figures, about 15 inches high, are rated from 16 to 20 guineas, and those of 5 or 6 inches as many pounds, and this proportion is pretty nearly observed in the measures between these sizes. When they exceed it, the figures grow much dearer.

"The porcelain entirely white, without the least painting, is the most esteemed of all, and with reason. It is not permitted to be sold, but reserved for the King's use, who makes very magnificent presents of it to foreign princes."

A note at the end of this account says, "It is with pleasure we can inform the publick, that an undertaking of this kind is carried on in the greatest perfection in our own country, so as to emulate the elegancies of Dresden or China porcelain, particularly at Chelsea and Stratford, near this metropolis."

This white porcelain was sometimes ornamented by private persons, especially by a Baron Busch, of Hildesheim, who was the only person possessed of the secret of engraving with a diamond on china. In an advertisement of a sale by auction at Golden Square by Mr. Owen in June 1767, we find a "tea set of the beautiful snow-white Dresden, with the hunt of the heron and falcon, most curiously engraved by Baron Busch. The valuable service now at Saltzdal, belonging to the Duke of Brunswick, esteemed at £10,000, was made a present to that Prince by the Baron, as were also the other curious pieces in the cabinets of most of the princes of the Empire. This set was brought into England by the secretary of a sovereign prince, and some plates framed as pictures, engraved by the same hand after Rembrandt," &c.

In the Schreiber Collection there was a cup and saucer etched with birds, trees, and ruins, which were stated to be by Busch; the etching does not appear to penetrate beneath the glaze, but it is unsigned. Busch also etched on glass, and some pieces we have seen have his name written on them. (*Ker. Gall.*, enlarged edition, fig. 217.) There is a saucer etched by Busch in the Franks Collection, which is signed "Busch" and dated 1749.

The description given by Sir J. C. Robinson in the Catalogue of the Uzielli Collection of a Dresden cup and saucer (No. 746) exactly applies to a cup and saucer, probably of the same set, in Mr. Borradaile's Collection: "Coffee-cup and saucer of old Dresden white porcelain, with flowers in low relief, the flowers filled in with a minute appliqué mosaic of black lacquer, mother-of-pearl, and gold piqué work. A rare and curious instance of the combination of lacquered-work and mosaics with porcelain, probably suggested by some Japanese examples, and by similar decorative processes to those in use by the 'tabatière' artists of the beginning of the eighteenth century."

In the Franks Collection there is a remarkable example of the combination of goldsmith's work with that of the potter.

The Japanese Palace of Dresden contained a very fine collection of every description of porcelain, especially Oriental. About 150 of the finest pieces of china in this Museum were the result of a singular bargain between Augustus the Strong of Saxony and the King of Prussia in 1717, by which, in exchange for some soldiers, the King of Prussia presented this fine collection of china. The "*acquits de livraison*," dated Oranienburg, the 29th April, and Charlottenburg, 1st May 1717, are still preserved among the archives of Dresden.

It may be stated that all the pieces of white Dresden porcelain sent from the Royal Manufactory are marked with a cut in the glaze above or through the two swords, so that those specimens which have been painted elsewhere are easily detected; faulty pieces are also marked with one or more cuts.

The mark adopted in or about 1716 was the arms of Saxony; Party per fess *sab.* and *arg.*, two swords in saltire *gules*, borne in an escutcheon by the Elector of Saxony as Grand-Marshal of the Empire, granted in 1423 to Frederick, Margrave of Misnia, surnamed the Warlike.

THE MARKS ON DRESDEN (MEISSEN) PORCELAIN.

The following marks which occur on specimens of old Dresden porcelain of different periods have been placed as nearly as possible in chronological order, commencing with the incised or impressed marks on Böttger's red ware, which preceded the white porcelain of a Venetian-like character. Several of these marks are very rare and may have been placed on trial or pattern pieces; others are not *fabrique* marks, but form part of the decoration of the specimen, and indicate a date or the name of the artist.   The general mark by which Dresden china is recognised is that of the crossed swords, and these vary according to period.   The Höroldt period is distinguished by the swords being smaller, and sometimes both points and hilts interlaced; on figures, birds, animals, groups, &c., intended for mounting, the mark frequently occurs very small, on the back of the foot of the piece and not on the bottom; this was to enable the part of the mark to be seen just above the rim or edging of the metal mount.   The period known as "Saxe au point," commencing 1763, is signified by a dot between the sword hilts, and that of the Marcolini period, from 1774-1814, by a star between the sword hilts.   After the Marcolini period was ended we find the swords larger and rather more freely drawn; and about fifty or sixty years ago, as the commercial importance of the Meissen factory increased, a reference number was incised in the paste in addition to the mark.   This number was for the purpose of enabling their trade customers to repeat their orders, and it naturally indicates that the manufactory was being carried on upon a business basis.   We may therefore consider as modern any specimen of Dresden (Meissen) porcelain which bears one of these numbers.   They are in cursive characters just incised in the paste with a pointed tool, and are of course in addition to the ordinary crossed swords in blue under the glaze.

 This mark, stamped in red paste of Böttger ware, is on a pair of small flat-shaped Pilgrim bottles with marks at sides, polished by the wheel, not glazed.   In Mr. Borradaile's Collection.   A similar pair, and also one of the later period ornamented with gilding and a square-shaped coffee-pot are in the Franks Collection; also on a pair of small candlesticks of same ware, which are similar in design to a pair of Queen Anne silver candlesticks of same time.   In the Collection of Mr. H. E. B. Harrison of Brighton.

 These marks (impressed) are on a quadrangular coffee-pot with rounded sides, the spout proceeding from a dragon's mouth, and on a very finely executed portrait medallion of John George, Duke of Saxe Weissenfels (1697-1712), of Böttger ware, both in the Franks Collection, which also contains a cup and saucer of the yellow Böttger ware with decorations in silver.

Several of the specimens of Böttger ware, and also two very early porcelain figures of Chinamen, which are in the Franks Collection, bear no *fabrique* mark, but are engraved with letters and numbers, which go to prove that they were originally in the Dresden Japanese Palace Collection. (See note on p. 480.)

This mark in blue occurs on a vase with globular body, canary coloured ground, with birds on branches, and butterflies in brilliant colours. Franks Collection.

ORIGINAL A.R. MARK.

DRESDEN. MEISSEN. *Hard paste.* The first mark used was the monogram A.R. (Augustus Rex), and was affixed to all pieces intended for royal use. It is found upon imitations of Oriental porcelain, and was in use from about 1710-12. The vase described in the Franks Collection is a

MODERN A.R. MARK.

typical specimen. This original mark should not be confused with the monogram placed upon modern Dresden, which is easily distinguished from the other. Both marks, original and counterfeit, are here placed one under the other for the reader's comparison. The china which until some recent litigation bore this monogram, and sometimes surmounted by a crown, was not made at the State factory of Meissen, but by a *private* firm named Wolfsohn in the *town* of Dresden. Since the litigation, which ended by the State factory obtaining an injunction against Wolfsohns, the latter firm have adopted a mark of the word "Dresden" surmounted by a crown.

Besides the "Dresden" fabrique of Wolfsohns there have been many others in the town of Dresden, some of whom used formerly to purchase from the State factory of Meissen faulty specimens in the white, and then decorate them in their workshops at Dresden; they also had models of their own which they made, baked, and decorated throughout. The chief of these was Meyers, who used a mark of crossed swords and placed his initial, M, between the sword-hilts. One named Thieme used a mark something like the head of a broad arrow, and also an imitation of the crossed swords, but without their being so exact a copy as to incur litigation; another firm stamped the word "MEISSEN" in the paste, and others have used marks which are colourable imitations of the crossed swords, more like the Limbach mark of two L's crossed or a bad example of the Courtille mark (two torches crossed). Only knowledge and the requisite experience of the models and their treatment, can in some cases determine which are the true Meissen and which the Dresden imitations. In many instances the models of some of the Dresden makers are very good, and from their having been made some forty or fifty years ago, they have acquired a tone which gives them an entrée into good collections.

The manufacturer of the greatest number of imitation of Dresden is, however, a Frenchman named Samson of the Rue Béranger, Paris, some of whose work has considerable merit. He used to place his initial letter S between the hilts of the crossed swords which he adopted as his mark, but he has also copied many other marks of the Meissen factory, and also that of nearly every other fabrique for the specimens of which there is a demand.

This very scarce and early mark, the monogram of Frederick Augustus, is also sometimes seen on pieces decorated in the Oriental taste.

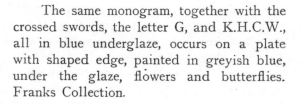

The same monogram, together with the crossed swords, the letter G, and K.H.C.W., all in blue underglaze, occurs on a plate with shaped edge, painted in greyish blue, under the glaze, flowers and butterflies. Franks Collection.

DRESDEN. The crossed swords and painter's mark of a square, in blue above the initials, which stand for the words *Königl. Hof. Conditorei Warschau*, are underneath portions of a service painted in blue *camaieu* with flowers and insects, and on the border is the monogram of Augustus Rex, and a crown above (King of Poland). The inscription in English is, "The King's Court Confectioner, Warsaw." One of his principal palaces was situated there; the service being made specially for his Majesty's use about A.D. 1720-30. In the possession of Herr Pollak of Vienna. A small flacon in the Franks Collection has the first three letters in purple. There is also a cream jug in the Franks Collection, painted in the Japanese (Kakiyemon) style, which bears the crown, as well as the monogram of Augustus Rex.

K.H.C.W. DRESDEN. These initials are on a porcelain statuette of a female allegorical figure, $3\frac{3}{4}$ inches high. (Bandinel Collection.) Sometimes the crossed swords are placed above, the whole enclosed in an oval. These letters occur with the crossed swords and H.F. combined on a blue and white cup decorated with the monogram of Augustus Rex, in the Franks Collection.

DRESDEN, of early date, from a specimen in the Museum at Dresden; quoted by Dr. Graesse, director. This mark is very similar to the crossed sceptres, occasionally used on Berlin porcelain. See *Berlin*.

DRESDEN. The caduceus mark, as it is termed, or rather the wand of Æsculapius, in allusion to the first profession of Böttger, was used from 1712-20, and is said to have been placed upon china intended for sale; it is found on pieces decorated in the Chinese style, as

well as others. This mark is on a small tray with scalloped edge painted in the Oriental style in the "Flying Fox" pattern formerly in Mr. Loraine Baldwin Collection. Sir A. W. Franks, Mr. Harrison of Brighton, Mr. Verschoyle, Mr. Hoskyns, Dr. Darmstaedter, and other collectors have specimens with this mark, several of which were formerly in Mr. Bohn's Collection, which was sold about thirty years ago.

This mark, which is another rendering of the above-named rod of Æsculapius, is on a beaker painted in colours, with gilding of Oriental pattern, consisting of a boy standing on a carpet, a kylin, a bunch of flowers, a bird on a branch, and scattered insects and flowers. Height 12 inches. Franks Collection.

DRESDEN. This rare mark is found in gold, with the swords in blue, on a service made expressly for the King's favourite, the Comtesse Cosel or Kosel. The Japanese Palace at Dresden possessed six pieces of it. She was a favourite of Augustus II., was disgraced in 1713, and died in 1733. Five pieces still remain in the Palace, the

sixth is in the Franks Collection. A mark similar but not exactly the same occurs in gold on a cup and saucer painted in Chinese subjects. Dr. Darmstaedter's Collection (Berlin).

DRESDEN. This early mark, of the Electoral swords crossed, in blue, with the date 1716, is on the bottom of a pure white porcelain female figure of one of the Muses; the date is impressed at the back. Berney Collection, Bracon Hall

*M.*P.*M.* DRESDEN. The initial letters of *Meissner Porzellan Manufactur.*

K.P.M. DRESDEN. The mark for royal pieces. The letters K.P.M. stand for *Königlichen Porzellan Manufactur;* marked in blue under the glaze. There is a fine tea and coffee service with this mark at Windsor Castle. Mr. Arthur Verschoyle has a teapot and saucer bearing this mark, which is rare.

K. P. M. This is another rendering of the same mark, and occurs on a teapot and cover, the lower part of the spout with a mask in relief, painted in colours, with gilding, two parts with scroll edges enclosing group of Chinese figures between them, sprigs of flowers. The number 86 is in gold, and probably indicates the number of the service. Franks Collection.

86.

K. P. M. DRESDEN. Another variety of the same mark. H., the painter's initial, in gold, the others blue.

H. Some of the early pieces of Dresden of the Höroldt period have gilders' marks or initials, in addition to the cross swords in blue.

z90. This mark is on a shaped oval box and cover, painted in colours in Japanese (Kakiyemon) style, with two figures; round the edge sprigs, inside the cover in black, 290 W. On the bottom the same number and letter, accompanied by the crossed swords in blue. Franks Collection.

W.

This is not a factory mark, but is part of the decoration of the tankard on which it occurs, being on a shield held by a Chinese soldier. It doubtless records the name of the painter, George Ernst Keil, at Meissen, July 6, 1724. The tankard is otherwise unmarked. Franks Collection.

This signature, which occurs on a tall cup and saucer, painted Chinese subjects in colours, is also given by Sir A. W. Franks in facsimile in his Catalogue of Continental Porcelain, and is said to be that of a painter living in Dresden, but probably not one of the regular employés. The specimen was formerly in the Collection of Sir Edward J. Dean Paul sold at Christie's in 1896.

These two initial letters occur on the saucers or stands of some exquisitely painted vases (marked with the cross swords) in His Majesty's collection at Windsor Castle.

DRESDEN. This mark and date is in red under a saucer painted with terminal figures of the heads and busts of Bacchus and Ariadne, and bold scrolls of gold shaded, between which is a panther; the cup has infant Bacchanals plucking grapes, and a goat. Now in the Franks Collection. The initial letter W under the crossed swords, also occurs on a fine cup and saucer painted with figures of angels in red *camaieu* (Dr. Darmstaedter's Collection); and the Editor possesses a good figure of a boy with tree stump, evidently Dresden, which has the W without the swords.

DRESDEN. On a cup, sea-green ground with a small medallion of Chinese figures in purple *camaieu*, gilt border; in the Sèvres Museum.

DRESDEN. A drinking-cup painted in blue and red *camaieu*, alternately with full-length Chinese figures and flowers between; the mark in gold.

This mark occurs on a cup and saucer with leaves in relief, painted in colours with Chinese figures, gilt lace-like borders. Franks Collection.

Note.—Sir A. W. Franks, in a marginal note, suggests that the factory was moved to Meissen in 1710; the word Dresden may indicate that these services were made for some official who lived at Dresden.

B. P. T.

Dresden. 17.39.

DRESDEN. On a square tray of white porcelain, with leaves in relief, marked at the back in blue under the glaze. (Bandinel Collection.) Victoria and Albert Museum. Mr. Sigismund Rücker had a cup and saucer of the same date, with leaves in relief, painted with figures in Oriental costume, but without the initials; and a teapot, same date, is in the Franks Collection. The same mark occurs on an *écuelle* with cover decorated with leaves in relief in gold with reddish-violet veins, and flowers painted in Japanese style. Collection of Dr. Darmstaedter (Berlin).

This is not a factory mark, but forms part of the decoration of a cup and saucer painted in colours with landscapes. The signpost on the cup bears the date 1741 with the crossed swords. The cup also bears the factory mark of the crossed swords in blue, and H in gold on the saucer, the swords in blue and 17 impressed. Franks Coll.

C. F Herold

invl; et fecit , a meisse

1750. 𝔍 12 Sept:

DRESDEN. A Meissen cup and saucer of exquisite workmanship, painted with brown and gilt medallions of ruins; on these are placed groups of classical figures of solid gold in high relief, the ground embossed with flowers; the inscription written above the crossed swords. This unique specimen was in the possession of Mr. H. G. Bohn, and is now in the Franks Collection. It may be noted that during the Herold or Höroldt period the crossed swords are smaller, and frequently have both the points and the hilts interlaced.

DRESDEN. Another variety, sometimes painted thicker; used about 1720, while Höroldt was director.

Alex Tromerij

a Berlin

DRESDEN. This name of a German artist is on a large oval box-cover, painted in enamel with the flight of Stanislaus Leckzinski, King of Poland, from Dantzig to Bar, in a carriage drawn by six horses, in 1736. The name of *Herold fecit* is written in the corner. Formerly in Lady C. Schreiber's Collection.

This mark is very unusual, as the lozenge appears between the points of the swords instead of the dot between the hilts, which is of a much later date (King's period). It is upon two tall cups painted in colours, with groups of flowers in Chinese style. Franks Collection.

DRESDEN. These varieties of the crossed swords with dot between the hilts, found on porcelain with Watteau subjects, &c., after 1763. This period is termed by collectors *Saxe au point*, and is also known as "King's period."

DRESDEN. Other varieties of the crossed swords, the arms of Saxony; on specimens formerly in the Collection of the Rev. T. Staniforth of Storrs, Windermere.

This mark occurs on a small cup, turquoise ground, with female bust in blue *camaieu*. This curious combination of letters, numbers, and the crossed swords with dots between the hilts, probably indicate a trial-piece. The crossed swords with dot were first used in 1763, and, as already observed, indicate the period known as *Saxe au point* or "King's period." Franks Collection.

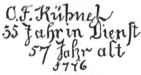

DRESDEN. This inscription is on a trial-piece. C. F. Kühnel, thirty-five years in service, fifty-seven years old, 1776. Mr. H. G. Bohn had a piece thus inscribed, which is now in the Franks Collection with another specimen having the same mark.

DRESDEN. Mr. Ditcham of Wisbech, Cambridgeshire, has two white biscuit figures of Paris and Venus, of Dresden manufacture, both marked as in the margin. Height, 11 inches. In the Museum at Dresden is another figure of the same set, with the Dresden numeral above, which the curator showed the Editor, saying they were all of the Dresden make, of about 1766 to 1780. This mark has by some authorities been erroneously attributed to Bristol.

This is a variation of the incised mark on biscuit ware, but the star on the apex of the triangle indicates the Marcolini period. It occurs on a cup and saucer (biscuit); the cup has the number 16 impressed. Franks Collection.

DRESDEN. A star between the handles is always found on pieces of the Marcolini period, 1774-1814.

Upon some of these Marcolini specimens we find occasionally a numeral ("4" is the most frequent) underneath the star as in the margin.

Mr. H. E. B. Harrison has two saucers very finely painted with the death of General Wolfe, and the Departure of the Regulars from Rome with this mark and also an *engraved* "2."

This mark has, combined with numbers and initials, the crossed swords with star between hilts, indicating the period of Marcolini's directorship, 1774-1814. The mark is in blue underglaze, except the number, 23, which is impressed and 97C added in black over the glaze. It occurs on a cup painted in greyish blue under the glaze, with groups of flowers, and is probably a pattern or trial-piece. Franks Collection.

This mark is on two plates with foliated edges of sixteen lobes, Japanese (Imari) pattern, richly painted in colours with gilding, bird, tree, with phœnix and flowers in the border.

Note.—These formed part of a large Japanese service of Imari porcelain, which they had been evidently made to match. One of these is in the Franks Collection.

ENGRAVED LETTERS AND NUMBERS.

It must have been frequently observed by collectors that underneath many pieces of Oriental and European china, Arabic numbers are deeply cut through the glaze. All these pieces were originally in the celebrated Dresden Collection at the Japanese Palace, but as the collection increased, it was considered desirable to sell the duplicate specimens; hence their dispersion throughout Europe. According to a former director of the Museum, Dr. Graesse, it was chiefly brought together by Augustus the Strong, King of Poland and Elector of Saxony, between 1694 and 1705, as we have before noted, which goes to show that the elector king was an amateur in china long before Böttger's invention. In order, it is said, to prevent the courtiers from making away with the royal property, every specimen was marked indelibly with a number, accompanied by a sign (cut through the glaze on the lathe), which referred to each particular class, thereby avoiding the use of high numbers. These must have been marked at an early date, being found only on the more ancient pieces of the Dresden porcelain. The Arabic numerals of course vary on every piece in rotation, agreeing with the inventory. Sir A. W. Franks, who examined the old inventories of the Collection, says the present copy, dated 1779, is from a still older document. There are five volumes. The pieces marked below are on specimens in Sir A. W. Franks' Historical Collection.

The first volume contains a list of miscellaneous objects, lacquers, carvings, &c.

Every piece in the Japanese Palace was marked in Arabic numerals separately.

2nd. Saxon or Meissen porcelain and Böttger ware, simply numbered.

$$N = 25-$$

3rd. Japanese porcelain, distinguished by the addition of a cross under the number.

$$N = 5o \\ +$$

4th. "Green Chinese porcelain," principally painted in green enamel, marked by an 丑.

$$N = 96 \\ 丑$$

White Chinese porcelain, marked with a triangle. This mark is useful to help us in distinguishing white Oriental from early Dresden, Fulham, or Plymouth porcelain, which were closely copied.

$$N = Z- \\ \triangle$$

Red Chinese porcelain, principally decorated in red, marked with an arrow.

$$N = 93-$$

5th. Blue and white "Indian porcelain," including crackle. Marked with a zigzag line.

$$N = 665.$$

"Old Indian porcelain," marked with a parallelogram.

$$N = 7- \\ \square$$

"Indian and Saxon black porcelain," marked with a P.

$$N = 5- \\ P$$

It may be observed, that nearly all the Japanese specimens are what we know as "Old Japan," made in Imari for exportation. The Collection, after being stowed away for many years in the vaults of the palace, has now been well arranged in the Johanneum.

There are in the Franks Collection some of these early Dresden copies of old Imari china plates, and exhibited in the same case for comparison is an original plate of Japanese make.

SALE MARKS.

On white porcelain vessels without defects. The mark across the swords was in reality a *nick* in the paste, not part of the mark. It was to indicate that the piece was sold *white* out of the factory, and therefore, if afterwards decorated, that the painting and gilding had been done outside the State factory. The sale of undecorated pieces was prohibited many years ago.

On porcelain, with trifling defects.

On porcelain defective. (*Brack.*)
[The Editor has always heard the three classes of quality called by the Meissen officials, Gut, Mittel, and Ausschuss—good, medium, and outcast.]

On porcelain tea and coffee services with defects, and vessels for the table, defective.

Do.   do.

ALT HALDENSLEBEN (Saxony). *Hard paste.* Manufactory of M. Nathusius; stamped in blue. Mr. Friedrich Hofmann gives the mark of this factory as the letter N., probably the initial of Nathusius.

Austria

VIENNA

HIS manufactory was established in 1718 by a Dutchman, Claude Innocent du Pasquier, who engaged a ceramist from Meissen named Stenzel to co-operate with him. With this object in view, Du Pasquier proceeded secretly to Meissen, where he contrived to scrape acquaintance with him in a coffee-house, and induced Stenzel to play a game of billiards, taking care to lose, and thus he secured his object. Stenzel, after some slight hesitation, accepted an offer of a thousand thalers to be paid yearly, with a carriage at his disposal, and forthwith proceeded to Vienna. Du Pasquier obtained a patent for twenty-five years, granted by the Emperor Charles VI., and signed by him at Luxembourg on the 27th of May 1718. In this patent it was distinctly notified that the factory was to receive no pecuniary aid from the Government, but an exclusive privilege was granted for the sale of porcelain, wholesale and retail, throughout the whole empire. The patent further stipulated that the ware should consist of the best material, and should display the most elegant and well-selected forms and colours, to which end neither labour nor expense was to be spared in the endeavour to produce patterns of original forms and fancy. This done, Du Pasquier entered into partnership with Heinrich Zerder, a merchant named Martin Peter, and an artist named Cristophe Conrad Hunger. Du Pasquier had many difficulties to contend with, and the productions not being equal to the Chinese, and inferior even to those of Meissen both as regards beauty and material, taste and decoration, and the sale consequently moderate, he was compelled to produce coarser articles; added to which Du Pasquier not being possessed of the secret, and the ceramist Stenzel, not having been paid regularly according to his contract, returned to Meissen, having maliciously destroyed many of the models. The works were therefore suspended at the end of the second year, without a knowledge of the secret or material. Du Pasquier, being a man of energy and determination, endeavoured by numerous experiments to discover the porcelain mixture, and his efforts were finally crowned with success.

The factory was at first established in a small house belonging to

Count Kufstein, and he worked with only ten assistants and one kiln; but in the year 1721 it was removed to a house belonging to Count Breuner; here the workmen were increased to twenty hands and more kilns were erected. Nevertheless the factory was not successful, and after twenty-five years' labour, Du Pasquier decided, in 1744, to offer it to the Government. The establishment was then in good working condition, and the workmen for the most part very efficient, and he proposed to take on himself the direction and management.

The young Empress, Maria Theresa, resolved to support the factory, which promised to give occupation and profit to her subjects, honour and gain to the state. She therefore commanded that it should be taken by state contract from its owner, that its debt of 45,449 florins should be paid off, and Du Pasquier receive the direction with a salary of 1500 florins a year. Modelling of groups and figures appears to have commenced when the factory became the property of the Government in 1747: Joseph Niedermeyer was the master-modeller and made the statuettes and figures. Count Philip Kinsky and Count Rudolph Cholert took great interest in the development of the factory, and in 1760, under Government control, it advanced rapidly to that perfection of art it subsequently maintained. In 1750 the workmen only numbered 40, eleven years later that number had increased to 140; in 1770 to 200, and in 1780 to 320. From 1747 to 1790 was the best period for figures and groups, while from 1780 to 1820 the painting on china became celebrated, the subjects being taken from Watteau, Lancret, Boucher, A. Kauffman, and others, as well as allegorical subjects. From 1747 to 1758 the chief direction of the works was given to Maierhoffer de Grünbühel. From 1758 to 1770 Joseph Wolf of Rosenfeld was director, and in 1770 Kessler was appointed; but the manufactory then began to decline, and it was not until 1785 that it again rose to importance. In 1785 the most important improvements were made under the direction of the Baron de Sorgenthal, artists of the highest talent being employed, and a first-rate chemist, named Leithner, was engaged to prepare the colours and gilding, and the *chefs-d'œuvre* of the early masters were copied, while the gilding was brought to a perfection which has never been surpassed. Sorgenthal made also, under the direction of Flaxman, some beautiful specimens of Wedgwood's jasper.

Among the principal artists employed at Vienna, Schindler was distinguished by his taste in designing ornaments, and George Perl, who followed Leithner, excelled in decorating the ware. Antone Grassi succeeded in substituting for the rococo style a purer classical taste: Foerstler was an admirable painter of mythological subjects: Lamprecht was celebrated for his paintings of animals in the style of Berghem: Joseph Nigg was a clever painter of flowers as well as classical subjects: Varsanni, J. Wech, and Perger were also exquisite painters of mythological and historical scenes, and K. Herr may be noticed as one of the best of this school of Viennese artists. We have met with several other names;

on a plate dated 1800 S. Raffey, another of 1805 signed Schallez, and 1856, L. Zetien.

On the death of Baron Sorgenthal in 1805, M. Neidermeyer became director; it continued its flourishing condition until about 1815. Leithner used the finest gold, which brought the gilding to the utmost perfection; moreover, he discovered a rich cobalt blue and a red-brown colour which no other factory could imitate. From the year 1784 to the date of its extinction it was the custom to mark every piece with the number of the year, which circumstance may be of great service to the connoisseur who seeks early specimens of Vienna porcelain; it is stamped without colour underneath the piece, or rather indented, the first numeral being omitted; thus, the number 792 stands for 1792, 802 for 1802, and so on. In 1827 it was under the direction of Benjamin Scholtz, who followed Neider-meyer; he died in 1834 and was succeeded by Baumgartner; in 1844 Baron Leithner took the direction, and in 1856 Alexander Loewe finished the list of directors. It was then on the decline, and economy, indifferent workmen, and bad artists copying from French models, sealed its doom; the splendid and expensive gilding, the exquisite paintings, &c., gave place to cheaper and less refined productions, and it dwindled down to a second-rate factory and became a burden to the state.

The statistics for 1861 are here given. The production of finished pieces from the kiln was 227,230 pieces, employing 200 workmen. The consumption of raw materials for the year was—

								Cwts.
China clay	.	.	.	.	.	.	.	1,564
Quartz	.	.	.	.	.	.	.	559
Felspar	.	.	.	.	.	.	.	282
Gypsum	.	.	.	.	.	.	.	199
Marble	.	.	.	.	.	.	.	80
Fire-proof clay for seggars	.	.	.	.	.	.	.	14,481

The porcelain kilns were heated with wood.

Douglas, speaking of Vienna in 1794, remarks, "In one of the suburbs is the manufactory of porcelain, which, though reckoned inferior to that of Dresden and Berlin, is executed with great beauty, but sold at an extravagant price. A service for Lord Spencer, and a still handsomer one for Sir F. M. Eden, I considered as elegant specimens of this fabric. All the porcelain manufactories which I have seen abroad appear to me useless and expensive sacrifices to vanity, as their produce is sold at such a price as must ever prevent its becoming an article of commerce."

The Imperial manufactory at Vienna was, in consequence of the great annual expense to the state, discontinued in 1864, and all the implements and utensils sold, the buildings being used for other purposes. The books on art, and all the drawings of its most successful period, many of its models, the library, and the ceramic collections, were given to the Austrian Museum, established about that time in Vienna, to be retained as a lasting memorial of its celebrity.

After the factory as a Government establishment was discontinued, a number of the old employés, who had bought undecorated china, painted and gilt the pieces in a similar manner to that in which the china had been decorated previous to 1864, and the merit of these decorators varies very considerably, from the best which equals the highest excellence of the state factory, to that which is unsatisfactory and meretricious by comparison.   When this supply of white china was exhausted, materials were procured elsewhere, and a production of so-called "Vienna" porcelain continued which for some time maintained a certain degree of excellence.   Gradually, however, with competition, prices of production became cheaper and cheaper, and vases, cups and saucers, and *cabarets*, which formerly cost considerable sums, were made so as to tempt a different class of dealer to buy them, than those who had dealt in the older and better class work.   Dutch metal was used instead of gold, elaborately painted subjects were produced by means of photographs transferred to the china and then painted, and in these latter days Vienna china has become a byword for over decorated, garish and tawdry work. Some of this work is done by two or three Dresden firms and a good deal is produced in Paris.

Upon some of the earlier productions the mark was a W, the initial letter of Wien, but specimens were generally unmarked until 1744.

The marks used from 1744, when the factory was acquired by the State, was a shield of the arms of Austria, painted in blue, occasionally impressed; and this simple mark has been continued to the present day.

VIENNA.   This mark is in blue, on an old Vienna *cabaret*, consisting of an oval tray with open-work edge, chocolate pot and cover, milk pot and cover, sucrier and cover, and cup and saucer, all decorated in *camaieu* with lustrous purple ground and rich gilding.   The design on each is a medallion with a bust supported by arabesque cupids.   Besides the *fabrique* mark, as in the margin, the number 85 is impressed.   This signifies the date of manufacture, 1785.   Franks Collection.

VIENNA.   On part of a service of Vienna porcelain : the A faintly stamped.

VIENNA.   On an old Vienna cup and saucer, coarsely painted with lake-colour festoons, edged with blue, gold border, and small detached flowers; the mark blue.

This mark is in lilac colour, on a flower-holder, painted in blue under glaze, and lilac. The body is an oval flask, from the upper edge of which proceed five radiating tubes, the two outer ones supported on camels' heads. The decoration is heraldic; height, 9¾ ins. Franks Collection.

Vienne 12 July 1771

In addition to the usual shield mark, the inscription and date occurs on a circular plaque from the centre of a dish painted in colours with two horsemen in a landscape. It has also the number 81 impressed.

Ant:ᵘˢ Anreiter
VZ: 1755

VIENNA. There are in the Sèvres Museum a cup and saucer, with compartments, of all the colours employed in the manufactory in 1806, and another cup, with those of 1838, and a plate painted with flowers, after Van Huysum, by Joseph Nigg, also a plaque by the same artist, about 1800. Mr. R. Napier, of West Shandon, had a plate painted with the Judgment of Paris, by Nigg.

Joseph Nigg.

VIENNA. There are some finely-painted pieces by an artist of the name of Lamprecht about 1796, who excelled in the representation of animals in the style of Berghem. A beautiful dessert service painted with birds in landscapes, many of the principal pieces being signed by him, is in the possession of Mr. W. Norris of Wood Norton, Norfolk. Lamprecht was afterwards engaged at Sèvres, and is yet remembered as having but one eye, and always working by candlelight.

LAMPRECHT.

VIENNA. The name of this artist is on a porcelain cup and saucer, finely painted with a nest of six cupids, some beginning to fly; drab ground, richly gilt border.

Perger.

VIENNA. This painter's name occurs on a beautifully painted plate, representing Ceres, in the Vallet Collection; and on other pieces with classical subjects.

Foerstler.

VIENNA. An artist's name on a porcelain plate, with highly-finished painting in the centre, of Perseus and Andromeda, rich gold border.

VARSANNI.

K. Herr. VIENNA. One of the best painters at this manufactory; his name is on highly-finished pieces of the beginning of this century, enriched with beautiful gilding; a charming specimen, a *cafétière*, rich gold ground, has a medallion painted with a gipsy showing a cage of three cupids to three young girls who are kneeling before it; formerly in Mr. J. Sanders' Collection; some of these pieces are dated 1814.

J. Wech. VIENNA. The name of a porcelain painter, on a plate; subject, a female clipping Cupid's wings; on others with Aurora, Orion, Apollo, and the Muses, &c.

VIENNA. The art of enamelling on copper was carried to great perfection; the principal artist was Christof Jünger. The Countess of Hopetoun has an enamelled tray, finely painted with a boy playing on the bagpipes and a girl with flowers dancing, inscribed, " *Foⁿ. Leopold Liebᵗ inven et pinxᵗ.*"

In 1907 an important monograph, profusely illustrated from the pens of J. Folnesics and Dr. E. W. Braun, was published, giving the full history of this important factory.

HEREND. HEREND (Hungary). There was a manufactory of porcelain here towards the end of the eighteenth

Herend. century, but we are not informed of its origin. The editor had in his possession a porcelain *cafétière*, or set of four covered pieces, viz., coffee and milk pots and two sugar vases, fitting into a stand, which has as many holes to receive them: painted with large red carnations, gold edges; marked as in the margin in incuse letters; date about 1800. Sometimes we find the word HEREND impressed, and the arms painted on the same pieces. See also mark of shield with crown given below.

HEREND. Porcelain manufactory carried on by Morice Fischer. The mark used by him is the shield of arms of Austria; established in 1839.

HEREND. Another mark of M. Fischer, on a modern porcelain cup and saucer formerly in the possession of Dr. Wadham; the Hungarian arms surmounted by a crown. Some of the porcelain produced here is of fine quality (*hard paste*), and the imitation of Oriental is very clever. There is a *cabaret* of white porcelain, with compartments in green, with flowers, &c., of the end of the eighteenth century; this was stated to have been bought in Ispahan in 1804, and purchased by the Victoria and Albert Museum in 1863 as Oriental; it is, however, now placed with the Hungarian productions. Specimens are also in the Franks Collection.

HEREND. This mark is used by Morice Fischer on his best porcelain; on a part of a service of yellow china formerly in Dr. Diamond's Collection.

Some of the most artistic productions of Morice Fischer were very carefully-finished imitations of old Sèvres: these either bore no mark or that of the fabrique counterfeited.

HEREND. This mark occurs on a cup and saucer, painted with groups in the Chinese style. Nineteenth century. (Victoria and Albert Museum.)

SOME MINOR FACTORIES OF BOHEMIA.

T the end of the eighteenth century there was a considerable industrial development as regards some minor potteries in the northern districts of Bohemia. Some of the factories still continue and others have ceased. They produced stoneware, fayence, and hard paste porcelain, but nothing of really first-class merit. Some exceptions may be made in favour of the Pirkenhammer, and occasionally one finds table services of Schlaggenwald of careful finish. To collectors of marks, however, the numerous signs, both *fabrique* marks and modellers' initials, and stamps afford a considerable field. For more convenient reference the following notices have been arranged under one heading.

SCHLAGGENWALD. *Hard paste.* This is the oldest porcelain manufactory in Austria, except that of Vienna; it was established about the year 1800. George Lippert was the owner in 1842, and much improved this industry; some pieces are marked "Lippert und Haas." There is in the Franks Collection a cylindrical cup and saucer, painted with medallions in colours, with the letter S in black and also the same letter incised. Sometimes the mark is in blue under glaze, and in red over glaze. Specimens occasionally have the S in gold.

S.   *S.*   *S.*   S

SCHLAGGENWALD. On a large cup and saucer, pink, white, and gold, painted with a girl holding a basket of flowers, inscribed "*Ich bringe was sich Freunde wunschen.*" Franks Collection.

SCHLAGGENWALD. The Editor is indebted to Herr Deneken, the curator of the Kaiser Wilhelm Museum in Crefeld, for the following additional marks, not hitherto published in any English book, on Schlaggenwald porcelain :—

ELBOGEN (Bohemia). *Hard paste*. Established 1815, for the manufacture of porcelain; it is celebrated especially by the works of its director and proprietor, M. Haidinger; the mark is an *elbow* or arm holding a sword, stamped without colour; heraldically : *or*, a dexter arm habited

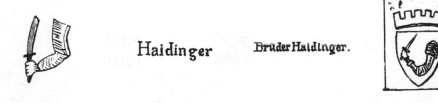

Haidinger   Bruder Haidinger.

gules, holding a scimitar *arg*. It is the sixth shield in the collar surrounding the arms of Austria for Sclavonia. There are several specimens in the Sèvres Museum, painted with landscapes, views of Prague, &c., with ornaments in relief coloured and gilt.

C.F.

F&R

XI   **XI**
CF   **F&B**
4   **4**

S.F.R

PIRKENHAMMER, near Carlsbad. *Hard paste.* Founded in 1802 by Frederick Hölke and J. G. List of Budstadt, in Saxony; they directed this manufactory for sixteen years. In 1818 it was bought by Christian Fischer of Erfurt, who improved it so much that since 1828 it has ranked as one of the first in Austria. The mark is C. F., stamped under the glaze; it was afterwards changed to F. & R., the initials of the proprietors Fischer & Reichembach; it is continued by MM. Fischer & Mieg. In the Franks Collection are two plates painted with fruit and flowers in bright colours, having the marks in the margin impressed.

PIRKENHAMMER. Two other marks of Messrs. Fischer & Reichembach.

The comparatively modern firm of Fischer & Mieg also adopted two hammers crossed as a fabrique mark of their goods.

K & G
PRAG

PRAGUE (Bohemia). The mark is stamped on the base of a statuette of a German warrior in white porcelain, also on some plates painted with figures of peasants, formerly in the Editor's possession. A manufactory carried on by MM. Kriegel & C[ie], successors of M. Prager.

The following additional marks are given on the authority of Dr. Pazaurek, who published, in 1905, the marks of several of these Bohemian minor factories :—

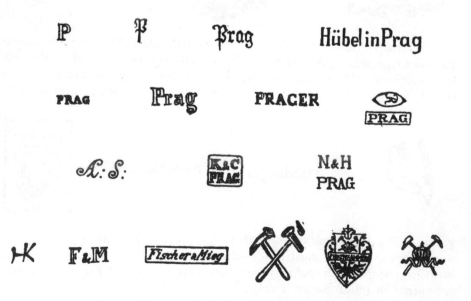

TEINITZ (Bohemia). A small town and castle, with a fine menagerie and convent, belonging to Count Traut-mansdorf, under whose protection this manufactory is carried on by a potter named Welby; we do not know the date of its establishment. This mark is stamped underneath a fine fayence plate, very well painted in bistre *camaieu*, with the discovery of Callisto by Diana, an elegant border in grey, with alternate square and oval white medallions of richly gilt designs; the gilding equals that of Vienna, which it closely resembles; date about 1800. In the Staniforth Collection. (*Ker. Gall.*, enlarged edition, fig. 169.)

TEINITZ. The Editor is indebted to Herr Denkenen of the Kaiser Wilhelm Museum, Crefeld, for the following additional marks found on Teinitz pottery. Some of these are evidently only modellers' stamps. These marks have not been hitherto published in an English book:—

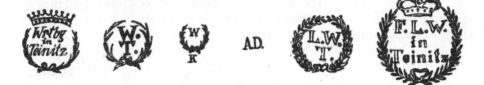

ZWEIBRÜCKEN or PFALZ-ZWEIBRÜCKEN (Bavaria). Nothing was known of any porcelain manufactory at this place until quite recently, and in the editions of Chaffers previous to the present (13th) the mark had been attributed to Strasbourg. In 1907 a monograph of the factory was published in Germany from the pen of Emil Heuser, and it is from this authority that the particulars in this notice have been taken.

Recent researches have brought to light evidence which proves that so early as 1740 attempts at porcelain making were made at Zweibrücken by a man called Councillor Paul, who died in 1753. A little later we hear of a physician named J. M. Stahl, a court favourite, who was associated with a potter named Russigu, formerly one of the modellers at Höchst, and they ultimately started the Zweibrücken porcelain factory under the protection of Christian IV., the reigning Prince. The exact date is not known, but it was flourishing about 1767, and declined in 1771, and after the death of Duke Christian in 1775 appears to have come to an end.

Only table services (hard paste) of quite ordinary quality as decoration, seem to have been produced, but the mark, both under and above the glaze in blue, has been hitherto wrongly attributed, and it is interesting to be able to give some record of a porcelain factory not recognised until now.

GIESSHÜBEL, near Carlsbad. A small factory appears to have been established here in 1803 by a merchant named Christian Nonne, whose name occurs in transactions relating to other Thuringian factories. After 1815 the factory was owned or managed by one Benedikt Knaute, whose initials impressed on specimens were used until 1835. About 1846 another period is denoted by an impressed N G, the initials of W. Ritter von Neuberg, "N" and the name of the place, Giesshübel, "G." The full name of Giesshübel also occurs on some specimens. In 1902 the factory was sold.

In appearance there is little or nothing except a mark to distinguish specimens from those of Closter Veilsdorf or any of the other small Thuringian factories.

The marks given in the margin come in the following order. The dart with two heads or barbs marks the earlier period, and is in blue under the glaze.

The dart with one head or barb comes next.

Then follows the mark of Benedikt Knaute, and afterwards that of Neuberg. In previous editions of Chaffers some of these marks have been erroneously attributed to Gräfenthal.

KLÖSTERLE. Another small Bohemian factory founded in 1793, of which very little seems to be known. The monogram $\mathcal{K}$, which is given by Dr. Gustav Pazaurek as one of the marks, is the same as appears on a Höchst figure (wheel mark) in the Franks Collection, Bethnal Green Museum, and the other marks are in blue under glaze, and also in red, orange, black, and gold over glaze.

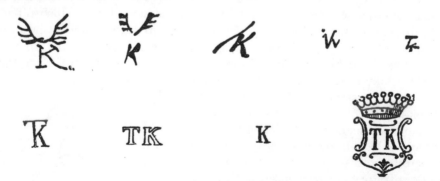

CHODAU, near Carlsbad. Another of the group of small Bohemian factories established in 1804, and of which little is known. The marks, hitherto unpublished in any English work, are given on the authority of Dr. Gustav Pazaurek, who tells us that the earliest is the word "Chodau"

impressed.   Dr. Pazaurek also states that there were four small factories in this place.   The initials P & S were for Portheim & Son, and the others were initials of potters.   There is really little merit in some of these minor factories, but the marks occasionally occur on unimportant specimens, and puzzle collectors.

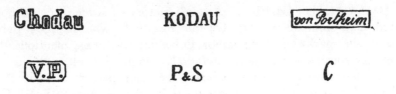

TANNOWA.   Another small and quite insignificant factory, whose marks are given by Dr. Gustav Pazaurek, who tells us that the pottery was started in 1813.

ALTROHLAU, near Carlsbad.   A small factory of *hard paste* porcelain, conducted by A. Nowotny, a short notice of which appeared in the previous edition of Chaffers under the heading "Alten-Rolhaw."   It was founded in 1813, and the marks are both impressed in the paste, and in blue under the glaze.

KLUM

J. Feresch

KLUM. These two marks are given by Dr. Pazaurek, the one, "KLUM," on a stoneware plate, the date of which he says is 1819, and the word Feresch is the name of the potter, impressed, who worked about 1835.

DALLWITZ, near Carlsbad. A small factory of stoneware and porcelain existed here from 1804. Dr. Gustav Pazaurek, who in 1905 published a list of the marks of these minor Bohemian factories, mentions that on the earlier specimens the name *Dalwitz* is stamped, spelt with one L, and that the name with two L's indicate the later period. About 1832 the works were managed by a potter named Lorenz (see mark W. W. L.), and about 1845 by Franz Urfus, whose name and initials appear in the following marks, which are impressed in the paste.

.D   DD   DALWITZ   W.W.L.   F.F.
                                   DALWITZ   D.

F&U   U   DALLWITZER
           DALWITZ   FABRIK
                          FRANZ URFUS

SUNDRY SMALL POTTERIES IN THE BOHEMIAN POTTERY DISTRICT.

The names, generally impressed in the paste of the stoneware and earthenware, with sundry modellers' marks, are given on the authority of Dr. Gustav Pazaurek, whose published list of marks has already been quoted.

Beyereck   BEIRECK. Date about 1824, impressed mark on stoneware only.

B:  AL   BUDAU. First date 1825, mark B, blue under glaze; later mark (impressed) about 1880; the initials of Anton Long.

SCHELTEN. First mark, "Palme" impressed; later mark "Ignaz Balle," 1851-60.

        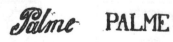   PALME

NEUMARK. Klattau district; impressed mark, date about 1832.

Neumark

KLENTSH. Klattau district; first date 1835; later under Anton Schmidt, 1889; impressed mark.

Klentsch

BUDWEIS. Established by Joseph Hardmuth, formerly in Vienna, 1818, and later carried on by Carl Hardmuth, 1846.

W   **WIEN**   **WIENER**   **HARDMUTH**

FISCHERN, near Carlsbad   First date 1848 (porcelain); impressed marks.

CARLSBAD

CARL KNOLL
CARLSBAD

AICH, near Carlsbad. Porcelain; first date 1849; impressed mark; the initials are modellers' marks.

Aich   **A M**   **AX**

HEGEWALD, near Friedland. First date 1850; impressed marks.

A P H   **R**      **RPM**

HOHENSTEIN, near Teplitz. Maiolica made here in 1850; impressed marks; that of Eichwald is since 1869.

V₃H   **B B**   *Eichwald*

BODENBACH. Imitation of Wedgwood ware, made since 1829. The initials impressed are those of Schiller and Gerbing.

S&G.   **Tetschen**

AUSSIG. First date 1841. The impressed mark being the initials of Joh Maresch; the factory afterwards conducted by Ferdinand Maresch.

J.M

Prussia

BERLIN

MANUFACTORY of porcelain *(hard paste)* was established here by William Gaspar Wegely in 1751, in the new Friedrich Strasse; his invention is thus alluded to in the *Gentlemen's Magazine* for 1753: "There has been discovered here (at Berlin) the whole art of making china-ware, without any particular kind of earth, from a kind of stone which is common enough everywhere. The fine glossy outward coat is prepared from this, as well as the substance of the china, over which, after it is painted, they throw a kind of varnish, which fixes the colouring, and make the figures look as if enamelled, without any mixture of metallic ingredients." The manufactory was carried on for about eight years, but it never remunerated the originator, and he abandoned it in 1761, when Gottskowski, a celebrated banker, became the purchaser; he removed the works to the Leipsiger Strasse; and, assisted by his capital, it was brought to great perfection.

John Ernest Gottskowski obtained the secret of porcelain from Ernest Heinrich Richard, who had been employed by Wegely, for which he received 4000 dollars, and was made director with a salary of 1200 dollars. Gottskowski did not personally manage the manufactory, but placed it under the management of the Commissioner Grunenger, which led to his employment from the year 1763-86 as the head of the Royal Porcelain Manufactory at Berlin. In 1763 Gottskowski gave up to the King the whole of his fabric of porcelain, receiving 225,000 dollars, and entering into a contract for the sale of his secrets. "Grunenger has recorded in his chronicle his labours to obtain the men best adapted for the different departments, among them Richard Bowman, and others of some note. From the specification and inventory drawn up on the occasion, some idea may be formed of the magnitude of his enterprise. There were— 7 administrators, 1 artist, 1 model-master, 2 picture-inspectors, 6 furnace-men, 3 glaze-workers, 5 lathe-turners, 3 potters, 6 mill-workers, 2 polishers, 6 sculptors, 6 embossers, 6 founders, 11 designers, 6 earthenware moulders, 13 potter wheelworkers, 3 model joiners, 1 girdler, 22 porcelain painters, 22 picture colourers, 3 colour makers, 4 packers and attendants, 8 wood-framers—making altogether 147 persons; the attendant expenses were 10,200 dollars. It is calculated that 29,516 red and coloured earthenware, 10,000 white vessels, and 4,866 painted porcelain—many of them of grotesque form, and many of the fashion of the day—were fabricated; articles of every description, groups, vases, flacons, statuary, snuff-boxes, fancy articles, earrings, lamps, and everything that the artist could suggest and the potter carry out. It is satisfactory to know that there exist at the present day 133 models from which these articles were fabricated, and the results of the labour, the energy, and the taste brought into play a hundred years ago may easily be studied" (*Major Byng Hall*). It was in September 1763 that Frederick the Great appeared for the first time in his manufactory, and Grunenger has recorded his Majesty's attentive examination of even the minutest details, and conversed with him on the improvements which might be made. Commissioner Grunenger, Mauritius Jacobi, Nogel, Eichman, Richard, Meyer, Claude, Böhme, and Kleppel continued at the head of the establishment and directed the different departments. A sum of 140,000 dollars was devoted to the improvement of the manufacture.

We read in the *Gentleman's Magazine* for 1764 that "the King of Prussia has at great expense introduced a porcelain manufactory into his dominions, and has already brought it to such perfection as to rival that at Meissen, near Dresden, which his Majesty, during the late war, in a manner ruined. With a view to encourage the manufacture in his kingdom, he made presents of superb services of Berlin china to several German princes in the year 1766. When Frederick the Great occupied Dresden in the Seven Years' War, he expatriated many of the best modellers and painters to form his Royal Manufactory. Among these were the celebrated enamel painter Jacques Claude, and Elias Meyer, the plastic modeller, Klipsel or Kleppel, and Böhme; there was also a modeller of birds and animals, who signs his pieces Efster. The King transported great quantities of the clay and a portion of the collection. Independent of this, and the better to ensure employment for five hundred persons engaged in the processes, he restricted the Jews resident in any part of his dominions from entering into the married state until each man had obtained a certificate from himself, which was only granted on the production of a voucher from the director of the manufactory that porcelain to a given amount had been purchased, and that there was reasonable cause for granting the indulgence. Of course the Jews more readily disposed of their purchases than the general dealers, and the device was attended with much success.[1] To ensure its prosperity and extend its operations, he embraced every opportunity that was presented; and the establishment was so well supported that in 1776 seven hundred men

---

[1] John Sebastian Hensell, in his book on the Mendelssohn family, relates that, in accordance with this degree, Moses Mendelssohn, a philosophical writer (who being a Jew, and not allowed a choice of objects), was "recommended," for due consideration in cash, by the authorities of the newly-founded Royal Porcelain Factory, to accept on his marriage *twenty massive porcelain apes*, each as large as life, some of which are still preserved in various branches of his family.

were constantly employed, and it is said that three thousand pieces of porcelain were made daily."

In 1769 an order was published permitting a lottery company to purchase annually to the amount of 90,000 dollars. In 1771, in the neighbourhood of Brackwitz, not far from Halle, a superior clay was discovered from which a porcelain of exquisite whiteness and beauty was obtained; somewhat later discoveries were made at Beerdersee and at Morland Seumwitz of material of the highest quality, sufficient for consumption during a century, and from thence, at the present day, the Royal Manufactory derives its most valuable material. In 1787 Frederick William II. appointed a commission, under the direction of the Minister Von Stemitz and Count Reden, and great improvements in the management were carried out. Up to the present period, the manufacture has not ceased to deserve the admiration of the public.

The late Mr. S. Rücker had a beautiful and interesting specimen, being a cup and saucer, part of the service presented by Frederick the Great to the Emperor Joseph II. on his coronation; the saucer has a highly-finished equestrian portrait, and the cup his initials, J. II., and the crowns of Austria, Bohemia, and Hungary on a velvet cushion. Mr. S. Rücker had also in his Collection a presentation piece of Berlin porcelain, a cup and saucer; the former has a highly-finished miniature portrait of Frederick the Great, and the latter his initials, F. W., equal in quality and finish to anything produced at Meissen.

In the Franks Collection is a minutely-painted cup and saucer with a portrait bust of Frederick and a tablet on which is inscribed: "*Nat.* 24 Jany. 1712; *Denat.* 17 Aug. 1786, signed, F. Berger, *fe.*" The mark is the usual sceptre in blue.

The Berlin Royal Porcelain Manufactory now works seven kilns, and employs three hundred workmen, the annual produce amounting, on an average, to half a million of finished articles, value 150,000 Prussian dollars. The superintendence is entrusted to M. Kolbe (who succeeded M. Frick in the direction), under whom are Dr. Elsner as chemist, M. Mantel as master-modeller, and M. Looschen as head-painter.

The porcelain manufactories of Berlin and Charlottenburg are both under the direction of M. Kolbe, Councillor of State, employing at the present time sixteen furnaces and about five hundred workmen. At Berlin wood is used for fuel; at Charlottenburg, coal.

At the Berlin manufactory *Lithophanie* was invented. It consisted of white biscuit plaques, the shadows being produced by the graduated thicknesses of the paste, which, when placed against a window, form transparent pictures; also *Lithogéognosie*, or transfer printing on porcelain, was perfected by a celebrated chemist named Pott, on which subject he published an illustrated book as early as 1753.

One of the finest products of Berlin is the magnificent service presented by the King of Prussia in 1818 to the Duke of Wellington.

The modern Berlin mark of the sceptre is sometimes covered with a large gold rose or a green leaf by trade impostors, to conceal it, or the mark is altogether removed by the action of hydrofluoric acid, which also destroys the glaze, and the blemish is concealed by a gold leaf or flower. Some of these pieces have a most imposing appearance, and are in close imitation of old Capo di Monte and other celebrated manufactories, which are frequently sold at high prices to the unwary. We know of a porcelain tankard with coloured nymphs and satyrs in relief, with imitation early silver mounts, and a counterfeit date, 1716, for which a high price was obtained; but there are plenty of others, moulded principally from ivory tankards. The deception may be traced to the neighbourhood of Frankfort, where so many falsifications have of late emanated. They are also made in considerable quantities in Paris.

Frederick, King of Prussia, was very desirous to produce china equal to that of Dresden, and the Berlin mark was frequently made to assimilate, as the following extract from a letter written by the Prince de Ligne to the King of Poland will prove: "One day I turned a plate to see what kind of china it was; on which the King of Prussia said, 'Of what manufacture do you suppose it to be?' I replied, 'Saxon, I think; but instead of two swords I perceive only one; that is fully as good as the two.' 'It is a sceptre,' said the King. 'I beg your Majesty's pardon, but it is so like a sword that one may easily mistake it.' This was indeed true in every respect."

BERLIN. The mark of Wegely from 1751 to 1761, two strokes of the W being longer and crossing each other. In the Franks Collection there is a white group marked with a W in blue, and the model of a lion on some rockwork, also in white, with the same initial boldly incised in the paste like the larger W in the margin. It should be observed that this W for Wegely is invariably accompanied by numbers impressed in the paste, this distinguishes specimens from those belonging to Wallendorf (*q.v.*), with which they are often confused.

This mark in blue is also found on specimens made during the time when the factory belonged to Gottskowski, 1761-63. In the Franks Collection is a cup and saucer painted with ducks and bunches of flowers. The cup is marked with the usual sceptre, and the saucer bears the "G." On both cup and saucer the figure 8 in gold.

BERLIN. In 1761, when it became a royal establishment, the sceptre was used, on painted and gilt porcelain in brown, on white china in blue; the letters KPM are sometimes placed below it, *Königlichen Preussische Manufactur*.

BERLIN. Another form of the sceptre, used about the same time; an eagle is sometimes added with F. on its breast.

KPM

BERLIN. A special mark in blue; it was first used about 1830 on small richly-decorated pieces. The letters represent *Königlichen Porzellan* or *Preussische Manufactur.*

W E

BERLIN. The mark of Wegely, being the first two letters of his name, impressed on an early Berlin vase, painted with a frieze of classical heads round the upper part and gilt leaves at bottom; also on a cup and saucer, dark blue ground with medallions of flowers, formerly in the Reynolds Collection and Lot 97 in the sale catalogue.

BERLIN. The crossed sceptres are sometimes found on the old Berlin ware, evidently to imitate the Dresden mark. This mark in blue, as in the margin, with the number 60 in gold, is on an octagonal sucrier and cover, painted with figures, of decided Saxon pattern. Was formerly in Mr. Loraine Baldwin's Collection.

BERLIN. On a German porcelain teapot decorated with floral arabesque in blue. This is another form of the crossed sceptres.

BERLIN. An early cup and saucer painted with figures and flowers; the crossed swords in blue, the letter red, for Wegely. Formerly in the late Mr. Joseph's Collection: the cup has W only.

BERLIN. These marks are found together on a *cabaret* of translucid porcelain; the pieces, of elegant form, are gilt inside and bordered with classic ornaments in gold, painted round the body with lilies of the valley and festoons upon a mat ground below, all carefully engraved. The marks are the Prussian eagle, with the initials of Frederick the Great on its breast, and KPM in brown, the sceptre in blue under the glaze, and the painter's mark in a neutral colour; also P. W. impressed upon the edge. In the possession of Mr. Lyndal Winthorp. (*Ker. Gall.*, enlarged edition, figs. 222, 3, 4.)

BERLIN. At the present day the porcelain is marked with the stamp annexed in blue, to which is sometimes added the painter's mark.

CHARLOTTENBURG, near Berlin (*hard paste*), established in 1760 by M. Pressel; the mark stamped in colours up to 1830. It now belongs to the Government, and both are directed by M. Kolbe. Ordinary porcelain is made, but of fine quality, for domestic use, which is called *Gesundheitsgeschirr* or *Hygiocérame;* it was intended to serve as a substitute for the pottery with a lead glaze, which was considered injurious from the poisonous nature of the ingredients.

"Charlottenburg was formerly only a small village called Lutzemburg, on the Spree, about two miles from Berlin. The consort of Frederick I., being pleased with its situation, began to build here, and after her death the works were continued by his Majesty, who named the place Charlottenburg, in memory of its having been the favourite retreat of his Queen, Sophia Charlotte. In this palace, one of the most considerable structures in Germany, is a closet furnished with the choicest porcelain, and a tea-table and equipage of solid gold" (*Royal Magazine*, 1759).

These letters are occasionally placed under the eagle to indicate the Berlin porcelain manufacture. Mr. W. Aylen of Southampton has a déjeûner service with the letters T. P. M. beneath the eagle.

B. P. M.

MOABIT, near Berlin. Established in 1835; M. Schumann, proprietor; the mark in blue.

BRANDENBOURG. In the commencement of the year 1713, Samuel Kempe, a miner of Freiberg, who had become one of the principal workmen of Böttger, escaped from Meissen, and offered his services to Frederic de Görne, a Minister of Prussia. A workshop was established at Plauen, on the Havel, near Brandenbourg, belonging to M. de Görne, and they made an inferior sort of porcelain, known as the "porcelain de Brandenbourg," which was taken to Leipzig fair, and sold from 1717 to 1729; after which time we have no further account of it.

WALDENBURG (Silesia). A manufactory of porcelain (*hard paste*), carried on by M. Krister.

ALTWASSER (Silesia). A manufactory of porcelain is still carried on by M. G. Tielsch & Co. There are some other potters at this place,— Messrs. Heuback, Kämpe, and Sontag.

HÖCHST (Mayence). *Hard paste.* Founded in 1720 by Gelz, a fayencier of Frankfort, assisted by Bengraf and Lowenfink; but they were unsuccessful, and called in Ringler of Vienna, who had escaped from that manufactory. In 1740, during the Electorate of John Frederick Charles, Archbishop of Mayence, their porcelain ranked among the first in Europe. About 1760 the celebrated modeller Melchior was engaged, and some very elegant statuettes were produced, also effective designs for vases, &c.; he left the manufactory about 1785, but his successor, Ries, was not so skilful, and his figures having disproportionate heads, the so-called "big-head" period commenced. Christian Gottlieb Kuntze is another celebrated enamel painter of this fabrique; he was born at Frankfort-on-the-Main in 1736, and worked at the porcelain fabriques of Höchst and of Hainau, and was especially celebrated for his beautiful blue and red enamels. On the invasion of the French in 1794, all the materials were sold by auction. Sir A. W. Franks puts the date of Melchior's work at Höchst from 1770 to 1780, when he says that he migrated to Frankenthal, and thence to Nymphenburg, where he died in 1825. There is apparent evidence of this in the great similarity of modelling in these three factories so far as the best class of figure work is concerned. They rank as the very best work of eighteenth century ceramic production, and when good specimens are offered for sale they realise very high prices. In the sale of Sir Walter Gilbey's Collection in 1909, Mr. Amor of St. James's Street gave 320 guineas for a pair of miniature Höchst groups not more than 3 inches high.

HÖCHST (Mayence). This mark is a wheel,—the arms of the Archbishop of Mayence,—sometimes surmounted by a crown, in gold, red, or blue, according to the quality. On a specimen in the Franks Collection bearing this mark there is also a monogram T.K. incised.

HÖCHST (Mayence). Usually the wheel is used without the crown.

HÖCHST (Mayence). Another wheel, with only five spokes; an early mark. Those pieces with the letter M. (Melchior) are very scarce.

HÖCHST (Mayence). Another mark of the manufactory in brownish-red, taken from Brongniart's work, and is very rare. It is probably an impressed mark. In the Franks Collection are some cleverly-modelled little figures, which, besides the wheel in blue, have letters scratched in the paste. One of these has I.K. in a monogram, another MAHM, and another MEILE. (*Ker. Gall.*, enlarged edition, figs. 225, 6, 7.)

The wheel is sometimes accompanied by the letter D. in blue; these are generally figures, the heads of which are rather large in proportion to their bodies, and are the work of a potter of later period, who has already been referred to under Höchst fayence, *q.v.*

This mark is on a cup and saucer painted in colours. On each a small landscape and sprigs. The wheel and I.K. are impressed, and the cypher L.S. is in purple. Franks Collection.

On a statuette of a little boy, with pale blue dress, yellow scarf round waist, pink hat and broken bow in hand. The wheel is in blue, and the figures and letters are incised. Franks Coll.

Bavaria

NUREMBERG

ILL recently the establishment of a porcelain factory was believed to have been founded at Nuremberg as early as 1712 on the authority of a director of the Berlin Museum, who attributed six oval plaques some 2 feet 6 inches in diameter, painted in blue *en camaieu*, four of them representing the Evangelists and the other two, with portraits of the founders themselves, inscribed on the back as follows: On the one, "*Herr Christoph Marz, Anfänger dieser alherlichen Nürnbergeschen porcelain-fabrique, an 1712, ætatis suæ* 60. *Georg Michael Tauber pinxit* A. 30. 0. 22. *November* 1720;" which in English reads thus: "M. Christoph Marz, founder of this magnificent Nuremberg fabrique of porcelain, in the year 1712," &c.; on the reverse of the other is written: "*Her Johann Conradt Romeli anfänger dieser allhiesigen porcelaine-fabrique, an* 1712. *In gott verschieden an* 1720*,*" with the name of the painter as before. Professor Brinckmann, the learned curator of the Hamburg Museum, has seen these plaques and is of positive opinion that they are of fine fayence and *not* of porcelain, and this opinion is quite in agreement with the belief of the Editor of Chaffers that porcelain was never made at Nuremberg. In the early part of the eighteenth century the word "porcelain" was used to describe a fine quality fayence with a beautiful glaze, and this term "porcelain" has doubtless been the cause of an erroneous attribution of such a factory. Mr. Reynolds possessed a large oval fayence plaque, with a portrait of another part proprietor of these works, inscribed on the back: "*Herr* JOHANN JACOB MAYER, *Erkauffer des Romelischen halben Antheils an dieser Porcelaine Fabrique. Año* 1720, *ætatis sue* 30. *Georg Michael Tauber pinxit Año* 1720 ♀ *di* 22 *November.*" "M. J. J. Mayer, purchaser of Romeli's half share of this fabrique in the year 1720, aged thirty." Marz died in 1731, when the establishment was sold, and it afterwards produced a common sort of pipeclay, ceasing entirely about the end of the eighteenth century. M. Demmin has also a square plaque, painted in blue, with the arms of Marz, inscribed as those just mentioned, but stating that he died on the 18th of March 1731. The plaque formerly in the Reynolds Collection described above is now in the Hamburg Museum.

FRANKENTHAL.

FRANKENTHAL (Palatinate, now Bavaria). *Hard paste.* Established in 1754 as a porcelain manufactory by Paul Hannong, who having discovered the secret of hard porcelain, offered it to the Royal Manufactory at Sèvres, but, not agreeing as to price, the offer was declined, and they commenced persecuting him. A decree of 1754 prohibited the manufacture of translucid ware in France except at Sèvres, and he was compelled to carry his secret to Frankenthal, and leave his fayence manufactory at Strasbourg in charge of his sons. Ringler, who had quitted Höchst in disgust after his secret had been divulged, became director. Paul Hannong, on the marriage of his eldest son, Joseph Adam Hannong, in June 1759, gave up to him, for a pecuniary consideration, all interest in the Frankenthal fabrique. Paul Hannong died at Strasbourg, 31st May 1768, ætat. 60. In 1761 it was purchased by the Elector Palatine Carl Theodor, and, by his patronage, attained great celebrity, which it maintained until he became Elector of Bavaria in 1798, when it greatly declined, and all the stock and utensils were sold in 1800, and removed to Greinstadt. The following chronogram denotes the year 1775 :—

VarIantIbVs·fLosCVLIs·DIVersI·CoLores,fabrICæ·
sVb·ReVIVIsCentIs·soLIs.hVIVs·raDIIs.eXVLtantIs·
In·FrankenthaL. ❋

It occurs on two porcelain plates, having in the centre the initials of Carl Theodor, interlaced and crowned, within a gold star of flaming rays; radiating from this are thirty divisions, and on the border thirty more, all numbered and painted with small bouquets *en camaïeu*, of all the various shades of colour employed in the manufactory; on the back is the usual monogram in blue, and "*N. 2.*" impressed. Formerly in the Collection of the Rev. T. Staniforth (*Ker. Gall.*, enlarged edition, fig. 288); and one of them is now in the Franks Collection.

This was one of the most important German factories, and here were made not only table services of both the ordinary and extraordinary descriptions, but every kind of group and figure, ornamental dishes, and vases in great variety. The groups and figures are particularly graceful, charmingly modelled and coloured, some of the more delicate ones being properly classed as Ceramic gems. Within the past twenty years the value of good Frankenthal groups and figures has increased enormously, as a reference to our prices at the end of this volume will indicate.

FRANKENTHAL. The early mark under Hannong was a lion rampant, the crest of the Palatinate, from 1755 to 1761; marked in blue. Collectors should beware of imitations bearing this rare mark, made by Samson of Paris.

FRANKENTHAL. The mark of Joseph Adam Hannong, and often found with the lion. (*Ker. Gall.*, enlarged edition, fig. 229.)

FRANKENTHAL. Second period, when it became a Government establishment. The initials of Carl Theodor under the Electoral crown. A vase and cover with a mythological subject, in the Victoria and Albert Museum, has both this and the preceding mark of Hannong. The Bavarian Government, whose factory at Frankenthal has been closed for nearly a century, have granted the right to use the mark to the present lessee of their Nymphenburg factory, and it therefore appears upon quite modern productions, generally white glazed groups and figures. This is very misleading. and for a Government a particularly unworthy and disingenuous proceeding.

NYMPHENBURG. The arms of Bavaria, impressed on the ware, and sometimes in blue colour (painted). This mark, formerly attributed to Nymphenburg, is, on the authority of the Museum expert of Munich, now included in the Frankenthal marks.

Dr. Darmstaedter has a rococo-shaped vase with red ornaments in relief, and painted in flowers, with this mark.

Dr. Darmstaedter has a group of mother and children with this mark (which by itself is not uncommon), and also $\mathcal{B}$ 6 and A.V. in red. The same collector has also a fine group of a lady scolding a servant for losing a piece of money, with the numeral "7" under the C.T. and "Me" in gold. These are potters' or decorators' marks. The numerals not infrequently found under the monogram C.T. denote the date: thus, 86 should be 1786, and so on.

There is in the Franks Collection an ecuelle, cover, and stand painted with a subject signed P. Hy. Gastel, also "Me" in gold; the former was a famous Frankenthal artist, and specimens signed G. in conjunction with the Frankenthal mark are by him.

FRANKENTHAL. The mark of Paul Hannong, frequently scratched under the glaze or pencilled.

FRANKENTHAL. A mark of Hannong, scratched under the glaze, on a figure formerly in the Collection of the Rev. T. Staniforth.

FRANKENTHAL. This mark has been attributed to Ringler, but not on good authority. Sir A. W. Franks catalogues a specimen with this mark as Frankenthal, but is not certain of its being so.

FRANKENTHAL. These two marks, of a lion rampant and monogram of Joseph Adam Hannong, are on a saucer painted with cattle; the letters beneath are impressed. Formerly in the Collection of the Rev. T. Staniforth, also on a well-modelled figure of a boy dancing, in Dr Darmstaedter's Collection.

FRANKENTHAL. This is probably a painter's mark or that of a modeller; it is placed by the side of the Carl Theodor monogram on a statuette of a man with two faces, holding a medallion on which is a nymph pouring water from an urn.

FRANKENTHAL. This mark is placed by Mr. Marryat as belonging to this manufactory, but it is very doubtful.

In *Altes Bayerisches Porzellan*, by Friedrich Hofmann of Munich, the following additional marks on Frankenthal porcelain are given:—

GREINSTADT. The stock and utensils of the Frankenthal manufactory were purchased in 1800 by M. Von Recum, of Greinstadt. This was recently carried on by Franz Bartolo, whose mark was F.B.

NEUDECH, on the Au, and NYMPHENBURG; established in 1747 by a potter named Niedermayer. The Comte de Hainshausen became patron in 1754, and in 1756 he sent for Ringler, who organised the establishment, and it was then placed under the protection of Maximilian Joseph, Elector of Bavaria. In 1758 this manufactory was altogether removed to Nymphenburg.   On the death of Carl Theodor, his successor, the Frankenthal manufactory was abandoned, and also transferred to Nymphenburg, together with some of the best modellers and painters.   The groups and figures, especially some of the little figures some two and a half or three inches high, are most delicately modelled and beautifully finished, and latterly when these have been offered for sale, have realised almost sensational prices, considering their size.   Some of these are copied from the pictures of the Bavarian artist Adler, and many of the best may be attributed to Melchior, whose work at Höchst and Frankenthal has already been referred to.   (*Ker. Gall.*, enlarged edition, figs. 230, 1, 2.)

The table services of Nymphenburg of the best period are also excellent in paste, painting and gilding.   Heintzmann and Lindeman were famous artists at this factory.

The works are still carried on a few miles from Munich, but the productions are chiefly turned out in the white, and decorated in Munich and elsewhere.   It is therefore not uncommon to find pieces so finished bearing the Nymphenburg impressed shield, which being colourless, escapes notice, and the mark of another factory added in blue.   The very objectionable practice of adding the mark of the old Frankenthal (Carl Theodor) monogram has been specially alluded to in the chapter on Imitations and Misleading Marks.

In the Sèvres Museum are three cups and saucers, with portraits of Maximilian Joseph, King of Bavaria, his Queen, and daughter, Princess Auguste-Amelie d'Eichstadt, painted by *Auer;* a cup, with a view of Munich, &c., obtained from the manufactory in 1808.

NYMPHENBURG, near Munich.   These marks, in blue, are on a cup of blue and red ornaments on white; the two L's impressed; the saucer has the arms of Bavaria only impressed.

This mark occurs on a tankard with the sides moulded in relief in panels painted in colours, with groups of flowers, pewter cover.   The shield is that of Bavaria impressed, the date 1765 is in gold, two leaves and I.A.H. in green.   Franks Collection.

This impressed form of the shield in a quatrefoil is on a cup and saucer with straight sides decorated in green and gold, silhouettes of lady and gentleman in oval frames, rich green festoons.   Franks Coll.

NYMPHENBURG.   This mark is on a pair of biscuit statu-ettes.   The shield impressed, and the letters C.A. and H. incised.   Franks Collection.

The following marks occur upon specimens of Nymphenburg porce-lain in the Franks Collection, some of the inscriptions are in colour (red or lilac); the shield is as usual impressed, and some of the letters are incised in the paste:—

NYMPHENBURG.   A tankard of porcelain, painted with figures emblematical of the four quarters of the globe: probably a painter's signature: it has the arms of Nymphenburg impressed.   Formerly in the Reynolds Collec-tion, and formed Lot 500 in the sale catalogue.

I.A.H
j778
D.17.8ᵉᵞ

NYMPHENBURG.   This word occurs on a plate of embossed basket pattern, painted with flowers inscribed on the back as in margin.

C. H. Silberkamer
1771.

The words mean "room for silver," and was probably marked on a ducal service, but it is certainly not the name of a person (artist or potter) as has been supposed.   The initials C. H. probably stand for Curfürstlich Hessich (Elector of Hesse).

NYMPHENBURG.   On a cup in the Collection of Mr. Revilliod of Geneva.

J. Willand Jⁿ

NYMPHENBURG.   The name of this artist occurs on a porcelain cup and saucer, painted with landscapes and figures, green and gold border; stamped with the shield, and name painted in full.   Formerly in the Reynolds Collection, and formed Lot 498 in the sale catalogue.

C. G. LINDEMAN
Pinxit.

62

Klein

77

NYMPHENBURG. The shield stamped, the name and figures in red, probably the painter's name.

NYMPHENBURG. This mark, painted in blue, of two intersecting triangles, with mystic characters at each point af the angle, varies on different specimens; probably Masonic. There are several specimens in the Franks Collection, and in addition to the impressed shield and the interlaced triangles the figure 5 or PD. incised.

These additional marks (generally impressed) are given on the authority of Friedrich Hofmann's catalogue of the collection in the Munich Museum : —

WURTZBURG (Bavaria). Hard paste. Eighteenth century; marked in blue with the mitre of the Prince-Bishop. No particulars are known.

Bäyreith

1744

BAYREUTH, formerly a Margraviate, under the same Government as Anspach, now annexed to Bavaria. *Hard paste.* There was a manufactory of pottery here as early as the sixteenth century, which has been noticed elsewhere. The town is about forty-one miles north-east of Nuremberg, and there still exists a manufactory, at which porcelain as well as fine fayence is made, at a village adjacent, called St. George-sur-l'Estang, on the opposite side of the Main. This mark, in gold letters, is on a cup, well painted with a view of the town, and figures in costume of the latter part of the last century; in the possession of Sir Henry B. Martin. The letters "F.M.," now defaced, are above, and "No. 24" below.

The making of *hard paste* porcelain is said by Dr. Brinckmann to have commenced here about 1766, although a previous attempt had been made some twenty years earlier. Very little is known of this factory, and the signature of "Metzsch" with date 1748, on a tall cup in the Franks Collection, is considered by Sir A. W. Franks to be that of a painter on and not a manufacturer of porcelain.

The making of *hard paste* porcelain is said to have commenced here in 1836 by a potter named Schmidt, who in that year presented some specimens to the Sèvres Museum, and a mark in margin appears with date 1744; on the tall cup in the Franks Collection is the date 1748, accompanied by the painter's signature, and a contraction of the word Bayreuth. Dr. Brinckmann thinks 1766 is the date of porcelain making, but reliable facts are unobtainable.

This mark is on a tall cup painted in colours, with a view of the terrace of a chateau, with group of courtly figures, large ship, &c., inside gilt. Franks Collection. *Ker. Gall.*, enlarged edition, fig. 234.

This mark on a small cup painted with rococo festoons in pink with gilding. Besides the C.B. in grey under glaze and H.B. there is a shield impressed indistinctly. Franks Coll.

BAYREUTH. Another mark; sometimes only the letter B is used.

BAYREUTH. On a well-painted porcelain cup, gilt fluted base, painted with landscapes and figures round the upper part in lake *camaieu*. In the Franks Collection.

ANSPACH. *Hard paste.* There was a factory here for fayence which has already been referred to in the section of the book dealing with German pottery, but at what date the manufacture of *hard paste* porcelain commenced is not known. Dr. Brinckmann thinks about 1760, although by some writers a date as early as 1718 has been named, but it is very improbable. The locality of the factory has also been in some doubt. Marryat mentions Anspach in Thuringia, but as there is no such place mentioned in the gazetteers as in Thuringia, it is almost certain that the Anspach meant is the former Margraviate in Bavaria, and Sir A. W. Franks in his notes

accompanying his catalogue of his collection of Continental porcelain tells us that the factory was removed in 1764 to the Margrave's schloss at Bruchberg. The eagle which surmounts the shield is one of the marks in the heraldic sign of Brandenburg, and the A is the initial letter of Anspach. It was not a factory of much importance, and its productions are similar to the old Hague porcelain. There are several excellent specimens in the Franks Collection, and these bear some of the marks given in the margin.

ANSPACH. This is another variety of the Anspach mark given above. It occurs on a cup and saucer in the Franks Collection.

ANSPACH. *Hard paste.* On a porcelain milk-ewer, beautifully painted in lake *camaieu*, with a landscape and richly-gilt scroll borders. In the Collection of the late Mr. Sigismund Rücker.

ANSPACH. Another modification of this mark, in blue under the glaze, which M. Greslou erroneously attributes to Meissen, as the monogram of Augustus, King of Poland, surmounted by the eagle. (*Ker. Gall.*, enlarged edition, fig. 233.)

ANSPACH. This mark is graved in the clay before baking, on a cup and saucer, painted with female portraits, formerly in the Collection of the Rev. T. Staniforth.

ANSPACH or BAYREUTH. On a German porcelain cup and saucer, painted with flowers and heart's-ease, in the Collection of the Rev. T. Staniforth.

Unknown mark. Germany, perhaps Anspach. On a decorative plate.

Brunswick, Wurtemberg, Baden, &c.

FÜRSTENBERG

THIS manufactory was established in 1750 by Bengraf, who came from Höchst : he died the same year, and Baron von Lang, a distinguished chemist, undertook the direction of the works under the patronage of Charles, Duke of Brunswick. The manufactory has been carried on by the Government up to the present time.

In 1807 a Sèvres Museum obtained from the manufactory a plate painted with classical subjects, by Brüning; a coffee-cup, decorated in gold by Heinze, and other specimens. M. Stünkel, director of the fabrique in 1840, also presented other pieces.

The porcelain is good, *hard paste*, but somewhat cold in effect. This factory produced some good busts in biscuit, and some of these, such as portrait medallions by well-known modellers of the time, Rombrich, Schubert and others have been made to form part of the decoration of vases and cups. Generally the appearance of Fürstenberg porcelain resembles the productions of Fulda and other similar German factories.

FÜRSTENBERG (Brunswick). *Hard paste.*
The mark is an F, of various forms, pencilled in blue. Initials are frequently seen below the letter of the fabrique, probably those of the painters; on one in the editor's possession are R.R.; on another A.C.; on a third the name *Beck.* This mark was originally given by Brongniart, but it is doubtful whether it was ever the fabrique mark of Fürstenberg. The Editor has reason to believe that it was the initial letter of a maker named Frankenheim, who made some passable groups and services about fifty years ago.

FÜRSTENBERG. On a plate, light green ground, perforated border, painted in the centre in purple *camaieu*, with figures after Watteau. Victoria and Albert Museum.

515

FÜRSTENBERG.   Other forms of the letter F; marked in blue.

A *specialité* of this factory was the production of portrait medallions of celebrities, and the busts of royal and noble personages in relief was a favourite decoration on vases, the relief parts being in *biscuit*.

There is in the Franks Collection an important bust in biscuit of Augusta, Duchess of Brunswick, grand-daughter of King George II.   The base bears the mark as in the margin at the bottom of the previous page,

but on the truncated part of the bust there is a very minute running horse, impressed with the letter W. The mark is so minute and indistinct that it might pass unnoticed, but that in the same collection there are some small oval portrait medallions which have 'the horse' more distinctly impressed.   In the previous edition of Chaffers this mark was attributed to Hesse-Cassel.   (*Ker. Gall.*, enlarged edition, fig. 245.)

HÖXTER.   One of the men who obtained the secret from Ringler, named Paul Becker, after having tried in vain to sell it in France and Holland, occupied the fabrique at Höxter, and produced some fine pieces, sufficient to arouse fears of rivalry on the part of the Duke of Brunswick, who made terms with him, so that his manufactory was abandoned; the mark used by him is unknown.   A painter of flowers, named Zieseler, made porcelain here about 1770; it did not succeed, and Paul Becker afterwards carried on the works.

NEUHAUS, near Paderborn.   1750.   Von Metzsh, a mixer of colours at the Fürstenberg manufactory, escaped with two others, and commenced making porcelain, but they were soon discovered, and obliged to discontinue it.   See notice of this painter in notice of Bayreuth, p. 513.

LUDWIGSBURG or LOUISBURG, called also KRONENBURG (Würtemberg). Porcelain *(hard paste)*.   This manufactory was established by Ringler in 1758, under the patronage of Charles Eugène, the reigning Duke.   It was celebrated for the fine paintings on its vases and services, as well as for its excellent groups, but the paste is coarse.   After Ludwigsburg ceased to be the ducal residence in 1775, the prosperity of the factory gradually declined, and it ceased in 1824.   The mark is the double C, for the name of Duke Charles, combined with a high German ducal crown

surmounted by a cross.   The mark of two C's with a Count's coronet, which is frequently attributed to this town, belongs to Niderviller.   Collectors are cautioned against very clever imitations of old Ludwigsburg groups and figures bearing a mark precisely the same as that on the genuine old productions; careful examination and comparison are necessary.

LUDWIGSBURG. Another mark; the double C surmounted by a crown and a cross. Sometimes an initial letter or monogram in red or blue, occurs in addition to this mark.

LUDWIGSBURG. Another mark of the cipher without a crown; must not be confounded with the interlaced C's of Niderviller.

Although Charles Eugène died in 1793, the same ciphers (CC) were used until 1806, when the letters under the crown were changed to T.R., and in 1818 to W.R., but these are rarely met with.

LUDWIGSBURG. These marks, in blue, are on the bottom of a cup and saucer, painted with the initials V and G in flowers; the cup has the L only, the saucer the arms of Würtemberg, the three stags' horns. In the Franks Collection.

LUDWIGSBURG. This shield and the letter K impressed are on a coffee-pot in the Victoria and Albert Museum, also on two cups and saucers, decorated with sprigs of flowers. Formerly in the Loraine Baldwin Collection.

LUDWIGSBURG. The letters T.R. under a crown were used from 1806 (the first year of the King's reign) until 1818.

LUDWIGSBURG or THURINGIAN. On a porcelain cup and saucer, drab ground, coarsely painted with Venus and Cupid, border of masks. Formerly in the Collection of the Rev. T. Staniforth, now in the Franks Collection. Sir A. W. Franks thinks it is Thuringian.

LUDWIGSBURG. On a porcelain cup and cover, painted with roses and other flowers, the mark in red, and a D impressed. Franks Collection. Also upon a custard cup painted with sprigs of flowers. This has the letters D.F. also incised as well as the mark. Franks Collection.

LUDWIGSBURG. This mark of the letters W.R. under a crown was used from 1818.

LUDWIGSBURG. This mark of a stag's horn, from the arms of Würtemberg, was used at a later period; a cup and saucer, light yellow ground with brown scroll border, has this mark in blue; also on a coffee-pot now in the Franks Collection. (*Ker. Gall.*, enlarged edition, figs. 247, 8, 9.)

HILDESHEIM (Hanover). *Hard paste.* Established about 1760, marked in blue; sometimes the letter A only.

FULDA (Hesse). Established about 1763 by Arnandus, Prince-Bishop of Fulda, for the manufacture of porcelain. *Hard paste.* The mark (in blue signifies *Fürstlich Fuldäisch* (belonging to the Prince of Fulda). The best artists were employed, and many grand vases, figures, and services produced, of a fine white paste, and handsomely decorated. The pieces are scarce, as the greater part were reserved for the Prince-Bishop, and they have lately increased enormously in value. The Prince's successor, Henri de Butler, in 1780 abandoned the manufacture, which, however, seems to have been carried on until about 1790. There is some evidence of this in an interesting cup and saucer in the Franks Collection, the cup being ornamented with the bust of an old man wearing an order, and on the saucer E.A.H.F.P. in cypher in a gilt frame. Sir A. W. Franks is probably correct in assuming these letters to signify Prince-Bishop Adalbert von Herstall, 1788-1814. The specimens are marked with the double F. under crown in blue as in the margin.

A cup and saucer, ornamented with a biscuit medallion portrait, is in the Victoria and Albert Museum. There are also some specimens with this mark in the Franks Collection.

FULDA. A cross, the arms of the Bishopric of Fulda, is frequently found upon groups of figures and other specimens. (*Ker. Gall.*, enlarged edition, figs. 241, 2, 3, 4.) In the Franks Collection there is a figure in Oriental costume well modelled in plain white porcelain, also a cup and saucer painted with landscapes bearing this mark.

This very rare mark is upon a conical cup with shaped handle, coarsely painted in flowers, and Sir A. W. Franks has considerable doubts in attributing it to Fulda, but thinks that it may have been a trial piece. Franks Collection.

BADEN. *Hard paste.* Established in 1753 as a porcelain manufactory by the Widow Sperl and some workmen from Höchst, with the patronage of the reigning Margrave, under the direction of Pfalzer; it ceased in 1778. The mark is an axe or the blade of an axe in gold.

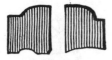

BADEN. The sign of the Widow Sperl, at the Grunenwinckel, in gold, on four porcelain figures of females, emblematical of Sculpture, Architecture, Poetry, and Painting; coloured and gilt, 10 inches high; in the Collections of the Rev. T. Staniforth and Mr. Bohn. M. Jacquemart gives this mark as two axe-*heads* only, without the handles, and the Editor thinks he is correct.

BADEN. This mark, the checks in gold, on blue ground, is on a china mug painted with flowers and birds, blue and gold border. It is very doubtful whether this mark is not a variation of that of Nymphenburg.

CASSEL or HESSE-CASSEL. A factory of *hard paste* porcelain is said to have been established here about 1766 as a development of a previously existing fayence factory, and to have carried on an extensive business chiefly in the production of table services, which were more of the domestic character than such as rank as cabinet specimens. A peculiarity of the decoration was a ribbed surface, and the painting generally of a slight character in flowers. Some groups and figures were also made, but no great excellence was ever attained. The mark of a running horse  (impressed), which in former editions of Chaffers was attributed to this factory, has now been rightly included in the Fürstenburg marks, *q.v.* Those in the margin of a lion rampant, which must not be confused with another lion rampant of Frankenthal, and the letter H.C. standing for Hesse-Cassel, are the usual marks on specimens of the factory, which ceased in 1788.

HESSE-DARMSTADT (Kelsterbach). The manufacture of porcelain here, as in so many other places, followed the making of fayence, and is believed to have only lasted from about 1758 until 1772. In general appearance there is little to distinguish specimens from those of the Fulda factory. This mark is attributed by M. A. Jacquemart to Hesse-Darmstadt; it occurs on a cup and saucer, with a black portrait of a gentleman and neat border of flowers; and the monogram of HD without the crown is on another cup and saucer, pink ground, with a view of a town. Franks Collection.

There is also in the Franks Collection a figure of a harlequin seated on the stump of a tree, wearing a lilac jerkin and yellow breeches, which bears this same mark, which is very rare, and signifies Hesse-Darmstadt. (*Ker. Gall.*, enlarged edition, fig. 236.)

Thuringia

HE group of about a dozen porcelain factories in the district of Thuringia have an interest not only for collectors of the older and more decorative specimens of these manufactories, but also because this pottery district has become quite an important centre of the German Ceramic industry. Little was known about these factories until the publication, in 1909, of an important work on the subject issued from the Leipzig press, and by the authority of the State Museum. It is entitled, "Alt thuringer Porzellan," by Richard Graul and Albrecht Kurzwelly, and gives an account of the development of the industry from small beginnings—a great many illustrations of specimens known to have been produced by the several fabriques, and the record of a great many marks and monograms which hitherto have been unpublished, and through insufficient knowledge have been wrongly attributed to other factories.

Until the first half of the eighteenth century had passed, there was no sign of any effort to make porcelain in this district. The great Meissen works under royal patronage, the factory of Berlin, and lesser ones at Frankenthal, Nymphenburg, Ludwigsburg, and many other places were all under royal or ducal protection, and the group of Thuringian factories differ in their origin from all of these, inasmuch as they appear to be the result of the enterprise and industry of merchants and potters of the time, taking advantage of the local resources of material suitable for the manufacture of true porcelain in this district, and were not carried on as the hobby or plaything of royal or noble amateur patrons. Gotthelf Greiner seems to have been the leading spirit of the enterprise, and Georg Heinrich Mackeleid, as an able chemist, seconded his efforts. Greiner was born February 22, 1732, the son of a glass blower, at Alsbach, and passed his youth at Limbach, where it was intended that he should follow the calling of his father, but he got into touch with the porcelain-making movement, and finding a potter named Dümmler to co-operate with him, they started in a small way, pipe-bowls and cups being their first productions. In 1762 a concession was obtained from the Duke of Saxe-Meiningen, and a potter named Hammann, from Katzhütte, being taken into partnership, the concern appears to have succeeded—the burning, turning, and painting being executed at Katzhütte, while the body and glaze were produced at Limbach. Greiner subsequently left Limbach and started other factories, and, as will be seen in the short notices of the individual factories which follow, he was apparently a man of restless energy, who did not remain long at any one place. He had sons who followed him, and these and his connections, nephews and sons-in-law, came eventually to own, or part own and manage, nearly all the china-making concerns in the district. The best of these factories may be given in the order adopted by the monograph already quoted:—1, Volkstedt; 2, Kloster Veilsdorf; 3, Gotha; 4, Wallendorf; 5, Gera; 6, Limbach; 7, Ilmenau; 8, Grossbreitenbach; 9, Rauenstein. There is mention of three or four smaller efforts, which only existed for a very short time, and scarcely survived the initial stages, namely, Tettau, Schney, and Kutzhütte.

In 1904 there was a special exhibition of Thuringian porcelain at Leipzig, which served to convey some idea of the importance of this local industry. If we compare the modelling of groups and figures of the Limbach, Volkstedt, and other contemporary factories named above, with the best of Meissen modelled by Kändler, of the Frankenthal, by Konrad Link, of Höchst, by Melchior, or of Nymphenburg by Bastelli, one misses the courtly grace, the delicacy or piquancy of these Ceramic gems, but one finds instead, careful work, strict attention to details, and an individuality which has much charm.

The paste or body of the porcelain, which is hard, is not pure white, like the fine old Meissen clay, but of a greyish tint, and the glaze is less transparent and not free from specks. As regards modelling, the figures are somewhat stiff, and the drawing a little out of proportion, but as types of peasant life these figures have quite a historic value. There were some good groups of mythological personages, many of musicians, actors, and soldiers, and that these forest potters were not deterred by the technical difficulties attending figures of unusual size, is evidenced by two statues in Limbach porcelain in the Weimar Museum of boys, which are about 36 inches high.

Table services and domestic ware were very largely produced, and flower-painting was a specialité. From 1760 to about 1780 those specimens which interest the collector, or what may be termed cabinet specimens, were made; after that time the conditions of these factories rendered it necessary that commercial standards should decide the character of the productions, and gradually the more artistic efforts were sacrificed to the useful and profitable.

Thuringia is still one of the great china-producing centres of Germany, and exports largely both to other parts of the empire and to foreign countries. As with certain exceptions, which will be mentioned in the following notices, the descriptions of the kind of china and class of decoration are common to nearly all this group of Thuringian factories, it will be unnecessary to give more than the dates of founding, changes of proprietorship, and illustrations of the various marks and monograms in use at the individual undertakings.

VOLKSTEDT. Although the factories of Gotha and Kloster Veilsdorf were in existence some few years before that at Volkstedt, this was the first of the Thuringian group which worked under State privilege. The founder, a chemist named Georg Heinrich Mackeleid, obtained State protection in 1760, and was joined by Johann Andreas Greiner, the Court painter, and later by his brother, Johann Georg Greiner, who appears to have undertaken the more technical management of the factory. He had, unknown to his partners, purchased the Gera factory, and he left Volkstedt to work at his own undertaking. Shortly afterwards both the Gera and Volkstedt factories became amalgamated.

VOLKSTEDT. This mark, a hayfork, is part of the arms of Schwartzburg (a hayfork and curry-comb); it is on a pair of candlesticks with blue flowers, formerly in possession of the author; also on a tankard in a mount of the last century. There is in the Franks Collection an oblong plateau painted with a medallion of a building near a stream bearing this mark.

VOLKSTEDT. The same mark, crossed, is on some pieces of porcelain, formerly in possession of the Rev. T. Staniforth. Dr. Darmstaedter of Berlin has a figure of a man with a basket of grapes, with this mark in blue, and "Greiner 1768" scratched in the paste.

VOLKSTEDT. This mark is made expressly to imitate the Dresden, the style of the Marcolini period being closely copied, as well as the form of the cup; gilt ring handle at top, and angular handle. It is on a cup, cover, and saucer, beautifully painted with groups of flowers.

The trefoil mark common to several of those Thuringian factories was also used, painted in different colours.

KLOSTER VEILSDORF. The founder of this factory was Prince Friedrich Wilhelm Eugene von Hildburghausen, who, owing to his position, was allowed to carry on the undertaking without the special State concession required in those days for a porcelain manufactory. The actual manager was a man named Bayer, and State protection was granted in 1765. Work of fairly artistic merit was produced, but the financial results were unsatisfactory, and in 1789 the services of Wilhelm Heinrich Greiner were obtained to improve the sales of the ware, as the losses were a heavy drain upon the Prince founder's income. The productions of the factory in 1790 amounted to about 13,000 florins, and, in the absence of customers, a huge stock was accumulated. The Prince died in 1795, and left the factory to his nephew, but a Government Commission would not recognise the bequest as valid, probably on account of the debts incurred in carrying on the factory, and it was sold in 1797 to the sons of Gotthelf Greiner, who was interested in several of the factories of this group.

KLOSTER VEILSDORF. *Hard paste.* The mark in the margin is upon a shaped tray with handles, edges moulded in rococo style and painted blue, bunches of flowers in centre. Franks Collection.

KLOSTER VEILSDORF. The letters C and V, sometimes interlaced.

KLOSTER VEILSDORF. Another mark, quoted by Mr. A. Joseph as unknown, but it is probably also of the same manufactory.

KLOSTER VEILSDORF. On a milkpot and cover painted with landscapes on a border of flowers. Victoria and Albert Museum. The arms are those of Saxe-Meiningen. (*Ker. Gall.*, enlarged edition, fig. 238.)

The following marks are given on the authority of Graul and Kurzwelly :—

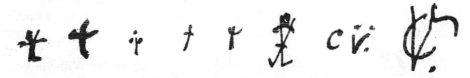

GOTHA. This is actually the oldest of the little group of Thuringian factories, and the actual date of its commencement is uncertain. In the monograph on these factories, which has already been quoted, there is a letter given from a Court official and statesman of the Duchy named Rotberg—written to a chemist named Paul, asking him to quit his employment at Fürstenburg and join him at Gotha, but Paul refused. This letter was dated 1758, and there is a specimen of Gotha porcelain in the Leipzig Museum bearing the mark of " R—g," the first and last letters of Rotberg's name, and also the date 1763. In 1767 the factory was enlarged and new buildings added, and the output must have been considerable, and this continued until 1805. The leading spirits of the undertaking were three craftsmen named Schulz, Gabel, and Brehm, who joined the staff in 1772, and remained until the beginning of the nineteenth century.

Rotberg died in 1795, and his widow sold the concern to Prince August of Gotha in 1802. The prince entrusted the management to

Schulz, Gabel and Brehm, and added to the directorate a former valet of his named Henneberg, who, about 1813, became sole proprietor, and it was by him that the factory was removed to its present site. He died in 1834, and was succeeded by sons and grandson, who directed until 1881, after which the factory passed to the possession of Simson Brothers.

The products of the Gotha factory were superior in quality to those of many of its kindred factories. They affected classic forms for the vessels of the table services, and a favourite decoration was to paint portraits, sometimes modelled in relief, in oval medallions. Silhouette portraits in black also occur. The mark of R—n, and of R, which stand for Rotberg, have been given erroneously in many books as indicating Rothenberg and Rudolstadt. This latter place was the seat of government, but not the site of a factory.

R   GOTHA. An early mark of the factory used previous to 1790.

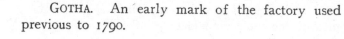

R. *g.*   ROTHENBERG (Gotha). The first and last letters of the name Rotberg, in blue, are on a cup and saucer, with landscapes in bistre on white ground; there is also the letter Z or N on both pieces, but it does not belong to the mark before mentioned, and may be the painter's initial. This mark was only used from 1790 until 1805, after which the cursive G became the mark. Previous to 1790 only the letter R was used. There are several pieces in the Franks Collection.

G
G   GOTHA. *Hard paste.* Founded by Wilhelm von Rotberg. The mark, a G of this form for the name of the town, was used after 1805.

Gotha.   GOTHA. The name thus on a cup and saucer, with two views of Gotha; marked in blue. (*Ker. Gall.*, enlarged edition, figs. 258, 9.)

        GOTHA. On a white porcelain tea service, with handsome gold pattern borders; in Dr. Diamond's Collection. This is a much later mark than the cursive G.

Sometimes the inscription is "PORZELLAN MANUFAKTUR GOTHA."

Herr Jännike mentions the mark of a firm named Simson Frères since 1875, whose mark is the word "Gotha" underneath a shield with the letter ⑀.

The following additional marks are given from Graul and Kurzwelly's monograph : —

WALLENDORF. This factory was founded by a potter named Hammann who had carried out some successful experiments at place called Katz-kütte in 1762, but further proceedings being forbidden, the necessary state patronage was obtained for carrying on a factory at Wallendorf in 1764. A company was formed by Hammann, his son and brother, and Gotthelf and Johann Greiner, but after seven years' working Gotthelf left the firm and started the Limbach factory in 1772. Other partners joined Hammann, but at the death of the latter in 1833 the factory was sold, and in 1897 it was worked by a limited company.

WALLENDORF (Saxe-Coburg). *Hard paste.* Established by Greiner and Hammann in 1762. This mark is given by Marryat, but there are so many W's that it is difficult to identify their locality with any degree of certainty. There is one distinction to be remarked between the two foreign marks of Wegely and Wallendorf, that specimens attributed to Wegely invariably have the W accompanied by numbers impressed in the paste.

Mr. H. E. B. Harrison has a can and saucer with this mark; the W varying on the can and the saucer, painted with a carefully executed miniature equestrian portrait of Frederick the Great. (*Ker. Gall.*, enlarged edition, figs. 261, 2.)

The following additional marks are given on authority of Graul and Kurzwelly's monograph : —

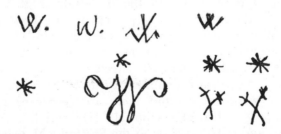

GERA. This factory was started in 1780 by a fayence maker named Johann Gottlob Ehwaldt, who found suitable clay near to the place where he lived, and having found a collaborator in a potter named Gottbrecht, they made some successful experiments. Two members of the Greiner family appear to have assisted them in obtaining the necessary privilege from the reigning Duke, and also to have been associated with the under-taking, for contemporary accounts show that Greiner had an angry cor-

respondence with Nonne and others of the Volkstedt factory, to whom he
was still bound. Eventually some compromise was arranged by an
amalgamation of the two concerns, but later on Gera again became independent under the ownership of the Greiners. Soon after 1782 we read
of a nett annual profit being made of 5000 to 7000 thalers, and of twelve
to sixteen turners being employed. After the Greiners death, a man
named Gustav Heinrich Leers appears to have owned the undertaking, and
obtained a privilege from the State to last for thirty years. The factory
is still in existence. A spécialité in the decoration of Gera porcelain is
the imitation of the graining of various woods, relieved by little pictures
like cards thrown on the surface. The mark of a G has sometimes a
peculiarity which will distinguish it from the Gotha G, by having a hook
at the upper part of the letter. The full word " Gera " is the mark of a
later period. There are two specimens in the Franks Collection. (*Ker.
Gall.*, enlarged edition, figs. 255, 7.)

The following marks are given on the authority of Messrs. Graul and
Kurzwelly's monograph :—

$$\mathcal{G} \quad \mathcal{G} \quad \mathcal{G} \quad \mathcal{G} \quad \mathrm{G} \quad \mathit{Gera} \quad \mathrm{C}$$

There is an important group of figures of Gera porcelain in the
Leipzig Museum, which is dated 1780.

LIMBACH. Some particulars of the early history of this factory,
which is one of the most important of the Thuringian group, have
been given in the notice at the commencement of this chapter. The
Greiners and Hammann were concerned in this and also with several
other kindred factories, and Gotthelf Greiner having severed his connection with Hammann started the undertaking at Limbach in 1772.
In 1781 a good reputation for porcelain had been established, and
some fifty people were employed. Greiner handed the management
over to his sons in 1792, and he died in 1797. Excellent figure
work of the distinctive character affected by these forest potters was
turned out at Limbach, and a painter of considerable merit named Heinrich
Elias Dressel worked here, and there are specimens marked with one
and sometimes with two of his initials, HD and D. A famous barber's
bowl, marked and dated 1778, is in the Stuttgart Museum. Flower painting was well executed, and many table services may still be seen, but so
many specimens of this and other Thuringian factories are unmarked that
it is difficult to attribute them. Some of the best modellers of the well-
known costume figures of peasants, musicians, and mythological personages were Jensel, Heumann, Kinzl, and Gabler. The earlier mark is
the monogram LB in two different formations. The crossed swords were
also used, but upon a threat of legal process by the Meissen authorities,

this was discontinued in favour of a trefoil, which one finds painted in different colours.

LIMBACH (Saxe-Meiningen). *Hard paste.* This manufactory was also under the direction of Gotthelf Greiner; established about 1761. The marks are said to be a single or double L; but there appears to be some confusion in the appropriation.

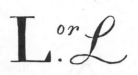

Mr. H. E. B. Harrison has a can and saucer, very carefully painted in animal subjects, marked with this L in blue, and there are also incised marks of H on the saucer and on the can. (*Ker. Gall.*, enlarged edition, figs. 253, 4.)

Mr. H. E. B. Harrison of Liverpool has two figures of men, in costumes of the later half of the eighteenth century, each holding a letter in his left hand, and on the cap of the one is a monogram

 (T.J.R.), and on that of the companion figure D.G. The mark is that in the margin painted in red.

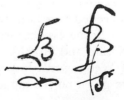

LIMBACH. On a cup and saucer painted in lake *camaieu*, with landscapes and figures; the mark also in red.

LIMBACH. This mark is on a cup and saucer painted with a cottage in a landscape in Indian-ink.

LIMBACH (?). This mark, in violet, is on a porcelain cup and saucer, painted in violet, and on a service formerly in the possession of Messrs. Litchfield and Radclyffe.

These marks occur on two custard or cream pots, with blue sprigs of flowers. Formerly in the Loraine-Baldwin Collection, now in the possession of his niece, Mrs. Millett.

LIMBACH. A double L, frequently found on German porcelain; it is probably Limbach.

LIMBACH.   On white porcelain; the mark in blue under the glaze.   Another variety of the L.

LIMBACH.   On porcelain painted with detached flowers in blue, dark blue edges; marked in blue.

LIMBACH.   On a porcelain cup and saucer painted with landscapes in lake *camaieu*, embossed borders; formerly in the Collection of the Rev. T. Staniforth.

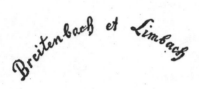

This inscription is scratched in the paste on a milkpot of grey-blue ware imitating Wedgwood, with designs in relief in white; on the one side a classical group, and on the other figures bearing between them a wreath with the cypher F.G.C. under a prince's crown.   Franks Collection.

ILMENAU.   A potter named Christian Zacharias Gräbners had commenced work at Grosbreitenbach, but was driven away by a more powerful rival named Major von Hopfgarten, and migrated to Ilmenau, where in 1777 he applied to the Grand Duke of Weimar for a concession. Gräbners, however, got into debt, and after financial assistance from the Duke had been granted for some years, he was obliged to assign his property to him, and remained as manager.   He appears to have broken his agreement with the Duke by assisting to start a porcelain factory in Russia.   Subsequently other managers were engaged, but the undertaking was not successful until 1786, when Gotthelf Greiner took it over and worked it for six years until he retired.   Christian Nonne of Volkstedt succeeded him, and in 1799 obtained a lease from the Duke, and managed it with the assistance of a son-in-law named Rösch, hence the mark N & R (Nonne and Rösch).   The chief specialité of Ilmenau was the imitation of Wedgwood's Jasper ware in portrait and subject plaques.   These marks are given on the authority of Messrs. Graul and Kurzwelly.

ILMENAU. Modern fabrique. The mark in the margin is that in use by a modern factory at Ilmenau.

GROSBREITENBACH. As noticed in the remarks on Ilmenau, the efforts of the potter Gräbners were succeeded by Major von Hopfgarten, who obtained a concession, and started a factory about 1777. His venture was unsuccessful, and he sold the whole concern to Gotthelf Greiner for 4000 thalers in 1783. Greiner entrusted the management to his son, and in 1787 there were twenty workmen, of whom six were painters. According to some writers only blue and white porcelain was made in 1812. There is considerable confusion between this and the Limbach factory on account of the same mark, a trefoil, having been used.

GROSBREITENBACH. *Hard paste.* Established about 1770 by Greiner. The demand for his porcelain was so great, that not being able to enlarge his works at Limbach, he purchased this as well at Veilsdorf and Volkstedt.

GROSBREITENBACH. This leaf is frequently imperfectly formed, and hardly to be recognised as a trefoil. The Rev. T. Staniforth had a case containing a white toy china tea and coffee service; on the outside of the case is a view of the manufactory and a trefoil leaf, with the letters G. G. & S., and above "Murrhin Spielzog." This is now in the Franks Collection. The trefoil is sometimes in pink or red, and on a specimen in the Franks Collection is in white in relief.

GROSBREITENBACH. Another mark of the same manufactory; it is usually in blue, but sometimes in red or gold. A great many specimens of the Thuringian manufacture have two or three rows of vertical ribs in slight relief over the surface, painted with flowers, &c.

GROSBREITENBACH. This mark, in blue, is found upon German porcelain. It is on a cup and saucer which was formerly in the possession of Mr. Reynolds, painted in purple *camaïeu*, with figures and views in Germany. Another cup and saucer with landscapes and flowers has the same in blue, accompanied by a small painter's mark of an arrow in red; formerly in the possession of the Marchese d'Azeglio. The Editor is inclined to think that this mark should be attributed to Limbach.

35

RAUENSTEIN. This was a very unimportant factory so far as the collector of cabinet specimens is concerned. Its products were chiefly the ordinary domestic china. The mark R—n given by Graul and Kurzwelly must not be confused with the somewhat similar sign of Gotha porcelain. The crossed swords were in imitation of Dresden, to which it is inferior. The marks occur in purple, blue, and red.

RAUENSTEIN, in Saxe-Meiningen, established 1760. *Hard paste.* Marked in blue on a cup and saucer painted with flowers, formerly in the Collection of the Right Hon. W. E. Gladstone. There is also one in the Franks Collection. (*Ker. Gall.*, enlarged edition, fig. 226.)

TETTAU. A small factory, the last and perhaps least of the Thuringian group, appears to have existed here.

The mark in the margin is given as that of Tettau by Professor Hofmann in his catalogue of the collection in the Munich Museum.

The reader should refer to the notice on the whole group of these Thuringian factories for information common to all of them, at the commencement of the chapter, pp. 520-21.

Switzerland

HE Nyon manufactory was in full work towards the end of the eighteenth century; it is said to have been established by a French flower-painter named Maubrée, and several Genevese artists painted on the porcelain, occasionally marking it with a " G " or " Geneve " in full, sometimes with and sometimes without the fish. There never was a manufactory of china at Geneva. The most celebrated painters were *Delarive, Hubert, Gide,* and *Pierre Mulhouser;* the monogram of the last named is here given; his paintings were good, with figures and flowers in the Dresden style.

This mark, in gold, is on a cup and saucer painted with a Swiss peasant and a lamb, and is probably the signature of Pierre Mulhouser, who painted the piece at Geneva. There was no porcelain made at Geneva, and this is almost certainly a Nyon specimen. Franks Collection.

NYON (Canton de Vaud). *Hard paste.* A cup and saucer of Gide's is signed thus. A descendant of his is a celebrated avocat at the present day. The late director was M. Gonin, who died 1863; he was succeeded by Burnand.

NYON. On a porcelain cup and saucer, bought at Geneva, and believed to be made at Nyon; the subjects are painted in bistre; the cup has a tablet inscribed " *Un cœur comme le votre*"; another on the saucer continues the sentence, " *est faite pour l'amitié.*"

NYON. These marks are those generally found on Nyon porcelain; sometimes the lines are so carelessly drawn as to make it difficult to identify the fish. (*Ker. Gall.,* enlarged edition, figs. 274, 5.) The late Mr. W. E. Gumbleton had a pretty inkstand, the pot formed as rosebuds, with this mark, and there is a specimen in the Franks Collection. An endeavour has been made to prove that there were two factories at

CM

P. M
Genève
—

Gide 1789.

G.

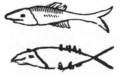

Nyon, but this is undoubtedly an error which probably arose from the fact that the mark varied in the drawing on different specimens.

ZURICH. *Hard paste.* The Zurich china factory was founded in 1763 by a few gentlemen of Zurich, amongst whom was the celebrated painter and poet Salomon Gessner, who not only furnished many designs, but painted himself at the factory. The managing director was a German named Spengler, who is supposed to have come from Höchst. The figures and groups were modelled by another German, a political refugee of the name of Sonnenschein, who left Zurich 1786 and became the first director of the Art Academy at Berne. Sonnenschein was a talented sculptor. The factory, where, besides china, pottery was also made, did not prosper; it changed hands in 1793, being then sold to a clever potter named Nehracher, after whose death in the year 1800 the manufacture of porcelain ceased. The painting on Zurich porcelain is generally very delicate and artistic, especially as regards the landscapes, which resemble those round the pretty Zurich lake with the chain of high mountains in the background. (*Ker. Gall.*, enlarged edition, figs. 276, 7.) Specimens are scarce, as the production was always very limited; hence numerous imitations made in Germany and also in Paris are frequently palmed upon the collector as genuine Zurich. The mark ℨ as in margin is in blue.

Sir Henry Angst, H.B.M. Consul-General at Zurich, made the most important collection of Zurich porcelain known; it consisting of more than 1500 specimens, which he presented to the Zurich Museum. The Editor is indebted to Sir Henry for some particulars in the notice of this factory.

Holland and Belgium

HE first manufactory of porcelain in Holland was at Weesp, near Amsterdam. It was established in 1764 by the Count Gronsveldt-Diepenbroek, who had by some means obtained the secret of the composition of hard paste. Having bought the materials of the old fayence works of Overtoom, he proceeded to make porcelain, and produced some fine white and transparent specimens; it only lasted seven years, and was closed in 1771 and the materials publicly sold. Notwithstanding the unsuccessful result from a commercial point of view, it was reopened by a Protestant minister, the Rev. De Moll of Oude Loosdrecht, associated with some capitalists of Amsterdam, but the next year it was removed to Loosdrecht. The decorations are very much of the Meissen character.

WEESP. *Hard paste*. The marks are a W and two crossed lines or swords, with dots, in blue. The latter has been assigned to Arnstadt, but is now authenticated as belonging to this manufactory.

WEESP. The crossed swords, in blue, on a porcelain teapot, painted with medallions of garden scenes and figures, blue borders and edges.

WEESP or WALLENDORF. These marks are on a cup and saucer; the W in blue, the name (perhaps that of the decorator) in gold. Sir A. W. Franks, in whose collection this specimen is, considers it to be Wallendorf. (See Wallendorf.)

WEESP. These letters are on a porcelain cup and saucer, canary-yellow ground and gilt borders, which seem to be of Dutch manufacture, and probably belong to this fabrique; in the Franks Collection.

WEESP or LOOSDRECHT. The same letters in red are on a hard paste cup and saucer, white ground, gilt borders; in front of the cup is a medallion in red with a black pencilled bust, inscribed underneath in gold letters "Doctor *ƒ*." The monogram ML. may be intended for Moll Loosdrecht and the W for Weesp, the manufacture of porcelain having commenced there, and within a year having been transferred to Loosdrecht. (*Ker. Gall.*, enlarged edition, figs. 278, 9.)

LOOSDRECHT *(hard paste)*, situate between Utrecht and Amsterdam, was the next town where porcelain was successfully made. It sprung from the ashes of Weesp, and in 1772 became a proprietary, with the Rev. De Moll at its head; after his death, in 1782, the concern passed into the hands of his partners, J. Rendorp, A. Dedel, C. Van der Hoop, Gysbz, and J. Hope, and was by them removed in 1784 to Amstel. The porcelain is of fine quality, decorated in the Meissen style; specimens are frequently met with, having gilt borders and a light blue flower between green leaves. The letters M. o. L. stand for "*Manufactur oude Loosdrecht*," marked in blue or impressed on the ware; the best pieces have a star also. By a singular coincidence it happened that the establishment was under the direction of the Rev. De Moll; sometimes the letter M is divided from the last two letters by two dots, which may mean "*Moll: oude Loosdrecht*." There was a set of five vases, painted with conversations from Watteau, the necks of openwork trellis, in Mr. Sigismund Rücker's Collection, thus marked. A specimen in the Franks Collection has this mark, accompanied by the M. o. L. and L. 48 incised in the paste. (*Ker. Gall.*, enlarged edition, figs. 280, 1.)

AMSTERDAM. There was a china manufactory here at the commencement of the nineteenth century (about 1810). This inscription is on a coffee-pot of a service, white ground, gold borders, and small detached flowers and medallions of coloured female heads, in Mr. Temple Frere's Collection.

AMSTERDAM. M. Jacquemart places this sign to Amsterdam, being the ancient arms of the United Provinces,—the Batavian lion traced in blue,—and quotes a specimen in the Museum of Sèvres. Mr. C. W. Reynolds had a pair of elegant bottles, painted in lake *camaieu* with birds and trees, bearing this mark in blue. Mr. Marryat gives this as a variety of the lion used in the Palatinate, and attributes it to Frankenthal, but the latter is always crowned, that of Holland never. This mark has been occasionally found accompanied by A. D., in a monogram, the initials of Daeuber, successor to the pasteur Moll. The Editor is strongly inclined to believe this to be a variation of the Frankenthal mark. The china and decoration are similar.

OUDE AMSTEL. *Hard paste.* In 1782, on the death of De Moll, the manufactory of Loosdrecht was removed to Oude Amstel (Old Amstel), near Amsterdam, and carried on with redoubled zeal by the same company, directed by a German named Daeuber, about 1784. It flourished under his direction for a few years, and a fine description of porcelain was produced; but it was not encouraged in Holland, and gradually declined, in consequence of the large importations from England which inundated the country. It was again offered for sale in 1789, and came into the hands of J. Rendorp, C. Van der Hoop, and Gysbz, still remaining under Daeuber's direction, but was entirely demolished at the close of the eighteenth century; sometimes the initials of the director, A. D., are found.

This mark in blue on a small teapot with a spout modelled as a pug-dog's head, and festoons of flowers painted on the body of the specimen. A very delicate little piece. Formerly in Mr. Loraine Baldwin's Collection.

NIEWER AMSTEL (New Amstel) *(hard paste)*, still nearer the capital, was established for the manufacture of porcelain, under the name of George Dommer & Co., which was in some degree supported by the King of Holland, and in 1808 a medal was awarded them by the first Industrial Exposition at Utrecht as an encouragement, theirs being the only porcelain fabrique in Holland. The King, wishing to save it, accorded an annual grant of 20,000 florins, but it was not the money so much as an experienced director that was required. It was of short duration, and ceased entirely about 1810.

LA HAYE (The Hague). Among the decrees *(arrêts)* of the States General of the 4th of April 1614, the following entry occurs, which is supposed to refer to an early manufactory of porcelain at the Hague: " Brevet d'invention de cinq ans pour tous les Pays-Bays accordé à Claes Jans. Z. Wytmans, natif de Bois le Duc, pour la fabrication de toutes sortes de *porcelaines*, pareilles en matières et en decors à celles des pays étrangers." M. Demmin, from whose pamphlet[1] this account is taken, observes: " It may be urged that the word porcelain was often used at this early period to describe all sorts of enamelled pottery, especially fine fayence. On the other hand, it must be remembered that the establishment of Delft had already, since 1530, been actively engaged in the

---

[1] *Recherches sur la Priorité de la Renaissance de l'Art Allemana, &c.* Paris, 1862. By Auguste Demmin.

fabrication of fayence, which would render inadmissible a brevet granted for the fabrication of this pottery. In any case, the manufactory here spoken of could not have been at Bois le Duc, for that town did not belong to Holland until 1629." This same Wytmans had already obtained, on the 9th of January of the same year, a brevet for twenty years for the manufacture of glass.

About the year 1775, a porcelain manufactory for both hard and soft paste was opened at the Hague, under the direction of a German named Leichner or Lynker; it was first situated in the *Bierkade*, and later in *Niewe Molstraat*. A correspondent in the *Navorscher* says: "In colour, painting, and whiteness, it is very much like the Saxon, but the substance is thicker. Tea and table services of this fabrique are to be met with, though scarce, for the undertaking failed, probably owing to the dearness of the material, or the wages; they were unable to compete with foreigners. The drawing and painting, both of landscapes and flowers, are in good taste. There are cups and saucers, on each of which the same group of flowers is represented from a different point of view; but the gilding, from being placed upon the edge instead of below it, is worn off. In 1809 or 1810, when it was the fashion for ladies to paint china, which was afterwards glazed, I remember seeing a workman in Amsterdam painting china who had formerly been painter at the Hague manufactory."

The trade-mark of the Hague manufactory is a stork, the *pia avis*, as it is termed by the old naturalists, and which is especially cherished in Holland. Meissen, writing in 1687, says: "It is but a league from Delft to the Hague. We scarce meet with any historian who mentions the city of Delft, without also speaking with admiration of what was observed not very long ago there, of two storks, the male and female, who, after many fruitless endeavours to save their young ones, which were in their nest on the top of a chimney, the house being at the time on fire, resolved at length to cover them with their own bodies, at the hazard of their lives, and to defend them from the flames or else to perish together." (*Ker. Gall.*, enlarged edition, fig. 282, 4.)

In the Victoria and Albert Museum are some specimens of this china; the decorations as well as the forms are of the Meissen character, and the

paintings well executed. It has been said that white porcelain, some even of soft paste, from Tournay and other places, was purchased by the director, and decorated by the Hague painters, marked with the stork, and sold as his own productions. The fabrique was not very important, there being only one furnace, employing from fifty to sixty workmen and painters. The works ceased in 1785 or 1786; the mark of the fabrique is a stork, the symbol of the town, in grey or gold. The value of Hague porcelain has considerably appreciated of late years, and services generally well painted in landscapes or fruits and flowers have fetched very high prices at Christie's.

LA HAYE. On a porcelain milk-jug, painted with flowers, lately in Captain Langford's Collection.

LA HAYE. Marked in blue on a tea-service, painted with medallions of figure subjects, formerly in the possession of the Editor. (*Ker. Gall.*, enlarged edition, figs. 285, 6.)

This mark in brownish-red appears on a plate which is part of a service with the ordinary Hague mark. It is painted with landscape in centre, with blue border and gilding, apparently soft paste. Franks Collection.

ROTTERDAM. There is no evidence of any porcelain having been made here, but this mark is on an oviform vase with lion's head handles, and painted with views. The F.L.S., which is in dark grey under the glaze, is probably the maker's mark, while the W. M., 1812, à Rotterdam, signifies that it was decorated there by the artist whose initials it bears. Franks Collection.

F. L. S.

A Rotterdam
W M: 1812

LILLE. *Pâte tendre*. This porcelain manufactory was established in 1711 by Sieurs Barthélémy Dorez and Pierre Pelissier, his nephew, natives of Lille. In their request for leave to found the manufactory, addressed to the Mayor and Council, they promised that it should be the second fabrique in Europe, where, up to that time, similar ware had been made out of China itself,—the first being St. Cloud. On the 25th of April 1711, their request was acceded to, and a house granted them, but, in consequence of its being unsuitable, another was accorded, situated on the Quai de la Haute-Deûle, and the privilege given for the fabrication of porcelain at Lille. A second request for the exclusive right of making porcelain was refused; but as it contains some interesting remarks, we give the following extract: "Il vous supplie, Messieurs, de lui accorder le privilège exclusif à tous autres, vous assurant être le seul, avec M. Chicanneau de St. Cloud, qui ait le véritable secret de la faire pareille aux échantillons qu'il a eu l'honneur de vous produire. Le maître de la manufacture de Rouen ayant cru avoir pénétré dans le secret s'était ingéré de faire et vouloir faire vendre à Paris, pour fabrique de St. Cloud, ce qui donnait une mauvaise réputation à cette dernière, par sa mauvaise qualité, l'abus s'étant découvert, il a été contraint de n'en plus fabriquer, et c'est à cette exemple que le suppliant vous supplie, Messieurs, de lui accorder le seul privilège en cette ville, et au Sieur Pelissier, son neveu." The potter of whom he so disdainfully speaks was Poterat of St. Sever, at Rouen. In the books of the receipts, the amount of 300 florins for rent appears annually in their joint names, but in the year 1717 the name of Dorez alone occurs. In an *Arrêt du Conseil l'Etat*, dated 1720, granting certain privileges, and being desirous of assisting the proprietors in so considerable an enterprise, a reduction of the tariff of 1664, in which they were excluded, was made (Lille belonging at that time to Holland, previous to the treaty of Utrecht, when Lille was ceded to France), and permission to introduce their wares into the kingdom of France at a reduced rate, so that they could fairly compete with foreign manufacturers, who were in a better position, being able to get the tin and lead from England at a cheaper rate. By this decree we find that porcelain was still made, but Barthélémy Dorez' two sons, François and Barthélémy, had succeeded him.

The porcelain (*pâte tendre*) of this time was like that of St. Cloud, but in the Delft style, the favourite ornamentation being Chinese designs.

L.L.
+

LILLE. Both Dorez and Pelissier, his nephew, being Frenchmen, they would naturally decorate their ware in the French style, like that of St. Cloud, and doubtless much of the Lille porcelain, from its similarity both in decoration and material, has been set down hitherto as St. Cloud. M. J. Houdoy as well as M. A. Jacquemart are of opinion that the pieces marked L. in the margin belong to Lille, and that about 1716 or 1717, when Dorez was the sole administrator, his own initial displaced that of the fabrique.

L

This single L occurs on an undoubted Lille plate with wavy edge, gadroon border, with band of basketwork near the edge, painted with flowers. It has also the letter A incised. Franks Collection.

D+.
ℬ
•L+

On the authority of MM. Chevagnac et de Grollier we give the three marks in the margin. The letter D being the initial of Dorez, and the monogram that of François and Barthélémy Dorez, while the letter L with dot and cross is another variation of the initial letter of Lille.

At a later period (in 1784) a manufactory of hard porcelain was established by Leperre Durot, under the patronage of the Dauphin; it was styled "Manufacture Royale de Monseigneur le Dauphin." Leperre Durot is thus spoken of in the decree: "Appliqué depuis sa jeunesse à la fabrication de poterie, terre de grès, faïences et même de la plus fine porcelaine;" and it goes on to state that, considering the immense expense in the consumption of wood employed as fuel, he has, after many attempts, succeeded in substituting coal, and he is authorised to manufacture porcelain and fayence at Lille, with exemption from duties and other exclusive privileges, for fifteen years. The porcelain of Leperre Durot is richly adorned with gold and carefully painted bouquets of flowers. There is a saucer in the Sèvres Museum bearing three rows of chemical characters and signs; under the foot it bears the following inscription: *Fait à Lille en Flandre, cuit au charbon de terre*, 1785.

In 1790 the manufactory changed hands, and several attempts were made to ensure its success, without avail, and about 1800 it altogether ceased. M. Roger succeeded Leperre Durot, and in 1792 he sold his interest in the works to Messieurs Regnault and Graindorge, who were ruined, and the establishment soon closed. There is an *écuelle* in the Sèvres Museum of Roger's fabrication, about 1795.

LILLE. The mark on the hard porcelain of Leperre Durot was a crowned dolphin, the emblem of the royal protection; it is in red, either pencilled or stencilled, but seldom seen so perfect as this. These pieces are rare in consequence of the short duration of the manufacture. They are sometimes marked "*à Lille*" only, and there is a custard cup with this inscription in black in the Franks Collection.

LILLE. Modern porcelain. On a compotier, with gold ornaments on white, and landscapes painted in Indian-ink. (*Ker. Gall.*, enlarged edition, fig. 319.)

fait par Lebrun à Lille

TOURNAY. *Soft paste.* A factory which subsequently developed into one of the first importance, was commenced here by a potter named François Carpentier, who, after a few months' proprietorship, sold his interest in 1751 to a merchant named Peterynk, who obtained special privileges and protection from the Empress Maria Theresa. He also was allowed to adopt the title of "Imperial and Royal" for his factory, and from about 1763, when the factory was enlarged, until 1777 or 1780, a very large turnout was made, and the sales in 1774 are said to have amounted to over 150,000 florins. There was a competition between this factory and Sèvres for the production of a service for the Duc d'Orleans, and Tournay succeeded in beating her rival, although it is said the service, which cost 60,000 florins, was never paid for by the Duke.

In 1793 the premises were burnt down, and from this time the factory experienced a succession of disasters, Peterynk himself dying in 1799 at a great age.

The business passed through different hands, and ultimately about 1850 was owned by the predecessors of the present proprietors, Messrs.

Boch Brothers, one of the most important firms of potters in Belgium for high-class table ware.

There is also another factory at Tournay which was established by a son of Peterynk, but although successful as a business enterprise, nothing of consequence from a collector's point of view has been produced.

The Tournay porcelain of the best period, 1755 or 1760, to 1777-80, is in the style of Sèvres, and a very characteristic decoration is a beautiful lustrous blue ground colour, and some fine bird paintings. An artist named Duvivier was famous for paintings of Italian landscapes, and Mayer, who also painted this kind of subject as well as others, was the decorator of the famous service mentioned above. Some of these landscapes are rendered in crimson, painted *en camaieu*, and this, with the beautiful blue in the borders, on the peculiar soft creamy paste, has a charming effect. One of the peculiarities of Mayer's bird decoration is the inscription underneath the specimen, of the names of the birds written in black ink, and another was the imitation of the grain and colour of different kinds of wood as a background, with a subject on a rectangular panel on a white relief. Basket pattern and trellis borders were also used as ornaments. Collectors who are acquainted with the peculiarities of Hague porcelain of the highest quality, will recognise a great similarity between it and that of Tournay.

TOURNAY. Marked in gold on a cup and saucer, painted with animals and birds illustrating Fontaine's Fables, formerly in the Collection of the Rev. T. Staniforth. (*Ker. Gall.*, enlarged edition, fig. 287.)

TOURNAY. On a plate painted with flowers and embossed wicker pattern border, in the Franks Collection. The above marks are found also in blue, black, violet, and red.

A variation of the Tournay mark; on two cups and saucers in the possession of Mr. J. W. Crowe, richly gilt and painted with brilliant blue flowers.

TOURNAY. This mark was used after 1755; in gold for the best quality, in blue or red for inferior specimens. Mr. Louis Huth had a dinner service so marked with blue flowers on a white creamy ground.

T° T^y   TOURNAY. These letters are said to be occasionally found placed separately on Tournay porcelain. In the Green Drawing-room at Windsor Castle there is a very beautiful service with rich border of blue and gold, and panels of birds, unmarked, and formerly described in the inventory as Chantilly, but with a note to the effect that in the opinion of the best experts it is Tournay. A triple salt-cellar of this service is in the Franks Collection. (*Ker. Gall.*, enlarged edition, fig. 290.)

BRUSSELS. *Hard paste.* There was a manufactory of porcelain here towards the end of the last century. This mark is on a teapot, with a band of roses in the centre and two belts of silver, with gold borders; on a cup and saucer of the same service is the name "*L. Cretté*," painted in red, formerly in Mr. Reynolds' Collection. The milkpot of this service was subsequently in the Staniforth, and is now in the Franks Collection. (*Ker. Gall.*, enlarged edition, fig. 292.)

BRUSSELS. This name is on a service, some pieces of which have only the name "*L. Cretté.*" Portions of another service, with the name and address, were in the Collection of the Rev. T. Staniforth, now in the Franks Collection. (*Ker. Gall.*, enlarged edition, fig. 291.)

L^r Cretté de Bruxelles rue D'Aremberg 1791.

BRUSSELS. The initials of L. Cretté on a cup and saucer; the former has a soldier with a musket, the latter the Belgian lion rampant holding a spear, on the end of which is the cap of liberty, marked in red; formerly in the possession of the Rev. T. Staniforth.

L.C.

BRUSSELS. The initials of L. Cretté alone in red, are on nearly all the pieces of a tea-service painted with military figures and trophies, and VIVE BRABANT; but one was signed with the painter's name, Ebenstein, as in the margin.

L.C.

Ebenstein

This monogram of the same painter, Ebenstein, in brown over glaze, is on a cylindrical cup and saucer, painted in colours, with birds on branches. Portions of the same service were marked with another Brussels mark. Franks Collection.

BRUSSELS or GERMAN. The first two marks are on a pair of porcelain candlesticks; the stand of each is marbled, with medallion bust of Neptune in pink; the upper part is formed of two dolphins, the tails twisted upwards; they were purchased in Belgium; afterwards in the Collection of Mr. Willett, Brighton. Sir A. W. Franks considers these specimens are of German origin. The third has been usually placed among the unknown marks, but most probably belongs to the Brussels manufactory.

LUXEMBOURG. An error of some importance appears to have arisen respecting the making of *porcelain* here in the eighteenth century. There is no mention of such a factory in MM. de Chavagnac et de Grollier's *Histoire des Manufactures Française*, and Sir A. W. Franks puts a note of interrogation in his notice in the *Catalogue of Continental Porcelain*. The monogram L.B., in various combinations, which was formerly attributed to Luxembourg, should be credited to the Thuringian factory of Limbach (*q.v.*), and the fine set of four figures of the Seasons, illustrated and described as Luxembourg in Chaffers' *Keramic Gallery*, are undoubtedly Limbach (see note on Luxembourg pottery, *Ker. Gall.*, enlarged edition, fig. 293.)

𝕽ussia and 𝕻oland

N Imperial china manufactory was established in 1744 by the Empress Elizabeth Petrowna, with workmen from Meissen. Catherine II. patronised the porcelain works, and in 1765 enlarged them considerably under the direction of the minister, J. A. Olsoufieff, since which time this fabrique has held a distinguished place among European manufactories. An artist named Swebach superintended the decorations, and in 1825 two workmen were sent from Sèvres to assist in the manufactory. The paste is hard, and of a bluish cast, finely glazed; it always shows its Dresden origin, and the imitations of the china of Saxony are very successful in making up portions of sets which have been broken.

We read in the *Connaissances Politiques de Beausobre*, Riga, 1773 (vol. i. pp. 210-218): "Il existe une fabrique de porcelaine, située sur la Néva, route de Schlüsselburg, à quatorze verstes de Pétersburg. Elle fabrique des porcelaines tellements belles et fines, qu'elle ne le cédent en rien à la porcelaine de Saxe, soit pour la blancheur et la finesse de l'émail, soit pour la beauté du décor. Sa blancheur est même supérieure à celle de Meissen. Le directeur, l'inspecteur, tous les maîtres et ouvriers sont à la solde de la cour," &c. &c.

ST. PETERSBURG. *Hard paste.* This mark of three parallel lines is in blue on two specimens in the Victoria and Albert Museum, formerly in the Collection of Mr. Bandinel, which he attributed to St. Petersburg. The former has in addition the letter K in gold. Mr. J. Loraine Baldwin had a cup and saucer painted with flowers bearing this mark in blue, which came from Russia, and evidently of that fabrique; it differs from this mark only in having a dot over the centre line.

This is a variety of a mark which we have frequently seen on Russian porcelain of early make; a Russian plate of this character, brought from St. Petersburg, thus marked, was formerly in the Loraine Baldwin Collection. The Editor thinks that this is probably a badly formed G, the initial of Gardner of Moscow.

ST. PETERSBURG. Another mark, said to be of the Imperial manufactory, in blue; but we have never met with a specimen.

ST. PETERSBURG. The cipher of the Empress Catherine II. *(Ekaterina)* from 1762 to 1796. It is on the back of a cup and cover, with well-painted figures, on dark blue ground, marked in blue. There is a teapot and a cup cover and saucer bearing this mark in the Victoria and Albert Museum.

ST. PETERSBURG. A porcelain dish, bearing the cipher of Catherine II. in blue, has also the letters $\Pi : K$ and a star in lake colour, probably the initials of the painter. In the Franks Collection.

ST. PETERSBURG. The cipher of the Emperor Paul, from 1796 to 1801.
At Knole House, Sevenoaks, there is a white and gold tea-service decorated with *fleur de lis* in a trellis, bearing this mark. The service was given to the Duke of Dorset by the Empress Catherine.

ST. PETERSBURG. This mark of the Emperor Paul is on a porcelain tureen painted with views in Italy, of the port of Alicant and the mole of Girgenti, with border of roses, formerly in the possession of Mr. A. Joseph; other portions of the same service were in the Collection of Mr. Reynolds, marked with the E. of Catherine II. Portions of this service are in the Franks Collection.
From the similarity of the decoration to that of the old Naples porcelain, and the mark somewhat resembling the N surmounted by a crown, specimens are sometimes mistaken for those of Naples, but the paste is hard, while that of Naples is soft.

ST. PETERSBURG. The cipher of the Emperor Alexander I., from 1801 to 1825; on a dessert plate of the service, part of which is in the Franks Collection, from which it would appear that the Imperial service was supplemented a few years later when Alexander succeeded Paul.

St. Petersburg. The cipher of Nicholas I., 1825 to 1855, marked in blue; it is on a cup and saucer, green ground, painted with flowers, in the Victoria and Albert Museum; and on a plate presented by the Emperor to the Sèvres Museum, finely painted by an artist named Stechetine.

St. Petersburg. Another mark of Nicholas I., on a pair of mayflower vases, formerly in the possession of Captain Langford. This mark is on a magnificent colossal vase, with paintings of the palaces of the Emperor of Russia dated 1844, in the Green Drawing-room of Windsor Castle.

St. Petersburg. The cipher of Alexander II., from 1855, marked in blue on a tea-service in the Sèvres Museum.

St. Petersburg. A manufactory of porcelain established in 1827 by the Brothers Korneloffe. On a specimen in the possession of M. Grigorovitch of St. Petersburg.

ВРАТЬЕВЪ
Корниловыхъ

Russia. This mark is on a green and gold cup and saucer painted with flowers, made by S. T. Kuznetsoff. Zaboda is the Russian for factory.

Moscow (1720). The potter Eggebrecht, who had undertaken a manufactory of Delft ware at Dresden, by direction of Böttger, had, after that was discontinued, left to go to Moscow, and being acquainted with some of the processes for making porcelain, commenced manufacturing it at Moscow. The Russians had in 1717 endeavoured to entice one of Böttger's best workmen, named Waldenstein, and were unsuccessful; but, it is said, another workman a few years after, named Richter, assisted them in their operations, but no traces are to be found of their subsequent history.

Moscow. A porcelain manufactory was established at Twer by an Englishman named Gardner in 1787; his name, in Russian letters, is

ГАРДНЕРЪ

found impressed on a porcelain cup and saucer, green and gold, ribbed. This mark is on a milk-pot decorated with flowers in gold and blue ornament, formerly in the possession of Mr. E. W. Craigie.

Moscow. This letter, in blue, is attributed to this manufacture; it is found on statuettes and groups. It is very probably the initial of Gardner.

Ç

A᷉

MOSCOW. The initials of A. Gardner, in monogram, are sometimes found alone.

ПОПОВЬІ

MOSCOW. Founded 1830. The mark of A. Popoff, who also signed his pieces with his initials in monogram. It is underneath a cup and saucer, painted with a view in Moscow, to which is attached a paper in Mr. Bandinel's writing: "Porcelain of the fabrique of A. Popove, warehouse No. 7, Moscow, on the river Fluxa, in the home of Buitschow." The view is of the Place Ronge at Moscow, to the right the monument of Minine and Pojarsky; the cathedral in the background. In the Victoria and Albert Museum. (*Ker. Gall.*, enlarged edition, fig. 297.)

АП

MOSCOW. This monogram of A. Popoff is on a fine specimen of a lobster lying on a dish shaped like a basket, in coloured porcelain, in perfect imitation of nature. The same mark is on a statuette of a Russian peasant making a list slipper, formerly in the Loraine Baldwin Collection. There are some figures of Russian peasants of this fabrique in the Franks Collection.

ФГ

ГУЛИНА

MOSCOW. Manufactory of porcelain by M. Gulena. The letters stand for "Fabrica Gospodina," followed by his name in Russian characters; the mark impressed and coloured. It is on a teapot coarsely painted with large roses and bluebells; brought from the Crimea on the 16th August 1854; purchased at the sale of the Crimean relics. Formerly in the possession of the author. (Specimens of Moscow porcelain illustrated *Ker. Gall.*, enlarged edition, figs. 294-6.)

This mark is printed in red over glaze. The Russian Eagle and initial of Emperor Alexander II. and a figure of St. George surrounded by a garter inscribed with A. Gardner's mark. It occurs on a statuette in biscuit of a Russian peasant breaking the ice with an iron-shod stick. Franks Collection.

KIEBZ.

13

II

KIEF, a town in the south of Russia, where there is a manufactory of fayence. The name is marked at the bottom of two specimens, one a large tazza-shaped vase, on pedestal of cream-coloured ware, 12 inches high, with ornaments etched or printed on it, and a blue line round the edge; and a very fine plate, with pierced border and basket pattern; date about 1780 or 1790.

KORZEC (Volhynia). POLAND. *Hard paste.* About 1803, Mérault, a chemist of the Sèvres manufactory, went to direct the fabrique at Korzec, taking with him an assistant in the laboratory named Petion. After carrying it on for a few years Mérault abandoned the direction and returned to France. Petion having suc-

ceeded him, sent a specimen of his manufacture to M. Brongniart in 1809, which is now in the Sèvres Museum, viz., a hard paste coffee-pot and saucer, decorated with gilding. The richness of the gilding equals that of Vienna; the paste is beautifully white, the decoration elegant. There is a cup and saucer in the Franks Collection.

KORZEC. This mark, of an eye within a triangle in blue, beneath the glaze, is very similar to the preceding, but more perfect. It occurs on a *pâte dure* cup and saucer, the cup

painted with a medallion portrait of a lady *en grisaille*, richly gilt borders and ornaments, doubtless executed by one of the Sèvres decorators taken there by Mérault; formerly in the possession of the Rev. T. Staniforth. (*Ker. Gall.*, enlarged edition, fig. 298.)

POLAND. Baranowka, or Baranufka, a town in the province of Volhynia, now belonging to Russia. This name is on a porcelain milkpot, hard paste, bluish white glaze, painted in bistre *camaieu* with flowers, outlined in gold, similar to Dresden; now in the Franks Collection.

Baranȯwka
II.

TURKEY. These marks in brown (under the glaze) are on a Turkish porcelain cup and cover, painted in rude flowers in red, blue, green, and yellow; the first mark is on the cup, the crescent on the cover. There is in the Franks Collection a large six-foil shaped cup cover and stand with a floral design in the body of the paste so arranged

that it is only visible when held up to the light (like a transparency); it was exhibited in the International Exhibition of 1851. It bears no mark, but Sir A. W. Franks has grounds for attributing it to Turkey.

Sweden, Denmark, and Norway

MARIEBERG. It is not known with certainty when true porcelain was first made at Marieberg. Under Sten, the director, it attained a considerable extension; he engaged a Frenchman named Huret in 1770, and another, Jacques Dortie, in 1777, to assist him in making porcelain, who remained until 1780. Fleurot, a modeller, was also employed. The sale of porcelain was never very important; it was very similar to the pieces made at Menneçy-Villeroy, evidencing its French origin. The little well-modelled cream-pots with covers, with fluted spirals and delicately-painted bouquets of flowers, are well known. There are also (although rare) occasionally seen porcelain statuettes of different sizes, and other objects, such as candelabra, in the rococo style; these pieces bear the letters MB. traced in the clay before baking. For the early history of the Marieberg fabrique the reader is referred to the notice on pottery made here in the earlier part of this volume. (*Ker. Gall.*, enlarged edition, fig. 300.)

MARIEBERG. This monogram is impressed under a porcelain compotier and cover, painted with flowers, and on another in the Victoria and Albert Museum, presented by M. Christian Hammer of Stockholm. The same mark occurs in a small cream-pot in the Menneçy style, in the Franks Collection.

MARIEBERG. On a porcelain compotier and cover formerly in the possession of Mr. Louis Huth. The mark is the three crowns of Sweden; the MB. for Marieberg, and F., probably the name of the decorator (Henri) Frantzen.

MARIEBERG. Another mark on a compotier and cover; the letter S. is probably the initial of Sten, the director. Formerly in the possession of Mr. Louis Huth.

MARIEBERG. This mark occurs on a porcelain compotier and cover, painted in pink *camaieu*, with roses and China asters, gilt-leaf borders, in the possession of Mr. Horace Marryat; another is in the Victoria and Albert Museum, presented by M. Christian Hammer of Stockholm. Other marks found on Marieberg porcelain are given by Mr. G. H. Strale in his notice of the Rörstrand and Marieberg ceramic fabriques of the eighteenth century.

Mr. W. E. Gumbleton has a cup and cover with the three crowns and a curious mark like a mushroom.

COPENHAGEN. (Fournier's *soft paste*.) A soft paste factory was started here about 1760 by a Frenchman named Louis Fournier, who, with the assistance of some clever painters, achieved some success, but the works ceased in 1768, and specimens are very rare, and the parts of the service in the Franks Collection described below are excellent representatives.

COPENHAGEN. (*Hard paste*.) The present hard paste manufactory was commenced by an apothecary of the name of Müller in 1772. The Baron von Lang, from the Fürstenberg manufactory, is said to have been instrumental in forming this at Copenhagen; it is at least known that he entered the Danish service about the same time. Among the artists employed in painting porcelain about the period of its first establishment were Gylding, Seipsius, and Ruch. The capital was raised in shares, but not being successful, the Government interfered, and it became a royal establishment in 1779, and was for several years maintained at considerable loss, and as a royal factory it came to an end in 1864, after the disastrous war. The mark is in blue, of three parallel wavy lines, signifying the Sound and the Great and Little Belts. There is a fine tea-service of Copenhagen china; the plateau has a beautifully-executed portrait of Raffaëlle, the other pieces painted with portraits of all the most celebrated painters; formerly in the possession of the Rev. T. Staniforth of Storrs. (*Ker. Gall.*, enlarged edition, fig. 301.)

COPENHAGEN. The name of a painter, pencilled in pink on a square jardinière, painted with figures and trophies of vases, garlands, &c., bearing also the three wavy lines in blue.

COPENHAGEN. This mark occurs on a china *déjeûner*, with portraits of the kings and queens of Denmark, probably made here, although not authenticated. When the Queen-Dowager of Denmark's effects were sold at Marlborough House, there were some curious specimens of Copenhagen china; black jugs, with a large gilt Latin cross on each side, embossed.

This mark in blue is on two parts of a beautiful service, a coffee-pot and sucrier painted in mythological subjects with gilding and ground of rose du Barri colour. The coffee-pot has also the mark repeated in gold under the spout. The mark is the initial of Frederick V. of Denmark, and probably this service was made for him. They are of the soft paste produced previous to the present factory of hard paste porcelain. These specimens were formerly in the Bohn Collection, now in the Franks Collection.

Mr. H. E. B. Harrison has also a small oval *écuelle* cover and stand with rich claret-coloured decorations, which has this mark in gold.

COPENHAGEN.   By the enterprise of some able men a new company was formed in 1888, and under the leadership of one Philip Schou they have produced a highly finished ware, decorated with subdued colours, with pearly tints, representations of snow-storms, rocks, sea-birds, and dancing waves, the whole scheme of decoration evidently influenced by the new Japanese school of artistic porcelain. The company is called "The Alumina."

COPENHAGEN.   There is also a rival to this modern company of considerable importance under the proprietorship of Bing & Geöndahl,

established in 1853, who, with a staff of clever artists, produce some novel ceramic effects. Mr. Pietro Krohn, curator of the Museum of Copenhagen, is one of the directors, Mr. Elias Peterson has made a reputation for fine coloured enamel glazes with the self colours of old Chinese porcelain, and an artist named Willumsen has achieved considerable success as a painter of vases. He is the art director of the factory. A specialité of their decoration is the modelling in relief of figures of animals and flowers round the sides of the vases. Independent allegorical figures and busts are also produced after the style of Thorwalsden. The mark of the fabric is in the margin.

A well-illustrated monograph entitled *Royal Copenhagen Porcelain*, by Arthur Hayden, published in 1911, gives some fuller particulars as to the Ceramic History of Copenhagen.

DENMARK.   Mr. Herman A. Kähler makes a lustred ware at Næstved in Denmark. This mark is incised on the plate.

UNCERTAIN MARKS.

Unknown marks.

Unknown.   Of some German manufactory; it occurs on an octagonal box and cover of Dresden pattern, painted with flowers, formerly in Mr. Loraine Baldwin's Collection.

This mark, hitherto classed as uncertain, may safely be attributed to Limbach, *q.v*

Unknown. This mark is on a German porcelain cup.

Unknown. On a cup and saucer; with cupids supporting a shield, and a French motto.

Unknown. On a German plate with landscapes in blue.

Unknown. On a German fayence jug, in the shape of a helmet, in blue *camaieu*, of the eighteenth century.

Unknown. On a tea-pot, of European manufacture, in imitation of Oriental; blue flowers and gold ornaments; the mark in gold.

Uncertain. The mark of a painter, on a German porcelain (?) cruche or mug, painted in purple *camaieu* with landscape and figures round the drum, and the monogram and date. Victoria and Albert Museum.

Unknown. On a German porcelain *écuelle*, painted in the Chinese style, the initials and date in red. Sèvres Museum.

Unknown. German porcelain. On an *écuelle*, beautifully painted with mythological subjects, signed at bottom in gold letters, G. B. F. (for *fecit*). Victoria and Albert Museum.

Unknown. On a German porcelain tea-service, green ground, gilt borders, with medallions painted with playing cards, formerly in the Collection of the Rev. T. Staniforth of Storrs; something like Hannong's mark.

Unknown (German). On a cup and saucer, plain white, moulded in the form of a leaf. Franks Collection.

France

SOFT PASTE PORCELAIN

 F Germany has the credit of the first introduction into Europe of the manufacture of hard paste porcelain, having many of the qualities of the Chinese productions of which it was an imitation, France may rightly claim the credit of the more beautiful if less serviceable *pâte tendre*, or soft paste china, the composition of which has been explained in other parts of this work. It only seems necessary to state here that a group of small factories under the protection of French noblemen existed during the first half of the eighteenth century, and gradually lapsed from various causes.

This cessation was partly due to the death of the patrons who found the necessary means for carrying on an expensive hobby, but it was also brought about by the personal interest which the King of France took in establishing the National and Royal Porcelain Factory at Sèvres which, as will be seen in the notice of Vincennes, caused the removal of that factory to larger and more important premises, and also attracted the best workmen from such factories as Menneçy, St. Cloud, Chantilly, and others of the soft paste group. The separate notices of these smaller factories will follow somewhat in their proper chronological order, and to the collector of marks it is very interesting to acquire specimens of these early productions in *pâte tendre* which culminated in the marvellous examples turned out by the Sèvres factory during its best period.

They may be placed thus:—

1. Rouen, supposed date of establishment	. .	1673
2. St. Cloud	. .	1690
3. Chantilly	. .	1725
4. Menneçy	. .	1735
5. Removal to Bourg-la-Reine	. .	1783
6. Vincennes (afterwards Sèvres)	. .	1738
7. Sceaux-Penthièvre	. .	1749
8. Sèvres, removal from Vincennes	. .	1756
9. Crépy-en-Valois	. .	1762

ROUEN. *Soft paste.* Louis Poterat, Sieur de St. Étienne, of St. Sever, at Rouen, obtained letters patent in 1673, stating that he had discovered processes for fabricating porcelain similar to that of China and wares resembling those of Delft, but the former was of a very rude character, and never arrived at any perfection. In the letters patent granted to the heirs of Chicanneau at St. Cloud, reference is made to the previous grant to Louis Poterat de St. Étienne in these terms : "We formerly considered the manufacture of porcelain so advantageous to our kingdom, that we accorded privileges to a person named St. Étienne at Rouen, but the said St. Étienne did nothing more than approach the secret, and never brought it to perfection these petitioners have acquired, and because they now only make fayence; and since his death, some years since, his widow has always continued to make fayence only, and as no person, on her part, has made any porcelain, we can without injury to the said St. Étienne accord the petitioners the like privilege, being sure that no persons in the kingdom can make, or ever did make, porcelain equal to theirs."

After the establishment at St. Cloud had commenced selling porcelain, the Rouen manufactory appears to have revived its porcelain in the hopes of competing with them, but with no good result. In the petition of Dorez and Pelissier to establish a similar manufactory at Lille in 1711, they speak very disdainfully of the Rouen fabrique, thus : "The master of the manufactory at Rouen having believed he had penetrated the secret, sent his ware to Paris, to sell as that of St. Cloud, which gave a bad reputation to the latter, in consequence of its bad quality, but the fraud being discovered, he was constrained to relinquish his fabrication."

In the Victoria and Albert Museum there is a tall cup of beautiful soft paste, if possible more tender and delicate than that of the St. Cloud and Menneçy factories, which it closely resembles, and this is said to be Rouen porcelain. It bears no mark, and specimens which can be attributed to Rouen are so scarce that comparisons cannot be made. It certainly does differ slightly from the other productions of the group of soft paste factories to which allusion has been made, and therefore the Editor does not challenge Mr. FitzHenry's attribution nor that of the museum authorities who have accepted it. The cup deserves the best attention of collectors.

M. de Chavagnac states that the mark assigned to Rouen porcelain is the letters A.P. with a star, the latter representing one of the three stars in the armorial shield of the Poterat family; but the attribution of this mark requires confirmation. The Editor has never seen a marked specimen of Rouen porcelain.

ST. CLOUD.

Dr. Martin Lister, an English physician and eminent naturalist, who visited Paris in 1698, says :

"I saw the Potterie of St. Clou, with which I was marvellously well pleased, for I confess I could not distinguish betwixt the Pots made there, and the finest China ware I ever saw. It will, I know, be easily granted me, that the Paintings may be better

designed and finisht, (as indeed it was), because our men are far better Masters in that
Art than the Chineses; but the Glazing came not the least behind them, not for whiteness nor the smoothness of running without Bubbles; again, the inward Substance and
Matter of the Pots was to me the very same, hard and firm as Marble, and the self-
same grain on this side vitrification. Further, the Transparency of the Pots the very
same.''

He adds, that although the proprietor, M. Morin, had been practising the
secret of his paste for more than twenty-five years, it was only within the
last three years that he had succeeded in bringing it to perfection;
we may therefore safely place its introduction in 1695. Although the
ware was so much praised by Lister, the specimens of that period in
the Sèvres Museum are very coarse and little better than fayence, and
no really fine porcelain was made until Chicanneau became director of
the works.

It must be observed that Lister only speaks of Morin as the proprietor, who was evidently living and carrying on the works at the time
of his visit in 1698. He was a chemist of Toulon, and although it is
difficult to reconcile this statement with the letters patent of 1702, it is
not improbable that Morin was actually proprietor, and supplied the
capital for the new speculation, and Chicanneau, father and son, had
been directors from the commencement. At his death or retirement,
about 1700, they became sole proprietors, Chicanneau himself dying
shortly after.

In the letters patent of 1702, granted to the heirs of Chicanneau, we
find this his widow, Barbe Courdray, and his children, Jean, Jean-Baptiste,
Pierre, and Geneviève Chicanneau, were interested in the works; that their
father had applied himself for many years past in the fabrication of
fayence, which he had brought to a high state of perfection, and had made
many experiments and attempts to discover the secret of true porcelain,
and from the year 1696 had produced some nearly equal to the porcelain
of China. His children, to whom he imparted the secret, had since his
death successfully continued the fabrication, and they were permitted,
individually or collectively, to fabricate porcelain at St. Cloud, or any
other part or parts of the kingdom, except Rouen and its faubourgs; this
privilege was for ten years. In 1712 a renewal took place for ten years,
and in the meantime the widow, Barbe Courdray, had married a M. Trou.
This document also informs us that a similar privilege was previously
granted in 1673 to Sieur de St. Étienne of Rouen (Louis Poterat).

In 1742 letters patent were granted for twenty years more to Jean
and Jean-Baptiste Chicanneau, Marie Moreau, the widow of Pierre
Chicanneau (third son), and Henri and Gabriel Trou, children of Barbe
Courdray by her second marriage. About this time serious disagreements
occurred between the two families, and they separated, Gabriel and Henri
Trou remaining at St. Cloud, patronised by the Duke of Orleans, while
Marie Moreau opened another establishment in the Rue de la Ville
l'Evêque, Faubourg St. Honoré, directed by Domenique François Chican-

neau. In 1772 another arrêt granted privileges for twenty years to both these establishments, Marie Moreau having died in 1743, and left Domenique her business.

This mark is given on the authority of MM. Chavagnac et de Grollier as being used at the branch factory established by Marie Moreau, the widow of Pierre Chicanneau, in 1711. After his death in 1743 Henri Trou succeeded after opposition in dispossessing the Chicanneaus, and carried on the works until 1764.

The manufactory of St. Cloud was destroyed by fire (the act of an incendiary) in 1773, and the manufacture ceased, the proprietors not being able to raise sufficient funds to rebuild it. In the Franks Collection there is a very dainty little pair of cream-pots decorated with appliqué ornament in thin gold touched with green enamel.

In the catalogue of the Strawberry Hill Collection, by Horace Walpole, 1784, we read of "a tea-pot, milk-pot, and ten cups and saucers of white quilted china of St. Cloud."

ST. CLOUD (Seine-et-Oise). *Soft paste.* The mark of this first period was the "sun in his splendour," in compliment to the king, and was used from about 1696 to 1732.

ST. CLOUD (? Naples). The fleur-de-lis impressed on the ware is on a cup and saucer of soft paste formerly in the possession of Mr. C. W. Reynolds. This same mark occurs on Neapolitan porcelain (see notice of Naples), and the Editor, not having seen the specimen herereferred to, is doubtful whether it is not of the latter fabrique.

ST. CLOUD. The mark used from about 1730 to 1762 was ST C, and T for Trou, the director, either blue or graved in the ware. There are several specimens bearing this mark in the Franks Collection. Very rarely one finds specimens marked with the ST C only without the letter T. This is said to be the first mark used.

This very unusual mark in blue under glaze occurs on cylindrical pot and cover with stiff arabesques in blue. It has only recently been attributed to this factory. Franks Collection. (See illustrations, *Ker. Gall.*, enlarged edition, figs. 303, 4.)

Uncertain. These marks are found upon porcelain similar to that of St. Cloud which belong to some of the successors or imitators of Trou.

CHANTILLY (Oise). *Soft paste.* This manufactory was founded in 1725 by Ciquaire Cirou, under the patronage of Louis-Henri, Prince de Condé, as appears by letters patent dated 5th October 1735. This porcelain was highly esteemed, and there was hardly any object which they did not produce, from the lofty vase to the simplest knife-handle; the Chantilly pattern was a great favourite for ordinary services, called also "Barbeau," a small blue flower running over the white paste. The

mark is a hunting-horn in blue or red, frequently accompanied by a letter, indicating the pattern or initial of the painter; sometimes the horn is impressed and marked in blue on the same piece, as on a specimen formerly in Mr. Baldwin's Collection. When Ciquaire Cirou died in 1751, the manufacture passed into the hands of Messrs. Peyrard, Aran, and Antheaume de Surval, who continued it successfully until the Revolution, when it was closed; subsequently Mr. Potter, a rich Englishman, already proprietor of the establishments at Montereau and Forges, attempted in 1793 to carry it on, with a view of employing the workmen who had been thrown out of employment, but the enterprise was abandoned in 1800. With the same generous view of employing the population, the Mayor of Chantilly, M. Pigorry, in 1803 opened a *new* fabrique, principally for domestic vessels, dinner and tea services, &c.; he was succeeded by MM. Bougon and Chalot, of whose productions there are some specimens at Sèvres, acquired in 1818. The list kept at Sèvres states that after the catastrophe of Potter, the old works were taken by Baynal and Lallement. In 1793, while under the direction of Potter, a fayence (*terre de pipe*) was produced in imitation of the English, and especially of the productions of Wedgwood. Mr. Marryat had a hard paste saucer marked "*Chantilly P. & V.*"

The decoration of Chantilly porcelain is very slight, generally in the old Japanese (Kakiyemon) style, or in detached sprigs of flowers and blue, but occasionally such subjects as a hawking party or landscape. Sir A. W. Franks mentions the mark of a P.L. combined as in the margin accompanying the horn, which differs from the cursive P. on the piece at South Kensington. The initial letter is in gold. The horn is sometimes in red and sometimes in blue.

Included in the recent gift of Mr. FitzHenry to the Victoria and Albert Museum there are some good costume figures of Chantilly porcelain. These are rare.

CHANTILLY. This mark with the name at length is on a porcelain plate, white ground, with blue sprigs of flowers, in the Victoria and Albert Museum.

CHANTILLY with the mark of Pigorry, who resuscitated the factory in 1803. (See illustrations in *Ker. Gall.*, enlarged edition, figs. 305, 6.)

MENNEÇY VILLEROY (Seine-et-Oise). *Soft paste* (1735). This important manufactory was established in 1735 by François Barbin, under the patronage of the Duc de Villeroy, at a spot called "Les Petites Maisons" on the Duke's estate. The early specimens are similar to the *porcelaine tendre* of St. Cloud, of a milky translucid appearance. There is in the Sèvres Museum a dish painted with a landscape in *camaieu*, marked in blue, with the initials of Barbin, composed of C. F. B. interlaced. He was succeeded about 1748 by Messieurs Jacques and Jullien, and the manufactory continued in a flourishing state until 1773, when, on the expiration of the lease, it was removed to Bourg-la-Reine. The mark is usually D. V. impressed, sometimes traced in colour; another mark, in blue, is on a soft paste egg-cup, of very early manufacture, formerly in Mr. Reynolds's Collection.   **. D.V.**   There is in the Franks Collection a very elegant little shaped vase, painted with a medallion of cupids, bearing this mark.

The productions of Menneçy are among the daintest and most charming of the collector's gems; the decoration is, as a rule, very slight, just a sprig of flowers, of the old Japanese ornament (Kakiyemon), but the beautiful, milky, soft paste sets off this enrichment to peculiar advantage; one finds little toilet pots of this ware which formed part of the fittings of a dressing-case or travelling box of the middle of the eighteenth century. In the Franks Collection are two cylindrical pots of this kind, which are incised with D. C. O., which Sir A. W. Franks says closely resembles Menneçy, and he also mentions that the numeral sometimes incised over the D. V. is a potter's mark. On some specimens above the D. V. is a faint imperfect impression of a coronet. Cte. de Chavagnac et Mis de Grollier mention a white Menneçy group which was sold in the Davillier sale, 1904, as fully marked "de Villeroy" written in the paste. The same authority also gives a cursive monogram D. V. and the letters D. V. F., D. V. L., P. D. V., and mentions several specimens of Menneçy biscuit. (See illustrations, *Ker. Gall.*, enlarged edition, figs. 308, 12.)

BOURG-LA-REINE (Seine). *Soft paste.* Established in 1773 by Messieurs Jacques and Jullien, who removed thither on the expiration of their lease at Menneçy, and the fabrication was continued, only changing the mark of D. V. to B. R. It was in active existence, making china purely of an industrial character, in 1788, for in that year M. Jacques, jun., the director, addressed the Minister complaining of the injury done to the French manufactures by the new treaty of commerce with England. A can and saucer, painted with exotic birds and sprigs of flowers, possess unusual interest, because the *two* pieces bear each one of these marks, the saucer B. R., the cup D. V.; they were probably made about the time of the removal of the works. Formerly in the Octavius Morgan Collection. These marks are given by Chavagnac et de Grollier :—

BOURG-LA-REINE. These marks are graved in the clay beneath the glaze on an early dish of hard paste, finely glazed, but covered with raised blemishes, painted in blue, with a Chinaman drawing a lady in a sort of palanquin; formerly in Mr. John J. Bagshaw's Collection.

In the Franks Collection these letters are incised or scratched in the paste of some little toilet pots, of the same character exactly as those of Menneçy. On some specimens of both Menneçy and Bourg-la-Reine the name of a modeller, MO, is also scratched.

MODERN BOURG-LA-REINE. Monsieur Dalpayrat and Madame Lesbros make stoneware at Bourg-la-Reine, near Paris. They are also now making other wares. This mark occurs impressed on a bottle, mottled in green and red.

VINCENNES.

The history of the premier soft paste of Vincennes is of especial importance because, as will be seen in the notice of Sèvres, it was here that the great royal and national porcelain manufactory had its cradle. The establishment of the Vincennes factory is said to have been due to the interest of M. Orry de Fulvi, Counsellor of State and Controller of Finance, who was induced to undertake the venture by the two brothers Robert and Gilles Dubois, who had learned the secrets of porcelain manufacture at Chantilly, and by permission of Louis XV. the factory was allowed to carry on work close to the Château of Vincennes. This occurred in 1738, and three years afterwards the brothers Dubois left the factory owing to misconduct, and the work was subsequently carried on under the direction of Charles Adam, with the assistance of men who had formerly been employed at Chantilly. Under a special grant of protection from the King a new company was formed in 1745, and with fresh capital the manufactory was considerably developed. Duplessis, a famous jeweller, directed the models, and Hellot, a noted chemist, superintended the selection of materials. The King granted to the factory a monopoly, and exempted from military service all the employés. While the King thus gave every encouragement to the workers, he on the other hand caused a strict law to be passed to prevent any of the employés offering their services to other factories. Under such royal encouragement and protection the success of the Vincennes factory was assured, while the delicate soft paste lent itself to the artistic decoration of the artists employed. At first the ornamentation was copied from Chinese models, but this was soon followed by the use of a rich cobalt blue, now known by collectors as "bleu de Vincennes," and this is accompanied by fine gilding, not only in the lines and scrolls which framed in the "reserves," but as an ornament to the "reserves." A little later cupids and children after Boucher appear, and a charming effect was produced by the painting of these subjects *en camaieu*. Madame Pompadour took great personal interest in the factory, and gave an order for the enormous sum of £32,000 to be expended on porcelain artificial flowers, which were used to make a bower in her garden at the Château of Bellevue. These flowers, charmingly modelled and daintily coloured, were a specialité of the Vincennes factory. We have already noticed the rich deep blue ground which was the first "ground" colour produced; this has a mottled or uneven appearance, from its being painted on the body with a brush. At a later date this process was altered by the colour being powdered, and afterwards fused by heat, but collectors prize the earlier mottled effect. About 1752 Hellot introduced the beautiful turquoise ground colour, and these two are the only ground colours one finds on Vincennes porcelain. The King had allowed the reversed "L" to be used as a mark, and this appears on specimens previous to 1753, sometimes with a dot between the letters and sometimes without. In 1753 the use of the letters of the alphabet commenced to indicate the date, thus 1753 is marked by the letter A, 1754 by B, and so on.

It was now determined to erect more suitable premises at Sèvres, and as soon as these were ready, the manufactory was removed from Vincennes to the new building, and the continuation of its history will be found under the notice of that factory.

Among the specimens of soft paste porcelain presented by Mr. FitzHenry to the Victoria and Albert Museum, there are some characteristic pieces of early Vincennes. There are also some good specimens in the Jones Bequest and in the Franks Collection.

The crown or fleur-de-lis placed over the mark denotes a piece intended for royal use or for presents. Sometimes on the Vincennes pieces of fine quality we find a very small fleur-de-lis placed away from the double L.

VINCENNES. The double L interlaced and traced in blue, from 1745-53, without any letters indicating the date; carried on by a company under the direction of Charles Adam at the Château de Vincennes, under the especial patronage of the King.

These marks occur on specimens of Vincennes soft paste. The double L reversed cypher with a dot between the letters is in gold and also in blue, and is the same mark as that adopted by the Royal Sèvres factory. It is, in fact, the same factory removed in 1756 from Vincennes to Sèvres. There are several specimens in the Franks Collection.

VINCENNES, afterwards removed to SÈVRES. The letter placed within the cipher denotes the year in which it was made: thus A signifies 1753, continuing the alphabet down to Z, 1777, and afterwards the double letter to 1793 (P.P.).

The signature of Taunay, a Sèvres painter, occurs on a leaf-shaped sauceboat of Vincennes porcelain. Taunay worked at Vincennes about 1750, and afterwards continued under the new regimé at Sèvres. Franks Collection.

This mark in blue, accompanied by a painter's mark, which is probably that of Chevalier (afterwards a Sèvres painter), is on one of the sugar-bowls of a fine service of Vincennes soft paste with rich bleu de Vincennes ground colour and excellent gilding, the decoration of the "reserves" being in exotic birds. Other pieces of the same service have no fabric mark, but some different painters' marks. The service was formerly in the Editor's possession, and is now in Captain Thistlethwayte's Collection.

HARD PASTE PORCELAIN AT VINCENNES.

At a much later date a hard paste factory appears to have been set up at Vincennes by Pierre Antoine Hannong, son of the famous Strasbourg potter, and he was allowed to make use of the premises formerly occupied by the soft paste factory. This occurred about 1765, and continued with indifferent success under a letter of protection which expired in 1788, when the works were closed. The mark of L.P. under a crown is attributed to this fabrique. We have met with some other marks on porcelain exactly similar in its peculiar felspar appearance, as well as in decoration; "*h et L*," in gold, as given in the margin, perhaps the initials of Hannong and Le Maire, on a ewer painted with arabesques and flowers in pale colours.

These initials in gold, which may be those of Hannong and Lemaire, but in a different variety, occur on a cup and saucer painted in colour with a double line of blue dots, with lace flounces dotted with gold, which is in the Franks Collection; its attribution to Vincennes is somewhat uncertain.

VINCENNES. This mark is in pink on a sugar-pot painted with flowers, something like the Marseilles porcelain. Baron Davillier.

VINCENNES. This mark in gold is on a cup and saucer, with a deep border of blue and gold, red flowers and gilt festoons, well painted; date about 1800. Franks Collection.

VINCENNES. M. Jacquemart thinks the L. P. under a crown belongs to this fabrique, under the protection of Louis Philippe, Duc de Chartres, afterwards King of the French, but in the latest authority on French porcelain, "Histoire des Manufactures Françaises," by MM. de Chavagnac et de Grollier, this seems to be satisfactorily disproved.

VINCENNES. The letter H with two tobacco pipes occurs with the letters L.P. on a plate of soft paste, painted with birds and butterflies; the mark probably of Hannong.

SCEAUX-PENTHIÈVRE (Seine), near Paris. *Soft paste.* This manufactory was established in 1750 by Jacques Chapelle; it was situated opposite the Petit Châtelet and was carried on by Glot in 1773, who in 1775 obtained the protection of the Duc de Penthièvre, at which time the manufacture of porcelain was revived and actively pursued.

These letters are engraved on the soft clay, and are the usual porcelain marks. The Prince-Protector died in 1794, but the production of *pâte tendre* ceased before that time. The painters Becquet and Taillandier left these works to go to Sèvres.

SCEAUX.

A later mark, painted in blue on a cup and saucer, lately in Mr. Reynolds's Collection. It occurs more frequently on fayence, accompanied by the letters S.X. for Sceaux, or S.P. for Sceaux-Penthièvre. The anchor is the ensign of the dignity of the High Admiral of France.

Specimens of Sceaux are rare, and they are so similar in every respect to those of Menneçy and Bourg-la-Reine that it is only by a mark one can distinguish them.

SÈVRES.

In the notice of the soft paste factory of Vincennes we have shown that the history of the great Sèvres manufactory commences with that of Vincennes, and in order that the reader may get a more complete story of this very important enterprise, we will again mention the leading facts concerning the making of soft paste china, first at Vincennes and afterwards at Sèvres.

In 1738 the secret of the manufacture was carried by some of the workmen to Chantilly, and works were commenced there by the Brothers Dubois. They subsequently left, taking with them the secret to Vincennes, where a laboratory was granted them, but after three years they were dismissed. In 1745 a sculptor named Charles Adam was instrumental in forming a company; the scheme was approved of by the King, and exclusive privileges were accorded them for thirty years, and a place granted for the prosecution of the manufacture in the Château de Vincennes. M. Jacquemart gives the following list of employees in the manufactory in 1750 :—

Le Sieur Boileau, directeur
Duplessis, orfèvre du Roi, composait les modèles.
Bachélier avait la direction de toutes les parties d'art.
Les modeleurs sculpteurs étaient Auger, Chabury et La Salle.
Les jeteurs des moules en plâtre : Michelin et Champagne.
Les mouleurs : Gallois et Moyer.
Les tourneurs : Vaudier, Corne, Goffart, De l'Atre, Gravant.
Les répareurs : Chenob chef, Gremont, Chanou, Bulidon, Wagon, Henry, Le Maitre, Lucas, Jame, Beausse, Varion, Misera, Paris, Melsens, Gerin, l'Auvergnat, Gambier, Joseph, Made Grémont, Made Wagon, Desnoyers, Goffat cadet, Gilloun, Marion, De l'Arte cadet, et Louis.
Les chimistes : Bailly et Jouenne.
Les peintres : Capelle, Armand cadet, Thevenet, Armand aiñé, Taunay, Caton, Cardin, Xhrouet, Chevalier, Yvernel, Touzez, Tabory, Pigal, Binet, Made Capelle, Bardet, Made Bailly.
Les brunisseuses : Mlles Bailly ainée et jeune.
Gravant façonnait les fleurs que Thevenet était chargé de peindre après la cussion en couverte.

It may interest some of our readers to know the remuneration accorded by the State to the principal persons employed about this time, bearing in mind that the equivalent value in the present day would be three times that amount; thus, 2000 livres or francs would be equal to 6000 francs, £240.

Le Sieur Boileau, director	2000 livres.
Le Sieur Duplessis, compositeur des modèles (c'était l'orfèvre du Roi), pour aller à Vincennes quatre jours par semaine . .	3600 ,,
Le Sieur Bachélier pour y aller un jour	2400 ,,
Le Frère Hyppolite pour ses voyages	100 ,,

The decorations, up to about 1753, were chiefly in the Chinese style. In 1753 the privilege of Charles Adam was purchased by Eloy Richard. Louis XV. took a third share, and it became a royal establishment. Madame de Pompadour greatly encouraged the ceramic art, and it arrived at great perfection. The buildings were found too small to meet the increasing demands for their beautiful productions, and in 1756 they removed to a large edifice at Sèvres, which had been built expressly for the company. In 1760 the King became sole proprietor, and M. Boileau was appointed director.

A decree of Council, dated 17th January 1760, ordains that after the 1st of October this manufacture and all its appurtenances belongs to his Majesty.

According to Article VIII., this manufacture shall continue to be worked under the title of "Manufacture de Porcelaine de France." It shall enjoy, conformably to the decrees of 24th July 1745 and 19th August 1753, the exclusive privilege of making every description of porcelain, plain or painted, gilt or ungilt, plain or in relief, sculpture, flowers, or figures.

It renews his Majesty's prohibition against any person or persons, of what condition or quality they may be, from making or causing to be made, or sculptured, painted, or gilt, any of the said works, of whatever form they may be, or to sell or barter them, on pain of confiscation of the said porcelain, and all matters and utensils employed therein, the destruction of the kilns, and 3000 livres (francs) penalty for each contravention, one-third to the informer, one-third to the General Hospital, and the other third to the said Royal Manufactory. His Majesty wishing, nevertheless, to favour the particular privileges hitherto granted, and which may be renewed in due course for the fabrication of certain ordinary porcelain and fayence, permits fabricants to continue the manufacture of white porcelain, and to paint in blue in the Chinese patterns only. His Majesty expressly prohibits the employment of any other colour, especially of gilding, and the making of figures, flowers, and sculpture, except to ornament their own wares. With regard to makers of fayence, His Majesty permits them to continue their works, without, however, the use of coloured grounds, in medallions or otherwise, or of gilding under the same penalties, &c. ·

About 1761 the secret of making hard porcelain was purchased of Pierre Antoine Hannong for 3000 livres annuity. It had been known for more than fifty years in Saxony, and the manufacture of the *pâte tendre* being expensive and liable to accidents in the furnace, it was deemed of great importance to be able to make what was considered the only true porcelain. Dr. Guettard, a naturalist, had discovered an inferior sort of kaolin at Alençon, of which he had made porcelain, but it was not equal to that of China or Saxony, and in 1765 he published "*Une Histoire de la Découverte faite en France de Matières semblables dont la Porcelaine de*

Chine est composée." Although possessed of the knowledge, they had not the means of producing it, being unable to procure the kaolin necessary, until accident led to the discovery of some quarries yielding it in abundance at St. Yrieix, near Limoges. Madame Darnet, the wife of a surgeon at St. Yrieix, having remarked in a ravine near the town a white unctuous earth, which she thought might be used as a substitute for soap in washing, showed it with that object to her husband, who carried it to a pharmacien at Bordeaux. This person, having probably heard of the researches to obtain a porcelain earth, forwarded the specimen to the chemist Macquer, who recognised it immediately as kaolin.

In the Sèvres Museum there is a small figure of Bacchus, made with this first specimen of St. Yrieix kaolin brought by Darnet in 1765. In 1769 the chemist Macquer, after repeated experiments, successfully established the manufacture of hard porcelain at Sèvres, and the two descriptions of china continued to be made until 1804. Of course the terms *pâte tendre* and *pâte dure* were unknown till then; the Sèvres porcelain was simply called *porcelaine Française.*

There was in the late Mr. Louis Huth's Collection a pair of very beautiful groups of cupids in white soft paste, having every appearance of early Sèvres porcelain, but unmarked. One of the cupids holds in his hand a scroll on which is etched in ink a building, and above it the words: *Manufacture Royale de Porcelaine de France*, underneath the building, *Sol du Bas Terrein, Méran fecit.* They are remarkable specimens.

By a decree of the 17th February 1760 it was ordered that the manufactory of Sèvres "continuera d'être exploitée sous le titre de *Manufacture Royale de Porcelaine de France*;" so it is alluded to in the earliest accounts as the *porcelaine de France.* About 1770 it was called *porcelaine du Roy*, and subsequently *porcelaine de Sèvres.*

Another decree of the 17th January 1787 ordains—

1st. All undertakers of the manufacture of porcelain established in the city and faubourg of Paris, within the distance of thirty leagues, except those established previous to May 1784, shall be compelled to place in the hands of the Controller of Finances the titles by which they were established within three months from the date of this decree: in default of which they shall not under any pretext continue the said works, unless otherwise ordained. His Majesty expressly prohibits all persons from working such manufactories in future without special authority from the Controller-General, after the advice taken of his Majesty's Commissioner of the Royal Manufactory, to whom the demand shall be addressed.

2nd. All persons having obtained permission previous to May 1784 to make porcelain, and have not availed themselves of it, or having established a manufactory have ceased to work it, cannot recommence without the authority before stated.

3rd. His Majesty prohibits undertakers of manufactories established before the said 16th May 1784, and which are now in operation, to transfer or dispose of the right accorded them, or continue the working thereof, except to their children and lineal descendants, or unless the persons to whom they propose to cede the said fabrique have previously obtained a decree authorising them to carry on the establishment.

4th. His Majesty also prohibits all undertakers of manufactures of porcelain from making any of the objects reserved by the Royal Manufactory by the decree of the 16th May 1784, unless they have actually obtained permission, which cannot be accorded them until the perfection of their fabrication has been tested in assembly which is held every year in the presence of Commissioners appointed by his Majesty; and nevertheless the Manufactures de la Reine, de Monsieur, et de M. le Comte d'Artois et de M. le Duc d'Angoulême having been recognised heretofore as having satisfied this proof, are at liberty to carry on their work, except that neither they nor any other are allowed to fabricate any works of *grand luxe*, such as tableaux of porcelain and sculptured works, whether it be vases, figures, or groups, exceeding 18 inches in height, including the stand, such being reserved exclusively for the Royal Manufactory.

5th. His Majesty prohibits all undertakers of the manufacture of porcelain established in his realm of counterfeiting any figures, groups, and animals of porcelain made at the Royal Manufactory on pain of seizure, confiscation, and penalty of 3000 livres; and they are expressly enjoined to place on each piece they make a distinctive mark to show the denomination of their fabrique and their residence.

6th. The said undertakers are restricted to let the persons they employ work only in the ateliers of their manufactory, and they shall not under any pretext give out work to be made in the town or elsewhere.

7th. Fayenciers, traders, or others are prohibited from erecting muffle kilns to bake in the colours on porcelain; also from keeping in their stock any unmarked merchandise, or counterfeiting or altering the marks they bear, on penalty of 3000 livres, interdiction of their commerce, and imprisonment.

8th. His Majesty also prohibits under penalty of 3000 livres to fayenciers, traders, and others the painting or decorating any white porcelain, whether it comes from the Royal Manufactory or any other similar establishment, or to bake or cause to be baked in their kilns any figures in imitation of biscuit.

In 1760 Boileau was made director. In 1773 Parent[1] succeeded Boileau, and in 1779 he was followed by Regnier, who was imprisoned in 1793. Three members of the Convention then administered the fabrique, leaving the inspection of it to Chanou; he was displaced by a triumvirate composed of MM. Salmon, Etlinger, and Meyer, who remained in the directory until 1800, in which year M. Brongniart was appointed sole director, and effected great improvements in the manufacture of hard porcelain. This position he retained nearly fifty years, until his death, which happened in 1847, when he was succeeded by M. Ebelman, and after him M. Regnault, succeeded by M. Baumgart.

M. Brongniart conceived the idea of forming a Museum of ceramic productions, in which he was encouraged by Napoleon, who applied to the various manufactories of Germany for specimens of their porcelain, and issued orders to all the Prefects of France to furnish collections from the several potteries in their Departments; these contributions from 1805 to 1812 formed the nucleus of the present extensive Museum. The late M. Riocreux, for so many years the Conservateur du Musée Céramique, ably carried out the intentions of M. Brongniart by arranging and classifying the various ceramic productions in such a way as to be of great service to amateurs, and his intimate knowledge of the subject to which he had devoted himself, his readiness to give information, and his

---

[1] Parent was discharged from his office in consequence of his misdoings; he disposed (on his own account) of the products of the manufacture, either to decorate his apartment or by presents to procure friends and protectors. Bachélier in his Memoirs says, "On a vu à sa vente le groupe des Graces de Claudion du prix de 192 livres, avec quatre divinités de 36 livres piece, vendues en bloc 45 livres. On peut juger de l'enorme quantité de porcelaines qu'il y avoit à cette vente."

affability, will be remembered and universally acknowledged by visitors; he was the able coadjutor of M. Brongniart in the *Catalogue du Musée Céramique* of Sèvres. The great work of M. Brongniart, *Traité des Arts Céramiques*, is well known; and those of our readers who wish for information on the details of the fabrication of pottery and porcelain will do well to consult this valuable treatise.

Under the denomination of *vieux Sèvres* is comprehended all porcelain, *pâte tendre*, made at the Royal Manufactory from the day of its foundation up to the end of the eighteenth century, or rather up to the days of the French Revolution. The different kinds of styles of form and ornamentation are thus distinguished: "Pompadour" or "Rocaille," from 1753 to 1763; style Louis XV., from 1763 to 1786; style Louis XVI., from 1786 to 1793. Those exquisite pieces of decorative furniture, such as cabinets, consoles, writing-tables, &c., inlaid with plaques of Sèvres porcelain, with their beautiful and highly-finished ormolu mounts of festoons of flowers, scrolls, borders, and caryatid supports, were doubtless completed in the manufactory itself, where a staff of experienced workmen were employed in producing them for royal presents. Even carriages were ornamented with plaques of porcelain. In speaking of the Longchamps of 1780, Madame du Barry mentions the equipage of the actress Mademoiselle Beaupré: "Nous la vimes paraître dans une voiture dont les panneaux étaient en porcelaine ornée de peintures délicieuses, les encadrements en cuivre surdoré," &c. The Comtesse de Valentinois had at the same time the panels of her carriage made of Sèvres porcelain.

They also produced at Sèvres medallions of white cameo-biscuit busts and figures, on blue ground, in imitation of Wedgwood's celebrated jasper, which were occasionally mounted in console tables and other pieces of furniture.

Besides the sales which took place at the manufactory, the King had expositions of Sèvres porcelain at Versailles, which furnished the grandees with an opportunity of making their court in purchasing the products of the royal fabrique. Every New Year's Day the new and choicest pieces were exposed for sale in a *salon* of the palace, the King himself presiding and making the distribution to the nobility and gentry in exchange for their money. Numerous anecdotes of occurrences at these displays are yet remembered. One day Louis XV. perceived the Comte de * * * take up a pretty cup and quietly deposit it in his pocket; the next day an employé waited upon him and presented the saucer, which he had forgotten, accompanied by the invoice. On New Year's Day, 1786, several pieces of porcelain having disappeared, a strict surveillance was instituted. A lady was observed, while the attendant's head was turned away, to secrete a piece of china; the man, politely offering her a small piece of money, said, "I beg your pardon, Madame, but I find I was mistaken; the cup which I sold you was only 21 livres, and I neglected to give you the change." The lady, disconcerted by his finesse and presence of mind, immediately handed him a louis-d'or.

The sales at Versailles were, however, of small importance compared with those of Sèvres, whether to the King for presents to sovereigns and ambassadors, &c., for his châteaux, or to the nobility and merchants. The royal family were large purchasers, and the great patronesses were Madame de Pompadour and, later, Madame du Barry, who expended immense sums at the manufactory. We find in the register of the sales of Sèvres many of the pieces fully described, from which we select the following : An Englishman named Morgan on one occasion in 1771 bought 35 vases, from 96 to 500 livres (francs) each, amounting altogether to 17,437 livres,[1] and he was a large buyer in succeeding years; he was probably a merchant. In 1782 we read, "Deux vases émaillées (fleurs en biscuit) donnés par le Roi au Comte et à la Comtesse du Nord, 2400 livres," and "Une toilette table et miroir en porcelaine, fond bleu, ornée d'émaux (jewelled), offerte par le Roi à la Comtesse du Nord, 75,000 livres." Among the presents from Louis XV. in 1758 we notice : To the King of Denmark, a service of green, with figures, flowers, and birds, 30,000 livres; in 1764, to the Emperor of China, vases, groups after Boucher, Oudry, &c., as well as goblets and various other pieces, which were renewed in 1772 and 1779; from Louis XVI. in 1778, to the Emperor of Morocco, dinner and tea services of *pâte tendre* amounting to 6948 livres; in 1786, to Archduke Ferdinand of Austria, a table service of turquoise with daisies and roses, with a sculptured centre; a blue carabet with miniatures, busts of the King and Queen, costing altogether 26,748 livres; in 1787, to the Comte d'Aranda, Spanish ambassador, a grand table service of *pâte tendre*, blue ground, with groups of flowers, of the value of 48,252 livres; in 1788, to Tippoo Sahib, the Sultan of Mysore, a table service, vases, cups, and busts, costing 33,126 livres. It should be added that for many years there have been no sales to the public of Sèvres porcelain from the State manufactory. The productions are made for presentation only.

We will conclude our quotations by describing a few well-known pieces of Sèvres porcelain, and the prices at which they were sold by auction a century ago.

"Un vase en formede navire de porcelaine de Sèvres, à cartouche fond bleu et fleurs naturelles, de 17 pouces de haut sur 14 de long. 279 livres 19 sous." (Catalogue du Marquis de Ménars, 1782.)

This is the famous *vaisseau à mat* or *nef* (the form of which is borrowed from the arms of the city of Paris), which at the present day would probably realise as much as fifty to a hundred thousand francs. (One of these *nefs* is represented in the *Ker. Gall.*, enlarged edition, fig. 348.)

"Trois vases, l'un desquels faisant milieu, de couleur bleu foncé, et orné d'un cartouche colorié représentant des soldats tirant l'epée près de la tente d'une

---

[1] The livre tournois of vingt sous is equal to a franc ; at the present day a livre of this period is equivalent to about three francs.

vivandière, qui s'occupe à les apaiser. Ce vase est richement orné d'anses et guirlandes de feuilles de chêne et autres ornements dorés, aussi bleu et or; le tout pris dans la masse et de porcelaine; hauteur 16 pouces, largeur 10 pouces. Les deux autres, de même genre, sont à quatre cartouches coloriés en relief, dont trois représentent des trophées de guerre, et le quatrième des soldats et vivandières; hauteur 20 pouces, largeur 8 pouces. 1100 livres " (£44). (Catalogue de la Duchesse de Mazarin, 1781.)

"Déjeûner avec plateau, etc., à personages Chinois. 600 livres. Cet article ordonné par Madame la Comtesse du Barry et livré à elle même, est du travail le plus exquise. Il a couté deux mois et demi de travail au premier peintre de la manufacture."

The painter here alluded to was probably Leguay, who painted Chinese subjects, miniatures, children, trophies, &c.; his works are much esteemed. A *cabaret* with *champêtre* scenes painted by him brought at the Bernal Sale in 1857 £465, and a cup and saucer with figures by the same artist was sold for £107.

To show how difficult was the operation of firing these vases of *pâte tendre*, and how liable to injury, we quote an observation made by the director on the invoice: "2 cuvettes Verdun à fleurs et oiseaux, 480 livres; 3 cuvettes Courteille de même à treillage, 654 livres; *ces cuvettes à mettre des fleurs ont été ordonnées par Mme. la Comtesse* (du Barry), *sur les dessins qu'elle a choisis, et elle n'ignore pas combien il en a péri au feu, avant de réussir à celles qu'on lui a livrée.*" MM. de Verdun and Barberie de Courteille, here mentioned as designers of these vases, were connected with the administration of affairs at Sèvres.

A small but very choice supper service of twenty-four pieces, painted with Chinese figures, flowers, and landscapes, was purchased for a special occasion at 3,804 livres by Madame du Barry, the invoice of which has the following remark: "This service was delivered at Lucienne the day the King supped there. The paintings are as exquisite and by the same painter as the Chinese déjeûner before described."

There is an album at Sèvres which contains several hundred drawings of plates in water-colours by the artists of the manufactory from 1750 to 1800. These are very carefully executed, of the size of the originals, accompanied by the prices, and occasionally by the names of the purchasers.

The painted plates cost ordinarily at Sèvres from 8 to 72 livres (francs), seldom more. However, we find that Madame du Barry ordered some at 140 livres, and those of the famous service of the Empress of Russia cost as much as 240 livres, but these are rare exceptions. We select a few examples:—

Plate painted with flowers, simple (for the Prince Louis de Rohan, 1772) . 12 livres.
Plate, with blue border and centre, with flowers and gilt ornaments (for the Princesse de Lamballe) . . . . 18 livres.
Plate, rose and foliage (for Madame du Barry, 1774) . . . . 27 livres.
Plate, white ground, with birds, flowers, quivers, flambeaux, doves, &c. . . 30 livres.
Plate, riband, pale blue, and garlands of flowers . . . . 30 livres.
Plate, ground "bleu céleste, oiseaux et chiffres" (for the Prince de Rohan, 1772), the San Donato service . . . . 36 livres.

Plate, turquoise border, garlands, bouquets, and medallions (for the Duke of Saxe-Teschen) .   .   .   .   36 livres.

Plate, small vases in bleu du Roi, garlands of flowers, and ciphers D B (for Madame du Barry) .   .   .   .   42 livres.

.* This service cost 21,500 livres.

Plate, painted with Chinese figures (for Madame du Barry) .   .   .   .   140 livres.

Plate, turquoise ground, medallions and cartouches of flowers and birds .   48 livres.

Plate, ground green œil de perdrix, birds and busts .   .   .   .   72 livres.

Plate, with three cartouches of military subjects, arms of Castile and cipher C L (for the Prince of Asturias) .   .   .   .   .   .   72 livres.

Plate, with birds after Buffon, the names underneath, bleu du Roi borders .   72 livres.

A service was made at Sèvres for the Prince de Rohan in 1772 of *bleu céleste* (turquoise) *oiseaux et chiffres*, consisting of 360 pieces, at the price of 20,700 livres (£828). A part of this service (172 pieces) was sold in one lot at the San Donato Sale on the 23rd March 1870, and bought by M. Rutter for the Earl of Dudley for £10,200, and the expenses.

These extracts are taken from a pamphlet entitled *Les Porcelaines de Sèvres*, by Baron C. Davillier, which contains an account of the purchases made at the manufactory by Madame du Barry, &c., in 1771, 1772, 1773, 1774, and sales of celebrated collections towards the end of last century.

It is a remarkable fact that the Sèvres Museum, so rich in specimens of other fabriques of Europe, possesses no collection of the grand Sèvres vases and groups made at the Royal Manufactory in the later half of the last century; but fortunately the moulds of them have been preserved, and many of the choicest pieces have been reproduced in plaster, to which we shall presently refer. There are, however, to be found many very interesting objects in connection with the manufacture; among these we may mention an assortment of detached flowers, enamelled and painted in close imitation of nature. The fabrication of these flowers originated at Vincennes, the fashion of wearing them as personal ornaments going out at the time the manufactory was transferred to Sèvres; they were the work of the wives of the workmen employed there. An idea of the high price of some of these bouquets may be formed from the statement of M. Brongniart, that the mounting of two groups, made for the King and Dauphiness in 1748, each cost the sum of 3000 livres (about £120); the equivalent value at the present day would be about £350; and in 1750 it is related that the King ordered at the Vincennes manufactory painted porcelain flowers with their vases for upwards of 800,000 livres (£32,000) for all his country houses, especially for the Château de Belle Vue and the Marquise de Pompadour; but this is doubtless an exaggeration, for M. Riocreux asserts that there never was made in one year more than 300,000 livres of flowers, and that the entire manufacture in one year never exceeded 1,800,000 (£72,000).

The Marquise de Pompadour, who, it is well known, took great interest in the fabrication, with an especial taste for these delicate porcelain flowers, knew well how to play her part in pleasing the King. One day she waited for him in the enchanting Château de Belle Vue, which had cost him so dearly, and on entering she received him in an apartment at the extremity of which was a large hothouse, and a parterre of flowers, although it was then in the midst of a rigorous winter; as the fresh roses, the lilies, and the pinks were in abundance, the King was delighted, and could not sufficiently admire the beauty and the sweet odour of the parterre. Nature was there only counterfeited; those vases, the flowers, the roses, pinks, lilies, the stalks, and the leaves were all of porcelain, and the odour of the various flowers was the effect of their volatile essences extracted by art.

There are also some minute imitations in porcelain of gems and engraved stones from the antique, modelled expressly for application by incrustation, on the magnificent table service executed in 1778 for the Empress Catherine II. of Russia. This famous service was of *pâte tendre* and consisted of 744 pieces; it cost 328,188 livres, or about £13,200, equivalent at the present day to nearly £40,000. The Czarina considered the price exorbitant, and a long diplomatic correspondence ensued. One hundred and sixty pieces were carried away during a fire at the palace of Tsarskoe-Selo and found their way to England; they were purchased by Mr. John Webb, but with a few exceptions they were repurchased by the late Emperor Nicholas and taken back to Russia a short time before the Crimean War. The description of a plate of this service in the possession of Robert Napier, Esq., of Shandon, may interest many of our readers: it is of turquoise ground with the letter E in the centre, formed of minute flowers and the Roman numeral II. interlaced (Ekaterina II.), surmounted by an imperial crown, enclosed by two branches, one of palm, the other laurel; the turquoise border has cameo medallions of portraits and antique gems on a jasper ground, and two narrow borders of white, with flowers and gilding; the whole covered with gold ornamentation. The marks of all the artists engaged are on the back of the plate, viz., Dodin for the cameos and busts, Niquet for the floreated initials, Boulanger the detached bouquets, and Prévost the gilding. It is dated 1777. The late Mr. Goode of South Audley Street possessed eleven specimens of this remarkable service, which are illustrated in Litchfield's *Pottery and Porcelain;* they were sold at Christie's in 1895, with the rest of his collection of Sèvres china, the plates above described realising about £160 each. An oval dish of the service is in the collection of Dr. Darmstaedter of Berlin.

Another very remarkable table service was the famous dessert set made originally for Louis XVI., and afterwards purchased by George IV., and placed in the Green Drawing-Room at Windsor Castle, where it is now. The ground colour is the rich *bleu du Roi*, and the medallions of mythological subjects are the work of Legay, Philippine, Dodin and Asselin. The value of the whole service has been assessed at £100,000. The late Mr. Goode possessed seventeen pieces, which were sold at Christie's in 1895. These are all illustrated in Litchfield's *Pottery and Porcelain.*

In the inventory of "Decorative China" at Windsor Castle, each piece of this famous service is specially described, together with the facsimile of its mark, subject, name of artist, and a small photograph for identification; and when Mr. Goode's Sèvres was exhibited in 1882, the subjects on the specimens noted in the Windsor Castle inventory as "missing" were carefully compared with those in Mr. Goode's Collection by Mr. Seabrook, and a note is placed in the inventory by that gentleman to the effect that they are in no single case the individual specimens missing from the Windsor Castle service. He suggests that they may have been extra pieces made at the time, or for some trifling defect placed on one side and sold. He also says that at the Loan Exhibition at South Kensington in 1862 there were fifteen pieces exhibited, and it is these and two others which Mr. Goode afterwards bought. There are twelve pieces missing from the Windsor Castle service. In the inventory mentioned above, there is a record of the actual cost of each piece at the Sèvres Factory, taken from the archives of that establishment, and as this has never yet been published, it is very interesting to compare the prices with those which such specimens now command by public auction.

The description of each piece is in curious terms; thus the seaux or ice-pails are called "pails for bottles"; this is probably the clumsy translation of the French term *seau* when the inventory was compiled some thirty or forty years ago. In each case the year of production at Sèvres is given :—

Plates	Original cost	480 francs each	
5 Pails for bottles	1787-9-90	960 ,, ,,	
1 Smaller	1786	840 ,, ,,	
10 Pails for glasses	1784-5-6-8-9-90	480 ,, ,,	
1 Oval pail with separation or glass-holder	1784	720 ,,	
1 Pail for ice, with cover	1785	840 ,,	
1 Punch-bowl	1788	4800 ,,	
1 Middling-sized bowl or mortar	1788	No price	
2 Salad-bowls	1787-9	720 francs each	
3 Round compotiers	1785-9	480 ,, ,,	
2 Long compotiers	1786	480 ,, ,,	
2 Butter dishes, covers, and stands	1785-7	600 ,, ,,	
2 Sugar-basins with covers and stands	1785-7	600 ,, ,,	
1 Mustard-pot with stand	1787	600 ,, ,,	
7 Cream-jugs	1787	84 ,, ,,	
14 Ice-cups	1784-6-7	72 ,, ,,	
10 Double salt-cellars	1785-6-7	72 ,, ,,	
4 Egg-cups	1785-7	30 ,, ,,	

The present value of these plates, which cost 480 francs, or less than £20, is now from £150 to £200 and of the seaux or "pails for bottles," which cost 1920 francs, or a little under £80, is now £500 to £700 the pair.

Some other remarkable services are in our best private collections.

Mr. Leopold de Rothschild has the fine turquoise ground service with bird paintings which was made for the Prince Cardinal de Rohan, and bears his monogram. The famous service made for Madame du Barry has been broken up, and one finds plates and dishes in various collections.

The beautiful jewelled Sèvres called in France *porcelain à émaux* is well known, being ornamented with appliqué gems in chaste gold settings, which appear to be the work at the same time of the porcelain-maker and the jeweller. According to the register of Sèvres, in 1784 the King presented to Prince Henry of Prussia "deux vases en pâte tendre ornés d'émaux, et un service de dessert, fond vert, orné de fleurs, de fruits et de diverses pièces de sculpture, dont quatorze représentant des française illustres. La valeur du présent était de . . . 28,052 livres" (£1122). The steel dies by which the gold mounts were stamped are still preserved at Sèvres. The jewelled Sèvres was first made in 1780 (CC), and as so many counterfeit examples are in existence, it may be well to caution the amateur that all pieces bearing an earlier date are false. A garniture of three oviform vases, rich gros bleu ground, jewelled and signed in gold, L. G. (Le Guay), are in Mr. Leopold de Rothschild's Collection, and are probably three of the finest specimens extant of this kind of Sèvres.

The models of the principal vases which have been made at the Sèvres manufactory were arranged by M. Riocreux in the Ceramic Museum. These models, preserved with so much diligence by the late M. Riocreux, it is feared, perished in the attack on Sèvres by the Prussians; the valuable Museum of pottery and porcelain having been fortunately removed previously, was preserved.

The forms from 1740 to 1800 are frequently named after the designers of the models, as the vase Falconnet, vase Clodion, vase La Rue, vase Duplessis, vase Boizot, vase Bachélier, vase Hébert, vase Pajou, vase Lefebvre, vase Bolvry, vase Daguerre, vase Grammont, vase Gardin, vase Madame Adelaide, vase Boileau, vase Lagrenée, vase La Riche, vase Madame Poupart, vase Moreau, &c.; others derived their names from their forms or ornamentation, as vaisseau à mât, vase grec à festons, vase gobelet, vase oignonnière, vase ovale cygne, vase à oreilles, vase cassolette, vase cornet, vase bouc, vase lézard, vase Angora, vase bouc à raisin, vase myrthe, vase à tête de morue, vase à panneaux, vase tête de lion, vase bourse, vase ruche, vase enfants, vase tulipe, vase à palme, vase rénard et raisins, vase militaire, vase solaire, vase torse, vase cuir, vase Syrène, vase serpent, vase pendule, vase antique ferré, vase œuf, vase fuseau, vase à l'amour Falconnet, vase fontaine à roseau, vase à ognon, vase tête d'éléphant Duplessis, a reproduction of which by Minton is at Windsor Castle, vase Bachélier de quatre saisons, vase à couronne, vase chinois, vase flacon à mouchoir, vase sphinx, vase caryatide, vase Mercure ovale, vase tourterelle, vase médaille, vase étrusque, vase Triton, vase colonne de Paris, &c. The principal groups and figures of which the moulds are still in existence at Sèvres are—la pêche et la chasse, le maître et la maîtresse d'école, une conversation espagnole, le flûteur et le hautbois espagnols, le déjeûner, la toilette, la nourrice; subjects from Don Quixote; fables of La Fontaine; la baigneuse, by Falconnet; la baigneuse aux roseaux, by Falconnet; Cupid, known as "Garde à vous," by the same; Leda; les enfants, by La Rue; le triomphe de la beauté; l'étude et la paresse, by Boizot; l'hommage à la beauté; le larcin de la rose; l'amour et la fidélité; la beauté couronnée par les Graces; l'amour remouleur, the last five by Boizot; and many classical subjects—the judgment of Paris, Achilles, Télémaque, &c.; busts of celebrated men; groups to commemorate events, as the marriage of the Dauphin, the birth of the Dauphin, by Pajou, 1781, &c.

Boizot was a sculptor, and designed many beautiful ornaments and friezes, many of which were executed in ormolu by Gouthière; a very fine clock in the Marquis of Hertford's Collection bears the following inscription: "Boizot fils sculpsit, et executé par Gouthière, cizeleur et doreur du roy, à Paris, Quay Pelletier, à la bouche d'or, 1771." In Sèvres we have the statuettes and groups of le triomphe de la beauté, l'étude et la paresse, l'hommage à la beauté, le larcin de la rose la beauté couronnée par les Graces, l'amour remouleur, &c.

Clodion was *sculpteur du Roi* and modeller, whose terra-cottas are well known; he also worked in marble the Sèvres group of the Graces.

Pajou, *sculpteur du Roi*, in marble and bronze groups in Sèvres—the birth of the Dauphin, the marriage of the Dauphin, and other historical groups.

Daguerre was a sculptor of ormolu ornaments and designer, *circa* 1775.

Bachélier, le vase de quatre saisons.

Duplessis was *sculpteur, fondeur, ciseleur et doreur du Roi, circa* 1775; he worked also in silver and bronze, and designed and ornamented with rich gilt mounts many vases of porphyry, agate, and Sèvres china, &c., he designed the vase Duplessis with the elephant-head handles.

Falconnet was a sculptor in marble; in Sèvres china his pieces were the vase à l'amour, statuettes of la baigneuse, la baigneuse aux roseaux, Cupid, known as the "Garde à vous," and the companion, &c.

Lagrenée, a painter, was employed at the Trianon to decorate the ceilings, &c.

La Rue, sculptor in marble, &c. In Sèvres biscuit we have a statuette of Leda and groups of children. The statuary work at Sèvres has always been executed in biscuit china in order to more closely resemble marble.

The signatures of several of these sculptors and modellers who worked at Sèvres will be found added to the present (13th edition) of Chaffers.

Pierre Gouthière was the most celebrated among the *ciseleurs* and *doreurs du Roy*, whose exquisite mountings are known to all the amateurs of our day, and much sought after, his choice bronze friezes and mouldings being literally worth their weight in gold. He was born about the year 1740. In 1771 he executed the ornamental work, such as clocks, candelabra, consoles, frames, fire-irons, bell-handles, cornices, locks, and all the fittings which adorned the Pavilion of Luciennes at Versailles and the hôtel of Madame du Barry; for three years' work in August 1773 he received no less than 124,000 livres, equivalent to about 350,000 francs of the present day.   Gouthière continued working for Madame du Barry, as shown by her Memoirs, down to 1793, the date of her execution, at which time a large sum was still owing, which he never recovered.   He also supplied Louis XVI. and Marie Antoinette with his chasings.   The Duc d'Aumont, the Duchesse de Mazarin, and all the principal people of the court patronised him.   In 1806 the poor artist, doubtless ruined long before, again applied for the liquidation of his claims against the Government without success, and he was reduced to solicit a home in the hospital, where he died in great distress.   Such was the end of the greatest chaser France ever produced, more unfortunate still than his contemporary, André Charles Boulle, who, having served the King and the richest people of the court, was allowed to die in poverty.

The feet or pedestals of the larger vases being made and baked separately and afterwards put together, to prevent confusion had occasionally the names of the corresponding portions scratched underneath to denote which they belonged to, as "pied de vase enfants," "pied de vase tête de lion," "pied de vase lézard," &c., inscriptions which have much puzzled some amateurs.

The principal colours used in decorating the ground of the Sèvres vases were:—

1. The "*bleu céleste*," or "*turquoise*," invented in 1752 by Hellot.
2. The rich deep cobalt blue, called "*bleu du Roi*," of which there were two varieties, the darker being designated "*gros bleu*."
3. The "*violet pensée*," a beautiful violet colour, from a mixture of manganese, one of the rarest decorations of the *pâte tendre*.
4. The "*rose Pompadour*,"[1] a charming pink or rose colour, invented in 1757 by Xhrouet of Sèvres.
5. The "*jaune clair*," or "*jonquille*," a sort of clear canary colour.
6. The "*verte pomme*," or apple green.
7. The "*verte pré*," or bright grass green.
8. The "*rouge de fer*," a brilliant red.
9. The "*gris d'agathe*," agate grey.
10. The "*pourpre*," purple.
11. The "*carmin*," carmine.
12. The "*bleu lapis*," or gros bleu, veined.
13. The "*bleu turc*," or "*turquin*," a pale greyish blue, which must not be confounded with the *turquoise*.

Many other grounds occur in inventories, among which are fond *vert sablé*, fond *rose tendre*, fond *vert rehaussé d'or*, fond *or riche*, fond *vert œil de perdrix*, fond *lapis caillouté*.

---

[1] This colour is called in England "*rose du Barry*," but it is not known by that name in France, being usually designated "*rose Pompadour*." It was discovered in the time of Madame de Pompadour, who greatly encouraged the ceramic manufactory at Sèvres, and it became her favourite colour.   The dates on the first specimens range from 1757 to about the time of her death. Xhrouet was an artist attached to the manufactory, and as a recompense for the discovery of this beautiful colour he received 150 livres (francs).   The orthography of his name is here correctly written, for a contemporary publisher of Paris, probably a relation, so spells it in an edition of Marmontel: his mark was a cross, which it is supposed alludes to the proper pronunciation of his name.

It may be useful to recount here a system of deception carried on to a great extent some years ago, namely, that of counterfeiting old Sèvres. Afted the discovery of French kaolin, the attention of the director was turned especially to the production of true china or hard paste, although soft paste was made simultaneously. When M. Brongniart became director, the hard paste was almost entirely made, sacrificing the old *pâte tendre*, which was declared to be useless in art, of expensive manipulation, dangerous to the workmen, subject to great risk in the furnace, &c.; a considerable accumulation, therefore, of white unfinished pieces remained stowed away in the warerooms, which greatly embarrassed them, and the glory of the *pâte tendre* having passed away, the director unwisely resolved to part with it all. In 1813 three dealers, named Pérès, Ireland, and Jarman, purchased the whole stock at a merely nominal price, and immediately took rooms close to the Sèvres factory and commenced decorating it, being assisted by many of the old painters of Sèvres. Here they soon completed vast quantities of pseudo-Sèvres, which soon spread over Europe; they were so well finished that even royalty itself was deceived. In the following year (1814) a nobleman purchased a déjeûner, beautifully gilt and ornamented with painted medallions of portraits of Louis XIV. and the principal persons of his court. In the same year it was presented to Louis XVIII. as a valuable family relic, and it remained for more than two years in the salon of the Tuileries. Some doubts of its genuineness having arisen, the Comte de Pradel sent the service to the Sèvres manufactory, and there more experienced persons soon discovered the deceit. The hybrid ornamentation soon betrayed its recent decoration; the principal plateau belonged to an epoch subsequent to the Revolution, the gilding was much inferior, the paintings too highly worked up for those of the eighteenth century, and the monograms of the painters fictitious : one of these was the letter S followed by points, not on the ancient list of painters' marks; it proved to be the mark of one Soiron, an enameller specially retained by the firm Pérès. The King then placed it in the Museum as a warning to others. At Sèvres every piece of ware is usually marked by the particular signs of the painter and gilder, accompanied by the double L and the letters denoting the date : a reference, therefore, to the Tables, observing where the signs of the painters agree with the subjects they painted, and if the dates correspond with the style in vogue at that particular time, will suffice to detect the false pieces. This system of fabricating old Sèvres from early *pâte tendre* has led to the destruction of many interesting pieces from the fabriques of Menneçy, Chantilly, Tournay, &c.

M. Arnoux ("Report on Pottery at the Paris Exhibition, 1867") relates : —

"About 1804, the person who presided over the mixture of the soft paste died, followed a few months afterwards by the head-fireman. These vacancies in his staff confirmed M. Brongniart in his resolution to suppress entirely the manufacture of soft porcelain, and give his attention wholly to the hard. M. Brongniart, certainly the most eminent and learned of all who have managed the Sèvres manufactory, cannot be blamed for this decision, which was in accordance with the tastes of the time; but towards the end of his career he was one of the first to recognise the mistake he had committed. M. Ebelman, his pupil and successor, in 1847 reproduced the *pâte tendre* during the four years of his management, but did not prepare the body of the soft paste he used, owing to a singular fact. In 1804 M. Brongniart requiring the cellar where the clay for the soft paste was stored, decided to have it thrown away. The order was received by an intelligent man, who put it aside in some covered tanks, where it remained unnoticed for forty-five years, till M. Ebelman manifested the wish to revive the old *pâte tendre*. It was then M. Riocreux revealed to him the existence of the hidden treasure. This unexpected help, besides saving the time spent in experiments and supplying material for immediate use, gave—what was more important—a standard for all the new mixtures. Since then Sèvres has continued to produce the soft paste, but in less quantity than could be wished."

FAMOUS COLLECTIONS OF OLD SÈVRES PORCELAIN.

The collection of H.M. the King at Windsor Castle and Buckingham Palace, containing about 300 specimens.

The collection of Sir Richard Wallace (now the property of the nation) at Hertford House, Manchester Square, London, containing 223 specimens.

The Jones Collection at the Victoria and Albert Museum.

The private collection of the Earl of Harewood at Harewood House, near Leeds, open to the public on Thursdays.

The collections of the Duke of Buccleuch, Lord Hillingdon, and some members of the Rothschild family.

Illustrations of specimens in *Ker. Gall.*, enlarged edition, coloured plate facing page 288, and figs. 345-47.

SÈVRES MARKS.

This manufactory was first established at Vincennes in 1740. The porcelain was not marked with letters to denote the date until 1753. On the 19th November of that year a decree of the King directed their use, in conjunction with the double L. In the Sèvres Museum is a specimen with the interlaced L's enclosing the letter A, and under it, in Arabic numerals, the date 1753. The works were carried on at Vincennes until 1756, therefore the letters A, B, and C denote the pieces actually made there; with D commenced the Sèvres porcelain, the manufactory being removed in 1756. Those pieces with the double interlaced L, and no letter enclosed, but merely a simple point, are by some considered to be of Vincennes previous to 1753. This is to a certain extent correct, but not invariably so, for there are many instances of subsequent pieces being also undated. In the Sèvres Museum is a basin thus marked, painted with a view of the Château de Vincennes.

There is a special feature in the decoration of the best Vincennes porcelain which should be observed. The beautiful rich dark blue ground is shaded and uneven from the colour having been applied to the surface with a brush, and it is known as "bleu de Vincennes." Afterwards, when the Sèvres factory had taken over the Vincennes works, the method of adding the colour by means of a powder was adopted, and the colour became more even in consequence.

THE FIRST ROYAL EPOCH, FROM 1745 TO 1792, INCLUDED THE EARLIER WORKS AT VINCENNES *(q.v.)*.

VINCENNES or SÈVRES. Marked in gold on a cup and saucer, green ground and flowers on border and gilding, formerly in the possession of Lady Palmerston; painted by Fumez, 1754.

SÈVRES. In 1764 the Pompadour period ended. In 1764 the gilding of porcelain in other French manufactories was prohibited. In 1769 hard paste was discovered; from this time until 1802 both hard and soft paste were made simultaneously. In 1780 jewelled porcelain was first made. The double L. was occasionally ornamented, as in the margin.

SÈVRES. These two marks, of 1770 and 1771, with their accompanying emblems, not being in the list of painters, have been considered allusive to the comet of 1769; but the first is found on pieces dated 1761, 1770, and 1776, and is probably the mark of a painter whose name is unknown. These occur on a cup and saucer formerly in the Collection of the Rev. T. Staniforth, and now in the Rev. A. H. S. Barwell's possession.

The double letters were used in 1778 and ended in 1795 with RR (see Table of Signs, p. 604). In 1784 the prohibition of gilding in other manufactories was removed. In 1786 the Louis Sixteenth style prevailed.

FIRST REPUBLICAN EPOCH, 1792 TO 1804.

"République Française," accompanied by the word "Sèvres." The mark traced with a brush in green, blue, or red, according to the fancy of the painter.

On a cup and saucer with Revolutionary emblems, dated 1795; in the Victoria and Albert Museum.

R.F
Sevres.

"République Française." The custom of marking the ware with the date of its manufacture ceased in 1795, and was not renewed until 1801.

$\mathcal{R}.\mathcal{F}$
Sevres.

"République Française." This mark is another variety of the same epoch.

Sèvres

These marks of the Republican period lasted from 1793 to 1800.

$MN^{\underline{\underline{le}}}$
Sèvres

This mark indicates the Consular period, and was first used in 1803, generally stencilled in red.

FIRST IMPERIAL EPOCH, 1804 TO 1814.

$M.Imp^{\underline{le}}$
de Sevres.

This mark (1806), varying the sign placed under the words, was used by Napoleon from 1804 to 1809, usually printed or stencilled in red. In 1805 the manufacture of soft paste was discontinued under Brongniart, director.

The Imperial Eagle, painted in red, was used in 1810, and continued until the abdication of the Emperor in 1814.

SECOND ROYAL EPOCH, 1814 TO 1848.

Louis XVIII., 1814 to 1824. The royal cipher revived, printed in blue; the fleur-de-lis, Sèvres, and 21 being the last two figures of the year 1821.

Reign of Charles X., 1824 to 1829. The ciphers CC interlaced, enclosing sometimes the numeral X., sometimes a fleur-de-lis, are painted in blue. The figures indicate the year: thus, 1824, 1827 and 1825.

Charles X. Mark used in 1829 and 1830; this was applied to porcelain merely gilt at the edges.

Used on decorated pieces. The mark printed in blue, for 1829 and 1830.

This mark, printed in blue, was only used from the beginning of August 1830 to the end of the year.

Louis Philippe. This mark was used from 1831 until November 1834, printed in blue.

Louis Philippe. These initials were used from November 1834 until July 1845. The mark is generally printed in blue or green for decorated pieces.

The Château d'Eu services of white and gold, dated 1837, bear this mark in addition.

This mark occurs on a pair of hard-paste vases beautifully painted in Raffaelesque ornament, and mounted by Gouthière with handles formed as goats, in His Majesty's Collection, Windsor Castle.

Services were made at Sèvres for all the royal palaces; we have met with many others: "CHÂTEAU DE COMPIÈGNE," "CHÂTEAU DE NEUILLY," "CHÂTEAU DE TUILERIES," "CHÂTEAU DE DREUX," "CHÂTEAU DE FONTAINEBLEAU" (1846), &c.

The double cipher of Louis Philippe, principally on white wares, impressed and printed in blue or green; used from 1845 to 1848.

After 1833 the last two numerals of date in an oval printed in chrome green were adopted for white porcelain.

SECOND REPUBLICAN EPOCH, 1848 TO 1851.

"République Française," 1851. The marks printed in red, used for decorated pieces from 1848 to 1851.

SECOND IMPERIAL EPOCH, 1852.

The mark used after the proclamation of the Empire in 1852.

Monogram of the Emperor Napoleon III., used in 1854 and continued. In 1854 the manufacture of soft paste, which had been abandoned for fifty years, was revived.

This mark is stencilled in green on ordinary white pieces for 1861; when scratched through, it denotes that the piece has been issued without decoration.

For the more recent marks of the Sèvres factory the editor is indebted to the valuable work of Cte de Chavagnac et Mis de Grollier, entitled *Histoire des Manufactures Françaises de Porcelaine.*

THIRD REPUBLICAN EPOCH.

Used in 1871. Printed in red.

1872-99. Printed in red.

1880-89. Printed in red.

1890-1904. Printed in red without date.

1888-91. Stamped in relief : a potter at work.

1848-99. Mark printed in green on pieces before firing.

Same mark, but scratched through to show that it was issued without decoration.

1860-99. Stamped on *biscuit* china.

1900-4. Mark in green to indicate year of manufacture.

1900-4. Mark stamped in *biscuit*.

1900-2. Mark in red to indicate date of decoration.

1900-2. Mark in red to indicate date of gilding.

1900. Mark used for large decorated specimens.

1902-4. Mark used to indicate year of decoration.

1902-4. Mark used to indicate date of gilding.

1898 and 1904. Marks used for specimens presented to ministers, ambassadors, &c.

TABLE OF MARKS AND MONOGRAMS

OF

PAINTERS, DECORATORS, AND GILDERS OF THE ROYAL MANUFACTORY OF SÈVRES,

FROM 1753 TO 1800.

Marks.	Names of Painters.	Subjects.	Period of Work, from
	ALONCLE, François	Birds, flowers, and emblems	1758-81
	ANTEAUME, Jean-Jacques	Landscapes and animals	1754-
	ARMAND, Pierre Louis Philippe	Birds, flowers, &c.	1746-85
	ASSELIN	Portraits, miniatures	1764-1803
	AUBERT ainé	Flowers	1754-
	BAILLY, fils	Flowers	1745-93
	BAR, or BARRE	Detached bouquets	1780-91
	BARDET	Flowers	1751-1800
	BARRAT	Garlands, bouquets	1769-
	BAUDOUIN	Ornaments; friezes; gilder of the second class	1750-
	BECQUET	Flowers	1748-
	BERTRAND	Detached bouquets	1750-1800
	BIENFAIT, J. B.	Gilding and painting	1755-59

Marks.	Names of Painters.	Subjects.	Period of Work, from
♈	BINET	Detached bouquets	1750-
S c	BINET, M^{dme}, *née* Sophie CHA-NOU; see also CHANOU.	Garlands, bouquets	1750-1800
(tree mark)	BOUCHET, Jean	Landscapes, animals, ornaments; also gilder	1757-93
B	BOUCOT	Birds and flowers	Before 1800
Pb or P B.	BOUCOT, P.	Flowers, arabesques and garlands	1785-91
Y.	BOUILLAT, fils	Flowers, landscapes	1800-11
R.B.	BOUILLAT, Rachel, afterwards M^{dme} MAQU-ERET	Detached bouquets	
B.	BOULANGER	Detached bouquets, and painter in gold of the first class	1779-85
&	BOULANGER, jun.	Children, rustic subjects	1770-81
Bn.	BULIDON	Detached bouquets	1763-
m.b or MB	BUNEL, M^{dme}, *née* BUTEUX, Manon	Detached bouquets	1778-1817
(anchor mark)	BUTEUX, sen.	Cupids, flowers, emblems, &c., *en camaieu*	1759-86
9.	BUTEUX, eld. son.	Detached bouquets &c.	1760-
(triangle with dot)	BUTEUX, yr. son	Pastorals, children, &c.; painter and gilder	1759-
(triangle)	CAPELLE, M^{dme}.	Various friezes	1749-

Marks.	Names of Painters.	Subjects.	Period of Work, from
	CARDIN	Detached bouquets; chief of painters in 1793	1749-
	CARRIER, or CARRIÉ	Flowers	1752-
c.	CASTEL	Landscapes, hunting subjects, birds, &c.; gilder in 1793	1771-
	CATON	Pastorals, children, portraits	1747-93
	CATRICE	Detached bouquets and flowers	Before 1800
ch.	CHABRY	Miniatures, pastorals; sculptor and modeller	1763-
Sc	CHANOU, Sophie, afterwards M^{dme} BINET	Garlands, bouquets, and landscapes; see also Binet	1750-1800
IC	CHANOU, Jean-Baptiste	*Chef des fours et pâtes*	1779-1825
	CHANOU, M^{dme}.	Flowers and ground colours	Before 1800
c.p:	CHAPUIS, sen.	Flowers, birds	1756-
j.c.	CHAPUIS, jun.	Detached bouquets	1800-
	CHAUVAUX, sen.	Gilding of first class	1752-93
j.n.	CHAUVAUX, jun.	Gilding and bouquets	1773-
	CHEVALIER, Pierre François	Flowers, bouquets	1755-
	CHOISY, DE	Flowers, arabesques	1770-
	CHULOT	Emblems, flowers, and arabesques	1755-93

Marks.	Names of Painters.	Subjects.	Period of Work, from
c .m . or **CM**	COMMELIN	Garlands, bouquets	1765-93
L. or	COUTURIER	Gilding	1783-

COTEAU of Geneva was one of the artists who decorated the *jewelled Sèvres;* he was an enameller, and his beautiful enamelled frames are much prized.

Marks.	Names of Painters.	Subjects.	Period of Work, from
♪	CORNAILLE	Flowers, bouquets	1755-
	DE L'ATRE	(Mark attributed only)	1754-
	DIEU	Chinese subjects, flowers, gilding	1780-90
k or **K.**	DODIN	Figures, various subjects portraits	1754-1803
	DRAND	Chinese subjects and gilding (formerly at Chantilly)	1761-
	DUBOIS, Jean René	Flowers and garlands	1756-57
	DUROSEY, Julia	Flowers, friezes, &c.	
	DUROSEY, Soph., afterwards M^{dme} NOUAILHER	Flowers, friezes, &c.	
	DUSOLLE	Detached bouquets	Before 1800
D T.	DUTANDA	Bouquets, garlands	1773-
	EVANS	Butterflies, landscapes, and animals later. Birds in 1780.	1752-93
F	FALOT	Arabesques, birds, butterflies	1764-80
	FONTAINE	Emblems, miniatures, and gilding	1752-

Marks.	Names of Painters.	Subjects.	Period of Work, from
♡	FONTELLIAU	Gilding	1753-
Y	FOURÉ	Flowers, bouquets	Previous to 1748
☀	FRITSCH	Figures, children	1763-65
ƒ z or ƒ. ✗.	FUMEZ	Flowers, arabes-ques, &c.	1776-93
❧	GAUTHIER	Landscapes, animals,	1787-91
G	GENEST	Figures, &c. (chief of painters)	1752-80
☨	GENIN, Charles	Figures, genre sub-jects	1756-58
G d.	GERARD, Claude Charles	Pastorals, minia-tures	1771-1825
ℒ.l or ℒₜ	GERARD, Mdme.	Flowers	-1792
ℛ	GIRARD	Arabesques, Chinese subjects	1771-93
☤	GOMERY	Birds	1756
G t.	GREMONT	Garlands, bouquets	1769-
X or X	GRISON	Gilding	1749-
J n.	HENRION	Garlands, bouquets	1768
h c.	HÉRICOURT	Garlands, bouquets	1755-
W or W	HILKEN	Figures, subjects, &c.	Previous to 1800
H	HOURY	Flowers	1747-
H.	HUNY	Flowers	Previous to 1800
Z.	JOYAU	Detached bouquets	Previous to 1800

Marks.	Names of Painters.	Subjects.	Period of Work, from
j.	JUBIN	Gilding	Previous to 1800
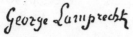	LAMPRECHT, George	Animals and figures	1784-93
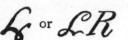 or *LR*	LA ROCHE	Bouquets, medallions, emblems	1758-
or	LEANDRE	Pastoral subjects	Previous to 1800
L	LE BEL, sen.	Figures and flowers	
LB or *LB*	LE BEL, jun.	Garlands, bouquets, insects (gilder in 1793)	1765-93
LL or **LL**	LECOT	Chinese subjects	1763-93
‿	LEDOUX, Jean Pierre	Landscapes and birds	1758-
LG or **LG**	LE GUAY, sen.	Famous gilder and painter in blue at Vincennes	1749-
	LE GUAY, Pierre André	Miniatures, children, trophies, Chinese; also gilder	1772-
L or *L* or *Levé*	LÉVÉ, père	Flowers, birds, and arabesques	1754-
f	LÉVÉ, Felix	Flowers, Chinese	Previous to 1800
R.B	MAQUERET, M^{dme}, *née* Rachel BOUILLAT	Flowers	Previous to 1800
M	MASSY	Flowers and emblems	1789-1802
∫ or *S*	MÉRAULT, sen.	Various friezes	1754

Marks.	Names of Painters.	Subjects.	Period of Work, from
9	MÉRAULT, jun.	Bouquets, garlands; also gilder	1759-90
X	MICHAUD	Flowers, bouquets, medallions	1757-80
m or *M*	MICHEL	Detached bouquets	Previous to 1800
M.	MOIRON	Detached bouquets	1790
5.	MONGENOT	Flowers, bouquets	1754-
H or *M*	MORIN	Marine and military subjects; famous artist	1754-80
A	MUTEL	Landscapes	1754-
n φ	NIQUET	Painter and gilder	1764
⊥	NOEL, Guillaume	Flowers, ornaments	1755-93
SD	NOUAILHER, M^{dme}, *née* Sophie DURO-SEY	Flowers	1780-
👁	PAJOU	Figures	1750-
P	PARPETTE, Philippe	Flowers and gilding	1755-93
L. S	PARPETTE, Louise	Flowers, garlands	Previous to 1880
P.T.	PETIT, Nicholas, sen.	Flowers	1756-
f	PFEIFFER	Detached bouquets; also gilder	1793-
PH	PHILIPPINE the elder	Children, *genre* subjects	1779-1823
p ᵃ or *p.*	PIERRE, sen.	Flowers, bouquets	Previous to 1880
P 7 or *p 7.*	PIERRE, Jean Jacques, jun.	Bouquets, garlands	1763-

Marks.	Names of Painters.	Subjects.	Period of Work. from
S.t	PITHOU, sen.	Portraits, historical subjects: consulting artist	1772-93
S.j.	PITHOU, jun.	Figures, ornaments, flowers	1749-93
HP.	PRÉVOST	Gilding; also flowers	1754-93
(vase) or (vase)	POUILLOT	Detached bouquets	1777-
(dots)	RAUX	Detached bouquets	Previous to 1800
XX	ROCHER	Figures and miniatures	1758-
M	ROSSET	Landscapes, flowers and animals	1753-93
R L	ROUSSEL	Detached bouquets	Previous to 1800
S. h .	SCHRADRE	Birds, landscapes	1783-
s s.p.	SINSSON, Jacques Nicholas, père	Flowers	1795-
(antlers) or (wreath)	SINSSON, Nicholas	Flowers, groups, and garlands	1773-
(mark) or (dots)	SIOUX, sen.	Bouquets, garlands formerly a fan painter	1752-80
O	SIOUX, jun.	Flowers and garlands *en camaieu*	1752-
◇ or ◇	TABARY	Birds, &c.	1754-
❀	TAILLANDIER	Bouquets, garlands	1753-90

Marks.	Names of Painters.	Subjects.	Period of Work, from
• • •	TANDART	Bouquets, garlands	1755-
	TARDI, Claude Antoine	Bouquets, garlands	1757-95
TANAY	TAUNAY	Famous as specialist in colours (carmine, violet, and pink)	1753-
• • • •	THEODORE	Gilding	Previous to 1800
or	THEVENET, sen.	Flowers, medallions, groups	
jt:	THEVENET, jun.	Flowers, ornaments, friezes	1752-59
VD	VANDÉ	Gilding, flowers	1755-
Y:t	VAUTRIN, afterwards Madame GERARD	Bouquets, friezes	
W	VAVASSEUR	Arabesques and flowers	1753-
or	VIELLARD	Emblems, ornaments	1752-
2000	VINCENT	Gilding (this mark is a pun on the painter's name)	1752-1803
3V	WEYDINGER, Pierre	Gilder	About 1780 -1817
or	XHROUET	Landscapes; said to be the inventor of the rose-coloured ground	1750
or +	YVERNEL	Landscapes, birds	1750

MARKS OF PAINTERS (UNKNOWN).

Marks.	Name of Painter.	Subjects.
L F or *LF*	Unknown	Cupids, &c.

J.F.   On a jonquil cup and saucer, beautifully painted with Leda and swan and emblems; date 1780.

ts   On a bleu du Roi cup and saucer, painted with pastoral figures and emblems; date 1764. (Probably a mark of Pajou.)

┃   On two cups and saucers, painted with small wreaths of flowers, festoons and decorations, dated 1770 and 1776; also on a saucer of similar decoration, delicately painted, lake, blue and gold borders. 1761.

VB   On a cup and saucer, turquoise, painted with interiors and women and children, the gilding by Prévost; dated 1781.

I.N.   On a cup and saucer, white ground with festoons and bouquets of flowers, bordered with green ovals and gold stars, painted by Tandart, 1780.

ᴟ   On an oval plateau, painted with a fisherman in landscape and ruins, deep turquoise border, date 1758; also on a cup and saucer, with medallions of children; date 1765.

Y⟩   On a cup and saucer, canary ground, in centre, a basket of flowers and fruit, the gilding by Vincent; date 1788.

FM   This mark of an acorn and oak leaf in blue, and FM in gold, are below the double L and date 1765. The former belongs to a painter, the latter to a gilder, both of which are unpublished; they occur on a gros bleu *trembleuse* with Vernet subjects, formerly in the Shandon Collection. Since ascribed by M. E. Garnier to Gauthier and inserted in the preceding list.

GI   Mark of a gilder employed at Sèvres, on a cup and saucer, 1790, painted by Lévé *père;* also on another cup and saucer, time of the Republic, painted by Commelin; in the possession of J. W. Crowe, Esq.

LATE PERIOD, 1800 TO ABOUT 1900.

Marks.	Names of Painters.	Subjects.	Period of Work, from
ℐ. A.	ANDRÉ, Jules	Landscapes	1843-69
A.R.	APOIL, Charles Alexis	Figures, subjects, &c.	1845-64
E.R.	APOIL, M^{dme}	Figures	1864-9
P.A	AVISSE, Alexandre Paul	Ornaments	1850-
B	BALDISSERONI	Figure subjects	1860-79
B	BALLANGER	Decorator	1902-04
B	BARBIN, François Hubert	Ornaments	1824-39
AB	BARRÉ, Louis Desiré	Flowers (chief of painters)	1881
B. or BARRIAT	BARRIAT, Charles	Figures and ornaments	1852-83
AB	BELET, Adolphe	Decorator	After 1800
B	BELET, Emile	Painter	1876-
B	BELET, Louis	Decorator	1879-1904
HB	BIENVILLE, H.	Decorator	1877-1904

Marks.	Names of Painters.	Subjects.	Period of Work. from
ᴜB	BLANCHARD, Louis Etienne	Gilder and painter	1849-67
A.B.	BLANCHARD, Alex.	Decorator and modeller	1878-1900
ᴜMB	BOCQUET	Decorator	1902-4
B.ϟ	BOITEL	Gilding	About 1800
ÆB	BONNIER, Achille	Decorations	After 1850
ÆB	BONNUIT	Decorations	1858-1904
ÆB	BOULLEMIER, A.	Gilding	About 1830 -42
F. B	BOULLEMIER, sen.	Gilding	1807-
B f	BOULLEMIER, jun.	Gilding	About 1830
(Ey)	BRECY, Paul	Decorator	1880-1904
Brunel.R	BRUNEL-ROCQUES, Antoiné	Painter	1863-
B	BULOT, Eugéne Alexandre	Flowers and birds	1862-1883
EB	BULOT, Eugène	Flowers and birds	1862-1883
B x.	BUTEUX, apprentice	Flowers	About 1800
Œ	CABAU	Flowers	1847-84
C.P	CAPRONNIER	Gilding	About 1814
Ch.C.	CATTEAU	Painter	1902-4

Marks.	Names of Painters.	Subjects.	Period of Work, from
I. G	CELOS	Decorations; *pâte sur pâte*	1865-94
L C	CHARPENTIER	Decorations	About 1850
F.C.	CHARRIN, D^{lle} Fanny	Figures, subjects, portraits	After 1800
C.C.	CONSTANT	Gilding	1804-15
C. T.	CONSTANTIN	Figures	1813-45
Ft FC	COURCY, A. F. de	Figures	1866-86
A	COURSAJET		Died in 1886
A	DAMMOUSE	Figures and ornaments; *pâte sur pâte*	About 1870-80
AD	DAVID, Alex.	Decorations; also gilding	1850-82
D. F.	DAVIGNON	Landscapes	Died 1812
De Gault.	DEGAULT, J. M.	Figures *en grisaille*	1808-17
D.F.	DELAFOSSE	Figures	1805-15
DC	DERICHSWEILER	Decorations	1858-88
D P.	DESPERAIS	Ornaments	1794-1812
D h	DEUTSCH	Gilder	1805-17
C D	DEVELLY, C.	Landscapes and figures	1813-48
Þ Þ	DEVICQ	Figures	1880-1904

Marks.	Names of Painters.	Subjects.	Period of Work, from
D.Ì.	DIDIER	Ornaments	1819-48
ℍₛ	DROUET, Emile	Figures and decorations	1879-1904
D.Ɡ	DROUET, Gilbert	Flowers and gilding	About 1800
Ac.D.	DUCLUZEAU, M^{dme}	Figures, subjects, portraits	1807-48
Dy	DUROSEY, C. C. M.	Gilding (chief of gilders)	1802-
ꞭD	EAUBONNE d'	Decorator	1904
ℑ	ESCALLIER, M^{dme} Marie	Flowers	1874-88
HF	FARAGUET, M^{dme}	Figures, subjects, &c.	1856-70
Ƒ	FICQUENET, Charles	Flowers and ornaments; *pâte sur pâte*	1864-81
Ꞙ.	FONTAINE, Jean Joseph	Flowers	1827-57
A.Fournier ⬡ or *A.F.*	FOURNIER, A.	Decorator	1878-1904
ꞮhꞖ.	FRAGONARD, E. T. E.	Figures, *genre*, &c.	1847-69
EF	FROMENT, E. J. V.	Figures and subjects	1853-84
Gu.	GANEAU, jun.	Gilding	After 1800
Ꞡ	BEBLEUX, Gustave		1883-1903

Marks.	Names of Painters	Subjects.	Period of Work, from
J.G.	GELY	Ornaments (*pâte sur pâte*)	1851-88
G. G.	GEORGET, Jean	Figures, portraits	1802-23
Gob.R	GOBERT, A. T.	Figures in enamel and on paste	Died about 1884
J.Goddé.	GODDÉ, A. J.	Decorator and enameller	1861-80
D.G.	GODIN, fils	Gilding and painting *en camaieu*	1792-1831
F. G. or	GOUPIL, Frederic	Figures	1860-79
	GUILLEMAIN	Decorations	1872-
	HALLION, Eug.	Landscapes	1870-
	HALLION, François	Gilding, decorations	1866-77
h. ϑ.	HUARD, Pierre	Ornaments	1811-46
.Є.Ӡ.	HUMBERT	Figures	1812-
Ꞓ	JARDEL	Decorator	1886-1904
Æ	JULIENNE, Eug.	Renaissance ornaments	About 1837
Lagrenée Jne	LA GRENÉE, the younger		After 1875
L.H.	LAMBERT	Flowers	1864-96
L G ce·	LANGLACE, J. B. G.	Landscapes	1807-44
P: Langlois	LANGLOIS	Landscapes	1847-72

Marks.	Names of Painters.	Subjects.	Period of Work, from
H	LASSERRE	Painter	1896-1904
L	LATACHE	Gilding	1870-79
L..B.	LE BEL, Nicholas	Landscapes	About 1823
L	LE CAT	Ground colours	1872-1904
L.	LEGAY, J. E.	Ornaments; *pâte sur pâte*	1866-84
A	LEGER	Painter	1902-4
L.G.	LEGRAND	Chinese subjects	About 1800
L.G.	LE GUAY, Et. Ch.	Figures, portraits Re-entered	1780-1782 1812-40
EL	LEROY, Eugène	Gilding	1864-88
AL	LIGUÉ, Denis	Painter	1881-1904
C.L.	LUCAS Charles C.	Painter; also modeller, *see list*	1877-1904
𝒩 or ⋔	MARTINET	Flowers	1861-70
E. de M	MAUSSION, Mlle de	Figures	1860-70
FM	MÉRIGOT, F.	Flowers and decorations	1848-70
AMouEXR	MEYER, Alfred	Figures, &c.	1863-71
MC	MICAUD	Gilding	About 1800
OM	MILET, Optat	Decorations on fayence and paste	1862-76
LM	MIMART	Decorator	1884-1904

Marks.	Names of Painters.	Subjects.	Period of Work, from
𝓜 𝓡	MOREAU, Louis Philippe Auguste	Gilder	1838-71
𝓜 𝓡	MOREAU, Denis Joseph	Gilding	1809-15
𝓜	MORIN	Gilder	1888-1904
AM	MORIOT, Nicolas Marie	Figures, &c.	1830-48
𝓜	MORIOT, M^dlle	Figures and subjects	After 1800
O. Ch	OUINT, Charles	Decorator	1879-82
O	OUINT, Emanuel	Ground layer	1877-89
𝓟	PAILLET, Fernand	Ornaments and figures	1879-88
P	PALLANDRE	Flowers and decorations	After 1850
𝓟.𝓢.	PARPETTE, D^lle	Flowers	1791-1825
P	PELUCHE	Decorator	1880-1904
𝓟.𝓱.	PHILIPPINE	Flowers and ornaments	1785-91
		Re-entered	1807-40
𝓟	PIHAN	Decorator	1888-1904
P	PLINE	Painter	1867
		Gilder	1870
𝓟	PORCHON	Ornament	After 1800
𝓡	POUPART, A.	Landscapes	1815-48
𝓠	QUENNOY	Decorator	1902
R or 𝓡.	REGNIER, F.	Figures, various subjects	1836-60

Marks.	Names of Painters.	Subjects.	Period of Work. from
ЈꞦ	REGNIER, Hya-cinthe	Figures, &c.	1825-63
ꞝꞦ	REJOUX, Emile	Decorations and gilding	1862-90
E 1,000	RENARD, Emile	Decorations	1846-
ℋℭꞦ.	RENARD, Henri	Landscapes	1881
ꞠꞚꞦ or ꞝꞦ	RICHARD, Emile	Flowers	1867-70
E.R	RICHARD, Eug.	Flowers	1838-72
Ꞧ or ꞝ	RICHARD, Fran-çois Gervais	Decorations	1833-78
ЈꞜ.Ꞧ.	RICHARD, Joseph	Decorations	1830-70
꭪ or ꭪	RICHARD, Paul	Gilding	1849-81
L R	RICHARD, Leon	Painter	1902-4
Ꞧ	RIOCREUX, Isi-dore	Landscapes	1847
Ꞧ	RIOCREUX, Dé-siré-Denis	Flowers	1807-
PR	ROBERT, Pierre	Landscapes	1815-30
ꞒR	ROBERT, M^{dme}	Flowers and land-scapes	After 1800
Ꞧ	ROBERT, Jean François	Landscapes	1806-43
PⱮR	ROUSSEL	Figures	1842-72

Marks.	Names of Painters.	Subjects.	Period of Work, from
Ab:Schilt	SCHILT, François Philippe Abel	Figures, subjects and portraits	1847-80
P.S.	SCHILT, Louis Pierre	Flowers	1818-55
ES	SIEFFERT, Louis Eugène	Figures	1882-88
ES	SIMARD, Eugène Alexandre		1880-94
S.S.p	SINSSON, Pierre	Flowers; also gilding	1796-1845
MS	SOLON[1] (Left for Mintons, *q.v.* 1870.)	Figures and ornaments	1862-71
S.W.	SWEBACH	Landscapes and figures	1803-14
HT	TRAGER, Henry	Painter	1887-1904
J.T. or *J.T*	TRAGER, Jules	Flowers, birds, ancient style	1897-
L	TRAGER, Louis	Painter	1888-1904
Pr:	TRISTAN, Etienne J.	Printer, painter, and gilder	1837-82
T.	TROYON	Ornaments and gilding	1802-
J-U	ULRICH	Painter	1889-1904
VG	VIGNOL, Gustave	Ornament	1882-1904
W	WALTER	Flowers	1867-70

[1] Solon worked for the trade in Paris as well as for the Sèvres factory. This "outside" work is signed Miles.

MARKS OF SOME OF THE MODELLERS EMPLOYED
AT SÈVRES.

Marks.	Names of Modellers.	Subjects.	Period of Work, from
B. r.	BÈRANGER, A.	Modeller and decorator	1807-46
(bird mark)	BOUCHER	Flower modeller	1754-
B r	BOURDOIS		1773-74
B			
Brachard uine F Juin 1823 Ser 2es *Brachard f. 1820*	BRACHARD, J. C. N.	Modeller	1776-[1]
AB	BRIFFAUT	Repairer	1837-
B	BULIDON, Henri	Modeller	1745-
	CELOS	Also painter, *see list*	1865-94
ch.	CHABRY, junior	Also painter	1763-
Chaudet f. (SÈVRES)	CHAUDET	And sculptor	About 1800
(Doat mark)	DOAT	Also sculptor	1879-1904
F	FALCONET	Celebrated for groups and figure-modelling, head of sculpture school formerly at Vincennes	1754-66

[1] The mark of Brachard occurs on a biscuit group of male and female figures embracing, with Cupid behind in the Victoria and Albert Museum.

Marks.	Names of Modellers.	Subjects.	Period of Work, from
F	FERNEX	Groups after Boucher	About 1750
E. forgeot	FORGEOT, Charles Ed.	Also sculptor	1862
J.G	GÉLY, Leopold J. J.	*Pâte sur pâte*	1851-88
LR	LE RICHE, Joseph	Head of sculpture studio	1757-92
L 1762	LE TOURNEUR	His mark is on La Baigneuse, famous statuette by Falconet, repaired by Le Tourneur	1762
LTne LT T T	LE TRONNE	Second-class sculpture	1753-
JL	LIANCE, senior	Also repairer of figures	1769-
JL	LUCAS, C. C.	Also painter, *see list*	1877-1904
NM NE	MAUGENDRE	Sculpture	1880-86
5.	MONGENOT	Flower modeller	1754-
P	PEROTTIN	Sculpture	1760-
JR	ROGER	Modeller of ornament	1862-

Marks.	Names of Modellers.	Subjects.	Period of Work, from
	SANDOZ, Alphonse	Assistant sculptor	1881-1904
	SOLON	Modeller of ornament, *pâte sur pâte*, left Sèvres for Mintons 1871	1862-71

CHRONOLOGICAL TABLE OF SIGNS EMPLOYED IN THE ROYAL MANUFACTORY OF SÈVRES.

By which the exact date of any piece may be ascertained. It differs from that before given by M. Brongniart in the addition of the letter J for 1762 and the JJ for 1787, which is now altered on the authority of the late M. Riocreux of the Sèvres Museum.

A	(Vincennes).	1753	O	. . . .	1767	DD	. . . .	1781
B	(ditto).	1754	P	. . .	1768	EE	. . . .	1782
C	(ditto).	1755	Q	. . .	.[1] 1769	FF	. . . .	1783
D	removed to Sèvres	1756	R	. . . .	1770	GG	. . . .	1784
E	. . . .	1757	S	. . . .	1771	HH	. . . .	1785
F	. . . .	1758	T	. . . .	1772	II	. . . .	1786
G	. . . .	1759	U	. . . .	1773	JJ	. . . .	1787
H	. . . .	1760	V	. . . .	1774	KK	. . . .	1788
I	. . . .	1761	X	. . . .	1775	LL	. . . .	1789
J	. . . .	1762	Y	. . . .	1776	MM	. . . .	1790
K	. . . .	1763	Z	. . . .	1777	NN	. . . .	1791
L	. . . .	1764	AA	. . . .	1778	OO	. . . .	1792
M	. . . .	1765	BB	. . . .	1779	PP	. . . .	1793
N	. . . .	1766	CC	. . . .	1780		To July 17th.

NOTE.—These letters are not always placed within the cypher, but occasionally outside, when the interlaced L's are too contracted to receive them; or if double letters, one on each side. It may also be observed that the date letters are sometimes capitals and sometimes small.

There was for some time a difference of opinion about the use of the letter J, both double and single, a well-known authority, M. Garnier, having omitted this letter from his list of marks, while Mr. Chaffers included it. The Editor's personal knowledge caused him to confirm Mr. Chaffers' contention, and this inclusion brought the end of the Royal period to P. P. 1793.

The researches of MM. Chavagnac et de Grollier now fully confirm this, and acting on their authority the Editor has now omitted the double letters QQ and RR 1794, 1795, believing that although some very few examples may be extant bearing such date marks, they are the result of

[1] The comet of 1769 furnished the Administration of the time with the idea of transmitting the recollection of the event by their productions. This comet was sometimes substituted for the ordinary mark.

accident, as according to an official letter fully quoted in the *Histoire des Manufactures Françaises de Porcelaine*, referred to above, the official date for the alteration of the mark was July 17, 1793.

King Louis XVI. was executed on 21st January 1793, and on 17th July of that year the Minister of Interior addressed an official letter to M. Regnier, the director of the Sèvres factory, ordering him with as little delay as possible to obliterate the double L, and to alter the mark.

During the Revolutionary changes the double letters were rarely used, and from 1793 to 1800 we meet with few examples, when they were replaced by the following signs :—

Year	IX (1801) indicated by	$T9$	1807	.	.	.	.	.	.	7
			1808	.	.	.	.	.	.	8
,,	X (1802) ,,	X	1809	.	.	.	.	.	.	9
			1810	.	.	.	.	.	.	10
,,	XI (1803) ,,	XI	1811 (onze)	.	.	.	.	.	.	o.z.
			1812 (douze)	.	.	.	.	.	.	d.z.
,,	XII (1804) ,,	$\div$	1813 (treize)	.	.	.	.	.	.	t.z.
			1814 (quatorze)	.	.	.	.	.	.	q.z.
,,	XIII (1805) ,,	$\dashv\vdash$	1815 (quinze)	.	.	.	.	.	.	q.n.
			1816 (seize)	.	.	.	.	.	.	s.z.
,,	XIV (1806) ,,	↓	1817 (dix sept)	.	.	.	.	.	.	d.s.

From this date the year is expressed by the last two figures only—thus, 18 for 1818, &c.—up to the present time.

CRÉPY EN VALOIS. *Soft paste.* Nothing was known of the existence of a soft paste factory here until it was revealed by the researches of MM. de Chavagnac et de Grollier, whose recent *Histoire* has already been quoted several times by the editor of this, the latest edition of Chaffers. The factory is said to have been founded by a potter who had previously worked at Menneçy, and the specimens which have been identified are similar to the productions of that factory. A mark C. P. was used, which hitherto had been listed as one of the uncertain marks; it is now assigned by the above-named authorities to this factory, but the full mark was the word Crépy. According to some records in the archives of Paris, discovered by the above-named expert writers, the factory was started in 1762, and was producing considerable quantities of both useful and ornamental porcelain from 1764-66. There was a depôt in Paris, and the sale books have been discovered and record during the years 1764-66 considerable sales of porcelain flowers, similar no doubt to those made at Vincennes and Sèvres, and also of groups, figures, and useful services and snuff-boxes. The mark was the word Crépy incised, but specimens are rare, and unless marked would probably be attributed to the better known factory of Menneçy.

Crepy

INCISED.

This mark is quoted by MM. de Chavagnac et de Grollier as being on a small figure seated on a couch. White fine soft paste, transparent lead glaze.

C. P.

INCISED.

Mark from same authority, on a small figure seated on a lion. The mark may be taken as an abbreviation of Crépy.

FRENCH FACTORIES, CHIEFLY OF HARD PASTE PORCELAINS.

"RÉAUMUR'S PORCELAIN" (1729). Réné-Anthony Ferchault, Lord of Réaumur, born at Rochelle in 1683, died 1758, made a great many experiments with a view of ascertaining the properties of Oriental porcelain between the years 1727 and 1729. Upon carefully observing fragments of glass, porcelain, and pottery, he became convinced that china was nothing more than a demi-vitrification, which might be obtained either by exposing a vitrifiable matter to the action of fire, and withdrawing it before it was perfectly vitrified, or by making a paste of two substances, one of which was vitrifiable, the other not. It was therefore very easy to discover by which of these methods the porcelain of China was made; nothing more was necessary than to urge it with a strong fire; if it consisted wholly of a vitrifiable matter half vitrified, it would be converted into glass; if of two substances, one of which was not vitrifiable, it would come out of the furnace the same as it went in. This experiment being made, the Chinese porcelain suffered no alteration, but all the European porcelain was changed into glass. But when the Chinese porcelain was thus discovered to consist of two different substances, it was further necessary to find out what they were and whether France produced them. M. de Réaumur subsequently procured from China the *petuntse* and *kaolin*, and although he did not perfectly succeed, he pointed out the way for the Comte de Brancas-Lauraguais, Macquer, and others, in the successful production of the hard paste or only true porcelain, which was introduced at Sèvres in 1769. He also contrived a new species of porcelain, which was called by his name, consisting only of glass annealed, a second time, or allowed to remain for a certain time in the oven at a red heat, when it became a milky white, much less beautiful than porcelain, but a discovery more curious than useful. This attempt at making porcelain was similar to some of the first essays at Meissen about the year 1707, but which were immediately abandoned as a bad fabrication, and not worthy the name of porcelain. The Germans call this substance *Milch Glass;* there is a specimen in the Japanese Palace at Dresden.

BRANCAS-LAURAGUAIS (1765). The Duke of Orleans, with the assistance of Guettard the chemist, and Le Guay, porcelain-maker, about 1758 made many attempts to produce hard paste with the *kaolin* of Alençon, but it does not appear that they succeeded. The Comte de Lauraguais in 1765, in conjunction with Darcet and Le Guay (the Prince's workman), were more fortunate, and specimens of the *pâte dure* made by them are much sought for; they are usually marked with the initials in cursive character of the Count's name, Brancas-Lauraguais.

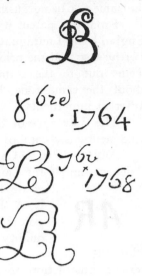

M. Jacquemart gives the marks in the margin from some medallions which are attributed to the Comte de Brancas-Lauraguais; the first, dated October 1764, is on an oval medallion with a peasant holding a pipe and pot of beer, after Teniers; the second is on a round medallion in the Rouen Museum, copied from a bust of Louis XIV. by Nini, the date, September 1768, is accompanied by two signatures; the L. B. is that of Lauraguais, the other, L. R., is perhaps the name of the modeller. It is known that the Count employed a workman named Leguay, and there may have been others.

M. Jacquemart thus describes the ware of Lauraguais: "La pâte est grossière, un peu bise et piqué de points noirs, les vases, peints en bleu (nous n'en avons rencontré aucun decoré en peintures polychrômes), sont évidemment inspirés par la porcelaine anglaise de Chelsea, avec les mêmes formes et une disposition semblable dans les bouquets," &c.

In the *Scots Magazine* for the year 1764 we find the following notice: "They write from Paris that after a number of chymical operations, the Count de Lauraguais has at last found out the true composition of the porcelain from China and Japan, which he can manufacture at a very cheap rate, as the materials are easy to be obtained. The Academy of Sciences have approved of his invention."

In a letter from Dr. Darwin to Josiah Wedgwood (Meteyard's *Life of Wedgwood*, vol. i., p. 436) dated April 27, 1766, he says: "Count Laragaut has been at Birmingham, and offered ye secret of making ye finest old China as cheap as your pots. He says ye materials are in England. That ye secret has cost £16,000, y^t he will sell it for £2000. He is a man of science, dislikes his own country, was six months in ye Bastile for speaking against ye Government—loves everything English. I suspect his scientific passion is stronger than perfect sanity."

In this year he seems to have brought his *pâte dure* to perfection, and in June 1766, "The Count de Lauraguais, *of London*," obtained a patent in England for his invention for fourteen years as "a new method of making porcelain ware in all its branches, viz., to make the coarser species of China, the more beautiful ones of the Indies, and the finest of Japan, in a manner different from any that is made in our dominions, and he having found the materials tryed in Great Britain, has brought the same to so great perfection that the porcelain made therewith after his new method far excels any that has hitherto been made in Great Britain, the same not being fusible by fire, as other china is."

From this patent it appears that *hard* porcelain was actually made in England by Lauraguais in 1766, two years before the date of Cookworthy's, so that the priority of the perfection of it with *kaolin* and *petuntse* seems due to the former, although the invention of both took place about the same time, having arrived at the same end by the use of different ingredients.

The Catalogue of the Collection at Strawberry Hill by Horace Walpole mentions a copy of the Bacchus of M. Angelo by Lauraguais.

ARRAS (Pas-de-Calais). Established 1782 by the Demoiselles Deleneur, under the patronage of M. de Colonne, Intendant de Flandre et de l'Artois; it only lasted a few years. The mark is A R, in blue under the glaze. It is a beautiful porcelain body, and many specimens are equal both in quality and decoration to the Sèvres. In 1785 they adopted coal instead of wood for baking the ware. From the imperfect construction of the kilns, small particles of coal were carried by the draught into the kiln, which even penetrated into the seggars and injured the surface of the ware. Dr. Diamond had a charming jug of Arras porcelain, painted with brilliant cobalt blue flowers, in which this defect is very perceptible, the minute rough fragments of coal still adhering to the glaze. The fabrication ceased altogether in 1786.

These specimens are valued very highly; they are brilliant in colour and have the qualities of old Sèvres, but the only ground colour known to the Editor is the beautiful cobalt blue mentioned above. In the Hawkins sale in 1904, four cups and saucers, a sucrier, and a plate of this porcelain realised £300. Two of the cups and saucers are in Mr. Herbert Young's Collection, and the sucrier in that of Mrs. Burns.

This variant of the usual mark is upon a saucer with blue trailing pattern painted round the sides, and C. S. is also scratched in the paste. Franks Collection.

M. le Baron Davillier had a saucer, soft paste, with this mark in pink, painted in various colours with flowers; sometimes the initials of painters occur underneath; P and the letter L, &c. (*Ker. Gall.*, enlarged edition, fig. 315.)

BOULOGNE (Pas-de-Calais). A few years since a manufactory of porcelain was established here by M. Haffringue with the *kaolin* of Limoges; a splendid white and transparent body was produced, and some clever Italian modellers engaged, but the sale was not remunerative and it was discontinued. The mark is a square tablet in relief with an anchor, and letters in the four corners. Lady Charlotte Schreiber had a tea-service, the medallions of cupids and emblems left unglazed, and a pair of biscuit plaques, each with a dead bird finely executed in high relief. (*Ker. Gall.*, enlarged edition, figs. 316-17.)

ETIOLLES (Seine-et-Oise), near Corbeil. *Soft paste.* Established 1768; Monnier manufacturer. The mark deposed by him at Sèvres was that adjoined; it lasted only a short time. The porce-

lain of St. Cloud was at first imitated, afterwards hard paste was made.

ETIOLLES. A hard-paste plate painted in landscape and figures, with rocks and mountain scenery, the place and maker's name scratched deeply into the paste, bears the date 1771; formerly in Mr. J. Loraine Baldwin's Collection. Another specimen, in M. Jacquemart's possession, is dated 1768; and a hard porcelain *theière* painted with flowers, the mark graved in the clay. A similar mark on a piece in the Sèvres Museum, dated 1779, and a service for- merly in Mr. Reynolds's Collection has "Etiolles, 1770, Pellevé," graved in the paste on each piece. This service, originally in an old French marque- terie fitted box, was purchased on the Continent

*Etiolles
1768
Pellevé*

by Mr. Samuel Litchfield (the Editor's father), and passed into Mr. C. W. Reynolds's Collection; at his sale it was bought by Mr. James Saunders, and when his Collection was dispersed the service was broken up into different lots and sold separately on account of the rareness of the mark. There is a cup and saucer of this factory in the Franks Collection; the cup is marked with a P, and the saucer is marked with the name E. Pellevé, with date 1770, all incised. (*Ker. Gall.*, enlarged edition, fig. 318.)

CLIGNANCOURT (Montmartre, Paris). *Soft and hard paste.* Estab- lished 1775 by Pierre Deruelle, under the patronage of Monsieur le Comte de Provence, brother of the King (afterwards Louis XVIII.), and under his powerful patronage, with the advantages of excellent material for paste and the command of the services of good artists, some excellent results were obtained, chiefly in table services, which in many respects rival those of Sèvres with white grounds, to which they are similar. After Deruelle's death or retirement the quality of the ware declined, in common with that of many other similar factories which enjoyed special protection and privileges for a short period. The first mark was a windmill in blue, which is rarely met with, being used so short a time. In Horace Walpole's description of objects at Strawberry Hill, 1780, we read of "a white and gold cup and saucer, with Chinese figures, of the porcelain of Clignancour, a new manufacture, estab- lished by the Comte de Provence, called Porcelaine de Monsieur."

CLIGNANCOURT. On a sucrier, with gold border, the mark painted in blue; formerly in Mr. Reynolds's Collection.

CLIGNANCOURT. An early mark, representing one of the primitive windmills which existed on the heights of Clignancourt; this mark is on a coffee-pot and cover decorated with gilding in the Franks Collection.

CLIGNANCOURT. This is a stencilled mark, in red, erroneously supposed to be that of Deruelle, used on pieces in the Chinese style, in hard paste, from 1775 to 1780. In more perfect marks we can trace the letters L. S. X., for the Prince's names, Louis Stanislas Xavier.

CLIGNANCOURT. Another better-defined monogram than the last of the Prince's initials, which clearly does not represent Deruelle's; it is stencilled in red on a cup and saucer which was in the author's possession. There is a specimen in the Franks Collection.

CLIGNANCOURT. L.S.X. surmounted by the Prince's crown. A square tray with border of gilt branches with this mark stencilled in red is in the Franks Collection.

CLIGNANCOURT. Another stencilled mark of Deruelle, but not so frequently met with.

CLIGNANCOURT. The initials of Louis Stanislas Xavier, L.S.X., or double C. and M. for Monsieur, both marked in gold on the back of a plate, painted in front with festoons and arabesque borders in gold and colours; in the centre a Chinaman riding on an ostrich.

CLIGNANCOURT. Used when under the patronage of Monsieur the King's brother, the mark being M and a crown, stencilled in red, called "Porcelaine de Monsieur." It ceased about 1790.

CLIGNANCOURT. A stencilled mark on an early piece in the Sèvres Museum.

Moitte. CLIGNANCOURT. Deruelle was succeeded by Moitte; his name is pencilled in red under a high French porcelain inkstand well painted with bold arabesques and scrolls in colour, fret border, in the late Mr. A. Joseph's Collection. (Specimens illustrated in *Ker. Gall.*, enlarged edition, figs. 321-24.)

ORLÉANS (Loiret). This manufactory of porcelain *pâte tendre* was established by M. Gérault Daraubert in 1753, under the protection of the Duc de Penthièvre, and the porcelain first made here was of soft paste, but they subsequently produced hard paste, and both kinds of body were produced concurrently.

In the list presented to the Intendant on the 8th June 1777 we find the following:—

"La naissance de la Manufacture Royale établie à Orléans est du 13 Mai 1753, sous permission accordée par le Roy pour l'espace de 20 années; le 7 Mai 1773, les bontés de Sa Majesté luy ont prorogé son privilége pour 15 ans; à cause que cette manufacture n'avait rien fait pour sa fortune n'y même pour son aisance. Les premières terres qu'elle a employées provenaient de Beylen près de la Flandre; en 1755 des environs de Paris; fin de 1756 de Saint Mamers près de Châteaudun. Les trois premières pâtes sont nommées par le public *porcelaine tendre*."

ORLÉANS. It is marked with a label of three points (*lambeau d'Orleans*) in blue, graved in the moist clay. Gérault Daraubert was succeeded in the direction of the manufactory of Orléans by Bourdon *fils* about 1788; Piedor, Dubois, and lastly, Benoist Le Brun, from 1808 to 1811. The mark on the *pâte tendre* is composed of a *lambel* of three points in outline, and C beneath; on hard porcelain, the *lambel* filled with colour. From 1808 to 1811 Benoist Le Brun marked the ware with his initials, in blue or gold, in form of a monogram.

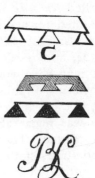

ORLÉANS. A cup and saucer, painted *en grisaille*, with a tomb and a willow tree; has this mark of Benoist Le Brun in gold.

This mark in blue is on a cup painted in blue, soft paste, very common, in the possession of M. le Baron Davillier; in red on a cup, hard paste, painted with flowers. In the same collection are other pieces of Orléans with the *lambel* and the *fleur-de-lis*.

There must necessarily be some confusion between the filled-in label of three points used for hard paste Orléans china, and the specimens of hard paste Vincennes during the proprietorship of Séguen, who adopted the same mark. (*Ker. Gall.*, enlarged edition, figs. 325-6.)

Herr Jännike also gives the mark in the margin and places the date of its use as from 1790 to 1800.

LUNÉVILLE (Meurthe). Established 1731. "Manufacture Stanislas." By the tenor of the letters patent of the Duke Francis III. granted to Jacques Chambrette, it appears that porcelain was made here as early as 1731; but if it were actually made, it could have lasted only a very short time, and gave place to a sort of half porcelain or *terre de pipe*.

The early attempts of the fabrique, made before Stanislas, Voltaire, and La Marquise du Chatelet, prove that the *terre de pipe* of the year 1748 acquired considerable reputation, and Stanislas accorded to it many privileges, according to the letters patent of 1749, "à cause de la bonne qualité de ses produits en terre de pipe ou demi-porcelaine."

LUNÉVILLE (Meurthe). Established 1769. Niderviller was not the only place in which the potters of Lorraine distinguished themselves, for Paul Louis Cyfflé, sculptor of Stanislas Leczinski, Duc de Lorraine, obtained in 1768 letters patent for fifteen years, by virtue of which he established another manufactory for superior vessels of the materials called *terre de Lorraine*, and in the following year a new privilege was granted for making groups and statuettes with his improved paste, under the name of *pâte de marbre*. Cyfflé was born at Bourges in January 1724, and resided at Lunéville as early as 1746, so that it is probable he may have worked at the Stanislas manufactory at Lunéville, his own not being established until 1768; the works of Cyfflé were of biscuit, that is, not covered with glaze, so that the delicacy of the work, for which he was remarkable, was not destroyed, giving it a greater resemblance to marble. The following important groups are by this artist: The pedestrian statue of Stanislas in the Bibliothèque Imperiale de Nancy; the group of Henry IV. and Sully, offered to the King of Denmark, when at Lunéville; and Belisarius. Cyfflé had three children—Stanislas, a painter; Joseph, who succeeded his father; and François, engineer.

Of the same character, and made in the same department, was the *biscuit de Nancy* (Nantes?), of which we have no particulars, except the reference made by Walpole in his Catalogue of Strawberry Hill, 1784. He describes "a bust of Voltaire in biscuit of Nancy," and "Rubens's Child in biscuit china of Nancy," both of which are well known to connoisseurs.

LUNÉVILLE. There are two biscuit figures of peasant boys; one, playing on the bagpipes, is stamped underneath as in the margin, the S scratched; the other is stamped "*Terre de Lorraine*," and underneath I. G. is scratched in the clay before firing.

LUNÉVILLE. The mark in the margin occurs on a fine group of Leda, formerly in the possession of Mr. Bryant of St. James's Street; the words "*Terre de Lorraine*" impressed on a tablet, and the name of the artist, "*Leopold*," scratched on the ware before firing. Another group in the Sèvres Museum, representing the "Dead Bird," has a similar stamp, but the name *François*. A biscuit figure of a boy holding a bird's nest in his hat, stamped "*Terre de Lorraine*," also with the name of the modeller, *Besle*, was in the Staniforth Collection.

NIDERVILLER (Meurthe), near Strasbourg. Established about 1760, by Jean Louis, Baron de Beyerlé, Councillor and Treasurer of the King, and Director of the Mint at Strasbourg. He purchased the manor and estate, and constructed buildings expressly for the manufacture of pottery. After successfully carrying on this branch for several years, he attempted hard porcelain in 1768, and procured potters and artists from Saxony. In his new enterprise he was equally successful, sparing no expense to procure the best modellers both in fayence and porcelain, assisted by Paul Louis Cyfflé, of Lunéville, and others. Three or four years before his death, which happened in 1784, the estate was bought by General de Custine. This new proprietor continued the fabrique, under the direction of M. Lanfray, who paid especial attention to the production of fine porcelain; the fabrication of statuettes was greatly increased, the best of which were modelled by MM. Lemire and Favot, from Lunéville. Among the artists who have contributed to the celebrity of the Niderviller manufacture was Joseph Deutsch, an excellent painter on pottery and porcelain, who afterwards directed the *atelier* of Madame Gérard at Paris. After the decapitation of the unfortunate M. de Custine, his estate, being forfeited to the Republic, was sold on the 25th Germinal An X. (1802) to M. Lanfray, and carried on by him until his death in 1827; his marks during this time on painted pieces and figures were the name of the town stamped, or his own initial stencilled. On the 15th November 1827 the manufactory was sold to M. L. G. Dryander of Saarbrück, who, for many years, continued to make porcelain as well as fayence groups and statuettes, but the distance of his fabrique from the kaolin of St. Yrieix prevented him from competing successfully with those of Limoges, and this branch was abandoned.

NIDERVILLER, near Strasbourg. Both fine fayence and hard porcelain were made here; the mark was B. and N. in monogram (Beyerlé, Niderviller), in blue.

NIDERVILLER. On a vase in the Sèvres Museum, which M. Riocreux attributes to Beyerlé.

NIDERVILLER. Monograms of Beyerlé of Niderviller, both on fayence and hard paste porcelain marked in brownish red.

NIDERVILLER. General de Custine. His first mark was the monogram C.N. (Custine, Niderviller) marked in blue.

NIDERVILLER. The mark of two C's under a Count's coronet was adopted in 1792, pencilled in blue; it has been erroneously attributed to Kronenberg or Louisberg, but that has an Imperial crown surmounted by a cross, whereas this is a Count's coronet.

NIDERVILLER. Marked in blue on a cup; the saucer belonging to it has only the two C's interlaced; of French manufacture.

NIDERVILLER. Two C's interlaced for Custine, sometimes found on this ware, without the coronet, marked in blue. This mark, minutely painted, is found both on fayence and porcelain services and figures. (*Ker. Gall.*, enlarged edition, figs. 327-28.)

NIDERVILLER. The letter N., for Niderviller, occurs on a set of plates, on one of which is the double C, and on another the letter N., in the Collection of the Rev. T. Staniforth of Storrs. It is quoted by Mr. Marryat, who places it as Louisberg, mistaking the interlaced C's for the mark of that manufactory, leaving this letter unexplained.

NIDERVILLER. The mark of F. C. Lanfray, successor to Custine, towards the end of the eighteenth century; F.C.L. in a monogram stencilled in blue, on a piece in the Sèvres Museum.

NIDERVILLER. Another mark of F. C. Lanfray, stencilled in blue, on a cup and saucer formerly in Mr. Reynolds's Collection.

NIDERVILLER. This mark is stamped in relief on the back of a biscuit group of a youth kissing a girl, in Mr. Danby Seymour's Collection.

The marks in the margin are added to those of Niderviller, on the authority of MM. de Chavagnac et de Grollier.

MONTREUIL (Seine). A fabrique of porcelain (*hard paste*), carried on by M. Tinet, in imitation of Oriental, sometimes in other styles. This mark is given by Jännike as used at this fabrique.

BOISSETTE (Seine-et-Marne), near Melun. Established in 1777 by Jacques Vermonet, *père et fils*, which lasted only a short time, and its productions, though of good quality, present no special features to distinguish them from those of similar hard paste Paris factories. Mr. H. E. B. Harrison has two plates well painted with flowers bearing this mark in blue under glaze.

This mark, which is the initial of Boissette, followed by two dots, is on a boat-shaped tray in the Franks Collection. There is also a shaped tureen cover stand and a cup and saucer in the Victoria and Albert Museum.

VAUX, near Melun. Established about 1770 (but was of short duration) by Hannong, Moreau being director; it belonged to Messrs. Laborde and Hocquart. M. Riocreux so attributes this mark. There is a specimen painted with bouquets of flowers, lately in Mr. Reynolds's Collection, marked in blue. The monogram contains all the letters of the name of the fabrique. This has been attributed by M. Jacquemart to Bordeaux, and Sir A. W. Franks agrees. According to our most recent authority, MM. Chavagnac et de Grollier, the proprietors of the hard paste porcelain factory at Vincennes applied to a M. Bertin in 1769 for the necessary permission to manufacture porcelain at this place, but whether they obtained it does not appear.

There must always be confusion between the records of this alleged factory and that of Bordeaux, since not only is the mark given by the different authorities identical with that used by Bordeaux for a time, but such specimens as are attributed to Vaux have the usual characteristics of French hard paste porcelain, and may have been made at Bordeaux.

LA SEINIE (Haute-Vienne). Established in 1774 by the Marquis de Beaupoil de St. Aulaire, the Chevalier Dugareau, and the Comte de la Seinie. It attained some success whilst under the direction of M. Bertin in 1778. In 1789 M. de la Seinie retired, and the works were farmed by M. Baignol of Limoges till 1793, when it was held by three Paris workmen, who gave it up in 1805; it was afterwards taken by M. Closterman of Limoges. It is said that the white china was bought from this factory and decorated in Paris. There is a tall cup with this mark (painted with a landscape very much in the style of Höchst) in the Franks Collection. The whole service was formerly in the Editor's possession.

CAEN (Calvados). This manufactory was established and supported by some of the principal inhabitants about 1798, for the manufacture of fayence of English character. Not being successful during two years of trial, they commenced making porcelain with the kaolin of Limoges, and they produced some good ornamental pieces, some clever painters being engaged. It was situated near the Church of Vaucelles, and the warehouse for selling the products was at the corner of the Rue de Bernières and Rue St. Jean; it was at first successful, and according to the *Annuaire du Calvados en l'An XII.* (1803-4), "En peu de temps, cette nouvelle fabrique a prospéré au point qu'elle rivalise avec les établissements les plus célèbres. A l'exposition qui eut lieu à la Municipalité, on a admiré la blancheur de la pâte, l'élégance des dessins et l'éclat des colors. La Société d'Agriculture et de Commerce lui décerna la première médaille d'encouragement. Elle occupe environ quarante ouvriers sous la direction du Citoyen Ducheval négociant." Under the ruinous condition of the war, the Caen porcelain was obliged to succumb at the end of eight or ten years of its existence. The china is hard paste, and equal to that of Sèvres, and of the same forms; the mark is stencilled in red on a cabaret,

caen   the plateau triangular, of pale yellow ground, handsomely gilt, painted *en grisaille* with birds and animals, a purple line round the edge, marked as in the margin on all the pieces except the cups. A tea-cup and saucer delicately painted with gold and green festoons and small square medallions

CAEN   of landscapes in Indian-ink, with the word "Caen" stencilled in red, was in the Collection of Rev. T. Staniforth. A tea-pot and a coffee-cup and saucer of this fabrique are in the Sèvres Museum, made while under the direction of M. D'Aigmont Desmares, about the year 1803. (*Ker. Gall.*, enlarged edition, fig. 330.) A sugar bowl and cover, painted in green and black and decorated with gilding, is in the Victoria and Albert Museum.

Le françois à Caen.   A more recent manufacture was carried on by M. Le François. We have seen services of fine china, white and gold, occasionally painted with flowers, of the first half of this century, the name stencilled in red or pencilled as in margin.

VALOGNES (Manche). About the year 1800 a company of land-owners of Cotentin was formed at Valognes for the manufacture of fayence, under the direction of M. Le Tellier de la Bertinière, a native of Bayeux; he was soon succeeded by M. Le Masson, who gave a fresh impetus to the concern, and having obtained from the Directory the temporary concession of the Convent of Cordeliers, the works were removed thither, and hard porcelain made with the kaolin of St. Yrieix, near Limoges. Unfortunately for the prosperity of the new fabrique, in about eighteen months M. Le Masson died, and it was thrown into confusion. In 1802 the shareholders confided the direction to M. Joachim Langlois, who knowing that the principal obstacle to success was the high price of kaolin brought from Limoges, and being a good mineralogist and chemist, discovered that material in the commune of Pieux, Cotentin. About 1805 they joined to the production of household ware, *articles de luxe*. At this period there were twelve painters and gilders, many from Sèvres; among these were MM. Zwinger and Camus. Up to 1809 many important pieces were made, some prices being as high as 800 francs. In 1810 the partnership expired, and declining to enter into any new contract with M. Langlois, and being deprived of the site of the fabrique, he transferred the manufacture to Bayeux.

BAYEUX (Calvados). Established 1810. At the expiration of his term with the proprietors of the manufactory of hard porcelain at Valognes, M. Joachim Langlois transported the manufacture to Bayeux, where he acquired a large piece of ground, the ancient Convent of Benedictines, the majority of the artists and workmen following him; it was carried on with considerable success, and several medals were obtained. In 1819 it occupied about eighty workmen, and M. Langlois, his wife and two daughters, were the principal painters and gilders. M. Langlois died in 1830, and the manufactory was carried on by his widow and his son, M. Frederick Langlois; the widow died in 1847. M. F. Gosse became proprietor in 1849, and joining to great intelligence considerable pecuniary resources, a new impulse was given to the manufactory; the number of workmen when he took the works numbered only thirty-five, but he afterwards employed one hundred and thirty, with three large furnaces. Independent of porcelain, a vast quantity of chemical vessels were made of every description, carrying out his maxim, *Progrès et reduction de prix*. M. Brongniart says this porcelain has justly the reputation of resisting fire to a greater degree than any other manufacture, except that of Sèvres. There are some specimens in the Sèvres Museum, acquired in 1819.

BAYEUX. The mark of M. Gosse, a manufacturer here; some pieces in the Victoria and Albert Museum.

BAYEUX. Another mark with lion passant and mural crown. In the same Collection.

ISIGNY (Calvados). A manufactory of hard porcelain and stoneware, conducted by M. F. Langlois. There are some specimens in the Sèvres Museum, acquired in 1843.

BORDEAUX (Gironde). The porcelain made here was under the direction of M. Veillard, a Frenchman, and Mr. Johnston, an Englishman; it is of fine quality and a very clear white, frequently decorated with bright blue. A pair of splendid vases nearly 5 feet high, painted in the best style of Moustiers ware, obtained the prize medal at the Exposition in London in 1862. The mark of the fabrique is the three intersecting crescents of Henri II. enclosing the words, *"Veillard," "Johnston," "Bordeaux."*

BORDEAUX. The porcelain manufactory here was, according to M. Jacquemart, carried on by a M. Verneuille, who used this mark and the A and V crossing each other, which was formerly attributed to Vaux, near Melun. There are some specimens in the Sèvres Museum, and M. de St. Leon possesses a service on some of the pieces of which both these marks occur.

TOURS (Indre-et-Loire). Established in 1762. Noel Sailly, a fayence maker of this place, applied for permission to make porcelain, having constructed a furnace for the purpose, which was granted. The demand is said to have exceeded the supply; he died in 1783, and the manufacture was continued by his son. We have not been able hitherto to identify any of the pieces.

VALENCIENNES (Nord), 1785. By an order of Council, dated 24th May 1785, M. Fauquez is permitted to carry on a manufacture of porcelain at Valenciennes. In 1775 he married a lady named Lamoninary, and her brother assisted in the management of the factory, and his initial L, together with F (Fauquez) and V (Valenciennes), appear on some specimens. M. Fauquez was originally established at St. Amand in the manufacture of fayence as early as 1740, and probably carried on the making of both wares simultaneously. M. Jacquemart says the permission was granted on condition that coal was used in his kilns, and that he was associated with a M. Vannier. A first-rate sculptor of the name of Verboeckhoven, called Fickaer, executed some biscuit groups, especially a Descent from the Cross. Among the collaborateurs of Lamoninary may be mentioned Anstett of Strasbourg, Joseph Fernig, painter and chemist, Gelez, Mester, and Poinbœuf.

The accompanying ciphers appear on pieces of the sams service, one in blue and the other in brown, under the glaze. Mr. W. E. Gumbleton had a cup and saucer fully marked with this monogram. In the Sèvres Museum are some pieces with the cipher L. V. and the word VALENCIEN, written in blue. The manufactory ceased about 1798. The last mark is on a chocolate pot formerly in Mr. Loraine Baldwin's Collection. The last two have the letter F for Fauquez omitted.

This mark in red over glaze is on a cup and saucer in the Franks Collection, and is attributed by Garnier to Valenciennes, but placed by Jacquemart among the uncertain French marks. (*Ker. Gall.*, enlarged edition, fig. 331.)

ST. AMAND-LÈ-EAUX (Nord), France. Founded by M. Maximilian de Bettignies in 1800, for the manufacture of porcelain *pâte tendre*, like the old Sèvres. He was formerly proprietor of the Tournay manufactory, which he ceded to his brother Henri when that city

became re-annexed to Belgium. Some specimens of modern manufacture were sent to the London Exposition in 1862. "M. de Bettignies of St. Amand-les-Eaux, where the manufacture of soft paste has never been discontinued from the last century, has furnished the Parisian trade with many of the vases painted in imitation of old Sèvres, thus proving that it was possible to manufacture soft paste china commercially on a small scale. However, the difficulties to be overcome in making large pieces, and particularly articles for use, such as dishes, rendered the workmanship very expensive. Fortunately the introduction of phosphate of lime, which is obtained from bones, in the paste of the porcelain—a discovery essentially English—has supplied a means to obtain a fine transparency, and, without affording all the plasticity of the hard porcelain, it does not prevent the mixture being cast, moulded, or turned easily by the ordinary processes."—Arnoux, *Report on Pottery*, Paris Exhibition, 1867.

The mark given above is generally in red and sometimes in blue. A later work is a seal in slight relief as in the margin.

A great many forgeries of old Sèvres have been perpetrated by unscrupulous dealers securing sparsely decorated pieces of St. Amand porcelain, grinding out the mark, and having the piece afterwards decorated in the manner of Sèvres, the soft paste helping in the deception. It has generally the appearance of Tournay porcelain.

CHATILLON (Seine). On a plate about 1775, hard paste, ornamented with flowers and gilding. There are many places of the same name in France, but this one is near Paris. In Baron

C. Davillier's Collection. Another similar is in the Sèvres Museum. M. Jacquemart gives the name of Roussel & Co., Lortz, and Rouget, as recent potters at this place.

NANTES (Loire-Inférieure). Porcelain manufactory, established 1780, by Jacques Fourmy, son of Mathurin Fourmy; he passed his youth in the Manufacture Royale de Faïence de Nantes, which was carried on by his father. In the year 1779 Nicolas Fournerat de la Chapelle, porcelain maker at Limoges, made attempts to produce hard porcelain like that of

Saxony, which succeeded to some extent.   From the 4th of January 1780 a contract of partnership was entered into for seven years between him and Pierre August de Rostaing de Nivas and Jacques Fourmy, under the title of "Fourmy fils, Fournerat et De Nivas"; the initials of each of their names interlaced into a monogram and traced in red, served as the mark of this Nantes porcelain. Fournerat, being of a restless disposition, seceded from the firm in 1781.   It went on prosperously until the insurrection of La Vendée and the Revolution entirely put a stop to the sale of objects of luxury, and the works were closed about the year 1790.

In 1809 some specimens of porcelain *pâte dure* (coffee-cups) were sent to the Sèvres Museum from the fabrique of M. Decan of Nantes.

CHOISY-LE-ROY. *Hard paste.* Established in 1786 by M. Clement; the manufactory belonged to M. Lefèvre. A record preserved at Sèvres indicates the existence at Choisy of another manufactory, directed by M. Seilletz, but whether he refers to this or a distinct fabrique is not known.

LIMOGES (Haute-Vienne).   M. Massie, who had obtained authority to establish a manufactory of fayence at Limoges, subsequently associated himself with a person named Fournerat and the brothers Grellet to extend his works to the making of porcelain. An Order of Council, dated December 1773, permitted him to found an establishment of which the products were to be marked C. D.; a former project for an Order of Council indicates the mark as having been G. R. et Cie;

G R et Cie   it was discontinued in 1788. Fournerat, in 1779, having discovered how to make *porcelaine dure*, left Limoges and entered into partnership with Jacques Fourmy and another at Nantes, the firm being Fourmy fils, Fournerat et De Nivas. The works were subsequently purchased by MM. Joubert and Cancate.   In 1794 M. Monnerie established, in the old Augustine convent at Limoges, a manufacture which continued in operation till 1800, when it declined. When M. Baignol left La Seinie he set up a manufacture on his own account, which was, next to that of M. Alluaud, the most considerable in the place.

LIMOGES. This mark, in red, is on a porcelain tureen, painted with flowers, gilt borders, having on the top a bunch of vegetables.

Also on a porcelain plate, with gold border and garlands of roses.

Another form of the same initials, given by Jännike.

LIMOGES. The fabrique of M. Alluaud is the most ancient in France for the manufacture of hard porcelain. In 1788 M. Alluaud was made director of the Royal Manufactory founded at Limoges four years previously, and its success was only interrupted for a time by the Revolution. He utilised the kaolin of the mines of Marcognac, of which he was the proprietor, and in 1797 it was again in full activity. He died in 1799, and was succeeded by his son François, who quitted the army and took the direction, and, being a scientific man, in a few years-obtained a thorough knowledge of chemistry and mineralogy; his discoveries are thus acknowledged by M. Brongniart: "M. François Alluaud possesses the kaolin mines of Marcognac and the felspar of Chanteloupe. Two workshops on the Vienne have 150 pairs of *meules* for the preparation of the ingredients, and two manufactories of porcelain at Limoges comprise eight kilns, six for coal and two for wood, employing 1000 workmen; half is consumed in France, the rest exported to America and Germany" (*Traité des Arts Céramiques*).

The following is a list of more recent manufacturers at Limoges:—

Fabrique of porcelain (*hard paste*), by M. Tharaud, about 1827.
Fabrique of porcelain (*hard paste*), by Messrs. Nenert & Ruault. Sèvres Museum, 1831.
Fabrique of porcelain (*hard paste*), by Messrs. Michel & Valin. Sèvres Museum, 1894.
Fabrique of porcelain, by M. Tathille & Co. Sèvres Museum, 1833.
A porcelain manufactory is now carried on by Messrs. Demartial & Talandier. Specimens in the Paris Exhibition, 1867.
Messrs. P. Guerry and R. Delinières. Table and breakfast services, white and painted, &c. Paris Exhibition, 1867.
A porcelain manufactory is carried on by Haviland & Co. Specimens in Paris Exhibition, 1867.

SARREGUEMINES (Moselle). Messrs. Utzchneider and Co. are now important manufacturers of porcelain *pâte tendre* and biscuit figures and groups; services painted in the English style, and frequently decorated with transfer pictures, artistic white stoneware, &c. In the Sèvres Museum is a bust *in biscuit* of the founder of the fabrique, François Paul Utzchneider, by F. François, sculptor to the firm; dated 1858.

The mark at present used is of a more complicated character, as shown in the margin. The manufactory still maintains its high character for porcelain and biscuit, and is one of the most important fabriques in France.

STRASBOURG (Bas Rhin), 1752. *Hard paste*. Established by Paul Hannong. About the year 1752 he obtained the secret of true porcelain from Ringler, but in consequence of the monopoly of Sèvres he was compelled to relinquish it, and in 1753 removed to Frankenthal, where he was received with open arms, and in 1761 greatly flourished under the protection of the Elector Palatine, Carl Theodore. The Strasbourg marks are those of Hannong, as

in the margin. The mark in the margin **Ḣ** is always impressed in the paste, and is accompanied by other letters and numbers. The former are V for vase, F for figure, and G for group, VC for plates, C and CC for cups, while the numbers refer to a factory list. (*Ker. Gall.*, enlarged edition, figs. 332-33.)

STRASBOURG. The monograms of Paul Antoine Hannong.

These marks in blue, both over and under the glaze, occur on specimens in the Franks Collection. The monogram of Joseph Hannong, and the initial of Valentin Guse.

The mark of the letter H and also of the monogram P. H. occur in infinite variety of form. In Messrs. Chavagnac and Grollier's *Histoire des Manufactures Françaises de Porcelaine* are given no less than thirty illustrations of different forms of this initial or monogram.

FRANCE. A caduceus on an embossed oval occurs on some French biscuit groups.

ST. DENIS-DE-LA-CHEVASSE (Poitou). Established in 1784 by the Marquis de Torcy. All we know of this fabrique is a request to establish a manufactory here, which was accorded.

ST. BRICE. Established in 1784 by Messrs. Gomon & Croasmen. In a letter dated 17th June 1784, M. Montaran announces to M. l'Intendant de Paris that these fabricants of porcelain and glass at St. Brice request permission to take the title of "Manufacture Royale de Monseigneur le Dauphin," which was refused, in consequence of his having about the same time patronised the fabrique of Lille. The enterprise was of short duration.

ISLE ST. DENIS (Seine). *Hard paste.* Established in 1778 by Laferté. There are no documents extant relating to this fabrique, which must have been in existence before 1778, for in that year there were received at the house of Nicolas Catrice, a painter of Sèvres, ready to be painted and falsely marked with the double L of Sèvres, seven pieces of the fabrique of St. Denis. It must therefore have been in full activity at that time, and the ware of sufficiently high quality to pass for porcelain of the Royal Manufactory. In the list kept at Sèvres denoting the condition of the factories we read: "Ile St. Denis, Laferté, à la suite de pertes enormes, la fabrique a été detruite." M. Riocreux has discovered two pieces made there, viz., two biscuit busts, life size; one of Louis XVI., signed, "*Gross, 1779*"; the other of Monsieur le Comte de Provence by the same artist, signed, "*Gross L'Isle Saint De * * *, 1780.*"

MARSEILLES (Bouches-du-Rhone). A manufactory of porcelain was established here by Joseph Gaspard Robert about 1766, and was in full activity on the visit of the Comte de Provence in 1777, who especially noticed a large vase, finely modelled, a complete service expressly made for England, and porcelain flowers delicately copied from nature, like those of Sèvres. The order from England, where so many important china manufactories already existed, shows it was renowned at that time. The factory was closed about the period of the French Revolution in 1793.

MARSEILLES. Joseph Gaspard Robert. M. le Baron Davillier had two fine specimens so signed; one is a sucrier and cover, with medallions, finely painted, of a view of the port of Marseilles and a promenade of figures in the national costume; the other a cup painted with bouquets of flowers. M. Montreuil and the Sèvres Museum have specimens.

MARSEILLES. Sometimes only marked R, on a cup decorated in blue, in the style of Japan, and on another painted with flowers in polychrome and other ornaments, finely gilt. In the Davillier Collection.

MARSEILLES. Robert *frère* or Robert *fils.* This mark is on the companion to the cup last mentioned, signed only R.; it is identical as to paste, touch, painting of flowers, and gilding, and was undoubtedly from the same fabrique; certainly not of Naples, as suggested by M. Jacquemart, who reads it as "*Re Ferdinando,*" but neither the mark nor quality of the porcelain favour such an attribution. The other is the monogram of Joseph Robert. Mr. W. E. Gubleton had a coffee-pot cover, and saucer decorated with wreaths of pink roses marked with the ℞, The mark is scarce. There is a specimen in the Franks Collection.

MARSEILLES. In gold, on a vase of hard porcelain, ornamented with flowers in relief forming garlands; beautiful paste and gilding, equal to Sèvres; it is the monogram of Joseph Gaspard Robert. Baron C. Davillier had numerous pieces of this fabrique, some of which are painted equal to the Meissen porcelain.

SOME MINOR PARIS FABRIQUES.

The notices and their distinguishing marks which follow under this heading are those of comparatively unimportant fabriques which sprung up quite at the end of the eighteenth, or commencement of the nineteenth century in Paris and its neighbourhood. Some of these only existed for a short time, just so long as they were supported by patrons of rank and means, or by the energy of an individual potter or proprietor. In many cases the china was obtained from Limoges, or Fontainebleau, or elsewhere, and only decorated at the Paris fabrique, and the mark, sometimes the name and address, is that of the decorator only. To collectors of "marks" the productions of these various potters and decorators are interesting; they are very similar in character, all of them being hard paste, like the late productions of Sèvres, and the shapes generally those which we recognise as prevailing during the period of the Directoire or the Empire which followed. They are generally table services, and occasionally vases, but very seldom groups or figures.

PARIS (Rue de la Ville l'Evêque, Faubourg St. Honoré, 1722). Marie Moreau, widow of Pierre Chicanneau (nephew of Jean), opened a manufactory here, with Domenique François Chicanneau as director, the proprietorship of the fabrique of St. Cloud being divided, leaving Gabriel and Henri Trou there. In 1742 an *arrêt* granted them the privilege of continuing the works for twenty years longer. Marie Moreau died in 1743, and they were then carried on by Domenique, and ceased probably at the expiration of the letters patent in 1762.

C M ☩　PARIS (Faubourg St. Honoré). The mark of Veuve Chicanneau, *née* Marie Moreau.

PARIS (Pont-aux-Choux). *Manufacture du Duc d'Orléans.* On the 22nd of April 1784, Louis Honoré de la Marre de Villars opened an

establishment for the manufacture of porcelain in the Rue des Boulets, Faubourg St. Antoine; the mark deposited was M.J., as in margin. It was afterwards disposed of to Jean Baptiste Outrequin de Montarcy and Edme Toulouse, who in August 1786 obtained a *brévet* from the Duc d'Orléans, Louis Philippe Joseph, and authority to sign the productions with the letters L. P. and take the title

of "Manufacture de M. le Duc d'Orléans." They were afterwards
established in the Rue Amelot, *au Pont-aux-Choux*, by which name the
porcelain is generally known. These letters alone
are mentioned in the official documents, which say
nothing about the letters being crowned. M. Jacquemart consequently says that Mr. Marryat is wrong
in assigning the P. L. crowned to this manufactory.
(See VINCENNES.) This mark ceased in 1793 with
the condemnation of the Duke of Orléans, and the
works subsequently produced were inscribed merely
"*Fabrique du Pont-aux-Choux*," as on a fountain
spoken of by M. Jacquemart. Outrequin de Montarcy
and Toulouse parted with the manufactory to a M. Werstock, who was
replaced by a M. Lemaire, and subsequently by Canon and Lefebvre.

PARIS (Pont-aux-Choux). Under Louis Philippe
Joseph, Duke of Orléans. Marked in blue beneath
a porcelain tea-pot, painted with sprigs and flowers,
in the Rev. T. Staniforth's Collection.

Two other marks of the same fabrique are here
given.

PARIS.   This mark, stencilled in red, is on a
French hard porcelain cup and saucer painted with
scrolls and festoons of flowers, gilt borders; also
stamped in red on a beautiful ewer (with old mount-
ing in silver gilt), and a basin ornamented with flowers, cameos, scrolls,
&c.; style of Sèvres, hard paste, about 1780. The beautiful service with
the same mark quoted by M. Jacquemart (*Merv. de la Céram.*, part iii.
p. 324), which he could not decipher, belongs no doubt to Paris, and very
likely *Pont-aux-Choux*, the M. O. being for the Outrequin de Montarcy or
Manufacture d'Orléans. A Sèvres cup with the same decoration appears
to be from the same hand, perhaps a painter from Sèvres. Baron C.
Davillier's Collection.

PARIS (Faubourg St. Antoine, Barrière de
Reuilly). *Hard paste.* Established in 1784 by
Henry Florentine Chanou, an old pupil of Sèvres.
There are some specimens in the Sèvres Museum,
the mark pencilled in red.

C.H

In the Franks Collection there is a cup with
this mark in gold, and the same letters are sometimes interlaced. The fabrique had a short life,
and specimens are scarce.

PARIS (Faubourg St. Antoine, Rue de Reuilly). *Hard paste.* Established in 1774 by Jean Joseph Lassia. M. Jacquemart also gives this last letter from a specimen of Lassia's porcelain in his own collection; a porcelain cup and saucer, pale yellow ground, gilt edges, with landscape in bistre, has this mark in gold.

PARIS (Rue Fontaine au Roi, called "De la Courtille"). *Hard paste.* This important manufactory was established in 1773 by Jean Baptiste Locré, afterwards joined by Russinger in 1784, who during the Revolution was sole director; it was also called "La Manufacture de Porcelain Allemande." In the *Porcelaine de Sèvres* by Baron C. Davillier, is a memorandum by Locré as follows: "Livrée à Mme la Comtesse du Barry par la manufacture de porcelaine allemande, établie à la Basse Courtille dès le mois de Decembre 1773. Une buste de porcelaine de grandeur naturelle, éxecuté d'après le model en plâtre que lui a été remis par M. Pajou, suivant les ordres de Mme la Comtesse, valant trois mille livres (£120). Signed LOCRÉ."

Pouyat
&
Puffinger
P.R.

This mark is composed of two flambeaux crossed in blue, and not two arrows, as usually given. It is frequently mistaken for that of Dresden, being also of hard paste. The mark sometimes appears in a more sketchy form, and is occasionally accompanied by letters. (*Ker. Gall.*, enlarged edition, fig. 337.)

PARIS (Rue Fontaine au Roi). De la Courtille. This mark is stencilled in red on a cup and saucer; the initials P.R., sometimes stencilled in red and sometimes in gold, belong to the same firm. In 1800 Pouyat was the only proprietor.

PARIS. De la Courtille. The name of a subsequent manufacturer. On a cup and saucer painted with a girl and pet lamb, the mark in gold, the flambeaux in blue as usual.

manufacture
A. Deltuf

PARIS. De la Courtille. The second mark, a sort of rest, is in blue *au grand feu* on the cup; the former is on a saucer.

This mark, which has the appearance of the letter A, is almost certainly the crossed torches badly formed. It occurs on some specimens in the Franks Collection.

Monginot
20 Boulevart
des Italiens.

PARIS (Boulevard des Italiens). The name engraved on a piece from Louis Philippe's sale. M. Monginot was probably a small manufacturer.

PARIS (Faubourg St. Antoine). *Hard paste.* Established 1773. The manufacturer's name was Morelle; the mark stands for "Morelle à Paris."

PARIS (Faubourg St. Lazare). *Hard paste.* Founded 1773 by Pierre Antoine Hannong or Hanüng, after his unsuccessful attempt to establish a manufactory of hard porcelain at Vincennes, which appears to have failed from want of resources.

These marks, which occur in blue and also in gold, are attributed by Sir A. W. Franks to this fabrique. There are specimens in the Franks Collection. The C. P. are the initials of Charles Philippe, Comte d'Artois, the patron of the factory. The " h " is one of the signatures of Hannong.

PARIS (Rue de la Roquette). *Hard paste.* Established in 1773. Souroux, manufacturer, succeeded by Ollivier, and afterwards by Pétry. There was a manufactory of fayence here as early as 1675.

This mark in blue under glaze is no doubt two varieties of the letter S for Souroux, and appears on a saucer and also on a sucrier in the Franks Collection.

PARIS (Faubourg St. Antoine, Rue de la Roquette). Established about 1773 for hard paste by Vincent Dubois à l'Hotel des Arbalètriers. The mark is two pointless arrows in blue. The Rev. A. H. S. Barwell has a finely painted écuelle cover and stand with this mark; it was formerly in the Staniforth Collection.

This mark stencilled in red on one of the cups of a coffee set of rich gros bleu and gold decoration, the style being of the first Empire. In the possession of Mr. St. J. Oscar Thompson, of Brentwood.

Mr. H. E. B. Harrison has a can and saucer red-orange ground with birds and gilding bearing this mark, obviously another mark of this potter.

PARIS (Rue de la Roquette). Manufacturer's name, M. Darté; a cup and saucer in the Sèvres Museum, bought in 1807.

PARIS (Rue Amelot). *Hard paste.* Fabrique of M. Lefebvre; cups and saucers, Sèvres Museum.

MAP

H

h   ᴄ.ᴘ.   CP

S

θ   *s'*

Lᴺ. DARTE Rue Vivienne N.

DARTE FRERES 4 PARIS

This mark is on a pair of plates painted with cupids playing games, and richly gilt, formerly in the Editor's possession.

PARIS (Gros Caillou). *Hard paste.* Established 1773 by Advenir Lamarre.

PARIS (Rue Thiroux). *Hard paste.* Established 1778 by André Marie Lebœuf, manufacturer. This factory produced during the first twenty years of its existence a great deal of well decorated and highly-finished porcelain, mostly table services, jardinières, and such pieces in the character of hard paste late Sèvres china. The mark is A. under a crown, for Antoinette (it was under the protection of Marie Antoinette), stencilled in red. The products of the factory are known as *Porcelaine de la Reine.*

Two other varieties of the mark of this fabrique. There are specimens in the Franks Collection. (*Ker. Gall.*, enlarged edition, fig. 334.)

M. Jacquemart has found this mark on pieces of the same service, bearing also the stencilled letter A crowned.

Housel

The successors of Lebœuf were Messrs. Guy and Housel. Guy was perhaps the son of the Widow Guy of the Petit Carousel. M. Housel signed his name alone probably when M. Guy succeeded his mother at the Petit Carousel; he remained proprietor from 1799 to 1804.

Rue Thirou
a Paris.

PARIS (Rue Thiroux). *Hard paste.* The initials of Guy and Housel, on a pair of seaux or jardinières, painted with roses and gilt borders, in the possession of the Countess Dowager of Lichfield.

LEVEILLE
12
Rue THIROUX

PARIS (No. 12 Rue Thiroux). Manufactory of M. Leveille. These letters are usually arranged in form of an oval.

PARIS (Rue Thiroux). *Hard paste.* This mark is in gold on a hard porcelain compotier, well painted with vignettes of nymphs bathing, forget-me-nots and roses round the border, finely gilt; very much like Dresden. The mark is M.A., probably for Marie Antoinette. Formerly in Mr. Bohn's Collection.

This mark, stencilled in red, is on a cup and saucer in the Franks Collection, and on the authority of Jacquemart is attributed with some doubt to this factory.

PARIS (Rue Faubourg St. Denis). About 1773. *Hard paste.* Established by M. Barrachin.

PARIS (Rue Faubourg St. Denis). The mark in gold; carried on by M. Flamen Fleury. Formerly the proprietors were Messrs. Latourville and Co.

FLEURY.

PARIS. This mark is stencilled imperfectly in red on a cup and saucer with purple and dark-blue decorations, on pale French grey ground with heavy gilding. In the possession of Mr. H. St. J. Oscar Thompson, of Brentwood. It is similar to the late hard paste productions of Sèvres.

Flamen
Fleury
Paris.

PARIS. This mark is in gold on the base of a small white and gold cup.

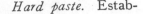

PARIS (Rue de Clichy). *Hard paste.* So placed by Mr. Marryat, but neither the name nor date of establishment are given; the mark A is in blue.

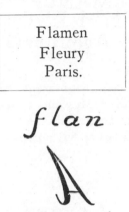

PARIS (Rue de Bondy). 1780. *Hard paste.* Dihl and Guerhard, manufacturers, under the patronage of the Duc d'Angoulême; called "Porcelaine d'Angoulême." This factory was one of the most important of its time, and under the able direction of Dihl produced table services and vases, also specimen pieces of the best kind, the character of decoration being generally that which we find on Sèvres of the late hard paste period. In Horace Walpole's Catalogue of the Strawberry Hill Collection, 1784, is described "a white cup and saucer with coloured flowers, made for the Comte d'Artois, and called *Porcelaine d'Angoulême.*" On the 10th November 1818, Moses Poole, of Lincoln's Inn, Middlesex, patent agent, took out a patent, in consequence of a communication made to him by Christopher Dihl, he being a foreigner, residing abroad, and being possessed of an invention as follows: "The application of known mastics or cements to various purposes, such as modelling statues, making slabs, raising or impressing figures, or other ornamental appearances, also to the covering of houses, or in any other matter in which mastic or cement may or can be applied." The first mark is painted in red on the plateau of a *cabaret;* some of the

smaller pieces have the monogram only, others have the monogram G.A. in an oval, surmounted by a coronet in gold; one stencilled in red. This service is beautifully painted with stags in Indian-ink, and formerly belonged to Mr. Reynolds. (*Ker. Gall.*, enlarged edition, figs 335-36.)

 Marked in gold on an Angoulême cup, the saucer having the inscription in full (as quoted below). In the Victoria and Albert Museum.

MANUF^{RE}
MGR le DUC
Angouleme
Paris.

PARIS (Rue de Bondy). Dihl & Guerhard. On an Angoulême cup and saucer, with forget-me-nots; the mark is stencilled in red, partly obliterated.

A magnificent vase of Angoulême porcelain is in the Victoria and Albert Museum, 3 feet 3 inches high, painted *en grisaille* with the Rape of the Sabines on a gold ground; it was purchased by the Department for £171 8s., and is worth three times that sum.

Dihl.

PARIS (Rue de Bondy). The mark of Dihl painted in blue on a can and saucer in the Franks Collection.
Mr. W. E. Gumbleton had a pair of vases with this mark of mottled brown glaze, which the Editor purchased at the Hamilton Palace Collection.

MANUF^{RE}
de M M^{rs}
Guerhard et
Dihl à Paris

PARIS. Messrs. Guerhard & Dihl. This mark, stencilled in red, is on a porcelain cup and saucer, yellow ground, with landscape and figures, in red *camaieu.*

REVIL
R^{ue} Neuve
des
Capucines

PARIS. "*Revil, Rue Neuve des Capucines*," is on a porcelain cup and saucer, pink ground, with broad gold border and small white oval medallions; the mark stencilled in red.

V^e M
& C

PARIS. Veuve M. & Co.; name unknown. The name stencilled in red on a cup and saucer with deep border of gold, painted festoons and scrolls.

DASTIN.

PARIS. The name is stencilled in red on a French porcelain cup and saucer, green ground, gold-leaf border.

PARIS (Faubourg Saint-Denis). Fabrique of Charles Philippe, Comte d'Artois, afterwards Charles X., 1769. *Hard paste.* We read in the *Guide des Amateurs*, printed in Paris, 1787: "This manufacture in the Rue du Faubourg St. Denis is the most ancient of all those established in Paris. Pierre Antoine Hannong of Strasbourg, who brought into France the secret of hard porcelain,

formed the first establishment in 1769. Having obtained the protection of Charles Philippe, Comte d'Artois, it is called by his name." It belonged actually to Louis Joseph Bourdon Desplanches, who continued the fabrication of hard porcelain. The subsequent proprietors were Messrs. Schmidt & Co., Rénard Houet, and Benjamin Schoelcher. This mark has already been given as probably that of another Paris manufactory (Paris, Faubourg, St. Lazare) on page 627.

PARIS (Boulevard des Italiens, No. 2). He is classed in *Galignani* among the dealers; his name occurs on some plates with richly-gilt borders, and

Schoelcher.

on a handsome white and gold dessert service in the Editor's possession. Sometimes the mark is *Schoelcher et fils.*

PARIS, FOESCY, MEHUN ET NOIRLAC. *Hard paste.* Established about 1817. It is one of the largest porcelain manufactories in France, employ-

C. H. PILLIVUT
& Cie Paris

ing 2000 workmen. Their products have been rewarded by medals of New York, Paris, and London; they make every description, both useful and ornamental. The mark is simply the name in an oval.

FOESCY (Cher, and at Paris, No. 5 Passage Violet, Rue Poissonnière). Fabrique of M. André Cottier. This mark is on a hard paste china bowl, painted with flowers and richly gilt. About the first quarter of the nineteenth century.

Manufre de Foëscy,
Passage Violet, No. 5,
R. Poissonnière, à Paris.

PARIS. The mark of M. Feuillet is sometimes in black, but usually marked in gold on the back of the plates; sometimes only one mark, the single letter in blue. These two together are on a plate painted with flowers in lake *camaieu* formerly in the Editor's possession. Mr. Cornwallis West had some plates, crimson borders with beautiful gilding and highly-finished paintings of flowers. A peculiarity in this fabrique is the three cockspur marks in the centre at back; it has a great similarity to Tournay porcelain, and is made to resemble that of Sèvres.

Feuillet

℉

PARIS. "*Feuillet*," written in gold, as well as the monogram in the margin, in imitation of the Sèvres mark. A handsome service in the Sèvres style, with rich green and gold border and painted in fruits, was in Sir Edward Dean Paul's Collection, sold at Christie's in 1896, marked with the name "Feuillet," and address, "Passage Landrix dans l'Impasse, Paris." As was the case with several of these Paris so called factories, the china was purchased from Limoges or Fontainebleau, or some other manufacturer, and there decorated and marked by the Paris artist.

J.P.

PARIS. Formerly Belleville, and now Fontainebleau. *Hard paste.* Established 1790 by Jacob Petit; the mark is blue in the moist clay. This manufactory is still carried on at 54 Rue Paradis Poissonnière, and the depôt, 32 Rue de Bondy. The products of the first period were much esteemed, being well painted and well modelled, bearing his mark, but recently the proprietor has unwisely altered his original plan and imitates Dresden, counterfeiting also the mark of the crossed swords; a practice which cannot be too much reprehended, as it is the cause of much deception. Jacob Petit also makes biscuit figures, birds' nests, flowers, &c. In 1853 he patented in England some improvements in porcelain, which consisted in having raised surfaces and painting the same, the combination being claimed. The initials J.P., as in the margin, are in blue.

R
C·P
1

PARIS (Rue de Crussol). *Hard paste.* Established 1789 by Charles Potter, an Englishman; called the "Prince of Wales's China"; the mark *in red*. A similar mark *in blue*, the top letter being B, is on a canary-coloured cup and saucer, painted with flowers and butterflies; in the Collection of the Rev. T. Staniforth.

B
Potter
42

PARIS (Rue de Crussol). These marks are on separate pieces of the same service, one marked in red, the others in blue. Specimens in the Franks Collection. Mr. W. Gumbleton had a cup and saucer bearing these marks. (*Ker. Gall.*, enlarged edition, fig. 340.)

PB

EB

PARIS (Rue de Crussol). The initials in blue under glaze occur on specimens in the Franks Collection, which are attributed to this factory.

PARIS. Manufacture de Petit Carousel. Established about 1775. We have no account of the establishment of this porcelain fabrique; the specimens appear to be of the epoch of the French Revolution. The Commercial Almanacks inform us that, 1798-99, the establishment was directed by the Widow Guy, and afterwards by her son, M. Guy, and it is supposed that his father was the founder about 1775. Three letters P.C.G. may refer to *Petit Carousel Guy*; another example reads, "*P.C.G. Manufacture du Petit Carousel à Paris.*" The annexed mark is stencilled in red on a French cup and saucer, painted with flowers in gold-bordered compartments.

P
C G
M^{re} du Pt.
Carousel
à Paris

PARIS. On a porcelain cup and saucer with gilt flowers and leaves, marked in red. Formerly in the possession of the Rev. T. Staniforth of Storrs.

T.G.
C.
Paris.

PARIS (Rue de Popincourt, 1780). This manufactory was either founded or purchased in 1783 by M. Nast, who after working in Paris as a saddler, became a potter at Vincennes, and then removed to Paris, where he achieved considerable success, and died in 1817. His sons carried on the concern with indifferent success until 1835. The works were in the Rue des Amandiers. One of Nast's specialities was a decoration in relief in white biscuit somewhat in the style of our Wedgwood, and also with coloured ground and white relief. The general character of Nast's china is that of the usual hard paste Paris factories. M. Jacquemart mentions a biscuit bust of Bonaparte in costume of a general, under the foot of which is written, "*Manf^re de Porcelaine du C^en Nast, Rue Des Amandiers D^on Popincourt.*"

Mr. B. Fillon has two biscuit busts, one of Hoche, the other of Bonaparte, with their names written under, and the inscription just given; he considers them to have been modelled by Houdin in 1797.

This inscription in gold is found on a basin and stand of pure white, with raised ornaments richly gilt, resting on a stand of three lions' feet. The Franks Collection.

*nast a paris
par brevet d'inv,^on*

PARIS. This mark is stencilled in red on a cup and saucer, with spiral gold lines crossing each other, flowers in the spaces between, and gold spots; the cup is also marked B. In Mr. Danby Seymour's Collection.

NAST.

PARIS. Nast, manufacturer. This mark is stencilled in red on a cup and saucer, painted with flowers. H. J. Nast is mentioned in the jury awards in 1851.

N . . .
à .
Paris

C. H. MENARD
Paris
72 Rue de Popincourt.

PARIS (Rue de Popincourt). *Hard paste.* Founded in 1796 by Le Sieur de Cœur d'Acier. The pieces are sometimes marked with a heart. It was carried on by Messrs. Darté in 1812, afterwards by Discry and Talmour; the present proprietor is M. Menard. The mark is oval.

PARIS. A novel style of decoration was patented in 1857 by Mons. Brianchon, which gives porcelain the lustrous appearance of mother-of-pearl; it is termed "*decor de couleurs nacrées à base de bismuth.*" The patent for London was granted to Jules Jos Henri Brianchon in 1857 for ornamenting porcelain, &c., with variegated reflections or coatings prepared with metallic fluxes and colouring matters. The fluxes are salts of bismuth, in certain proportions, and "essence of lavender, or any other essence which does not cause any precipitation in the mixture. The metallic salts and oxides, which assist in colouring, are salts of platina, silver, antimony, cobalt, chrome, copper, iron, &c., and sometimes salts of gold in order to produce the rich tint of shells or the reflection of the prism." The name of the firm was Gillet & Brianchon.

This beautiful ware is still made, and the manufacture is carried on by M. Brianchon, 222 Rue de Lafayette; but the patent for England having expired, this lustrous glaze has been recently adopted both at Belleek in Ireland, and at Worcester.

PARIS. This mark, incised in the paste, occurs on some figures of coloured biscuit china made at one of the Paris factories. They are simply of the "cheap ornament" character, and have no merit from the collector's point of view, but as the mark occasions inquiry it is added here for identification.

Dagoty
à paris

Manufacture
de S.M.L'Imperatrice.
P.L DAGOTY
à Paris.

PARIS (Boulevard Poissonnière). *Hard paste.* Established by P. L. Dagoty towards the end of the last century; he sent some specimens to the Sèvres Museum in 1804; his fabrique was called "L'Impératrice." This mark, stencilled in red, is on a set of china, green borders, painted with classical figures, also on four cups and saucers in the Windsor Castle Collection.

F. M. HONORÉ.

M^{ture} de MADAME
Duchesse d'Angoulême
Dagoty E. Honoré,
PARIS.

F. D. HONORÉ
à Paris.

PARIS (50 Boulevard St. Antoine). Established about 1785. *Hard paste.* The two sons, Edward and Theodore, went into partnership with P. L. Dagoty at La Seinie and Paris, Rue de Chevreuse, about 1812. It was then styled "*Manufacture de Madame la Duchesse d'Angoulême.*" In 1820 this partnership was dissolved, and the brothers Honoré kept the fabrique in Paris—Boulevard Poissonnière.

PARIS (Rue St. Honoré). A specimen so marked in the Bandinel Collection.

R. F. DAGOTY

PARIS. This mark is on an écuelle of porcelain, gilt all over with scrolls and bees, and medallions of coloured subjects of children; the name unknown. In the possession of Mr. Lermitte.

PARIS. This name occurs on a china *cabaret (hard paste)*, decorated with flowers in the Sèvres style, but of ordinary character (nineteenth century). In Mr. Hawkins of Grantham's Collection.

L' Gardie,
a Paris

PARIS. Established by M. Lerosey. On a modern china dessert service, deep rose-coloured border, and a cipher in the centre in pink ribbon.

Lerosey
11 Rue de la paix

PARIS. Two porcelain plates with printed plans of the cities of St. Petersburg and Moscow, and numerous annotations, also inscribed "*Gravée à Paris, par R. F. Tardieu, Place de l'Estrapade, No. 1.*"

PARIS. Delaherche (Auguste) makes stoneware. The mark in question occurs on a stoneware vase, covered with green, purple and brown glaze. Monsieur Delaherche has a depôt at 1 Rue Halévy, Paris.

This signature in red occurs on a cup and saucer, with gilded ornaments in the late Louis Seize taste, and panels of views in sepia, with insects painted in centre of saucer. Hard paste, and similar in character to other Paris factories. Howard Paget of Tamworth.

In possession of Mr. T.

PARIS. Monsieur E. Samson fils ainé makes pottery in imitation of old wares, not only European, but also Oriental, with the greatest skill. This mark occurs on an enamelled earthenware plate painted with geometrical and scroll ornament in imitation of Rouen ware. His factory is in Paris, and he has a depôt in the Avenue de l'Opera, Paris.

PARIS. Monsieur Clément Massier makes a lustred ware at Golfe-Juan (Alpes Maritimes), and has a depôt in the Rue de Rivoli, Paris. This mark occurs on a vase lustred, with floral decoration.

On some of the pieces from this factory the name of L. Levy also occurs.

Clement-Massier
Golfe-Juan. A.M

L Levy.

The following porcelain manufactories are mentioned by M. Brongniart :—

LURCY LÉVY (Allier), Porcelain (*hard paste*), Fab. Marquis de Sinety, 1814, and M. Burguin, 1834.

VILLEDIEU (Indre), Porcelain (*hard paste*), Fab. M. Bernard, 1830.

VILLEDIEU, Porcelain (*hard paste*), Fab. de M. Louault. M. Lalouette was director in 1823, and designed a large Medici vase, which at the Exposition was bought by the King and given to the Sèvres Museum.

VIERZON (Cher), Porcelain, Fab. de Messrs. Pétry & Ronsse, 1844.

ORCHAMPS (Jura), Porcelain, Fab. de M. Barré-Russin, 1729.

NEVERS (Nièvre), Porcelain, Messrs. Neppel & Bonnot, 1844.

ST. YRIEIX-LA-PERCHE (Vienne), Porcelain, Fab. de M. Denuelle, 1829.

MAGNAG-BOURG (Vienne), Porcelain, Fab. M. Boilleau-Gauldrée, 1827.

PLOMBIÈRES (Vosges), Porcelain, M. Hevisé & Co., director M. Troté.

The following modern fabriques are briefly noticed by M. A. Jacquemart :—

PARIS, Faubourg St. Denis, 92, Bernard & Co., Le Cointre & Co., Lefèvre, Lebourgeois.

PARIS, Rue de la Pepinière, 16, Chevalier Frères, Marchand, Fourmy, Potter & Co., Tregent.

PARIS, Rue de Charonne, Lévy & Co., Pressinger, Massonet, Dartés Frères, the last removed to Rue de la Roquette.

PARIS, Rue de la Roquette, 98, Robillard.

PARIS, Petite-Pologne, Rue du Rocher, 12, Betz & Co., Nicolet & Greder, Reville, Pérè.

PARIS, Rue des Marais, Toulouse, Mercier.

PARIS, Butte de Belleville, Pétry, Guy, Desfossés.

PARIS, Rue Baffroy, Dubois, Hannong.

PARIS, Rue Baffroy, 32, L'Hote.

PARIS, Rue Neuve Saint Gilles, Lortz, Rouget, Lebon, Savoie, Honoré.

PARIS, Rue Folie, Méricourt, Cremière, Freund.

PARIS, Rue des Récollets, 2, Desprès, *cameos*.

PARIS, Rue Ménilmontant, Cossart.

PARIS, Rue de Crussol, Constant, *fabrique de biscuit*.

VERSAILLES (Seine-et-Oise), Panckoucke, Roger, Teingout.

FONTAINEBLEAU (Seine-et-Oise), Benjamin, Baruchweil.

LORIENT (Morbihan), Hervé, Sauvageau.

BOURBONNAIS, Senetti, Deruelle fils.

GOURNAY (Seine-Inférieure), Wood.

NANTES (Loire-Inférieure), Decaen.

COLMAR (Haut-Rhin), fayence and porcelain, signed *Colmar*.

VIERZON (Cher), Hache & Pepin, Lehalleurs.

PARIS. To the above list may be added Stône, Coquerell et Le Gros. Mr. H. E. B. Harrison has a pair of plates painted in mythological subjects in brown colour and borders of Empire style which. bear the name of this firm. There are others, but it is difficult to say which are the names of makers and which those of decorators only who have marked the pieces at the time of painting.